READER IN TRAGEDY

Marcus Nevitt is Senior Lecturer in English Literature at the University of Sheffield, UK. He is the author of *Women and the Pamphlet Culture of Revolutionary England, 1640–1660* (2006) and is a contributing editor to the *Cambridge Edition of the Works of Aphra Behn* (2019).

Tanya Pollard is Professor of English at Brooklyn College and the Graduate Center, City University of New York, USA. Her books include *Greek Tragic Women on Shakespearean Stages* (2017), *Drugs and Theater in Early Modern England* (2005), and *Shakespeare's Theater: A Sourcebook* (2003).

Related Titles

VISIONS OF TRAGEDY IN MODERN AMERICAN DRAMA
Edited by David Palmer
ISBN 978-1-4742-7693-1

READER IN COMEDY: AN ANTHOLOGY OF THEORY AND CRITICISM
Edited by Magda Romanska and Alan Ackerman
ISBN 978-1-4742-4789-4

Forthcoming

A CULTURAL HISTORY OF TRAGEDY
Edited by Rebecca Bushnell
ISBN 978-1-4742-8814-9

SHAKESPEAREAN TRAGEDY: HAMLET, OTHELLO, KING LEAR, MACBETH
Kiernan Ryan
ISBN 978-1-4725-8698-8

READER IN TRAGEDY

AN ANTHOLOGY OF CLASSICAL CRITICISM TO CONTEMPORARY THEORY

Edited by Marcus Nevitt and Tanya Pollard

methuen | drama

LONDON • NEW YORK • OXFORD • NEW DELHI • SYDNEY

METHUEN DRAMA
Bloomsbury Publishing Plc
50 Bedford Square, London, WC1B 3DP, UK
1385 Broadway, New York, NY 10018, USA

BLOOMSBURY, METHUEN DRAMA and the Methuen Drama logo are trademarks of
Bloomsbury Publishing Plc

First published in Great Britain 2019

Selection, editorial matter and introductions © Marcus Nevitt and Tanya Pollard, 2019

Marcus Nevitt and Tanya Pollard have asserted their right under the Copyright, Designs and Patents Act,
1988, to be identified as the editors of this work.

For legal purposes the Acknowledgements on pp. vii, 329–31 constitute an extension of this
copyright page.

Cover image: Antoni Brodowski, *Oedipus and Antigone* (© ART Collection / Alamy Stock Photo)

A catalogue record for this book is available from the British Library.

A catalog record for this book is available from the Library of Congress.

ISBN: HB: 978-1-4742-7043-4
PB: 978-1-4742-7042-7
ePDF: 978-1-4742-7045-8
eBook: 978-1-4742-7044-1

Typeset by Deanta Global Publishing Services, Chennai, India
Printed and bound in India

To find out more about our authors and books visit www.bloomsbury.com and
sign up for our newsletters.

CONTENTS

Contents

ACKNOWLEDGEMENTS

The editors would like to thank Rob Yates and Woo Ree Heor for invaluable assistance in preparing the manuscript for publication, and to Dan Jacobson for crucial assistance with research at an earlier stage. We're also particularly grateful to Biodun Jeyifo for personal permission to reproduce his essay 'Tragedy, History and Ideology'. Exchanges with the following colleagues and friends have helped inform our understanding of the historical development of tragedy: Frances Babbage, Anna Barton, Joe Bray, Sam Durrant, Jane Plastow, Jonthan Rayner, Amber Regis, Cristiana Sogno, Will Stenhouse, Robert Stern, Gillian Woods, Angela Wright, and Andrew Van der Vlies. For crucial support with turning this material into a book, we are grateful to Mark Dudgeon, Lara Bateman, and Susan Furber at Bloomsbury.

NOTE ON THE TEXTS

The writings on tragedy gathered in this volume are reproduced from previous publications, with permission from the relevant copyright holders. (A number of selections have been omitted because of costs and/or restrictions on permissions.) For the most part, these texts appear here as they did in those editions, but we have added our own annotations to make the texts and their allusions more easily accessible for readers; when texts included their own annotations, we have also changed the numbering of the notes for clarity and simplicity. When references in original notes have been incomplete and/or abbreviated, we have silently expanded them. In order to distinguish between original notes and our own additions, we have labelled original authorial notes with the authors' names, for example 'Freud's note'; when translators have added their own annotations, we have labelled them 'translator's note'. Throughout this book, unlabelled notes represent our own additions. In the cases of early printed texts, such as those of Stephen Gosson, Philip Sidney, and Thomas Heywood, extracts here are taken from original editions but have been lightly modernized as well as annotated.

GENERAL INTRODUCTION

The painting reproduced on this book's cover presents one of tragedy's most iconic families. Antoni Brodowski's *Edyp i Antygona*, which now hangs in the National Museum in Warsaw, first appeared as a submission to an 1823 Polish painting competition where the myth of Oedipus and Antigone was one of the three specified themes.[1] Taking this scene from Sophocles' tragedy *Oedipus at Colonus*, Brodowski depicts Antigone and her blind father Oedipus wandering in exile outside of their former home in Thebes. The pair offers stark challenges to conventional models of family. Cursed for marrying his mother and killing his father, Oedipus undermines kinship roles and rules, just as Antigone, who is both his daughter and his sister, disrupts generational lines. Despite their uncomfortable breaks with family laws, they are bound and defined by their filial ties. As this painting shows, they enter their new banished state together, even as they seem to plot different responses to their banishment. Brodowski's Oedipus, figured as a serene and vigorous Stoic rather than a shambling, mutilated old man, is a hero who turns inward as he takes the air; he is supported by a daughter who seems less concerned for her father's well-being than in taking steps in a different direction, looking beyond the frame of the painting. In marked contrast to other entries to the competition, which variously show Antigone gazing directly at her father in pity, sympathy or love, Brodowski emphasizes Oedipus's heroic fortitude in the face of tragedy's disasters in dialogue with Antigone's own resolve, her ability to support her father while turning from him to face the encroaching darkness alone.[2] In having his subjects gaze in different directions, with different expressions, and towards different futures, Brodowski joins an ongoing conversation about tragedy. His painting becomes part of the tragedy's afterlife, and accordingly one of this family's many descendants.

We begin this book with an arresting and unfamiliar image of one of tragedy's most famous families in order to highlight the flexible and often unorthodox bonds that join people together both within tragedies and in the broader conversations that the genre has sparked. Aristotle declared that the best tragedies involve family (literally *oikos*, or household), and in particular feature a small number of families well known from myth (extract 1.2). His preferred households offer stories of extraordinary catastrophes, inherited and adapted from one generation to the next. Aristotle attributes these families' tragic power to their special capacity to rouse emotions, but they also illustrate the complex processes of transmission that have shaped the body of writings we know as tragedies. Just as families are marked by

---

[1]On Brodowski and the 1823 painting competition organized by the Polish Commission for Religious Denominations and Public Enlightenment see http://culture.pl/pl/tworca/antoni-brodowski; Elizabeth W. Scharffenberger, 'Oedipus at Colonus', in *Brill's Companion to the Reception of Sophocles*, ed. Rosanna Lauriola and Kyriaskos N. Demetrious (Leiden: Brill, 2017), 326–88, 354.
[2]Compare, for example, Brodowski's painting with Aleksander Kokular's submission to the same 1823 competition: http://cyfrowe.mnw.art.pl/dmuseion/docmetadata?id=5150&show_nav=true.

resemblances, reactions, and rebellions towards shared histories, the same is true of tragedies themselves. Makers of tragedy are haunted by the ghosts of earlier writers, subjects, characters, and plots, even when they pursue new directions. Similar patterns shape the enormous body of writings about tragedy. For as long as tragedies have been written, people have wondered about what they are, what they do, and the nature of their peculiar attractions. When they put their questions and responses into writing, they join a long-standing set of conversations. Like Brodowski, they become part of tragedy's afterlife, part of its expanded family.

The language of family has a long history of overlap with the vocabulary of literary categories. Literary kinds share etymological roots with kin; similarly, genres share roots with genus, genealogy, and genetics. These words are members of the same lexical family: rooted in the Anglo-Saxon *cynn*, kin and kind are the Germanic equivalents of the Latin *genus* and Greek *genos*, sharing roots in the Aryan *gen-*, 'to produce, engender, beget'. Like the related words 'gender', 'generation', 'genesis', and 'genes', the words 'kin', 'kind', 'genre', and 'genealogy' imply processes of production and reproduction, creation and procreation, with all their attendant pleasures, anxieties, and complexities.

This book presents a family tree of sorts, not of tragedies themselves, but of reflections on the genre of tragedy. At times responses to tragedies have taken the form of reimagining tragic figures and scenarios in original plays, operas, poems, novels, films, and works of visual art, such as Brodowski's painting. At other times they have taken the form of philosophical, critical, and theoretical writings, which are our focus here. These writings are often seen as accessories, tools for understanding tragedies, but they also form a literary tradition of their own, with their own internal continuities, shifts, alliances, tensions, and breaks. Although they form a very different genre from the plays they discuss, their shared themes and investments also bind them together into an extended literary family. In some cases, the same writers have contributed to both of these genres. Among those included in this volume, Giraldi Cinthio, Stephen Gosson, Thomas Heywood, Pierre Corneille, John Milton, John Dryden, Percy Shelley, Bertolt Brecht, William Butler Yeats, Athol Fugard, and Hélène Cixous have all written tragedies as well as critical reflections on the genre. Other writers represented here, such as Horace, Philip Sidney, Samuel Johnson, Voltaire, William Hazlitt, George Eliot, and Virginia Woolf, are known for their contributions to other literary genres, including lyric poetry, satire, and fiction. For many of them, ideas about tragedy have served not simply as responses to pre-existing entities, but also as engines for producing new and experimental versions of the genre. Similarly, while only some of the writers represented here have written tragedies, all of them have watched, read, and thought about tragedies. As a result, these writings represent one of tragedy's most complex and enduring features: its relationship with its audiences. The history of ideas about tragedy, then, forms a crucial part of the history of tragedy itself.

In the millennia since its earliest developments in ancient Athens, tragedy has spread from a small handful of poets and themes to encompass multiple authors, subjects, continents, and forms. Throughout its changes and expansions, however, it has drawn upon its primary identity as a theatrical form that portrays suffering, and involves audiences in the vicarious experience of another's pain. The sympathetic transmission of emotions at the genre's heart has haunted critics, many of whom have reflected on its strangeness. Why do audiences enjoy experiencing others' pain, and how do plays lure us into doing so? Many kinds of literature elicit imaginative identification, but tragedy's distinctive form – in which actors ventriloquize fictional characters' sufferings to listening audiences – enforces especially immediate forms of interpersonal contact. This formal structure often finds a mirror within the plays' story lines; characters respond to each other's suffering within the play, while audiences outside the play do the same, whether in similar or different ways.

Family relations offer a useful model for the mixture of proximity and separation that marks responses to tragedies both within plays and outside them. Observing that tragic incidents must take place between either enemies, those indifferent to each other, or intimates (*philoi*, those bound by affection), Aristotle insists that conflicts between intimates make for the most tragic plots, because of their greater potential for eliciting emotion (extract 1.2). Although *philoi* do not need to be family members, this premise – that suffering is especially wrenching when caused and/or witnessed by people closely tied to each other – resonates with his similar claim, mentioned above, that the best tragedies depict a small number of families. Aristotle is often seen as prescribing rules, but his account primarily documents the practice of the period's tragic playwrights. As he suggests, most ancient tragedies dramatized a few specific families from Greek legend: in particular, the house of Cadmus (featuring Oedipus, Jocasta, Antigone, and Creon), the house of Atreus (including Agamemnon, Clytemnestra, Iphigenia, Electra, and Orestes), and the house of Priam (with Hecuba, Hector, Paris, Cassandra, and Polyxena). Together, these three families feature in two-thirds of extant Greek tragedies.

The prominence of these particular families responds in part to relations between writers. The earliest extant tragedies are acutely self-conscious of their relationship both to previous tragedies and to the epic traditions that preceded them. The Athenian playwrights Euripides and Sophocles responded to their predecessor, Aeschylus, as well as to each other, and all three of these tragedians self-consciously drew on Homer and other early poets for subject matter, characters, and themes. Unlike the houses of Atreus and Priam, the house of Cadmus – the family depicted on this book's cover – was not part of the Trojan War, but the legend of Oedipus appears in both the *Iliad* and the *Odyssey*, as well as in Hesiod's *Works and Days*. Rooted in the epic tradition, Oedipus evokes the struggles of that genre's itinerant warrior-heroes, but his defiant daughter Antigone does not appear in these earlier texts. Part of a subsequent generation, she is firmly tied to the later and more domestic genre of Attic tragedy. Both she and her father/brother have become associated especially with Sophocles: most famously his *Oedipus Tyrannus* and *Antigone*, and secondarily *Oedipus at Colonus*. Yet their extended family sprawls across generations of tragic playwrights, featuring in Aeschylus' *Seven against Thebes*, Euripides' *Phoenician Women*, and many other plays from antiquity that are now lost. Since then, they have continued to appear in new plays over the centuries. Among many later versions, the Roman tragic playwright Seneca wrote an *Oedipus* (first century CE), as did John Dryden (1678), Voltaire (1718), Frank McGuinness (2008), and Luis Alfaro (2010). Antigone has similarly inspired plays by writers including Robert Garnier (1580), Jean Cocteau (1922), Jean Anouilh (1944), Bertolt Brecht (1948), Félix Morisseau-Leroy (1953), Luis Rafael Sánchez (1968), José Watanabe (2000), Lynn Nottage (2004), and Caridad Svich (2004), as well as numerous films, operas, translations, and adaptations.

Although the stories of Oedipus and Antigone culminate in their deaths, both characters remain eerily undead, reviving periodically in new plays and debates. This uncanny persistence, as well as the strangeness and intensity of their suffering, has attracted the attention of critics and theorists as well as playwrights. The two figures experience very different crises: Oedipus must accept responsibility for terrible things that he did unwittingly, while Antigone deliberately chooses to disobey the law of the *polis*, or city-state, in order to give her brother an honourable burial. Old and young, male and female, powerful and powerless, ignorant and self-aware, both find themselves caught in unresolvable conflicts. As such, they have animated a wide range of critical perspectives and conversations. Among the writings collected in this volume, one or both of these characters feature prominently in the selections by Aristotle (extract 1.2), Longinus (extract 1.4), René Rapin (extract 2.8), John Dryden (extract 2.9), G.W.F. Hegel (extract 4.6), George Eliot (extract 4.7), Sigmund Freud (extract 5.1), George Steiner (extract 5.7), René Girard (extract 6.1), Nicole Loraux (extract 6.5), and Judith Butler (extract 6.8), as well as in many influential accounts that we have not been able to include here.

Although these writers are drawn to the distinctive electricity generated by this particular tragic household, the different kinds of arguments they explore point more broadly to some of the primary territories charted out by critical approaches to tragedy. The emotional complexity embedded in family structures, as well as the ferocity of the sexual politics they inevitably encompass, has occupied psychoanalytic writers such as Freud and Lacan, and feminist critics such as Loraux and Butler. Yet tragedy's long-running focus on the household, or *oikos*, has implications far beyond the recognizably domestic areas of family, emotion, and eros. As the etymological root of both 'ecology' and 'economics', the *oikos* also represents the broader environmental context explored by ecocritical writers such as Joseph Meeker (extract 6.3), as well as the social and economic contexts probed by Marxist-inspired writers such as Bertolt Brecht (extract 5.5) and Augusto Boal (extract 6.2).

Because of its inevitable battles for power, moreover, the *oikos* also serves as microcosm for the *polis*, or city-state, especially when the household in question has a public status as the seat of a ruler. Tragedy's origins in emerging Athenian democracy linked the genre with political debates and consequences: Athenians proudly saw their new democratic system as a triumph over the threat of tyranny, and tragic playwrights routinely depicted the dangers and defeats of tyrants.[3] In his 1570 commentary on Aristotle's *Poetics*, Italian writer Lodovico Castelvetro went so far as to assert that tragedies and monarchies cannot coexist: 'for a king is very jealous of his royal condition, and is careful about putting before the humble and before individuals examples that may arouse and direct their spirits towards innovations and a change of rulers. On the contrary, because the king knows that the common people delight in and enjoy the evil fortunes of the great, they do not ever have tragedies produced in public.'[4] These backdrops have inspired theories of the genre focused on its political affinities and consequences, such as Raymond Williams' discussion of tragedy and revolution (extract 5.9), or Biodun Jeyifo's account of the historical underpinnings of postcolonial tragedy (extract 6.6). The public aftershocks of tragedies' struggling households suggest the multivalent meanings of families, not only for their intimate psychological domain, but also for the broader social, legal, political, and cosmic structures they inhabit, and for which they serve as microcosm.

As conversations about tragedy have grown, the issues and controversies they raise have evolved in response to other social, political, and intellectual developments. Early debates about the consequences of participating in fictional suffering have expanded into different questions

---

[3]On the relationship between Athenian politics and the development of tragedy, see David M. Carter, ed. *Why Athens?: A Reappraisal of Tragic Politics* (Oxford: Oxford University Press, 2011).
[4]Castelvetro, *On the Poetics*, trans. Allen H. Gilbert, in *Literary Criticism: Plato to Dryden*, ed. Allan H. Gilbert (New York: American Book Company, 1940), 305–57, 331.

about the genre's potential dangers and virtues, the abuses and repressions it contains, and the possibilities that it might express or occlude for resisting the will of the powerful. In the spirit of a family tree, we have organized the writings in this volume by generations, moving chronologically to trace a history of ideas about tragedy in response to other thinkers. At least as early as Aristotle's response to his teacher Plato, writers on tragedy have looked back to their predecessors, at times reverentially, at times defiantly, and frequently a mixture of the two. This history is neither comprehensive nor authoritative. Instead, we highlight some influential and provocative original voices, ones that have shaped conversations about the genre. Beginning with the earliest responses to tragedy in ancient Greece, Chapter 1 explores perspectives from classical antiquity and the Middle Ages. Subsequent chapters collect writings from the early modern period, the eighteenth century, the nineteenth century, twentieth century, and recent decades. Because these conversations are ongoing, the book will never be complete. We look forward to seeing this history continue to be rewritten.

CHAPTER 1
ANTIQUITY AND THE MIDDLE AGES

When charting the terrain of tragedy, all roads lead to Greece. Classical antiquity is not only the genre's point of origin; it has also remained the primary touchstone for defining, admiring, and condemning the tragic theatre's unsettling power. For many, tragedy will evoke plays such as Aeschylus' *Agamemnon*, Sophocles' *Oedipus the King*, or Euripides' *Medea*: dramas focused on a powerful protagonist whose life will be destroyed over the course of the action in large part because of his or her own actions. It might also call to mind forceful secondary characters who support or challenge the protagonist; gods who prove unpredictably vicious, indifferent, or instrumental; and a chorus of onlooking witnesses, at first bemused and then increasingly anxious and stricken. This pattern does not fit all Greek tragedies – among other things, as Aristotle observed, some in fact end happily – but it has achieved an indelible stamp on our collective imaginations. From the brief but striking moment of its Greek beginnings, tragedy developed its primary identity as a dramatic genre associated with anguish, error, and inevitability, all on a grand scale.

The earliest tragedies that have survived were written in Athens in the fifth century BCE, during a time of social and political transition. Amid the developing institutions of democracy, the city reflected on its evolving identity at the civic and religious festivals where tragedies were staged. As public, city-sponsored events, the plays responded to both of these contexts. Although tragedies did not directly dramatize current events, they explored political and philosophical questions through their depictions of the mythological past, and their recurring interest in the fall of proud rulers has been linked with Athenian democracy's hostility to tyrants.[1] The plays also reflect their identification with religious ritual in their attention to prophesies, sacrifices, and the dangerous omnipotence of the gods, whose irrational and incomprehensible power contrasts starkly with the powerlessness of the human world.[2] By depicting the catastrophes of ancient myth through the intimate frameworks of personal passions, crises, and retaliations, playwrights elicited identification with past imagined worlds, raising questions about ongoing struggles between the sexes and between the generations, and reminding audiences of the precariousness of their own domestic worlds.

One thing that Greek tragedies did not do was invent new stories. Although tragic playwrights adapted and tinkered, they took their material from a well-known stock of myths that audiences would have known. Many of their stories came from Homer, the revered figure

---

[1]See Paula Debnar, 'Fifth-Century Athenian History and Tragedy', in *A Companion to Greek Tragedy*, ed. Justina Gregory (Oxford: Blackwell, 2005), 1–22; David Carter, 'Was Attic Tragedy Democratic?' *Polis* 21, no. 1–2 (2004): 1–25; and Richard Seaford, 'Tragic Tyranny', in *Popular Tyranny: Sovereignty and Its Discontents in Ancient Greece*, ed. Kathryn Morgan (Austin: University of Texas Press, 2003), 95–115.
[2]See Christiane Sourvinou-Inwood, 'Greek Tragedy and Ritual', in *A Companion to Tragedy*, ed. Rebecca Bushnell (Oxford: Blackwell, 2005), 7–24; Scott Scullion, 'Tragedy and Religion: The Problem of Origins', in *A Companion to Greek Tragedy*, 23–37.

identified with epic poems on the Trojan War and its aftermath. Aeschylus, Sophocles, and Euripides all wrote tragedies about the legendary traumas of Troy, in which they responded directly to Homer as well as to each other; Aeschylus reportedly claimed that 'all of our tragedies are slices from Homer's great banquets'.[3] Even beyond this shared subject matter, early critics saw tragedy as building on epic's literary strategies. Plato noted with disapproval that Homer's epics, like tragedies, rely heavily on direct first-person speech and dialogue; he described Homer as the 'first teacher and leader' of tragedy, and referred to heroes from 'Homer or some other of the makers of tragedy', suggesting that they were in the same category (extract 1.1).[4] Aristotle similarly, though more approvingly, described Homer as the father of tragedy, and observed that his epics joined tragedy in depicting serious, heroic men entangled in struggles (extract 1.2).[5] Sung by skilled actors called rhapsodes, epic poems also offered a prototype for dramatic performances. Yet while Homer's stories played out against the vast backdrops of Trojan battlefields and Mediterranean seas, tragedies took a miniaturizing lens to focus on the *oikos*, or household, where they could dissect the fault lines that shaped and resulted from these mythic collisions. Contained within one act and the finite space of the stage, these plays were marked by compression, brevity, and intensity, serving as microcosms for the larger existential crises they illuminated.

Just as tragedies revolve around violent opposition, from very early on they sparked violent opposition as well.[6] Despite the genre's prestige and prominence in Athens, the earliest extant philosophical account of tragedy condemned it, arguing that plays should be banned for harming their listeners. In *The Republic* (*c*.380–360 BCE), Plato's Socrates described tragedy's emotional intensity as irresistibly pleasurable, but concluded that surrendering to it threatened the rational self-control necessary to a stable and just society. Writing a generation later, Plato's student Aristotle came to a nearly opposite stance, describing tragedy's pleasures as beneficial and instructive. In his *Poetics* (*c*.350–330 BCE), Aristotle agreed with his former teacher that tragedy aroused the passions, but argued that it could productively transform them. In particular, he argued that by producing pity and fear, tragedy could bring about a *catharsis* of these emotions, prompting centuries of debate over a term whose meanings could encompass purgation, purification, transformation, and more. In contrast to Plato's heated and lyrical attack, Aristotle adopted a characteristically methodological approach, anatomizing tragedy by breaking it down into what he saw as its essential parts, and analysing how each of these parts could contribute most fully to its *telos*, or goal. He observed that tragedy could take many forms, but claimed that to best elicit the pity and fear conducive to tragic pleasure and catharsis, it should depict a reversal of fortune from happiness to suffering, brought about by error rather than by accident or evil, and accompanied by a recognition or revelation. The protagonist who commits the error and experiences the resulting suffering should be ethically good enough to earn the audience's concern and empathy, but imperfect enough to bear some responsibility for the terrible events that unfold.

---

[3] Athenaeus, *The Deipnosophists*, trans. Charles Duke Yonge (London, 1853), 8.347C.
[4] *Republic*, 595C, 605C.
[5] *Poetics*, 1448b34.
[6] For an overview of early responses, see Stephen Halliwell, 'Learning from Suffering: Ancient Responses to Tragedy', in *A Companion to Greek Tragedy*, 394–412.

Despite their disagreements, Plato and Aristotle agreed that tragedy was defined especially by its status as *mimesis*, another multivalent Greek word that refers to imitation, representation, and fiction. Both thinkers were interested in the effects of allowing characters to speak directly in their own voices, drawing playwrights, actors, and audience members into their minds, and eliciting a potent form of identification. The experience of imaginative alignment with a fictional character would become one of tragedy's most compelling and contentious aspects. For Plato, identification endangers listeners, by invading our hard-earned rationality and restraint with another's experience of intolerable pain. For Aristotle, on the other hand, this participation in another's suffering is the crucial element necessary for the tragic pleasure and catharsis that make playgoing valuable. As additional writers began weighing in on the nature of tragedy, debates continued to centre on this imaginative identification and its attendant emotional intensity, as well as on the structural principles that might most effectively conjure its force.

Although Athenian tragedy was a local and historically specific phenomenon, it was preserved, revived, and performed throughout the Greek-speaking world and beyond. As the rival civilization of Rome began to develop its own tradition of tragedy, after a similar political transition from monarchy to republic, it turned to Greek models. Romans not only staged Greek tragedies, but also began writing their own tragedies in conversation with Greek originals.[7] The earliest known playwright to write tragedies in Latin, Livius Andronicus (*c*.284–*c*.205 BCE), was himself Greek, and began his literary career translating Greek texts into Latin. His plays, which have not survived, showcase Greek tragic subjects in their titles, which include *Achilles*, *Aegisthus*, and *Aiax*. The best known Roman tragic playwright, Seneca (*c*.4 BCE–65 CE), similarly looked to Greek tragic models in his plays, which include *Agamemnon*, *Oedipus*, *Medea*, *Hippolytus*, *Hercules*, and *The Trojan Women*. As theatrical traditions continued to develop, conventionally Greek tragic plays were joined by alternate tragic forms, such as pantomimes featuring dance, concerts featuring song, and solo aria performances.[8]

Just as Roman playwrights began their ventures into the genre by looking to the authority of Greek tragic traditions, Roman poets and philosophers did the same when reflecting on the nature of tragedy. In his *Ars Poetica* (Art of Poetry), the Roman poet Horace (65–8 BCE) turns to Greek authors, plays, and myths to illustrate how to write tragedies; less directly, he draws on Aristotle as a model in formulating a set of rules that tragedies should follow in order to be effective (extract 1.3). Horace describes emotional involvement as a constituent part of tragedy; he explains that playwrights should depict emotions onstage in order to move their audiences, since these emotions will spread contagiously to those who watch them. Although he does not advocate emotion for its own sake, he builds on Aristotle's idea that each genre has a proper *telos*, or goal, and that eliciting emotion is appropriate for tragedy. His emphasis on consistency, decorum, and rules contrasts strikingly with another critic of the Roman era, who also draws on Greek tragic examples but towards a very different end. The Greek author of *On the Sublime*, conventionally referred to as Longinus, argued that literary

---

[7]See Vassiliki Panoussi, 'Polis and Empire: Greek Tragedy in Rome', *A Companion to Greek Tragedy*, 413–27; Gesine Manuwald, *Roman Republican Theatre* (Cambridge: Cambridge University Press, 2011); and Ingo Gildenhard and Martin Revermann, ed. *Beyond the Fifth Century: Interactions with Greek Tragedy from the Fourth Century BCE to the Middle Ages* (Berlin and New York: de Gruyter, 2010).

[8]H.A. Kelly, 'Tragedy and the Performance of Tragedy in Late Roman Antiquity', *Traditio* 35 (1979): 21–44.

greatness requires violence and disorientation (extract 1.4). Although Longinus advises on how to construct lofty or sublime language, he insists that rules are meant to be broken. Citing poets whose work is correct, meticulous, and flawless, he points out that they are not the ones we remember: instead, it is the messy, inconsistent, sprawling writers whose powerful effects show literary genius. Tragedy is only one of the literary forms in which Longinus identifies sublimity, but tragic playwrights have an important place in his account. In his preference for boldly overwhelming audiences with awe rather than inspiring pity and fear, he suggests a very different sense of tragedy's goals than earlier writers.

After the heyday of Greek and Roman antiquity, evolving conversations about tragedy continued to revisit terms and questions established by Plato and Aristotle. Latin scholars of late antiquity, such as the fourth-century grammarians Diomedes, Donatus, and Evanthius, returned to classical models to explain tragedy's Greek origins and rules, with an eye both to structural principles and to the moral lessons that they saw the plays as illustrating (extract 1.5). In particular, these writers emphasized a particular understanding of Aristotle's recommendations. Eliding his discussions of tragic pleasure, dramatic performance, and the variety of possible plot structures, they came to link tragedy specifically with nobility and unhappy endings.[9] Later medieval approaches to the genre, by writers including Boethius, Boccaccio, Chaucer, and Lydgate, extended these emphases, applying the word 'tragedy' to narrative stories as well as drama, identifying it specifically with the fall of kings and princes, and shifting the cause of tragic suffering to Providence or Fortune rather than the protagonist's error. The idea of tragedy became simultaneously narrower, in the range of plots it could encompass, and more capacious, in that it could refer to terrible events more broadly rather than only staged performances.

Alongside evolving reconceptions of classical tragic models, the growing influence of Christianity raised new questions, subjects, and forms for the genre, shadowed by suspicions about the moral influence of pagan traditions. In particular, the religion introduced new variations on Plato's concerns about tragedy's effects on the soul. For early Christian authors such as Tertullian (c.155–c.240 CE) and Lactantius (c.250–c.325 CE), tragedy was a pagan relic redolent of idolatry, and its scandalous traffic in sins such as violence and lust threatened audiences' spiritual purity. The Christian theologian and philosopher Augustine (354–430 CE) revisited Plato's concerns about the danger of tragic emotions within this religious framework (extract 1.6). In repenting the sins he had committed before converting to Christianity, Augustine responded with a particular revulsion to his youthful passion for plays. Unlike some Christian moralists who condemned the theatre, he was not primarily concerned with the stage's erotic allure, or its glamourization of violent and destructive behaviour. Instead, he attacked the grief, pity, and misery he experienced on behalf of tragic characters. Although most would consider these emotional responses to be charitable and even Christian, their artificial construction and misdirection struck him as damning. Unlike Aristotle, Horace, or Longinus, he was not concerned about tragedies that are badly written or insufficiently affecting; instead, like Plato, he feared tragedy that is dangerously effective at conjuring passionate emotion.

---

[9]On late antique and medieval ideas of tragedy, see Henry Ansgar Kelly, *Ideas and Forms of Tragedy from Aristotle to the Middle Ages* (Cambridge: Cambridge University Press, 1993).

Just as the playwrights of classical antiquity established a lasting template for the genre of tragedy, the period's philosophers similarly established the foundation for later debates about tragedy, and their arguments are still surprisingly urgent even after thousands of years. Roman interest in Greek models inspired new plays and new theories, and Christian concerns introduced additional concerns that similarly continue to resonate. Throughout these conversations, the ethical status of imaginative identification with tragic speakers has remained a consistent source of both fascination and controversy. To those approaching these conversations for the first time, it might seem strange that the stakes should be so high. Why should Plato, writing about ideal civic structure, be disturbed enough by tragedy to ban its poets from his imagined state? Why should Aristotle feel compelled to make a public refutation of his teacher's conclusions? And of all the past sins for which he repented, why should Augustine have felt such an anguished guilt about his attendance at plays? Why, for that matter, have so many later writers reflecting on tragedy felt compelled to return to the earliest formulations of these debates, and why should we be still reading them now? All of these questions ultimately circle around the larger question of why tragedy has made such an indelible cultural mark, one that prompted potent responses in its earliest onlookers and still continues to occupy our thoughts. Just as the experience of watching tragedy draws us into identifying with its speakers, similarly the experience of reading Plato, Aristotle, and subsequent critics of tragedy pushes us to ask their questions ourselves, and to enter the still-unfolding conversation they began.

1.1 PLATO, *THE REPUBLIC* (C.380–360 BCE)

Plato (*c.*429–347 BCE) was an influential Greek philosopher who founded the Academy, a school for philosophy. He wrote philosophical dialogues, many of which featured a fictionalized version of his teacher, Socrates. *The Republic*, the most famous of his dialogues, presents an account of the ideal city-state, and reflects on the role of the arts in it. Plato's Socrates determines that although some arts may be allowed in this city, tragedy must be banned. Because it is fiction, tragedy encourages lies, which he ascribes to essentially all poetry. Tragedy is more dangerous than other literary forms, however, because it relies on direct representation (*mimesis*) – allowing characters to speak for themselves – rather than indirect narration. For Plato, this formal quality leads to tragedy's most unsettling feature: by inviting listeners to identify with passionate, suffering speakers, it encourages surrender to pleasurable emotional intensity, which undermines the rationality of the ideal city.

[Book Three.]

I don't understand what you mean by form, said Adeimantus.[10]

I must explain, then, said I. Let me put it in this way. Any story in prose or verse is always a setting forth of events, past, present, or future, isn't it?

Yes.

And that can be done either in pure narrative or by means of representation or in both ways.

I am still rather in the dark.

I seem to be a poor hand at explaining; I had better give a particular illustration.[11] You remember the beginning of the *Iliad*, which describes how Chryses[12] begged Agamemnon to release his daughter, and Agamemnon was angry, and Chryses called on his god to avenge the refusal on the Greeks. So far the poet speaks in his own person, but later on he speaks in the character of Chryses and tries to make us feel that the words come, not from Homer, but from an aged priest. Throughout the *Iliad* and *Odyssey*, the events are set forth in these two different forms. All the time, both in the speeches and in the narrative parts in between, he is telling his story; but where he is delivering a speech in character, he tries to make his manner resemble that of the person he has introduced as speaker. Any poet who does that by means of voice and gesture, is telling his story by way of dramatic representation; whereas, if he makes no such attempt to suppress his own personality, the events are set forth in simple narrative.

Now I understand.

Observe, then, that, if you omit the intervening narrative and leave only the dialogue, you get the opposite form.

Yes, I see; that occurs in tragedy, for instance.

---

[10]**Adeimantus:** one of Plato's brothers, presented as one of Socrates' primary interlocutors in the *Republic*.

[11]**[Translator's note]:** The explanation, necessitated by the ambiguity of the Greek *mimesis*, is shortened in the translation.

[12]**Chryses:** Trojan priest of Apollo in Homer's *Iliad*. After Agamemnon took his daughter Chryseis as a war prize, Chryses begged for her release, enlisting Apollo's help. Agamemnon's eventual replacement of Chryseis with Achilles' war prize Briseis prompted the rage of Achilles that begins the *Iliad*.

Exactly, said I. Now I think you see the distinction I failed to make clear. All story-telling, in prose or poetry, is in one of three forms. It may be wholly dramatic: tragedy, as you say, or comedy. Or the poet may narrate the events in his own person; perhaps the best example of that is the dithyramb.[13] Or again both methods may be used, as in epic and several other kinds of poetry.

Yes, he said, I see now what you meant.

Remember, too, I began by saying that, having done with the content, we had still to consider the form. I meant that we should have to decide whether to allow our poets to tell their story in dramatic form, wholly, or in part (and, if so, in what parts), or not at all.

You mean, I suspect, the question whether we shall admit tragedy and comedy into our commonwealth.

Perhaps, I replied, or the question may be wider still. I do not know yet; but we must go wherever the wind of the argument carries us.[14]

That is good advice.

Here then, Adeimantus, is a question for you to consider: Do we want our Guardians[15] to be capable of playing many parts? Perhaps the answer follows from our earlier principle that a man can only do one thing well; if he tries his hand at several, he will fail to make his mark in any of them. Does not that principle apply to acting? The same man cannot act many parts so well as he can act one.

No, he cannot.

Then he will hardly be able to pursue some worthy occupation and at the same time represent a variety of different characters. Even in the case of two forms of representation so closely allied as tragedy and comedy, the same poet cannot write both with equal success. Again, the recitation of epic poetry and acting on the stage are distinct professions; and even on the stage different actors perform in tragedy and comedy.

That is so.

And human talent, Adeimantus, seems to be split up into subdivisions even minuter than these; so that no man can successfully represent many different characters in the field of art or pursue a corresponding variety of occupations in real life.

Quite true.

If, then, we are to hold fast to our original principle that our Guardians shall be set free from all manual crafts to be the artificers of their country's freedom, with the perfect mastery which comes of working only at what conduces to that end, they ought not to play any other part in dramatic representation any more than in real life; but if they act, they should, from childhood upward, impersonate only the appropriate types of character, men who are brave, religious, self-controlled, generous. They are not to do anything mean or dishonourable; no more should they be practised in representing such behaviour, for fear of becoming infected with the reality. You must have noticed how the reproduction of another person's gestures or tones of voice or states of mind, if persisted in from youth up, grows into a habit which becomes second nature.

Yes, I have.

---

[13][**Translator's note**]: The most important type of lyric poetry in Plato's time.
[14][**Translator's note**]: In Chapter XXXV poetry and painting will in fact be criticized as 'representation' in a wider sense.
[15]**Guardians:** Plato's Socrates uses this term to designate the philosophers responsible for ruling the city.

So these charges of ours, who are to grow up into men of worth, will not be allowed to enact the part of a woman, old or young, railing against her husband, or boasting of a happiness which she imagines can rival the gods', or overwhelmed with grief and misfortune; much less a woman in love, or sick, or in labour; nor yet slaves of either sex, going about their menial work; nor men of a low type, behaving with cowardice and all the qualities contrary to those we mentioned, deriding one another and exchanging coarse abuse, whether drunk or sober, and otherwise using language and behaviour that are an offence against themselves as well as their neighbours; nor must they copy the words and actions of madmen. Knowledge they must have of baseness and insanity both in men and women, but not reproduce such behaviour in life or in art.

Quite true.

[…]

Suppose, then, that an individual clever enough to assume any character and give imitations of anything and everything should visit our country and offer to perform his compositions, we shall bow down before a being with such miraculous powers of giving pleasure; but we shall tell him that we are not allowed to have any such person in our commonwealth; we shall crown him with fillets of wool, anoint his head with myrrh, and conduct him to the borders of some other country. For our own benefit, we shall employ the poets and story-tellers of the more austere and less attractive type, who will reproduce only the manner of a person of high character and, in the substance of their discourse, conform to those rules we laid down when we began the education of our warriors.

[…]

Book Ten

And if, as we think, the part of us which is ready to act upon these reflections is the highest, that other part which impels us to dwell upon our sufferings and can never have enough of grieving over them is unreasonable, craven, and faint-hearted.

Yes.

Now this fretful temper gives scope for a great diversity of dramatic representation; whereas the calm and wise character in its unvarying constancy is not easy to represent, nor when represented is it readily understood, especially by a promiscuous gathering in a theatre, since it is foreign to their own habit of mind. Obviously, then, this steadfast disposition does not naturally attract the dramatic poet, and his skill is not designed to find favour with it. If he is to have a popular success, he must address himself to the fretful type with its rich variety of material for representation.

Obviously.

We have, then, a fair case against the poet and we may set him down as the counterpart of the painter, whom he resembles in two ways: his creations are poor things by the standard of truth and reality, and his appeal is not to the highest part of the soul, but to one which is equally inferior. So we shall be justified in not admitting him into a well-ordered commonwealth, because he stimulates and strengthens an element which threatens to undermine the reason. As a country may be given over into the power of its worst citizens while the better sort are ruined, so, we shall say, the dramatic poet sets up a vicious form of government in the individual soul: he gratifies that senseless part which cannot distinguish great and small, but regards the same things as now one, now the other; and he is an image-maker whose images are phantoms far removed from reality.

Quite true.

But, I continued, the heaviest count in our indictment is still to come. Dramatic poetry has a most formidable power of corrupting even men of high character, with a few exceptions.

Formidable indeed, if it can do that.

Let me put the case for you to judge. When we listen to some hero in Homer or on the tragic stage[16] moaning over his sorrows in a long tirade, or to a chorus beating their breasts as they chant a lament, you know how the best of us enjoy giving ourselves up to follow the performance with eager sympathy. The more a poet can move our feelings in this way, the better we think him. And yet when the sorrow is our own, we pride ourselves on being able to bear it quietly like a man, condemning the behaviour we admired in the theatre as womanish. Can it be right that the spectacle of a man behaving as one would scorn and blush to behave oneself should be admired and enjoyed, instead of filling us with disgust?

No, it really does not seem reasonable.

It does not, if you reflect that the poet ministers to the satisfaction of that very part of our nature whose instinctive hunger to have its fill of tears and lamentations is forcibly restrained in the case of our own misfortunes. Meanwhile the noblest part of us, insufficiently schooled by reason or habit, has relaxed its watch over these querulous feelings, with the excuse that the sufferings we are contemplating are not our own and it is no shame to us to admire and pity a man with some pretensions to a noble character, though his grief may be excessive. The enjoyment itself seems a clear gain, which we cannot bring ourselves to forfeit by disdaining the whole poem. Few, I believe, are capable of reflecting that to enter into another's feelings must have an effect on our own: the emotions of pity our sympathy has strengthened will not be easy to restrain when we are suffering ourselves.

That is very true.

Does not the same principle apply to humour as well as to pathos? You are doing the same thing if, in listening at a comic performance or in ordinary life to buffooneries which you would be ashamed to indulge in yourself, you thoroughly enjoy them instead of being disgusted with their ribaldry. There is in you an impulse to play the clown, which you have held in restraint from a reasonable fear of being set down as a buffoon; but now you have given it rein, and by encouraging its impudence at the theatre you may be unconsciously carried away into playing the comedian in your private life. Similar effects are produced by poetic representation of love and anger and all those desires and feelings of pleasure or pain which accompany our every action. It waters the growth of passions which should be allowed to wither away and sets them up in control, although the goodness and happiness of our lives depend on their being held in subjection.

I cannot but agree with you.

If so, Glaucon,[17] when you meet with admirers of Homer who tell you that he has been the educator of Hellas[18] and that on questions of human conduct and culture he deserves

---

[16]**Homer … stage:** Plato's Greek specifies 'Homer or some other of the tragedy-makers', implicitly identifying Homer as one of the writers of tragedy.

[17]**Glaucon:** Plato's older brother, presented in the dialogue as one of Socrates' primary interlocutors.

[18]**Hellas:** Greece.

to be constantly studied as a guide by whom to regulate your whole life, it is well to give a friendly hearing to such people, as entirely well-meaning according to their lights, and you may acknowledge Homer to be the first and greatest of the tragic poets; but you must be quite sure that we can admit into our commonwealth only the poetry which celebrates the praises of the gods and of good men. If you go further and admit the honeyed muse in epic or in lyric verse, then pleasure and pain will usurp the sovereignty of law and of the principles always recognized by common consent as the best.

Quite true.

So now, since we have recurred to the subject of poetry, let this be our defence: it stands to reason that we could not but banish such an influence from our commonwealth. But, lest poetry should convict us of being harsh and unmannerly, let us tell her further that there is a long-standing quarrel between poetry and philosophy. There are countless tokens of this old antagonism, such as the lines which speak of 'the cur which at his master yelps,' or 'one mighty in the vain talk of fools' or 'the throng of all-too-sapient heads,' or 'subtle thinkers all in rags.'[19] None the less, be it declared that, if the dramatic poetry whose end is to give pleasure can show good reason why it should exist in a well-governed society, we for our part should welcome it back, being ourselves conscious of its charm; only it would be a sin to betray what we believe to be the truth. You too, my friend, must have felt this charm, above all when poetry speaks through Homer's lips.

I have indeed.

It is fair, then, that before returning from exile poetry should publish her defence in lyric verse or some other measure; and I suppose we should allow her champions who love poetry but are not poets to plead for her in prose, that she is no mere source of pleasure but a benefit to society and to human life. We shall listen favourably; for we shall clearly be the gainers, if that can be proved.

Undoubtedly.

But if it cannot, then we must take a lesson from the lover who renounces at any cost a passion which he finds is doing him no good. The love for poetry of this kind, bred in us by our own much admired institutions, will make us kindly disposed to believe in her genuine worth; but so long as she cannot make good her defence we shall, as we listen, rehearse to ourselves the reasons we have just given, as a counter-charm to save us from relapsing into a passion which most people have never outgrown. We shall reiterate that such poetry has no serious claim to be valued as an apprehension of truth. One who lends an ear to it should rather beware of endangering the order established in his soul, and would do well to accept the view of poetry which we have expressed.

I entirely agree.

Yes, Glaucon; for much is at stake, more than most people suppose: it is a choice between becoming a good man or a bad; and poetry, no more than wealth or power or honours, should tempt us to be careless of justice and virtue.

Your argument has convinced me, as I think it would anyone else.

---

[19][**Translator's note**]: The source of these poetical attacks on philosophy is unknown. The earliest philosophers to denounce Homer and Hesiod had been Xenophanes and Heraclitus, about the beginning of the fifth century.

Further reading

Elizabeth Asmis, 'Plato on Poetic Creativity', in *The Cambridge Companion to Plato*, ed. R. Kraut (Cambridge: Cambridge University Press, 1992), 338–64.

Pierre Destrée, 'Poetry, Thumos and Pity in the *Republic*', in *Plato and the Poets*, ed. Pierre Destrée and Fritz-Gregor Herrmann (Leiden: Brill, 2011), 267–82.

Jessica Moss, 'What Is Imitative Poetry and Why Is It Bad?', in *The Cambridge Companion to Plato's Republic*, ed. G.R.F. Ferrari (Cambridge: Cambridge University Press, 2007), 415–44.

1.2 ARISTOTLE, *POETICS* (C.350–330 BCE)

Aristotle (384–322 BCE) was a Greek philosopher who studied with Plato and later served as tutor to Alexander the Great. A prolific and influential writer on a wide variety of philosophical, scientific, and political topics, Aristotle explains tragedy by dividing it into key parts – spectacle, character, plot, language, song, and thought – and analysing how each can best support the genre's functions. In contrast to Plato's claim that tragedy's power of conjuring painful emotions is the genre's most dangerous trait, Aristotle argues that arousing pity and fear is tragedy's central purpose, and that this emotional engagement is valuable not only because of its strange pleasures, but also because it can lead to a catharsis, a cleansing, purification, or purgation of these feelings. In order to achieve this goal, he explains, tragedies must follow certain structural rules. Although his pragmatic, confident tone suggests a straightforward and objective description, his account of the genre diverges sharply from the model developed by his teacher. His claims that tragedy is educational, and that the pleasure it produces is valuable, similarly oppose Plato's suspicion of poetry's appeal. A crucial touchstone for later discussions of tragedy, Aristotle can seem deceptively familiar, but repays close and repeated readings.

4.

It is clear that the general origin of poetry was due to two causes, each of them part of human nature. Imitation[20] is natural to man from childhood, one of his advantages over the lower animals being this, that he is the most imitative creature in the world, and learns at first by imitation. And it is also natural for all to delight in works of imitation. The truth of this second point is shown by experience: though the objects themselves may be painful to see, we delight to view the most realistic representations of them in art, the forms for example of the lowest animals and of dead bodies. The explanation is to be found in a further fact: to be learning something is the greatest of pleasures not only to the philosopher but also to the rest of mankind, however small their capacity for it; the reason of the delight in seeing the picture is that one is at the same time learning – gathering the meaning of things, e.g. that the man there is so-and-so;[21] for if one has not seen the thing before, one's pleasure will not be in the picture as an imitation of it, but will be due to the execution or colouring or some similar cause. Imitation, then, being natural to us – as also the sense of harmony and rhythm, the metres being obviously species of rhythms – it was through their original aptitude, and by a series of improvements for the most part gradual on their first efforts, that they created poetry out of their improvisations.

Poetry, however, soon broke up into two kinds according to the differences of character in the individual poets; for the graver among them would represent noble actions, and those of noble personages; and the meaner sort the actions of the ignoble. The latter class produced invectives[22] at first, just as others did hymns and panegyrics.[23] We know of no such poem by

---

[20]**Imitation:** the Greek word *mimesis* can refer to simple imitation as well as to all forms of representational art.
[21]**That ... so-and-so:** that is, identifying the subject of a portrait.
[22]**Invectives:** satirical attacks.
[23]**Panegyrics:** poems of praise.

any of the pre-Homeric poets, though there were probably many such writers among them; instances, however, may be found from Homer downwards, e.g. his *Margites*,[24] and the similar poems of others. In this poetry of invective its natural fitness brought an iambic metre[25] into use; hence our present term 'iambic', because it was the metre of their 'iambs' or invectives against one another.[26] The result was that the old poets became some of them writers of heroic and others of iambic verse. Homer's position, however, is peculiar: just as he was in the serious style the poet of poets, standing alone not only through the literary excellence, but also through the dramatic character of his imitations,[27] so too he was the first to outline for us the general forms of Comedy by producing not a dramatic invective, but a dramatic picture of the Ridiculous; his *Margites* in fact stands in the same relation to our comedies as the *Iliad* and *Odyssey* to our tragedies. As soon, however, as Tragedy and Comedy appeared in the field, those naturally drawn to the one line of poetry became writers of comedies instead of iambs, and those naturally drawn to the other, writers of tragedies instead of epics, because these new modes of art were grander and of more esteem than the old.

[...]

6.

Reserving hexameter poetry[28] and Comedy for consideration hereafter, let us proceed now to the discussion of Tragedy; before doing so, however, we must gather up the definition resulting from what has been said. A tragedy, then, is the imitation of an action that is serious and also, as having magnitude, complete in itself; in language with pleasurable accessories, each kind brought in separately in the parts of the work; in a dramatic, not in a narrative form; with incidents arousing pity and fear, wherewith to accomplish its catharsis of such emotions. Here by 'language with pleasurable accessories' I mean that with rhythm and harmony or song superadded; and by 'the kinds separately' I mean that some portions are worked out with verse only, and others in turn with song.

I. As they act the stories, it follows that in the first place the Spectacle (or stage-appearance of the actors) must be some part of the whole; and in the second Melody and Diction, these two being the means of their imitation. Here by 'Diction' I mean merely this, the composition of the verses; and by 'Melody', what is too completely understood to require explanation. But further: the subject represented also is an action; and the action involves agents, who must necessarily have their distinctive qualities both of character and thought, since it is from these that we ascribe certain qualities to their actions. There are in the natural order of things, therefore, two causes, Character and Thought, of their actions, and consequently of their success or failure in their lives. Now the action (that which was done) is represented in the play by the Fable or Plot. The Fable, in our present sense of the term, is simply this, the combination of the incidents, or things done in the story; whereas Character is what makes us ascribe certain moral qualities to the agents; and Thought is shown in all they say when proving a particular point or, it may be, enunciating a general truth. There are six parts consequently of every tragedy, as a whole, that is, of such or such quality, viz. a Fable or Plot, Characters, Diction, Thought, Spectacle and

---

[24]*Margites*: a lost mock-epic that Aristotle attributed to Homer.
[25]**Iambic metre**: an iamb is a metrical foot composed of two syllables, the first unstressed, the second stressed.
[26]**'iambs' … one another:** the Greek verb *iambizein* means to mock or lampoon.
[27]**Dramatic … imitations:** referring to the extensive direct speech, in contrast to indirect narrative, in Homer's epics.
[28]**Hexameter poetry:** i.e. epic, which was written in hexameter, verse lines composed of six metrical feet.

Melody; two of them arising from the means, one from the manner, and three from the objects of the dramatic imitation; and there is nothing else besides these six. Of these, its formative elements, then, not a few of the dramatists have made due use, as every play, one may say, admits of Spectacle, Character, Fable, Diction, Melody, and Thought.

II. The most important of the six is the combination of the incidents of the story.

Tragedy is essentially an imitation not of persons but of action and life, of happiness and misery. All human happiness or misery takes the form of action; the end for which we live is a certain kind of activity, not a quality. Character gives us qualities, but it is in our actions – what we do – that we are happy or the reverse. In a play accordingly they do not act in order to portray the Characters; they include the Characters for the sake of the action. So that it is the action in it, i.e. its Fable or Plot, that is the end and purpose of the tragedy; and the end is everywhere the chief thing. Besides this, a tragedy is impossible without action, but there may be one without Character. The tragedies of most of the moderns are characterless – a defect common among poets of all kinds, and with its counterpart in painting in Zeuxis[29] as compared with Polygnotus;[30] for whereas the latter is strong in character, the work of Zeuxis is devoid of it. And again: one may string together a series of characteristic speeches of the utmost finish as regards Diction and Thought, and yet fail to produce the true tragic effect; but one will have much better success with a tragedy which, however inferior in these respects, has a Plot, a combination of incidents, in it. And again: the most powerful elements of attraction in Tragedy, the Peripeties[31] and Discoveries, are parts of the Plot. A further proof is in the fact that beginners succeed earlier with the Diction and Characters than with the construction of a story; and the same may be said of nearly all the early dramatists. We maintain, therefore, that the first essential, the life and soul, so to speak, of Tragedy is the Plot; and that the Characters come second – compare the parallel in painting, where the most beautiful colours laid on without order will not give one the same pleasure as a simple black-and-white sketch of a portrait. We maintain that Tragedy is primarily an imitation of action, and that it is mainly for the sake of the action that it imitates the personal agents. Third comes the element of Thought, i.e. the power of saying whatever can be said, or what is appropriate to the occasion. This is what, in the speeches in Tragedy, falls under the arts of Politics and Rhetoric; for the older poets make their personages discourse like statesmen, and the moderns like rhetoricians. One must not confuse it with Character. Character in a play is that which reveals the moral purpose of the agents, i.e. the sort of thing they seek or avoid, where that is not obvious – hence there is no room for Character in a speech on a purely indifferent subject. Thought, on the other hand, is shown in all they say when proving or disproving some particular point, or enunciating some universal proposition. Fourth among the literary elements is the Diction of the personages, i.e. as before explained, the expression of their thoughts in words, which is practically the same thing with verse as with prose. As for the two remaining parts, the Melody is the greatest of the pleasurable accessories of Tragedy. The Spectacle, though an attraction, is the least artistic of all the parts, and has least to do with the art of poetry. The tragic effect is quite possible without

---

[29]**Zeuxis:** a fifth-century painter known for his realism.
[30]**Polygnotus:** also a fifth-century painter, born in Thasos but made an Athenian citizen in honour of his artistic skill and contributions to the city.
[31]**Peripeties:** reversals, from the Greek word *peripeteia*.

a public performance and actors; and besides, the getting-up of the Spectacle is more a matter for the costumier[32] than the poet.

7.

Having thus distinguished the parts, let us now consider the proper construction of the Fable or Plot, as that is at once the first and the most important thing in Tragedy. We have laid it down that a tragedy is an imitation of an action that is complete in itself, as a whole of some magnitude; for a whole may be of no magnitude to speak of. Now a whole is that which has beginning, middle, and end. A beginning is that which is not itself necessarily after anything else, and which has naturally something else after it; an end is that which is naturally after something itself, either as its necessary or usual consequent, and with nothing else after it; and a middle, that which is by nature after one thing and has also another after it. A well-constructed Plot, therefore, cannot either begin or end at any point one likes; beginning and end in it must be of the forms just described. Again: to be beautiful, a living creature, and every whole made up of parts, must not only present a certain order in its arrangement of parts, but also be of a certain definite magnitude. Beauty is a matter of size and order, and therefore impossible either (1) in a very minute creature, since our perception becomes indistinct as it approaches instantaneity; or (2) in a creature of vast size – one, say, 1,000 miles long – as in that case, instead of the object being seen all at once, the unity and wholeness of it is lost to the beholder.

Just in the same way, then, as a beautiful whole made up of parts, or a beautiful living creature, must be of some size, a size to be taken in by the eye, so a story or Plot must be of some length, but of a length to be taken in by the memory. As for the limit of its length, so far as that is relative to public performances and spectators, it does not fall within the theory of poetry. If they had to perform a hundred tragedies, they would be timed by water-clocks, as they are said to have been at one period. The limit, however, set by the actual nature of the thing is this: the longer the story, consistently with its being comprehensible as a whole, the finer it is by reason of its magnitude. As a rough general formula, 'a length which allows of the hero passing by a series of probable or necessary stages from misfortune to happiness, or from happiness to misfortune', may suffice as a limit for the magnitude of the story.

8.

The Unity of a Plot does not consist, as some suppose, in its having one man as its subject. An infinity of things befall that one man, some of which it is impossible to reduce to unity; and in like manner there are many actions of one man which cannot be made to form one action. One sees, therefore, the mistake of all the poets who have written a *Heracleid*, a *Theseid*,[33] or similar poems; they suppose that, because Heracles was one man, the story also of Heracles must be one story. Homer, however, evidently understood this point quite well, whether by art or instinct, just in the same way as he excels the rest in every other respect. In writing an *Odyssey*, he did not make the poem cover all that ever befell his hero – it befell him, for instance, to get wounded on Parnassus[34] and also to feign madness at the time of the call to arms, but the two

---

[32]**Costumier:** designer responsible especially for the performers' masks.
[33]*Heracleid ... Theseid:* epic poems based on the lives of Heracles and Theseus, respectively.
[34]**Parnassus:** mountain near Delphi, sacred to Apollo, and home of the Muses. Towards the end of the *Odyssey*, Odysseus recalls having been wounded there by a boar.

incidents had no probable or necessary connexion with one another – instead of doing that, he took an action with a Unity of the kind we are describing as the subject of the *Odyssey*, as also of the *Iliad*. The truth is that, just as in the other imitative arts one imitation is always of one thing, so in poetry the story, as an imitation of action, must represent one action, a complete whole, with its several incidents so closely connected that the transposal or withdrawal of any one of them will disjoin and dislocate the whole. For that which makes no perceptible difference by its presence or absence is no real part of the whole.

9.

From what we have said it will be seen that the poet's function is to describe, not the thing that has happened, but a kind of thing that might happen, i.e. what is possible as being probable or necessary. The distinction between historian and poet is not in the one writing prose and the other verse – you might put the work of Herodotus[35] into verse, and it would still be a species of history; it consists really in this, that the one describes the thing that has been, and the other a kind of thing that might be. Hence poetry is something more philosophic and of graver import than history, since its statements are of the nature rather of universals, whereas those of history are singulars. By a universal statement I mean one as to what such or such a kind of man will probably or necessarily say or do – which is the aim of poetry, though it affixes proper names to the characters; by a singular statement, one as to what, say, Alcibiades[36] did or had done to him. In Comedy this has become clear by this time; it is only when their plot is already made up of probable incidents that they give it a basis of proper names, choosing for the purpose any names that may occur to them, instead of writing like the old iambic poets about particular persons. In Tragedy, however, they still adhere to the historic names;[37] and for this reason: what convinces is the possible; now whereas we are not yet sure as to the possibility of that which has not happened, that which has happened is manifestly possible, else it would not have come to pass. Nevertheless even in Tragedy there are some plays with but one or two known names in them, the rest being inventions; and there are some without a single known name, e.g. Agathon's *Antheus*,[38] in which both incidents and names are of the poet's invention; and it is no less delightful on that account. So that one must not aim at a rigid adherence to the traditional stories on which tragedies are based. It would be absurd, in fact, to do so, as even the known stories are only known to a few, though they are a delight none the less to all.

It is evident from the above that, the poet must be more the poet of his stories[39] or Plots than of his verses, inasmuch as he is a poet by virtue of the imitative element in his work, and it is actions that he imitates. And if he should come to take a subject from actual history, he is none the less a poet for that; since some historic occurrences may very well be in the probable and possible order of things; and it is in that aspect of them that he is their poet.

Of simple Plots and actions the episodic are the worst. I call a Plot episodic when there is neither probability nor necessity in the sequence of episodes. Actions of this sort bad poets construct through their own fault, and good ones on account of the players. His work being for

---

[35]**Herodotus:** Greek historian (*c.*484–*c.*425 BCE) known as 'the father of history'.
[36]**Alcibiades:** prominent Athenian politician and general (*c.*450–404 BCE).
[37]**Historic names:** i.e. names from myth, which Aristotle identifies with history.
[38]**Agathon's *Antheus*:** Agathon (*c.*448–400 BCE) was an Athenian tragic playwright; his play *Antheus* (*The Flower*) has not survived.
[39]**Poet … stories:** the Greek word *poiētēs* means both poet and maker, two senses that Aristotle merges in this phrase.

public performance, a good poet often stretches out a Plot beyond its capabilities, and is thus obliged to twist the sequence of incident.

Tragedy, however, is an imitation not only of a complete action, but also of incidents arousing pity and fear. Such incidents have the very greatest effect on the mind when they occur unexpectedly and at the same time in consequence of one another; there is more of the marvellous in them then than if they happened of themselves or by mere chance. Even matters of chance seem most marvellous if there is an appearance of design as it were in them; as for instance the statue of Mitys at Argos killed the author of Mitys' death by falling down on him when a looker-on at a public spectacle;[40] for incidents like that we think to be not without a meaning. A Plot, therefore, of this sort is necessarily finer than others.

10.

Plots are either simple or complex, since the actions they represent are naturally of this twofold description. The action, proceeding in the way defined, as one continuous whole, I call simple, when the change in the hero's fortunes takes place without Peripety or Discovery; and complex, when it involves one or the other, or both. These should each of them arise out of the structure of the Plot itself, so as to be the consequence, necessary or probable, of the antecedents. There is a great difference between a thing happening *propter hoc* and *post hoc*.[41]

11.

A Peripety is the change from one state of things within the play to its opposite of the kind described, and that too in the way we are saying, in the probable or necessary sequence of events; as it is for instance in *Oedipus*: here the opposite state of things is produced by the Messenger, who, coming to gladden Oedipus and to remove his fears as to his mother, reveals the secret of his birth. And in *Lynceus*:[42] just as he is being led off for execution, with Danaus at his side to put him to death, the incidents preceding this bring it about that he is saved and Danaus put to death. A Discovery is, as the very word implies, a change from ignorance to knowledge, and thus to either love or hate, in the personages marked for good or evil fortune. The finest form of Discovery is one attended by Peripeties, like that which goes with the Discovery in *Oedipus*. There are no doubt other forms of it; what we have said may happen in a way in reference to inanimate things, even things of a very casual kind; and it is also possible to discover whether some one has done or not done something. But the form most directly connected with the Plot and the action of the piece is the first-mentioned. This, with a Peripety, will arouse either pity or fear – actions of that nature being what Tragedy is assumed to represent; and it will also serve to bring about the happy or unhappy ending. The Discovery, then, being of persons, it may be that of one party only to the other, the latter being already known; or both the parties may have to discover themselves. Iphigenia, for instance, was discovered to Orestes by sending the letter; and another Discovery was required to reveal him to Iphigenia.[43]

Two parts of the Plot, then, Peripety and Discovery, are on matters of this sort. A third part is Suffering; which we may define as an action of a destructive or painful nature, such

---

[40]**Mitys … spectacle:** this is the only record of this event.

[41]*propter hoc* and *post hoc*: because of the thing, and after the thing.

[42]*Lynceus*: Lynceus was king of Argos after Danaus; the play has not survived.

[43]**Orestes … Iphigenia:** this summary describes the plot of Euripides' *Iphigenia in Tauris* (*c*.414 BCE).

as murders on the stage, tortures, woundings, and the like. The other two have been already explained.

12.

The parts of Tragedy to be treated as formative elements in the whole were mentioned in a previous Chapter. From the point of view, however, of its quantity, i.e. the separate sections into which it is divided, a tragedy has the following parts: Prologue, Episode, Exode,[44] and a choral portion, distinguished into Parode[45] and Stasimon;[46] these two are common to all tragedies, whereas songs from the stage and Commoe are only found in some. The Prologue is all that precedes the Parode of the chorus; an Episode all that comes in between two whole choral songs; the Exode all that follows after the last choral song. In the choral portion the Parode is the whole first statement of the chorus; a Stasimon, a song of the chorus without anapaests or trochees; a Commas, a lamentation sung by chorus and actor in concert. The parts of Tragedy to be used as formative elements in the whole we have already mentioned; the above are its parts from the point of view of its quantity, or the separate sections into which it is divided.

13.

The next points after what we have said above will be these: (1) What is the poet to aim at, and what is he to avoid, in constructing his Plots? and (2) What are the conditions on which the tragic effect depends?

We assume that, for the finest form of Tragedy, the Plot must be not simple but complex; and further, that it must imitate actions arousing pity and fear, since that is the distinctive function of this kind of imitation. It follows, therefore, that there are three forms of Plot to be avoided. (1) A good man must not be seen passing from happiness to misery, or (2) a bad man from misery to happiness.

The first situation is not fear-inspiring or piteous, but simply odious to us. The second is the most untragic that can be; it has no one of the requisites of Tragedy; it does not appeal either to the human feeling in us, or to our pity, or to our fears. Nor, on the other hand, should (3) an extremely bad man be seen falling from happiness into misery. Such a story may arouse the human feeling in us, but it will not move us to either pity or fear; pity is occasioned by undeserved misfortune, and fear by that of one like ourselves; so that there will be nothing either piteous or fear-inspiring in the situation. There remains, then, the intermediate kind of personage, a man not pre-eminently virtuous and just, whose misfortune, however, is brought upon him not by vice and depravity but by some error of judgement, of the number of those in the enjoyment of great reputation and prosperity; e.g. Oedipus, Thyestes,[47] and the men of note of similar families. The perfect Plot, accordingly, must have a single, and not (as some tell us) a double issue; the change in the hero's fortunes must be not from misery to happiness, but on the contrary from happiness to misery; and the cause of it must lie not in any depravity, but in

---

[44]**Exode:** the final scene after the chorus leaves the stage.
[45]**Parode:** the song sung by the chorus as they enter.
[46]**Stasimon:** a song sung by the chorus while staying in place in the stage.
[47]**Thyestes:** in Greek myth, king of Olympia, son of Pelops and Hippodamia. A feud between him and his brother Atreus culminated with Atreus killing Thyestes' sons, baking them into a pie, and feeding them to him. The curse on their house shadowed Atreus' sons Agamemnon and Menelaus, as well as Thyestes' later son Aegisthus.

some great error[48] on his part; the man himself being either such as we have described, or better, not worse, than that. Fact also confirms our theory. Though the poets began by accepting any tragic story that came to hand, in these days the finest tragedies are always on the story of some few houses, on that of Alcmeon,[49] Oedipus, Orestes, Meleager,[50] Thyestes, Telephus,[51] or any others that may have been involved, as either agents or sufferers, in some deed of horror. The theoretically best tragedy, then, has a Plot of this description. The critics, therefore, are wrong who blame Euripides for taking this line in his tragedies, and giving many of them an unhappy ending. It is, as we have said, the right line to take. The best proof is this: on the stage, and in the public performances, such plays, properly worked out, are seen to be the most truly tragic; and Euripides, even if his execution be faulty in every other point, is seen to be nevertheless the most tragic certainly of the dramatists. After this comes the construction of Plot which some rank first, one with a double story (like the *Odyssey*) and an opposite issue for the good and the bad personages. It is ranked as first only through the weakness of the audiences; the poets merely follow their public, writing as its wishes dictate. But the pleasure here is not that of Tragedy. It belongs rather to Comedy, where the bitterest enemies in the piece (e.g. Orestes and Aegisthus[52]) walk off good friends at the end, with no slaying of any one by any one.

14.

The tragic fear and pity may be aroused by the Spectacle; but they may also be aroused by the very structure and incidents of the play – which is the better way and shows the better poet. The Plot in fact should be so framed that, even without seeing the things take place, he who simply hears the account of them shall be filled with horror and pity at the incidents; which is just the effect that the mere recital of the story in *Oedipus* would have on one. To produce this same effect by means of the Spectacle is less artistic, and requires extraneous aid. Those, however, who make use of the Spectacle to put before us that which is merely monstrous and not productive of fear, are wholly out of touch with Tragedy; not every kind of pleasure should be required of a tragedy, but only its own proper pleasure.

The tragic pleasure is that of pity and fear, and the poet has to produce it by a work of imitation; it is clear, therefore, that the causes should be included in the incidents of his story. Let us see, then, what kinds of incident strike one as horrible, or rather as piteous. In a deed of this description the parties must necessarily be either friends,[53] or enemies, or indifferent to one

---

[48]**Error:** the Greek word *hamartia*, which means missing the mark, is an important part of Aristotle's theory of tragedy, and receives much discussion from later commentators.

[49]**Alcmeon:** in Greek myth, son of Amphiaraus and Eriphyle. After Amphiaraus died in a battle against Thebes to which he was prompted by Eriphyle, Alcmeon led the Argives in attacking Thebes in retaliation. He then killed his mother in revenge for her betrayal, and was subsequently set upon by Furies and driven mad.

[50]**Meleager:** in Greek myth, son of Althea and Oeneus. When he was born, his mother was told that he would die when a log in their hearth was consumed by fire. She removed it from the fire to preserve his life, but eventually killed him by burning it after he killed her brother and his own brother in a fight over the huntress Atalanta.

[51]**Telephus:** son of Heracles and Auge, he was exposed on a mountain as an infant after an oracle said he would kill his uncles. He survived, eventually became king of Mysia, was wounded by Achilles when the Greeks accidentally landed there on their way to Troy, and later sought out Achilles after learning from an oracle that he could only be cured by the person who wounded him.

[52]**Aegisthus:** the son of Thyestes, and cousin of Agamemnon, he become the lover of Agamemnon's wife Clytemnestra while Agamemnon was fighting in Troy. Upon Agamemnon's return, Aegisthus helped Clytemnestra murder her husband, and was subsequently killed by Agamemnon's son Orestes in revenge.

[53]**Friends:** the Greek word *philoi* refers to people bound by strong ties, including family, which Aristotle goes on to

another. Now when enemy does it on enemy, there is nothing to move us to pity either in his doing or in his meditating the deed, except so far as the actual pain of the sufferer is concerned; and the same is true when the parties are indifferent to one another. Whenever the tragic deed, however, is done within the family – when murder or the like is done or meditated by brother on brother, by son on father, by mother on son, or son on mother – these are the situations the poet should seek after. The traditional stories, accordingly, must be kept as they are, e.g. the murder of Clytaemnestra by Orestes and of Eriphyle by Alcmeon.[54] At the same time even with these there is something left to the poet himself; it is for him to devise the right way of treating them. Let us explain more clearly what we mean by 'the right way'. The deed of horror may be done by the doer knowingly and consciously, as in the old poets, and in Medea's murder of her children in Euripides.[55] Or he may do it, but in ignorance of his relationship, and discover that afterwards, as does the *Oedipus* in Sophocles.[56] Here the deed is outside the play; but it may be within it, like the act of the Alcmeon in Astydamas,[57] or that of the Telegonus in *Ulysses Wounded*.[58] A third possibility is for one meditating some deadly injury to another, in ignorance of his relationship, to make the discovery in time to draw back. These exhaust the possibilities, since the deed must necessarily be either done or not done, and either knowingly or unknowingly.

The worst situation is when the personage is with full knowledge on the point of doing the deed, and leaves it undone. It is odious and also (through the absence of suffering) untragic; hence it is that no one is made to act thus except in some few instances, e.g. Haemon and Creon in *Antigone*.[59] Next after this comes the actual perpetration of the deed meditated.[60] A better situation than that, however, is for the deed to be done in ignorance, and the relationship discovered afterwards, since there is nothing odious in it, and the Discovery will serve to astound us. But the best of all is the last; what we have in *Cresphontes*, for example, where Merope, on the point of slaying her son, recognizes him in time;[61] in *Iphigenia*, where sister and brother are in a like position;[62] and in *Helle*, where the son recognizes his mother,[63] when on the point of giving her up to her enemy.

---

emphasize in upcoming examples.

[54]**Clytaemnestra … Alcmeon:** two murders of mothers by their sons; see notes above.

[55]**Medea's … Euripides:** Euripides' *Medea* (431 BCE) features Medea's murder of her sons in revenge against her husband Jason's betrayal of her.

[56]**Oedipus … Sophocles:** in Sophocles' play, as in the legend, Oedipus has killed his father Laius, and married his mother Jocasta, without realizing who either was.

[57]**Alcmeon … Astydamas:** there were two tragic poets named Astydamas, both in the fourth century BCE; the younger one, cited here, was one of the most successful poets of his day, winning numerous victories. His *Alcmaeon* survives only in a fragment.

[58]**Telegonus … Wounded:** alternate title of a play by Sophocles, *Odysseus Akanthoplex*, that has survived only in fragments. In it, Odysseus has a son by Circe, Telegonus, who unwittingly kills his father in combat.

[59]**Haemon … Antigone:** towards the end of Sophocles' *Antigone* (c.441 BCE), a messenger describes Haemon, Antigone's betrothed, attempting to stab his father Creon before missing him and instead killing himself.

[60]**Perpetration … meditated:** that is, in full knowledge.

[61]**Cresphontes … time:** in Euripides' lost play by this name, Cresphontes presents himself to his father's murderer under pretence of being his own killer, in order to avenge his father's death. His mother, Merope, recognizes him when she is on the verge of killing him in his sleep.

[62]**Iphigenia … position:** in Euripides' *Iphigenia in Tauris* (c.414 BCE), the priestess Iphigenia is about to have Orestes killed before she realizes he is her brother.

[63]**Helle … mother:** in Greek myth, Helle and her twin brother Phrixus were rescued from being murdered by their stepmother Ino when their mother Nephele sent a golden ram. Helle fell into the Hellespont, named after her, while Phrixus survived, preserving the ram's fleece, which became the Golden Fleece sought by Jason and the Argonauts. The play has not survived.

This will explain why our tragedies are restricted (as we said just now) to such a small number of families. It was accident rather than art that led the poets in quest of subjects to embody this kind of incident in their Plots. They are still obliged, accordingly, to have recourse to the families in which such horrors have occurred.

On the construction of the Plot, and the kind of Plot required for Tragedy, enough has now been said.

15.

In the Characters there are four points to aim at. First and foremost, that they shall be good. There will be an element of character in the play, if (as has been observed) what a personage says or does reveals a certain moral purpose; and a good element of character, if the purpose so revealed is good. Such goodness is possible in every type of personage, even in a woman or a slave, though the one is perhaps an inferior, and the other a wholly worthless being. The second point is to make them appropriate. The Character before us may be, say, manly; but it is not appropriate in a female Character to be manly, or clever. The third is to make them like the reality, which is not the same as their being good and appropriate, in our sense of the term. The fourth is to make them consistent and the same throughout; even if inconsistency be part of the man before one for imitation as presenting that form of character, he should still be consistently inconsistent. We have an instance of baseness of character, not required for the story, in the Menelaus in *Orestes*;[64] of the incongruous and unbefitting in the lamentation of Ulysses in *Scylla*,[65] and in the (clever) speech of Melanippe;[66] and of inconsistency in *Iphigenia at Aulis*, where Iphigenia the suppliant is utterly unlike the later Iphigenia.[67] The right thing, however, is in the Characters just as in the incidents of the play to endeavour always after the necessary or the probable; so that whenever such-and-such a personage says or does such-and-such a thing, it shall be the probable or necessary outcome of his character; and whenever this incident follows on that, it shall be either the necessary or the probable consequence of it. From this one sees (to digress for a moment) that the Denouement also should arise out of the plot itself, and not depend on a stage-artifice, as in *Medea*,[68] or in the story of the (arrested) departure of the Greeks in the *Iliad*.[69] The artifice must be reserved for matters outside the play – for past events beyond human knowledge, or events yet to come, which require to be foretold or announced; since it is the privilege of the Gods to know everything. There should

---

[64]**Menelaus in *Orestes*:** in Euripides' *Orestes* (408 BCE), Menelaus (the brother of Agamemnon and uncle of Orestes) refuses to help Orestes based on political calculations about his standing among his allies, leading Orestes to declare him the worst of men.

[65]**Ulysses in *Scylla*:** Scylla was a sea monster known from Homer's *Odyssey*, when Odysseus has to navigate a narrow strait between her and another sea monster, Charybdis. Aristotle refers here to Odysseus' laments in a dithyramb by the poet Timotheus.

[66]**Melanippe:** Euripides wrote two tragedies, both of which survive only in fragments, about Melanippe, the daughter of Aeolus and Hippe, and granddaughter of the centaur Chiron. Aristotle refers to *Melanippe the Wise*, in which Melanippe, after being seduced by Poseidon and giving birth to twins, persuades her father not to kill the twins through a philosophical argument that Aristotle criticizes as overly sophisticated for her character.

[67]**Inconsistency ... Iphigenia:** in Euripides' *Iphigenia in Aulis* (405 BCE), Iphigenia is at first fearful of dying and pleads to live, but then changes her mind and announces that she will give herself voluntarily as a sacrifice.

[68]**Stage-artifice ... *Medea*:** at the end of Euripides' *Medea*, Medea escapes by means of a chariot above the stage, like a *deus ex machina*.

[69]**Departure ... *Iliad*:** in Book Two of the *Iliad*, the goddess Athena confronts Odysseys and stops the Greeks from leaving Troy.

be nothing improbable among the actual incidents. If it be unavoidable, however, it should be outside the tragedy, like the improbability in the *Oedipus* of Sophocles. But to return to the Characters. As Tragedy is an imitation of personages better than the ordinary man, we in our way should follow the example of good portrait-painters, who reproduce the distinctive features of a man, and at the same time, without losing the likeness, make him handsomer than he is. The poet in like manner, in portraying men quick or slow to anger, or with similar infirmities of character, must know how to represent them as such, and at the same time as good men, as Agathon and Homer have represented Achilles.

All these rules one must keep in mind throughout, and further, those also for such points of stage-effect as directly depend on the art of the poet, since in these too one may often make mistakes. Enough, however, has been said on the subject in one of our published writings.

Further reading

Elizabeth Belfiore, 'Pleasure, Tragedy and Aristotelian psychology', *The Classical Quarterly* 35, no. 2 (1985): 349–61.

Stephen Halliwell, 'Pleasure, Understanding, and Emotion in Aristotle's *Poetics*', in *Essays on Aristotle's Poetics*, ed. Amélie Oksenberg Rorty (Princeton: Princeton University Press, 1992), 315–40.

David Wiles, 'Aristotle's *Poetics* and Ancient Dramatic Theory', in *The Cambridge Companion to Greek and Roman Theatre*, ed. Marianne McDonald and J. Michael Walton (Cambridge: Cambridge University Press, 2007).

1.3 HORACE, *THE ART OF POETRY* (C.10 BCE)

Unlike the two previous treatises, both prose works by philosophers, the *Ars Poetica* (Art of Poetry) is a poem, written by a poet reflecting on best practices in his craft. Horace (65–8 BCE) was a prominent lyric poet in Augustan Rome, during the uneasy transition from a republic to an empire. He wrote the *Ars Poetica* (*c.*10 BCE) as a verse letter to a Roman senator, Lucius Calpurnius Piso, and his two sons. The poem does not focus exclusively on tragedy, but tragedy features prominently in its discussion of the rules, styles, and subject matters appropriate to poetic genres. Like Aristotle, Horace argues that poetry should be both pleasurable and educational. Towards this end, he prescribes specific rules to achieve the correct effect and decorum. In his emphasis on appropriateness and consistency, Horace advises his readers not only on how to write poetry, but also more broadly on how to conduct and present oneself in the theatre of Roman politics and society.

The Art of Poetry

Why hail me poet, if I fail to seize
The shades of style, its fixed proprieties?
Why should false shame compel me to endure
An ignorance which common pains would cure?

A comic subject steadily declines
To be related in high tragic lines.
The Thyestean feast[70] no less disdains
The vulgar vehicle of comic strains.
Each has its place allotted; each is bound
To keep it, nor invade its neighbour's ground.
Yet Comedy sometimes will raise her note:
See Chremes,[71] how he swells his angry throat!
And when a tragic hero tells his woes,
The terms he chooses are akin to prose.
Peleus or Telephus,[72] suppose him poor

---

[70]**Thyestean feast:** in Greek myth, a feud between Thyestes and his brother Atreus culminated with Atreus killing Thyestes' sons, baking them into a pie, and feeding them to him. Horace invokes this horror to emphasize the impossibility of treating tragic material in comic form.

[71]**Chremes:** a character in the comedy *The Self-Tormentor* (*c.*163 BCE), by Roman comic playwright Terence.

[72]**Peleus or Telephus:** in Greek myth, Peleus married the sea nymph Thetis, and was father to the hero Achilles. Telephus, king of Mysia, son of Heracles and Auge, was wounded by Achilles when the Greeks accidentally landed there on their way to Troy, and later sought out Achilles after learning from an oracle that he could only be cured by the person who wounded him. Both represent the material of tragedy.

Or driven to exile, talks in tropes no more;
His yard-long words desert him, when he tries
To draw forth tears from sympathetic eyes.

Mere grace is not enough: a play should thrill
The hearer's soul, and move it at its will.
Smiles are contagious; so are tears;[73] to see
Another sobbing, brings a sob from me.
No, no, good Peleus; set the example, pray,
And weep yourself; then weep perhaps I may:
But if no sorrow in your speech appear,
I nod or laugh; I cannot squeeze a tear.
Words follow looks: wry faces are expressed
By wailing, scowls by bluster, smiles by jest,
Grave airs by saws,[74] and so of all the rest.
For nature forms our spirits to receive
Each bent that outward circumstance can give:
She kindles pleasure, bids resentment glow,
Or bows the soul to earth in hopeless woe;
Then, as the tide of feeling waxes strong,
She vents it through her conduit-pipe, the tongue.
Unless the speaker's words and fortune suit,
All Rome will join to jeer him, horse and foot.
Gods should not talk like heroes, nor again
Impetuous youth like grave and reverend men;
Lady and nurse a different language crave,
Sons of the soil and rovers o'er the wave;
Assyrian, Colchian, Theban, Argive,[75] each
Has his own style, his proper cast of speech.

Or study keeping in the type you frame:
If great Achilles[76] figure in the scene,
Make him impatient, fiery, ruthless, keen;
All laws, all covenants let him still disown,
And test his quarrel by the sword alone.
Still be Medea[77] all revenge and scorn,

---

[73]**Smiles … tears:** the idea that emotions can be transferred from speaker to audience is central to Horace's theory of tragedy's effectiveness.

[74] **Saws:** that is, "sawing" the air with one's hands, indicating melodramatic stage gesture.

[75]**Assyrian, Colchian, Theban, Argive:** according to conventions of antiquity, those from Assyria and Colchis would both be barbarians, with Assyrians expected to be effeminate, while those from Colchis would be bolder. Thebans would evoke tyranny, while Argives should be heroic and reserved.

[76]**Achilles:** as the fiercest warrior of the Trojan War, the hero Achilles was known for his rage and pride.

[77]**Medea:** from her depiction in Euripides' tragedy, Medea was known for taking revenge on her husband Jason, who abandoned her to marry another woman, by killing their children.

Ino[78] still sad, Ixion[79] still forsworn,
Io[80] a wanderer still, Orestes[81] still forlorn.

[…]

Thespis[82] began the drama: rumour says
In travelling carts[83] he carried round his plays,
Where actors, smeared with lees,[84] before the throng
Performed their parts with gesture and with song.
Then Aeschylus[85] brought in the mask and pall,
Put buskins[86] on his men to make them tall,
Turned boards into a platform, not too great,
And taught high monologue and grand debate.
The elder Comedy had next its turn,
Nor small the glory it contrived to earn:
But freedom passed into unbridled spite,
And law was soon invoked to set things right:
Law spoke: the chorus lost the power to sting,
And (shame to say) thenceforth refused to sing.

[…]

A bard will wish to profit or to please,
Or, as a tertium quid,[87] do both of these.
Whene'er you lecture, be concise: the soul
Takes in short maxims, and retains them whole:
But pour in water when the vessel's filled,
It simply dribbles over and is spilled.

Keep near to truth in a fictitious piece,
Nor treat belief as matter of caprice.

---

[78]**Ino:** in Greek myth, Ino was daughter of Cadmus and Harmonia, and queen of Thebes. She attempted to kill her stepchildren, Phrixus and Helle, who were rescued by a golden ram sent by their mother Nephele. By helping to raise the god Dionysus, child of her sister Semele by Zeus, she incurred the jealousy of Hera, who punished her by maddening her husband Athamas, resulting in his murder of their sons.

[79]**Ixion:** in Greek myth, Ixion went mad after murdering his father-in-law in response to a feud. Although Zeus took pity on him and brought him to Olympus, Ixion abused his hospitality by trying to seduce Zeus's wife Hera, after which he was expelled from Olympus and bound to a burning wheel for eternity.

[80]**Io:** a priestess of Hera, with whom Zeus fell in love; she was turned into a cow and followed by a stinging gadfly sent by Hera, forcing her to wander the world until she was eventually rescued and restored to human form by Zeus.

[81]**Orestes:** the son of Agamemnon and Clytemnestra, he killed his mother in revenge for her murder of his father, after which he was maddened and pursued by Furies.

[82]**Thespis:** known as the first actor (sixth century BCE), representing tragedy.

[83]**Travelling carts:** Thespis was believed to have traveled to perform in different cities, carrying his masks and props in horse-drawn wagons.

[84]**Smeared with lees:** in the comedy *Acharnians* (425 BCE), Aristophanes coined the term *trugodia* – comedy, or mock-tragedy – which he linked etymologically with *trux*, or wine-lees.

[85]**Aeschylus:** Greek tragic playwright (*c.*525–*c.*455 BCE) often called the father of tragedy.

[86]**Buskins:** high-laced boots identified with Greek tragic actors.

[87]**Tertium quid:** a third thing (Latin).

If on a child you make a vampire sup,
It must not be alive when she's ripped up.
Dry seniors scout an uninstructive strain;
Young lordlings treat grave verse with tall disdain:
But he who, mixing grave and gay, can teach
And yet give pleasure, gains a vote from each:
His works enrich the vendor, cross the sea,
And hand the author down to late posterity.

[…]

Orpheus,[88] the priest and harper, pure and good,
Weaned savage tribes from deeds and feasts of blood,
Whence he was said to tame the monsters of the wood.
Amphion[89] too, men said, at his desire
Moved massy stones, obedient to the lyre,
And Thebes arose. 'Twas wisdom's province then
To judge 'twixt states and subjects, gods and men,
Check vagrant lust, give rules to wedded folk,
Build cities up, and grave a code in oak.
So came great honour and abundant praise,
As to the gods, to poets and their lays.
Then Homer and Tyrtaeus,[90] armed with song,
Made manly spirits for the combat strong:
Verse taught life's duties, showed the future clear,
And won a monarch's favour through his ear:
Verse gave relief from labour, and supplied
Light mirth for holiday and festal tide.
Then blush not for the lyre: Apollo sings
In unison with her who sweeps its strings.

But here occurs a question some men start,
If good verse comes from nature or from art.
For me, I cannot see how native wit
Can e'er dispense with art, or art with it.
Set them to pull together, they're agreed,
And each supplies what each is found to need.

---

[88]**Orpheus:** famous musician of Greek myth, known for mesmerizing audiences, and for his attempt to rescue his wife Eurydice from the underworld.
[89]**Amphion:** another musician of Greek myth, known for building the walls around Thebes by playing music to the stones.
[90]**Homer and Tyrtaeus:** Homer is known for the epic poems the *Iliad* and the *Odyssey*; Tyrtaeus was a Greek lyric poet from Sparta.

Further reading

Andrew Laird, 'The *Ars Poetica*', in *The Cambridge Companion to Horace*, ed. Stephen Harrison (Cambridge: Cambridge University Press, 2007), 132–43.

Ellen Oliensis, 'The Art of Self-Fashioning in the *Ars Poetica*', in *Horace and the Rhetoric of Authority* (Cambridge: Cambridge University Press, 1998), 198–223.

Tobias Reinhardt, 'The *Ars Poetica*', in *Brill's Companion to Horace*, ed. Hans-Christian Günther (Leiden: Brill, 2013), 499–526.

1.4 LONGINUS, *ON THE SUBLIME* (C.50–70 CE)

Although the author of *On the Sublime* is unknown, he is conventionally referred to as Longinus or Pseudo-Longinus. The name persists because of an early identification with Cassius Longinus (third century CE), although this attribution has been generally discredited, as scholars now typically date the text to the first century CE. The treatise's Greek title, *Peri Hypsous*, literally means 'On Height'; it explores literary pursuit of sublime height or grandeur, described as a violent force that captivates, enthrals, and subjugates audiences. Although tragedy is not the only vehicle for the sublime, it is an important one, and Longinus draws heavily on tragic playwrights for examples of literary sublimity. The treatise's celebration of poetry's wild and unruly possibilities distinguishes it sharply from the structural and tonal rules praised by Aristotle and Horace. Like Plato, Longinus identifies tragic power with violence, irrationality, and ecstasy; unlike Plato, he praises these effects as triumphant achievements to be sought, rather than moral failures to be avoided. His account of the sublime came to exert a powerful influence on some later theorists of tragedy, including Edmund Burke (extract 3.5) and Friedrich Nietzsche (extract 4.8).

VIII

There are, it may be said, five principal sources of elevated language. Beneath these five varieties there lies, as though it were a common foundation, the gift of discourse, which is indispensable. First and most important is the power of forming great conceptions, as we have elsewhere explained in our remarks on Xenophon.[91] Secondly, there is vehement and inspired passion. These two components of the sublime are for the most part innate. Those which remain are partly the product of art. The due formation of figures deals with two sorts of figures, first those of thought and secondly those of expression. Next there is noble diction, which in turn comprises choice of words, and use of metaphors, and elaboration of language. The fifth cause of elevation – one which is the fitting conclusion of all that have preceded it – is dignified and elevated composition. Come now, let us consider what is involved in each of these varieties, with this one remark by way of preface, that Caecilius[92] has omitted some of the five divisions, for example, that of passion. 2. Surely he is quite mistaken if he does so on the ground that these two, sublimity and passion, are a unity, and if it seems to him that they are by nature one and inseparable. For some passions are found which are far removed from sublimity and are of a low order, such as pity, grief and fear; and on the other hand there are many examples of the sublime which are independent of passion, such as the daring words of Homer with regard to the Aloadae,[93] to take one out of numberless instances,

---

[91]**Xenophon:** ancient Greek philosopher and student of Socrates (*c.*430–354 BCE); Longinus's remarks on him have been lost.
[92]**Caecilius:** Caecilius of Caleacte in Sicily was a Greek rhetorician in Rome during the reign of Augustus (27 BCE–14CE); he wrote a lost treatise on the sublime.
[93]**Aloadae:** in Greek myth, the giants Otus and Ephialtes, Poseidon's sons with Iphimedia, wife of Aloeus; fired by pride, they tried to attack Mount Olympus, the seat of the gods, but ended up destroying each other.

Yea, Ossa in fury they strove to upheave on Olympus on high,
With forest-clad Pelion above, that thence they might step to the sky.[94]

And so of the words which follow with still greater force: –

Ay, and the deed had they done.[95]

3. Among the orators, too, eulogies and ceremonial and occasional addresses contain on every side examples of dignity and elevation, but are for the most part void of passion. This is the reason why passionate speakers are the worst eulogists, and why, on the other hand, those who are apt in encomium are the least passionate. 4. If, on the other hand, Caecilius thought that passion never contributes at all to sublimity, and if it was for this reason that he did not deem it worthy of mention, he is altogether deluded. I would affirm with confidence that there is no tone so lofty as that of genuine passion, in its right place, when it bursts out in a wild gust of mad enthusiasm and as it were fills the speaker's words with frenzy.

[…]

XV

Images, moreover, contribute greatly, my young friend, to dignity, elevation, and power as a pleader. In this sense some call them mental representations. In a general way the name of *image* or *imagination* is applied to every idea of the mind, in whatever form it presents itself, which gives birth to speech. But at the present day the word is predominantly used in cases where, carried away by enthusiasm and passion, you think you see what you describe, and you place it before the eyes of your hearers. 2. Further, you will be aware of the fact that an image has one purpose with the orators and another with the poets, and that the design of the poetical image is enthralment, of the rhetorical – vivid description. Both, however, seek to stir the passions and the emotions.

Mother! – 'beseech thee, hark not thou on me
Yon maidens gory-eyed and snaky-haired!
Lo there! – lo there! – they are nigh – they leap on me![96]

And:

Ah! she will slay me! whither can I fly?[97]

In these scenes the poet himself saw Furies, and the image in his mind he almost compelled his audience also to behold. 3. Now, Euripides is most assiduous in giving the utmost tragic effect to these two emotions – fits of love and madness. Herein he succeeds more, perhaps, than in any other respect, although he is daring enough to invade all the other regions of the

---

[94][**Translator's note:**] *Odyssey*, XI, 315–6.
[95][**Translator's note:**] *Odyssey*, XI, 317.
[96][**Translator's note:**] Euripides, *Orestes*, 255.
[97][**Translator's note:**] Euripides, *Iphigenia in Tauris*, 291.

imagination. Notwithstanding that he is by nature anything but elevated, he forces his own genius, in many passages, to tragic heights, and everywhere in the matter of sublimity it is true of him (to adopt Homer's words) that

> The tail of him scourgeth his ribs and his flanks to left and to right,
> And he lasheth himself into frenzy, and spurreth him on to the fight.[98]

4. When the Sun hands the reins to Phaethon, he says

> 'Thou, driving, trespass not on Libya's sky,
> Whose heat, by dews uptempered, else shall split
> Thy car asunder.'

And after that,

> 'Speed onward toward the Pleiads seven thy course.'
> Thus far the boy heard; then he snatched the reins:
> He lashed the flanks of that wing-wafted team;
> Loosed rein, and they through folds of cloudland soared.
> Hard after on a fiery star his sire
> Rode, counselling his son – 'Ho! thither drive!
> Hither thy car turn – hither!'[99]

Would you not say that the soul of the writer enters the chariot at the same moment as Phaethon and shares in his dangers and in the rapid flight of his steeds? For it could never have conceived such a picture had it not been borne in no less swift career on that journey through the heavens.

The same is true of the words which Euripides attributes to his Cassandra: –

> O chariot-loving Trojans.[100]

5. Aeschylus, too, ventures on images of a most heroic stamp. An example will be found in his *Seven against Thebes*, where he says

> For seven heroes, squadron-captains fierce,
> Over a black-rimmed shield have slain a bull,
> And, dipping in the bull's blood each his hand,
> By Ares and Enyo, and by Panic
> Lover of blood, have sworn.[101]

---

[98] [**Translator's note:**] *Iliad*, XX, 170–1.

[99] [**Translator's note:**] Euripides, *Phaethon*, 168–77.

[100] [**Translator's note:**] Euripides, fragment, possibly from *Alexandros*.

[101] [**Translator's note:**] Aeschylus, *Seven against Thebes*, 42.

In mutual fealty they devoted themselves by that joint oath to a relentless doom. Sometimes, however, he introduces ideas that are rough-hewn and uncouth and harsh; and Euripides, when stirred by the spirit of emulation, comes perilously near the same fault, even in spite of his own natural bent. 6. Thus in Aeschylus the palace of Lycurgus at the coming of Dionysus is strangely represented as *possessed*: –

A frenzy thrills the hall; the roofs are bacchant
With ecstasy:[102]

an idea which Euripides has echoed, in other words, it is true, and with some abatement of its crudity, where he says: –

The whole mount shared their bacchic ecstasy.[103]

7. Magnificent are the images which Sophocles has conceived of the death of Oedipus, who makes ready his burial amid the portents of the sky.[104] Magnificent, too, is the passage where the Greeks are on the point of sailing away and Achilles appears above his tomb to those who are putting out to sea[105] – a scene which I doubt whether anyone has depicted more vividly than Simonides.[106] But it is impossible to cite all the examples that present themselves. 8. It is no doubt true that those which are found in the poets contain, as I said, a tendency to exaggeration in the way of the fabulous and that they transcend in every way the credible, but in oratorical imagery the best feature is always its reality and truth. Whenever the form of a speech is poetical and fabulous and breaks into every kind of impossibility, such digressions have a strange and alien air. For example, the clever orators forsooth of our day, like the tragedians, see Furies, and – fine fellows that they are – cannot even understand that Orestes when he cries

Unhand me! – of mine Haunting Fiends thou art –
Dost grip my waist to hurl me into hell![107]

has these fancies because he is mad. 9. What, then, can oratorical imagery effect? Well, it is able in many ways to infuse vehemence and passion into spoken words, while more particularly when it is combined with the argumentative passages it not only persuades the hearer but actually makes him its slave. Here is an example. 'Why, if at this very moment,' says Demosthenes, 'a loud cry were to be heard in front of the courts, and we were told that the prison-house lies open and the prisoners are in full flight, no one, whether he be old or young, is so heedless as not to lend aid to the utmost of his power; aye, and if any one came forward and said that yonder stands the man who let them go, the offender would be promptly put to death without

---

[102][**Translator's note:**] Aeschylus, fragment, from the *Lycurgeia*.
[103][**Translator's note:**] Euripides, *Bacchae*, 726.
[104][**Translator's note:**] Sophocles, *Oedipus at Colonus*, 1586.
[105][**Translator's note:**] Sophocles, fragment, *Polyxena*.
[106][**Translator's note:**] Simonides, fragment.
[107][**Translator's note:**] Euripides, *Orestes*, 264.

a hearing.'[108] 10. In the same way, too, Hyperides on being accused, after he had proposed the liberation of the slaves subsequently to the great defeat, said 'This proposal was framed, not by the orator, but by the battle of Chaeroneia.'[109] The speaker has here at one and the same time followed a train of reasoning and indulged a flight of imagination. He has, therefore, passed the bounds of mere persuasion by the boldness of his conception, 11. By a sort of natural law in all such matters we always attend to whatever possesses superior force; whence it is that we are drawn away from demonstration pure and simple to any startling image within whose dazzling brilliancy the argument lies concealed. And it is not unreasonable that we should be affected in this way, for when two things are brought together, the more powerful always attracts to itself the virtue of the weaker. 12. It will be enough to have said thus much with regard to examples of the sublime in thought, when produced by greatness of soul, imitation, or imagery.

[…]

XXXIII

Come, now, let us take some writer who is really immaculate and beyond reproach. Is it not worth while, on this very point, to raise the general question whether we ought to give the preference, in poems and prose writings, to grandeur with some attendant faults, or to success which is moderate but altogether sound and free from error? Aye, and further, whether a greater number of excellences, or excellences higher in quality, would in literature rightly bear away the palm? For these are inquiries appropriate to a treatise on the sublime, and they imperatively demand a settlement. 2. For my part, I am well aware that lofty genius is far removed from flawlessness; for invariable accuracy incurs the risk of pettiness, and in the sublime, as in great fortunes, there must be something which is overlooked. It may be necessarily the case that low and average natures remain as a rule free from failing and in greater safety because they never run a risk or seek to scale the heights, while great endowments prove insecure because of their very greatness, 3. In the second place, I am not ignorant that it naturally happens that the worse side of human character is always the more easily recognised, and that the memory of errors remains indelible, while that of excellences quickly dies away. 4. I have myself noted not a few errors on the part of Homer and other writers of the greatest distinction, and the slips they have made afford me anything but pleasure. Still I do not term them wilful errors, but rather oversights of a random and casual kind, due to neglect and introduced with all the heedlessness of genius. Consequently I do not waver in my view that excellences higher in quality, even if not sustained throughout, should always on a comparison be voted the first place, because of their sheer elevation of spirit if for no other reason. Granted that Apollonius in his *Argonautica*[110] shows himself a poet who does not trip, and that in his pastorals Theocritus[111] is, except in a few externals, most happy, would you not, for all that, choose to be Homer rather than Apollonius? 5. Again: does Eratosthenes in the *Erigone*[112] (a little poem which is altogether free from flaw)

---

[108][**Translator's note:**] Demosthenes, *Oration*, 24.208.

[109][**Translator's note:**] *Hyperides* (see Plutarch, *Lives of the Ten Orators*, 849A)..

[110]**Apollonius … Argonautica:** Apollonius of Rhodes (third century BCE) was a Greek poet; the *Argonautica* is an epic poem narrating the travels of Jason and the Argonauts to Colchis to get the Golden Fleece.

[111]**Theocritus:** Greek poet (third century BCE) known especially for pastoral lyric poems.

[112]**Eratosthenes … Erigone:** Eratosthenes of Cyrene (*c.*276 BCE–*c.*195 BCE) was a Greek mathematician, scholar, and poet; the *Erigone* was an epic poem describing the suicide of Erigone, daughter of Icarius, after her father's death.

show himself a greater poet than Archilochus[113] with the rich and disorderly abundance which follows in his train and with that outburst of the divine spirit within him which it is difficult to bring under the rules of law? Once more: in lyric poetry would you prefer to be Bacchylides rather than Pindar?[114] And in tragedy to be Ion of Chios[115] rather than – Sophocles? It is true that Bacchylides and Ion are faultless and entirely elegant writers of the polished school, while Pindar and Sophocles, although at times they burn everything before them as it were in their swift career, are often extinguished unaccountably and fail most lamentably. But would anyone in his senses regard all the compositions of Ion put together as an equivalent for the single play of the *Oedipus*?

Further reading

Robert Doran, 'Defining the Longinian Sublime', in *The Theory of the Sublime from Longinus to Kant* (Cambridge: Cambridge University Press, 2015), 27–57.

Suzanne Guerlac, 'Longinus and the Subject of the Sublime', *New Literary History* 16, no. 2 (1985): 275–89.

Neil Hertz, 'A Reading of Longinus', in *The End of the Line: Essays on Psychoanalysis and the Sublime* (New York: Columbia University Press, 1985), 1–20.

---

[113]**Archilochus:** Archaic Greek lyric poet (*c*.680–*c*.645 BC); his poems only survive in fragments, but in ancient Greece he was widely admired, on a par with Homer.

[114]**Bacchylides … Pindar:** Bacchylides was a Greek lyric poet (fifth century BCE) known for elegance and polish but criticized as superficial, especially relative to his contemporary Pindar (*c*.522–*c*.443 BCE), whom Quintilian pronounced Greece's best lyric poet.

[115]**Ion of Chios:** Greek poet and playwright (*c*.490–*c*.420 BCE), whose work survives only in fragments.

1.5 EVANTHIUS, 'ON DRAMA' (FOURTH CENTURY CE)

Evanthius (fourth century CE) was a Latin grammarian who worked in Constantinople. His treatise *De Fabula* (On Drama) served as the basis for the *De Comoedia* (On Comedy) by Aelius Donatus (also fourth century CE), a Roman grammarian and teacher. The two treatises were frequently conflated together into the *De Comoedia et Tragoedia* [On Comedy and Tragedy], which circulated throughout the medieval and early modern periods. *De Fabula* primarily offers an explanatory history of comedy and tragedy, modelled loosely on those presented by Aristotle and Horace. Its influential account of the distinction between tragedy and comedy is primarily structural: tragedies begin well but end badly, while comedies begin badly but end well. Building on a distinction drawn by Aristotle, Evanthius also establishes the role of social class in defining the two genres: comedies depict the middle or lower classes, while tragedies present great men. This distinction features prominently in later accounts of the genres.

Tragedy and comedy began in religious ceremonies which the ancients held to give thanks for a good harvest.

The sort of song which the sacred chorus offered to Father Bacchus[116] when the altars had been kindled and the sacrificial goat brought in was called tragedy. This is from *apo tou tragou kai tes oides*[117] – that is, from 'goat', an enemy of vineyards, and from 'song'. There is a full reference to this in Vergil's *Georgics* [II.380 ff.], either because the poet of this sort of song was given a goat, or because a goatskin full of new wine was the usual reward to the singers; or else because the players used to smear their faces with wine-lees prior to the introduction of masks by Aeschylus.[118] 'Wine-lees' in Greek is *truges*. And the word 'tragedy' was invented for these reasons.

But while the Athenians were not yet confined to the city and Apollo was called 'Nomius' [shepherd] and 'Aguieus' [guardian] – that is, guardian of shepherds and villages – they erected altars for divine worship around the hamlets, farms, villages, and crossroads of Attica and solemnly chanted a festival song to him. It was called comedy *apo ton komon kai tes oides*[119] – the name composed, as I think, from 'villages' [*komai*] and 'song' [*oide*]. Or else it was composed *apo tou komazein kai aidein*[120] – going to a revel singing. This is not unlikely since the comic chorus was drunk or engaged in love making on the sacred day.

And once the historical sequence has been established, it is clear that tragedy appeared first. For man moved little by little from barbarism and brutality to a civilized condition. Later towns were founded and life became more mild and easier. Thus the matter of tragedy was discovered long before the matter of comedy.

---

[116]**Bacchus:** Roman name for the Greek god Dionysus, the god of wine and theatre. In ancient Athens, tragedies were performed at the Festival of Dionysus, divided between a City Dionysia and Rural Dionysia.

[117]*Apo tou tragou kai tes oides:* from the goat and song (Greek).

[118]**Aeschylus:** earliest Greek tragic playwright whose plays are still extant (*c.*525–*c.*455 BCE).

[119]*Apo ton komon kai tes oides:* from the villages and song (Greek).

[120]*Apo tou komazein kai aidein:* from revelling and singing.

Thespis[121] is thought to be the inventor of tragedy by those who study ancient history. And Eupolis, along with Cratinus and Aristophanes,[122] is thought to be the father of old comedy. But Homer, who is, as it were, the copious fountainhead of all poetry, provided exemplars for these sorts of poetry and established almost a law for their composition. We know that he wrote the *Iliad* in the form of a tragedy and that the *Odyssey* has the form of a comedy. In the beginning such poems were crude and not all polished and graceful as they later became. And after Homer's excellent and copious work they were regularized in their structure and parts by clever imitators.

[...]

Of the many differences between tragedy and comedy, the foremost are these: In comedy the fortunes of men are middle-class, the dangers are slight, and the ends of the actions are happy; but in tragedy everything is the opposite – the characters are great men, the fears are intense, and the ends disastrous. In comedy the beginning is troubled, the end tranquil; in tragedy events follow the reverse order. And in tragedy the kind of life is shown that is to be shunned; while in comedy the kind is shown that is to be sought after. Finally, in comedy the story is always fictitious; while tragedy often has a basis in historical truth.

Further reading

Chrysanthi Demetriou, 'Aelius Donatus and His Commentary on Terence's Comedies', in *The Oxford Handbook of Greek and Roman Comedy*, ed. Michael Fontaine and Adele C. Scafuro (Oxford: Oxford University Press, 2014), 782–802.

Marvin Herrick, *Comic Theory in the Sixteenth Century* (Urbana: University of Illinois Press, 1950), 57–60.

Henry Ansgar Kelly, 'The Roman Tradition', in *Ideas and Forms of Tragedy from Aristotle to the Middle Ages* (Cambridge: Cambridge University Press, 1993), 5–15.

[121]**Thespis:** known as the first actor (sixth century BCE), representing tragedy.
[122]**Eupolis ... Cratinus ... Aristophanes:** ancient Greek comic playwrights associated with Old Comedy.

1.6 AUGUSTINE, 'ON STAGE-PLAYS' (397–400 CE)

Augustine (354–430 CE), bishop of Hippo, was an influential Christian philosopher. In his *Confessions* (397–400 CE), he repents his youthful devotion to sensual pleasures. Having forsworn his wife, mistress, and other love affairs in order to become an ascetic and celibate Christian, he also swore off his love of the tragic theatre, which he came to see not only as pagan, but also as feeding a dangerous addiction to emotional intensity. Influenced by Stoic and Platonic philosophy as well as Christian thought, Augustine condemns the vicarious sympathies instilled by watching tragedies as fostering an immoral pleasure in others' sorrows. Pity, sorrow, and compassion, he explains, should be invested in helping people who genuinely suffer; to waste these emotions on fictional constructs, where they can do no good, is dangerous as well as indulgent. By encouraging this wastefulness, as well as by nurturing the instinct to luxuriate in depraved emotions, the tragic theatre appeals to all that is worst in the soul.

Chap. II. – In public spectacles he is moved by an empty compassion. He is attacked by a troublesome spiritual disease.

2. Stage-plays also drew me away, full of representations of my miseries and of fuel to my fire. Why does man like to be made sad when viewing doleful and tragical scenes, which yet he himself would by no means suffer? And yet he wishes, as a spectator, to experience from them a sense of grief, and in this very grief his pleasure consists. What is this but wretched insanity? For a man is more affected with these actions, the less free he is from such affections. Howsoever, when he suffers in his own person, it is the custom to style it 'misery;' but when he compassionates others, then it is styled 'mercy.' But what kind of mercy is it that arises from fictitious and scenic passions? The hearer is not expected to relieve, but merely invited to grieve; and the more he grieves, the more he applauds the actor of these fictions. And if the misfortunes of the characters (whether of olden times or merely imaginary) be so represented as not to touch the feelings of the spectator, he goes away disgusted and censorious; but if his feelings be touched, he sits it out attentively, and sheds tears of joy.

3. Are sorrows, then, also loved? Surely all men desire to rejoice? Or, as man wishes to be miserable, is he, nevertheless, glad to be merciful, which, because it cannot exist without passion, for this cause alone are passions loved? This also is from that vein of friendship. But whither does it go? Whither does it flow? Wherefore runs it into that torrent of pitch, seething forth those huge tides of loathsome lusts into which it is changed and transformed, being of its own will cast away and corrupted from its celestial clearness? Shall, then, mercy be repudiated? By no means. Let us, therefore, love sorrows sometimes. But beware of uncleanness, O my soul, under the protection of my God, the God of our fathers, who is to be praised and exalted above all for ever, beware of uncleanness. For I have not now ceased to have compassion; but then in the theatres I sympathized with lovers when they sinfully enjoyed one another, although this was done fictitiously in the play. And when they lost one another, I grieved with them, as if pitying them, and yet had delight in both. But now-a-days I feel much more pity for him that delighteth in his wickedness, than for him who is counted as enduring hardships by failing to obtain some pernicious pleasure, and the loss of some miserable felicity. This, surely, is the

truer mercy, but grief hath no delight in it. For though he that condoles with the unhappy be approved for his office of charity, yet would he who had real compassion rather there were nothing for him to grieve about. For if good-will be ill-willed (which it cannot), then can he who is truly and sincerely commiserating wish that there should be some unhappy ones, that he might commiserate them. Some grief may then be justified, none loved. For thus dost Thou, O Lord God, who lovest souls far more purely than do we, and art more incorruptibly compassionate, although Thou art wounded by no sorrow. 'And who is sufficient for these things?'

4. But I, wretched one, then loved to grieve, and sought out what to grieve at, as when, in another man's misery, though feigned and counterfeited, that delivery of the actor best pleased me, and attracted me the most powerfully, which moved me to tears. What marvel was it that an unhappy sheep, straying from Thy flock, and impatient of Thy care, I became infected with a foul disease? And hence came my love of griefs – not such as should probe me too deeply, for I loved not to suffer such things as I loved to look upon, but such as, when hearing their fictions, should lightly affect the surface; upon which, like as with empoisoned nails, followed burning, swelling, putrefaction, and horrible corruption. Such was my life! But was it life, O my God?

Further reading

Pat Easterling and Richard Miles, 'Dramatic Identities: Tragedy in Late Antiquity', in *Constructing Identities in Late Antiquity*, ed. Richard Miles (London: Routledge, 1999), 95–111.

Donnalee Dox, 'The Idea of a Theater in Late Antiquity: Augustine's Critique and Isidore's History', in *The Idea of the Theater in Latin Christian Thought: Augustine to the Fourteenth Century* (Ann Arbor: University of Michigan Press, 2004), 11–42.

Jennifer Herdt, 'The Theater of the Virtues: Augustine's Critique of Pagan Mimesis', in *Augustine's City of God: A Critical Guide*, ed. James Wetzel (Cambridge: Cambridge University Press, 2012), 111–29.

CHAPTER 2
THE EARLY MODERN PERIOD

After classical antiquity, the sixteenth and seventeenth centuries gave rise to some of tragedy's most celebrated traditions. Although Aeschylus, Sophocles, and Euripides represent the genre's origins, Shakespeare has come to rival and perhaps even overtake their place in the tragic canon; plays such as *Hamlet* and *King Lear* have become some of its most familiar exemplars. While Shakespeare's popular renown is exceptional, his historical moment also gave rise to other important tragic playwrights including Christopher Marlowe, Thomas Kyd, Thomas Middleton, and John Webster in England, as well as Félix Lope de Vega in Spain, and, just slightly later, Pierre Corneille and Jean Racine in France. In part because of this profusion of literary creativity, the early modern period has often been called the Renaissance, a term coined to celebrate what was seen by many as a rebirth of classical humanism. In conjunction with medieval ideas of tragedy, rising awareness of Greek theatre prompted new conversations about both why and how one might recreate new versions of antiquity's legendary plays.

Early modern writers inherited medieval models of tragedy developed by writers such as Boethius, Boccaccio, Chaucer, and Lydgate. In particular, the genre came to be associated especially with stories of the falls of famous men, sometimes called *de casibus* narratives after Boccaccio's fourteenth-century *De Casibus Virorum Illustrium*.[1] As Greek texts acquired new visibility after the fifteenth-century collapse of the Byzantine Empire, however, their forms began to both contest and merge with evolving medieval models. The new resources of the printing press helped humanist scholars circulate emerging Greek texts to broader audiences, translators, writers, and readers, prompting heated debates about the plays associated with tragedy's origins.[2] Conversations about the tragic theatre began in Italian cities, where scholars produced the earliest printed editions of Greek plays, but they quickly travelled, expanded, and evolved. In France, classical study inspired imitation, resulting in neoclassical plays and dramatic theories; in England, playwrights and critics simultaneously revered and rebelled against the authority linked with antiquity. Throughout these and other European literary traditions, the ethical and theological impact of classical tragedy both resonated and competed with the teachings of the New Testament, also originally written in Greek, and also newly available for scrutiny – and controversy – in the wake of emerging philological scholarship.[3]

Sixteenth-century writers began experimenting with new, old, and hybrid tragic forms in conversation with a surge of writings about tragedy. In many cases, these debates responded to

---

[1]See Henry Ansgar Kelly, *Ideas and Forms of Tragedy from Aristotle to the Middle Ages* (Cambridge: Cambridge University Press, 1993), and Kelly, *Chaucerian Tragedy* (Cambridge: D.S. Brewer, 1997).
[2]See Robert Garland, *Surviving Tragedy* (London: Duckworth, 2004), and N.G. Wilson, *From Byzantium to Italy: Greek Studies in the Italian Renaissance* (Baltimore: Johns Hopkins University Press, 1992).
[3]On the period's rising tensions between Greek scholarship and Christian thought, see Simon Goldhill, 'Learning Greek Is Heresy! Resisting Erasmus', in *Who Needs Greek?: Contests in the Cultural History of Hellenism* (Cambridge: Cambridge University Press, 2002), 14–59.

the new visibility of Aristotle's *Poetics*, which was published in Latin in 1498 and in Greek in 1508. This intellectual traffic, however, had multiple sources and directions. New engagement with genre theory also followed rising attention to Greek dramatic genres, as writers turned to Aristotle's guidelines in order to rethink and rewrite newly popular Greek plays.[4] While some sixteenth-century continental writers, such as Julius Caesar Scaliger and Lodovico Castelvetro (extract 2.2), are known for their literary criticism, many others who participated in these debates identified primarily as playwrights and poets, including Lodovico Dolce, Ludovico Ariosto, Giambattista Giraldi (extract 2.1), and Giambattista Guarini. These writers typically claimed Aristotle's mandate in order to justify their literary strategies, while quietly filtering his recommendations through more recent and/or eclectic ideas about the genre's moral purpose. Alongside claims of fostering Christian virtue, the tragic plays and *novelle* (prose fictions) that these authors produced were often bloody, bawdy, and sensational, featuring murder, suicide, infanticide, dismemberment, adultery, and incest. As both advocates and critics observed, these works appealed to audiences especially through visceral engagement of their emotions, especially horror, fear, pity, sympathy, and desire. Although the period's Italian writings have not left their mark on the tragic canon as visibly or memorably as their English and French contemporaries, they left an influential legacy especially through their impact on early modern English writers. Shakespeare, in particular, took many of his plots from Italian sources; perhaps most notably, his *Othello* rewrote a *novella* by Giraldi.

With their eloquent soliloquies, spectacular violence, erotic crises, and failures of justice, English tragedies from the late sixteenth and early seventeenth centuries have achieved a particularly vivid hold in the cultural imagination. Because so many of the best-known English plays came from the popular realm of the emerging commercial theatres, scholars have usually seen them as firmly removed from the more elite theoretical conversations about the genre that flourished in continental Europe. Just as English plays drew on Italian literary sources, however, English writers also responded to emerging debates about the tragic genre more broadly. Early English humanist scholars participated in transnational conversations about classical models, resulting in a similar set of translations, adaptations, and new tragedies that merged neoclassical structures with medieval *de casibus* narrative. As interest grew, playwrights increasingly experimented with new possibilities for tragic forms. Performances, meanwhile, began moving from schools, universities, and aristocratic homes into new and increasingly public spaces. The construction of commercial playhouses in London, beginning in the 1560s, encouraged productions of plays directed at large audiences, prompting playwrights to enliven tragedies with popular elements from other genres including mystery plays, moralities, satire, and especially comedy. As tragedies became both more visible and further unmoored from their classical roots, they sparked controversy from many of the genre's defenders as well as its attackers.

Many English critics, schooled in classical and continental literary traditions, advocated models of tragedy adhering strictly rooted to what they saw as ancient rules. George Puttenham's *Art of English Poesy* (1589) and William Scott's *The Model of Poesy* (1599) both

---

[4]See Daniel Javitch, 'The Emergence of Poetic Genre Theory in the Sixteenth Century', *Modern Language Quarterly* 59, no. 2 (1998): 139–69; Nicholas Cronk, 'Aristotle, Horace, and Longinus: The Conception of Reader Response', in *The Cambridge History of Literary Criticism: Vol. 3, The Renaissance*, ed. Glyn P. Norton (Cambridge: Cambridge University Press, 1999), 199–204.

drew on Aristotle and Italian literary theorists in defining tragedy, as did neo-Latin academic writings such as Alberico Gentili's *Commentario* (1593); although they defended tragedy, these accounts of the genre did not necessarily resemble the versions presented by contemporary plays. Meanwhile, moralists hostile to the growing success of the commercial theatre complained about its growing liberties and improprieties.[5] As playwrights increasingly engaged the attractions of sensational subjects – including the spectacular array of vices dramatized by their Italian precursors – larger populations of theatregoers became increasingly attracted to them for entertainment, and critics became increasingly enraged about their incendiary effects on audiences' souls. Following more general attacks such as preacher John Northbrooke's *A Treatise Against Dicing, Dancing, Plays, and Interludes* (1577), the classically schooled author Stephen Gosson wrote a series of antitheatrical invectives between 1579 and 1582 (extract 2.3). Echoing Plato's concerns about the theatre's dangerous power to mould audiences in its own images (extract 1.1), Gosson argued that contemporary tragedies appealed to playgoers' worst instincts and appetites by seducing them into lust, grief, and violent rage.

As was the case in Italy and earlier in antiquity, writers of literary criticism often also wrote plays and poems themselves. Gosson had written plays before turning against them, and he dedicated his first treatise, *The School of Abuse* (1579), to the poet and statesman Philip Sidney, presumably in hopes of sympathy and patronage. Despite Sidney's commitment to moral concerns, however, he was a passionate supporter of the literary arts, and shortly after the appearance of Gosson's treatise he wrote a *Defense of Poetry* (*c*.1580, published 1595) at least partly as a rebuke to Gosson (extract 2.4). Like Thomas Lodge, another poet who quickly stood up to counter Gosson ('A Reply to Stephen Gosson's School of Abuse', in *Defense of Poetry, Music, and Stage Plays*, 1579), Sidney drew on Aristotle's *Poetics* in his *Defense*, though he also counterintuitively cited Plato, inverting his moral logic to present poetry as supporting rather than undermining the pursuit of goodness.[6] Sidney's praise for tragedy was qualified by his ambivalence about the contemporary stage, which he often found unseemly for its breaches from classical decorum, but his broader claims about its potential moral and pedagogical virtues established an important foundation for ongoing defences of the medium.

Sidney wrote poetry and prose, but other contemporaries who defended the theatre had more direct ties to it. The actor and playwright Nathan Field wrote an impassioned 1616 defence of plays to a preacher who railed against the medium. More influentially, Thomas Heywood, a playwright and former actor, published a book titled *Apology for Actors* (1612), in which he turned directly to the literary and moral authority of the ancient Greek world to argue for the redemptive power of theatrical performance (extract 2.5). Although Heywood does not limit his focus to tragedy, the genre occupies an important place in his account. He agreed with Gosson's essential charge, borrowed from Plato, that tragic performances propelled audiences to identify with their protagonists. Like Sidney, however, Heywood argued that this identification could be a powerful force for self-improvement: watching performances of heroism could inspire heroic instincts, while the shame generated by recognizing a protagonist's

---

[5]On early modern England's antitheatricalism, see Jonas A. Barish, *The Antitheatrical Prejudice* (Berkeley: University of California Press, 1981), and Leah S. Marcus, 'Antitheatricality: The Theater as Scourge', in *A New Companion to Renaissance Drama*, ed. Arthur Kinney and Thomas Warren Hopper (Oxford: Wiley-Blackwell, 2017), 182–92.
[6]Micha Lazarus, 'Sidney's Greek Poetics', *Studies in Philology* 112, no. 3 (2015): 504–36; Morriss Partee, 'Sir Philip Sidney and the Renaissance Knowledge of Plato', *Journal of English Studies* 51, no. 5 (1970): 411–24.

flaws could lead audiences to confront and mend the same vices in themselves. Despite his insistence on the theatre's fundamental goodness, Heywood's defence suggests grounds for ambivalence. By emphasizing the medium's power to mould viewers in the image of what they watch, he implicitly acknowledges the potential for dangerous forms of imitation as well.

Perhaps surprisingly, we can see similar ambivalence in the most substantial body of writings reflecting on the theatre around the turn of the seventeenth century: the plays themselves. As many scholars have noted, the plays of Shakespeare and his contemporaries are self-consciously metatheatrical, persistently reflecting on their own medium. Hamlet stages a tragedy to trap his villainous uncle (*c*.1599); the rude mechanicals of *Midsummer Night's Dream* rehearse a performance of a would-be tragedy to celebrate a wedding (*c*.1595); and the maddened mourner Hieronimo carries out a violent revenge by performing a tragic play in Thomas Kyd's *The Spanish Tragedy* (*c*.1587). Sometimes these inset tragedies turn out to have positive consequences, such as prompting confessions and revelations, but they often have terrible effects, ending in mockery, misery, and/or death. By staging scenes of spectatorship, and crafting elaborate extended theatrical conceits, these and other plays engage deliberately in contemporary debates about possible motives, strategies, and consequences of performing and watching plays. It is impossible to extrapolate a unified theory of tragedy from the many and complex metatheatrical moments presented by the period's plays, but they share a heightened sense of the genre's charged capacity to transform its audiences, for better and for worse.

The concerns about literary and moral authority that consumed playwrights during the development of the early commercial theatres took new forms in the English tragedy of the later seventeenth century, which had to negotiate the political revolutions and regime changes that threatened its very right to exist. Shortly after the outbreak of the English Civil War (1642–9), parliament issued an ordinance which officially put an end to the system of public theatre which had nurtured Shakespeare's tragedies as well as the classic Jacobean and Caroline revenge tragedies of Thomas Middleton, John Webster, Francis Beaumont, and John Fletcher. Parliament closed the playhouses by asserting that 'public sports do not well agree with public calamities, nor public stage-plays with seasons of humiliation, this being an exercise of sad and pious solemnity, and the other being spectacles of pleasure, too commonly expressing lascivious mirth and levity'.[7] The rationale for the closure was partly pragmatic – it was in no one's interest to have large groups of people congregating together for several hours during a time of civil unrest – but also ideological and religious.[8] Public theatre, of whatever genre, was deemed insufficiently serious, sad, or pious for a nation facing God's immediate judgement in the form of bloody civil war.

With a few renegade or privileged exceptions, the closure of the public theatres held throughout the Cromwellian Commonwealth and Protectorate, for the best part of 18 years until the Restoration of the monarchy in 1660. During that period, when tragedies were printed and read rather than staged, the English theatre-loving public, of necessity, developed a taste for reading plays as much as seeing them; this partly drove the Puritan John Milton's famous insistence (extract 2.7) that contemporary tragedy could still do Christian moral work

---

[7]'An Ordinance of the Lords and Commons concerning stage places, 2 September 1642', in *Theatre in Europe, A Documentary History: English Professional Theatre, 1530–1660*, ed. Glynne Wickham, Herbert Berry and William Ingram (Cambridge: Cambridge University Press, 2000), 132.

[8]See Martin Butler, *Theatre and Crisis 1632–1642* (Cambridge: Cambridge University Press, 1984).

if it was raised above 'common interludes' and was reimagined as a dramatic poem rather than as a stage play.[9] After the reopening of theatres, however, this proved to be a minority view; for all of Restoration drama's later reputation for moral decadence and sexual permissiveness, the official warrant announcing the reopening of the public playhouses actually insisted that a new generation of tragedians – unlike their Elizabethan, Jacobean and Caroline forbears – needed to improve as well as entertain its spectators: 'all … Tragedies & Comedies … shall be purged and freed from all obsenenese and profanes & soe become instructive to Morality in Our People'.[10]

Since English theatre had lost a generation of working tragedians during the 1640s and 1650s, it had to turn to reworkings of pre-war, Shakespearean English stage classics and contemporary continental (especially French) dramas in order to assemble a repertoire of producible tragic work when this warrant came into effect. This process of adaptation meant that long-standing continental debates about neoclassical rules for tragedy were encountered afresh in England and became centrally, if belatedly, important on English shores at the same time as the principles of Restoration theatrical decorum were being fleshed out.[11]

The most influential codifications of neoclassical theatrical rules such as François Hédelin, abbé D'Aubinac's *La Pratique du Theatre* (1657) or Corneille's *Trois Discours Sur Le Poème Dramatique* (1660) (extract 2.6) were forged in the same theatrical culture that produced the magnificent tragedies of Corneille (1606–54) and Racine (1639–99). French neoclassical criticism of tragedy sought to clarify and establish the rules that enabled entertaining and serious theatre which could stand alongside that of classical antiquity in terms of symmetry of design as well as ethical complexity. In the same theatrical culture that saw Corneille and Racine return to the tragedies of Euripides in plays like *Médée* (1635) and *Phèdre* (1677), French neoclassical critics re-examined Aristotle's *Poetics*, looking to update its insights for a modern world with very different ideas of agency, decorum and hierarchy from those of Greek or Roman antiquity. If on occasion this criticism can make the *Poetics* sound much more prescriptive than it ever actually was, these commentators insisted that Aristotle's reading of tragedy's ethical potential still had currency in the seventeenth century. Thus the Jesuit René Rapin (1621–87) was adamant that an Aristotelian view of tragedy could be assimilated to a Christian world view (extract 2.8). In an argument imitated by the English poet-dramatist John Dryden (1631–1700) (extract 2.9), Rapin argued that catharsis was a means through which the sin of pride could be tempered, and that the purgation of pity and fear was an enthralling recalibration of our capacity for moral action. Tragedy in the early modern period thus remained a touchstone for discussions about entertainment, ethics, and individual responsibility central to societies across Europe.

---

[9]On English theatrical culture during the interregnum see Maureen Bell, 'Booksellers Without an Author, 1627–1685', in *Thomas Middleton and Early Modern Textual Culture: A Companion to the Collected Works*, ed. Gary Taylor and John Lavagnino (Oxford: Oxford University Press, 2007), 260–85; Janet Clare, *Drama of the English Republic, 1649–1660* (Manchester: Manchester University Press, 2002); and Susan J. Wiseman, *Drama and Politics in the English Civil War* (Cambridge: Cambridge University Press, 1998).

[10]Quoted in Leslie Hotson, *The Commonwealth and Restoration Stage* (Cambridge, MA: Harvard University Press, 1928), 209.

[11]On neoclassical idea of tragedy in the early modern period see Raphael Lyne, 'Neoclassicisms', in *Tragedy in Transition*, ed. Sarah Annes Brown and Catherine Silverstone (Malden, MA and Oxford: Wiley-Blackwell, 2007), 123–40; John D. Lyons, *Kingdom of Disorder: The Theory of Tragedy in Classical France* (West Lafayette: Purdue University Press, 1999).

2.1 GIOVAN BATTISTA GIRALDI CINTHIO, *DISCOURSE OR LETTER ON THE COMPOSITION OF COMEDIES AND TRAGEDIES* (1555)

Giovanni Battista Giraldi (1504–73), known as Cinthio, wrote plays and *novelle* (short fiction) as well as literary criticism. Born and educated in Ferrara, he taught at its university before taking subsequent teaching posts in Mondovi and Pavia. Although his writings are no longer widely known, they were influential in his time; his 1565 story collection *Hecatommithi* provided the plots of Shakespeare's *Othello* and *Measure for Measure*. In his critical writings, Giraldi entered contemporary debates about dramatic genres, which responded to the new availability of Aristotle's *Poetics* and ancient Greek plays. His 1555 *Discourse on the Composition of Comedies and Tragedies* reflects his experience as a playwright, and his interest in audiences' reactions and preferences. In contrast to critics who insisted on what they saw as classical rules, Giraldi took a pragmatic approach focused on what succeeded at moving audiences. Towards this end, he defended the aesthetic value of what he called 'tragedy with a happy ending', now better known as tragicomedy.

The imitation of an action is one feature that comedy and tragedy have in common; but they are different, in that tragedy imitates an illustrious and royal action and comedy an ordinary and private one, which is why Aristotle claimed that comedy imitated worse actions. He didn't mean by this that it should imitate vile and vicious actions but less illustrious ones, which, in terms of nobility, are worse if they are compared with royal ones. Both actions should be complete, and given proper size as they are brought to an end (I said proper size because if the actions are smaller than they should be they cannot be beautiful) since there is no beauty in things that are of lesser size than what is appropriate for their kind; and if they are too extended (beside being disproportionate, and thus not beautiful) they bore the auditors. The appropriate size of each then will be, for tragedy, when the action will have progressed from a state of unhappiness to one of happiness, or else from happiness to wretchedness without interposing any unrelated matters in between; and for comedy when, thanks to the poet's wit, the action will have progressed by proper means from disorders and troubles to peace and tranquillity. And if you wish to know the ascribed time for the entire representation, I say that we don't have it the way the ancients did, for whom the duration was determined at the public games by a water clock, which was called a 'clepsidra.'[12] But I deem it a good thing for the poet to measure time with his judgment, in such a way that he ends the play without annoying the spectators. I believe that the representation of a comedy calls for no less than three hours, and tragedy no less than four. I saw, from the plays I composed, that such duration was appropriate for one and the other genre because the attention of the auditors indicated to me that the representation onstage for those stretches of time did not seem too long for them. And to conclude this section, I say, Mr. Giulio, that, rather than wanting to make the action somewhat longer, it is better to leave a little desire in the minds of the spectators, keeping a check on the time instead of leaving the spectators bored by prolonging it.

---

[12]**Clepsidra:** ancient clock that measures time by the flow of water.

Now returning to where we started, these two types of plots are, in part, different in the means by which they imitate, and in part similar. Tragedy and comedy imitates with sweet speech, that is, with verse (called 'meter' by Aristotle) and not with prose. Neither genre can be composed without verse and merit praise. Verse is one of the constitutive parts of their bodies, and thus both comedy and tragedy cannot but be defective and lame whenever they lack verse. If, in ancient times, there were possibly some, among the Greeks, who wrote them in prose, that's because matters are not perfect at their beginnings and need our diligence and labor to arrive at their proper end and reach perfection. Just as back then, writing these plays in prose was not reproached because no one knew any better, so now that the two genres have achieved their proper form not writing them in verse cannot but be reproached.

[…]

Besides the aforementioned similarities, tragedy and comedy have in common their purpose because both aim to introduce good morals, but they do so diversely. Comedy is without terror and pity (since in comedy there are no deaths, nor terrible events; it seeks rather to achieve its end with pleasure or some festive jests), whereas tragedy, both the kind that ends happily and the one that ends unhappily, with its wretched and terrible events, purges minds of vices and inspires good morals.

[…]

Even though the plot is a feature common to tragedy and comedy, some desire nonetheless that the tragic plot be taken from history and that the comic plot be invented by the poet. This difference, it seems, can be explained reasonably; that is, comedy must make recourse to private and ordinary actions and tragedy to royal and exalted ones; to private citizens in one case and to kings and persons of high rank in the other; and since the latter are in the public eye, not to have heard of any singular action of theirs as soon as it is performed by them seems to lie outside the bounds of probability. Therefore, tragedies being numbered among illustrious actions because of the persons who give rise to them, it seems unlikely that they could be brought onto the stage without some prior knowledge of them. Private events, on the other hand, can easily be invented because in general they seldom go beyond their own households and are soon forgotten. In this case the poet can therefore have a wider field in which to invent what he wants and to invent new plots for the stage. But even though this reasoning seems solid, I still maintain that, as in comedy, tragic plots can also be invented by the poet; in addition to the fact that Aristotle, judicious about this matter no less than he is about others, allows it in more than one place in his *Poetics*, Cornutus states the same after him, telling us that comedy invents its plot, whereas tragedy frequently draws it from history, thus indicating that it not always necessary for tragedy to take its plot from history.[13] It appears to me also that reason is able to present the same truth with much probability because the power of moving tragic feelings depends only on imitation, which does not depart from probability, and facts as such do not move the feelings without words fitly and metrically joined together. It therefore seems to me that it is within the power of the poet to move the tragic passions as he will in a tragedy of his own invention, the action of which he invents on the basis of natural types of behavior and which stays within the range of what usually happens or might happen. And

---

[13][**Translator's note:**] Lucius Annaeus Cornutus (born *c*.AD 20), Stoic philosopher and mentor of Persius, was included in titles of early modern editions of Terence's comedies as one of the ancient commentators and was sometimes confused with Evanthius, who himself was not distinguished from Donatus by sixteenth century readers.

perhaps a newly invented tragedy can move the emotions (in order to implant good morals) even more because, striking the souls of the spectators as new, it commands more attention. Aware that the action about to be represented can be known only through the representation, the spectator no sooner tastes the plot and thinks that it might be ingeniously constructed than he concentrates his attention and tries not to lose one word. And this might be the reason that led Aristotle (when he allowed us to invent plots) to say that, among those taken from history, the least known are more pleasing and effective. However much pity and terror come from the [impact of the] plot, they lack any power if the poet's talent doesn't add to it sweet and efficacious words. That a feigned plot can have this power, experience has shown in the case of my *Orbecche*[14] (such as it is) every time it has been played. Not only new spectators (let it be allowed me, Mr. Giulio, to talk about this with you not in order to praise myself but to confirm with the newest of examples what I am presently discussing) but those who came to see it every time the tragedy was acted were unable to restrain their sighs and sobs. And you, Mr. Giulio, among others know it, since you played the role of Oronte and saw the tears of the lady you love so much every time you mourned your fate as that dramatic character, tears you could never see in the real quarrels between you. Our most gentle Flaminio [Ariosti][15] saw the same in his beloved, that sweet foe, when he played Orbecche with such grace and verisimilitude that he gave a very clear indication of his most noble soul.

[…]

Here it should be observed that even though double tragedies are little praised by Aristotle (though some think otherwise), double plotting is greatly praised in comedy and made the plays of Terence succeed wonderfully.[16] I call that plot double which has in its action diverse kinds of persons of the same kind, as two lovers of different wit, two old men of varied nature, two servants with opposite characters, and others such, as may be seen in the *Andria*[17] and in other plays of the same poet, where it is clear that these like persons but different in character make the knot and the denouement of the plot most pleasing. And I believe that if this were well imitated in tragedy by a good poet, and the knot so arranged that its untying will not generate confusion, the double structure will be no less pleasing than in comedy (ever saving due reverence to Aristotle). If there have been some who favored this method and held different opinions than Aristotle, they are not, I think, to be blamed, especially if the tragedy has a happy ending. For this kind of end is much like that of comedy, and thus such tragedy can also be alike in its imitation of the action. Let what I have said about the weaving and the untying of the plot suffice for now.

Since only action is imitated in both comedy and tragedy, and since the action of comedy is about ordinary people, and it doesn't deal with the pitiful or the terrible, the choice of characters in comedy is not as difficult as it is for tragedy. And all the more so because comedy admits the representation not only of respectable citizens but [also of] servants, parasites, prostitutes, cooks, pimps, soldiers – in short, all the sorts of ordinary people that inhabit a city. But tragedy requires more care.

---

[14]*Orbecche*: Giraldi's best-known play, a 1541 tragedy in which Orbecche, daughter of the Persian king Sulmone, secretly marries Oronte and has two children by him, spurring a violent revenge from her father when he learns of the unauthorized marriage. Orbecche responds by carrying out her own violent revenge upon her father.

[15]**Flaminio**: actor who performed in *Orbecche*; apparently a boy actor, since he played a female role.

[16]**Terence's comedies**: Roman comic playwright Terence (*c.*190–*c.*159 BCE) was extremely popular in the sixteenth century.

[17]*Andria*: popular comedy of romantic intrigue by Terence (166 BCE).

In this regard one should know that lofty and royal actions can be of three kinds since they can involve either good persons, or wicked ones, or persons in between. However, one needs to consider which of these will act in ways that best suit tragedy. Because this kind of play aims to produce terror and pity, to instill good morals the poet must choose actions apt to produce this didactic effect. The actions of good men ending wretchedly will never arouse fear and pity because the afflictions that befall them will display a cruelty that will produce so much horror that pity will be virtually extinguished, and this will fail to instill any good morals. Since tragedy purges the souls of men by the fear and pity produced by the sorrows men undergo because of their faults, tragedy cannot achieve its end when those who suffer adversity have not committed a sinful action. Similarly, the actions of wicked individuals will not produce this effect because the evil that befalls them is seen to be just punishment for their wickedness. Those who live uprightly wish to see the wicked suffer, and [the upright] experience no pity nor terror from their [the wicked's] punishment. However, our common humanity (a wicked man is still human) makes us feel something unpleasant about their punishment.

Persons, then, of high station who are halfway between the good and the wicked awaken marvelous pity if something horrible befalls them. The cause of this is that it appears to the spectator that the person who suffers may deserve some sort of penalty, but not such a heavy one. And this justice combined with the weight of the punishment induces that fear and that pity which is necessary to tragedy.

[…]

As for tragedies, there are two sorts: one kind that ends in sorrow, the other that ends happily. The latter, in bringing about this end, does not abandon the terrible or the pitiful, for without these there cannot be a good tragedy. This type of tragedy, which Aristotle called mixed, was revealed to us by Plautus in the prologue of the *Amphitryon*, when he said that in this play less noble persons were mingled with great and royal ones.[18] This he took from the *Poetics* of Aristotle, where there is a passage on this sort of tragedy.[19] It is in its nature more pleasing to the spectators because it ends in happiness. In this kind of tragedy the recognition of persons has an important role; through the recognition those for whom we feel dread and compassion are saved from perils and from death. Among all the recognitions which Aristotle teaches us (for it does not appear to me pertinent to speak of all of them) the most praiseworthy is the one by means of which there is a change of fortune from wretched to happy, as in its place we shall explain. But this noble kind of recognition is not so closely connected with tragedy that ends happily that it is not also very suitable to tragedies with an unhappy ending, in which it produces an opposite effect to that just mentioned; that is, it makes the happy become wretched and turns friends into enemies.

Among the Latins, Seneca never undertook tragedies with a happy ending but devoted himself to those with sad endings.[20] Which he did with such excellence that in nearly all his tragedies (it seems to me) he surpasses in prudence, gravity, decorum, majesty, and skill in the

---

[18]**Plautus' *Amphitryon*:** *Amphitryon* is a Roman comedy by comic playwright Plautus (*c*.254–184 BCE), dramatizing the birth of Hercules. At the play's start, Mercury describes the play as a tragedy, and then announces that to please the audience, he will make it a tragicomedy.

[19]**Aristotle … tragedy:** Aristotle discusses tragedy with a happy ending as a subset of the genre in *Poetics*, 1453a30–9.

[20]**Seneca … tragedies:** Roman playwright Seneca (*c*.4 BCE–*c*.65 CE), who wrote tragedies based on Greek models, was a popular authority on tragedy in the sixteenth century.

use of maxims all the Greeks who ever wrote, though in his use of language he might have been chaster and more painstaking. Yet in spite of that I have composed some tragedies with happy endings – the *Altile*, the *Selene*, the *Antivalomeni*,[21] and others – merely as a concession to the spectators and to make the plays appear more pleasing on the stage, and to conform with the custom of our times. Although Aristotle says this is to cater to the ignorance of the spectators, and the other method has its defenders, I have still thought it better to satisfy the audience with less excellence (if the opinion of Aristotle is to be accepted as the better) than with a little more loftiness to displease those for whose pleasure the play is put on the stage. It would be of little use to compose a play a little more praiseworthy that would then be odious when performed. Tragedies that end terribly can serve for texts to be read (if it appears that spectators hate them); those that end happily can be for the stage.

[…]

Yet even among such base auditors, grave matters can sometimes have such effect that even though their condition makes them lack the capacity for gravity possessed by judicious hearers, they are nonetheless awed by it. They willingly come to hear a frightful and tearful action if it is skillfully handled on the stage. In trying to figure out the reason for this, I have decided that tragedy also has its particular delight: in this weeping is found a secret pleasure which delights its auditors and makes their minds attentive and fills them with marvel, which, in turn, makes them keen to learn, by means of fear and pity, what they don't know, namely, to flee wickedness and pursue virtue. In addition to which, the disposition that human beings have to tearful events draws them quite willingly to watch the spectacle which reveals to us our nature and which makes the humanity that is in us have ample reason to pity the woes of the afflicted. Thus it happens that because the tragic fable makes man experience that which is proper to him, having compassion for the miseries of others, viewers will return eager to rewitness a tragedy if it is performed several times. This occurred, as I said above with my *Orbecche*.

Further reading

Alexandra Coller, 'Friendship, Gender, and Virtue in the Renaissance: The Tragedies of Giambattista Giraldi Cinzio', *Italica* 92, no. 3 (2015): 600–12.

Philip Russell Horne, *The Tragedies of Giambattista Cinthio Giraldi* (Oxford: Oxford University Press, 1962).

Daniel Javitch, 'Introduction to Giovan Battista Giraldi Cinthio's "Discourse or Letter on the Composition of Comedies and Tragedies"', *Renaissance Drama* 39 (2011): 197–206.

---

[21]*Altile … Antivalomeni*: tragedies by Giraldi featuring happy endings.

2.2 LODOVICO CASTELVETRO, *THE POETICS OF ARISTOTLE* (1570)

Lodovico Castelvetro (1505–71) is best known for his 1570 Italian commentary on Aristotle's *Poetics*; he is also known for being charged with heresy after translating writings by the Protestant author Philip Melanchthon, after which he was excommunicated and exiled from Italy. Castelvetro describes his commentary as explaining Aristotle's literary theory, but he makes notable departures from the *Poetics*. He famously proclaims that pleasure is the only purpose of poetry, rebutting Aristotle's suggestion that audiences should also learn from it. Despite his emphasis on delight, the Christian framework through which Castelvetro filters the *Poetics* leads him to morally inflected criticisms and corrections, including a revised understanding of catharsis. Most influentially, he developed the idea that tragedy should feature unity of action, time, and place. These so-called Aristotelian unities came to command considerable authority among playwrights in early modern France, and to a lesser extent in England, but they represent a particular tradition of Aristotelian interpretation rather than Aristotle himself.

I.9. History and the Arts and Sciences Not Fit Subjects for Poetry

But there is another and more obvious reason why the arts and sciences cannot supply matter for poetry. It is that poetry was invented for the sole purpose of providing pleasure and recreation, by which I mean to provide pleasure and recreation to the souls of the common people and the rude multitude, who are incapable of understanding the rational proofs, the distinctions, and the arguments, all of them subtle and nothing like the talk normally heard among the unlearned, which philosophers make use of in their investigations of the truth of things and students of the arts in constituting the arts; and, not understanding them, it is only natural that they should hear them with annoyance and displeasure, for we are all naturally annoyed beyond measure when others speak of matters exceeding our intellectual reach. And so if we conceded that the arts and sciences could supply proper matter to the poets, we should be obliged to concede also either that poetry was not invented to give pleasure or that it was not invented for the ignorant, but that its purpose was to teach and its only audience persons disciplined by the study of letters and exercised in disputations. That these views are false will be proved in the pages that follow.

Now since poetry was invented for the pleasure and recreation of the common people, its subjects must be things suited to their understanding and therefore capable of giving them pleasure. Such things are the everyday happenings that are talked about among the people, the kind that resemble those reported in any one day's news and in histories. This is the reason for our contention that as regards its matter poetry is an image or an imitation of history. And being an imitation of history, poetry not only brings glory to its inventor and entitles him to the name of poet, but offers more pleasure than the histories of actual events. The reasons for this will be given in the proper place. To the matter of poetry is added metre, a marvelous and delightful mode of speech. One of the reasons why poetic matter is treated metrically has already been given; it is that metre renders it possible for the speaker on the stage to speak without impropriety in a loud voice and so to make himself quite easily heard by his audience. ... (III.5d; 1.253). But if the arts and sciences lie beyond the intellectual reach of the common people, poets should not only refrain from taking artistic and scientific matters as subjects of whole poems, but should also guard against introducing such matters into any part of them. In this regard Lucan and Dante[22] are especially and needlessly at fault, for they both made use of astronomical lore to designate the seasons of the year and the hours of the day and night, a fault that cannot be imputed to Homer or to Virgil in his *Aeneid*.[23] For this reason I cannot but wonder a little at Quintilian, who asserts (*Inst. Or.* 1. 4. 4) that one cannot be a good student of the poets unless he is schooled in both astronomy and philosophy.[24]

[...]

III.11 Happiness and Misery as Ends of Tragedy and Comedy

The end of tragedy is happiness or misery, but not happiness or misery of every kind, for as we shall see these differ according as they are produced by tragic or comic incidents. The happiness produced by tragedy is the kind a person knows when he himself or some one dear to him is saved from death or is released from suffering or avoids a fall from the rank of royalty. Tragic misery, on the other hand, is restricted to the kind a person knows when he himself or some one dear to him suffers death or is plunged into suffering or falls from the rank of royalty. The happiness produced by comedy is the kind a person knows when he has succeeded in putting an end to the scorn to which he himself or persons dear to him have been subjected, in blotting out some disgrace which had been thought ineffaceable, in recovering some lost person or thing dear to him, or in achieving the satisfaction of amorous desire. Comic misery, on the other hand, is restricted to the misery a person knows when he himself or some one dear to him is made the object of mild scorn, suffers some mild disgrace or the loss of a few possessions, is thwarted in love, or is otherwise made somewhat unhappy.

[...]

III.14.

Returning to our subject, I am unable to understand why the fall of a man of very holy life from happiness to misery should not arouse pity and fear; why it should not, in fact, arouse greater pity and fear than the fall of a man of ordinary virtue, for those whose lives are not of a holiness comparable to his, as the lives of the common people generally are not, are more terrified and dismayed by the sufferings of one better than themselves than by those of one of their own kind. The experience of such a fall would fill them with the fear that they may

---

[22]**Lucan and Dante:** Roman poet Marcus Annaeus Lucanus (39–65 CE) was best known for his *Pharsalia*, an epic poem about the wars between Julius Caesar and Pompey. Florentine poet Dante Alighieri (1265–1321) is known especially for his *Divine Comedy*, a trilogy including the *Inferno*, *Purgatorio*, and *Paradisio*.

[23]**Homer ... Virgil:** Homer's *Iliad* and *Odyssey* were known as the original models of the epic genre; Virgil's *Aeneid* was the most influential epic in the early modern period.

[24]**Quintilian:** Roman rhetorician Quintilian (*c*.35–*c*.100 CE) is best known for his *Institutio Oratoria*, on how to be a successful orator.

well be visited by a similar misfortune, bringing before their minds the Gospel text (Luke 23:31), 'For if they do these things in green tree, what should be done in the dry?' And who shall be pitied if not the saintly man who falls into misfortune? For if we are moved to pity by those who suffer unjustly, who deserves misfortune less than the man of most saintly life? None assuredly, and the representation of a supremely saintly man falling from happiness to misery should not therefore have been rejected as incapable of moving audiences to pity and fear. Yet Aristotle asserts that the fall of such a man does not fill us with pity and fear but with indignation against God, which is a blasphemous state of mind. To which I reply that if we are filled with indignation against God it does not follow that we are not also filled with pity and fear. The indignation does not extinguish the pity and fear. When, for example, a person of ordinary virtue is unjustly injured by some one, we feel indignation against the latter, but do not for that reason fail to be moved to pity and fear by the undeserved suffering of the injured man. Who is there that does not hate Phaedra, the false accuser of Hippolytus to his father, and is not at the same time moved to pity and fear by Hippolytus' death, which is a consequence of that accusation?[25]

At this point someone may protest, 'I concede to you that the fall of a man of holy life from happiness to misery will move people to pity and fear if you will concede to me that it will also move them to indignation against God. But that indignation is blasphemous, and to avoid it we must eschew the kind of reversal involving that kind of person and renounce all the pity and all the fear that it might generate.' To which one may briefly reply that the common people, who believe that God rules the world and watches over all individual things, exercising a special care over each, believe also that He is just in all his actions and makes all things redound to His own glory and to the good of His faithful servants. Therefore when they witness the suffering of a holy man they do not forthwith revile and blaspheme God and accuse Him of injustice, but turning their hate against the immediate causes which by God's permissive will had the power to work the holy man's hurt, they absolve God of all blame, and unable to conceive of Him as the author of evil, explain the holy man's suffering in one of a number of ways. They may imagine that he appears to be more holy than he really is and that he is justly punished as a hypocrite. Or, since no one is quite without sin, they may believe that he has fallen into sins which God as a just judge will not allow to go unpunished. Or they may think that he has been tried by misfortune so that he may become more perfect, as gold is refined in the fire. Or they may reason that he has been ill treated because God chose this way to manifest His glory, making his fall the occasion of raising him up again in this world or of reserving greater rewards for him in the next. In short they will ascribe the good man's suffering to any cause except God's injustice and will humble themselves before His might without resistance and without struggle. The fact is that if, on witnessing the fall of a just man, the people were truly moved to indignation and truly fixed the blame on God, they would respond in precisely the same manner to the unjust sufferings of a person of ordinary virtue, for in so far as the latter suffers unjustly he does so by God's permissive will. Yet Aristotle never asserts that the suffering of such a man is an abomination.

---

[25] **Phaedra ... accusation:** In Euripides' tragedy *Hippolytus*, Aphrodite punishes Hippolytus for his rejection of passion by forcing his stepmother, Phaedra, to fall in love with him. When he learns of her passion from her nurse, his anger and contempt drive Phaedra to commit suicide, leaving a message for her husband that his son raped her; in response Hippolytus is exiled, cursed, and killed by a sea monster.

III.5b, 'It Must Have Magnitude'

Let us now investigate the proper magnitude of poetic plots. A plot may be considered in two ways, as something that may be apprehended by the intellect alone, without the aid of the media that convey it to the senses, and again as something conveyed to the senses by the media of imitation, and to be apprehended by both sight and hearing, or by the hearing only. The magnitude of a plot may be considered in the same two ways. Reserving consideration of the magnitude of plots of the first type to a later page, we observe that the magnitude of the plots that are apprehended by both sight and hearing should be equal to that of an actual event worthy of being recorded by history; for since the imaginary action from which the plot is formed represents words directly with words and things with things, it must of necessity fill as many hours on the stage as the imaginary action it represents would have filled or would fill in the world if it had actually occurred or were to occur there. Hence we may say that the magnitude of an imaginary plot considered as something that can be apprehended by the senses should equal that of the event it represents, and that it stands in the same relation to that event as, say, a portrait to its original when the latter's dimensions are preserved. Now a plot that is apprehended by sight and hearing must not exceed twelve hours, as we have argued elsewhere in support of Aristotle. This limitation holds for both tragic and comic plots. But the magnitude of the plot that is apprehended by the hearing only does not conform to that of the event it represents, nor is there a single measuring rod that can be applied to both; for narrative plots disregard the time element in the events they represent, and any of their episodes may be of longer or shorter duration than its historical counterpart. (This would seem to be true of dithyrambic poetry as well, at least in so far as it employs language as a medium.) It is of longer duration when the treatment of its subject is particularized and detailed; of shorter duration when it is generalized and succinct. The longer plot may be compared to a portrait that is larger than life and the shorter to one that is of the same dimensions.

[…]

III.5c, It Must Have Unity

[I.233] The third requirement of the plot is that it have unity. A plot, Aristotle asserts (8. 51a 16–35), may be said to have unity if it consists of a single action of a single person.[26] and not

---

[26][**Translator's note:**] 'Of a single person' is not an Aristotelian requirement. Having said (8. 51a 30–31) that in the imitative arts other than poetry the single imitation is always of one thing, A. adds ὄντω χαὶ τὸν μῦθον, ἐπεὶ πράξεως μίμησίς ἐστι, μιᾶς τε εἶναι. . ., which C. correctly translates (R. 1.233) '[Bisogna] cosi anchora la favola, che è rassomiglianza d' attione, sia d'una. . . .' ([It is necessary]. . .too, that the plot, which is the imitation of an action, should be the imitation of one action). In the commentary C. arbitrarily adds 'of one person' to 'a single action' (una sola attione d' una persona). This last phrase is omitted later in the paragraph, but the conception of the poem as representing the single action of a single person remains constant in C.'s conception of unity. Further on in this chapter he will deny that a poem may not contain more than one action and will assert that every well-constructed tragedy or comedy (ogni tragedia et comedia bene ordinata) contains not one action but two, though one of them 'seems' (pare) to be subordinate to the other. But in the end he will conclude that poets are free to make a plot consisting of a number of actions of a single person, or a single action of a whole people, or a number of actions of a whole people, or many actions of many persons or many peoples. Yet poets will normally restrict themselves to the representation of the single actions of single persons: tragic and comic poets because they labour under severe restrictions of time and place

all the actions of one person's life. This contradicts the opinion held by some that a plot may be said to have unity if it simply relates the actions of a single person, which assumes that the unity of the plot results from its having a single hero and not a single action. The statement of this requirement gives Aristotle the occasion for censuring poets who, holding an erroneous opinion of the matter, composed a *Herculeid* or a *Theseid,* that is, poems relating all the actions of Hercules or Theseus, and for praising Homer, whose *Iliad* and *Odyssey* each contains a single action. Not content with having proved his point by invoking the authority of Homer, he seeks to reinforce his proof by invoking theory, saying that just as in the other imitative arts the imitation is one if its object is a single thing, so in poetry if the plot, which is the imitation of an action, has unity, it follows that the action it imitates is a single action. Finally he says that the plot represents a whole action, and this leads him to speak of the disposition of the parts, showing how we may ascertain whether they are in the proper order and whether any one of them is or is not indispensable to the whole. These last observations, like much else in the *Poetics,* are out of their proper order, for they hark back to the first requirement of the plot, that it must be a whole and should have been incorporated in the discussion of that requirement.

[...]

III.10. Tragic Pleasure and the Spectacle

At this point some one may ask what kind of pleasure it is that we feel in seeing a good man falling unjustly from happiness to misery. A story of this kind, they say, should normally be the cause not of pleasure but of sorrow. Now there is not the shadow of a doubt that by 'pleasure' Aristotle means the purgation and expulsion of pity and fear from human souls by the action, which we have already described at some length (III.1), of these same emotions. But if this purgation and expulsion are effected, as he affirms, by the action of pity and fear, it is patently absurd to speak of it as a kind of pleasure. It is rightly to be designated, rather, as a moral benefit, for its effect is by nature health of soul produced by the action of very bitter medicine. The authentic pleasure which derives from the experience of pity and fear we ourselves have called 'indirect pleasure' (p. 164). We call it indirect because it is not the *direct* result of the experience of a tragic event. The immediate effect upon us of such events, which depict the unjust sufferings of others, is, in fact, one of sadness; this sadness, however, being caused, as it is, by injustice, brings us to a recognition of our goodness, and it is this recognition that, thanks to the love we naturally bear ourselves, becomes the cause of very great pleasure. To this pleasure is added another that is not inconsiderable and springs from the private and unarticulated discovery, occasioned by our observation of the unjust sufferings of other men that may also visit us and others like us, that we are subject to many misfortunes and that no man should rest his trust in a tranquil course of the things of this world. Discovering these truths by our own effort yields a greater pleasure than learning them from someone who should impart them to us verbally and in public in the capacity of a master, for the experience

---

and epic poets because though not subject to those restrictions they welcome the opportunities that the difficulties of producing a notable epic on so limited a subject afford them for displaying the excellence of their genius. For the frequent use of the double plot by Italian tragic writers see Marvin T. Herrick, *Italian Tragedy in the Renaissance* (Urbana: University of Illinois Press, 1965), p. 282.

of actualities imprints doctrine on the soul more deeply than the mere voice of any master. Then, too, it gives us greater pleasure to learn a little by our own efforts than a great deal from others, for we cannot begin to learn from others without first confessing our ignorance of that which we desire to know and then being left with a sense of obligation to them for what they have taught us. It is perhaps with an eye to all this that the Preacher (Eccl. 7:2) has said that it is better to go to the house of mourning than to the house of feasting.

[...]

At this point someone may protest, 'I concede to you that the fall of a man of holy life from happiness to misery will move people to pity and fear if you will concede to me that it will also move them to indignation against God. But that indignation is blasphemous, and to avoid it we must eschew the kind of reversal involving that kind of person and renounce all the pity and all the fear that it might generate.' To which one may briefly reply that the common people, who believe that God rules the world and watches over all individual things, exercising a special care over each, believe also that He is just in all his actions and makes all things redound to His own glory and to the good of His faithful servants. Therefore when they witness the suffering of a holy man they do not forthwith revile and blaspheme God and accuse Him of injustice, but turning their hate against the immediate causes which by God's permissive will had the power to work the holy man's hurt, they absolve God of all blame, and unable to conceive of Him as the author of evil, explain the holy man's suffering in one of a number of ways. They may imagine that he appears to be more holy than he really is and that he is justly punished as a hypocrite. Or, since no one is quite without sin, they may believe that he has fallen into sins which God as a just judge will not allow to go unpunished. Or they may think that he has been tried by misfortune so that he may become more perfect, as gold is refined in the fire. Or they may reason that he has been ill treated because God chose this way to manifest His glory, making his fall the occasion of raising him up again in this world or of reserving greater rewards for him in the next. In short they will ascribe the good man's suffering to any cause except God's injustice and will humble themselves before His might without resistance and without struggle. The fact is that if, on witnessing the fall of a just man, the people were truly moved to indignation and truly fixed the blame on God, they would respond in precisely the same manner to the unjust sufferings of a person of ordinary virtue, for in so far as the latter suffers unjustly he does so by God's permissive will. Yet Aristotle never asserts that the suffering of such a man is an abomination.

[...]

V.2a. Epic poetry

[1.148] The actions adopted by tragedy were not and, as we shall show, could not in the nature of things have been of the same length as those proper to epic poetry, that is to say, they did not extend over a longer period of time than one revolution of the sun. The fact is, however, that tragedy at first adopted actions of a length suited to epic poetry, but that it later rejected them as unsuited to dramatic treatment. This explains why Aristotle takes pains to specify the maximum period of time over which a tragic action may extend, which is one revolution of the sun, but leaves the time limits of epic poetry indeterminate. For epic poetry tells its story through the single medium of language, and since language has the power to set all kinds of things, however remote in time and space, before our intellect, it can, without violence to its nature, recount an action that happened in different places over many years. This cannot be done by tragedy, for a tragic action may not extend beyond quite narrow limits of time or place – to be more precise, it must be set in a place no larger than the stage on which the actors perform and in a period of time no longer than that which is filled by their performance. But just as the place in question is limited by the stage, so the time is limited by the period within which the audience may sit in the theatre without discomfort, and this period, as Aristotle tells us and I myself believe, cannot be longer than one revolution of the sun, or twelve hours, for people cannot go without food, drink, and sleep and without relieving their bowels and their bladders and attending to other bodily needs for longer than twelve hours. Nor can they be deceived into believing that the action extends over a number of days and nights when they can tell by the testimony of their senses that they have been sitting in the theatre only a few hours. That being so, let Plautus and Terence[27] find what justifications they can for those comedies of their authorship in which the actions fill more than a single day.

---

[27]**Plautus and Terence:** Plautus (*c*.254–184 BCE) and Terence (*c*.195–*c*.159 BCE) were the most prominent comic playwrights of ancient Rome.

2.3 STEPHEN GOSSON, *PLAYS CONFUTED IN FIVE ACTIONS* (1582)

Stephen Gosson (1554–1624), an English writer and minister, was one of the most influential attackers of the early modern stage. Classically educated at Canterbury's Cathedral School and Oxford, he became an actor and playwright in London in the 1570s, but turned against the theatre in his treatises *The School of Abuse* (1579), *An Apology of the School of Abuse* (also 1579), and *Plays Confuted in Five Actions* (1582). After going on to become ordained as a minister, he held a series of posts culminating in his 1600 appointment as rector of the prestigious St. Botolph's. Gosson's account of tragedy is indebted especially to Plato and the Christian church fathers. He argues that plays are the work of the devil, seducing viewers into blasphemy, idolatry, and sin through appealing to pleasure. He holds that reading and writing plays can be acceptable, but that performances are immoral, because self-transformation, impersonation, and deception violate God's will.

That stage plays are the doctrine and invention of the devil may be gathered by Tertullian,[28] who notes very well that the devil, foreseeing the ruin of his kingdom, made these shows in order to enlarge his dominion and pull us from God.

And Thomas Lodge,[29] in that patched pamphlet of his wherein he takes upon him the defense of plays, little perceiving how lustily the chips fly in his face whilst he hews out timber to make the frame, confesses openly that plays were consecrated by the heathens to the honor of their gods, which in deed is true, yet serves it better to overthrow them than establish them: for whatsoever was consecrated to the honor of heathen gods was consecrated to idolatry; stage plays, by his own confession, were consecrated to the honor of heathen gods, therefore consecrated to idolatry. Being consecrated to idolatry, they are not of God; if they proceed not from God, they are the doctrine and inventions of the devil. ...

The argument of tragedies is wrath, cruelty, incest, injury, murder either violent by mighty men. The ground work of comedies is love, cozenage,[30] flattery, bawdry,[31] sly conveyance of whoredom; the persons, cooks, queans,[32] knaves, bawds, parasites, courtesans, lecherous old men, amorous young men. ... The best play you can pick out is but a mixture of good and evil; how can it be then the schoolmistress of life? The beholding of troubles and miserable slaughters that are in tragedies drive us to immoderate sorrow, heaviness, womanish weeping and mourning, whereby we become lovers of dumps and lamentation, both enemies to fortitude. Comedies so tickle our senses with a pleasanter vein that they make us lovers of laughter and pleasure without any mean,[33] both foes to temperance; what schooling is this? ...

---

[28]**Tertullian:** Christian church father (*c.*160–240 CE) from Carthage; author of theological and moral works, including tracts against the theatre. Gosson cites him here from *De Spectaculis*, II.

[29]**Thomas Lodge:** English author (1558–1625) of plays, poems, prose romances, and pamphlets. Gosson studied at Oxford at the same time as Lodge and probably knew him; he refers here to Lodge's 1579 *Defence of Poetry, Music and Stage Plays*, which he wrote in reply to Gosson's first antitheatrical treatise, *The School of Abuse* (1579).

[30]**Cozenage:** trickery, deception.

[31]**Bawdry:** lewd and lascivious material.

[32]**Queans:** impudent women, strumpets.

[33]**Mean:** moderation.

Upon this consideration, Aristotle[34] utterly forbids young men of plays till they be settled in mind and immovable in affection, lest, coming to the stage to fetch physic for love, they quench their heat with a pint of water and a pottle[35] of fire; partly because that which is learned must be learned of the best, lest the example of ungodly masters poison us rather than instruct us. But whether plays, for the matter, or players, for their manners, be fit schoolmasters of honesty, I report me to them that by frequenting theaters they are very well acquainted with the argument of the one, the life of the other. If any goodness were to be learned at plays it is likely that the players themselves, which commit every syllable to memory, should profit most, because that as every man learns, so he lives; and as his study is, such are his manners. But the daily experience of their behaviour shows that they reap no profit by the discipline themselves. How, then, can they put us in any good hope to be instructed thereby, when we have the sight of such lessons, but an hour or two as they study and practice every day, yet are never the better?

[...]

So subtle is the devil that, under the colour of recreation in London, and of exercise of learning in the universities, by seeing of plays, he makes us to join with the Gentiles[36] in their corruption. Because the sweet numbers of poetry flowing in verse do wonderfully tickle the hearers' ears, the devil hath tied this to most of our plays, that whatsoever he would have stick fast to our souls might slip down in sugar by this enticement, for that which delights never troubles our swallow. Thus when any matter of love is interlarded,[37] though the thing itself be able to allure us, yet it is so set out with sweetness of words, fitness of epithets, with metaphors, allegories, hyperboles, amphibologies,[38] similitudes, with phrases so picked, so pure, so proper; with action so smooth, so lively, so wanton; that the poison, creeping on secretly without grief, chokes us at last, and hurls us down in a dead sleep. As the devil hath brought in all that poetry can sing, so hath he sought out every strain that music is able to pipe, and drawn all kind of instruments into that compass, simple and mixed.

[...]

It may easily be gathered by the end of plays that comedies and tragedies are the fittest devises he could strew behind him to stop us of passage and break our order. Not that he meaneth to take his heels, but to kill us by subtlety when we straggle. What brings disorder more then sin? That plays are set out for a sinful delight may be gathered partly by Menander,[39] partly by Terence,[40] partly by the manner of penning in these days, partly by the object of plays. By Menander because Vives[41] affirms that he, perceiving the Macedons[42] wholly given over to love and wantonness, wrote comedies of love to feed their humor. By Terence because

---

[34]**Aristotle:** the Greek philosopher Aristotle makes this recommendation in his *Politics*, VII, xv, 9–10. For Aristotle's views on the theatre, see extract 1.2.

[35]**Pottle:** little pot; half-gallon measure.

[36]**Gentiles:** heathens, idolaters.

[37]**Interlarded:** mixed.

[38]**Amphibologies:** ambiguities.

[39]**Menander:** Greek playwright (*c.*344–*c.*292 BCE), best-known author of Greek New Comedy.

[40]**Terence:** Roman playwright (185–159 BCE) known for Roman New Comedy.

[41]**Vives:** Juan Luis Vives (1493–1540) was a humanist scholar from Valencia, Spain. Gosson here cites his commentary on Augustine's *De Civitate Dei*, II.viii.

[42]**Macedons:** inhabitants of Macedonia, ancient kingdom to the north of Greece.

he confesses of himself that all that he sought was but to close with the common people.[43] By the manner of penning in these days, because the poets send their verses to the stage upon such feet as continually are rolled up in rhyme at the fingers' ends, which is plausible to the barbarous, and carries a sting into the ears of the common people. By the object, because tragedies and comedies stir up affections, and affections are naturally planted in that part of the mind that is common to us with brute beasts.

He that travails to advance the worst part of the mind is like unto him that in government of cities gives all the authority to the worst men which, being well weighed, is to betray the city, and the best men, into the hands of the wicked. But the poets that write plays, and they that present them upon the stage, study to make our affections overflow, whereby they draw the bridle from that part of the mind that should ever be curbed, from running on head: which is manifest treason to our souls, and delivers them captive to the devil.

[...]

Therefore as I have already discovered the corruption of plays by the corruption of their causes – the efficient, the matter, the form, the end – so will I conclude the effects that this poison works among us. The devil is not so ignorant how mightily these outward spectacles effeminate and soften the hearts of men; vice is learned with beholding, sense is tickled, desire pricked, and those impressions of mind are secretly conveyed over to the gazers, which the players do counterfeit on the stage. As long as we know ourselves to be flesh, beholding those examples in theaters that are incident to flesh, we are taught by other men's examples how to fall. And they that came honest to a play may depart infected. Lactantius[44] doubts whether any corruption can be greater than that which is daily bred by plays, because the expressing of vice by imitation brings us by the shadow, to the substance of the same. Whereupon he affirms them necessary to be banished, lest wickedness be learned, or with the custom of pleasure, by little and little we forget God. What force there is in the gestures of players may be gathered by the tale of Bacchus and Ariadne, which Xenophon[45] reports to be played at a banquet by a Syracusan and his boy and his dancing trull.[46] In came the Syracusan, not unlike to prologue of our plays, discoursing the argument of the fable; then entered Ariadne,[47] gorgeously attired like a bride, and sat in the presence of them all; after came Bacchus[48] dancing to the pipe. Ariadne, perceiving him, though she neither rose to meet him nor stirred from the place to welcome him, yet she showed by her gesture that she sat upon thorns.

When Bacchus beheld her, expressing in his dance the passions of love, he placed himself somewhat near to her, and embraced her: she, with an amorous kind of fear and strangeness, as though she would thrust him away with the little finger and pull him again with both her hands, somewhat timorously and doubtfully entertained him.

---

[43]**Terence … people:** see Terence, *Andria*, Prologue, 1–3.

[44]**Lactantius:** Christian church father (*c.*250–325 CE) from North Africa; Gosson here cites his *Divine Institutes*, VI, xx, 27.

[45]**Xenophon:** ancient Greek philosopher and student of Socrates (*c.*430–354 BCE); this anecdote comes from his *Symposium*, IX, ii–vii.

[46]**Trull:** prostitute.

[47]**Ariadne:** in Greek myth, daughter of King Minos of Crete; she ran away with Theseus after helping him escape the Minotaur's labyrinth, but was abandoned by him on the island of Naxos, where she was claimed by Dionysus/Bacchus, the god of wine, madness, and theatre.

[48]**Bacchus:** Roman name for Dionysus.

At this the beholders began to shout; when Bacchus rose up, tenderly lifting Ariadne from her seat, no small store of courtesy passing between them, the beholders rose up. Every man stood on tip toe, and seemed to hover over the prey; when they swore, the company swore; when they departed to bed, the company presently was set on fire; they that were married posted home to their wives; they that were single vowed very solemnly to be wedded.

As the sting of phalangion[49] spreads her poison through every vein when no hurt is seen, so amorous gesture strikes to the heart when no skin is razed. Therefore Cupid is painted with bow and arrows, because it is the property of lust to wound aloof.[50] Which being well weighed, Saint Cyprian[51] had very good cause to complain that players are spots to our manners, nourishers of vice, and corrupters of all things by their gestures. The godly Father, knowing the practice of playing to be so evil, and the inconveniences so monstrous that grew thereby, thinks the majesty of God to be stained, the honor of his church defaced, when players are admitted to the table of the Lord. Neither was this the opinion of Saint Cyprian alone, but of the whole assembly of learned fathers in the counsel held under Constantius the emperor.[52]

Further reading

Jonas A. Barish, *The Antitheatrical Prejudice* (Berkeley: University of California Press, 1981).

Stephen S. Hilliard, 'Stephen Gosson and the Elizabethan Distrust of the Effects of Drama', *English Literary Renaissance* 9, no. 2 (1979): 225–39.

Efterpi Mitsi, 'Myth and Metamorphosis in Stephen Gosson's *Schoole of Abuse*', *English* 60, no. 229 (2011): 108–23.

[49]**Phalangion:** spider.

[50]**Aloof:** from afar.

[51]**Saint Cyprian:** Christian church father (*c.*200–58 CE), bishop of Carthage; he attacks playgoing in letters to Eucratius and Donatus.

[52]**Constantius the emperor:** Constantius II (317–61 CE) was Roman Emperor from 337 to 361 CE. The counsel cited is the Synod of Arles, 353 CE.

2.4 PHILIP SIDNEY, *DEFENSE OF POETRY* (1595)

Sir Philip Sidney (1554–86) was an English courtier, poet, and critic best known for his sonnet sequence *Astrophil and Stella*, prose romance *The Arcadia*, and *Defence of Poesy* (written *c*.1580, published 1595). Educated at Oxford, Sidney draws on ideas from Plato, Aristotle, Horace, and Italian Renaissance critics in his *Defence*, which promotes literature's moral value in response to attacks such as Stephen Gosson's. Sidney overturns Plato's criticism of imitation by arguing that poetry bypasses the physical world to reach the metaphysical. Echoing Horace's dictum that poetry should be *dulce et utile* (pleasurable and useful), he asserts that its appeal to pleasure heightens its educational power; following Aristotle, he describes poetry as more philosophical than history. Sidney expresses ambivalence about drama, warning against bawdry, mockery, and contemporary playwrights' failures to follow classical rules. Despite these concerns, he honours 'the high and excellent tragedy' for inspiring awe and moral improvement.

So that the right use of comedy will, I think, by nobody be blamed; and much less of the high and excellent tragedy, that openeth the greatest wounds and showeth forth the ulcers that are covered with tissue, that maketh kings fear to be tyrants, and tyrants manifest their tyrannical humors, that with stirring the effects of admiration and commiseration teacheth the uncertainty of this world, and upon how weak foundations gilded roofs are built: that maketh us know, *Qui sceptra duro saevus imperio regit, Timet timentes; metus in auctorem redit.*[53] But how much it can move, Plutarch yieldeth a notable testimony of the abominable tyrant Alexander Phaeraeus,[54] from whose eyes a tragedy well made and represented drew abundance of tears, who without all pity had murdered infinite numbers, and some of his own blood: so as he that was not ashamed to make matters for tragedies, yet could not resist the sweet violence of a tragedy. And if it wrought no further good in him, it was that he in despite of himself withdrew himself from hearkening to that which might mollify[55] his hardened heart. But it is not the tragedy they do mislike, for it were too absurd to cast out so excellent a representation of whatsoever is most worthy to be learned.

[...]

Our tragedies and comedies, not without cause cried out against, observing rules neither of honest civility, nor skillful poetry: excepting *Gorboduc*[56] (again I say of those that I have seen), which, notwithstanding as it is full of stately speeches and well sounding phrases, climbing to the height of Seneca's style,[57] and as full of notable morality which it doth most delightfully

---

[53]***Qui ... redit:*** He who wields the sceptre harshly, with tyrannic force, fears those who fear; fear rebounds on its author; Seneca, *Oedipus*, 705–6.

[54]**Plutarch ... Phaeraeus:** Alexander, the tyrant of Pherae, was reported to have wept at the sufferings of Euripides' *Hecuba*. The Greek historian Plutarch (*c*.46–120 CE) recounted this scene in both his *Life of Alexander* and his *Life of Pelopidas.*

[55]**Mollify:** soften.

[56]**Gorboduc:** *Gorboduc*, by Thomas Sackville and Thomas Norton (1561), was the first English tragedy written in blank verse.

[57]**Seneca's style:** Roman author Lucius Annaeus Seneca (*c*.4 BCE–65 CE) wrote elaborately rhetorical tragedies that were widely read, translated, and admired in the sixteenth century.

teach, and so obtain the very end of poesy. Yet in truth, it is very defective in the circumstances, which grieves me, because it might not remain as an exact model of all tragedies. For it is faulty both in place and time, the two necessary companions of all corporal actions. For where the stage should always represent but one place, and the uttermost time presupposed in it should be, both by Aristotle's precept and common reason, but one day, there is both many days and places inartificially imagined.[58] But if it be so in *Gorboduc*, how much more in all the rest, where you shall have Asia of the one side, and Africa of the other, and so many other under kingdoms that the player, when he comes in, must ever begin with telling where he is, or else the tale will not be conceived. Now you shall have three ladies walk to gather flowers, and then we must believe the stage to be a garden. By and by we hear news of shipwreck in the same place; then we are to blame if we accept it not for a rock. Upon the back of that comes out a hideous monster with fire and smoke, and then the miserable beholders are bound to take it for a cave; while, in the meantime, two armies fly in, represented with four swords and bucklers, and then what hard heart will not receive it for a pitched field?

Now, of time, they are much more liberal. For ordinary it is that two young princes fall in love; after many traverses she is got with child, delivered of a fair boy; he is lost, groweth a man, falleth in love, and is ready to get another child, and all this in two hours' space. Which, how absurd it is in sense, even sense may imagine, and art hath taught, and all ancient examples justified, and at this day the ordinary players in Italy will not err in. Yet will some bring in an example of *Eunuch* in Terence[59] that containeth matter of two days, yet far short of twenty years. True it is, and so was it to be played in two days, and so fitted to the time it set forth. And though Plautus have in one place done amiss, let us hit it with him, and not miss with him.

But they will say, how then shall we set forth a story which contains both many places and many times? And do they not know that a tragedy is tied to the laws of poesy and not of history? Not bound to follow the story, but having liberty either to feign a quite new matter, or to frame the history to the most tragical convenience. Again, many things may be told which cannot be shown, if they know the difference betwixt reporting and representing. As, for example, I may speak, though I am here, of Peru, and in speech digress from that to the description of Calcutta; but in action, I cannot represent it without Pacolet's horse.[60] And so was the manner the ancients took, by some Nuntius,[61] to recount things done in former time or other place. Lastly, if they will represent an history, they must not (as Horace saith) begin *ab ovo*,[62] but they must come to the principal point of that one action which they will represent.

By example this will be best expressed. I have a story of young Polydorus, delivered for safety's sake, with great riches, by his father Priam to Polymnestor, King of Thrace, in the Trojan war time.[63] He, after some years, hearing the overthrow of Priam, for to make the

---

[58]**Aristotle's precept:** the neoclassical unities of time, action, and place, were widely attributed to Aristotle, but were formulated in the sixteenth century; see Castelvetro (extract 2.2).

[59]***Eunuch* in Terence:** Roman comic playwright Terence (*c*.195–*c*.159 BCE), born in North Africa, was much admired in sixteenth century Europe. In his *Eunuch* (161 BCE) a young man pretends to be a eunuch in order to gain access to a beautiful young woman.

[60]**Pacolet's horse:** in the popular medieval romance *Valentine and Orson*, the dwarf Pacolet had a magic horse.

[61]**Nuntius:** Latin for messenger, a common source for reported action in ancient plays.

[62]***Ab ovo*:** from the egg (Latin). In his *Art of Poetry*, Horace commented that the good poet would not tell the story of the Trojan War *ab ovo*, from the egg (of which Helen was born), but would start in the middle; see *Art of Poetry*, 125–52.

[63]**Polydorus ... time:** Sidney recounts here the plot of Euripides' *Hecuba* (*c*.424), which was the most frequently

treasure his own, murdereth the child; the body of the child is taken up by Hecuba; she, the same day, findeth a sleight to be revenged most cruelly of the tyrant. Where now would one of our tragedy writers begin, but with the delivery of the child? Then should he sail over into Thrace, and so spend I know not how many years, and travel numbers of places. But where doth Euripides? Even with the finding of the body, the rest leaving to be told by the spirit of Polydorus. This needs no further to be enlarged; the dullest wit may conceive it.

But besides these gross absurdities, how all their plays be neither right tragedies, nor right comedies, mingling kings and clowns, not because the matter so carrieth it, but thrust in the clown by head and shoulders to play a part in majestical matters, with neither decency nor discretion: so as neither the admiration and commiseration, nor the right sportfulness, is by their mongrel tragicomedy obtained. I know Apuleius[64] did somewhat so, but that is a thing recounted with space of time, not represented in one moment; and I know the ancients have one or two examples of tragicomedies, as Plautus hath *Amphitryo*.[65] But if we mark them well, we shall find that they never, or very daintily, match hornpipes and funerals. So falleth it out that having indeed no right comedy in that comical part of our tragedy, we have nothing but scurrillity unworthy of any chaste ears, or some extreme show of doltishness, indeed fit to lift up a loud laughter and nothing else: where the whole tract of a comedy should be full of delight, as the tragedy should be still maintained in a well raised admiration.

But our comedians think there is no delight without laughter, which is very wrong: for though laughter may come with delight, yet commeth it not of delight, as though delight should be the cause of laughter. But well may one thing breed both together. Nay, rather in themselves they have, as it were, a kind of contrariety. For delight we scarcely do but in things that have a convenience to ourselves, or to the general nature; laughter almost ever commeth of things most disproportioned to ourselves and nature. Delight hath a joy in it, either permanent or present; laughter hath only a scornful tickling.

For example, we are ravished with delight to see a fair woman, and yet are far from being moved to laughter. We laugh at deformed creatures, wherein certainly we cannot delight. We delight in good chances; we laugh at mischances. We delight to hear the happiness of our friends and country, at which he were worthy to be laughed at that would laugh. We shall contrarily laugh sometimes to find a matter quite mistaken, and go down the hill against the bias, in the mouth of some such men as, for the respect of them, one shall be heartily sorry he cannot choose but laugh, and so is rather pained than delighted with laughter. Yet deny I not but that they may go well together, for as in Alexander's picture, well set out, we delight without laughter, and in twenty mad antics, we laugh without delight. So in Hercules, painted with his great beard and furious countenance, in a woman's attire, spinning at Omphale's commandment,[66] it breeds both delight and laughter: for the representing of so strange a power in love procures delight, and the scornfulness of the action stirreth laughter.

But I speak to this purpose, that all the end of the comical part be not upon such scornful matters as stir laughter only, but mix with it that delightful teaching which is the end of poesy.

---

published and translated Greek play in the sixteenth century.

[64]**Apuleius:** Roman author (*c.*124–*c.*170 CE) best known for his prose fiction *Metamorphoses*, or *The Golden Ass.*

[65]**Plautus … Amphitryo:** in the prologue to *Amphitryo*, by Roman comic playwright Plautus (*c.*254–184 BCE), Mercury pronounces the play a tragicomedy; this was the first recorded use of the term.

[66]**Hercules … commandment:** Hercules was forced into this role when enslaved to Omphale, Queen of Lydia.

And the great fault even in that point of laughter, and forbidden plainly by Aristotle,[67] is that they stir laughter in sinful things, which are rather execrable than ridiculous: or in miserable, which are rather to be pitied then scorned. For what is it to make folks gape at a wretched beggar and a beggarly clown, or, against law of hospitality, to jest at strangers because they speak not English so well as we do? What do we learn, since it is certain *nil habet infelix paupertas durius in se, quam quod ridiculos homines facit?*[68] But rather a busy loving courtier, a heartless threatening Thraso,[69] a self-wise seeming schoolmaster, a wry transformed traveller: these if we saw walk in stage-names, which we play naturally, therein were delightful laughter, and teaching delightfulness, as in the other tragedies of Buchanan[70] do justly bring forth a divine admiration. But I have lavished out too many words of this play-matter; I do it because as they are excelling parts of poesy, so is there none so much used in England, and none can be more pitifully abused: which, like an unmannerly daughter, showing a bad education, causeth her mother poesy's honesty to be called in question.

Further reading

Gavin Alexander, 'Introduction', in *Sidney's The Defence of Poesy and Selected Renaissance Literary Criticism* (London: Penguin, 2004), xvii–lxxx.

Micha Lazarus, 'Sidney's Greek Poetics', *Studies in Philology* 112, no. 3 (2015): 504–36.

Donald V. Stump, 'Sidney's Concept of Tragedy in the *Apology* and in the *Arcadia*', *Studies in Philology* 79, no. 1 (1982): 41–61.

---

[67]**Forbidden … by Aristotle:** Aristotle criticizes humour through mockery in *Poetics*, 1449a31–3.
[68]*nil … faci:* Does luckless poverty have nothing harder to bear than that it makes men ridiculous? Juvenal, *Satires*, III, 152–3.
[69]**Thraso:** a bragging soldier in Terence's *Eunuch*.
[70]**Buchanan:** George Buchanan (1506–82) was a Scottish poet, scholar, and translator; he produced Latin translations of Euripides' *Medea* and *Alcestis*, and wrote Latin neoclassical tragedies imitating Greek models.

2.5 THOMAS HEYWOOD, *THE APOLOGY FOR ACTORS* (1612)

Thomas Heywood (*c*.1574–1641) was an English playwright and actor who claimed to have had a part in writing of over two hundred plays; the twenty-three that survive include comedies, tragedies, romances, pageants, masques, mythological cycles, and history plays. In *The Apology for Actors* (1612), Heywood defended plays against their detractors by advocating the transformative effects of acting. In contrast to critics such as Gosson who follow Plato in condemning imitation as dangerous, Heywood argues that imitation lies at the heart of theatre's moral value. Drawing on both classical antiquity and recent history, he describes heroic figures whom actors and audiences can benefit from imitating; he also argues that watching villainy prompts moral horror that reforms sinners and deters wrongdoers. In response to Christian concerns about the theatre, Heywood points out that the New Testament never condemns acting, despite the lively classical drama during the time of Christ and his apostles.

Amongst many other things tolerated in this peaceable and flourishing state, it hath pleased the high and mighty princes of this land to limit the use of certain public theaters, which since many of these over-curious heads have lavishly and violently slandered,[71] I hold it not amiss to lay open some few antiquities to approve the true use of them, with arguments (not of the least moment) which, according to the weakness of my spirit and infancy of my judgment, I will (by God's grace) commit to the eyes of all favorable and judicial readers, as well to satisfy the requests of some of our well qualified favorers, as to stop the envious acclamations of those who challenge to themselves a privilege invective, and against all free estates a railing liberty.

[…]

In the first of the Olympiads,[72] amongst many other active exercises in which Hercules ever triumphed as victor, there was in his nonage[73] presented unto him by his tutor in the fashion of a history, acted by the choice of the nobility of Greece, the worthy and memorable acts of his father Jupiter. Which, being personated with lively and well-spirited action, wrought such impression in his noble thoughts that in mere emulation of his father's valor (not at the behest of his stepdame Juno), he performed his twelve labors: him valiant Theseus followed, and Achilles, Theseus, which bred in them such haughty and magnanimous attempts that every succeeding age hath recorded their worths, unto fresh admiration.

[…]

A description is only a shadow received by the ear, but not perceived by the eye; so, lively portraiture is merely a form seen by the eye, but can neither show action, passion, motion, or any other gesture, to move the spirits of the beholder to admiration. But to see a soldier shaped like a soldier, walk, speak, act like a soldier; to see a Hector[74] all besmeared in blood, trampling

---

[71]**Over-curious … slandered:** referring to antitheatricalists such as Stephen Gosson (see extract 2.3).
[72]**Olympiads:** four-year epochs used in ancient Greece to date historical events; the first Olympiad would have begun in 776 BCE.
[73]**Nonage:** childhood.
[74]**Hector:** Trojan hero, son of King Priam.

upon the bulks of kings; a Troilus[75] returning from the field in the sight of his father Priam, as if man and horse even from the steed's rough fetlocks to the plume in the champion's helmet had been together plunged into a purple ocean; to see a Pompey[76] ride in triumph, then a Caesar[77] conquer that Pompey; laboring Hannibal[78] alive, hewing his passage through the Alps; to see as, I have seen, Hercules in his own shape hunting the boar, knocking down the bull, taming the hart, fighting with Hydra, murdering Geryon, slaughtering Diomedes, wounding the Stimphalides, killing the Centaurs, pashing the lion, squeezing the dragon, dragging Cerberus in chains, and lastly, on his high pyramids writing *Nil ultra*:[79] oh, these were sights to make an Alexander.

To turn to our domestic histories: what English blood, seeing the person of any bold English man presented and doth not hug his fame, and hunny[80] at his valor, pursuing him in his enterprise with his best wishes, and as being rapt in contemplation, offers to him in his heart all prosperous performance, as if the personater were the man personated: so bewitching a thing is lively and well spirited action, that it hath power to new mold the hearts of the spectators and fashion them to the shape of any noble and notable attempt. What coward to see his countryman valiant would not be ashamed of his own cowardice? What English prince should he behold the true portraiture of that famous King Edward the third,[81] foraging France, taking so great a king captive in his own country, quartering the English lions with the French flower-de-lyce,[82] and would not be suddenly inflamed with so royal a spectacle, being made apt and fit for the like achievement?

[…]

Art thou addicted to prodigality? envy? cruelty? perjury? flattery? or rage? Our scenes afford thee store of men to shape your lives by, who be frugal, loving, gentle, trusty, without soothing, and in all things temperate. Wouldst thou be honourable? Just, friendly, moderate, devout, merciful, and loving concord? Thou mayest see many of their fates and ruins who have been dishonourable, unjust, false, gluttonous, sacrilegious, bloody-minded, and broachers of dissention. Women likewise that are chaste, are by us extolled, and encouraged in their virtues, being instanced by Diana, Belphebe, Matilda, Lucrece, and the Countess of Salisbury.[83]

---

[75]**Troilus:** another Trojan warrior, also a son of King Priam.

[76]**Pompey:** Gnaeus Pompeius Magnus, known as Pompey the Great (106 BCE–48 BCE), was a Roman general and rival to Julius Caesar; he was defeated by Caesar in 48 BCE after the collapse of the First Triumvirate (Pompey, Caesar, and Marcus Licinius Crassus).

[77]**Caesar:** Julius Caesar (100 BCE–44 BCE) was a Roman politician and general who became dictator and consul of the Roman Republic before his assassination brought on the civil wars that ended the Republic and began the rise of the Roman Empire.

[78]**Hannibal:** Carthaginian general (247 BCE–*c*.182 BCE); he famously surprised Rome by invading Italy through crossing the Alps with an army and a herd of elephants, beginning the second Punic War.

[79]*Nil ultra:* no more. Heywood here recounts the labours of Hercules.

[80]**Hunny:** marvel, delight.

[81]**King Edward the third:** (1312–77), known for his long-running reign over England (1327 until his death) and for military triumphs over France.

[82]**Flower-de-lyce:** fleur-de-lis, heraldic lily worn on royal arms of France.

[83]**Diana … Countess of Salisbury:** Diana was the Roman goddess of virginity. Belphebe, a character in Spenser's *Faerie Queene* (1590), was raised as a virgin by Diana. Matilda was a virgin Matilda of medieval legend, as well as an alternate name for the chaste Maid Marian of the Robin Hood legend. The Roman Lucretia, wife of Collatine, stabbed herself after being raped by Tarquin. Margaret Pole, Countess of Salisbury, became a famous martyr after being beheaded by Henry VIII in 1541.

The unchaste are by us showed their errors, in the persons of Phrine, Lais, Thais, Flora: and amongst us, Rosamond, and Mistress Shore.[84] What can sooner print the modesty in the souls of the wanton than by discovering unto them the monstrousness of their sin? It follows that we prove these exercises to have been the discoverers of many notorious murders, long concealed from the eyes of the world. To omit all far-fetched instances, we will prove it by a domestic and home-born truth, which within these few years happened. At Lynn in Norfolk, the then Earl of Sussex's players[85] acting the old history of Friar Francis,[86] and presenting a woman who, insatiately doting on a young gentleman, had (the more securely to enjoy his affection) mischievously and secretly murdered her husband, whose ghost haunted her, and at diverse times in her most solitary and private contemplations, in most horrid and fearful shapes, appeared and stood before her. As this was acted, a townswoman (till then of good estimation and report) finding her conscience (at this presentment) extremely troubled, suddenly screeched and cried out Oh my husband, my husband! I see the ghost of my husband fiercely threatening and menacing me. At which shrill and unexpected outcry, the people about her, moved to a strange amazement, inquired the reason of her clamor, when presently, unurged, she told them that seven years ago she, to be possessed of such a gentleman (meaning him) had poisoned her husband, whose fearful image personated itself in the shape of that ghost: whereupon the murderess was apprehended, before the Justices further examined, and by her voluntary confession after condemned. That this is true, as well by the report of the actors as the records of the town, there are many eye-witnesses of this accident yet living, vocally to confirm it.

As strange an accident happened to a company of the same quality some twelve years ago, or not so much, who playing late in the night at a place called Perin in Cornwall, certain Spaniards were landed the same night unsuspected, and undiscovered, with intent to take in the town, spoil, and burn it, when suddenly, even upon their entrance, the players (ignorant as the townsmen of any such attempt) presenting a battle on the stage with their drum and trumpets struck up a loud alarm: which the enemy hearing, and fearing they were discovered, amazedly retired, made some few idle shot in a bravado, and so in a hurly-burly fled disorderly to their boats. At the report of this tumult, the townsmen were immediately armed, and pursued them to the sea, praying God for their happy deliverance from so great a danger, who by his providence made these strangers the instrument and secondary means of their escape from such imminent mischief, and the tyranny of so remorseless an enemy.

Another of the like wonder happened at Amsterdam in Holland. A company of our English comedians (well known) travelling those countries, as they were before the Burgers and the other chief inhabitants, acting the last part of the *Four Sons of Aymon*,[87] towards the last act of the history, where penitent Renaldo, like a common laborer, lived in disguise, vowing as his last penance to labor and carry burdens to the structure of a goodly church there to be erected: whose diligence the laborers envying, since by reason of his stature and strength, he

---

[84]**Phrine … Mistress Shore:** Phryne was a courtesan in ancient Greece (fourth century BCE), as was Lais of Corinth (fifth century BCE). Thais was a courtesan and the mistress of Ptolemy, as well as a prostitute in Terence's *Eunuch*. Flora, Roman goddess of flowering plants, was associated with fertility and sexual excess; Rosamond Clifford was the mistress of King Henry II, and Jane Shore was the mistress of King Edward IV.

[85]**Earl of Sussex's players:** an English theatre company, active 1569–1618.

[86]**History of Friar Francis:** this play has been lost.

[87]*Four Sons of Aymon:* popular contemporary romance translated from a French medieval source.

did usually perfect more work in a day than a dozen of the best (he working for his conscience, they for their lucres[88]). Whereupon by reason his industry had so much disparaged their living, conspired amongst themselves to kill him, waiting for some opportunity to find him asleep, which they might easily do, since the sorest laborers are the soundest sleepers, and industry is the best preparative to rest. Having spied their opportunity, they drove a nail into his temples, of which wound immediately he died. As the actors handled this, the audience might on a sudden understand an outcry, and loud shriek in a remote gallery, and pressing about the place, they might perceive a woman of great gravity, strangely amazed, who with a distracted and troubled brain oft sighed out these words: 'Oh my husband, my husband!' The play, without further interruption, proceeded; the woman was to her own house conducted, without any apparent suspicion, every one conjecturing as their fancies led them. In this agony she some few days languished, and on a time, as certain of her well-disposed neighbors came to comfort her, one amongst the rest being church-warden, to him the sexton posts, to tell them of a strange thing happening him in the ripping up of a grave: see here (quoth he) what I have found, and shows them a fair skull, with a great nail pierced quite through the brain-pan, but we cannot conjecture to whom it should belong, nor how long it hath lain in the earth, the grave being confused, and the flesh consumed. At the report of this accident, the woman, out of the trouble of her afflicted conscience, discovered a former murder. For twelve years ago, by driving that nail into that skull, being the head of her husband, she had treacherously slain him. This being publicly confessed, she was arraigned, condemned, adjudged, and burned. But I draw my subject to greater length then I purposed: these therefore out of other infinites, I have collected, both for their familiarness and lateness of memory.

Further reading

Jean Howard, 'Thomas Heywood: Dramatist of London and Playwright of the Passions', in *The Cambridge Companion on Shakespeare and Contemporary Dramatists*, ed. Ton Hoenselaars (Cambridge: Cambridge University Press, 2012), 120–33.

Richard Rowland, *Thomas Heywood's Theatre, 1599–1639* (Aldershot: Ashgate, 2010).

Ronald Bedford, 'On Being a Person: Elizabethan Acting and the Art of Self-Representation', in *Early Modern Autobiography: Theories, Genres, Practices*, ed. Ronald Bedford, Lloyd Davis and Philippa Kelly (Ann Arbor: University of Michigan Press, 2006), 49–61.

[88]**Lucres:** money.

2.6 PIERRE CORNEILLE, *THREE DISCOURSES ON DRAMATIC POETRY* (1660)

Pierre Corneille (1606–84) was one of the foremost dramatists of seventeenth-century Europe and, before Jean Racine (1639–99), established the benchmark for French classical tragedy. While he wrote over 30 plays in a variety of genres, he was most famed for his composition of tragedies, especially those four regarded as his most brilliant mature works: *Le Cid* (1636–7), *Horace* (1640), *Cinna* (1640–1), and *Polyeucte* (1641–2). The first of these plays provoked a notorious controversy, known as the 'Querelle Du Cid', centring upon the structure and morality of tragedy in contemporary France, with the Académie française eventually determining in 1637 that *Le Cid* had violated not just neoclassical rules concerning time and plotting but also the most basic ethical standards (since the play's heroine, Chimène, wishes to marry her father's murderer). Corneille returned to these debates about tragic decorum later in his career when he included three short essays on tragedy in a collected edition of works in 1660. These essays meditated upon Aristotle's importance for seventeenth-century French theatre, contested some key ideas of the *Poetics*, and distinguished Aristotle's original positions from those of later generations of interpreters.

'On Tragedy and the Means of Treating It according to Verisimilitude[89] or "the Necessary"'

Tragedy has this special use that 'through pity and fear, it purges similar emotions.' These are the terms Aristotle uses in his definition[90] and which teach us two things: one that tragedy arouses pity and fear; two, that by means of pity and fear, it purges similar emotions ....

'We pity,' he says, 'those whom we see suffering an undeserved misfortune and we fear that the same may happen to us when we see people similar to ourselves suffering.' Thus pity includes a concern for the person whom we see suffering, the fear which follows concerns us, and just this passing from one to the other gives us enough of an opening to find the manner in which the purgation of the emotions in tragedy takes place. Pity for a misfortune into which we see people like ourselves fall brings us to the fear of something similar happening to us, this fear leads to the desire to avoid it, and this desire leads us to purge, moderate, rectify, and even to root out in ourselves this passion, which before our very eyes plunges into misfortune the people we pity. The reason for this is ordinary, but natural and indubitable: to avoid the effect, we have to eliminate the cause ... It is true that, ordinarily, only kings are the leading characters in a tragedy and that the audience, not having royal power, has no reason to fear the misfortunes that happen to them. But these kings are men just like the audience and fall into their misfortunes through a transport of passion, of which the spectators themselves are capable. They even give a rationale which easily stretches from the greatest to the least; and the spectator can readily conceive that if a king gives himself up to an excess of ambition, love, hate,

---

[89]**verisimilitude:** in French neoclassical terms, 'verisimilitude' or 'vraisemblance' refers to the degree that a tragic plot conforms to what its audience might be assumed to expect.
[90]**Aristotle ... definition:** see extract 1.2.

or vengeance and falls into a misfortune so great that one pities him, he [the spectator] who is only a commoner has all the more reason to bridle such passions for fear that they may sink him in a similar misfortune. Moreover, it is not necessary to show only the misfortunes of kings in the theatre. Those of other men could find a place there if they were sufficiently illustrious and sufficiently extraordinary to merit it and if history cared enough to inform us about them....

If the purgation of emotions is achieved in tragedy, I insist that it must be done in the manner that I am going to explain. But I doubt that it is ever achieved even in those [tragedies] which fulfill the conditions Aristotle demanded. They are to be found in *Le Cid*[91] and are the reason for its great success: Rodrigue and Chimène have this integrity subject to passions and these passions cause their misfortune since they are only unhappy inasmuch as they are passionate for each other. They fall into unhappiness through this human weakness of which we, like them, are capable. Their misfortune invariably arouses pity and it has cost the spectators enough tears that it cannot be disputed. This pity must [if Aristotle is correct] make us fear falling into the same misfortune and purge in us this excess of love which causes their misfortune, and makes us pity them. But I do not know if pity either instills fear or purges love and I am very much afraid that Aristotle's reasoning on this point is only a beautiful idea which never has its effect in reality....

Nevertheless, whatever difficulty there might be in finding this effective and palpable purgation of passions by means of pity and fear, it is easy for us to agree with Aristotle. We have only to say that in this way of expressing himself he did not mean that these two means [pity and fear] always act together; and that according to him[92] one of the two is sufficient to produce this purgation, with the difference, however, that pity cannot occur without fear and that fear can occur without pity. The death of the Count in *Le Cid* causes no pity, and can, nevertheless, better purge in us this sort of arrogance that is envious of the glory of others than all the compassion we feel for Rodrigue and Chimène can purge the emotions attached to this violent love which arouses pity for both of them ....

To oppose the feelings of one's nature to the raptures of passion or to the severity of duty will create a powerful agitation, which will please the audience ....

In the tragic actions which take place between people who are close to each other, it is necessary to consider if he who wishes to kill the other knows him or does not know him, or if he carries out the deed or fails to do so. The diverse combinations of these two ways to act form four sorts of tragedies to which our philosopher[93] attributes various degrees of perfection. The least perfect is the play in which 'one knows whom one wishes to kill, and in fact has him killed, as in the case of Medea who kills her children, Clytemnestra her husband, Orestes his mother'.[94] And the second type has something more elevated than the first according to [Aristotle]. 'One character has another die without knowing him, and recognizes him with

---

[91]*Le Cid*: the title of Corneille's first influential tragedy of 1636–7. Rodrigue and Chimène are the play's tragic protagonists; they love each other but are bound by various honour codes to seek each other's ruin. The Count of Gormas is Chimène's father whom Rodrigue kills as revenge for dishonouring his family.

[92][**Translator's note**]: Corneille is boldly distorting Aristotle.

[93]**our philosopher:** Aristotle.

[94]**Medea ... Orestes his mother:** In Euripides' tragedy *Medea* (431 BCE), Medea kills her own children in revenge for Jason's abandonment of her; in Aeschylus's *Oresteia* (458 BCE), Clytemnestra murders Agamemnon because of his willingness to sacrifice their daughter Iphigenia, after which Clytemnestra's son, Orestes, plots with his other sister, Electra, to kill their mother.

profound pain after having slain him; and this happens,' he says, 'either before the tragedy as with Oedipus, or during the tragedy.' … The third kind has a high degree of excellence; [it is] to be found 'when one is ready to kill someone close to oneself without knowing it, and when one recognizes this person soon enough to save him, such as when Iphigenia recognizes Orestes[95] as her brother just as she is going to sacrifice him to Diana, and escapes with him.' … He entirely condemns the fourth type which consists of those who knowingly undertake the deed and do not carry it through, which he says 'are rather unsuccessful and not at all tragic'. He gives as an example Haemon in *Antigone*,[96] who pulls his sword on his father and only uses it to kill himself. But if this condemnation were not modified it would be taken too far and would include not only *Le Cid* but *Cinna*, *Rodogune*, *Héraclius*, and *Nicomède*.[97]

Let us then say that [the condemnation] applies only to those [characters] who know the person they want to be rid of, and fail to act, by a simple change of mind, without there being any important event which obliges them to do so and without any loss of power on their part. I have already classed this sort of ending as faulty. But when the characters do all they can and are prevented from arriving at a result by some superior power or by some change in fortune which makes them perish themselves, or puts them under the power of those whom they would like to ruin, there is no doubt that this creates a tragedy of a type perhaps even more sublime than the three types that Aristotle admits; and if he did not speak of it, it is because he saw no examples of it in the theatre of his own time, where it was not the fashion to save good people through the death of bad ones unless one tarnished them with some crime, as with Electra,[98] who frees herself from oppression by the death of her mother, which she encourages her brother to bring about and for which she helps him to find the means ….

The poet's goal is to please according to the rules of his art. In order to please he sometimes has to heighten the brilliance of great actions and to extenuate the horror of fatal ones. These are necessities of embellishment in which he can violate the particular verisimilitude by some alteration of history, but he cannot do without the general verisimilitude, except rarely, and then for things which are of the utmost beauty and so brilliant that they dazzle. Above all, he must never push them [the embellishments] beyond an extraordinary verisimilitude, because these ornaments which he adds from his own invention are not absolutely necessary and it is better to dispense with them completely than to adorn his play with them contrary to all types of verisimilitude. In order to please according to the rules of his art he has to confine his action to unity of time and place; and as this is an absolute and indispensable necessity, he has much greater freedom in these two items than in those of embellishments.

Given the difficulty of finding in history or human imagination enough of these illustrious events worthy of tragedy, whose resolutions and effects could happen at the same place and on the same day, without slightly violating the usual order of things, I cannot believe that this kind of violation is completely condemnable, provided it does not extend to the impossible. There

---

[95]**Iphigenia recognizes Orestes:** at a key point in Euripides' tragedy *Iphigenia in Tauris* (c.414 BCE), the siblings Iphigenia and Orestes eventually recognize one another and this recognition prevents Orestes from being sacrificed.

[96]**Haemon in *Antigone*:** Haemon is the son of the Theban king Creon in Sophocles's tragedy *Antigone* (c.441 BCE). He kills himself, rather than his father, after his father refuses to let Antigone bury her brother Polynices.

[97]***Cinna … Nicomède*:** a selection of Corneille's own tragedies – *Cinna* (1640–1); *Rodogune* (1645); *Héraclius* (1647); *Nicomède* (1651).

[98]**Electra:** daughter of Agamemnon and Clytemnestra in Greek mythology. Following the murder of Agamemnon, she plotted with her brother Orestes to kill her mother in revenge.

are excellent subjects where one cannot avoid it; and a scrupulous playwright would deprive himself of a fine opportunity for fame, and the public of a great deal of satisfaction, if he did not dare to be bold enough to put them on stage, for fear of having to make them move faster than verisimilitude permits. In this case I will give him some advice which he might perhaps find beneficial: he should not specify a fixed time in his play, nor any specific place where he puts his characters. The imagination of the spectator will have more liberty to let itself drift with the flow of the action, if it is not fixed by these boundaries; and he might not notice this haste, if the boundaries did not remind him and focus his attention on it despite himself. I have always regretted having made the King say, in *Le Cid*, that he wanted Rodrigue to wait an hour or two after the defeat of the Moors before fighting Don Sanche. I had done it to show that the play took place within twenty-four hours; and this only served to alert the audience to the constraint to which I submitted the action. If I had ended this fight without designating the time, perhaps no one would have noticed it.

I do not think that in comedy the playwright has this liberty to compress the action, out of the necessity of reducing it to fit the unity of time. Aristotle wants all actions included in it to be verisimilar, and he does not by any means add the words: 'or necessary', as he does for tragedy. Also the difference is quite great between the actions of one and the other. Those of comedy stem from ordinary people and consist only of love intrigues and deceptions, which develop so easily in a day that quite often, in the plays of Plautus and Terence,[99] the time of their duration scarcely exceeds that of their performance. But in tragedy public affairs are usually intermingled with the private interests of the illustrious people who appear in them. There are battles, the capture of cities, great dangers, revolutions of states; and all this is hard to reconcile with the promptitude that the rule obliges us to impose on what happens on stage ….

From 'On the Three Unities: Of Action, of Time, and of Place'

Thus I maintain, as I have already said, that in comedy unity of action consists of unity of intrigue or of hindrance to the schemes of the protagonists. In tragedy it consists of unity of danger, whether the hero succumbs to it or escapes from it. I do not claim that one cannot allow several dangers in the latter, and several intrigues or obstacles in the former, provided that one leads necessarily into the other ….

There must be only one complete action, which leaves the spectator with a calm mind; but it can only evolve through several other incomplete actions, which serve as progressions, and keep the spectator in an agreeable state of suspense. This is what must be done at the end of every act in order to render the action continuous. It is not necessary to know precisely everything the characters do in the intervals between the acts, nor what they are doing when they do not appear on stage, but it is necessary that every act leave an expectation of something that must happen in the following act ….

This leads me to remark that the playwright is not obliged to present to view all the particular actions which lead to the main one. He must choose those which for him are the most worthwhile to show, either because of the beauty of the spectacle, or because of the

---

[99]**Plautus and Terence:** Plautus (*c*.254–184 BCE) and Terence (*c*.195–*c*.159 BCE) were the most prominent comic playwrights in ancient Rome.

brilliance and vehemence of the passions which they produce, or because of some other charm which is attached to them; and he must hide the other [actions] backstage so as to reveal them to the spectator either through narration or through some other exercise of art. Above all, he must bear in mind that particular actions and the main action have to be linked together in such a way that the last actions portrayed are produced by the preceding ones and that all actions have their origin in the protasis which must end with the first act ....

The liaison between the scenes which unites all the particular actions of every act ... is a great ornament in a play which greatly serves to give continuity in the performance; but finally it is only an ornament and not a rule ....

The rule regarding unity of time is founded on these words of Aristotle, 'that a tragedy must contain the duration of its action within one revolution of the sun, or try not to go much beyond it'. These words give rise to this famous dispute as to whether they should be understood as meaning a natural day of twenty-four hours, or an artificial day of twelve: these are two opinions each of which has a considerable following. For myself, I find that there are subjects so difficult to contain in so short a time, that not only would I give them a full twenty-four hours, but I would even permit myself the same licence that this philosopher gives in exceeding this a little, and without scruple would push it as far as thirty. There is a maxim in law that one must stretch favor and restrain rigor ... and I find that an author is rather bothered by this constraint, which has forced some of the writers of antiquity to go as far as the impossible. Euripides in *The Suppliant Women*[100] has Theseus of Athens leave with an army, do battle before the walls of Thebes (which are about twelve or fifteen leagues away), and come back victorious in the following act. And from the moment he leaves until the arrival of the messenger, who comes to give an account of his victory, Aethra and the Chorus have only thirty-six lines to speak. That is a lot to do in so short a time. ...

Many inveigh against this rule which they call tyrannical and they would be right if it were founded only on Aristotle's authority. But what must make it acceptable is the common sense that supports it. The play is an imitation or, more properly put, a portrayal of the actions of men, and there is no doubt that portraits are all the more excellent, the more they resemble the original. The performance lasts two hours, and if the action therein represented did not need more [time] in reality, it would resemble it perfectly. Thus we stop neither at twelve hours, nor at twenty-four, but contain the action of the play in the least amount of time possible, so that its performance better resembles reality and is more perfect ....

Above all I would like to leave this duration [of the action] to the imagination of the spectators and never to fix the time needed, unless required by the subject, principally when its verisimilitude is a little forced, as in *Le Cid*, because this [definiteness] only serves to warn the audience of this precipitateness. What need is there to remark at the beginning of a play that the sun is coming up, that it is midday in the third act, and that the sun is setting at the end of the last act, even when no violence is done to anything in a play by the necessity of obeying this rule? It is an affectation which merely serves to annoy an audience; it is sufficient to establish the possibility of the thing within the time that contains it, so that one may follow [the passage of time] easily if one wants to pay attention to it, without having to apply one's mind to it despite

---

[100] *The Suppliant Women*: a tragedy by Euripides (*c.*424 BCE) in which a group of Argive women ask the Athenian King Theseus to enable their sons' burial when they are denied it by the Theban ruler Creon. Theseus defeats the Theban army in combat and allows the corpses to be laid to rest.

oneself. Even in actions which have no more duration than their actual performance, it would be tasteless to note from act to act that half an hour has passed between one and the other ....

When we take a longer time, such as ten hours, I would like to see the eight that we have to lose be consumed in the intervals between acts, and that each of the acts contains only the time that the performance uses up, especially when there is a constant liaison between scenes; for this liaison does not tolerate a gap between two scenes. Nonetheless I think that the fifth act, because of a particular privilege, has the right to hurry time on a little, so that the part of the action that it represents takes more than is needed for its performance. The reason for this is that the spectator is impatient to see the ending, and when the ending depends on actors who have left the stage, all the conversation one gives to those who remain on stage awaiting news of the others only drags and seems to be without action ....

I cannot forget that although we must compress all the tragic action into the space of a day, this does not prevent the tragedy revealing what its heroes have been doing for several years through a narration or in some other more artful manner, since there are tragedies the crux of which consists in the obscurity of the hero's birth which needs to be explained, as in *Oedipus*. ... But I cannot forget that the choice of an illustrious and much awaited day is a great ornament to any play. Occasions do not always present themselves....

As for unity of place, I can find no precept either in Aristotle or Horace.[101] This has led some people to believe that the rule was only established as a consequence of the unity of time, and they have consequently persuaded themselves that this unity extends as far as a man can come and go in twenty-four hours. This opinion is a little free, and if one made a character travel by coach the two sides of the stage could represent Paris and Rouen.

[...]

To rectify in some fashion this duplication of places when it is unavoidable, I would like two things to be done: first, that the setting never change in the same act, but only between one act and another, as is done in the first three acts of *Cinna*;[102] secondly, that the two places never need different sets and that neither of the two is ever named, but only the general place where both are contained, such as Paris, Rome, Lyon, Constantinople, etc. This will help to deceive the spectator who, seeing nothing that makes him notice the diversity of places, will not notice any (unless through a malicious and critical reflection, of which few are capable), the majority wholeheartedly following the action that they see presented.

Further reading

Marvin A. Carlson, *Theories of the Theatre: A Historical and Critical Survey, from the Greeks to the Present* (Ithaca, NY and London: Cornell University Press, 1993).

John D. Lyons, *Kingdom of Disorder: The Theory of Tragedy in Classical France* (West Lafayette: Purdue University Press, 1999).

Gordon Pocock, *Corneille and Racine: Problems of Tragic Form* (Cambridge: Cambridge University Press, 1973).

---

[101] [**Translator's note:**] It appeared first in Castelvetro.
[102] *Cinna*: Corneille's own tragedy of this name, first performed in 1640–1.

2.7 JOHN MILTON, 'OF THAT SORT OF DRAMATIC
POEM WHICH IS CALLED TRAGEDY' (1671)

John Milton (1608–74), English poet and pamphleteer, was a prodigious student of Greek tragedy (his heavily annotated copy of a 1602 edition of Euripides' plays survives in the Bodleian Library, Oxford). This extract, originally printed as a prefatory epistle to *Samson Agonistes* (1671) shows how he was drawn to classical and European rather than contemporary English standards of tragedy and worked carefully with Aristotelian conventions throughout *Samson Agonistes* – all action takes place in twenty-four hours and is conveyed in a variety of meters; all violence against the protagonist is reported. Milton was at pains, however, to emphasize the congeniality of classical ideas of tragedy and a Christian world view, asserting that St Paul quoted Euripides and that the great German biblical scholar, David Pareus (1548–1622), read the *Book of Revelation* as being structured like a tragedy.

This question of discerning tragic patterns of suffering in Old Testament narrative had obsessed Milton since the late 1630s. A manuscript of his works in the library of Trinity College, Cambridge, shows him making notes about the tragic potential in the stories of Abraham fleeing Egypt, Noah and the Flood, and the destruction of Sodom and Gomorrah; it also reveals how his great *Genesis* poem, *Paradise Lost* (1667), was initially imagined not as an epic but as a tragedy. Unlike later generations of writers on tragedy, therefore, Milton evidently saw no unworkable contradiction between the world described by tragedy and one controlled by a beneficent Christian God.

Tragedy, as it was antiently compos'd, hath been ever held the gravest, moralest, and most profitable of all other Poems: therefore said by *Aristotle* to be of power by raising pity and fear, or terror, to purge the mind of those and such like passions, that is to temper and reduce them to just measure with a kind of delight, stirr'd up by reading or seeing those passions well imitated. Nor is Nature wanting in her own effects to make good his assertion: for so in Physic things of melancholic hue and quality are us'd against melancholy, sowr against sowr, salt to remove salt humours. Hence Philosophers and other gravest Writers, as *Cicero*, *Plutarch* and others, frequently cite out of Tragic Poets, both to adorn and illustrate thir discourse. The Apostle *Paul* himself thought it not unworthy to insert a verse of *Euripides* into the Text of Holy Scripture, 1 *Cor.* 15. 33.[103] and *Pareus*[104] commenting on the *Revelation*, divides the whole

---

[103]**I Cor 15.33.:** 'Be not deceived: evil communications corrupt good manners'; The line is a maxim from lost plays by Menander (most likely his *Thaïs*) and Euripides.

[104]**Pareus:** David Pareus (1548–1622), German Calvinist and biblical scholar. For the passage Milton is referring to, see Elias Arnold's English translation of Pareus's *A Commentary upon the Divine Revelations of the Apostle and Evangelist* (1644), 20: 'But that which beginneth at the fourth Chapter (which is the first propheticall Vision) and the following unto the end, … have plain|ly a *Dramaticall* forme, hence the Revelation may truely be called a *Propheticall Drama*, show, or representation. For as in humane Tragedies, diverse persons one after another come upon the Theater to represent things done, and so again depart: diverse Chores [Choruses] also or Companies of Musitians and Harpers distinguish the diversity of the *Acts*, and while the *Actors* hold up, do with musicall accord sweeten the wearinesse of the Spectators, and keepe them in attention: so verily the thing it selfe speaketh that in this Heavenly Interlude, by diverse *shewes* and *apparitions* are represented diverse, or rather (as we shall see) the same things touching the Church, not past, but to come, and that their diverse *Acts* are renewed by diverse *Chores* or Companies'.

Book as a Tragedy, into Acts distinguisht each by a Chorus of Heavenly Harpings and Song between. Heretofore Men in highest dignity have labour'd not a little to be thought able to compose a Tragedy. Of that honour *Dionysius* the elder[105] was no less ambitious, then before of his attaining to the Tyranny. *Augustus Caesar*[106] also had begun his *Ajax*, but unable to please his own judgment with what he had begun, left it unfinisht. *Seneca* the Philosopher[107] is by some thought the Author of those Tragedies (at lest the best of them) that go under that name. *Gregory Nazianzen*[108] a Father of the Church, thought it not unbeseeming the sanctity of his person to write a Tragedy, which he entitl'd, *Christ suffering*. This is mention'd to vindicate Tragedy from the small esteem, or rather infamy, which in the account of many it undergoes at this day with other common Interludes; hap'ning through the Poets error of intermixing Comic stuff with Tragic sadness and gravity; or introducing trivial and vulgar persons, which by all judicious hath bin counted absurd; and brought in without discretion, corruptly to gratifie the people. And though antient Tragedy use no Prologue,[109] yet using sometimes, in case of self defence, or explanation, that which *Martial* calls an Epistle;[110] in behalf of this Tragedy coming forth after the antient manner, much different from what among us passes for best, thus much before-hand may be Epistl'd; that *Chorus* is here introduc'd after the Greek manner, not antient only but modern, and still in use among the *Italians*. In the modelling therefore of this Poem, with good reason, the Antients and *Italians* are rather follow'd, as of much more authority and fame. The measure of Verse us'd in the Chorus is of all sorts, call'd by the Greeks *Monostrophic*,[111] or rather *Apolelymenon*,[112] without regard had to *Strophe*, *Antistrophe* or *Epod*, which were a kind of Stanza's fram'd only for the Music, then us'd with the Chorus that sung; not essential to the Poem, and therefore not material; or being divided into Stanza's or Pauses, they may be call'd *Allaeostropha*.[113] Division into Act and Scene referring chiefly to the Stage (to which this work never was intended) is here omitted.

It suffices if the whole Drama be found not produc't beyond the fift Act, of the style and uniformitie, and that commonly call'd the Plot, whether intricate or explicit, which is nothing indeed but such oeconomy, or disposition of the fable as may stand best with verisimilitude and

---

[105]**Dionysius the elder:** Dionysius I of Syracuse (*c*.431–367 BCE), commonly regarded as one of the most despotic tyrants of antiquity. His political self-presentation was self-consciously theatrical. He was notorious for wearing a tragic actor's royal robe and is also reported to have written several tragedies.

[106]**Augustus Caesar:** Macrobius (dates uncertain) and Suetonius (*c*.69–*c*.140 CE) both reported that Augustus Caesar (63 BCE–14 CE) enthusiastically began writing a tragedy about the Greek hero Ajax but destroyed it because he was unhappy with his writing style; Macrobius, *Saturnalia*, 2.4. 1–2; Suetonius, *Life of Augustus*, 71.

[107]**Seneca the Philosopher:** Lucius Annaeus Seneca (4 BCE–65 CE), also known as Seneca the Younger, was a Roman statesman, philosopher and sometime advisor to Emperor Nero. He wrote at least 8 tragedies, including *Phaedra*, *Oedipus*, and *Medea*, the texts of which are the only complete Roman tragedies to survive from antiquity.

[108]**Nazianen:** Gregory Nazianzen (325?–390?) was bishop of Constantinople. In Milton's lifetime the influential Byzantine tragic poem on subject of the Passion, *Christus Patiens* (eleventh or twelfth century), was attributed to him.

[109]**Prologue:** 'Prologue', here, in the Restoration sense of a direct opening address to a theatre audience rather than that which precedes the chorus's entrance in classical tragedy.

[110]**Epistle:** The Roman poet Martial (*c*.38–*c*.104 CE) in the prefatory epistle to his second book of *Epigrams* suggested that ancient tragedies, as well as comedies, needed prefatory prologues or epistles because, unlike more singular-voiced poetic forms like epigram or lyric, 'they [plays] cannot speak for themselves'; Martial, *Epigrams*, 17.

[111]**Monostrophic:** Of a single metrical pattern used in all strophes or line arrangements in Greek choral and lyric poetry.

[112]**Apolelymenon:** An irregular arrangement of lines as opposed to the typical organizational structure of choral odes in Greek tragedy: Strophe (turn), Antistrophe (counter-turn), and Epode (after-song).

[113]**Allaeostropha:** Irregular strophic patterning, that is, verse in irregular stanza patterns.

decorum; they only will best judge who are not unacquainted with *Aeschylus*, *Sophocles*, and *Euripides*, the three Tragic Poets unequall'd yet by any, and the best rule to all who endeavour to write Tragedy. The circumscription of time wherein the whole Drama begins and ends, is according to antient rule, and best example, within the space of 24 hours.

Further reading

Hannah Crawford, 'The Politics of Greek Tragedy in *Samson Agonistes*', *The Seventeenth Century* 31, no. 2 (2016): 239–60.

W.R. Parker, *Milton's Debt to Greek Tragedy in Samson Agonistes* (Hamden, CT: Archon Books, 1963).

Andrew Zurcher, 'Milton on Tragedy, Law, Hypallage and Participation', in *Young Milton: The Emerging Author*, ed. Edward Jones (Oxford: Oxford University Press, 2012), 182–205.

2.8 RENÉ RAPIN, *REFLECTIONS ON ARISTOTLE'S TREATISE OF POESIE* (1674)

René Rapin (1621–87) was a French Jesuit writer whose literary critical works were well known throughout late seventeenth-century Europe. His *Reflexions sur la Poétique d'Aristote* were published in Paris in 1674 with an English translation by the critic and historian Thomas Rymer (1641–1713) appearing in London in the same year. Rapin found keen English audiences for his ideas, who – for nationalistic rather than strictly literary critical reasons – were especially receptive to his denunciations of the supposedly effeminate state of contemporary French stage tragedy. It is, however, as a vernacularizer of Aristotle's ideas of tragedy that Rapin is perhaps best remembered today. Rapin was at the forefront of the French neoclassical interpretation of Aristotle which insisted that the *Poetics* was a series of trans-historical prescriptions or rules for composing the ideal tragedy rather than a set of brilliant observations about the ways in which classical tragedy had worked in a particular culture at a particular time. He enlisted Aristotle, too, to insist upon the ethical nature of tragedy, claiming that catharsis is, above all else, a means of facilitating the most appropriate moral responses to different kinds of human behaviour.

Since it is not so much to instruct, as to exercise the *Wits*, that I make these *Reflections* publick; I am not so vain to think them *necessary*, nor yet humble enough to believe them altogether *unprofitable*. This *Treatise* is no *New Model* of *Poesie*; for that of *Aristotle* onely is to be adhered to, as the exactest Rule for governing the *Wit*. In effect this *Treatise* of *Poesie*, to Speak properly, is nothing else, but *nature* put in method, and *good sense* reduc'd to principles. There is no arriving at perfection but by these Rules, and they certainly go astray that take a different course. What faults have not most of the *Italian*, *Spanish*, and other Poets fallen into, through their ignorance of these principles. And if a *Poem* made by these Rules fails of success, the fault lies not in the Art, but in the Artist; all who have writ of this Art have followed no other *Idea* but that of Aristotle.

[…]

XVII

Tragedy, of all parts of *Poesie*, is that which Aristotle has most discuss'd;[114] and where he appears most exact. He alledges that *Tragedy* is a *publick Lecture*, without comparison more *instructive* than *Philosophy*; because it teaches the *mind* by the sense, and rectifies the passions, by the passions themselves, in calming by their emotion the troubles they excite in the heart. The Philosopher had observ'd two important faults in man to be regulated, *pride*, and *hardness of heart*, and he found for both Vices a cure in *Tragedy*. For it makes man modest, by representing the *great masters of the earth humbled*; and it makes him tender and merciful, by shewing him on the Theatre the strange accidents of life, and the unforeseen disgraces to which the most important persons are subject.

---

[114]*Aristotle* **has most discussed:** even though Rapin appears to be quoting and translating Aristotle directly in this section, he is actually offering a loose, paraphrased interpretation which enables the Christianized, moral reading of the *Poetics* to follow. For a more precise translation see extract 1.2.

But because man is naturally timorous, and compassionate, he may fall into another extreme, to be either too fearful, or too full of pity; the too much fear may shake the constancy of mind, and the too great compassion may enfeeble the equity.[115] 'Tis the business of *Tragedy* to regulate these two weaknesses; it prepares and arms him against disgraces, by shewing them so frequent in the most considerable persons; and he shall cease to fear ordinary accidents, when he sees such extraordinary happen to the *highest part* of Mankind. But as the end of *Tragedy* is to teach men not to fear too weakly the common misfortunes, and manage their fear; it makes account also to teach them to spare their compassion, for objects that deserve it. For there is an injustice in being mov'd at the afflictions of those who deserve to be miserable. One may see without pity Clytemnestra slain by her son Orestes in Aeschylus, because she had cut the throat of Agamemnon her husband;[116] and one cannot see Hippolytus dye by the plot of his stepmother Phedra in Euripides, without compassion; because he dyed not but for being chaste and virtuous.[117] This to me seems, in short, the design of *Tragedy*, according to the *system* of Aristotle, which to me appears admirable, but which has not been explain'd as it ought by his Interpreters; they have not, it may seem, sufficiently understood the mystery, to unfold it well.

XVIII

But it is not enough that *Tragedy* be furnish'd with all the most moving and terrible Adventures, that *History* can afford, to stir in the heart those motions it pretends, to the end, it may cure the mind of those *vain fears* that may annoy it, and of those *childish compassions* that may soften it. 'Tis also necessary, says the Philosopher,[118] that every Poet employ these great objects of terrour and pity, as the two most powerful springs, in art, to produce that pleasure which *Tragedy* may yield. And this pleasure which is properly of the mind, consists in the agitation of the Soul mov'd by the passions. *Tragedy* cannot be delightful to the Spectator, unless he become sensible to all that is represented, he must *enter* into all the different thoughts of the Actors, *interest* himself in their Adventures, *fear, hope, afflict* himself, and *rejoyce* with them. The Theatre is dull and languid, when it ceases to produce these motions in the Soul of those that stand by. But as of all passions *fear* and *pity* are those that make the strongest impressions on the heart of man, by the natural disposition he has of being afraid, and of being mollifi'd; Aristotle has chosen these amongst the rest, to move more powerfully the Soul, by the tender *sentiments* they cause, when the heart admits, and is pierced by them. In effect, when the Soul is shaken, by motions so natural and so humane, all the impressions it feels, become delightful; its trouble pleases, and the emotion it finds, is a kind of charm to it, which does cast it into a sweet and profound meditation, and which insensibly does engage it in all the interests that are managed on the Theatre. 'Tis then that the heart yields it self over to all the objects that are propos'd, that all images strike it, that it espouses the sentiments of all those that speak, and becomes susceptible of all the passions that are presented, because 'tis mov'd. And in this *agitation* consists all the pleasure that one is capable to receive from *Tragedy*; for the spirit of man does please itself with the different *situations*, caus'd by the different objects, and the various passions that are represented.

---

[115]**equity:** the ability to judge and act fairly.
[116]**Clytemnestra … Agamemnon:** a plot outline for Aeschylus's trilogy of tragedies, *The Oresteia* (c.458 BCE).
[117]**Hippolytus … Euripides:** a summary of the plot of Euripides's tragedy *Hippolytus* (428 BCE).
[118]**the philosopher:** Aristotle.

XIX

It is by this admirable spring, that the Oedipus of Sophocles (of which Aristotle speaks continually, as of the most perfect Model of a *Tragedy*) wrought such great effects on the people of Athens, when it was represented. The truth is, all is *terrible* in that piece, and all there is *moving*. See the Subject. *The Plague destroying* Thebes, Oedipus *the King concerned at the loss of his Subjects, causes the Oracle to be consulted, for a remedy. The Oracle ordains him to revenge the assassinat[119] committed on the person of his Predecessor King* Laius. Oedipus *rages in horrible imprecations against the author of the crime, without knowing him; he himself makes a strict search to discover him; he questions* Creon, Tiresias, Jocasta, *and a man of* Corinth *for intelligence; and it appear'd by the account that this Prince received, that he himself committed the murder, he would punish.* The minds of the Spectators are in a perpetual suspense; all the words of Tiresias, Iocasta, and the Corinthian, as they give light to the *discovery*, cause *terrours* and surprises; and clear it by little and little. Oedipus finding it to be himself that was Author of the *assassinat*, by evidence of the testimonies, at the same time understood that Laius whom he had slain, was his Father; and that Iocasta, whom he had married, is his Mother, which he knew not till then; because he had from his Infancy been brought up in the Court of the King of Corinth. This *discovery* is like a Thunderclap that oblig'd him to abandon himself to all the despair that his Conscience inspir'd; he tears out both his eyes, to punish himself the more cruelly with his own hands. But this *Criminal* whom all the world *abhors* before he is known, by a return of *pity* and tenderness, becomes an object of *compassion* to all the Assembly; now he is bemoan'd, who a moment before pass'd for execrable; and they melt at the misfortunes of the person they had in horror; and excuse the most abominable of all Crimes, because the Author is an *Innocent unfortunate*, and fell into this crime, that was foretold him, notwithstanding all the precautions he had taken to avoid it; and what is most strange, is, that all the steps he made to carry him from the murder, brought him to commit it. Finally, this flux and reflux of indignation, and of pity, this revolution of horror and of tenderness, has such a wonderful effect on the minds of the Audience; all in this piece moves with an *air* so delicate and passionate, all is *unravel'd* with so much art, the suspensions manag'd with so much *probability*; there is made such an universal *emotion* of the Soul, by the *surprises, astonishments, admirations*; the sole *incident* that is form'd in all the piece, is so natural, and all tends so in a direct line to the *discovery* and *catastrophe*; that it may not only be said, that never *Subject* has been better devised than this, but that never can be invented a better, for *Tragedy*.
   [...]

XX

Modern Tragedy turns on other principles; the *Genius* of our (the *French*) Nation is not strong enough, to sustain an action on the Theatre by moving only *terror* and *pity*. These are *Machins[120]* that will not *play* as they ought, but by great thoughts, and noble expressions, of which we are not indeed altogether so capable, as the *Greeks*. Perhaps our Nation, which is naturally *gallant*, has been oblig'd by the necessity of our Character to frame for our selves a new *system* of *Tragedy* to suit with our humour. The *Greeks*, who were *popular* Estates,[121] and who hated

---

[119]**assassinat:** assassination.
[120]**Machins:** machines.
[121]**popular Estates:** democratic.

Monarchy, took delight in their spectacles, to see Kings humbled, and high Fortunes cast down, because the exaltation griev'd them. The *English*, our Neighbours, love blood in their sports, by the quality of their temperament: these are Insulaires,[122] separated from the rest of men; we are more humane. *Gallantry* moreover agrees with our *Manners*; and our Poets believ'd that they could not succeed well on the Theatre, but by sweet and tender *sentiments*; in which, perhaps, they had some reason: for, in effect, the passions represented become deform'd and insipid, unless they are founded on *sentiments* conformable to those of the *Spectator*. 'Tis this that obliges our Poets to stand up so strongly for the priviledge of *Gallantry* on the Theatre, and to bend all their Subjects to love and *tenderness*; the rather, to please the *Women*, who have made themselves Judges of these divertisements, and usurped the right to pass sentence. And some besides have suffer'd themselves to be prepossess'd, and led by the *Spaniards*, who make all their *Cavaliers* amorous. 'Tis by them that *Tragedy* began to degenerate; and we by little and little accustom'd to see *Heroes* on the Theatre, smitten with another love than that of *glory*; and that by degrees all the *great men* of Antiquity have lost their characters in our hands. 'Tis likewise perhaps by this *gallantry* that our Age would devise a colour to excuse the feebleness of our wit; not being able to sustain always the same action by the greatness of words and thoughts. However it be; for I am not hardy enough, to declare my self against the publick; 'tis to degrade *Tragedy* from that *majesty* which is proper to it, to mingle in it love, which is of a character alwayes *light*, and little sutable to that *gravity* of which *Tragedy* makes profession. Hence it proceeds, that these *Tragedies* mixed with *gallantries*, never make such admirable impressions on the spirit, as did those of Sophocles and Euripides; for all the bowels were moved by the great objects of *terrour* and *pity* which they proposed. 'Tis likewise for this, that the reputation of our modern *Tragedies* so soon decays, and yield but small delight at *two years end*; whereas the Greek please yet to those that have a good taste, after two thousand years; because what is not grave and serious on the Theatre, though it give delight at present, after a short time grows distasteful, and unpleasant; and because, what is not proper for great thoughts and great figures in *Tragedy* cannot support it self. The Ancients who perceiv'd this, did not interweave their *gallantry* and love, save in *Comedy*. For love is of a character that always degenerates from that *Heroick air*, of which *Tragedy* must never divest it self. And nothing to me shews so mean and sensless, as for one to amuse himself with whining about frivolous kindnesses, when he may be admirable by great and noble *thoughts*, and sublime expressions. But I dare not presume so far on my own capacity and credit, to oppose my self of my own head against a usage so established. I must be content modestly to propose my doubts; and that may serve to exercise the *Wits*, in an Age that onely wants *matter*. But to end this *Reflection* with a touch of *Christianism*, I am persuaded, that the innocence of the Theatre might be better preserv'd according to the *Idea* of the *ancient* Tragedy: because the *new* is become too effeminate, by the softness of latter Ages; and the Prince de Conty who signaliz'd his zeal against the *modern* Tragedy, by his Treatise on that Subject,[123] would, without doubt, have allowed the *ancient*, because that has nothing that may seem dangerous.

---

[122]**insulaires:** islanders.

[123]**Prince de Conty … Treatise on that Subject:** Armand de Bourbon, Prince of Conti (1629–66) who wrote the antitheatrical *Traité de la comédie et des spectacles* (1666).

XXI

The other faults of *modern* Tragedy are ordinarily that either the *subjects* which are chosen are mean and frivolous; or the *Fable* is not well wrought, and the *contrivance* not regular; or that they are too much crowded with *Episodes*; or that the *Characters* are not preserv'd and sustain'd; or that the *incidents* are not well prepar'd; or that the *Machins* are forced; or that, what is *admirable* fails in the *probability*, or the *probability* is too plain and flat; or that the *surprises* are ill managed, the *knots* ill tyed, the *loosing* them not natural, the *Catastrophe's* precipitated, the *Thoughts* without elevation, the *Expressions* without majesty, the *Figures* without grace, the *Passions* without colour, the *Discourse* without life, the *Narrations* cold, the *Words* low, the *Language* improper, and all the *Beauties* false. They speak not enough to the heart of the Audience, which is the onely Art of the Theatre, where nothing can be delightful but that which moves the affections, and which makes impression on the Soul; little known is that *Rhetorick* which can lay open the passions by all the natural degrees of their birth, and of their progress: nor are those Morals at all in use, which are proper to mingle these *different interests*, those *opposite glances*, those *clashing maxims*, those *reasons* that destroy each other, to ground the incertitudes and irresolutions, and to animate the Theatre. For the Theatre being essentially destined for *action*, nothing ought to be idle, but all in agitation, by the thwarting of passions that are founded on the different interests, that arise; or by the embroilment that follows from the *intrigue*. Likewise there ought to appear no *Actor*, that carries not some design in his head, either to cross the designs of others, or to support his own; all ought to be in trouble, and no calm to appear, till the *action* be ended by the *Catastrophe*. Nor finally, is it well understood that it is not the admirable intrigue, the surprising and wonderful events, the extraordinary incidents that make the beauty of a Tragedy, it is the *discourses* when they are natural and passionate. Sophocles was not more successful than Euripides on the Theatre at Athens, but by the *discourse*, though the Tragedies of Euripides have more of *action*, of *morality*, of wonderful *incidents*, than those of Sophocles. It is by these faults, more or less great, that *Tragedy* in these dayes has so little effect on the mind; that we no longer feel those agreeable *trances*, that make the pleasure of the Soul, nor find those *suspensions*, those *ravishments*, those *surprises·* those *admirations* that the *ancient* Tragedy caus'd; because the *modern* have nothing of those astonishing and terrible objects that *affrighted*, whilst they *pleas'd*, the Spectators, and made those great impressions on the Soul, by the ministry of the passions. In these dayes men go from the Theatre as little mov'd as when they went in and carry their *heart* along with them, *untoucht* as they brought it: so that the pleasure they receive there, is become as superficial, as that of *Comedy*, and our gravest Tragedies are (to speak properly) no more but *heighten'd Comedies*.

Further reading

Thora Burnley Jones and Bernard de Bear Nicol, *Neo-Classical Dramatic Criticism 1560–1770* (Cambridge: Cambridge University Press, 1976).

John D. Lyons, 'The Barbarous Ancients: French Classical Poetics and the Attack on Ancient Tragedy', *MLN* 110, no. 5 (1995): 1135–47.

2.9 JOHN DRYDEN, 'THE GROUNDS OF CRITICISM IN TRAGEDY' (1679)

John Dryden (1631–1700), English poet, playwright, and critic, was one of the most influential arbiters of literary taste in Restoration society. He was one of the first truly professional – as opposed to aristocratic amateur – playwrights of the Restoration. Appointed Poet Laureate in 1668, he wrote plays in all genres but was especially famed for his work in two related genres: tragedy and the heroic play. The latter was a form of serious drama composed in heroic couplets which, in its recounting of moral stories of heroism and glorious foundational myths of national origins, had as much in common with epic poetry as theatrical tragedy. Heroic plays such as Dryden's own two-part *The Conquest of Granada* (1670–1) were especially popular in the early years of the Restoration, but began to fall from favour in the mid-1670s, when critics began to object to their leaden moralism and heavy-handed bombast. In response to such criticism, Dryden began to develop a new kind of pathetic tragedy which sought to meld Shakespearean tragedy with more recent French examples of the genre established by Jean Racine (1639–99). Dryden's adaptation of *Troilus and Cressida* (1679) was one such play; he altered the Shakespearean original to ensure that Cressida remained true to Troilus throughout the drama but committed suicide to become a more recognizably virtuous tragic heroine. Conscious that his re-writing provoked important questions about the relationships between English and continental models of tragedy he included 'The Grounds of Criticism in Tragedy' as a preface to the play.

Tragedy is thus defin'd by Aristotle, (omiting what I thought unnecessary in his Definition.) 'Tis an imitation of one intire, great, and probable action; not told but represented, which by moving in us fear and pity, is conducive to the purging of those two passions in our minds. More largely thus, Tragedy describes or paints an Action, which Action must have all the proprieties above nam'd. First, it must be one or single, that is, it must not be a History of one Mans life: Suppose of Alexander the Great, or Julius Cæsar, but one single action of theirs. This condemns all Shakespears Historical Plays, which are rather Chronicles represented, than Tragedies, and all double action of Plays.[124] As to avoid a satire upon others, I will make bold with my own *Marriage-a-la-Mode*,[125] where there are manifestly two Actions, not depending on one another: but in *Oedipus*[126] there cannot properly be said to be two Actions, because the love of Adrastus and Euridice[127] has a necessary dependence on the principal design, into which it is woven. The natural reason of this Rule is plain, for two different independent actions, distract the attention and concernment of the Audience, and consequently destroy the intention of the Poet: If his business be to move terror and pity, and one of his Actions be Comical, the other Tragical, the former will divert the people, and utterly make void his

---

[124]**double action of Plays**: double plotting.
[125]*Marriage-A-la-Mode*: the title of one of Dryden's own comedies, first performed in London in 1671.
[126]*Oedipus*: a reference to Dryden and Nathaniel Lee's own tragedy *Oedipus* (1678).
[127]**Adrastus and Euridice**: Adrastus, prince of Argos and Eurydice, Oedipus's daughter, are young lovers who feature in the plot of Dryden and Lee's adaptation of the Oedipus tragedy.

greater purpose. Therefore as in Perspective, so in Tragedy, there must be a point of sight in which all the lines terminate: Otherwise the eye wanders, and the work is false. This was the practice of the Grecian Stage. But Terence[128] made an innovation in the Roman: all his Plays have double Actions; for it was his custome to Translate two Greek Comedies, and to weave them into one of his, yet so, that both the Actions were Comical; and one was principal, the other but secondary or subservient. And this has obtain'd on the English Stage, to give us the pleasure of variety.

As the Action ought to be one, it ought as such, to have Order in it, that is, to have a natural beginning, a middle, and an end: A natural beginning says Aristotle, is that which could not necessarily have been plac'd after another thing, and so of the rest. This consideration will arraign all Plays after the new model of Spanish Plots, where accident is heap'd upon accident, and that which is first might as reasonably be last: an inconvenience not to be remedyed, but by making one accident naturally produce another, otherwise 'tis a Farce, and not a Play. Of this nature, is *The Slighted Maid*;[129] where there is no Scene in the first Act, which might not by as good reason be in the fifth. And if the Action ought to be one, the Tragedy ought likewise to conclude with the Action of it. Thus in *Mustapha*,[130] the Play should naturally have ended with the death of Zanger, and not have given us the grace Cup after Dinner, of Solyman's divorce from Roxolana.

The following properties of the Action are so easy, that they need not my explaining. It ought to be great, and to consist of great Persons, to distinguish it from Comedy; where the Action is trivial, and the persons of inferior rank. The last quality of the action is, that it ought to be probable, as well as admirable and great. 'Tis not necessary that there should be Historical truth in it; but always necessary that there should be a likeness of truth, something that is more then barely possible, probable being that which succeeds or happens oftner than it misses. To invent therefore a probability, and to make it wonderfull, is the most difficult undertaking in the Art of Poetry: for that which is not wonderfull, is not great, and that which is not probable, will not delight a reasonable Audience. This action thus describ'd, must be represented and not told, to distinguish Dramatic Poetry from Epic: but I hasten to the end, or scope of Tragedy; which is to rectify or purge our passions, fear and pity.

To instruct delightfully is the general end of all Poetry: Philosophy instructs, but it performs its work by precept: which is not delightfull, or not so delightfull as Example. To purge the passions by Example, is therefore the particular instruction which belongs to Tragedy. Rapin a judicious Critic, has observ'd from Aristotle, that pride and want of commiseration are the most predominant vices in Mankinde:[131] therefore to cure us of these two, the inventors of Tragedy, have chosen to work upon two other passions, which are fear and pity. We are wrought to fear, by their setting before our eyes some terrible example of misfortune, which happened to persons of the highest Quality; for such an action demonstrates to us, that no condition is privileg'd from the turns of Fortune: this must of necessity cause terror in us, and consequently

---

[128]**Terence:** Publius Terentius (185 BCE–159 BCE), Roman playwright, famed for his development of classical comedy.
[129]*The Slighted Maid*: Robert Stapylton's comedy *The Slighted Maid* was first performed in 1663.
[130]*Mustapha*: Roger Boyle, first Earl of Orrery's *Mustapha* (1665) was an immensely popular Restoration tragedy, centring on the lives of the Turkish emperor Solyman the Magnificent, his wife Roxolana and his sons Mustapha and Zanger.
[131]**Rapin … Mankinde:** René Rapin (1621–87), French Jesuit theologian, poet and historian. For a contemporary translation of the exact passage that Dryden is referring to here, see extract 2.8.

abate our pride. But when we see that the most virtuous, as well as the greatest, are not exempt from such misfortunes, that consideration moves pity in us: and insensibly works us to be helpfull to, and tender over the distress'd, which is the noblest and most God-like of moral virtues. Here 'tis observable, that it is absolutely necessary to make a man virtuous, if we desire he should be pity'd: We lament not, but detest a wicked man, we are glad when we behold his crimes are punish'd, and that Poetical justice is done upon him. Euripides was censur'd by the Critics of his time, for making his chief characters too wicked: for example, Phædra though she lov'd her Son-in-law with reluctancy, and that it was a curse upon her Family for offending Venus; yet was thought too ill a pattern for the Stage. Shall we therefore banish all characters of villany? I confess I am not of that opinion; but it is necessary that the Hero of the play be not a Villain: that is, the characters which should move our pity ought to have virtuous inclinations, and degrees of morall goodness in them. As for a perfect character of virtue, it never was in Nature; and therefore there can be no imitation of it: but there are allays of frailty to be allow'd for the chief Persons, yet so that the good which is in them, shall outweigh the bad; and consequently leave room for punishment on the one side, and pity on the other.

After all, if any one will ask me, whether a Tragedy cannot be made upon any other grounds, than those of exciting pity and terror in us? Bossu,[132] the best of modern Critics, answers thus in general: That all excellent Arts, and particularly that of Poetry, have been invented and brought to perfection by men of a transcendent Genius; and that therefore they who practice afterwards the same Arts, are oblig'd to tread in their footsteps, and to search in their Writings the foundation of them: for it is not just that new Rules should destroy the authority of the old. But Rapin writes more particularly thus: That no passions in a story are so proper to move our concernment as Fear and Pity; and that it is from our concernment we receive our pleasure, is undoubted; when the Soul becomes agitated with fear for one character, or hope for another; then it is that we are pleas'd in Tragedy, by the interest which we take in their adventures.

[...]

The difference between Shakespeare and Fletcher[133] in their Plotting seems to be this, that Shakespeare generally moves more terror, and Fletcher more compassion: For the first had a more Masculine, a bold and more fiery Genius; the Second a more soft and Womanish. In the mechanic beauties of the Plot, which are the Observation of the three Unities, Time, Place, and Action, they are both deficient; but Shakespeare most. Ben Jonson reform'd those errors in his Comedies, yet one of Shakespeare's was Regular before him: which is, *The Merry Wives of Windsor*.[134]

[...]

After the Plot, which is the foundation of the play, the next thing to which we ought to apply our Judgment is the manners, for now the Poet comes to work above ground: the ground-work indeed is that which is most necessary, as that upon which depends the firmness of the whole

---

[132]**Bossu:** René Le Bossu (1631–80), French critic whose *Traité du poëme épique* was published in Paris in 1675.

[133]**Fletcher:** John Fletcher (1579–1625): Jacobean playwright. His plays – especially his collaborations with Francis Beaumont (1584–1616) – remained in the repertory after the Restoration.

[134]***Merry Wives of Windsor*:** one of Shakespeare's late Elizabethan comedies (*c*.1597–1601). Its observation of the neoclassical Unities of Time, Place, and Action meant that it was extremely popular in the late seventeenth and early eighteenth centuries.

Fabric; yet it strikes not the eye so much, as the beauties or imperfections of the manners, the thoughts and the expressions.

The first Rule which Bossu, prescribes to the Writer of an Heroic Poem, and which holds too by the same reason in all Dramatic Poetry, is to make the moral of the work; that is, to lay down to your self what that precept of morality shall be, which you would insinuate into the people: as namely, Homer's, (which I have Copy'd in my *Conquest of Granada*)[135] was, that Union preserves a Common-wealth, and discord destroys it. Sophocles, in his *OEdipus*, that no man is to be accounted happy before his death. 'Tis the Moral that directs the whole action of the Play to one center; and that action or Fable, is the example built upon the moral, which confirms the truth of it to our experience: when the Fable is design'd, then and not before, the Persons are to be introduc'd with their manners, characters and passions.

The manners in a Poem, are understood to be those inclinations, whether natural or acquir'd, which move and carry us to actions, good, bad, or indifferent in a Play; or which incline the persons to such, or such actions: I have anticipated part of this discourse already, in declaring that a Poet ought not to make the manners perfectly good in his best persons, but neither are they to be more wicked in any of his characters, than necessity requires. To produce a Villain, without other reason than a natural inclination to villany, is in Poetry to produce an effect without a cause: and to make him more a Villain than be has just reason to be, is to make an effect which is stronger then the cause.

The manners arise from many causes: and are either distinguish'd by complexion, as choleric and phlegmatic, or by the differences of Age or Sex, of Climates, or Quality of the persons, or their present condition: they are likewise to be gather'd from the several Virtues, Vices, or Passions, and many other common-places which a Poet must be suppos'd to have learn'd from natural Philosophy, Ethics, and History; of all which whosoever is ignorant, does not deserve the Name of Poet.

[...]

The chief character or Hero in a Tragedy, as I have already shown, ought in prudence to be such a man, who has so much more in him of Virtue than of Vice, that he may be left amiable to the Audience, which otherwise cannot have any concernment for his sufferings: and 'tis on this one character that the pity and terror must be principally, if not wholly founded. A Rule which is extreamly necessary, and which none of the Critics that I know, have fully enough discover'd to us. For terror and compassion work but weakly, when they are divided into many persons. If Creon had been the chief character in *Oedipus*,[136] there had neither been terror nor compassion mov'd; but only detestation of the man and joy for his punishment; if Adrastus and Euridice had been made more appearing characters, then the pity had been divided, and lessen'd on the part of Oedipus: but making Oedipus the best and bravest person, and even Jocasta but an underpart to him; his virtues and the punishment of his fatall crime, drew both the pity, and the terror to himself.

By what had been said of the manners, it will be easy for a reasonable man to judge, whether the characters be truly or falsely drawn in a Tragedy; for if there be no manners appearing in

---

[135]*Conquest of Granada*: a two-part tragedy (1670–1) in heroic couplets by Dryden. Dryden preferred the label 'heroic drama' to the play, arguing for the affinities of tragedy with epic.

[136]**Creon … *Oedipus*:** Dryden again has in mind his and Nathaniel Lee's dramatization of the Oedipus myth. Creon, King of Thebes, was the brother of Jocasta (Oedipus's wife and mother).

the characters, no concernment for the persons can he rais'd: no pity or horror can be mov'd, but by vice or virtue, therefore without them, no person can have any business in the Play. If the inclinations be obscure, 'tis a sign the Poet is in the dark, and knows not what manner of man he presents to you; and consequently you can have no Idea, or very imperfect, of that man: nor can judge what resolutions he ought to take; or what words or actions are proper for him: Most Comedies made up of accidents, or adventures, are liable to fall into this error: and Tragedies with many turns are subject to it: for the manners never can be evident, where the surprises of Fortune take up all the business of the Stage; and where the Poet is more in pain, to tell you what happened to such a man, than what he was. 'Tis one of the excellencies of Shakespeare, that the manners of his persons are generally apparent; and you see their bent and inclinations. Fletcher comes far short of him in this, as indeed he does almost in every thing: there are but glimmerings of manners in most of his Comedies, which run upon adventures: and in his Tragedies, *Rollo, Otto*, the *King and No King, Melantius*,[137] and many others of his best, are but Pictures shown you in the twilight; you know not whether they resemble vice, or virtue, and they are either good bad, or indifferent, as the present Scene requires it. But of all Poets, this commendation is to be given to Ben Jonson, that the manners even of the most inconsiderable persons in his Plays are every where apparent.

[…]

The Passions, as they are consider'd simply and in themselves, suffer violence when they are perpetually maintain'd at the same height; for what melody can be made on that Instrument all whose strings are screw'd up at first to their utmost stretch, and to the same sound? But this is not the worst; for the Characters likewise bear a part in the general calamity, if you consider the Passions as embody'd in them: for it follows of necessity, that no man can be distinguish'd from another by his discourse, when every man is ranting, swaggering, and exclaiming with the same excess: as if it were the only business of all the Characters to contend with each other for the prize at Billingsgate;[138] or that the Scene of the Tragedy lay in Bet'lem.[139] Suppose the Poet should intend this man to be Cholerick, and that man to be patient; yet when they are confounded in the Writing, you cannot distinguish them from one another: for the man who was call'd patient and tame, is only so before he speaks; but let his clack be set a going, and he shall tongue it as impetuously, and as loudly as the errantest Hero in the Play. By this means, the characters are only distinct in name; but in reality, all the men and women in the Play are the same person. No man should pretend to write, who cannot temper his fancy with his Judgment: nothing is more dangerous to a raw horse-man, than a hot-mouth'd Jade without a curb.

[…]

The next necessary rule is to put nothing into the discourse which may hinder your moving of the passions. Too many accidents as I have said, encumber the Poet, as much as the Arms of Saul did David;[140] for the variety of passions which they produce, are ever crossing and jostling each other out of the way. He who treats of joy and grief together, is in a fair way of causing neither

---

[137]***Rollo, Otto*, the *King and No King, Melantius*:** In addition to *A King and No King* (1611), Dryden refers here to two other Fletcher tragedies. Rollo and Otto are characters from *The Bloody Brother* (1617), whereas Melantius is a young general in *The Maid's Tragedy* (c.1611).

[138]**Billingsgate:** the location of a famous London fish market, proverbially home to the most vulgar and abusive speech.

[139]**Bet'lem:** Bedlam, or Bethlehem Hospital, a London psychiatric hospital.

[140]**Arms of Saul did David:** 1 Samuel 17 records how, when going into battle with the Philistine Champion Goliath, David refused King Saul's offer of armour, in order to remain more agile.

of those effects. There is yet another obstacle to be remov'd, which is pointed Wit, and Sentences affected out of season; these are nothing of kin to the violence of passion: no man is at leisure to make sentences and similes, when his soul is in an Agony. I the rather name this fault, that it may serve to mind me of my former errors; neither will I spare myself, but give an example of this kind from my *Indian Emperor*:[141] Montezuma, pursu'd by his enemies, and seeking Sanctuary, stands parlying without the Fort, and describing his danger to Cydaria, in a simile of six lines;

> As on the sands the frighted Traveller
> Sees the high Seas come rowling from afar, &c.

My Indian Potentate was well skill'd in the Sea for an Inland Prince, and well improv'd since the first Act, when he sent his son to discover it. The Image had not been amiss from another man, at another time: Sed nunc non erat hisce locus:[142] he destroy'd the concernment which the Audience might otherwise have had for him; for they could not think the danger near, when he had the leisure to invent a Simile.

If Shakespeare be allow'd, as I think he must, to have made his Characters distinct, it will easily be infer'd that he understood the nature of the Passions: because it has been prov'd already, that confus'd passions make undistinguishable Characters: yet I cannot deny that he has his failings; but they are not so much in the passions themselves, as in his manner of expression: he often obscures his meaning by his words, and sometimes makes it unintelligible. I will not say of so great a Poet, that he distinguish'd not the blown puffy stile, from true sublimity; but I may venture to maintain that the fury of his fancy often transported him, beyond the bounds of Judgment, either in coyning of new words and phrases, or racking words which were in use, into the violence of a Catachresis:[143] 'Tis not that I would explode the use of Metaphors from passions, for Longinus[144] thinks 'em necessary to raise it; but to use 'em at every word, to say nothing without a Metaphor, a Simile, an Image, or description, is I doubt to smell a little too strongly of the Buskin.[145] ...

Further reading

John C. Sherwood, 'Precept and Practice in Dryden's Criticism', *The Journal of English and Germanic Philology* 68, no. 3 (1969): 432–40.

Christopher J. Wheatley, 'Tragedy', in *The Cambridge Companion to English Restoration Theatre*, ed. Deborah Payne Fisk (Cambridge: Cambridge University Press, 2000), 70–85.

---

[141]**my *Indian Emperor*:** *The Indian Emperour, or the Conquest of Mexico by the Spaniards* (1665), one of Dryden's rhymed heroic tragedies. Montezuma is the Emperor of Mexico in Dryden's play; Cydaria is his daughter.

[142]**Sed nunc non erat hisce locus:** 'For such things there is a place, but not just now', from Horace's *Ars Poetica*, 1.19.

[143]**Catachresis:** a tortured, over-elaborate metaphor.

[144]**Longinus:** the author of the treatise *On the Sublime* (extract 1.4) was thought in Dryden's period to be the Greek rhetorician and philosopher Cassius Longinus (213–73).

[145]**Buskin:** a theatrical boot, long associated with tragedy. Dryden argues that Shakespeare's over-use of metaphors made some of his characters overly theatrical rather than believable or life-like.

CHAPTER 3
THE EIGHTEENTH CENTURY

A military dictator has won a bloody civil war and pursues a rebellious resistance movement through northern Africa. The rebel leader knows that the dictator will find them soon and consults with his comrades as to whether it would be more virtuous to resist him unto death, certain of defeat, or spare further bloodshed and submit to the new regime. Opting for neither of these courses of action, the rebel leader counsels his fighters to wait it out and see what happens; as the dictator's forces move ever closer, the rebel leader kills himself, not knowing whether his suicide is impetuously self-defeating or an exemplary act of heroism.

Although this description might have some resonances with today's global political situation, it is actually a précis of the plot of Joseph Addison's tragedy *Cato* (1713). Addison's play was perhaps the most popular English stage tragedy of the eighteenth century; it was lauded by Voltaire (see extract 3.3) and was performed more than 20 times in London in its first year. By the end of the century there were 26 English editions of it and it had been translated into Dutch, French, German, Italian, and Polish.[1] Its emphasis on the conflict between liberty and tyranny meant that it also became a signal text during the American Revolution (Benjamin Franklin committed parts of it to memory and it was reputed to be George Washington's favourite play).[2]

What Addison's immediate European contemporaries found most appealing about the tragedy, however, was its staging of the relationship between reason and the passions, or emotions. Cato the Younger, the eponymous tragic hero, sustains his wait-it-out-and-see attitude to the dictatorial advances of Julius Caesar on the grounds that it is a rational middle way rather than an extreme emotional response to crisis. 'Let not a torrent of impetuous zeal / Transport [us] beyond the bounds of reason,' he counsels his auditors, 'While there is yet hope, do not distrust the Gods.'[3] But the gods in Addison's play ultimately do nothing to salvage or worsen Cato's cause; the audience are actually, like Cato himself, left profoundly uncertain about supernatural involvement in earthly affairs and whether our agency ultimately has any bearing on the meaning of our lives. Even though Cato's suicide was one of antiquity's most celebrated heroic deaths – in Book IX of Lucan's *Pharsalia*, for instance, it showed how republican values remained resolutely undimmed despite the advances of Roman imperialism – in Addison's hands it looks much more like the considered but finally uncertain choice of an honourable man. After he has stabbed himself, Addison's Cato still has a moment to gasp one last reflection on human fallibility: 'O when shall I get loose from this vain world / … And yet methinks a beam of light breaks in/on my departing soul. Alas, I fear / I have been too hasty. … The best may erre.'[4]

---

[1] Joseph Addison, *Cato: A Tragedy and Selected Essays*, ed. Christine Dunn Henderson and Mark E. Yellin, with a Foreword by Forrest McDonald (Indianapolis: Liberty Fund, 2004), xi, http://oll.libertyfund.org/titles/1229.

[2] Addison, *Cato: A Tragedy and Selected Essays*, viii.

[3] Joseph Addison, *Cato: A Tragedy. As It Is Acted at the Theatre-Royal in Drury-Lane, by Her Majesty's Servants* (London, 1713), 19.

[4] Addison, *Cato: A Tragedy*, 62.

Cato's rather messy end, his parting sense of the indeterminate and the contingent nature of earthly endeavour, clearly reveals Addison's commitment to classical ideas of tragedy (see extract 3.1). There is no providential consolation from Christian or pagan deities here, no act of moral accounting or the meting out of poetic justice at the close of his play. The good end unhappily as well as uncertainly, even though there had been a theatrical fashion emerging since the late seventeenth century for tragedians to ensure that their morally upright protagonists were rewarded rather than desolated. Instead, Addison's audiences were confronted with the senselessness and waste examined by his tragedy and reflected upon the affective consequences of such desolation. They considered how the intensely passionate response to tragedy was intensely contradictory, too, inspiring both grief and a sense of wonder; at such moments its effects edge towards what contemporaries such as Edmund Burke thought of as the sublime (see extracts 3.5 and 3.9). As one of Addison's early critics put it:

> Yet with such wond'rous art your skilful hand
> Does all the passions of the soul command,
> That even my grief to praise and wonder turn'd.[5]

It is important to reflect upon the high contemporary estimation of Addison's *Cato* since it calls into question an instrumental theory about tragedy in the eighteenth century. Addison's *Cato* was really very successful in a century in which tragedy is commonly thought to have died or failed (and it is only in recent years that such a picture has begun to be questioned).[6] There are myriad reasons why tragedy is supposed by some to have gone into terminal decline in this period: playwrights pedantically observing neoclassical 'rules' for the Aristotelian unities of time and place; the rise of middle-class or bourgeois theatre audiences and their reputed mania for happy endings and poetic justice; the unstoppable rise of the novel.[7] However, the grandest narrative for the supposed decline of tragedy takes an epochal perspective. The eighteenth century was the period of the Enlightenment, and Enlightenment values – such as belief in human perfectibility, continual progress in knowledge and understanding, freedom of thought and action, the triumphant powers of Reason – were inimical to tragedy. George Steiner, for example, used the great Enlightenment thinker, Jean-Jacques Rousseau, to explain the decline of tragedy in the following terms:

> Tragic drama tells us that the spheres of reason, order, and justice are terribly limited and that no progress in our science or technical resources will enlarge their relevance. ... Things are as they are, unrelenting and absurd. We are punished far in excess of our guilt. ... [However] Rousseau implied a radical critique of the notion of guilt. In the

---

[5]Bonamy Dobrée, ed., *Five Restoration Tragedies* (Oxford: Oxford University Press, 1955), 379.

[6]Eugene Hnatko, 'The Failure of Eighteenth-Century Tragedy', *SEL* 11, no. 3 (1971): 459–68; George Steiner, *The Death of Tragedy* (London: Faber, 1982); Susan Staves, 'Tragedy', in *The Cambridge Companion to British Theatre, 1730–1830*, ed. Jane Moody and Daniel O'Quinn (Cambridge: Cambridge University Press, 2007), 87–102. For persuasive overviews which problematize such readings see Felicity A. Nussbaum, 'The Challenge of Tragedy', in *The Oxford Handbook of the Georgian Theatre, 1737–1832*, ed. Julia Swindells and David Francis Taylor (Oxford: Oxford University Press, 2014), 368–89 and Felicity A. Nussbaum, 'The Unaccountable Pleasure of Eighteenth-Century Tragedy', *PMLA* 129, no. 4 (2014): 688–707.

[7]See Hnatko, 'Failure of Eighteenth-Century Tragedy', 459–60, 68.

Rousseauist mythology of conduct, a man could commit a crime either because his education had not taught him to distinguish good and evil, or because he had been corrupted by society. ... And because the individual is not wholly responsible, he cannot be wholly damned. Rousseauism closed the doors of hell. ... In authentic tragedy, the gates of hell stand open and damnation is real.[8]

Such an interpretation fails to take account of the lack of progression and the profound notes of uncertainty sounded at the end of a tragedy like Addison's *Cato* (which Steiner brusquely dismisses as 'cold, lifeless stuff' when compared to the 'authentic tragedy' of antiquity).[9] This is because Steiner's reading of tragedy is wedded to a vision of the eighteenth century as the Age of Reason in which rationalist Enlightenment values triumph over and tidy up everything in their path. However, as historians and philosophers now routinely remark, the age was as much preoccupied with bodily, emotional, non- or anti-rational ways of knowing and being as it was with a solely rationalist understanding of the world. In the seventeenth century, philosophers like René Descartes and Baruch Spinoza presented the human subject as bedevilled by a conflict between reason and the passions – a battle which reason must win if we are to act and understand, rather than be passive and misunderstand, the world.[10] By contrast, a significant number of their Enlightenment counterparts re-interrogated the relationship between body and mind in order to question whether reason really did remain our uncorrupted, sovereign guide in the universe and whether our passions were indeed as corrupting and destructive as had previously been claimed.[11] Francis Hutcheson's *An Essay on the Nature and Conduct of the Passions* (1742) and Adam Smith's *Theory of Moral Sentiments* (1759) were landmark texts in the philosophical re-evaluation of the relationship between thought and feeling and how we might perceive and understand our relationship with society. Working within the same philosophical tradition, David Hume famously declared in the *Treatise of Human Nature* (1739) that a strictly rationalist philosophy of the human subject looked at the issue the wrong way round: 'Reason is, and ought only to be the slave of the passions, and can never pretend to any other office than to serve and obey them.'[12] Rousseau likewise maintained in *A Discourse on the Origin of Inequality* (1755) that 'it is by the activity of the passions that our reason is improved'.[13]

---

[8]Steiner, *Death of Tragedy*, 8–9, 127–8.

[9]Ibid., 265.

[10]Susan James, *Passion and Action: The Emotions in Seventeenth-Century Philosophy* (Oxford: Oxford University Press, 1999), 124–57.

[11]See Ildiko Csengei, *Sympathy, Sensibility and the Literature of Feeling in the Eighteenth Century* (Basingstoke: Palgrave, 2012); Adela Pinch, *Strange Fits of Passion: Epistemologies of Emotion, Hume to Austen* (Stanford, CA: Stanford University Press, 1996), 17–50; Jonathan Lamb, *The Evolution of Sympathy in the Long Eighteenth Century* (London: Pickering and Chatto, 2009); James A. Harris, 'The Government of the Passions', in *The Oxford Handbook of Eighteenth-Century British Philosophy*, ed. James A. Harris (Oxford: Oxford University Press, 2013), 270–90; and Laura J. Rosenthal, 'Adam Smith and the Theatre in *Moral Sentiments*', in *Passions, Sympathy and Print Culture: Public Opinion and Emotional Authenticity in Eighteenth-Century Britain*, ed. Heather Kerr, David Lemmings and Robert Phiddian (Basingstoke: Palgrave, 2016), 122–4.

[12]David Hume, *A Treatise of Human Nature*, ed. Ernest Mossner (Harmondsworth: Penguin, 1985), 462.

[13]Jean-Jacques Rousseau, *The Social Contract; and, Discourses*, trans. G.D.H. Cole, Rev. J.H. Brumfitt, and J.C. Hall (London: Everyman, 1973), 61.

Ever since Aristotle announced in the *Poetics* (extract 1.2) that tragic pleasure resided in the audience's experiences of pity and fear, theories of tragedy have circled around our affective responses to the genre and what these might reveal about our relationship to each other and our place in the cosmos. The eighteenth-century obsession with the passions aroused by tragedy scratched a similar itch. While philosophers like Burke (extract 3.5), Hume (extract 3.4), and Rousseau (extract 3.6) each had profoundly different takes on the usefulness of tragic theatre and the passions it provoked, their interest in tragedy and the passions was shared by every writer in this chapter, regardless of occupation, social class, or gender. The dramatist and poet Joanna Baillie, for instance, probed the quotidian, passionate blocks to rational action – and how these had a particular upon the lives of women – in her psychologically-driven tragedies (see extract 3.9). Baillie's work shows that a desire to discuss and understand the tragic passions was much more than a narrowly philosophical exercise in debating why we take pleasure in artistic representations of terrible events or how a single aesthetic object can provoke simultaneous, apparently antithetical affective responses (such as pity and delight or fear and pleasure). Rather, eighteenth-century discourses of tragedy and the passions were part of a widespread attempt to understand the interplay between art, reason, feeling, and action, to probe, in other words, the extent and limits of our agency, and how good art might relate to the good life.

These had long been the grand stakes of the grand old genre of tragedy, but in the eighteenth century it was no longer just the grand, or the nobly born, who could play for them. While, two centuries later, Steiner opined that the bourgeois encroachment upon tragedy had negative effects on theatrical output in the eighteenth century – 'the liberalisation of the audience led to the lowering of dramatic standards' because middle-class spectators, preferring pat, easily moralized endings, 'would not take the risk of terror and revelation implicit in tragedy' – the audiences for and authors of tragedy who feature in this chapter did not necessarily share this view.[14] Even if George Lillo (extract 3.2), in his bourgeois tragedy *The London Merchant* (1731), did indeed emphasize a straightforwardly moral scheme for the interpretation of tragic catastrophe, other commentators and playwrights, such as Joseph Addison in *The Spectator* (extract 3.1), a key source for any understanding of English middle-class values in the period, railed against a contemporary taste for poètic justice in tragedy. Addison argued instead, both in his literary periodical and in *Cato*, that classical ideas of tragedy still had some currency in the eighteenth century.

But it was not just classical ideas of tragedy that were fêted by eighteenth-century commentators. In France as well as England, Shakespeare's tragedies were prized for asserting an important modern standard of what tragedy might be and do. Elizabeth Montagu (extract 3.8) thought Shakespeare's understanding of the passions unparalleled and saw his plays as offering the basis for a move to more naturalistic – and less hyperbolic or histrionic – styles of tragic acting. Voltaire, too (extract 3.3), for all of his criticism of the absurdities of Shakespeare's theatrical plotting, regarded his use of soliloquy as affording a vast expansion of the possibilities for exploring the psychology of tragic heroism. For the great lexicographer and Shakespeare editor, Samuel Johnson (extract 3.7), Shakespeare, while not the greatest observer of neoclassical rules for tragedy, was perhaps the greatest observer of nature; his characteristic

---

[14]Steiner, *Death of Tragedy*, 115.

mixing of high and low, the intermingling of serious with comic scenes, established the standard whereby tragedy could thumb its nose at neoclassical prescriptions, and be moral theatre without having recourse to leaden didacticism. Johnson's sense that tragedy might instruct precisely because it entertains, that reason was intimately related to tragedy's ability to rouse different passions, gets to the heart of what the genre meant for its eighteenth-century audiences; like every extract in this chapter, it also suggests that reports of tragedy's death in this period have been greatly exaggerated.

3.1 JOSEPH ADDISON AND RICHARD STEELE, *THE SPECTATOR* (1711–14)

The Spectator (1711–14) was an English periodical produced by Joseph Addison (1672–1719) and Richard Steele (1672–1729). Originally envisaged as a continuation of Steele's *The Tatler* (1709–11), *The Spectator* appeared six days a week, sold up to 4000 copies a day and played a key role in shaping public opinion in eighteenth-century England. Addison and Steele adopted the persona of Mr Spectator, a wealthy English country gentleman, to offer their readers short essays on familiar and important topics such as education, religion, literature, and the family. Their aim was to entertain and inform but also to improve the manners and morality of polite society; this has led later commentators to analyse *The Spectator*'s importance in the formation of bourgeois or middle-class values in the period. One of *The Spectator*'s moral concerns – which also prompted Addison's own tragedy *Cato* (1713) – was the state of contemporary tragedy which, in its insistence upon poetic justice, was regarded as falling short of the ethical standards set by classical tragedy.

No. 39: Saturday, 14 April 1711

As a perfect tragedy is the noblest production of human nature, so it is capable of giving the mind one of the most delightful and most improving entertainments. 'A virtuous man' (says Seneca) 'struggling with misfortunes, is such a spectacle as gods might look upon with pleasure';[15] and such a pleasure it is which one meets with in the representation of a well-written tragedy. Diversions of this kind wear out of our thoughts every thing that is mean and little. They cherish and cultivate that humanity which is the ornament of our nature. They soften insolence, soothe affliction, and subdue the mind to the dispensations of Providence.

It is no wonder, therefore, that in all the polite nations of the world, this part of the drama has met with public encouragement.

The modern tragedy excels that of Greece and Rome in the intricacy and disposition of the fable; but, what a Christian writer would be ashamed to own, falls infinitely short of it in the moral part of the performance.

This I may show at large hereafter: and in the mean time, that I may contribute something towards the improvement of the English tragedy, I shall take notice, in this and in other following papers, of some particular parts in it that seem liable to exception.

Aristotle observes, that the Iambic verse in the Greek tongue was the most proper for tragedy; because at the same time that it lifted up the discourse from prose, it was that which approached nearer to it than any other kind of verse. 'For,' says he, 'we may observe that men in ordinary discourse very often speak iambics without taking notice of it.'[16] We may make the same observation of our English blank verse, which often enters into our common discourse,

---

[15]**says Seneca:** in *De Providentia*, 2.7; Lucius Annaeus Seneca, *Moral Essays*, trans. John Basore (Cambridge, MA: Harvard University Press, 1994), I:11.
[16]**ordinary discourse … speak iambics:** from Aristotle's *Poetics*. See extract 1.2.

though we do not attend to it, and is such a due medium between rhyme and prose, that it seems wonderfully adapted to tragedy. I am therefore very much offended when I see a play in rhyme; which is as absurd in English, as a tragedy of hexameters would have been in Greek or Latin. The solecism is, I think, still greater in those plays that have some scenes in rhyme and some in blank verse, which are to be looked upon as two several languages; or where we see some particular similes dignified with rhyme at the same time that every thing about them lies in blank verse. I would not however debar the poet from concluding his tragedy, or if he pleases, every act of it, with two or three couplets, which may have the same effect as an air in the Italian opera after a long recitativo, and give the actor a graceful exit. Besides that, we see a diversity of numbers in some parts of the old tragedy in order to hinder the ear from being tired with the same continued modulation of voice. For the same reason I do not dislike the speeches in our English tragedy that close with a hemistich,[17] or half verse, notwithstanding the person who speaks after it begins a new verse, without filling up the preceding one; nor with abrupt pauses and breakings off in the middle of a verse, when they humour any passion that is expressed by it.

Since I am upon this subject, I must observe that our English poets have succeeded much better in the style than in the sentiment of their tragedies. Their language is very often noble and sonorous, but the sense either very trifling or very common. On the contrary, in the ancient tragedies, and indeed in those of Corneille and Racine,[18] though the expressions are very great, it is the thought that bears them up and swells them. For my own part, I prefer a noble sentiment that is depressed with homely language, infinitely before a vulgar one that is blown up with all the sound and energy of expression. Whether this defect in our tragedies may arise from want of genius, knowledge, or experience in the writers, or from their compliance with the vicious taste of their readers, who are better judges of the language than of the sentiments, and consequently relish the one more than the other, I cannot determine. But I believe it might rectify the conduct both of the one and of the other, if the writer laid down the whole contexture of his dialogue in plain English, before he turned it into blank verse: and if the reader, after the perusal of a scene, would consider the naked thought of every speech in it, when divested of all its tragic ornaments. By this means, without being imposed upon by words, we may judge impartially of the thought, and consider whether it be natural or great enough for the person that utters it, whether it deserves to shine in such a blaze of eloquence, or show itself in such a variety of lights as are generally made use of by the writers of our English tragedy.

I must in the next place observe, that when our thoughts are great and just, they are often obscured by the sounding phrases, hard metaphors, and forced expressions in which they are clothed. Shakspeare is often very faulty in this particular. There is a fine observation in Aristotle to this purpose, which I have never seen quoted. 'The expression,' says he, 'ought to be very much laboured in the unactive parts of the fable, as in descriptions, similitudes, narrations, and the like; in which the opinions, manners, and passions of men are not represented; for these (namely, the opinions, manners, and passions) are apt to be obscured by pompous phrases and

---

[17]**hemistich:** a half line of verse divided by a caesura.
[18]**Corneille and Racine:** Pierre Corneille (1606–84) and Jean Racine (1639–99), the foremost French stage tragedians of the seventeenth century.

elaborate expressions.'[19] Horace, who copied most of his criticisms after Aristotle, seems to have had his eye on the foregoing rule, in the following verses:

Et tragicus plerumque dolet sermone pedestri:
Telephus et Peleus, cum pauper et exuluterque,
Projicit ampullas et sesquipedalia verba,
Si curat cor spectantis tetigisse querela.

Hor. Ars Poet. ver. 95

Tragedians, too, lay by their state to grieve:
Peleus and Telephus,[20] exil'd and poor,
Forget their swelling and gigantic words.

Roscommon.[21]

Among our modern English poets, there is none who has a better turn for tragedy than Lee;[22] if, instead of favouring the impetuosity of his genius, he had restrained it, and kept it within its proper bounds. His thoughts are wonderfully suited to tragedy, but frequently lost in such a cloud of words that it is hard to see the beauty of them. There is an infinite fire in his works, but so involved in smoke that it does not appear in half its lustre. He frequently succeeds in the passionate parts of the tragedy, but more particularly where he slackens his efforts, and eases the style of those epithets and metaphors in which he so much abounds. What can be more natural, more soft, or more passionate, than that line in Statira's speech where she describes the charms of Alexander's conversation?

Then he would talk—Good gods! how he would talk![23]

That unexpected break in the line, and turning the description of his manner of talking into an admiration of it, is inexpressibly beautiful, and wonderfully suited to the fond character of the person that speaks it. There is a simplicity in the words that outshines the utmost pride of expression.

Otway[24] has followed nature in the language of his tragedy, and therefore shines in the passionate parts more than any of our English poets. As there is something familiar and domestic in the fable of his tragedy, more than in those of any other poet, he has little pomp, but great force in his expressions. For which reason, though he has admirably succeeded in the tender and melting part of his tragedies, he sometimes falls into too great familiarity of

---

[19]**elaborate expressions:** The quotation is Addison's translation of Aristotle *Poetics*, XXIV; see Stephen Halliwell, ed. and trans., *Aristotle Poetics* (Cambridge, MA: Harvard University Press, 1995), 125.

[20]**Peleus and Telephus:** In Greek mythology Peleus, husband of the sea nymph Thetis and father of Achilles, was sent into exile for killing his stepbrother Phocus. In Euripdes's lost tragedy, *Telephus*, Telephus, king of the Mysians, pretended to be a beggar in order to get Clytemnestra to help heal a wound he had sustained in battle with Achilles.

[21]**Roscommon:** Wentworth Dillon, fourth earl of Roscommon (1637–85), eminent member of the court of Charles II. His *Horaces Art of Poetry* (1679) was the most influential Restoration translation of Horace's *Ars Poetica*.

[22]**Lee:** Nathaniel Lee (*c*.1645–92), Restoration playwright and poet who wrote several successful tragedies including *The Rival Queens* (1677) and with John Dryden, a version of *Oedipus* (1679).

[23]**Statira's speech:** Statira (*c*.340 BCE–323 BCE) was the wife of Alexander the Great; the quotation is from Lee's tragedy *The Rival Queens* (London, 1677), sig. C2r.

[24]**Otway:** Thomas Otway (1652–85), English Restoration playwright most famous in the eighteenth century for his tragedies *The Orphan* (1680) and *Venice Preserv'd* (1683).

phrase in those parts, which, by Aristotle's rule, ought to have been raised and supported by the dignity of expression.

It has been observed by others, that this poet has founded his tragedy of *Venice Preserv'd* on so wrong a plot, that the greatest characters in it are those of rebels and traitors. Had the hero of this play discovered the same good qualities in the defence of his country that he showed for its ruin and subversion, the audience could not enough pity and admire him; but as he is now represented, we can only say of him what the Roman historian says of Catiline, that his fall would have been glorious (*si pro patria sic concidisset*)[25] had he so fallen in the service of his country.

No. 40: Monday, 16 April 1711

The English writers of tragedy are possessed with a notion, that when they represent a virtuous or innocent person in distress, they ought not to leave him till they have delivered him out of his troubles, or made him triumph over his enemies. This error they have been led into by a ridiculous doctrine in modern criticism, that they are obliged to an equal distribution of rewards and punishments, and an impartial execution of poetical justice. Who were the first that established this rule I know not; but I am sure it has no foundation in nature, in reason, or in the practice of the ancients. We find that good and evil happen alike to all men on this side the grave; and as the principal design of tragedy is to raise commiseration and terror in the minds of the audience, we shall defeat this great end, if we always make virtue and innocence happy and successful. Whatever crosses and disappointments a good man suffers in the body of the tragedy, they will make but a small impression on our minds, when we know that in the last act he is to arrive at the end of his wishes and desires. When we see him engaged in the depth of his afflictions, we are apt to comfort ourselves, because we are sure he will find his way out of them; and that his grief, how great soever it may be at present, will soon terminate in gladness. For this reason, the ancient writers of tragedy treated men in their plays, as they are dealt with in the world, by making virtue sometimes happy and sometimes miserable, as they found it in the fable which they made choice of, or as it might affect the audience in the most agreeable manner. Aristotle considers the tragedies that were written in either of these kinds, and observes, that those which ended unhappily had always pleased the people, and carried away the prize in the public disputes of the stage, from those that ended happily. Terror and commiseration leave a pleasing anguish on the mind, and fix the audience in such a serious composure of thought, as is much more lasting and delightful than any little transient starts of joy and satisfaction. Accordingly we find, that more of our English tragedies have succeeded, in which the favourites of the audience sink under their calamities, than those in which they recover themselves out of them. The best plays of this kind are *The Orphan, Venice Preserv'd, Alexander the Great, Theodosius, All for Love, Oedipus, Oroonoko, Othello,* etc.[26] *King Lear* is an admirable tragedy of the same kind, as Shakespeare wrote it; but as it is reformed according

---

[25]**si pro Patria …:** Addison here translates a line on the death of the Roman Senator Catiline from Lucius Annaeus Florus, *Epitome of Roman History*, II.xii.12.

[26]***The Orphan … Othello:*** Alongside a Restoration production of Shakespeare's *Othello*, Addison lists a number of Restoration tragedies: Thomas Otway, *The Orphan* (1680) and *Venice Preserv'd* (1683); Nathaniel Lee, *The Rival Queens: Or, the Death of Alexander the Great* (1677) and *Theodosius: Or, the Force of Love* (1680); John Dryden, *All for Love* (1677); John Dryden and Nathaniel Lee, *Oedipus, a Tragedy* (1678–9); Thomas Southerne, *Oroonoko, A Tragedy* (1695).

to the chimerical notion of poetical justice, in my humble opinion it has lost half its beauty.[27] At the same time I must allow, that there are very noble tragedies which have been framed upon the other plan, and have ended happily; as indeed most of the good tragedies, which have been written since the starting of the above-mentioned criticism, have taken this turn; as *The Mourning Bride, Tamerlane, Ulysses, Phaedra and Hippolytus*, with most of Mr. Dryden's.[28] I must also allow, that many of Shakespeare's, and several of the celebrated tragedies of antiquity, are cast in the same form. I do not therefore dispute against this way of writing tragedies, but against the criticism that would establish this as the only method; and by that means would very much cramp the English tragedy, and perhaps give a wrong bent to the genius of our writers.

The tragi-comedy, which is the product of the English theatre, is one of the most monstrous inventions that ever entered into a poet's thoughts. An author might as well think of weaving the adventures of Aeneas and Hudibras into one poem,[29] as of writing such a motley piece of mirth and sorrow. But the absurdity of these performances is so very visible, that I shall not insist upon it.

The same objections which are made to tragi-comedy, may in some measure be applied to all tragedies that have a double plot in them; which are likewise more frequent upon the English stage, than upon any other; for though the grief of the audience, in such performances, be not changed into another passion, as in tragi-comedies; it is diverted upon another object, which weakens their concern for the principal action, and breaks the tide of sorrow, by throwing it into different channels. This inconvenience, however, may in a great measure be cured, if not wholly removed, by the skilful choice of an under plot, which may bear such a near relation to the principal design, as to contribute towards the completion of it, and be concluded by the same catastrophe.

There is also another particular, which may be reckoned among the blemishes, or rather the false beauties of our English tragedy: I mean those particular speeches which are commonly known by the name of Rants. The warm and passionate parts of a tragedy are always the most taking with the audience; for which reason we often see the players pronouncing, in all the violence of action, several parts of the tragedy which the author writ with great temper, and designed that they should have been so acted. I have seen Powell[30] very often raise himself a loud clap by this artifice. The poets that were acquainted with this secret, have given frequent occasion for such emotions in the actor, by adding vehemence to words where there was no passion, or inflaming a real passion into fustian. This hath filled the mouths of our heroes with bombast; and given them such sentiments as proceed rather from a swelling than a greatness of mind. Unnatural exclamations, curses, vows, blasphemies, a defiance of mankind, and an

---

[27]*King Lear ... reformed:* a reference to Nahum Tate's *The History of King Lear* (1681), a re-writing of Shakespeare's tragedy which avoided the innocent Cordelia's death and introduced a romantic plot in which she is happily married. Tate's *Lear* was preferred to Shakespeare's throughout the eighteenth century in Britain and America.

[28]*The Mourning Bride ... Mr Dryden's:* Addison is comparing eighteenth-century tragedies with the Restoration productions of John Dryden. He lists William Congreve, *The Mourning Bride* (1697); Nicholas Rowe, *Tamerlaine* (1701) and *Ulysses: A Tragedy* (1706); Edmund Smith, *Phaedra and Hippolytus* (1707).

[29]**Aeneas and Hudibras:** Aeneas was the hero of Virgil's epic *The Aeneid* (c.29–19 BCE) whereas Hudibras was the eponymous comic hero of Samuel Butler's popular mock-epic poem *Hudibras* (1684).

[30]**Powell:** Martin Powell (d. c. 1725), impresario and puppet showman who devised an immensely popular brand of puppet theatre. A key stage in the development of the Punch-and-Judy tradition, it relied on the exaggerated delivery of lines for its effects.

outraging of the gods, frequently pass upon the audience for towering thoughts, and have accordingly met with infinite applause.

I shall here add a remark, which I am afraid our tragic writers may make an ill use of. As our heroes are generally lovers, their swelling and blustering upon the stage very much recommends them to the fair part of the audience. The ladies are wonderfully pleased to see a man insulting kings, or affronting the gods, in one scene, and throwing himself at the feet of his mistress in another. Let him behave himself insolently towards the men, and abjectly towards the fair one, and it is ten to one but he proves a favourite with the boxes. Dryden and Lee, in several of their tragedies, have practised this secret with good success.

No. 418. Monday, 30 June 1712

There is yet another Circumstance which recommends a Description more than all the rest, and that is if it represents to us such Objects as are apt to raise a secret Ferment in the Mind of the Reader, and to work, with Violence, upon his Passions. For, in this Case, we are at once warmed and enlightened, so that the Pleasure becomes more Universal, and is several ways qualified to entertain us. Thus in Painting, it is pleasant to look on the Picture of any Face, where the Resemblance is hit, but the Pleasure increases, if it be the Picture of a Face that is Beautiful, and is still greater, if the Beauty be softened with an Air of Melancholy or Sorrow. The two leading Passions which the more serious Parts of Poetry endeavour to stir up in us, are Terror and Pity. And here, by the way, one would wonder how it comes to pass, that such Passions as are very unpleasant at all other times, are very agreeable when excited by proper Descriptions. It is not strange, that we should take Delight in such Passions as are apt to produce Hope, Joy, Admiration, Love, or the like Emotions in us, because they never rise in the Mind without an inward Pleasure which attends them. But how comes it to pass, that we should take delight in being terrified or dejected by a Description, when we find so much Uneasiness in the Fear or Grief which we receive from any other Occasion?

If we consider, therefore, the Nature of this Pleasure, we shall find that it does not arise so properly from the Description of what is terrible, as from the Reflection we make on our selves at the time of reading it. When we look on such hideous Objects, we are not a little pleased to think we are in no Danger of them. We consider them at the same time, as Dreadful and Harmless; so that the more frightful Appearance they make, the greater is the Pleasure we receive from the Sense of our own Safety. In short, we look upon the Terrors of a Description, with the same Curiosity and Satisfaction that we survey a dead Monster. ...

It is for the same Reason that we are delighted with the reflecting upon Dangers that are past, or in looking on a Precipice at a distance, which would fill us with a different kind of Horror, if we saw it hanging over our Heads.

In the like manner, when we read of Torments, Wounds, Deaths, and the like dismal Accidents, our Pleasure does not flow so properly from the Grief which such melancholy Descriptions give us, as from the secret Comparison which we make between our selves and the Person who suffers. Such Representations teach us to set a just Value upon our own Condition, and make us prize our good Fortune, which exempts us from the like Calamities. This is, however, such a kind of Pleasure as we are not capable of receiving, when we see a Person actually lying under the Tortures that we meet with in a Description; because in this case, the Object presses too close upon our Senses, and bears so hard upon us, that it does not give us Time or Leisure to reflect on our selves. Our Thoughts are so intent upon the Miseries of the Sufferer, that we cannot turn them upon our own Happiness. Whereas, on the contrary, we consider the Misfortunes we read in History or Poetry, either as past, or as fictitious, so that the Reflection upon our selves rises in us insensibly, and over-bears the Sorrow we conceive for the Sufferings of the Afflicted.

But because the Mind of Man requires something more perfect in Matter, than what it finds there, and can never meet with any Sight in Nature which sufficiently answers its highest Ideas of Pleasantness; or, in other Words, because the Imagination can fancy to itself Things more Great, Strange, or Beautiful, than the Eye ever saw, and is still sensible of some Defect in what it has seen; on this account it is the part of a Poet to humour the Imagination in its own Notions, by mending and perfecting Nature where he describes a Reality, and by adding greater Beauties than are put together in Nature, where he describes a Fiction.

Further reading

Lisa A. Freeman, *Character's Theater: Genre and Identity on the Eighteenth-Century English Stage* (Philadelphia: University of Pennsylvania Press, 2002).

Donald J. Newman (ed.), *The Spectator: Emerging Discourses* (Newark, NJ: University of Delaware Press, 2005).

Felicity A. Nussbaum, 'The Unaccountable Pleasure of Eighteenth-Century Tragedy', *PMLA* 129, no. 4 (2014): 688–707.

3.2 GEORGE LILLO, 'THE DEDICATION' AND 'PROLOGUE'
TO *THE LONDON MERCHANT* (1731)

George Lillo (*c.*1691–1739) was a jeweller who only turned to writing for the theatre in his late thirties. His second play, *The London Merchant* (1731), was much admired by Diderot, and was instrumental in popularizing English domestic tragedy in the eighteenth century. It dramatizes the story of the apprentice George Barnwell who, seduced and exploited by Sarah Millwood, a sex worker, turns thief and murderer. Both are executed for their crimes but a repentant Barnwell meets his fate piously and without fear: 'This Justice, in Compassion to Mankind, cuts off a Wretch like me, by one such example to secure thousands from future ruin' (V.x). Lillo had great faith in the ethical and reformist potential of tragedy, its capacity to moderate an audience's passions. That potential was enhanced, he contended, when tragedy's cast of characters was extended from the aristocracy to 'the Generality of Mankind', or the mercantile and working classes.

To *Sir* John Eyles, *Baronet.* Member of Parliament for, and Alderman of the City of *London*, and Sub-Governor of the *South-Sea* Company.[31]

SIR,

If Tragick Poetry be, as Mr. *Dryden* has some where said, the most excellent and most useful Kind of Writing,[32] the more extensively useful the Moral of any Tragedy is, the more excellent that Piece must be of its Kind. I hope I shall not be thought to insinuate that this, to which I have presumed to prefix your Name, is such; that depends on its Fitness to answer the End of Tragedy, the exciting of the Passions, in order to the correcting such of them as are criminal, either in their Nature, or through their Excess. Whether the following Scenes do this in any tolerable Degree, is, with the Deference, that becomes one who wou'd not be thought vain, submitted to your candid and impartial Judgment.

What I wou'd infer is this, I think, evident Truth; that Tragedy is so far from losing its Dignity, by being accommodated to the Circumstances of the Generality of Mankind, that it is more truly august in Proportion to the Extent of its Influence, and the Numbers that are properly affected by it.[33] As it is more truly great to be the Instrument of Good to many, who stand in need of our Assistance, than to a very small Part of that Number. If Princes, &c. were alone liable to Misfortunes, arising from Vice, or Weakness in themselves, or others, there wou'd be good Reason for confining the Characters in Tragedy to those of superior Rank; but, since the contrary is evident, nothing can be more reasonable than to proportion the Remedy to the Disease.

I am far from denying that Tragedies, founded on any instructive and extraordinary Events in History, or a well-invented Fable, where the Persons introduced are of the highest Rank, are

---

[31]**Sir John Eyles:** Sir John Eyles (1683–1745), financier and director of the Bank of England from 1715–7. He was MP for the City of London between 1727 and 1734.
[32]**Tragick Poetry ... Dryden:** see extract 2.9.
[33]**Generality of Mankind:** the mercantile and working classes. Lillo here suggests that tragedy has more influence when it connects directly with the lived experiences of greater numbers of people.

without their Use, even to the Bulk of the Audience. The strong Contract between a *Tamerlane* and a *Bajazet*, may have its Weight with an unsteady People, and contribute to the fixing of them in the Interest of a Prince of the Character of the former, when, thro' their own Levity, or the Arts of designing Men, they are render'd factious and uneasy, tho' they have the highest Reason to be satisfied.[34] The Sentiments and Example of a *Cato*, may inspire his Spectators with a just Sense of the Value of Liberty, when they see that honest Patriot prefer Death to an Obligation from a Tyrant, who wou'd sacrifice the Constitution of his Country, and the Liberties of Mankind, to his Ambition or Revenge.[35] I have attempted, indeed, to enlarge the Province of the graver Kind of Poetry, and should be glad to see it carried on by some abler Hand. Plays, founded on moral Tales in private Life, may be of admirable Use, by carrying Conviction to the Mind, with such irresistable Force, as to engage all the Faculties and Powers of the Soul in the Cause of Virtue, by stifling Vice in its first Principles. They who imagine this to be too much to be attributed to Tragedy, must be Strangers to the Energy of that noble Species of Poetry. *Shakespeare*, who has given such amazing Proofs of his Genius, in that as well as in Comedy, in his *Hamlet*, has the following Lines.

> *Had he the Motive and the Cause for Passion*
> *That I have; he wou'd drown the Stage with Tears*
> *And cleave the general Ear with horrid Speech;*
> *Make mad the Guilty, and appal the Free,*
> *Confound the Ignorant, and amaze indeed*
> *The very Faculty of Eyes and Ears.*

And farther, in the same Speech,

> *I've heard that guilty Creatures at a Play,*
> *Have, by the very cunning of the Scene,*
> *Been so struck to the Soul, that presently*
> *They have proclaim'd their Malefactions.*[36]

Prodigious! yet strictly just. But I shan't take up your valuable Time with my Remarks; only give me Leave just to observe, that he seems so firmly perswaded of the Power of a well wrote Piece to produce the Effect here ascribed to it, as to make *Hamlet* venture his Soul on the Event, and rather trust that, than a Messenger from the other World, tho' it assumed, as he

---

[34]**Tamerlane and Bajazet:** Timur (1336–1405), Mongol warrior and founder of Timurid empire. Commonly known in European culture as Tamerlane, his conquering of the Turkish emperor Bajazet or Bayezid I (1354–1403) was the subject of the first of Christopher Marlowe's *Tamburlaine* plays (*c.*1587). These historical figures were given new currency for eighteenth-century English audiences by Nicholas Rowe's tragedy *Tamerlane* (*c.*1701) and Handel's opera *Tamerlano* (1724).

[35]**Cato:** Marcus Porcius Cato, or Cato the Younger (95–46 BCE), Roman statesman and staunch defender of the values of the Roman Republic. He killed himself rather than accept the imperial authority of Julius Caesar and was commonly regarded as a hero of classical Republicanism. He was the subject of Joseph Addison's immensely successful stage tragedy *Cato* (1713).

[36]***Hamlet:*** Lillo here slightly misquotes the 'what a rogue or peasant slave soliloquy' from Act 2 of Shakespeare's *Hamlet* (1601). It is the 'cue', not 'cause' of passion in Folio and Quarto editions of the play.

expresses it, his noble Father's Form, and assured him, that it was his Spirit. I'll have, says *Hamlet*, Grounds more relative

> ---*The Play's the Thing,*
> *Wherein I'll catch the Conscience of the King.*[37]

Such Plays are the best Answers to them who deny the Lawfulness of the Stage.

Considering the Novelty of this Attempt, I thought it would be expected from me to say something in its Excuse; and I was unwilling to lose the Opportunity of saying something of the Usefulness of Tragedy in general, and what may be reasonably expected from the farther Improvement of this excellent Kind of Poetry.

Prologue

Spoke by Mr. Cibber, Jun.[38]

> *The Tragick Muse, sublime, delights to show*
> *Princes distrest, and Scenes of Royal Woe;*
> *In awful Pomp, Majestick, to relate*
> *The Fall of Nations, or some Heroe's Fate:*
> *That Scepter'd Chiefs may by Example know*
> *The strange Vicissitude of Things below:*
> *What Dangers on Security attend;*
> *How Pride and Cruelty in Ruin end:*
> *Hence Providence Supream to know; and own*
> *Humanity adds Glory to a Throne.*
>   *In ev'ry former Age, and Foreign Tongue,*
> *With Native Grandeur thus the Goddess sung.*
> *Upon our Stage indeed, with wish'd Success,*
> *You've sometimes seen her in a humbler Dress;*
> *Great only in Distress. When she complains*
> *In Southern's, Rowe's, or Otway's moving Strains,*[39]
> *The Brillant Drops, that fall from each bright Eye,*
> *The absent Pomp, with brighter Jems, supply.*
>   *Forgive us then, if we attempt to show,*
> *In artless Strains, a Tale of private Woe.*
> *A London Prentice ruin'd is our Theme,*
> *Drawn from the fam'd old Song, that bears his Name.*

---

[37]**Play's the Thing:** the concluding couplet to Hamlet's 'what a rogue and peasant slave' soliloquy: *Hamlet* 2.2. 606-7.

[38]**Mr Cibber:** Theophilus Cibber (1703–58), actor, playwright and theatre manager. Cibber played the tragic protagonist George Barnwell in Lillo's play. He is described here as 'Jun', or 'Junior', because he was the son of famous actor and poet laureate Colley Cibber (1671–1757).

[39]**Southern's, Rowe's, or Otway's:** the playwrights Thomas Southerne (1660–1746), Nicholas Rowe (1674–1718), and Thomas Otway (1682–5). All experimented by occasionally composing tragedies with non-aristocratic protagonists.

We hope your Taste is not so high to scorn
A moral Tale, esteem'd e'er you were born;
Which for a Century of rolling Years,
Has fill'd a thousand-thousand Eyes with Tears.
    If thoughtless Youth to warn, and shame the Age
From Vice destructive, well becomes the Stage;
If this Example Innocence secure,
Prevent our Guilt, or by Reflection cure;
If Millwood's dreadful Guilt, and sad Despair,[40]
Commend the Virtue of the Good and Fair,
Tho' Art be wanting, and our Numbers fail,[41]
Indulge th' Attempt in Justice to the Tale.

Further reading

Roberta F.S. Borkat, 'The Evil of Goodness: Sentimental Morality in *The London Merchant*', *Studies in Philology* 76, no. 3 (1979): 288–312.

Stephen L. Trainor, 'Tears Abounding: *The London Merchant* as Puritan Tragedy', *Studies in English Literature 1500–1900* 18, no. 3 (1978): 509–21.

David Wallace, 'Bourgeois Tragedy or Sentimental Melodrama? The Significance of George Lillo's *The London Merchant*', *Eighteenth Century Studies* 25, no. 2 (1991–2): 123–43.

---

[40]**Millwood:** Sarah Millwood, the villain of Lillo's tragedy who leads George Barnwell to his ruin.
[41]**Numbers:** poetic metre. In keeping with his goal of communicating tragedy clearly to the 'Generality of Mankind', Lillo composed his play entirely in prose rather than verse.

3.3 VOLTAIRE, 'LETTER XVIII. ON TRAGEDY' (C.1733)

François-Marie Arouet (1694–1778), known as Voltaire, was a giant of European theatre and Enlightenment philosophy. He wrote 49 plays, 27 of which were tragedies. Despite his criticism of Shakespearean and Restoration tragedy for failing to observe neoclassical 'rules' of the tragic unities (a criticism which offended many English readers), Voltaire was an Anglophile who sought to use aspects of English tragedy, especially its use of soliloquy, to remodel contemporary French tragic theatre. Thus, even though he criticized the absurdity of Desdemona's death in Shakespeare's *Othello* (1604), his tragedy of jealousy in the Christian–Islamic encounters *Zaïre* (1732) is heavily indebted to the earlier play. Voltaire wrote his *Letters Concerning the English Nation* in English following his stay in London between 1726 and 1728. When it was translated into French as *Lettres Philosophiques* (1733), it was censored because of its implied wholesale criticism of French society in matters of literature, religion, science, and trade.

The English as well as the Spaniards were possessed of theatres at a time when the French had no more than moving, itinerant stages. Shakespeare, who was considered as the Corneille of the first-mentioned nation, was pretty nearly contemporary with *Lopez de Vega*,[42] and he created, as it were, the English theatre. Shakespeare boasted a strong fruitful Genius: He was natural and sublime, but had not so much as a single spark of good Taste, or knew one Rule of the Drama. I will now hazard a random, but, at the same time, true reflection, which is, that the great merit of this dramatic poet has been the ruin of the English stage. There are such beautiful, such noble, such dreadful scenes in this writer's monstrous farces, to which the name of tragedy is given, that they have always been exhibited with great success. Time, which alone gives reputation to writers, at last makes their very faults venerable. Most of the whimsical gigantic images of this poet, have, through length of time (it being a hundred and fifty years since they were first drawn) acquired a right of passing for sublime. Most of the modern dramatic writers have copied him; but the touches and descriptions which are applauded in Shakespeare, are hissed at in these writers; and you will easily believe that the veneration in which this author is held, increases in proportion to the contempt which is shown to the moderns. Dramatick writers don't consider that they should not imitate him; and the ill-success of Shakespeare's imitators produces no other effect, than to make him be considered as inimitable. You remember that in the tragedy of *Othello, Moor of Venice*, a most tender piece, a man strangles his wife on the stage, and that the poor woman, whilst she is strangling, cries aloud that she dies very unjustly. You know that in *Hamlet, Prince of Denmark*, two grave-diggers make a grave, and are all the time drinking, singing ballads, and making humorous reflections (natural indeed enough to persons of their profession) on the several skulls they throw up with their spades; but a circumstance which will surprise you is, that this ridiculous incident has been imitated. In the reign of King Charles II, which was that of

---

[42]**Lopez de Vega:** Lope Félix de Vega Carpio (1562–1635), Spanish playwright, poet and prose writer, commonly regarded as the most prodigious dramatist of the Spanish Golden Age.

politeness, and the Golden Age of the liberal arts; Otway, in his *Venice Preserv'd*,[43] introduces Antonio the senator, and Naki, his courtesan, in the midst of the horrors of the Marquis of Bedemar's conspiracy. Antonio, the superannuated senator plays, in his mistress's presence, all the apish tricks of a lewd, impotent debauchee, who is quite frantic and out of his senses. He mimics a bull and a dog, and bites his mistress's legs, who kicks and whips him. However, the players have struck these buffooneries (which indeed were calculated merely for the dregs of the people) out of Otway's tragedy;[44] but they have still left in Shakespeare's *Julius Cæsar* the jokes of the Roman shoemakers and cobblers, who are introduced in the same scene with Brutus and Cassius. You will undoubtedly complain, that those who have hitherto discoursed with you on the English stage, and especially on the celebrated Shakespeare, have taken notice only of his errors; and that no one has translated any of those strong, those forcible passages which atone for all his faults. But to this I will answer, that nothing is easier than to exhibit in prose all the silly impertinences which a poet may have thrown out; but that it is a very difficult task to translate his fine verses. All your junior academical sophs,[45] who set up for censors of the eminent writers, compile whole volumes; but methinks two pages which display some of the beauties of great geniuses, are of infinitely more value than all the idle rhapsodies of those commentators; and I will join in opinion with all persons of good taste in declaring, that greater advantage may be reaped from a dozen verses of Homer or Virgil, than from all the critiques put together which have been made on those two great poets. …

It is in these detached passages[46] that the English have hitherto excelled. Their dramatic pieces, most of which are barbarous and without decorum, order, or verisimilitude, dart such resplendent flashes through this gleam, as amaze and astonish. The style is too much inflated, too unnatural, too closely copied from the Hebrew writers, who abound so much with the Asiatic fustian.[47] But then it must be also confessed that the stilts of the figurative style, on which the English tongue is lifted up, raises the genius at the same time very far aloft, though with an irregular pace. The first English writer who composed a regular tragedy, and infused a spirit of elegance through every part of it, was the illustrious Mr. Addison.[48] His *Cato* is a masterpiece, both with regard to the diction and to the beauty and harmony of the numbers. The character of Cato is, in my opinion, vastly superior to that of Cornelia in the *Pompey* of Corneille, for Cato is great without anything like fustian, and Cornelia, who besides is not a necessary character, tends sometimes to bombast. Mr. Addison's Cato appears to me the greatest character that was ever brought upon any stage, but then the rest of them do not correspond to the dignity of it, and this dramatic piece, so excellently well writ, is disfigured by a dull love plot, which spreads a certain languor over the whole, that quite murders it.

---

[43] *Venice Preserv'd*: Thomas Otway's popular Restoration tragedy, *Venice Preserv'd* (1682).

[44] **struck … out of Otway's tragedy**: Restoration and eighteenth-century versions of Otway's tragedy were much reduced from the 1682 quarto. The cuts were chiefly to passages of comic fooling and were driven by the actors. By the early nineteenth century the performed text was some 900 lines shorter than Otway's original. See Aline Mackenzie Taylor, *Next to Shakespeare: Otway's 'Venice Preserv'd' and 'The Orphan' and Their History on the London Stage* (Durham, CA: Duke University Press, 1950), 276–81.

[45] **sophs**: abbreviation of 'sophisters'; people who reason and argue speciously.

[46] **detached passages**: soliloquies.

[47] **Asiatic fustian**: inappropriately bombastic language.

[48] **Mr Addison**: Joseph Addison (1672–1719), English poet, playwright and editor of *The Spectator*. Voltaire was an avid reader of *The Spectator* during his London years. See extract 3.1.

The custom of introducing love at random and at any rate in the drama passed from Paris to London about 1660, with our ribbons and our peruques.[49] The ladies who adorn the theatrical circle there, in like manner as in this city, will suffer love only to be the theme of every conversation. The judicious Mr. Addison had the effeminate complaisance to soften the severity of his dramatic character, so as to adapt it to the manners of the age, and, from an endeavour to please, quite ruined a masterpiece in its kind. Since his time the drama is become more regular, the audience more difficult to be pleased, and writers more correct and less bold. I have seen some new pieces that were written with great regularity, but which, at the same time, were very flat and insipid. One would think that the English had been hitherto formed to produce irregular beauties only. The shining monsters of Shakespeare give infinite more delight than the judicious images of the moderns. Hitherto the poetical genius of the English resembles a tufted tree planted by the hand of Nature, that throws out a thousand branches at random, and spreads unequally, but with great vigour. It dies if you attempt to force its nature, and to lop and dress it in the same manner as the trees of the Garden of Marli.[50]

Further reading

Nicholas Cronk (ed.), *Voltaire, Letters Concerning the English Nation* (Oxford: World's Classics, 2005).

Eva Jacobs, *Voltaire and Tragedy* (London: ProQuest Information and Learning, 1987).

---

[49]**peruques:** wigs. Like the ribbons used to adorn clothing, these were originally a French fashion imported into English courtly society.

[50]**Garden of Marli:** the park and palace of Marly; 7 km west of Versailles and built in 1679, they were the leisure palace and pleasure gardens of Louis XIV (1638–1715).

3.4 DAVID HUME, 'OF TRAGEDY' (1757)

David Hume (1711–76) was one of the foremost British philosophers and historians of the eighteenth century and a key figure of the Scottish Enlightenment. His philosophy as expressed in masterworks like *A Treatise of Human Nature* (1739–40) was staunchly empiricist in outlook, rejecting the abstractions of metaphysics in favour of the observation of human experience as the source of all ideas and knowledge. Hume was primarily interested in tragedy for what it revealed about our ability to experience apparently contradictory affective responses – for example, both pleasure and sorrow – to a single aesthetic object. Offering a psychological rather than a historical, literary, or philosophical theory of tragedy in this short essay, he contended that it was the style and eloquence of tragic art which converted the anxiety or terror we might feel for its protagonists into pleasure.

It seems an unaccountable pleasure, which the spectators of a well-wrote tragedy receive from sorrow, terror, anxiety, and other passions, which are in themselves disagreeable and uneasy. The more they are touched and affected, the more are they delighted with the spectacle, and as soon as the uneasy passions cease to operate, the piece is at an end. One scene of full joy and contentment and security is the utmost, that any composition of this kind can bear; and it is sure always to be the concluding one. If in the texture of the piece, there be interwoven any scenes of satisfaction, they afford only faint gleams of pleasure, which are thrown in by way of variety, and in order to plunge the actors into deeper distress, by means of that contrast and disappointment. The whole art of the poet is employed, in rouzing and supporting the compassion and indignation, the anxiety and resentment of his audience. They are pleased in proportion as they are afflicted; and never are so happy as when they employ tears, sobs, and cries to give vent to their sorrow, and relieve their heart, swoln with the tenderest sympathy and compassion.

The few critics, who have had some tincture of philosophy, have remarked this singular phænomenon, and have endeavoured to account for it. L'abbe *Dubos*,[51] in his reflections on poetry and painting, asserts, that nothing is in general so disagreeable to the mind as the languid, listless state of indolence, into which it falls upon the removal of every passion and occupation. To get rid of this painful situation, it seeks every amusement and pursuit; business, gaming, shows, executions; whatever will rouze the passions, and take its attention from itself. No matter, what the passion is: Let it be disagreeable, afflicting, melancholy, disordered; it is still better, than that insipid languor, which arises from perfect tranquillity and repose.

It is impossible not to admit this account, as being, at least, in part satisfactory. You may observe, when there are several tables of gaming, that all the company run to those, where the deepest play is, even tho' they find not there the finest players. The view, or at least, imagination of high passions, arising from great loss or gain, affects the spectators by sympathy, gives them

---

[51]**L'abbe *Dubos*:** Jean-Baptiste Dubos (1670–1742), French diplomat, historian and philosopher. His *Reflexions critique sur la poésie et sur la peinture* (1719) was instrumental in the development of aesthetic theory in the eighteenth century. It was translated into English as *Critical Reflections on Poetry, Painting and Music* (1748).

some touches of the same passions, and serves them for a momentary entertainment. It makes the time pass the easier with them, and is some relief to that oppression, under which men commonly labour, when left entirely to their own thoughts and meditations.

We find, that common lyars always magnify, in their narrations, all kinds of danger, pain, distress, sickness, deaths, murders, and cruelties; as well as joy, beauty, mirth, and magnificence. It is an absurd secret, which they have for pleasing their company, fixing their attention, and attaching them to such marvellous relations, by the passions and emotions, which they excite.

There is, however, a difficulty of applying to the present subject, in its full extent, this solution, however ingenious and satisfactory it may appear. It is certain, that the same object of distress which pleases in a tragedy, were it really set before us, would give the most unfeigned uneasiness tho' it be then the most effectual cure of languor and indolence. Monsieur *Fontenelle*[52] seems to have been sensible of this difficulty; and accordingly attempts another solution of the phænomenon; at least, makes some addition to the theory abovementioned.[53]

'Pleasure and pain,' says he, 'which are two sentiments so different in themselves, differ not so much in their cause. From the instance of tickling, it appears, that the movement of pleasure pushed a little too far, becomes pain; and that the movement of pain, a little moderated, becomes pleasure. Hence it proceeds, that there is such a thing as a sorrow, soft and agreeable: It is a pain weakened and diminished. The heart likes naturally to be moved and affected. Melancholy objects suit it, and even disastrous and sorrowful, provided they are softened by some circumstance. It is certain, that on the theatre the representation has almost the effect of reality; but yet is has not altogether that effect. However we may be hurried away by the spectacle; whatever dominion the senses and imagination may usurp over the reason, there still lurks at the bottom a certain idea of falshood in the whole of what we see. This idea, tho' weak and disguised, suffices to diminish the pain which we suffer from the misfortunes of those whom we love, and to reduce that affliction to such a pitch as converts it into a pleasure. We weep for the misfortune of a hero, to whom we are attached: In the same instant we comfort our selves, by reflecting, that it is nothing but a fiction: And it is precisely, that mixture of sentiments, which composes an agreeable sorrow, and tears that delight us. But as that affliction, which is caused by exterior and sensible objects, is stronger than the consolation, which arises from an internal reflection, they are the effects and symptoms of sorrow, which ought to prevail in the composition.'

This solution seems just and convincing; but perhaps it wants still some new addition, in order to make it answer fully the phænomenon, which we here examine. All the passions, excited by eloquence, are agreeable in the highest degree, as well as those which are moved by painting and the theatre. The epilogues of *Cicero*[54] are, on this account chiefly, the delight of every reader of taste; and it is difficult to read some of them without the deepest sympathy and sorrow. His merit as an orator, no doubt, depends much on his success in this particular. When he had raised tears in his judges and all his audience, they were then the most highly delighted, and expressed the greatest satisfaction with the pleader. The pathetic description

---

[52]**Monsieur *Fontenelle*:** Bernard Le Bovier de Fontenelle (1657–1757), French dramatist, scientist and man of letters. His *Reflexions sur La Poetique* (1742) was an important work of French theatre history.
[53]**[Hume's note]:** Reflexions sur la poetique. p. 36. (A citation for the long quotation from Fontenelle in the next paragraph.)
[54]**Cicero:** Marcus Tullius Cicero (106–43 BCE), Roman philosopher, lawyer and orator, renowned for his eloquence.

of the butchery made by *Verres* of the *Sicilian* captains is a master-piece of this kind:[55] But I believe none will affirm, that the being present at a melancholy scene of that nature would afford any entertainment. Neither is the sorrow here softened by fiction: For the audience were convinced of the reality of every circumstance. What is it then, which in this case raises a pleasure from the bosom of uneasiness, so to speak; and a pleasure, which still retains all the features and outward symptoms of distress and sorrow?

I answer: This extraordinary effect proceeds from that very eloquence, with which the melancholy scene is represented. The genius required to paint objects in a lively manner, the art employed in collecting all the pathetic circumstances, the judgment displayed in disposing them; the exercise, I say, of these noble talents, along with the force of expression, and beauty of oratorial numbers, diffuse the highest satisfaction on the audience, and excite the most delightful movements. By this means, the uneasiness of the melancholy passions is not only overpowered and effaced by something stronger of an opposite kind; but the whole movement of those passions is converted into pleasure, and swells the delight, which the eloquence raises in us. The same force of oratory, employed on an uninteresting subject, would not please half so much, or rather would appear altogether ridiculous; and the mind, being left in absolute calmness and indifference, would relish none of those beauties of imagination or expression, which, if joined to passion, give it such exquisite entertainment. The impulse or vehemence, arising from sorrow, compassion, indignation, receives a new direction from the sentiments of beauty. The latter, being the predominant emotions, seize the whole mind, and convert the former into themselves, or at least, tincture them so strongly as totally to alter their nature: And the soul, being, at the same time, rouzed by passion, and charmed by eloquence, feels on the whole a strong movement, which is altogether delightful.

The same principle takes place in tragedy; along with this addition, that tragedy is an imitation, and imitation is always of itself agreeable. This circumstance serves still farther to smooth the motions of passion, and convert the whole feeling into one uniform and strong enjoyment. Objects of the greatest terror and distress please in painting, and please more than the most beautiful objects, that appear calm and indifferent.[56] The affection, rouzing the mind, excites a large stock of spirit and vehemence; which is all transformed into pleasure by the force of the prevailing movement. It is thus the fiction of tragedy softens the passion, by an infusion of a new feeling, not merely by weakening or diminishing the sorrow. You may by degrees weaken a real sorrow, till it totally disappears; yet in none of its gradations will it ever give pleasure; except, perhaps, by accident, to a man sunk under lethargic indolence, whom it rouzes from that languid state.

---

[55]**Verres of the Sicilian:** Gaius Verres (ca. 120–43 BCE), a notoriously corrupt governor of Sicily. Cicero prosecuted Verres for corruption and extortion; his speeches denouncing Verres' behaviour were collected in 70 BCE as *In Verrem* ('Against Verres').

[56]**[Hume's note]:** Painters make no scruple of representing distress and sorrow as well as any other passion: But they seem not to dwell so much on these melancholy affections as the poets, who, tho' they copy every emotion of the human breast, yet pass very quickly over the agreeable sentiments. A painter represents only one instant; and if that be passionate enough, it is sure to affect and delight the spectator: But nothing can furnish to the poet a variety of scenes and incidents and sentiments, except distress, terror, or anxiety. Compleat joy and satisfaction is attended with security, and leaves no farther room for action.

To confirm this theory, it will be sufficient to produce other instances, where the subordinate movement is converted into the predominant, and gives force to it, tho' of a different, and even sometimes tho' of a contrary nature.

Novelty naturally excites the mind and attracts our attention; and the movements, which it causes, are always converted into any passion, belonging to the object, and join their force to it. Whether an event excites joy or sorrow, pride or shame, anger or goodwill, it is sure to produce a stronger affection, when new and unusual. And tho' novelty, of itself, be agreeable, it enforces the painful, as well as agreeable passions.

Had you any intention to move a person extremely by the narration of any event, the best method of encreasing its effect would be artfully to delay informing him of it, and first excite his curiosity and impatience before you let him into the secret. This is the artifice, practiced by *Iago* in the famous scene of *Shakespeare*; and every spectator is sensible, that *Othello's* jealousy acquires additional force from his preceding impatience, and that the subordinate passion is here readily transformed into the predominant.

Difficulties encrease passions of every kind; and by rouzing our attention, and exciting our active powers, they produce an emotion, which nourishes the prevailing affection.

Parents commonly love that child most, whose sickly infirm frame of body has occasioned them the greatest pains, trouble, and anxiety in rearing him. The agreeable sentiment of affection here acquires force from sentiments of uneasiness.

Nothing endears so much a friend as sorrow for his death. The pleasure of his company has not so powerful an influence.

Jealousy is a painful passion, yet without some share of it, the agreeable affection of love has difficulty to subsist in its full force and violence. Absence is also a great source of complaint amongst lovers, and gives them the greatest uneasiness: Yet nothing is more favorable to their mutual passion than short intervals of that kind. And if long intervals be pernicious, it is only because, thro' time, men are accustomed to them, and they cease to give uneasiness. Jealousy and absence in love compose the *dolce piccante*[57] of the *Italians*, which they suppose so essential to all pleasure.

There is a fine observation of the elder *Pliny*,[58] which illustrates the principle here insisted on. *It is very remarkable*, says he, *that the last works of celebrated artists, which they left imperfect, are always the most prized, such as the* Iris *of* Aristides, *the* Tyndarides *of* Nicomachus, *the* Medea *of* Timomachus, *and the* Venus *of* Apelles.[59] *These are valued even above their finished productions: The broken lineaments of the piece and the half formed idea of the painter are carefully studied; and our very grief for that curious hand, which had been stoped by death, is an additional encrease to our pleasure.*

These instances (and many more might be collected) are sufficient to afford us some insight into the analogy of nature, and to show us, that the pleasure, which poets, orators, and

---

[57] *dolce piccante*: pleasantly bitter (Italian).

[58] **elder Pliny:** Gaius Plinius Secundus (*c*.23–79 CE), or Pliny the Elder, Roman philosopher and naturalist. Hume here translates a passage from Pliny's *The Natural History* (*c*.77–9 CE), book 35, chapter 40.

[59] **Iris of Aristides ... Apelles:** Aristides of Thebes (fl. 360–330 BCE) a Greek painter, reputed to have died leaving a beautiful painting of Iris incomplete; Nicomachus (fl. 60 BCE) a Theban artist died before having had chance to finish his Tyndarides. Timomachus of Byzantium (fl. *c*.3–1 BCE) reportedly left his famous painting of Medea (now lost) incomplete. Apelles of Kos (fl. *c*.330 BCE) was one of the most renowned painters of Ancient Greece. He is reported to have been working on a painting of Aphrodite of Kos when he died.

musicians give us, by exciting grief, sorrow, indignation, compassion, is not so extraordinary nor paradoxical, as it may at first sight appear. The force of imagination, the energy of expression, the power of numbers, the charms of imitation; all these are naturally, of themselves, delightful to the mind; and when the object presented lays also hold of some affection, the pleasure still rises upon us, by the conversion of this subordinate movement, into that which is predominant. The passion, tho', perhaps, naturally, and when excited by the simple appearance of a real object, it may be painful; yet is so smoothed, and softened, and mollified, when raised by the finer arts, that it affords the highest entertainment.

To confirm this reasoning, we may observe, that if the movements of the imagination be not predominant above those of the passion, a contrary effect follows; and the former, being now subordinate, is converted into the latter, and still farther encreases the pain and affliction of the sufferer.

Who could ever think of it as a good expedient for comforting an afflicted parent, to exaggerate, with all the force of oratory, the irreparable loss, which he has met with by the death of a favorite child? The more power of imagination and expression you here employ, the more you encrease his despair and affliction.

The shame, confusion, and terror of *Verres*, no doubt, rose in proportion to the noble eloquence and vehemence of *Cicero*: So also did his pain and uneasiness. These former passions were too strong for the pleasure arising from the beauties of elocution; and operated, tho' from the same principle, yet in a contrary manner, to the sympathy, compassion, and indignation of the audience.

Lord *Clarendon*,[60] when he approaches the catastrophe of the royal party, supposes, that his narration must then become infinitely disagreeable; and he hurries over the King's death, without giving us one circumstance of it. He considers it as too horrid a scene to be contemplated with any satisfaction, or even without the utmost pain and aversion. He himself, as well as the readers of that age, were too deeply interested in the events, and felt a pain from subjects, which an historian and a reader of another age would regard as the most pathetic and most interesting, and by consequence, the most agreeable.

An action, represented in tragedy, may be too bloody and atrocious. It may excite such movements of horror as will not soften into pleasure; and the greatest energy of expression bestowed on descriptions of that nature serves only to augment our uneasiness. Such is that action represented in the *Ambitious Stepmother*,[61] where a venerable old man, raised to the height of fury and despair, rushes against a pillar, and striking his head upon it, besmears it all over with mingled brains and gore. The *English* theatre abounds too much with such images.

Even the common sentiments of compassion require to be softened by some agreeable affection, in order to give a thorough satisfaction to the audience. The mere suffering of plaintive virtue, under the triumphant tyranny and oppression of vice, forms a disagreeable spectacle, and is carefully avoided by all masters of the theatre. In order to dismiss the audience

---

[60]**Lord Clarendon:** Edward Hyde, first Earl of Clarendon (1609–74), seventeenth-century English statesman and favourite of the Stuart kings Charles I and Charles II. His *History of the Rebellion* (1702–4) was published posthumously but remains one of the most authoritative early accounts of the English civil war.

[61]**ambitious Stepmother:** Nicholas Rowe's *The Ambitious Stepmother* (1700), an extremely popular and violent stage tragedy.

with entire satisfaction and contentment, the virtue must either convert itself into a noble courageous despair, or the vice receive its proper punishment.

Most painters appear in this light to have been very unhappy in their subjects. As they wrought for churches and convents, they have chiefly represented such horrible subjects as crucifixions and martyrdoms, where nothing appears but tortures, wounds, executions, and passive suffering, without any action or affection. When they turned their pencil from this ghastly mythology, they had recourse commonly to *Ovid*,[62] whose fictions, tho' passionate and agreeable, are scarce natural or probable enough for painting.

The same inversion of that principle, which is here insisted on, displays itself in common life, as in the effects of oratory and poetry. Raise so the subordinate passion that it becomes the predominant, it swallows up that affection, which it before nourished and encreased. Too much jealousy extinguishes love: Too much difficulty renders us indifferent: Too much sickness and infirmity disgusts a selfish and unkind parent.

What so disagreeable as the dismal, gloomy, disastrous stories, with which melancholy people entertain their companions? The uneasy passion, being there raised alone, unaccompanied with any spirit, genius, or eloquence, conveys a pure uneasiness, and is attended with nothing that can soften it into pleasure or satisfaction.

Further reading

E.M. Dadlez, 'Pleased and Afflicted: Hume on the Paradox of Tragic Pleasure', *Hume Studies* 30, no. 2 (2004): 213–36.

Elisa Galgut, 'The Poetry and the Pity: Hume's Account of Tragic Pleasure', *British Journal of Aesthetics* 41, no. 4 (2001): 411–24.

Alex Neill, '"An Unaccountable Pleasure": Hume on Tragedy and the Passions', *Hume Studies* 24, no. 2 (1998): 335–54.

Dabney Townsend, *Hume's Aesthetic Theory: Taste and Sentiment* (New York: Routledge, 2001).

---

[62]**Ovid:** Publius Ovidius Naso (43 BCE–17 CE), one of the foremost poets of the classical Roman world.

3.5 EDMUND BURKE, 'SYMPATHY', 'OF THE EFFECTS OF TRAGEDY' AND 'THE SUBLIME' (1757)

Edmund Burke (*c*.1729–79) was an Irish-born historian, philosopher, politician, and political theorist. *A Philosophical Enquiry* (1757), his second printed work, was a hugely influential study of aesthetic taste. Key to Burke's aesthetics was his theory of the sublime (for an important philosophical precursor to Burke's theory, see Longinus's *On the Sublime*, extract 1.4.). Burke's sublime is a quality of greatness which provokes astonishment, fear, uncertainty and a desire for self-preservation (unlike the beautiful which prompts more social forms of joy and pleasure). The mind and the senses, alike, are unable fully to grasp the sublime in nature, such is its size or force. Because tragedy always conjures with terror and uncertainty, Burke argued, it produces passions and attitudes intimately associated with our experience of the sublime. He claimed that the best tragedies are those which are most realistic and life-life because humans are drawn to recognizable suffering and distress in the world partly as a means of experiencing the pleasure of our God-given capacity for sympathy.

PART I

SECT. XIII: Sympathy

It is by the first of these passions that we enter into the concerns of others; that we are moved as they are moved, and are never suffered to be indifferent spectators of almost any thing which men can do or suffer. For sympathy must be considered as a sort of substitution, by which we are put into the place of another man, and affected in many respects as he is affected; so that this passion may either partake of the nature of those which regard self-preservation, and turning upon pain may be a source of the sublime; or it may turn upon ideas of pleasure; and then, whatever has been said of the social affections, whether they regard society in general, or only some particular modes of it, may be applicable here. It is by this principle chiefly that poetry, painting, and other affecting arts, transfuse their passions from one breast to another, and are often capable of grafting a delight on wretchedness, misery, and death itself. It is a common observation, that objects which in the reality would shock, are in tragical, and such like representations, the source of a very high species of pleasure. This taken as a fact, has been the cause of much reasoning. The satisfaction has been commonly attributed, first, to the comfort we receive in considering that so melancholy a story is no more than a fiction; and next, to the contemplation of our own freedom from the evils which we see represented. I am afraid it is a practice much too common in inquiries of this nature, to attribute the cause of feelings which merely arise from the mechanical structure of our bodies, or from the natural frame and constitution of our minds, to certain conclusions of the reasoning faculty on the objects presented to us; for I should imagine, that the influence of reason in producing our passions is nothing near so extensive as it is commonly believed.

SECT. XIV: The effects of sympathy in the distresses of others

To examine this point concerning the effect of tragedy in a proper manner, we must previously consider, how we are affected by the feelings of our fellow creatures in circumstances of real distress. I am convinced we have a degree of delight, and that no small one, in the real misfortunes and pains of others; for let the affection be what it will in appearance, if it does not make us shun such objects, if on the contrary it induces us to approach them, if it makes us dwell upon them, in this case I conceive we must have a delight or pleasure of some species or other in contemplating objects of this kind. Do we not read the authentic histories of scenes of this nature with as much pleasure as romances or poems, where the incidents are fictitious? The prosperity of no empire, nor the grandeur of no king, can so agreeably affect in the reading, as the ruin of the state of Macedon,[63] and the distress of its unhappy prince. Such a catastrophe touches us in history as much as the destruction of Troy does in fable. Our delight in cases of this kind, is very greatly heightened, if the sufferer be some excellent person who sinks under an unworthy fortune. Scipio and Cato[64] are both virtuous characters, but we are more deeply affected by the violent death of the one, and the ruin of the great cause he adhered to, than with the deserved triumphs and uninterrupted prosperity of the other; for terror is a passion which always produces delight when it does not press too close, and pity is a passion accompanied with pleasure, because it arises from love and social affection. Whenever we are formed by nature to any active purpose, the passion which animates us to it, is attended with delight, or a pleasure of some kind, let the subject matter be what it will; and as our Creator has designed we should be united by the bond of sympathy, he has strengthened that bond by a proportionable delight; and there most where our sympathy is most wanted, in the distresses of others. If this passion was simply painful, we would shun with the greatest care all persons and places that could excite such a passion; as, some who are so far gone in indolence as not to endure any strong impression actually do. But the case is widely different with the greater part of mankind; there is no spectacle we so eagerly pursue, as that of some uncommon and grievous calamity; so that whether the misfortune is before our eyes, or whether they are turned back to it in history, it always touches with delight. This is not an unmixed delight, but blended with no small uneasiness. The delight we have in such things, hinders us from shunning scenes of misery; and the pain we feel, prompts us to relieve ourselves in relieving those who suffer; and all this antecedent to any reasoning, by an instinct that works us to its own purposes, without our concurrence.

SECT. XV: Of the effects of tragedy

It is thus in real calamities. In imitated distresses the only difference is the pleasure resulting from the effects of imitation; for it is never so perfect, but we can perceive it is an imitation,

---

[63]**ruin of the state of Macedon:** the Macedonian empire, established and maintained by Philip II of Macedonia (382–336 BCE) and his son Alexander the Great (356–323 BCE), was the largest empire of antiquity until the advent of the Roman empire. It was divided up when Alexander the Great died without an heir and was eventually destroyed in a series of wars with the Roman Republic and its allies (214–148 BCE).

[64]**Scipio and Cato:** Publius Cornelius Scipio (236–183 BCE), also known as Scipio Africanus, was a Roman general and master military tactician, famed for his victory over Hannibal in the Second Punic War (218–201 BCE). Marcus Porcius Cato, or Cato the Younger (95–46 BCE) was a Roman statesmen and staunch defender of the values of the Roman Republic. He killed himself rather than accept the imperial authority of Julius Caesar and was commonly regarded as a hero of classical Republicanism.

and on that principle are somewhat pleased with it. And indeed in some cases we derive as much or more pleasure from that source than from the thing itself. But then I imagine we shall be much mistaken if we attribute any considerable part of our satisfaction in tragedy to a consideration that tragedy is a deceit, and its representations no realities. The nearer it approaches the reality, and the further it removes us from all idea of fiction, the more perfect is its power. But be its power of what kind it will, it never approaches to what it represents. Chuse a day on which to represent the most sublime and affecting tragedy we have; appoint the most favourite actors; spare no cost upon the scenes and decorations; unite the greatest efforts of poetry, painting and music; and when you have collected your audience, just at the moment when their minds are erect with expectation, let it be reported that a state criminal of high rank is on the point of being executed in the adjoining square; in a moment the emptiness of the theatre would demonstrate the comparative weakness of the imitative arts, and proclaim the triumph of the real sympathy. I believe that this notion of our having a simple pain in the reality, yet a delight in the representation, arises from hence, that we do not sufficiently distinguish what we would by no means chuse to do, from what we should be eager enough to see if it was once done. We delight in seeing things, which so far from doing, our heartiest wishes would be to see redressed. This noble capital, the pride of England and of Europe, I believe no man is so strangely wicked as to desire to see destroyed by a conflagration or an earthquake, though he should be removed himself to the greatest distance from the danger. But suppose such a fatal accident to have happened, what numbers from all parts would croud to behold the ruins, and amongst them many who would have been content never to have seen London in its glory? Nor is it either in real or fictitious distresses, our immunity from them which produces our delight; in my own mind I can discover nothing like it. I apprehend that this mistake is owing to a sort of sophism, by which we are frequently imposed upon; it arises from our not distinguishing between what is indeed a necessary condition to our doing or suffering any thing in general, and what is the cause of some particular act. If a man kills me with a sword, it is a necessary condition to this that we should have been both of us alive before the fact; and yet it would be absurd to say, that our being both living creatures was the cause of his crime and of my death. So it is certain, that it is absolutely necessary my life should be out of any imminent hazard before I can take a delight in the sufferings of others, real or imaginary, or indeed in anything else from any cause whatsoever. But then it is a sophism to argue from thence, that this immunity is the cause of my delight either on these or on any occasions. No one can distinguish such a cause of satisfaction in his own mind I believe; nay when we do not suffer any very acute pain, nor are exposed to any imminent danger of our lives, we can feel for others, whilst we suffer ourselves; and often then most when we are softened by affliction; we see with pity even distresses which we would accept in the place of our own.

PART II

SECT. I: Of the passion caused by the sublime

The passion caused by the great and sublime in *nature*, when those causes operate most powerfully, is astonishment: and astonishment is that state of the soul in which all its motions are suspended, with some degree of horror. In this case the mind is so entirely filled with its object, that it cannot entertain any other, nor by consequence reason on that object which employs it. Hence arises the great power of the sublime, that, far from being produced by them, it anticipates our reasonings, and hurries us on by an irresistible force. Astonishment, as I have said, is the effect of the sublime in its highest degree; the inferior effects are admiration, reverence, and respect.

SECT. II: Terror

No passion so effectually robs the mind of all its powers of acting and reasoning as *fear*. For fear being an apprehension of pain or death, it operates in a manner that resembles actual pain. Whatever therefore is terrible, with regard to sight, is sublime too, whether this cause of terror be endued with greatness of dimensions or not; for it is impossible to look on anything as trifling, or contemptible, that may be dangerous. There are many animals, who, though far from being large, are yet capable of raising ideas of the sublime, because they are considered as objects of terror. As serpents and poisonous animals of almost all kinds. And to things of great dimensions, if we annex an adventitious idea of terror, they become without comparison greater. A level plain of a vast extent on land, is certainly no mean idea; the prospect of such a plain may be as extensive as a prospect of the ocean; but can it ever fill the mind with anything so great as the ocean itself? This is owing to several causes; but it is owing to none more than this, that the ocean is an object of no small terror. Indeed terror is in all cases whatsoever, either more openly or latently, the ruling principle of the sublime.

SECT. III: Obscurity

To make anything very terrible, obscurity seems in general to be necessary. When we know the full extent of any danger, when we can accustom our eyes to it, a great deal of the apprehension vanishes. Every one will be sensible of this, who considers how greatly night adds to our dread, in all cases of danger, and how much the notions of ghosts and goblins, of which none can form clear ideas, affect minds which give credit to the popular tales concerning such sorts of beings. Those despotic governments which are founded on the passions of men, and principally upon the passion of fear, keep their chief as much as may be from the public eye. The policy has been the same in many cases of religion. Almost all the heathen temples were dark. Even in the barbarous temples of the Americans at this day, they keep their idol in a dark part of the hut, which is consecrated to his worship. For this purpose too the Druids performed all their ceremonies in the bosom of the darkest woods, and in the shade of the oldest and most spreading oaks. No person seems better to have understood the secret of heightening, or of setting terrible things, if I may use the expression, in their strongest light, by the force of a judicious obscurity than Milton.[65] His description of death in the second book is admirably studied; it is astonishing with what a gloomy pomp, with what a significant and expressive uncertainty of strokes and coloring, he has finished the portrait of the king of terrors:

---

[65]**Milton:** John Milton, English poet and pamphleteer (1608–74).

> The other shape,
> If shape it might be called that shape had none
> Distinguishable, in member, joint, or limb;
> Or substance might be called that shadow seemed;
> For each seemed either; black he stood as night;
> Fierce as ten furies; terrible as hell;
> And shook a deadly dart. What seemed his head
> The likeness of a kingly crown had on.[66]

In this description all is dark, uncertain, confused, terrible, and sublime to the last degree.

SECT. IV: Of the differences between clearness and obscurity with regard to the passions

It is one thing to make an idea clear, and another to make it *affecting* to the imagination. If I make a drawing of a palace, or a temple, or a landscape, I present a very clear idea of those objects; but then (allowing for the effect of imitation which is something) my picture can at most affect only as the palace, temple, or landscape, would have affected in the reality. On the other hand, the most lively and spirited verbal description I can give raises a very obscure and imperfect *idea* of such objects; but then it is in my power to raise a stronger *emotion* by the description than I could do by the best painting. This experience constantly evinces. The proper manner of conveying the *affections* of the mind from one to another is by words; there is a great insufficiency in all other methods of communication; and so far is a clearness of imagery from being absolutely necessary to an influence upon the passions, that they may be considerably operated upon, without presenting any image at all, by certain sounds adapted to that purpose; of which we have a sufficient proof in the acknowledged and powerful effects of instrumental music. In reality, a great clearness helps but little towards affecting the passions, as it is in some sort an enemy to all enthusiasms whatsoever.

[...]

Painting, when we have allowed for the pleasure of imitation, can only affect simply by the images it presents; and even in painting, a judicious obscurity in some things contributes to the effect of the picture; because the images in painting are exactly similar to those in nature; and in nature, dark, confused, uncertain images have a greater power on the fancy to form the grander passions, than those have which are more clear and determinate. But where and when this observation may be applied to practice, and how far it shall be extended, will be better deduced from the nature of the subject, and from the occasion, than from any rules that can be given.

I am sensible that this idea has met with opposition, and is likely still to be rejected by several. But let it be considered that hardly anything can strike the mind with its greatness, which does not make some sort of approach towards infinity; which nothing can do whilst we are able to perceive its bounds; but to see an object distinctly, and to perceive its bounds, is one

---

[66]**The other shape … kingly crown had on:** John Milton, *Paradise Lost* (1667), 2. 666–73. The quotation describes the personified appearance of Death.

and the same thing. A clear idea is therefore another name for a little idea. There is a passage in the book of Job amazingly sublime, and this sublimity is principally due to the terrible uncertainty of the thing described: *In thoughts from the visions of the night, when deep sleep falleth upon men, fear came upon me and trembling, which made all my bones to shake. Then a spirit passed before my face. The hair of my flesh stood up. It stood still,* but I could not discern the form thereof; *an image was before mine eyes; there was silence; and I heard a voice – Shall mortal man be more just than God?*[67] We are first prepared with the utmost solemnity for the vision; we are first terrified, before we are let even into the obscure cause of our emotion: but when this grand cause of terror makes its appearance, what is it? Is it not wrapt up in the shades of its own incomprehensible darkness, more awful, more striking, more terrible, than the liveliest description, than the clearest painting, could possibly represent it? When painters have attempted to give us clear representations of these very fanciful and terrible ideas, they have, I think, almost always failed; insomuch that I have been at a loss, in all the pictures I have seen of hell, to determine whether the painter did not intend something ludicrous. Several painters have handled a subject of this kind, with a view of assembling as many horrid phantoms as their imagination could suggest; but all the designs I have chanced to meet of the temptations of St. Anthony were rather a sort of odd, wild grotesques, than any thing capable of producing a serious passion. In all these subjects poetry is very happy. Its apparitions, its chimeras, its harpies, its allegorical figures, are grand and affecting; and though Virgil's Fame and Homer's Discord[68] are obscure, they are magnificent figures. These figures in painting would be clear enough, but I fear they might become ridiculous.

Further reading

David Bromwich, *The Intellectual Life of Edmund Burke* (Cambridge, MA and London: The Belknap Press of Harvard University Press, 2014).

Terry Eagleton, 'Aesthetics and Politics in Edmund Burke', *History Workshop* no. 28 (1989): 53–62.

Stephen K. White, *Edmund Burke: Modernity, Politics and Aesthetics* (New York: Rowman and Littlefield, 2002).

---

[67] *Shall mortal man … God*: Job 4.13–7.

[68] **Virgil's Fame and Homer's Discord:** The all-powerful, personified figures of Fame and Discord appear in Book IV of Virgil's *Aeneid* (*c.*29–19 BCE), and Book IV of Homer's *Iliad* (*c.*eighth century BCE).

3.6 JEAN-JACQUES ROUSSEAU, *LETTER TO M. D'ALEMBERT ON THE THEATRE* (1758)

Jean-Jacques Rousseau (1712–78), Swiss-born composer, novelist, philosopher, and political theorist, was one of the instrumental thinkers of the Enlightenment. A key tenet of his thought, as espoused in *A Discourse on the Origin of Inequality* (1755), is that humanity is good by nature but is corrupted by society. In 1758, Rousseau was alarmed by an essay about his native Geneva published in one of the most important organs of French Enlightenment and radical thought, *L'Encyclopédie, ou Dictionnaire Raisonné des, Sciences, des Arts et des Métiers* (1751–72). The essay which he objected to, written by the *Encyclopédie*'s co-founder Jean le Rond d'Alembert (1717–83), called for the establishment of a system of civilizing and morally improving drama in Geneva (which, as a strictly Calvinist city, had no theatre). Rousseau's response to D'Alembert suggested that such a theatre would actually make Genevans less virtuous since tragedy weakened its spectators' natural ethical capacities. Rousseau's anti-theatricalism bears a striking resemblance to that of Plato (extract 1.1) and Augustine (extract 1.6).

The theatre, I am told, directed as it can and ought to be, makes virtue lovable and vice odious. What? Before there were dramas, were not virtuous men loved, were not the vicious hated, and are these sentiments feebler in the places that lack a theatre? The theatre makes virtue lovable. ... It accomplishes a great miracle in doing what nature and reason do before it! The vicious are hated on the stage. ... Are they loved in society when they are known to be such? Is it quite certain that this hate is the work of the author rather than of the crimes that he makes the vicious commit? Is it quite certain that the simple account of these crimes would produce less horror in us than all the colors with which he has painted them? If his whole art consists in producing malefactors for us in order to render them hateful, I am unable to see what is so admirable in this art, and we get, in this regard, only too many lessons without need of this one. Dare I add a suspicion which comes to me? I suspect that any man, to whom the crimes of Phaedra or Medea[69] were told beforehand, would hate them more at the beginning of the play than at the end. And if this suspicion is well founded, then what are we to think of this much-vaunted effect of the theatre?

I should like to be clearly shown, without wasting words, how it could produce sentiments in us that we did not have and could cause us to judge moral beings otherwise than we judge them by ourselves? How puerile and senseless are these vain pretensions when examined closely! If the beauty of virtue were the product of art, virtue would have long since been disfigured! As for me, even if I am again to be regarded as wicked for daring to assert that man is born good, I think it and believe that I have proved it.[70] The source of the concern which

---

[69]**Phaedra and Medea:** In Euripides' *Hippolytus* (428 BCE), Phaedra hanged herself after she had falsely accused her stepson, Hippolytus, of rape. Her husband Theseus believed the accusation and prayed to Poseidon to destroy his son, who was then killed in a chariot accident. According to Euripides' *Medea* (431 BCE), Medea fell in love with Jason on his quest for the Golden Fleece. But when Jason turned his affections to Glauce, daughter of Creon, king of Corinth, Medea killed them both and slew two of the sons she had with Jason.

[70]**believe that I have proved it:** Rousseau had already made such an argument in *A Discourse on the Origin of Inequality* (1755).

attaches us to what is decent and which inspires us with aversion for evil is in us and not in the plays. There is no art for producing this concern, but only for taking advantage of it. The love of the beautiful[71] is a sentiment as natural to the human heart as the love of self; it is not born out of an arrangement of scenes; the author does not bring it; he finds it there; and out of this pure sentiment, to which he appeals, are born the sweet tears that he causes to flow.

Imagine a play as perfect as you like. Where is the man who, going for the first time, does not go already convinced of what is to be proved in it and already predisposed toward those whom he is meant to like? But this is not the question; what is important is to act consistently with one's principles and to imitate the people whom one esteems. The heart of man is always right concerning that which has no personal relation to himself. In the quarrels at which we are purely spectators, we immediately take the side of justice, and there is no act of viciousness which does not give us a lively sentiment of indignation so long as we receive no profit from it. But when our interest is involved, our sentiments are soon corrupted. And it is only then that we prefer the evil which is useful to us to the good that nature makes us love. Is it not a necessary effect of the constitution of things that the vicious man profits doubly, from his injustice and the probity of others? What more advantageous treaty could he conclude than one obliging the whole world, excepting himself, to be just, so that everyone will faithfully render unto him what is due him, while he renders to no one what he owes? He loves virtue, unquestionably; but he loves it in others because he hopes to profit from it. He wants none of it for himself because it would be costly to him. What then does he go to see at the theatre? Precisely what he wants to find everywhere: lessons of virtue for the public, from which he excepts himself, and people sacrificing everything to their duty while nothing is exacted from him.

I hear it said that tragedy leads to pity through fear. So it does; but what is this pity? A fleeting and vain emotion which lasts no longer than the illusion which produced it; a vestige of natural sentiment soon stifled by the passions; a sterile pity which feeds on a few tears and which has never produced the slightest act of humanity. Thus, the sanguinary Sulla cried at the account of evils he had not himself committed.[72] Thus, the tyrant of Phera hid himself at the theatre for fear of being seen groaning with Andromache and Priam, while he heard without emotion the cries of so many unfortunate victims slain daily by his orders.[73] Tacitus reports that Valerius Asiaticus, calumniously accused by the order of Messalina, who wanted him to perish, defended himself before the emperor in a way that touched this prince very deeply and drew tears from Messalina herself.[74] She went into the next room in order to regain her

---

[71][Rousseau's note]: We have to do with the morally beautiful here. Whatever the philosophers may say of it, this love is innate to man and serves as principle to his conscience. (I can cite as an example of this the little play *Nanine* [by Voltaire], which has caused the audience to grumble and is only protected by the great reputation of its author. All this is only because honor, virtue, and the pure sentiments of nature are preferred in it to the impertinent prejudice of social station.)

[72]**Sanguinary Sulla:** Lucius Cornelius Sulla Felix (*c.*138–78 BCE), Roman military and political leader turned dictator. Plutarch's *Life of Sulla* paints him as a commander of uncommon cruelty who, during the Siege of Athens, bathed the city in blood; Plutarch, *Lives*, trans. Bernadotte Perrin (Cambridge, MA: Harvard University Press, 1916), IV:371.

[73]**tyrant of Phera … orders:** Plutarch's life of *Pelopidas* reports that Alexander, the tyrant of Phera, left a production of Euripides' *Trojan Women* because he did not want to be seen crying at the tragedy in front of the audience. Plutarch, *Lives*, trans. Bernadotte Perrin (Cambridge, MA: Harvard University Press, 1917), V:415.

[74]**Tacitus … Messalina:** Messalina (*c.*17 BCE–48 CE), wife of Roman Emperor Claudius, was regarded as a duplicitous sexual prodigy by the Roman historian Tacitus (56–120 CE). She was instrumental in a plot whereby Valerius Asiaticus (*c.*5 BCE–47 CE) was falsely accused of conspiracy. Asiaticus was permitted to plead his case before the Emperor

composure after having, in the midst of her tears, whispered a warning to Vitellius not to let the accused escape. I never see one of these weeping ladies in the boxes at the theatre, so proud of their tears, without thinking of the tears of Messalina for the poor Valerius Asiaticus.[75]

If, according to the observation of Diogenes Laertius,[76] the heart is more readily touched by feigned ills than real ones, if theatrical imitations draw forth more tears than would the presence of the objects imitated, it is less because the emotions are feebler and do not reach the level of pain, as the Abbé du Bos[77] believes,[78] than because they are pure and without mixture of anxiety for ourselves. In giving our tears to these fictions, we have satisfied all the rights of humanity without having to give anything more of ourselves; whereas unfortunate people in person would require attention from us, relief, consolation, and work, which would involve us in their pains and would require at least the sacrifice of our indolence, from all of which we are quite content to be exempt. It could be said that our heart closes itself for fear of being touched at our expense.

In the final accounting, when a man has gone to admire fine actions in stories and to cry for imaginary miseries, what more can be asked of him? Is he not satisfied with himself? Does he not applaud his fine soul? Has he not acquitted himself of all that he owes to virtue by the homage which he has just rendered it? What more could one want of him? That he practice it himself? He has no role to play; he is no actor.

The more I think about it, the more I find that everything that is played in the theatre is not brought nearer to us but made more distant. When I see the *Comte d'Essex*,[79] the reign of Elizabeth is ten centuries removed in my eyes, and, if an event that took place yesterday at Paris were played, I should be made to suppose it in the time of Molière.[80] The theatre has rules, principles, and a morality apart, just as it has a language and a style of dress that is its own. We say to ourselves that none of this is suitable for us, and that we should think ourselves as ridiculous to adopt the virtues of its heroes as it would be to speak in verse or to put on Roman clothing. This is pretty nearly the use of all these great sentiments and of all these brilliant maxims that are vaunted with so much emphasis – to relegate them forever to the stage, and to present virtue to us as a theatrical game, good for amusing the public but which it would be folly seriously to attempt introducing into society. Thus the most advantageous impression of the best tragedies is to reduce all the duties of man to some passing and sterile emotions

---

and Messalina and moved them to tears. He was spared execution to be allowed to commit suicide. The episode is recounted in Tacitus, *Annals: Books 4–6, 11–12*, trans. John Jackson (Cambridge, MA: Harvard University Press, 1937), XI. 1–3, 249–53.

[75][**Translator's note**]: This passage was added later and appeared in the edition of 1782.

[76]**Diogenes Laertius:** Diogenes Laërtius (fl. third century CE) was an early historian of ancient Greek philosophers; his *Lives of the Eminent Philosophers* (*c.*third century CE) was a storehouse of philosophical sayings and commonplaces.

[77]**Abbé du Bos:** Jean-Baptiste Dubos (1670–1742), French diplomat, historian and philosopher. His *Reflexions critique sur la poésie et sur la peinture* (1719) was instrumental in the development of aesthetic theory in the eighteenth century.

[78][**Rousseau's note**]: He says that the poet afflicts us only so much as we wish, that he makes us like his heroes only so far as it pleases us. This is contrary to all experience. Many people refrain from going to tragedy because they are moved to the point of discomfort; others, ashamed of crying at the theatre, do so nevertheless in spite of themselves; and these effects are not rare enough to be only exceptions to the maxim of this; *Reflexions critique sur la poesie et la peinture* (Paris, 1719), part I, section 3.

[79]**Comte d'Essex:** 1678 tragedy by French playwright Thomas Corneille (1625–1709), brother of the better-known playwright Pierre Corneille.

[80]**Moliere:** the stage name of Jean-Baptiste Poquelin (1622–73), French playwright commonly regarded as one of the greatest dramatists of the seventeenth century.

that have no consequences, to make us applaud our courage in praising that of others, our humanity in pitying the ills that we could have cured, our charity in saying to the poor, God will help you!

To be sure, a simpler style can be adopted on the stage, and the tone of the theatre can be reconciled in the drama with that of the world. But in this way, morals [manners] are not corrected; they are depicted, and an ugly face does not appear ugly to him who wears it. If we wish to correct them by caricaturing them, we leave the realm of probability and nature, and the picture no longer produces an effect. Caricature does not render objects hateful; it only renders them ridiculous. And out of this arises a very great difficulty; afraid of being ridiculous, men are no longer afraid of being vicious. The former cannot be remedied without promoting the latter. Why, you will ask, must I suppose this to be a necessary opposition? Why, Sir? Because the good do not make evil men objects of derision, but crush them with their contempt, and nothing is less funny or laughable than virtue's indignation. Ridicule, on the other hand, is the favorite arm of vice. With it, the respect that the heart owes to virtue is attacked at its root, and the love that is felt for it is finally extinguished.

[...]

What do we learn from *Phèdre* and *Œdipe* other than that man is not free and that heaven punishes him for crimes that it makes him commit? What do we learn in *Médée*[81] other than how cruel and unnatural a mother can be made by the rage of jealousy? Look at most of the plays in the French theatre; in practically all of them you will find abominable monsters and atrocious actions, useful, if you please, in making the plays interesting and in giving exercise to the virtues; but they are certainly dangerous in that they accustom the eyes of the people to horrors that they ought not even to know and to crimes they ought not to suppose possible. It is not even true that murder and parricide are always hateful in the theatre. With the help of some easy suppositions, they are rendered permissible or pardonable. It is hard not to excuse Phaedra, who is incestuous and spills innocent blood.[82] Syphax poisoning his wife, the young Horatius stabbing his sister, Agamemnon sacrificing his daughter, Orestes cutting his mother's throat, do not fail to be figures who arouse sympathy.[83] Add that the author, in order to make each speak according to his character, is forced to put into the mouths of villains their maxims and principles clad in the magnificence of beautiful verse and recited in an imposing and sententious tone for the instruction of the audience.[84]

---

[81]*Phèdre* **and** *Œdipe* **...** *Médée*: Jean Racine's *Phèdre* (1677), Voltaire's *Oedipe* (1718), and Pierre Corneille's *Médée* (1635) were all French theatrical adaptations of classical Greek tragedies.

[82]**Phaedra ... innocent blood:** see note 1. In Racine's 1677 version of Euripides' tragedy, Phaedra only commits suicide after she has learned of the death of Hippolytus; Rousseau argues that this change elicits much sympathy from the audience.

[83]**Syphax ... Orestes:** Syphax was king of Numidia who, in Jean Mairet's tragedy *Sophonisbe* (1634), encouraged his wife Sophonisbe to poison herself. The Roman warrior Horace stabbed his sister Camille for preferring family to nation in Pierre Corneille's tragedy *Horace* (1640). Jean Racine's *Iphigénie* (1674), adapting Euripides' *Iphigenia in Aulis*, dramatizes the Greek leader Agamemnon's attempts to sacrifice his daughter Iphigenia as propitiatory offering to the gods in preparation for the war with Troy. Orestes was one of the most famous matricides of antiquity; he killed his mother Clytemnestra for her involvement in the murder of his father Agamemnon. In Voltaire's *Oreste* (1750), however, Orestes stabs Clytemnestra accidentally.

[84]**[Translator's note:]** The French word translated here and elsewhere by *audience* is *parterre*. Its exact English equivalent is *pit*, the word denoting the part of the theatre in which the poor paid low admission for the right to stand. It has, hence, a derogatory sense implying the tasteless mob, the *hoi polloi*.

If the Greeks tolerated such theatre it was because it represented for them national traditions which were always common among the people, which they had reasons to recall constantly; and even its hateful aspects were part of its intention. Deprived of the same motives and the same concern, how can the same tragedy find, in your country, spectators capable of enduring the depictions it presents to them and the characters which are given life in it? One kills his father, marries his mother, and finds himself the brother of his children; another forces a son to slay his father; a third makes a father drink the blood of his son. We shudder at the very idea of the horrors with which the French stage is decked out for the amusement of the gentlest and the most humane people on earth! No … I maintain, and I bring in witness the terror of my readers, that the massacres of the gladiators were not so barbarous as these frightful plays. At the circus one saw blood flowing, it is true; but one did not soil his imagination with crimes at which nature trembles.

Further reading

David Marshall, 'Rousseau and the State of the Theatre', *Representations* 13 (1986): 84–114.

Vickie Sullivan and Katherine Balch, 'Spectacles and Sociability: Rousseau's Response in His *Letter to M. D'Alembert* to Montesquieu's Treatment of the Theatre and of French and English Society', *History of European Ideas* 41, no. 3 (2015): 357–74.

3.7 SAMUEL JOHNSON, 'PREFACE TO SHAKESPEARE' (1765)

Samuel Johnson (1709–84) was an English critic, essayist, fiction writer, lexicographer, and poet, best remembered for his magisterial *Dictionary* (1755). He had long been interested in tragedy; the only play he wrote, *Irene* (1749), was a heavily moralistic tragedy about Christian–Islamic relations which depicted the murder of its eponymous Greek-Christian heroine following the renunciation of her faith for fame and favour at the court of Mehmed the Conqueror. The play conformed to Johnson's *Dictionary* definition of 'tragedy' as '1. a dramatick representation of a serious action 2. any mournful or dreadful event,' but fell far short of the theatrical standards Johnson thought set by Shakespeare. In the preface to his edition of Shakespeare's plays, Johnson argued that Shakespeare's theatrical strength lay in his ability to be moral without being didactic, to compose tragedy that was more truthful because it 'mingled' weighty topics with comic materials and did not slavishly follow neo-classical prescriptions about the unities of dramatic action.

Shakespeare's plays are not in the rigorous and critical sense either tragedies or comedies, but compositions of a distinct kind; exhibiting the real state of sublunary nature, which partakes of good and evil, joy and sorrow, mingled with endless variety of proportion and innumerable modes of combination; and expressing the course of the world, in which the loss of one is the gain of another; in which, at the same time, the reveller is hasting to his wine, and the mourner burying his friend; in which the malignity of one is sometimes defeated by the frolick of another; and many mischiefs and many benefits are done and hindered without design.

Out of this chaos of mingled purposes and casualties the ancient poets, according to the laws which custom had prescribed, selected some the crimes of men, and some their absurdities; some the momentous vicissitudes of life, and some the lighter occurrences; some the terrours of distress, and some the gayeties of prosperity. Thus rose the two modes of imitation, known by the names of tragedy and comedy, compositions intended to promote different ends by contrary means, and considered as so little allied, that I do not recollect among the Greeks or Romans a single writer who attempted both.

Shakespeare has united the powers of exciting laughter and sorrow not only in one mind, but in one composition. Almost all his plays are divided between serious and ludicrous characters, and, in the successive evolutions of the design, sometimes produce seriousness and sorrow, and sometimes levity and laughter.

That this is a practice contrary to the rules of criticism will be readily allowed; but there is always an appeal open from criticism to nature. The end of writing is to instruct; the end of poetry is to instruct by pleasing.[85] That the mingled drama may convey all the instruction of tragedy or comedy cannot be denied, because it includes both in its alterations of exhibition, and approaches nearer than either to the appearance of life, by shewing how great machinations

---

[85]**Instruct by pleasing:** this commonplace formulation is indebted to Horace's *Ars Poetica* (*c.*10 BCE), which holds that poetry should be '*dulce et utile*,' pleasurable and useful; see extract 1.3.

and slender designs may promote or obviate one another, and the high and the low co-operate in the general system by unavoidable concatenation.

It is objected, that by this change of scenes the passions are interrupted in their progression, and that the principal event, being not advanced by a due gradation of preparatory incidents, wants at last the power to move, which constitutes the perfection of dramatick poetry. This reasoning is so specious, that it is received as true even by those who in daily experience feel it to be false. The interchanges of mingled scenes seldom fail to produce the intended vicissitudes of passion. Fiction cannot move so much, but that the attention may be easily transferred; and though it must be allowed that pleasing melancholy be sometimes interrupted by unwelcome levity, yet let it be considered likewise, that melancholy is often not pleasing, and that the disturbance of one man may be the relief of another; that different auditors have different habitudes; and that, upon the whole, all pleasure consists in variety.

The players, who in their edition[86] divided our authour's works into comedies, histories, and tragedies, seem not to have distinguished the three kinds, by any very exact or definite ideas.

An action which ended happily to the principal persons, however serious or distressful through its intermediate incidents, in their opinion constituted a comedy. This idea of a comedy continued long amongst us, and plays were written, which, by changing the catastrophe, were tragedies to-day and comedies to-morrow.

Tragedy was not in those times a poem of more general dignity or elevation than comedy; it required only a calamitous conclusion, with which the common criticism of that age was satisfied, whatever lighter pleasure it afforded in its progress.

History[87] was a series of actions, with no other than chronological succession, independent of each other, and without any tendency to introduce or regulate the conclusion. It is not always very nicely distinguished from tragedy.[88] There is not much nearer approach to unity of action in the tragedy of *Antony and Cleopatra*, than in the history of *Richard the Second*. But a history might be continued through many plays; as it had no plan, it had no limits.

Through all these denominations of the drama, Shakespeare's mode of composition is the same; an interchange of seriousness and merriment, by which the mind is softened at one time, and exhilarated at another. But whatever be his purpose, whether to gladden or depress, or to conduct the story, without vehemence or emotion, through tracts of easy and familiar dialogue, he never fails to attain his purpose; as he commands us, we laugh or mourn, or sit silent with quiet expectation, in tranquillity without indifference. …

Shakespeare engaged in dramatick poetry with the world open before him; the rules of the ancients were yet known to few; the publick judgment was unformed; he had no example of such fame as might force him upon imitation, nor criticks of such authority as might restrain his extravagance: He therefore indulged his natural disposition, and his disposition, as Rhymer

---

[86]**players … edition:** Shakespeare died without leaving a collected edition of his works. The First Folio of 1623 was produced seven years after his death, under the auspices of his playing company, the King's Men. It organized all of Shakespeare's theatrical output under three headings: comedies, histories, and tragedies.

[87]**History:** History plays. This theatrical genre flourished in English in the early modern period; Shakespeare was one of its most skilled exponents.

[88]**distinguished from tragedy:** Shakespeare's history plays *Richard II, Richard III and 3 Henry VI* were all described as tragedies on the title pages of some of their earliest printings. Likewise, the quarto of *King Lear* (1608) proclaimed that the play was a 'True Chronicle Historie'.

has remarked,[89] led him to comedy. In tragedy he often writes with great appearance of toil and study, what is written at last with little felicity; but in his comick scenes, he seems to produce without labour, what no labour can improve. In tragedy he is always struggling after some occasion to be comick, but in comedy he seems to repose, or to luxuriate, as in a mode of thinking congenial to his nature. In his tragick scenes there is always something wanting, but his comedy often surpasses expectation or desire. His comedy pleases by the thoughts and the language, and his tragedy for the greater part by incident and action. His tragedy seems to be skill, his comedy to be instinct. ...

In tragedy his performance seems constantly to be worse, as his labour is more. The effusions of passion which exigence forces out are for the most part striking and energetick; but whenever he solicits his invention, or strains his faculties, the offspring of his throes is tumour, meanness, tediousness, and obscurity. ...

To the unities of time and place he has shewn no regard, and perhaps a nearer view of the principles on which they stand will diminish their value, and withdraw from them the veneration which, from the time of Corneille,[90] they have very generally received by discovering that they have given more trouble to the poet, than pleasure to the auditor.

The necessity of observing the unities of time and place arises from the supposed necessity of making the drama credible. The criticks hold it impossible, that an action of months or years can be possibly believed to pass in three hours; or that the spectator can suppose himself to sit in the theatre, while ambassadors go and return between distant kings, while armies are levied and towns besieged, while an exile wanders and returns, or till he whom they saw courting his mistress, shall lament the untimely fall of his son. The mind revolts from evident falsehood, and fiction loses its force when it departs from the resemblance of reality.

From the narrow limitation of time necessarily arises the contraction of place. The spectator, who knows that he saw the first act at Alexandria, cannot suppose that he sees the next at Rome, at a distance to which not the dragons of Medea[91] could, in so short a time, have transported him; he knows with certainty that he has not changed his place; and he knows that place cannot change itself; that what was a house cannot become a plain; that what was Thebes can never be Persepolis.[92]

Such is the triumphant language with which a critick exults over the misery of an irregular poet, and exults commonly without resistance or reply. It is time therefore to tell him, by the authority of Shakespeare, that he assumes, as an unquestionable principle, a position, which, while his breath is forming it into words, his understanding pronounces to be false. It is false, that any representation is mistaken for reality; that any dramatick fable in its materiality was ever credible, or, for a single moment, was ever credited.

The objection arising from the impossibility of passing the first hour at Alexandria, and the next at Rome, supposes, that when the play opens the spectator really imagines himself at

---

[89]*Rhymer* **has remarked:** Thomas Rymer (1643–1713), English literary critic and historian. Rymer's *A Short View of Tragedy* (1693) criticized Shakespeare for his plot improbabilities and the comic turns of his tragedies. For Rymer's translation of René Rapin's *Reflections of Aristotles Treatise of Poesie* (1674), see extract 2.8.

[90]**Corneille:** Pierre Corneille (1606–84), French tragedian (see extract 2.6). Corneille, like Shakespeare, was criticized in the late seventeenth century for not observing the unities of time, place and action in his tragedies.

[91]**dragons of Medea:** in Greek mythology Medea's chariot was pulled by a pair of dragons or giant serpents.

[92]**Thebes ... Persepolis:** Thebes is a city in central Greece and was one of the most powerful city states of the ancient world; Persepolis is the Greek name for Parsa in present-day Iran and was the capital of the Persian Empire.

Alexandria, and believes that his walk to the theatre has been a voyage to Egypt, and that he lives in the days of Antony and Cleopatra. Surely he that imagines this, may imagine more. He that can take the stage at one time for the palace of the Ptolemies, may take it in half an hour for the promontory of Actium.[93] Delusion, if delusion be admitted, has no certain limitation; if the spectator can be once persuaded, that his old acquaintance are Alexander and Caesar, that a room illuminated with candles is the plain of Pharsalia, or the bank of Granicus,[94] he is in a state of elevation above the reach of reason, or of truth, and from the heights of empyrean poetry, may despise the circumscriptions of terrestrial nature. There is no reason why a mind thus wandering in extasy should count the clock, or why an hour should not be a century in that calenture of the brains that can make the stage a field.

The truth is, that the spectators are always in their senses, and know, from the first act to the last, that the stage is only a stage, and that the players are only players. They come to hear a certain number of lines recited with just gesture and elegant modulation. The lines relate to some action, and an action must be in some place; but the different actions that compleat a story may be in places very remote from each other; and where is the absurdity of allowing that space to represent first Athens, and then Sicily, which was always known to be neither Sicily nor Athens, but a modern theatre?

By supposition, as place is introduced, time may be extended; the time required by the fable elapses for the most part between the acts; for, of so much of the action as is represented, the real and poetical duration is the same. If, in the first act, preparations for war against Mithridates are represented to be made in Rome, the event of the war may, without absurdity, be represented, in the catastrophe, as happening in Pontus;[95] we know that there is neither war, nor preparation for war; we know that we are neither in Rome nor Pontus; that neither Mithridates nor Lucullus[96] are before us. The drama exhibits successive imitations of successive actions, and why may not the second imitation represent an action that happened years after the first; if it be so connected with it, that nothing but time can be supposed to intervene? Time is, of all modes of existence, most obsequious to the imagination; a lapse of years is as easily conceived as a passage of hours. In contemplation we easily contract the time of real actions, and therefore willingly permit it to be contracted when we only see their imitation.

It will be asked, how the drama moves, if it is not credited. It is credited with all the credit due to a drama. It is credited, whenever it moves, as a just picture of a real original; as representing to the auditor what he would himself feel, if he were to do or suffer what is there feigned to be suffered or to be done. The reflection that strikes the heart is not, that the evils before us are real evils, but that they are evils to which we ourselves may be exposed. If there be any fallacy, it is not that we fancy the players, but that we fancy ourselves unhappy for a moment; but we

---

[93]**palace of the Ptolemies … Actium:** the settings for much of Shakespeare's tragedy *Antony and Cleopatra* (c.1606). The Ptolemaic palace in Alexandria, Egypt, was, for a time home to Cleopatra; Mark Antony and Cleopatra's navy were eventually defeated off the coast of Actium in the Ionian Sea by the future Augustus Caesar.
[94]**Pharsalia … Granicus:** Pharsalus in central Greece was the location of epochal battle between Julius Caesar and Pompey during the Roman Civil War in 48 BCE; the Granicus River was a key battle site during conflict between Alexander the Great and the Persian Empire in 334 BCE.
[95]**Mithridates … Pontus:** Mithridates VI (135–63 BCE) was Emperor of Pontus (a kingdom in present-day Turkey). He resisted the eastern expansion of the Roman Republic.
[96]**Lucullus:** Lucius Licinius Lucullus (118 BCE–56 BCE) was a skilled Roman General who defeated Mithridates and forced him back into Pontus during the Eastern Wars (73–67 BCE).

rather lament the possibility than suppose the presence of misery, as a mother weeps over her babe, when she remembers that death may take it from her. The delight of tragedy proceeds from our consciousness of fiction; if we thought murders and treasons real, they would please no more.

Imitations produce pain or pleasure, not because they are mistaken for realities, but because they bring realities to mind. When the imagination is recreated by a painted landscape, the trees are not supposed capable to give us shade, or the fountains coolness; but we consider, how we should be pleased with such fountains playing beside us, and such woods waving over us. We are agitated in reading the history of 'Henry the Fifth', yet no man takes his book for the field of Agencourt. A dramatick exhibition is a book recited with concomitants that encrease or diminish its effect. Familiar comedy is often more powerful on the theatre, than in the page; imperial tragedy is always less. The humour of Petruchio may be heightened by grimace; but what voice or what gesture can hope to add dignity or force to the soliloquy of Cato.[97]

A play read, affects the mind like a play acted. It is therefore evident, that the action is not supposed to be real, and it follows that between the acts a longer or shorter time may be allowed to pass, and that no more account of space or duration is to be taken by the auditor of a drama, than by the reader of a narrative, before whom may pass in an hour the life of a hero, or the revolutions of an empire.

Whether Shakespeare knew the unities, and rejected them by design, or deviated from them by happy ignorance, it is, I think, impossible to decide, and useless to inquire. We may reasonably suppose, that, when he rose to notice, he did not want the counsels and admonitions of scholars and criticks, and that he at last deliberately persisted in a practice, which he might have begun by chance. As nothing is essential to the fable, but unity of action, and as the unities of time and place arise evidently from false assumptions, and, by circumscribing the extent of the drama, lessen its variety, I cannot think it much to be lamented, that they were not known by him, or not observed: Nor, if such another poet could arise, should I very vehemently reproach him, that his first act passed at Venice, and his next in Cyprus.[98] Such violations of rules merely positive, become the comprehensive genius of Shakespeare, and such censures are suitable to the minute and slender criticism of Voltaire:

Non usque adeo permiscuit imis
Longus summa dies, ut non, si voce Metelli
Serventur leges, malint a Caesare tolli.[99]

Yet when I speak thus slightly of dramatick rules, I cannot but recollect how much wit and learning may be produced against me; before such authorities I am afraid to stand, not that

---

[97]**Petruchio... Cato:** Johnson here contrasts the acting styles required to bring Petruchio, the comic hero of Shakespeare's *The Taming of the Shrew*, into being with those needed of actor playing the eponymous protagonist of Joseph Addison's tragedy *Cato* (1713).

[98]**Venice … Cyprus:** Johnson refers here to the settings of Shakespeare's *Othello* (*c*.1604).

[99]**Non usque …:** The quotation comes from Book III of Lucan's unfinished epic poem *Pharsalia* (*c*.65 CE) where Julius Caesar dismisses Metellus: 'The course of time has not wrought such confusion that the laws would not rather be trampled on by Caesar than saved by Metellus'; Marcus Annaeus Lucanus, *Pharsalia*, trans. J.D. Duff (Cambridge, MA: Harvard University Press, 1928), 125. The quotation suggests that Shakespeare will ignore all known laws for tragedy and, like Caesar, will be remembered throughout history.

I think the present question one of those that are to be decided by mere authority, but because it is to be suspected, that these precepts have not been so easily received but for better reasons than I have yet been able to find. The result of my enquiries, in which it would be ludicrous to boast of impartiality, is, that the unities of time and place are not essential to a just drama, that though they may sometimes conduce to pleasure, they are always to be sacrificed to the nobler beauties of variety and instruction; and that a play, written with nice observation of critical rules, is to be contemplated as an elaborate curiosity, as the product of superfluous and ostentatious art, by which is shewn, rather what is possible, than what is necessary.

He that, without diminution of any other excellence, shall preserve all the unities unbroken, deserves the like applause with the architect, who shall display all the orders of architecture in a citadel, without any deduction from its strength; but the principal beauty of a citadel is to exclude the enemy; and the greatest graces of a play, are to copy nature and instruct life.

Further reading

R.D. Stock, *Samuel Johnson and Neoclassical Dramatic Theory* (Lincoln: University of Nebraska Press, 1973).

Edward Tomarken, *Samuel Johnson on Shakespeare: The Discipline of Criticism* (Athens, GA: University of Georgia Press, 1991).

3.8 ELIZABETH MONTAGU, *AN ESSAY ON THE WRITINGS AND GENIUS OF SHAKESPEARE* (1769)

Elizabeth Montagu (1718–1800) was an English author, literary hostess, and founder of the elite Bluestocking Society, one of the most important women's literary and intellectual circles of the eighteenth century. Montagu was in the vanguard of an English response to Voltaire's criticism of Shakespearean tragedy for its failure to observe neoclassical rules (see extract 3.3); her essay is frequently nationalistic in tone, lauding Shakespeare's intimate knowledge of human passions above that of French tragedians. Montagu's blueprint for the genre called for less hyperbole, more natural styles of acting and a clearer expression of genuine sentiment as a means of exciting a passionate response to human suffering in art. Her defence of Shakespeare and her ideas about tragedy were extremely well known even if they have later been overshadowed by those of other male guests invited to Bluestocking meetings such as Edmund Burke (extract 3.5) and Samuel Johnson (extract 3.7). The *Essay on the Writing and Genius of Shakespear* was reissued or reprinted 7 times and translated into French and German during her lifetime.

It is as a moral philosopher, not as the mere connoisseur in a polite art, that Aristotle gives the preference, above all other modes of poetic imitation, to tragedy, as capable to purge the passions, by the means of pity and terror. The object of the epic poem is to inspire magnanimity; to give good documents of life; to induce good habits; and like a wholesome regimen,[100] to preserve the whole moral economy in a certain soundness and integrity. But it is not composed of ingredients of such efficacy, as to mitigate the violent distempers of the mind, nor can apply its art to the benefit of the ignorant vulgar, where those distempers are in their most exasperated state. An epic poem is too abstruse for the people; the moral is too much enveloped, the language too elevated for their apprehension; nor have they leisure, or application, to trace the consequences of ill-governed passions, or erroneous principles, through the long series of a voluminous work. The Drama is happily constituted for this purpose. Events are brought within the compass of a short period: precepts are delivered in the familiar way of discourse: the fiction is concealed, the allegory is realized; and representation and action take the place of cold unaffecting narration. A tragedy is a fable exhibited to the view, and tendered palpable to the senses; and every decoration of the stage is contrived to impose the delusion on the spectator, by conspiring with the imitation. It is addressed to the imagination, through which it opens to itself a communication with the heart, where it is to excite certain passions and affections; each character being personated, and each event exhibited, the attention of the audience is greatly captivated, and the imagination so far assists in the delusion, as to sympathize in the representation.

[...]

According to Aristotle, there can be no tragedy without action. Mr. Voltaire confesses, that some of the most admired tragedies in France, are rather conversations, than representations of an action.[101] It will hardly be allowed to those who fail in the most essential part of an

---

[100]**regimen:** a course of behaviour, diet, or exercise usually prescribed to improve health.
[101]**Voltaire ... action:** 'We have tragedies in France that are esteemed, which are conversations, rather than a representation of facts'; Voltaire, *Critical Essays on Dramatic Poetry* (London, 1761), 9.

art, to set up their performances as models. Can they who have robbed the Tragic Muse of all her virtue, and divested her of whatsoever gives her a real interest in the human heart, require, we should adore her for the glitter of a few false brilliants, or the nice arrangement of frippery ornaments? If she wears any thing of intrinsic value, it has been borrowed from the ancients; but by these artists it is so fantastically fashioned to modern modes, as to lose all its original graces, and even that necessary qualification of all ornaments, fitness and propriety. A French tragedy is a tissue of declamations, and laboured recitals of the catastrophe, by which the spirit of the Drama is greatly weakened and enervated, and the theatrical piece is deprived of that peculiar influence over the mind, which it derives from the vivid force of representation. …

The business of the Drama is to excite sympathy; and its effect on the spectator depends on such a justness of imitation, as shall cause, to a certain degree, the same passions and affections, as if what was exhibited were real. We have observed narrative imitation to be too faint and feeble a means to excite passion: declamation, still worse, plays idly on the surface of the subject, and makes the poet, who should be concealed in the action, visible to the spectator. In many works of art, our pleasure arises from a reflection on the art itself; and in a comparison, drawn by the mind, between the original and the copy before us. But here the art and the artist must not appear; for, as often as we recur to the Poet, so often our sympathy with the action on the stage is suspended. The pompous declamations of the French theatre are mere rhetorical flourishes, such as an uninterested person might make on the state of the persons in the drama. They assume the office of the spectator by expressing his feelings, instead of conveying to us the strong emotions and sensations of the persons under the pressure of distress. Experience informs us, that even the inarticulate groans and involuntary convulsions of a creature in agonies, affect us much more, than any eloquent and elaborate description of its situation, delivered in the properest words, and most significant gestures. Our pity is then attendant on the passions of the unhappy person, and on his own sense of his misfortunes. From description, from the report of a spectator, we may make some conjecture of his internal state of mind, and so far we shall be moved: but the direct and immediate way to the heart is by the sufferer's expression of his passion. As there may be some obscurity in what I have said on this subject, I will endeavour to illustrate the doctrine by examples.

Sophocles, in his admirable tragedy of *Oedipus Coloneus*,[102] makes Oedipus expostulate with his undutiful son. The injured parent exposes the enormity of filial disobedience; sets forth the duties of this relation in a very strong and lively manner; but it is only by the vehemence with which he speaks of them, and the imprecations he utters against the delinquent son, that we can guess at the violence of his emotions; therefore he excites more indignation at the conduct of Polynices, than sympathy with his own sorrow; of which we can judge only as spectators: for he has explained to us merely the external duties and relations of parent and child. The pangs of paternal tenderness, thus wounded, are more pathetically expressed by King Lear, who leaves out whatever of this enormity is equally sensible to the spectator, and

---

[102]*Oedipus Coloneus*: Sophocles' final Theban play, *Oedipus at Colonus* (c.406 BCE), which recounts the death of Oedipus.

immediately exposes to us his own internal feelings, when, in the bitterness of his soul, cursing his daughter's offspring, he adds:

> That she may feel,
> How sharper than a serpent's tooth it is,
> To have a thankless child.[103]

By this we perceive, how deeply paternal affection is wounded by filial ingratitude.

[...]

Shakespeare was born in a rank of life, in which men indulge themselves in a free expression of their passions, with little regard to exterior appearance. This perhaps made him more acquainted with the emotions of the heart, and less knowing or observant of outward forms: against the one he often offends, he very rarely misrepresents the other. The French tragedians, on the contrary, attend not to the nature of the man, whom they represent, but to the decorums of his rank: so that their best tragedies are made ridiculous, by changing the condition of the persons of the drama; which could not be so easily effected if they spoke the language of passion, which in all ranks of men is much alike. This kind of exterior representation falls intirely short of the intention of the Drama: and indeed many plays are little more than poems rehearsed; and the theatrical decorations are used rather to improve the spectacle, than to assist the drama, of which the poet remains the apparent hero.

[...]

Sophocles certainly unfolds the fatal mystery of the birth of Oedipus, with great art:[104] but our interest in the play arises not from reflection on the conduct of the poet, but is the effect of his making us alternately hope and fear for this guiltless, unhappy man. We wait with trembling expectation for the answer of the oracle, and for the testimony of Phorbas,[105] because we imagine that the destiny of Oedipus, and the fate of Thebes, depend on them; if we considered it merely as the contrivance of the poet, we should be as unconcerned at the unravelling of the plot, as about the explication of a riddle.

The affectation of elaborate art is certainly among the false refinements of the modern Stage. The first masters in theatrical representations made use of a diction, which united the harmony of verse to the easy and natural air of prose,[106] and was suited to the movement and bustle of action, being considered only as subservient to the fable, and not as the principal object of the poet or the audience.

[...]

To write a perfect tragedy, a poet must be possessed of the Pathetic or the Sublime; or perhaps, to attain the utmost excellence, must, by a more uncommon felicity, be able to give the Sublime the finest touches of passion and tenderness, and to the Pathetic the dignity of the Sublime. The straining a moderate or feeble genius to these arduous tasks, has produced the

---

[103]**thankless child:** William Shakespeare, *King Lear* (c.1605), 1.4.242–4.

[104]**birth of Oedipus:** Oedipus's knowledge that he is the biological son of Jocasta (his wife) and Laius is withheld until the final quarter of Sophocles' *Oedipus Rex* (c.429 BCE).

[105]**Phorbas:** Phorbas is the shepherd who finds the baby Oedipus on a hillside after he has been abandoned and rejected by his birth parents, Laius and Jocasta.

[106]**verse ... prose:** see Aristotle's remarks about iambics in extract 1.2.

most absurd bombast, and the most pitiable nonsense that has ever been uttered. Aristotle's rules, like Ulysses' bow, are held forth to all pretenders to Tragedy, who, as unfortunate as Penelope's suitors, only betray their weakness by an attempt superior to their strength, or ill adapted to their faculties.[107] Why should not Poetry, in all her different forms, claim the same indulgence as her sister art? The nicest connoisseurs in Painting have applauded every master, who has justly copied nature. Had Michael Angelo's bold pencil been dedicated to drawing the Graces, or Rembrandt's to trace the soft bewitching smile of Venus, their works had probably proved very contemptible. Fashion does not so easily impose on our sense, as it misleads our judgment. Truth of design, and natural colouring, will always please the eye: we appeal not here to any set of rules; but in an imitative art we require only just imitation, with a certain freedom and energy, which is always necessary to form a complete resemblance to the pattern, which is borrowed from nature.

Further reading

Elizabeth Eger, '"Out Rushed a Female to Protect the Bard": The Bluestocking Defense of Shakespeare', *Huntington Library Quarterly* 65, no. 1 (2002): 127–51.

Judith Hawley, 'Shakespearean Sensibilities: Women Writers Reading Shakespeare, 1753–1808', in *Shakespearean Continuities: Essays in Honour of E.A.J. Honigmann*, ed. John Batchelor, Tom Cain and Claire Lamont (Basingstoke and New York: Palgrave Macmillan, 1997), 290–304.

---

[107]**Aristotle's rules … Penelope's suitors:** Montagu depicts tragedy as the classical epic heroine Penelope fending off unworthy pursuers after her affections, imagined here as slavish adherents to neoclassical Aristotelian 'rules'. In Book XXI of Homer's *The Odyssey* Ulysses' bow was a weapon which only its owner could wield but which inferior heroes tried and failed to use.

3.9 JOANNA BAILLIE, 'INTRODUCTORY DISCOURSE' (1798)

Joanna Baillie (1762–1851) was a Scottish-born poet and dramatist, author of 26 plays. Although she was fêted in literary circles, none of her plays were runaway theatrical successes and she had to contend with the everyday sexism of a male-dominated industry. George Gordon, Lord Byron (1788–1824), a fan of her tragedy *De Monfort* (1798), recounted an anecdote about Voltaire who when 'asked why no woman has ever written a tolerable tragedy' replied that 'the composition of tragedy requires testicles'. 'If this be true,' Byron quipped, 'Lord knows what Joanna Baillie does – I suppose she borrows them.'[108] Baillie theorized her own practice of writing psychological rather than plot-driven tragedies by rejecting a tradition of heroic drama with its focus on histrionics, intrigue, and rhyming couplets in favour of careful, blank verse observations of the ways in which the passions could impede the operations of reason in quotidian, domestic contexts. In this way she hoped to expand the possibilities of tragedy for women. Although critics routinely position Baillie's writings on tragedy among Romantic or nineteenth-century responses to the genre, her 'Introductory Discourse' is included here because it grows directly out of her observations regarding eighteenth-century performance styles of the period's greatest Shakespearean actor, David Garrick (1717–89).[109]

In whatever age or country the Drama might have taken its rise, tragedy would have been the first-born of its children. For every nation has its great men, and its great events upon record; and to represent their own forefathers struggling with those difficulties, and braving those dangers, of which they have heard with admiration, and the effects of which they still, perhaps, experience, would certainly have been the most animating subject for the poet, and the most interesting for his audience, even independently of the natural inclination we all so universally shew for scenes of horrour and distress, of passion and heroick exertion. Tragedy would have been the first child of the Drama, for the same reasons that have made heroick ballad, with all its battles, murders, and disasters, the earliest poetical compositions of every country.

We behold heroes and great men at a distance, unmarked by those small but distinguishing features of the mind, which give a certain individuality to such an infinite variety of similar beings, in the near and familiar intercourse of life. They appear to us from this view like distant mountains, whose dark outlines we trace in the clear horizon, but the varieties of whose roughened sides, shaded with heath and brushwood, and seamed with many a cleft, we perceive not. When accidental anecdote reveals to us any weakness or peculiarity belonging to them, we start upon it like a discovery. They are made known to us in history only, by the great events they are connected with, and the part they have taken in extraordinary or important transactions. Even in poetry and romance, with the exception of some love story interwoven with the main events of their lives, they are seldom more intimately made known to us. To

---

[108]Ellen Donkin, *Getting into the Act: Women Playwrights in London, 1776–1829* (London and New York: Routledge, 1995), 178.

[109]E.J. Clery, *Women's Gothic: From Clara Reeve to Mary Shelley* (Tavistock: Northcote House, 2000), 17.

Tragedy it belongs to lead them forward to our nearer regard, in all the distinguishing varieties which nearer inspection discovers; with the passions, the humours, the weaknesses, the prejudices of men. It is for her to present to us the great and magnanimous hero, who appears to our distant view as a superior being, as a God, softened down with those smaller frailties and imperfections which enable us to glory in, and claim kindred to his virtues. It is for her to exhibit to us the daring and ambitious man, planning his dark designs, and executing his bloody purposes, mark'd with those appropriate characteristicks, which distinguish him as an individual of that class; and agitated with those varied passions, which disturb the mind of man when he is engaged in the commission of such deeds. It is for her to point out to us the brave and impetuous warrior struck with those visitations of nature, which, in certain situations, will unnerve the strongest arm, and make the boldest heart tremble. It is for her to shew the tender, gentle, and unassuming mind animated with that fire which, by the provocation of circumstances, will give to the kindest heart the ferocity and keenness of a tiger. It is for her to present to us the great and striking characters that are to be found amongst men, in a way which the poet, the novelist, and the historian can but imperfectly attempt. But above all, to her, and to her only it belongs to unveil to us the human mind under the dominion of those strong and fixed passions, which, seemingly unprovoked by outward circumstances, will from small beginnings brood within the breast, till all the better dispositions, all the fair gifts of nature are borne down before them. Those passions which conceal themselves from the observation of men; which cannot unbosom themselves even to the dearest friend; and can, often times, only give their fulness vent in the lonely desert, or in the darkness of midnight. For who hath followed the great man into his secret closet, or stood by the side of his nightly couch, and heard those exclamations of the soul which heaven alone may hear, that the historian should be able to inform us? and what form of story, what mode of rehearsed speech will communicate to us those feelings, whose irregular bursts, abrupt transitions, sudden pauses, and half-uttered suggestions, scorn all harmony of measured verse, all method and order of relation?

On the first part of this task her Bards have eagerly exerted their abilities: and some amongst them, taught by strong original genius to deal immediately with human nature and their own hearts, have laboured in it successfully. But in presenting to us those views of great characters, and of the human mind in difficult and trying situations which peculiarly belong to Tragedy, the far greater proportion, even of those who may be considered as respectable dramatick poets, have very much failed. From the beauty of those original dramas to which they have ever looked back with admiration, they have been tempted to prefer the embellishments of poetry to faithfully delineated nature. They have been more occupied in considering the works of the great Dramatists who have gone before them, and the effects produced by their writings, than the varieties of human character which first furnished materials for those works, or those principles in the mind of man by means of which such effects were produced. Neglecting the boundless variety of nature, certain strong outlines of character, certain bold features of passion, certain grand vicissitudes, and striking dramatick situations have been repeated from one generation to another; whilst a pompous and solemn gravity, which they have supposed to be necessary for the dignity of tragedy, has excluded almost entirely from their works those smaller touches of nature, which so well develop the mind; and by showing men in their hours of state and exertion only, they have consequently shewn them imperfectly. Thus, great and magnanimous heroes, who bear with majestick equanimity every vicissitude of fortune; who in every temptation and trial stand forth in unshaken virtue, like a rock buffeted by the waves;

who encompast with the most terrible evils, in calm possession of their souls, reason upon the difficulties of their state; and, even upon the brink of destruction, pronounce long eulogiums on virtue, in the most eloquent and beautiful language, have been held forth to our view as objects of imitation and interest; as though they had entirely forgotten that it is only from creatures like ourselves that we feel, and therefore, only from creatures like ourselves that we receive the instruction of example.[110] Thus, passionate and impetuous warriors, who are proud, irritable, and vindictive, but generous, daring, and disinterested; setting their lives at a pin's fee for the good of others, but incapable of curbing their own humour of a moment to gain the whole world for themselves; who will pluck the orbs of heaven from their places, and crush the whole universe in one grasp, are called forth to kindle in our souls the generous contempt of every thing abject and base; but with an effect proportionably feeble, as the hero is made to exceed in courage and fire what the standard of humanity will agree to.[111] Thus, tender and pathetick lovers, full of the most gentle affections, the most amiable dispositions, and the most exquisite feelings; who present their defenceless bosoms to the storms of this rude world in all the graceful weakness of sensibility, are made to sigh out their sorrows in one unvaried strain of studied pathos, whilst this constant demand upon our feelings makes us absolutely incapable of answering it.[112] Thus, also, tyrants are represented as monsters of cruelty, unmixed with any feelings of humanity; and villains as delighting in all manner of treachery and deceit, and acting upon many occasions for the very love of villainy itself; though the perfectly wicked

---

[110][**Baillie's note**]: To a being perfectly free from all human infirmity our sympathy refuses to extend. Our Saviour himself, whose character is so beautiful, and so harmoniously consistent; in whom, with outward proofs of his mission less strong than those that are offered to us, I should still be compelled to believe, from being utterly unable to conceive how the idea of such a character could enter into the imagination of man, never touches the heart more nearly than when he says, 'Father, let this cup pass from me' (Mark 14: 35–6). Had he been represented to us in all the unshaken strength of these tragick heroes, his disciples would have made fewer converts, and his precepts would have been listened to coldly. Plays in which heroes of this kind are held forth, and whose aim is, indeed, honourable and praise worthy, have been admired by the cultivated and refined, but the tears of the simple, the applauses of the young and untaught have been wanting.

[111][**Baillie's note**]: In all burlesque imitations of tragedy, those plays in which this hero is pre-eminent, are always exposed to bear the great brunt of the ridicule; which proves how popular they have been, and how many poets, and good ones too, have been employed upon them. That they have been so popular, however, is not owing to the intrinsick merit of the characters they represent, but their opposition to those mean and contemptible qualities belonging to human nature, of which we are most ashamed. Besides, there is something in the human mind, independently of its love of applause, which inclines it to boast. This is ever the attendant of that elasticity of soul, which makes us bound up from the touch of oppression; and if there is nothing in the accompanying circumstances to create disgust, or suggest suspicions of their sincerity (as in real life is commonly the case), we are very apt to be carried along with the boasting of others. Let us in good earnest believe that a man is capable of achieving all that human courage can achieve, and we will suffer him to talk of impossibilities. Amidst all their pomp of words, therefore, our admiration of such heroes is readily excited (for the understanding is more easily deceived than the heart), but how stands our sympathy affected? As no caution nor foresight, on their own account, is ever suffered to occupy the thoughts of such bold disinterested beings, we are the more inclined to care for them, and take an interest in their fortune through the course of the play: yet, as their souls are unappalled by anything; as pain and death are not at all regarded by them; and as we have seen them very ready to plunge their own swords into their own bosoms, on no very weighty occasion, perhaps, their death distresses us but little, and they commonly fall unwept.

[112][**Baillie's note**]: Were it not, that in tragedies where these heroes preside, the same soft tones of sorrow are so often repeated in our ears, till we are perfectly tired of it, they are more fitted to interest us than any other: both because in seeing them, we own the ties of kindred between ourselves and the frail mortals we lament; and sympathize with the weakness of mortality unmixed with anything to degrade or disgust; and also, because the misfortunes, which form the story of the play, are frequently of the more familiar and domestick kind. A king driven from his throne, will not move our sympathy so strongly, as a private man torn from the bosom of his family.

are as ill fitted for the purposes of warning, as the perfectly virtuous are for those of example.[113] This spirit of imitation, and attention to effect, has likewise confined them very much in their choice of situations and events to bring their great characters into action; rebellions, conspiracies, contentions for empire, and rivalships in love have alone been thought worthy of trying those heroes; and palaces and dungeons the only places magnificent or solemn enough for them to appear in.

They have, indeed, from this regard to the works of preceding authors, and great attention to the beauties of composition, and to dignity of design, enriched their plays with much striking, and sometimes sublime imagery, lofty thoughts, and virtuous sentiments; but in striving so eagerly to excell in those things that belong to tragedy in common with many other compositions, they have very much neglected those that are peculiarly her own. As far as they have been led aside from the first labours of a tragick poet by a desire to communicate more perfect moral instruction, their motive has been respectable, and they merit our esteem. But this praise-worthy end has been injured instead of promoted by their mode of pursuing it. Every species of moral writing has its own way of conveying instruction, which it can never, but with disadvantage, exchange for any other. The Drama improves us by the knowledge we acquire of our own minds, from the natural desire we have to look into the thoughts, and observe the behaviour of others. Tragedy brings to our view men placed in those elevated situations, exposed to those great trials, and engaged in those extraordinary transactions, in which few of us are called upon to act. As examples applicable to ourselves, therefore, they can but feebly effect us; it is only from the enlargement of our ideas in regard to human nature, from that admiration of virtue, and abhorrence of vice which they excite, that we can expect to be improved by them. But if they are not represented to us as real and natural characters, the lessons we are taught from their conduct and their sentiments will be no more to us than those which we receive from the pages of the poet or the moralist.

[The] last part of the task which I have mentioned as peculiarly belonging to tragedy, unveiling the human mind under the dominion of those strong and fixed passions, which seemingly unprovoked by outward circumstances, will from small beginnings brood within the breast, till all the better dispositions, all the fair gifts of nature are borne down before them, her poets in general have entirely neglected, and even her first and greatest have but imperfectly attempted. They have made use of the passions to mark their several characters, and animate their scenes, rather than to open to our view the nature and portraitures of those great disturbers of the human breast, with whom we are all, more or less, called upon to contend. With their strong and obvious features, therefore, they have been presented to us, stripped almost entirely of those less obtrusive, but not less discriminating traits, which mark them in their actual operation. To trace them in their rise and progress in the heart, seems but

---

[113][**Baillie's note**]: I have said nothing here in regard to female character, though in many tragedies it is brought forward as the principal one of the piece, because what I have said of the above characters is likewise applicable to it. I believe there is no man that ever lived, who has behaved in a certain manner, on a certain occasion, who has not had amongst women some corresponding spirit, who on the like occasion, and every way similarly circumstanced, would have behaved in the like manner. With some degree of softening and refinement, each class of the tragick heroes I have mentioned has its corresponding one amongst the heroines. The tender and pathetick no doubt has the most numerous, but the great and magnanimous is not without it, and the passionate and impetuous boasts of one by no means inconsiderable in numbers, and drawn sometimes to the full as passionate and impetuous as itself.

rarely to have been the object of any dramatist. We commonly find the characters of a tragedy affected by the passions in a transient, loose, unconnected manner; or if they are represented as under the permanent influence of the more powerful ones, they are generally introduced to our notice in the very height of their fury, when all that timidity, irresolution, distrust, and a thousand delicate traits, which make the infancy of every great passion more interesting, perhaps, than its full-blown strength, are fled. The impassioned character is generally brought into view under those irresistible attacks of their power, which it is impossible to repell; whilst those gradual steps that led him into this state, in some of which a stand might have been made against the foe, are left entirely in the shade. These passions that may be suddenly excited, and are of short duration, as anger, fear, and oftentimes jealousy, may in this manner be fully represented; but those great masters of the soul, ambition, hatred, love, every passion that is permanent in its nature, and varied in progress, if represented to us but in one stage of its course, is represented imperfectly. It is a characteristick of the more powerful passions that they will encrease and nourish themselves on very slender aliment; it is from within that they are chiefly supplied with what they feed on; and it is in contending with opposite passions and affections of the mind that we least discover their strength, not with events. But in tragedy it is events more frequently than opposite affections which are opposed to them; and those often of such force and magnitude that the passions themselves are almost obscured by the splendour and importance of the transactions to which they are attached. But besides being thus confined and mutilated, the passions have been, in the greater part of our tragedies, deprived of the very power of making themselves known. Bold and figurative language belongs peculiarly to them. Poets, admiring those bold expressions which a mind, labouring with ideas too strong to be conveyed in the ordinary forms of speech, wildly throws out, taking earth, sea, and sky, every thing great and terrible in nature to image forth the violence of its feelings, borrowed them gladly, to adorn the calm sentiments of their premeditated song. It has therefore been thought that the less animated parts of tragedy might be so embellished and enriched. In doing this, however, the passions have been robbed of their native prerogative; and in adorning with their strong figures and lofty expressions the calm speeches of the unruffled, it is found that, when they are called upon to raise their voice, the power of distinguishing themselves has been taken away. This is an injury by no means compensated, but very greatly aggravated by embellishing, in return, the speeches of passion with the ingenious conceits, and compleat similies of premeditated thought.[114] ...

From this general view, which I have endeavoured to communicate to my reader, of tragedy, and those principles in the human mind upon which the success of her efforts depends, I have been led to believe, that an attempt to write a series of tragedies, of simpler construction, less embellished with poetical decorations, less constrained by that lofty seriousness which has so generally been considered as necessary for the support of tragick dignity, and in which the chief object should be to delineate the progress of the higher passions in the human breast, each play exhibiting a particular passion, might not be unacceptable to the publick. And I have been the more readily induced to act upon this idea, because I am confident, that tragedy,

---

[114][**Baillie's note**]: This, perhaps, more than anything else has injured the higher scenes of tragedy. For having made such free use of bold hyperbolical language in the inferior parts, the poet when he arrives at the highly impassioned sinks into total inability: or if he will force himself to rise still higher on the wing, he flies beyond nature altogether, into the regions of bombast and nonsense.

written upon this plan, is fitted to produce stronger moral effect than upon any other. I have said that tragedy in representing to us great characters struggling with difficulties, and placed in situations of eminence and danger, in which few of us have any chance of being called upon to act, conveys its moral efficacy to our minds by the enlarged views which it gives to us of human nature, by the admiration of virtue, and execration of vice which it excites, and not by the examples it holds up for our immediate application. But in opening to us the heart of man under the influence of those passions to which all are liable, this is not the case. Those strong passions that, with small assistance from outward circumstances, work their way in the heart, till they become the tyrannical masters of it, carry on a similar operation in the breast of the Monarch, and the man of low degree. It exhibits to us the mind of man in that state when we are most curious to look into it, and is equally interesting to all.

Further reading

C.B. Burroughs, *Closet Stages: Joanna Baillie and the Theater Theory of British Romantic Women Writers* (Philadelphia: University of Pennsylvania Press, 1997).

Christine A. Colòn, *Joanna Baillie and the Art of Moral Influence* (New York: Peter Lang, 2006).

CHAPTER 4
THE NINETEENTH CENTURY

There is a deeply moving moment in the second book of George Eliot's masterpiece, *Middlemarch* (1871–2), where the novel's narrator pauses over the sight of a young woman weeping controllably to herself and asks us to consider the spectacle in generic terms. The woman in distress is Eliot's heroine, Dorothea, who is honeymooning in Rome with her middle-aged husband the Reverend Edward Casaubon and has been left alone once again while he pursues research into a never-to-be finished book in the Vatican library. Confronted with the cultural and historical superabundance of the imperial city, unable to process the excessive meanings of its art, history, and religion, she simultaneously experiences a dawning realization that the man she has married may not be the pious, intellectual hero of her generous, hopeful imagination but a selfish pedant. As the broad sweep of European history and a familial past become intertwined and rush past, Dorothea begins to sense with us that her marriage may not just be a dreadful mistake but also a waste of youth, hope, and love. Eliot's narrator, however, is uncertain whether this spectacle of suffering and partial recognition of both a grave error and the true nature of reality – something approaching *anagnorisis* in strictly Aristotelian terms – conforms to a recognizable pattern of tragedy:

> Nor can I suppose that when Mrs Casaubon is discovered in a fit of weeping six weeks after her wedding, the situation will be regarded as tragic. Some discouragement, some faintness of heart at the new real future which replaces the imaginary, is not unusual, and we do not expect people to be deeply moved by what is not usual. That element of tragedy which lies in the very fact of frequency, has not yet wrought itself into the coarse emotions of mankind; and perhaps our frames could hardly bear much of it. If we had a keen vision and feeling of all ordinary human life, it would be like hearing the grass grow and the squirrel's heart beat, and we should die of that roar which lies on the other side of silence. As it is, the quickest of us walk about well wadded with stupidity.[1]

Eliot's readers are here asked to weigh whether earlier ideas of tragedy – in which audiences are 'deeply moved by what is not usual' in the sufferings of great individuals mired in epochal crises – were merely a useful means of concealing or sublimating the frequently unbearable, potentially tragic nature of daily existence. What if tragedy is actually all around us, but is occluded by our propensity to see it only in the aestheticized struggle of, say, Antigone in the royal house of Thebes, rather than in the quotidian disasters of 'ordinary' women, like Dorothea, struggling to make their way in the world from their bit of the Midlands? Are the ideas about tragedy that we have encountered in the first three chapters of this anthology, then,

---

[1]George Eliot, *Middlemarch*, ed. W. J. Harvey (Harmondsworth: Penguin, 1985), 226.

nothing more than a kind of textual wadding that renders us stupid or insensible to what life is really like, that tragedy is here and now as well as there and then?

Even though *Middlemarch*, an epic novel about provincial life, is far too hopeful to be regarded as tragic – second chances do come around, Dorothea can enjoy reciprocated love after the death of her first husband – the novel poses a question that, in different ways, preoccupied each of the writers in this chapter. How might an individual experience tragedy in a recognizably modern world, where old certainties about how we relate to each other, where we come from, and where we are going to are no longer shared? Writers in this chapter turned to this question, in part, because of the transformative influence exercised by the late eighteenth-century philosophy of Immanuel Kant (1724–1804). Kant's philosophy radically restructured the relationship between the cognitive and the ethical. Reading his three Critiques – the *Critique of Pure Reason* (1781), the *Critique of Practical Reason* (1788), and the *Critique of Judgment* (1790) – it became possible to insist that universal values, such as the value of autonomy and freedom to set our own ends, might persist even if religion might be regarded as a matter of faith rather than knowledge.[2] The period that saw the reception and dissemination of Kant's ideas also witnessed the American (1775–83), French (1787–99), and Haitian (1791–1804) revolutions. These revolutionary conflicts are commonly regarded as watershed moments marking the birth of modernity, since – at least in principle, if not always the brutalizing, bloody reality of revolutionary practice – they offered the prospect of human existence in which the pursuit of equality, freedom, or happiness, none of which were, necessarily, tied to a shared belief in the same God, could be regarded as rational ends in themselves.[3]

In the nineteenth century, then, the audiences for tragedy had fresh and urgent imperatives to return to a genre which, since antiquity, had probed the limits of human agency, the place of suffering, and the (frequently illusory) promises of freedom. Tragedy continued to thrive, assume hybrid forms and develop as stage spectacle during this period, as authors and playwrights as diverse as Joanna Baillie, Charlotte Mary Sanford Barnes, Samuel Taylor Coleridge, Alexandre Dumas, fils, Victor Hugo, Henrik Ibsen, Heinrich von Kleist, Estelle Lewis, and August Strindberg explored the place and limits of irony, naturalism, and the passions in tragedy, and all had influential serious dramas performed at key moments in their careers.[4] This was also the century in which Richard Wagner explored the revolutionary vistas that music might open up for tragedy in the epic-historical sweep of his operas.[5] Amid this explosion of theatrical experimentation with tragedy there remained an enduring fascination with tragedies from antiquity and Shakespeare, although the currents of pan-European Romanticism – with its emphasis on individual genius, the imagination and the intersubjective

---

[2]Paul Guyer, *The Virtues of Freedom: Selected Essays on Kant* (Oxford: Oxford University Press, 2016); Andrew Bowie, *German Philosophy: A Very Short Introduction* (Oxford: Oxford University Press, 2010), 6–20; J.B. Schneewind, *The Invention of Autonomy* (Cambridge: Cambridge University Press, 1998).

[3]Hannah Arendt, *On Revolution* (New York: Viking, 1963); David Scott, *Conscripts of Modernity: The Tragedy of Colonial Enlightenment* (Durham and London: Duke University Press, 2004).

[4]See Barbara T. Cooper, 'French Romantic Tragedy', in *A Companion to Tragedy*, 452–68; Stephan Hulfeld, 'Modernist Theatre', in *The Cambridge Companion to Theatre History*, ed. David Wiles and Christine Dymkowski (Cambridge: Cambridge University Press, 2012), 15–32; Staves, 'Tragedy'.

[5]Eric Chafe, *The Tragic and the Ecstatic: The Musical Revolution of Wagner's Tristan und Isolde* (Oxford: Oxford University Press, 2005); Daniel H. Foster, *Wagner's Ring Cycle and the Greeks* (Cambridge: Cambridge University Press, 2010).

potential of sympathy – meant that there was a growing emphasis on reading tragedy rather than seeing it performed or staged.[6] Thus Charles Lamb and Mary Lamb wrote a series of prose retellings of Shakespeare's plays for children, *Tales from Shakespeare* (1807), with a clear sense that the lessons of tragedy were not too terrible to bear for their young readership; rather, they thought that reading good tragedy quickened the imagination and elevated a Romantic idea of vision above the mere senses (extract 4.2). Such ideas drew upon a Romantic conceptualization of the imagination as a faculty which, unlike Reason, enabled us to transcend our immediate concerns and circumstances, to imagine life as it might be and not just as it is. Thus the English Romantic poet Percy Bysshe Shelley (extract 4.5), following the founding father of German Romanticism A.W. Schlegel (extract 4.1), thought that the best tragedy expanded the capacity of the imagination by avoiding didacticism and probing the nature of moral freedom. But it was the English essayist William Hazlitt who did most to popularize the view that the capacities of our imaginations were best exercised by reading rather than watching tragedy. In his *Characters of Shakespeare's Plays* (1817), Hazlitt argued – again drawing upon A.W. Schlegel's emphasis on the moral freedoms afforded by tragedy – that reading tragedy was key for developing the imagination and the public's capacity for sympathy (extract 4.3). Internalizing and recreating the struggle of Shakespeare's tragic protagonists via the act of reading – rather than having those struggles externalized for us in transporting acts of performance – enabled our own imagination to carry us out of ourselves and into the feelings of others, thus purging us of selfishness.

This belief that unspectacularly private and readerly experiences of tragedy might drive imaginative moments of sympathy – and that such moments might form the basis for ethical behaviour – is precisely the aspiration that we saw George Eliot's narrator expressing in *Middlemarch*. Eliot's version of that idea was influenced by her own interest in the reading of classical tragedy (extract 4.7), in the ways that the tragic conflicts of a play like Sophocles's *Antigone* might be reanimated for women and men in the drawing rooms, parlours, and studies of Victorian England. Such concerns were, of course, the lifeblood of the novel in this period. Even though the eighteenth century witnessed the first tragic novels – Goethe's *The Sorrows of Young Werther* (1774) and Samuel Richardson's *Clarissa* (1747–8) chief among them – it was only in the nineteenth century that tragedy and the novel became habitual and eager bedfellows. Any brief list of the major novelists of the nineteenth century is also, necessarily, a thumbnail sketch of the development and migration of tragedy into prose fiction: Honoré de Balzac's *Le Pere Goriot* (1834–5), Emily Bronte's *Wuthering Heights* (1847), Joseph Conrad's *Lord Jim* (1900), Fyodor Dostoevsky's *Crime and Punishment* (1866), George Eliot's *The Mill on the Floss* (1860), Gustav Flaubert's *Madame Bovary* (1857), Thomas Hardy's *Jude the Obscure* (1894–5), Alessandro Manzoni's *The Betrothed* (1825–6), Herman Melville's *Moby Dick* (1851), Leo Tolstoy's *Anna Karenina* (1875–7), and Emile Zola's *L'Assommoir* (1877), for all of their infinite variety, each strive to accommodate the ambition and heft of tragic sense of existence into the recognizable, grindingly workaday settings of the modern world.

---

[6]On Romanticism and tragedy see Jeffrey N. Cox, especially *In the Shadow of Romance: Romantic Tragic Drama in Germany, England and France* (Athens: Ohio University Press, 1987) and idem., 'Romantic Redevelopment of the Tragic', in *Romantic Drama*, ed. Gerald Gillespie (Amsterdam and Philadelphia: John Benjamins Publishing Company, 1993), 153–66.

Whether they were successful in honouring a classical or even an early modern conception of tragedy, however, has been a matter of much critical debate.[7] As we will see in the next chapter, modern critics like George Steiner (extract 5.7) regarded Enlightenment and Romantic values – with their insistence on reason, order, perfectibility, and justice – as antithetical to a classically tragic sense of the universe in which the origins of catastrophe are either accidental or inexplicable. But there were proponents of this view in the nineteenth century, too. The philosopher Friedrich Nietzsche, for instance, a passionate devotee of the tragedies of Aeschylus and Sophocles, thought that the contemporary realist novel – which explained the whys and wherefores for characters' successes or misadventures, the chains of historical and personal causes for behaviour and suffering – had a fundamentally anti-tragic outlook, which he linked back to Plato's faith in the ability of reason and knowledge to master an understanding of the universe. Classical tragedy was valuable, on the other hand, Nietzsche argued (extract 4.8), because its depictions of irrationality and unintelligibility at the heart of the universe acted as important reminders of the immovable impediments to understanding the nature of being.

Nietzsche's contribution to contemporary debates about tragedy took place within a discursive context that was absolutely unprecedented and unique to this period. As Joshua Billings, Miriam Leonard, Peter Szonzi, and others have argued, it was only in the nineteenth century, specifically in the wake of the emergence of the philosophy of German Idealism, that discussions of tragedy could be used to frame the explicitly existential and metaphysical questions posed by European philosophy after Kant and the sociopolitical revolutions of the previous century (whereas previously such concerns had been extrapolated from philosophical works that were primarily studies of poetics and rhetoric).[8] The material constraints of a transhistorical anthology of this kind mean that we cannot do full justice to the richness of this philosophical tradition; Friedrich Hölderlin, Søren Kierkegaard, and Friedrich Wilhelm Joseph Schelling are three of the more notable absentees from what follows. But at the centre of this tradition is G.W.F. Hegel's magisterial account of classical and Romantic tragedy from his *Aesthetics* (extract 4.6) based upon his students' notes from a series of lectures he gave on fine art in the 1820s. After Aristotle's *Poetics* (extract 1.2), Hegel's thoughts on tragedy are perhaps the most influential of all of those extracted in this anthology; in place of Aristotle's emphasis on tragic plot focussing on the demise of a central hero, Hegel posited a dialectical structure in classical tragedy which saw a central tragic collision or conflict between two equally justified sets of values or powers. This collision produces not just tragic catastrophes but also the knowledge and historico-political progress borne of those catastrophes. For later philosophers like Arthur Schopenhauer (extract 4.4), Hegel's reading of tragedy was far too optimistic and purposive (i.e. it conformed to some obscure but carefully ordered scheme). Schopenhauer

---

[7]Sandra Macpherson, *Harm's Way: Tragic Responsibility and the Novel Form* (Baltimore: Johns Hopkins University Press, 2010); Terry Eagleton, *Sweet Violence: The Idea of the Tragic* (Oxford: Blackwell Publishing, 2003), 178–202; Jeannette King, *Tragedy and the Victorian Novel: Theory and Practice in the Novels of George Eliot, Thomas Hardy and Henry James* (Cambridge: Cambridge University Press, 1978).

[8]See Miriam Leonard, *Tragic Modernities* (Cambridge, MA: Harvard University Press, 2015); Joshua Billings and Miriam Leonard, eds., *Tragedy and the Idea of Modernity* (Oxford: Oxford University Press, 2015); Joshua Billings, *Genealogy of the Tragic: Greek Tragedy and German Philosophy* (Princeton and Oxford: Princeton University Press, 2014); Vassilis Lambropoulos, *The Tragic Idea* (London: Duckworth, 2006); David Farrell Krell, *The Tragic Absolute: German Idealism and the Languishing of God* (Bloomington: Indiana University Press, 2005); Peter Szondi, *An Essay on the Tragic*, trans. Paul Fleming (Stanford: Stanford University Press, 2002); Dennis J. Schmidt, *On Germans and Other Greeks: Tragedy and Ethical Life* (Bloomington: Indiana University Press, 2001).

argued, by contrast, that there was nothing benign, coherent, or rational in the universe and that tragedy is valuable because it provides fleeting escape from misery by fostering a quietness of mind, an honest estimation of where we are really at, through its representation of the truly terrible side of life.

Such pessimism is not where Eliot wanted us to be when we see Dorothea crying to herself in her comfortable rented apartment on the Via Sistina in Rome. But she did want us to recognize that the sufferings of tragedy are more continuous and ubiquitous than most accounts of it dare acknowledge, and that knowledge of this fact – in a world where instinctive and consoling shared beliefs in God or the stabilizing hierarchies of traditional patriarchal societies were beginning to recede – was probably more than we could bear. Nietzsche and Schopenhauer both thought that tragedy could indeed help us to live with such awful knowledge; each of the other writers in this chapter, by contrast, found within tragedy the most profound reserves of fellow feeling, the energy to help us move forward together, not alone.

4.1 AUGUST WILHELM SCHLEGEL, *A COURSE OF LECTURES ON DRAMATIC ART AND LITERATURE* (1809–11)

August Wilhelm Schlegel (1767–1845), academic, essayist, poet, philosopher, and translator, was one of the founders of the German Romantic movement. His *Course of Lectures on Dramatic Art and Literature* (1809–11), translated into Dutch, English, French, and Italian in his lifetime, was based upon a lecture series he gave in Vienna in 1808 and has subsequently been read as being instrumental in the emergence of Comparative Literature as a discipline. These lectures became the foremost theory of tragedy in early nineteenth-century Europe. A great student of classical tragedies as well as those of Calderón and Shakespeare – his translation of Shakespeare's plays, *Shakespeare's Dramatische Werke* (1825–33), is still regarded as one of the most important in German – Schlegel thought that tragedy's primary appeal lay in its universality. It depicted a primary conflict between human will and fate, forcing us to recognize the insignificance of earthly existence, that all misfortune may be endured or overcome, and, in the process, revealed our dependence on inscrutable higher powers. Such revelations were, for Schlegel, consoling rather than merely terrifying and placed him at odds with those Aristotelian and neoclassical interpretations of tragedy which saw either the audience experience of pity and fear or the meting out of poetic justice as the chief locus of tragic pleasure.

Lecture V

We come now to the essence of Greek tragedy. That in conception it was ideal, is universally allowed; this, however, must not be understood as implying that all its characters were depicted as morally perfect. In such a case what room could there be for that contrast and collision which the very plot of a drama requires? – They have their weaknesses, errors, and even crimes, but the manners are always elevated above reality, and every person is invested with as high a portion of dignity as was compatible with his part in the action. But this is not all. The ideality of the representation chiefly consisted in the elevation of every thing in it to a higher sphere. Tragic poetry wished to separate the image of humanity which it presented to us, from the level of nature to which man is in reality chained down, like a slave of the soil. … The Greeks … in their artistic creations, succeeded most perfectly, in combining the ideal with the real, or, to drop school terms, an elevation more than human with all the truth of life, and in investing the manifestation of an idea with energetic corporeity.[9] They did not allow their figures to flit about without consistency in empty space, but they fixed the statue of humanity on the eternal and immovable basis of moral liberty; and that it might stand there unshaken, formed it of stone or brass, or some more massive substance than the bodies of living men, making an impression by its very weight, and from its very elevation and magnificence only the more completely subject to the laws of gravity.

---

[9]**corporeity:** bodily substance.

Inward liberty and external necessity are the two poles of the tragic world. It is only by contrast with its opposite that each of these ideas is brought into full manifestation. As the feeling of an internal power of self-determination elevates the man above the unlimited dominion of impulse and the instincts of nature; in a word, absolves him from nature's guardianship, so the necessity, which alongside of her he must recognize, is no mere natural necessity, but one lying beyond the world of sense in the abyss of infinitude; consequently it exhibits itself as the unfathomable power of Destiny. Hence this power extends also to the world of gods: for the Grecian gods are mere powers of nature; and although immeasurably higher than mortal man, yet, compared with infinitude, they are on an equal footing with himself. In Homer and in the tragedians, the gods are introduced in a manner altogether different. In the former their appearance is arbitrary and accidental, and communicate to the epic poem no higher interest than the charm of the wonderful. But in Tragedy the gods either come forward as the servants of destiny, and mediate executors of its decrees; or else approve themselves godlike only by asserting their liberty of action, and entering upon the same struggles with fate which man himself has to encounter.

This is the essence of the tragical in the sense of the ancients. We are accustomed to give to all terrible or sorrowful events the appellation of tragic, and it is certain that such events are selected in preference by Tragedy, though a melancholy conclusion is by no means indispensably necessary; and several ancient tragedies, viz., the *Eumenides*, *Philoctetes*, and in some degree also the *Oedipus Colonnus*,[10] without mentioning many of the pieces of Euripides, have a happy and cheerful termination.

But why does Tragedy select subjects so awfully repugnant to the wishes and the wants of our sensuous nature? This question has often been asked, and seldom satisfactorily answered. Some have said that the pleasure of such representations arises from the comparison we make between the calmness and tranquillity of our own situation, and the storms and perplexities to which the victims of passion are exposed. But when we take a warm interest in the persons of a tragedy, we cease to think of ourselves; and when this is not the case, it is the best of all proofs that we take but a feeble interest in the exhibited story, and that the tragedy has failed in its effect. Others again have had recourse to a supposed feeling for moral improvement, which is gratified by the view of poetical justice in the reward of the good and the punishment of the wicked. But he for whom the aspect of such dreadful examples could really be wholesome, must be conscious of a base feeling of depression, very far removed from genuine morality, and would experience humiliation rather than elevation of mind. Besides, poetical justice is by no means indispensable to a good tragedy; it may end with the suffering of the just and the triumph of the wicked, if only the balance be preserved in the spectator's own consciousness by the prospect of futurity. Little does it mend the matter to say with Aristotle, that the object of tragedy is to purify the passions by pity and terror. In the first place commentators have never been able to agree as to the meaning of this proposition, and have had recourse to the most forced explanations of it. Look, for instance, into the *Dramaturgie* of Lessing.[11] Lessing

---

[10]***Eumenides ... Oedipus Colonnus:*** *The Eumenides* (*c.*458 BCE) is the third of Aeschylus's *Oresteia* tragedies; *Philoctetes* (409 BCE) and *Oedipus at Colonus* (*c.*406 BCE) are both tragedies by Sophocles.

[11]***Dramaturgie* of Lessing:** *Die Hamburgische Dramaturgie* (1767–9), was an influential collection of essays on theatre by Gotthold Ephraim Lessing (1729–81). Lessing adapted Aristotle's idea of catharsis to suggest that the pity and fear produced by tragedy might prompt its audience to virtuous action.

gives a new explanation of his own, and fancies he has found in Aristotle a poetical Euclid.[12] But mathematical demonstrations are liable to no misconception, and geometrical evidence may well be supposed inapplicable to the theory of the fine arts. Supposing, however, that tragedy does operate this moral cure in us, still she does so by the painful feelings of terror and compassion: and it remains to be proved how it is that we take a pleasure in subjecting ourselves to such an operation.

Others have been pleased to say that we are attracted to theatrical representations from the want of some violent agitation to rouse us out of the torpor of our every-day life. Such a craving does exist; I have already acknowledged the existence of this want, when speaking of the attractions of the drama; but to it we must equally attribute the fights of wild beasts among the Romans, nay, even the combats of the gladiators. But must we, less indurated,[13] and more inclined to tender feelings, require demi-gods and heroes to descend, like so many desperate gladiators, into the bloody arena of the tragic stage, in order to agitate our nerves by the spectacle of their sufferings? No: it is not the sight of suffering which constitutes the charm of a tragedy, or even of the games of the circus, or of the fight of wild beasts. In the latter we see a display of activity, strength, and courage; splendid qualities these, and related to the mental and moral powers of man. The satisfaction, therefore, which we derive from the representation, in a good tragedy, of powerful situations and overwhelming sorrows, must be ascribed either to the feeling of the dignity of human nature, excited in us by such grand instances of it as are therein displayed, or to the trace of a higher order of things, impressed on the apparently irregular course of events, and mysteriously revealed in them; or perhaps to both these causes conjointly.

The true reason, therefore, why tragedy need not shun even the harshest subject is, that a spiritual and invisible power can only be measured by the opposition which it encounters from some external force capable of being appreciated by the senses. The moral freedom of man, therefore, can only be displayed in a conflict with his sensuous impulses: so long as no higher call summons it to action, it is either actually dormant within him, or appears to slumber, since otherwise it does but mechanically fulfil its part as a mere power of nature. It is only amidst difficulties and struggles that the moral part of man's nature avouches itself. If, therefore, we must explain the distinctive aim of tragedy by way of theory, we would give it thus: that to establish the claims of the mind to a divine origin, its earthly existence must be disregarded as vain and insignificant, all sorrows endured and all difficulties overcome. With respect to everything connected with this point, I refer my hearers to the Section on the Sublime in Kant's *Kritik der Urtheilskraft*,[14] to the complete perfection of which nothing is wanting but a more definite idea of the tragedy of the ancients, with which he does not seem to have been very well acquainted.

---

[12]**poetical Euclid:** Euclid (323–285 BCE) was a Greek mathematician most famous for his work of geometry, *The Elements* (*c*.300 BCE). Schlegel is ridiculing Lessing's assessment of Aristotle's *Poetics* as if it laid bare the foundational principles of all literary expression rather than being just one philosopher's influential interpretation of the way tragedy worked in antiquity.

[13]**indurated:** hardened, callous.

[14]**Kant's *Kritik der Urtheilskraft*:** Immanuel Kant's *Critique of Judgment* (1790), in which Kant distinguished the sublime from the agreeable, the beautiful, and the good as a reflective judgement. Kant's sublime is something that is beyond the limits of comprehension and thus combines both pleasure and fear.

I come now to another peculiarity which distinguishes the tragedy of the ancients from ours, I mean the Chorus. We must consider it as a personified reflection on the action which is going on; the incorporation into the representation itself of the sentiments of the poet, as the spokesman of the whole human race. This is its general poetical character; and that is all that here concerns us, and that character is by no means affected by the circumstance that the Chorus had a local origin in the feasts of Bacchus, and that, moreover, it always retained among the Greeks a peculiar national signification.

[...]

Whatever it might be and do in each particular piece, it represented in general, first the common mind of the nation, and then the general sympathy of all mankind. In a word, the Chorus is the ideal spectator.[15] It mitigates the impression of a heart-rending or moving story, while it conveys to the actual spectator a lyrical and musical expression of his own emotions, and elevates him to the region of contemplation.

Modern critics have never known what to make of the Chorus; and this is the less to be wondered at, as Aristotle affords no satisfactory solution of the matter. Its office is better painted by Horace,[16] who ascribes to it a general expression of moral sympathy, exhortation, instruction, and warning. But the critics in question have either believed that its chief object was to prevent the stage from ever being altogether empty, whereas in truth the stage was not at all the proper place for the Chorus; or else they have censured it as a superfluous and cumbersome appendage, expressing their astonishment at the alleged absurdity of carrying on secret transactions in the presence of assembled multitudes. They have also considered it as the principal reason with the Greek tragedians for the strict observance of the unity of place, as it could not be changed without the removal of the Chorus; an act, which could not have been done without some available pretext. Or lastly, they have believed that the Chorus owed its continuance from the first origin of Tragedy merely to accident; and as it is plain that in Euripides, the last of the three great tragic poets, the choral songs have frequently little or no connexion with the fable, and are nothing better than a mere episodical ornament, they therefore conclude that the Greeks had only to take one more step in the progress of dramatic art, to explode the Chorus altogether. To refute these superficial conjectures, it is only necessary to observe that Sophocles wrote a Treatise on the Chorus,[17] in prose, in opposition to the principles of some other poets; and that, far from following blindly the practice which he found established, like an intelligent artist he was able to assign reasons for his own doings.

Modern poets of the first rank have often, since the revival of the study of the ancients, attempted to introduce the Chorus in their own pieces, for the most part without a correct, and always without a vivid idea of its real import. They seem to have forgotten that we have neither suitable singing or dancing, nor, as our theatres are constructed, any convenient place for it. On these accounts it is hardly likely to become naturalized with us.

[...]

---

[15]**ideal spectator:** for a refutation of Shlegel's reading of the role of the chorus in classical tragedy see extract 4.8 from Nietzsche's *The Birth of Tragedy*.

[16]**better painted by Horace:** In his *Ars Poetica* (c.10 BCE), the Roman poet Horace declared that the chorus should side with the good, offer sound advice and moderate excessive passions; Horace, *Ars Poetica*, 193–201. See extract 1.3.

[17]**Sophocles ... Treatise on the Chorus:** Sophocles is reputed to have written a prose treatise, now lost, entitled *On the Chorus*.

I have called mythology the chief materials of tragedy ... The marvellous possesses the advantage that it can, in some measure, be at once believed and disbelieved: believed in so far as it is supported by its connexion with other opinions; disbelieved while we never take such an immediate interest in it as we do in what wears the hue of the every-day life of our own experience. The Grecian mythology was a web of national and local traditions, held in equal honour as a sequence of religion, and as an introduction to history; everywhere preserved in full vitality among the people by ceremonies and monuments, already elaborated for the requirements of art and the higher species of poetry by the diversified manner in which it has been handled, and by the numerous epic or merely mythical poets. The tragedians had only, therefore, to engraft one species of poetry on another. Certain postulates, and those invariably serviceable to the air of dignity and grandeur, and the removing of all meanness of idea, were conceded to them at the very outset. Everything, down to the very errors and weaknesses of that departed race of heroes who claimed their descent from the gods, was ennobled by the sanctity of legend. Those heroes were painted as beings endowed with more than human strength; but, so far from possessing unerring virtue and wisdom, they were even depicted as under the dominion of furious and unbridled passions. It was an age of wild effervescence; the hand of social order had not as yet brought the soil of morality into cultivation, and it yielded at the same time the most beneficent and poisonous productions, with the fresh luxuriant fulness of prolific nature. Here the occurrence of the monstrous and horrible did not necessarily indicate that degradation and corruption out of which alone, under the development of law and order, they could arise, and which, in such a state of things, make them fill us with sentiments of horror and aversion. The guilty beings of the fable are, if we may be allowed the expression, exempt from human jurisdiction, and amenable to a higher tribunal alone. Some, indeed, have advanced the opinion, that the Greeks, as zealous republicans, took a particular pleasure in witnessing the representation of the outrages and consequent calamities of the different royal families, and are almost disposed to consider the ancient tragedy in general as a satire on monarchical government. Such a party-view, however, would have deadened the sympathy of the audience, and consequently destroyed the effect which it was the aim of the tragedy to produce.

[...]

To the very different relations of the age in which those heroes lived, the standard of mere civil and domestic morality is not applicable, and to judge of them the feeling must go back to the primary ingredients of human nature. Before the existence of constitutions, – when as yet the notions of law and right were undeveloped, – the sovereigns were their own lawgivers, in a world which as yet was dependent on them; and the fullest scope was thus given to the energetic will, either for good or for evil. Moreover, an age of hereditary kingdom naturally exhibited more striking instances of sudden changes of fortune than the later times of political equality. It was in this respect that the high rank of the principal characters was essential, or at least favourable to tragic impressiveness; and not, as some moderns have pretended, because the changing fortunes of such persons exercise a material influence on the happiness or misery of numbers, and therefore they alone are sufficiently important to interest us in their behalf; nor, again, because internal elevation of sentiment must be clothed with external dignity, to call forth our respect and admiration. The Greek tragedians paint the downfall of kingly houses without any reference to its effects on the condition of the people; they show us the man in the king, and, far from veiling their heroes from our sight by their purple mantles, they allow us to look, through their vain splendour, into a bosom torn and harrowed with grief and passion. That the main essential was not so much the regal dignity as the heroic costume, is evident from those tragedies of the moderns which have been written under different circumstances indeed, but still upon this supposed principle: such, I mean, as under the existence of monarchy have taken their subject from kings and courts. From the existing reality they dare not draw, for nothing is less suitable for tragedy than a court and a court life. Wherever, therefore, they do not paint an ideal kingdom, with the manners of some remote age, they invariably fall into stiffness and formality, which are much more fatal to boldness of character, and to depth of pathos, than the monotonous and equable relations of private life.

[…]

We must, however, principally explain the prolific capability of mythology, for the purposes of tragedy, by the principle which we observe in operation throughout the history of Grecian mind and art; that, namely, the tendency which predominated for the time, assimilated everything else to itself. As the heroic legend with all its manifold discrepancies was easily developed into the tranquil fulness and light variety of epic poetry, so afterwards it readily responded to the demands which the tragic writers made upon it for earnestness, energy, and compression; and whatever in this sifting process of transformation fell out as inapplicable to tragedy, afforded materials for a sort of half sportive, though still ideal representation, in the subordinate species called the *satirical drama*.

I hope I shall be forgiven, if I attempt to illustrate the above reflections on the essence of Ancient Tragedy, by a comparison borrowed from the plastic arts, which will, I trust, be found somewhat more than a mere fanciful resemblance.

The Homeric epic is, in poetry, what bas-relief is in sculpture, and tragedy the distinct isolated group.[18]

The poetry of Homer, sprung from the soil of legend, is not yet wholly detached from it, even as the figures of a bas-relief adhere to an extraneous backing of the original block. These figures are but slightly raised, and in the epic poem all is painted as past and remote. In bas-relief the figures are usually in profile, and in the epos[19] all are characterized in the simplest manner in relief; they are not grouped together, but follow one another; so Homer's heroes advance, one by one, in succession before us. It has been remarked that the *Iliad* is not definitively closed, but that we are left to suppose something both to precede and to follow it. The bas-relief is equally without limit, and may be continued *ad infinitum*, either from before or behind, on which account the ancients preferred for it such subjects as admitted of an indefinite extension, sacrificial processions, dances, and lines of combatants, &c. Hence they also exhibited bas-reliefs on curved surfaces, such as vases, or the frieze of a rotunda,[20] where, by the curvature, the two ends are withdrawn from our sight, and where, while we advance, one object appears as another disappears. Reading Homer is very much like such a circuit; the present object alone

---

[18]**epic … bas-relief, tragedy … isolated group:** Schlegel here opposes epic and tragedy by comparing them to two different kinds of classical structure. The former is associated with bas-relief, a type of carved work in which the figures, shown in profile, project just half of their true proportion from out of the surface on to which they are carved. Tragedy, on the other hand, is like a group of three-dimensional statues.

[19]**epos:** heroic narrative poems.

[20]**rotunda:** a circular building.

arresting our attention, we lose sight of that which precedes, and do not concern ourselves about what is to follow.

But in the distinct outstanding group, and in Tragedy, sculpture and poetry alike bring before our eyes an independent and definite whole. To distinguish it from natural reality, the former places it on a base as on an ideal ground, detaching from it as much as possible all foreign and accidental accessories, that the eye may rest wholly on the essential objects, the figures themselves. These figures the sculptor works out with their whole body and contour, and as he rejects the illusion of colours, announces by the solidity and uniformity of the mass in which they are constructed, a creation of no perishable existence, but endowed, with a higher power of endurance.

Beauty is the aim of sculpture, and repose is most advantageous for the display of beauty. Repose alone, therefore, is suitable to the single figure. But a number of figures can only be combined together into unity, *i.e., grouped* by an action. The group represents beauty in motion, and its aim is to combine both in the highest degree of perfection. This can be effected even while portraying the most violent bodily or mental anguish, if only the artist finds means so to temper the expression by some trait of manly resistance, calm grandeur, or inherent sweetness, that, with all the most moving truth, the lineaments of beauty shall yet be undefaced. The observation of Winckelmann on this subject is inimitable.[21] He says, that 'beauty with the ancients was the tongue on the balance of expression,' and in this sense the groups of Niobe and Laocoön are master-pieces; the one in the sublime and severe; the other in the studied and ornamental style.[22]

The comparison with ancient tragedy is the more apposite here, as we know that both Aeschylus and Sophocles produced a Niobe, and that Sophocles was also the author of a Laocoön.[23] In the group of the Laocoön the efforts of the body in enduring, and of the mind in resisting, are balanced in admirable equipoise. The children calling for help, tender objects of compassion, not of admiration, recall our eyes to the father, who seems to be in vain uplifting his eyes to the gods. The wreathed serpents represent to us that inevitable destiny which often involves all the parties of an action in one common ruin. And yet the beauty of proportion, the agreeable flow of the outline, are not lost in this violent struggle; and a representation, the most appalling to the senses, is yet managed with forbearance, while a mild breath of gracefulness is diffused over the whole.

In the group of Niobe there is the same perfect mixture of terror and pity. The upturned looks of the mother, and the mouth half open in supplication, seem yet to accuse the invisible wrath of heaven. The daughter, clinging in the agonies of death to the bosom of her mother, in her childish innocence has no fear but for herself: the innate impulse of self-preservation was never more tenderly and affectingly expressed. On the other hand, can there be a more

---

[21]**Winkelmann:** the German art historian Johann Joachim Winckelmann (1717–68). Schlegel's ensuing quotation is from Winckelmann's *Gerschichte der Kunst des Alterhums* (1764), book IV, chapter 3, para 5.

[22]**Groups of Niobe and Laocoön:** Winckelmann was enraptured by statues of the mythic figures of Niobe, prototypical proud, bereaved mother, and Laocoön, killed by the gods for breaking a vow of celibacy. For Winckelmann, the former was a figure of the female sublime whereas the latter represented a very different kind of heroic masculinity; Alex Potts, *Flesh and the Ideal: Winckelmann and the Origins of Art History* (New Haven and London: Yale University Press, 1994), 136.

[23]**Aeschylus ... Laocoön:** only fragments survive of Aeschylus's tragedy of *Niobe*; Sophocles is also reputed to have written a lost tragedy of Laocoön.

beautiful image of self-devoting, heroic magnanimity than Niobe, as she bends forward to receive, if possible, in her own body the deadly shaft? Pride and defiance dissolve in the depths of maternal love. The more than earthly dignity of the features are the less marred by the agony, as under the rapid accumulation of blow upon blow she seems, as in the deeply significant fable, already petrifying into the stony torpor. But before this figure, thus *twice* struck into stone, and yet so full of life and soul, – before this stony terminus of the limits of human endurance, the spectator melts into tears.

Amid all the agitating emotions which these groups give rise to, there is still a something in their aspect which attracts the mind and gives rise to manifold contemplation; so the ancient tragedy leads us forward to the highest reflections involved in the very sphere of things it sets before us – reflections on the nature and the inexplicable mystery of man's being.

Further reading

Joshua Billings, *Genealogy of the Tragic: Greek Tragedy and German Philosophy* (Princeton and Oxford: Princeton University Press, 2014).
Ralph W. Ewton, *The Literary Theories of August Wilhelm Schlegel* (The Hague and Paris: Mouton & Co., 1972).

4.2 CHARLES LAMB, 'ON THE TRAGEDIES OF SHAKESPEARE CONSIDERED WITH REFERENCE FOR THEIR FITNESS FOR STAGE REPRESENTATION' (1811)

Charles Lamb (1775–1834), English essayist and poet, was one of the foremost popularizers of Shakespeare's works in the nineteenth century. He co-authored, with his sister, Mary Lamb (1764–1847), the immensely popular *Tales from Shakespeare* (1807), a series of prose retellings of all of Shakespeare's plays. (Even though the work appeared under his name until the seventh edition of 1838, Charles wrote half of the preface and half a dozen tales while Mary completed the other 14 plays in the book.) The views on tragedy outlined in this essay on Shakespeare's tragedies – that Shakespearean tragedy is best read and that its performance is reductively or showily artificial – were first published in Leigh Hunt's quarterly magazine *The Reflector* in 1811. Lamb was not, however, anti-theatre or anti-performance; he was the author of four plays and more than half of his critical output was devoted to drama and the theatre. Rather, his view was part of a Romantic position which sought to elevate the imagination and vision above the senses (and especially sight); reading good tragedy quickened the imagination, whereas seeing it acted chained one to a merely sensory realm. While in marked contrast to views on Shakespearean tragedy espoused by A.W. Schlegel (4.1) and certainly a minority opinion in Shakespeare studies today, Lamb's opinion was echoed by contemporaries such as William Hazlitt (1778–1839) – see extract 4.3 – and Johann Wolfgang von Goethe (1749–1816) whose essay 'Shakespeare and No End!' (1815) advanced a similar opinion.

It may seem a paradox, but I cannot help being of opinion that the plays of Shakespeare are less calculated for performance on a stage than those of almost any other dramatist whatever. Their distinguished excellence is a reason that they should be so. There is so much in them, which comes not under the province of acting, with which eye, and tone, and gesture, have nothing to do.

The glory of the scenic art is to personate passion, and the turns of passion; and the more coarse and palpable the passion is, the more hold upon the eyes and ears of the spectators the performer obviously possesses. For this reason, scolding scenes, scenes where two persons talk themselves into a fit of fury, and then in a surprising manner talk themselves out of it again, have always been the most popular upon our stage. And the reason is plain, because the spectators are here most palpably appealed to, they are the proper judges in this war of words, they are the legitimate ring that should be formed round such 'intellectual prize-fighters.' Talking is the direct object of the imitation here. But in the best dramas, and in Shakespeare above all, how obvious it is, that the form of speaking, whether it be in soliloquy or dialogue, is only a medium, and often a highly artificial one, for putting the reader or spectator into possession of that knowledge of the inner structure and workings of mind in a character, which he could otherwise never have arrived at in that form of composition by any gift short of intuition. We do here as we do with novels written in the epistolary form. How many improprieties, perfect solecisms in letter-writing, do we put up with in *Clarissa*[24] and other books, for the sake of the delight which that form upon the whole gives us.

---

[24]***Clarissa***: Samuel Richardson's monumental tragic novel *Clarissa, or the History of a Young Lady* (1747–8).

But the practice of stage representation reduces everything to a controversy of elocution. … The character of Hamlet is perhaps that by which, since the days of Betterton,[25] a succession of popular performers have had the greatest ambition to distinguish themselves. The length of the part may be one of their reasons. But for the character itself, we find it in a play, and therefore we judge it a fit subject of dramatic representation. The play itself abounds in maxims and reflections beyond any other, and therefore we consider it as a proper vehicle or conveying moral instruction. But Hamlet himself – what does he suffer meanwhile by being dragged forth as a public schoolmaster, to give lectures to the crowd! Why, nine parts in ten of what Hamlet does, are transactions between himself and his moral sense, they are the effusions of his solitary musings, which he retires to holes and corners and the most sequestered parts of the palace to pour forth; or rather, they are the silent meditations with which his bosom is bursting, reduced to words for the sake of the reader, who must else remain ignorant of what is passing there. These profound sorrows, these light-and-noise-abhorring ruminations, which the tongue scare dares utter to deaf walls and chambers, how can they be represented by a gesticulating actor, who comes and mouths them out before an audience, making four hundred people his confidants at once? I say not that it is the fault of the actor so to do; he must pronounce them *ore rotundo*,[26] he must accompany them with his eye, he must insinuate them into his auditory by some trick of eye, tone, or gesture, or he fails. *He must be thinking all the while of his appearance, because he knows that all the while the spectators are judging of it.* And this is the way to represent the shy, negligent, retiring Hamlet.

It is true that there is no other mode of conveying a vast quantity of thought and feeling to a great portion of the audience, who otherwise would never learn it for themselves by reading, and the intellectual acquisition gained this way may, for aught I know, be inestimable; but I am not arguing that Hamlet should not be acted, but how much Hamlet is made another thing by being acted. I have heard much of the wonders which Garrick[27] performed in this part; but as I never saw him, I must have leave to doubt whether the representation of such a character came within the province of his art. Those who tell me of him, speak of his eye, of the magic of his eye, and of his commanding voice: physical properties, vastly desirable in an actor, and without which he can never insinuate meaning into an auditory, – but what have they to do with Hamlet? what have they to do with intellect? In fact, the things aimed at in theatrical representation, are to arrest the spectator's eye upon the form and the gesture, and so to gain a more favourable hearing to what is spoken: it is not what the character is, but how he looks; not what he says, but how he speaks it. I see no reason to think that if the play of Hamlet were written over again by some such writer as Banks or Lillo,[28] retaining the process of the story, but totally omitting all the poetry of it, all the divine features of Shakespeare,

---

[25]**Betterton:** Thomas Betterton (*c.*1635–1710), actor and theatre manager, one of the foremost English actors of the Restoration.

[26]***ore rotundo:*** sonorously enunciated, literally translated 'with round mouth'.

[27]**Garrick:** David Garrick (1717–79), actor, playwright, and theatre manager, commonly regarded as the foremost English actor of the eighteenth century and a great Shakespearean. Performance records show that he played the part of Hamlet at least ninety times.

[28]**Banks or Lillo:** John Banks (1652–1706), Restoration playwright especially famed for tragedies based on historical figures, such as *The Unhappy Favourite, or, The Earl of Essex* (1681) and *The Innocent Usurper: Or, the Death of the Lady Jane Gray* (1693); George Lillo (1691–1739), dramatist, whose second play, *The London Merchant* (1731), popularized English domestic tragedy. For Lillo see extract 3.2.

his stupendous intellect; and only taking care to give us enough of passionate dialogue, which Banks or Lillo were never at a loss to furnish; I see not how the effect could be much different upon an audience, nor how the actor has it in his power to represent Shakespeare to us differently from his representation of Banks or Lillo. Hamlet would still be a youthful accomplished prince, and must be gracefully personated; he might be puzzled in his mind, wavering in his conduct, seemingly cruel to Ophelia, he might see a ghost, and start at it, and address it kindly when he found it to be his father; all this in the poorest and most homely language of the servilest creeper after nature that ever consulted the palate of an audience; without troubling Shakespeare for the matter; and I see not but there would be room for all the power which an actor has, to display itself. All the passions and changes of passion might remain; for those are much less difficult to write or act than is thought; it is a trick easy to be attained, it is but rising or falling a note or two in the voice, a whisper with a significant foreboding look to announce its approach, and so contagious the counterfeit appearance of any emotion is, that let the words be what they will, the look and tone shall carry it off and make it pass for deep skill in the passions.

[…]

Some dim thing or other they [the audience] see, they see an actor personating a passion, of grief, or anger, for instance, and they recognize it as a copy of the usual external effects of such passions; or at least as being true to that symbol of the emotion which passes current at the theatre for it, for it is often no more than that: but of the grounds of the passion, its correspondence to a great or heroic nature, which is the only worthy object of tragedy, – that common auditors know anything of this, or can have any such notions dinned into them by the mere strength of an actor's lungs, – that apprehensions foreign to them should be thus infused into them by storm, I can neither believe, nor understand how it can be possible.

[…]

So to see Lear acted, – to see an old man tottering about the stage with a walking-stick, turned out of doors by his daughters in a rainy night, has nothing in it but what is painful and disgusting. We want to take him into shelter and relieve him. That is all the feeling which the acting of Lear ever produced in me. But the Lear of Shakespeare cannot be acted. The contemptible machinery by which they mimic the storm which he goes out in, is not more inadequate to represent the horrors of the real elements, than any actor can be to represent Lear: they might more easily propose to personate the Satan of Milton upon a stage, or one of Michael Angelo's terrible figures. The greatness of Lear is not in corporal dimension, but in intellectual: the explosions of his passion are terrible as a volcano: they are storms turning up and disclosing to the bottom that sea his mind, with all its vast riches. It is his mind which is laid bare. This case of flesh and blood seems too insignificant to be thought on; even as he himself neglects it. On the stage we see nothing but corporal infirmities and weakness, the impotence of rage; while we read it, we see not Lear, but we are Lear, – we are in his mind, we are sustained by a grandeur which baffles the malice of daughters and storms; in the aberrations of his reason, we discover a mighty irregular power of reasoning, immethodised from the ordinary purposes of life, but exerting its powers, as the wind blows where it listeth, at will upon the corruptions and abuses of mankind. What have looks, or tones, to do with that sublime identification of his age with that of the heavens themselves, when in his reproaches to them for conniving at the injustice of his children, he reminds them that 'they themselves are old?'[29] What gestures shall we appropriate to this? What has the voice or the eye to do with such things? But the play is beyond all art, as the tamperings with it show: it is too hard and stony; it must have love-scenes, and a happy ending. It is not enough that Cordelia is a daughter, she must shine as a lover too. Tate has put his hook in the nostrils of this Leviathan, for Garrick and his followers, the showmen of scene, to draw the mighty beast about more easily.[30] A happy ending! – as if the living martyrdom that Lear had gone through, – the flaying of his feelings alive, did not make a fair dismissal from the stage of life the only decorous thing for him. If he is to live and be happy after, if he could sustain this world's burden after, why all this pudder[31] and preparation, – why torment us with all this unnecessary sympathy? As if the childish pleasure of getting his gilt-robes and sceptre again could tempt him to act over again his misused station, – as if at his years, and with his experience, anything was left but to die.

[…]

I remember the last time I saw Macbeth played, the discrepancy I felt at the changes of garment which he varied, – the shiftings and re-shiftings, like a Romish priest at mass.[32] The luxury of stage improvements, and the importunity of the public eye, require this. The coronation robe of the Scottish monarch[33] was fairly a counterpart to that which our King wears when he goes to the Parliament-house, – just so full and cumbersome, and set out with ermine and pearls. And if things must be represented, I see not what to find fault with in this. But in reading, what robe are we conscious of? Some dim images of royalty – a crown and sceptre may float before our eyes, but who shall describe the fashion of it? Do we see in our mind's eye what Webb[34] or any other robe-maker could pattern? This is the inevitable consequence of imitating everything, to make all things natural. Whereas the reading of a tragedy is a fine abstraction. It presents to the fancy just so much of external appearances as to make us feel that we are among flesh and blood, while by far the greater and better part of our imagination is employed upon the thoughts and internal machinery of the character. But in acting, scenery, dress, the most contemptible things, call upon us to judge of their naturalness.

Perhaps it would be no bad similitude, to liken the pleasure which we take in seeing one of these fine plays acted, compared with that quiet delight which we find in the reading of it, to the different feelings with which a reviewer, and a man that is not a reviewer, reads a fine poem. The accursed critical habits, – the being called upon to judge and pronounce, must make it quite a different thing to the former. In seeing these plays acted, we are affected just as judges. When Hamlet compares the two pictures of Gertrude's first and second husband, who

---

[29]**'they themselves are old':** Shakespeare's Lear reminds his daughter Goneril 'if you yourselves are old, / Make it your cause'; Shakespeare, *King Lear*, 2.2.364–5.

[30]**Tate … Garrick:** Nahum Tate (*c*.1652–1715), Restoration playwright whose re-writing of Shakespeare *The History of King Lear* (1681) kept Cordelia alive and introduced a romantic plot in which she is happily married at the play's close. Tate's *Lear* was the most commonly performed version of the play throughout the eighteenth century. Lamb claims that Tate's revisions, as opposed to the Shakespearean original, enabled later generations of actors to showcase their talents above those of the playwright.

[31]**pudder:** fuss

[32]**Romish priest at mass:** Lamb appeals to his readers' Protestant prejudices by comparing Macbeth's costume to the vestments of a Roman Catholic priest.

[33]**the Scottish monarch:** Macbeth.

[34]**Webb:** William Webb, royal robe maker, who was responsible for much of the costuming at the coronation of George IV in 1821.

wants to see the pictures?[35] But in the acting, a miniature must be lugged out; which we know not to be the picture, but only to show finely a miniature may be represented. This shewing of everything, levels all things: it makes tricks, bows, and curtseys, of importance. Mrs. S.[36] never got more fame by anything than by the manner in which she dismisses the guests in the banquet-scene in *Macbeth*: it is as much remembered as any of her thrilling tones or impressive looks. But does such a trifle as this enter into the imaginations of the reader of that wild and wonderful scene? Does not the mind dismiss the feasters as rapidly as it can? Does it care about the gracefulness of the doing it? But by acting, and judging of acting, all these non-essentials are raised into an importance, injurious to the main interest of the play.

Further reading

John I. Ades, 'Charles Lamb, Shakespeare, and Early Nineteenth-Century Theater', *PMLA* 85, no. 3 (1970): 513–26.

Jonathan Bate, *Shakespeare and the English Romantic Imagination* (Oxford: Clarendon Press, 1989).

Roy Park, 'Lamb, Shakespeare, and the Stage', *Shakespeare Quarterly* 33, no. 2 (1982): 164–77.

---

[35]**Hamlet ... two pictures:** In Act 3, Scene 4 of Shakespeare's *Hamlet*, Hamlet asks Gertrude to compare the portrait of his dead father with that of his murderous stepfather Claudius.

[36]**Mrs S:** Sarah Siddons (1755–1831), renowned actor, most famous for her performance of Lady Macbeth. For George Henry Harlow's portrait of Siddons in this role in 1814 see https://www.bl.uk/collection-items/portrait-of-sarah-siddons-as-lady-macbeth-by-george-henry-harlow-1814.

4.3 WILLIAM HAZLITT, *CHARACTERS OF SHAKESPEARE'S PLAYS* (1817)

Characters of Shakespeare's Plays (1817) by William Hazlitt (1778–1830) – English Romantic critic, essayist, journalist, and painter – became a canonical work of nineteenth-century literary criticism. Hazlitt's views on the ethics of tragedy were indebted to those of August Wilhelm Schlegel – see extract 4.1 – a translation of whose *Lectures on Dramatic Art and Literature* (1809–11) he reviewed favourably in the *Edinburgh Review*. Hazlitt thought that tragedy was uniquely important in the way that it developed the imagination and the public capacity for sympathy. The 'imagination', he argued in his important *Essay on the Principles of Human Action* (1805), 'must carry me out of myself into the feelings of others'. Catharsis, became for Hazlitt, therefore, the purging of selfishness rather than involving any Aristotelian rebalancing of pity and fear. However, as revealed in his *Lectures on the Dramatic Literature of the Age of Elizabeth* (1820) he thought that capacity best cultivated by the reading rather than the performance of tragedy since when we read a work we internalize the tragic protagonist's struggle and 'feel that it has happened to ourselves' whereas performance can distract from or merely externalize tragic struggle.[37]

The object of the volume here offered to the public, is to illustrate these remarks in a more particular manner by a reference to each play. … The only work which seemed to supersede the necessity of an attempt like the present was Schlegel's very admirable *Lectures on the Drama*, which give by far the best account of the plays of Shakespeare that has hitherto appeared.[38] The only circumstances in which it was thought not impossible to improve on the manner in which the German critic has executed this part of his design, were in avoiding an appearance of mysticism in his style, not very attractive to the English reader, and in bringing illustrations from particular passages of the plays themselves, of which Schlegel's work, from the extensiveness of his plan, did not admit. We will at the same time confess, that some little jealousy of the character of the national understanding was not without its share in producing the following undertaking, for 'we were piqued' that it should be reserved for a foreign critic to give 'reasons for the faith which we English have in Shakespeare'. Certainly, no writer among ourselves has shown either the same enthusiastic admiration of his genius, or the same philosophical acuteness in pointing out his characteristic excellences.

[…]

OTHELLO

It has been said that tragedy purifies the affections by terror and pity. That is, it substitutes imaginary sympathy for mere selfishness. It gives us a high and permanent interest, beyond

---

[37] *The Complete Works of William Hazlitt*, ed. P.P. Howe (London: J.M. Dent, 1931), 6:247.

[38] **Schlegel's … Lectures on the Drama**: August Wilhelm Schlegel (1767–1845), German academic, translator. His *Course of Lectures on Dramatic Art and Literature* (1809–11) – see extract 4.1 – offered one of the most well-known theories of tragedy in the nineteenth century. Even though he disliked some of Schlegel's abstractions – dismissed here as 'mysticism' – Hazlitt was, along with Samuel Taylor Coleridge, instrumental in extending Schlegel's influence in England in the early nineteenth century.

ourselves, in humanity as such. It raises the great, the remote, and the possible to an equality with the real, the little and the near. It makes man a partaker with his kind. It subdues and softens the stubbornness of his will. It teaches him that there are and have been others like himself, by showing him as in a glass what they have felt, thought, and done. It opens the chambers of the human heart. It leaves nothing indifferent to us that can affect our common nature. It excites our sensibility by exhibiting the passions wound up to the utmost pitch by the power of imagination or the temptation of circumstances; and corrects their fatal excesses in ourselves by pointing to the greater extent of sufferings and of crimes to which they have led others. Tragedy creates a balance of the affections. It makes us thoughtful spectators in the lists of life. It is the refiner of the species; a discipline of humanity. The habitual study of poetry and works of imagination is one chief part of a well-grounded education. A taste for liberal art is necessary to complete the character of a gentleman, Science alone is hard and mechanical. It exercises the understanding upon things out of ourselves, while it leaves the affections unemployed, or engrossed with our own immediate, narrow interests. – *Othello* furnishes an illustration of these remarks. It excites our sympathy in an extraordinary degree. The moral it conveys has a closer application to the concerns of human life than that of any other of Shakespeare's plays. 'It comes directly home to the bosoms and business of men.'[39] The pathos in *Lear* is indeed more dreadful and overpowering: but it is less natural, and less of every day's occurrence. We have not the same degree of sympathy with the passions described in *Macbeth*. The interest in *Hamlet* is more remote and reflex. That of *Othello* is at once equally profound and affecting.

[…]

The movement of the passion in *Othello* is exceedingly different from that of *Macbeth*. In *Macbeth* there is a violent struggle between opposite feelings, between ambition and the stings of conscience, almost from first to last: in *Othello*, the doubtful conflict between contrary passions, though dreadful, continues only for a short time, and the chief interest is excited by the alternate ascendancy of different passions, the entire and unforeseen change from the fondest love and most unbounded confidence to the tortures of jealousy and the madness of hatred. The revenge of Othello, after it has once taken thorough possession of his mind, never quits it, but grows stronger and stronger at every moment of its delay. The nature of the Moor is noble, confiding, tender, and generous; but his blood is of the most inflammable kind; and being once roused by a sense of his wrongs, he is stopped by no considerations of remorse or pity till he has given a loose to all the dictates of his rage and his despair. It is in working his noble nature up to this extremity through rapid but gradual transitions, in raising passion to its height from the smallest beginnings and in spite of all obstacles, in painting the expiring conflict between love and hatred, tenderness and resentment, jealousy and remorse, in unfolding the strength and the weaknesses of our nature, in uniting sublimity of thought with the anguish of the keenest woe, in putting in motion the various impulses that agitate this our mortal being, and at last blending them in that noble tide of deep and sustained passion, impetuous but majestic, that 'flows on to the Propontic, and knows no ebb',[40] that

---

[39]**bosoms and business of men:** a rephrasing of Francis Bacon's 'it seems they came near to Mens Businesse and Bosomes' when referring to the popularity of his *Essays* in 1625; Francis Bacon, *The Essayes* (London, 1625), sig. A3v.
[40]**'flows on to the Propontic and knows no ebb':** the Propontic is the Sea of Marmara, between the Black Sea and the Aegean sea. The 'quotation' is an echo of Othello's reflections on his restless mind which he likens to a sea 'whose icy current and compulsive course / Ne'er feels retiring ebb, but keeps due on / To the Propontic'; Shakespeare, *Othello*, 3.4.457–9.

Shakespeare has shown the mastery of his genius and of his power over the human heart. The third act of *Othello* is his masterpiece, not of knowledge or passion separately, but of the two combined, of the knowledge of character with the expression of passion, of consummate art in the keeping up of appearances with the profound workings of nature, and the convulsive movements of uncontrollable agony, of the power of inflicting torture and of suffering it. Not only is the tumult of passion heaved up from the very bottom of the soul, but every the slightest undulation of feeling is seen on the surface, as it arises from the impulses of imagination or the different probabilities maliciously suggested by Iago. The progressive preparation for the catastrophe is wonderfully managed from the Moor's first gallant recital of the story of his love, of 'the spells and witchcraft he had used',[41] from his unlooked-for and romantic success, the fond satisfaction with which he dotes on his own happiness, the unreserved tenderness of Desdemona and her innocent importunities in favour of Cassio, irritating the suspicions instilled into her husband's mind by the perfidy of Iago, and rankling there to poison, till he loses all command of himself, and his rage can only be appeased by blood.

[…]

LEAR

It has been said, and we think justly, that the third act of *Othello*, and the three first acts of *Lear*, are Shakespeare's great masterpieces in the logic of passion: that they contain the highest examples not only of the force of individual passion, but of its dramatic vicissitudes and striking effects arising from the different circumstances and characters of the persons speaking. We see the ebb and flow of the feeling, its pauses and feverish starts, its impatience of opposition, its accumulating force when it has time to recollect itself, the manner in which it avails itself of every passing word or gesture, its haste to repel insinuation, the alternate contraction and dilatation of the soul, and all 'the dazzling fence of controversy'[42] in this mortal combat with poisoned weapons, aimed at the heart, where each wound is fatal. We have seen in *Othello*, how the unsuspecting frankness and impetuous passions of the Moor are played upon and exasperated by the artful dexterity of Iago. In the present play, that which aggravates the sense of sympathy in the reader, and of uncontrollable anguish in the swollen heart of Lear, is the petrifying indifference, the cold, calculating, obdurate selfishness of his daughters. His keen passions seem whetted on their stony hearts. The contrast would be too painful, the shock too great, but for the intervention of the Fool, whose well-timed levity comes in to break the continuity of feeling when it can no longer be borne, and to bring into play again the fibres of the heart just as they are growing rigid from over-strained excitement. The imagination is glad to take refuge in the half-comic, half-serious comments of the Fool, just as the mind under the extreme anguish of a surgical operation vents itself in sallies of wit. The character was also a grotesque ornament of the barbarous times, in which alone the tragic ground-work of the story could be laid. In another point of view it is indispensable, inasmuch as while it is a diversion to the too great intensity of our disgust, it carries the pathos to the highest pitch of which it

---

[41]'**spells and witchcraft he had used**': another 'quotation' which merely echoes the conclusion to Othello's speech relating the stories he used to woo Desdemona; 'This only is the witchcraft I have used'; Shakespeare, *Othello*, 1.3.170.
[42]'**dazzling fence of controversy**': a paraphrase rather than a quotation from John Milton's *Masque Presented at Ludlow Castle* (1634) where the Lady describes the combative nature of Comus's seductive rhetoric as 'dazzling fence'; *John Milton: The Complete Shorter Poems* ed. John Carey (Harlow: Pearson Education, 2007), 220.

is capable, by showing the pitiable weakness of the old king's conduct and its irretrievable consequences in the most familiar point of view. Lear may well 'beat at the gate which let his folly in',[43] after, as the Fool says, 'he has made his daughters his mothers'.[44] The character is dropped in the third act to make room for the entrance of Edgar as Mad Tom, which well accords with the increasing bustle and wildness of the incidents; and nothing can be more complete than the distinction between Lear's real and Edgar's assumed madness, while the resemblance in the cause of their distresses, from the severing of the nearest ties of natural affection, keeps up a unity of interest. Shakespeare's mastery over his subject, if it was not art, was owing to a knowledge of the connecting links of the passions, and their effect upon the mind, still more wonderful than any systematic adherence to rules, and that anticipated and outdid all the efforts of the most refined art, not inspired and rendered instinctive by genius.

Four things have struck us in reading *Lear*:

1. That poetry is an interesting study, for this reason, that it relates to whatever is most interesting in human life. Whoever therefore has a contempt for poetry, has a contempt for himself and humanity.

2. That the language of poetry is superior to the language of painting; because the strongest of our recollections relate to feelings, not to faces.

3. That the greatest strength of genius is shown in describing the strongest passions: for the power of the imagination, in works of invention, must be in proportion to the force of the natural impressions, which are the subject of them.

4. That the circumstance which balances the pleasure against the pain in tragedy is, that in proportion to the greatness of the evil, is our sense and desire of the opposite good excited; and that our sympathy with actual suffering is lost in the strong impulse given to our natural affections, and carried away with the swelling tide of passion, that gushes from and relieves the heart.

Further reading

Janet Ruth Heller, *Coleridge, Lamb, Hazlitt, and the Reader of Drama* (Columbia: University of Missouri Press, 1990).

Uttara Natarajan, *Hazlitt and the Reach of Sense: Criticism, Morals and the Metaphysics of Power* (Oxford: Oxford University Press, 1998).

E.W. Schneider, *The Aesthetics of William Hazlitt: A Study of the Philosophical Basis of His Criticism* (Philadelphia: University of Pennsylvania Press, 1933).

---

[43]**'beat at the gate which let his folly in':** when Lear begins to realize that Goneril and Regan may not have his interests at heart, he strikes his head and cries: 'Beat at this gate that let thy folly in and thy judgment out'; *King Lear*, 1.4.270–2.
[44]**made his daughters his mothers':** echoing the Fool's observation 'ever since thou madest thy daughters thy mothers'; *King Lear*, 1.4.153–4.

4.4 ARTHUR SCHOPENHAUER, *THE WORLD AS WILL AND REPRESENTATION* (1819)

Arthur Schopenhauer (1788–1860) was a German philosopher whose magnum opus *The World as Will and Representation* (sometimes translated as *The World as Will and Idea*) first appeared in 1819, with a greatly expanded second edition in 1844. Schopenhauer's philosophy was profoundly pessimistic in outlook; he defined the essence of the universe, an essence which is objectified in everything around us as well as in the more abstract Ideas that underpin reality, as Will. However, unlike German Idealists such as Georg Wilhelm Friedrich Hegel (see extract 4.6), Schopenhauer saw nothing benign, coherent, designed, or rational in the supreme principle of universe. Rather, Will is directionless, irrational, motiveless, all of which is revealed in the conflict and misery of existence. All art is important within this world view because it provides fleeting escape from the suffering of life, but tragedy is especially prized because it encourages tranquillity of mind by showing (rather than concealing or sublimating) 'the terrible side of life', thus enabling us to reflect upon and compose ourselves in the face of our knowledge of suffering in the world.

In the more objective kinds of poetry, especially in the romance, the epic, and the drama, the end, the revelation of the Idea of man,[45] is principally attained by two means, by true and profound representation of significant characters, and by the invention of pregnant situations in which they disclose themselves. For as it is incumbent upon the chemist not only to exhibit the simple elements, pure and genuine, and their principal compounds, but also to expose them to the influence of such reagents[46] as will clearly and strikingly bring out their peculiar qualities, so is it incumbent on the poet not only to present to us significant characters truly and faithfully as nature itself; but, in order that we may get to know them, he must place them in those situations in which their peculiar qualities will fully unfold themselves, and appear distinctly in sharp outline; situations which are therefore called significant. In real life, and in history, situations of this kind are rarely brought about by chance, and they stand alone, lost and concealed in the multitude of those which are insignificant. The complete significance of the situations ought to distinguish the romance, the epic, and the drama from real life as completely as the arrangement and selection of significant characters. In both, however, absolute truth is a necessary condition of their effect, and want of unity in the characters, contradiction either of themselves or of the nature of humanity in general, as well as impossibility, or very great improbability in the events, even in mere accessories, offend just as much in poetry as badly drawn figures, false perspective, or wrong lighting in painting. For both in poetry and painting we demand the faithful mirror of life, of man, of the world, only made more clear by the representation, and more significant by the arrangement.

For there is only one end of all the arts, the representation of the Ideas; and their essential difference lies simply in the different grades of the objectification of will to which the Ideas

---

[45]**Idea of man:** an abstract, timeless essence or pattern of what it is to be human, which lies behind every human being.
[46]**reagents:** substances or compounds used to cause or test for chemical reactions.

that are to be represented belong.[47] This also determines the material of the representation. Thus the arts which are most widely separated may yet throw light on each other. For example, in order to comprehend fully the Ideas of water it is not sufficient to see it in the quiet pond or in the evenly-flowing stream; but these Ideas disclose themselves fully only when the water appears under all circumstances and exposed to all kinds of obstacles. The effects of the varied circumstances and obstacles give it the opportunity of fully exhibiting all its qualities. This is why we find it beautiful when it tumbles, rushes, and foams, or leaps into the air, or falls in a cataract of spray; or, lastly, if artificially confined it springs up in a fountain. Thus showing itself different under different circumstances, it yet always faithfully asserts its character; it is just as natural to it to spout up as to lie in glassy stillness; it is as ready for the one as for the other as soon as the circumstances appear. Now, what the engineer achieves with the fluid matter of water, the architect achieves with the rigid matter of stone, and just this the epic or dramatic poet achieves with the Idea of man. Unfolding and rendering distinct the Idea expressing itself in the object of every art, the Idea of the will which objectifies itself at each grade, is the common end of all the arts. The life of man, as it shows itself for the most part in the real world, is like the water, as it is generally seen in the pond and the river; but in the epic, the romance, the tragedy, selected characters are placed in those circumstances in which all their special qualities unfold themselves, the depths of the human heart are revealed, and become visible in extraordinary and very significant actions. Thus poetry objectifies the Idea of man, an Idea which has the peculiarity of expressing itself in highly individual characters.

Tragedy is to be regarded, and is recognized as the summit of poetical art, both on account of the greatness of its effect and the difficulty of its achievement. It is very significant for our whole system, and well worthy of observation, that the end of this highest poetical achievement is the representation of the terrible side of life. The unspeakable pain, the wail of humanity, the triumph of evil, the scornful mastery of chance, and the irretrievable fall of the just and innocent, is here presented to us; and in this lies a significant hint of the nature of the world and of existence. It is the strife of will with itself, which here, completely unfolded at the highest grade of its objectivity, comes into fearful prominence. It becomes visible in the suffering of men, which is now introduced, partly through chance and error, which appear as the rulers of the world, personified as fate, on account of their insidiousness, which even reaches the appearance of design; partly it proceeds from man himself, through the self-mortifying efforts of a few, through the wickedness and perversity of most. It is one and the same will that lives and appears in them all,[48] but whose phenomena fight against each other and destroy each other. In one individual it appears powerfully, in another more weakly; in one more subject to reason, and softened by the light of knowledge, in another less so, till at last, in some single case, this knowledge, purified and heightened by suffering itself, reaches the point at which the phenomenon, the veil of Mâya,[49] no longer deceives it. It sees through the form of the phenomenon, the *principium individuationis*.[50] The egoism which rests on this perishes with

---

[47]**objectification of will ... belong:** the translation of Will, for Schopenhauer the essence of the universe, into different objects of perception.

[48]**will that lives and appears in them all:** all characters, whether good or bad, are objectifications of will – the essence of the universe – in Schopenhauer's scheme.

[49]**veil of Mâya:** veil of illusion, from the Sanskrit word 'maya' for 'illusion' or 'unreality'.

[50]***principium individuationis:*** the principle of individuation, that which distinguishes one thing or being from another.

it, so that now the *motives* that were so powerful before have lost their might, and instead of them the complete knowledge of the nature of the world, which has a *quieting* effect on the will, produces resignation, the surrender not merely of life, but of the very will to live. Thus we see in tragedies the noblest men, after long conflict and suffering, at last renounce the ends they have so keenly followed, and all the pleasures of life for ever, or else freely and joyfully surrender life itself. So is it with the steadfast prince of Calderón;[51] with Gretchen in *Faust*;[52] with Hamlet, whom his friend Horatio would willingly follow, but is bade remain a while, and in this harsh world draw his breath in pain, to tell the story of Hamlet, and clear his memory; so also is it with the Maid of Orleans, the Bride of Messina;[53] they all die purified by suffering, *i.e.*, after the will to live which was formerly in them is dead. In the *Mohammed* of Voltaire[54] this is actually expressed in the concluding words which the dying Palmira addresses to Mohammad: 'The world is for tyrants: live!'[55] On the other hand, the demand for so-called poetical justice rests on entire misconception of the nature of tragedy, and, indeed, of the nature of the world itself. It boldly appears in all its dullness in the criticisms which Dr. Samuel Johnson made on particular plays of Shakespeare, for he very naïvely laments its entire absence.[56] And its absence is certainly obvious, for in what has Ophelia, Desdemona, or Cordelia offended?[57] But only the dull, optimistic, Protestant-rationalistic, or peculiarly Jewish view of life will make the demand for poetical justice, and find satisfaction in it. The true sense of tragedy is the deeper insight, that it is not his own individual sins that the hero atones for, but original sin, *i.e.*, the crime of existence itself:

'Pues el delito mayor
Del hombre es haber nacido;'
('For the greatest crime of man
Is that he was born;')

as Calderón exactly expresses it.[58]

I shall allow myself only one remark, more closely concerning the treatment of tragedy. The representation of a great misfortune is alone essential to tragedy. But the many different ways in which this is introduced by the poet may be brought under three specific conceptions. It may happen by means of a character of extraordinary wickedness, touching the utmost limits

---

[51]**steadfast prince of Calderón:** Prince Fernando of Portugal, the protagonist of Pedro Calderón de la Barca's tragedy *El Principe Constante* [The Steadfast Prince] (*c.*1629).

[52]**Gretchen in *Faust*:** Gretchen, or Margarete, is seduced and abandoned by Faust in the first part of Johann Wolfgang von Goethe's tragedy *Faust* (1808).

[53]**the Maid of Orleans, the Bride of Messina:** tragic protagonists in Friedrich Schiller's *The Maid of Orleans* (1801) and *The Bride of Messina* (1803).

[54]***Mohammed* of Voltaire:** a reference to Voltaire's tragedy *Fanaticism, or Mahomet the Prophet* (1741).

[55]**Palmira ... live!:** just before her death in the final moments of Voltaire's *Fanaticism or Mahomet*, Mahomet's slave, Palmira, stabs herself, embracing death while denouncing Mahomet as a tyrant.

[56]**Dr. Samuel Johnson ... absence:** Samuel Johnson (1709–84), English critic, essayist, and lexicographer. He was more ambivalent on the question of poetic justice than Schopenhauer allows here. See extract 3.7.

[57]**Ophelia ... Cordelia:** the tragic heroines of, respectively, William Shakespeare's *Hamlet* (1601), *Othello* (1604) and *King Lear* (1605).

[58]**as Calderón exactly expresses it:** the quotation is spoken by the Polish prince Segismundo in the first act of Calderón's tragedy *La vida es sueño* [Life is a Dream] (1635).

of possibility, who becomes the author of the misfortune; examples of this kind are Richard III., Iago in *Othello*, Shylock in *The Merchant of Venice*, Franz Moor,[59] Phædra of Euripides, Creon in the *Antigone*, &c., &c. Secondly, it may happen through blind fate, *i.e.*, chance and error; a true pattern of this kind is the *Œdipus Rex* of Sophocles, the *Trachiniæ*[60] also; and in general most of the tragedies of the ancients belong to this class. Among modern tragedies, *Romeo and Juliet*, *Tancred* by Voltaire, and *The Bride of Messina*, are examples. Lastly, the misfortune may be brought about by the mere position of the *dramatis personæ* with regard to each other, through their relations; so that there is no need either for a tremendous error or an unheard-of accident, nor yet for a character whose wickedness reaches the limits of human possibility; but characters of ordinary morality, under circumstances such as often occur, are so situated with regard to each other that their position compels them, knowingly and with their eyes open, to do each other the greatest injury, without any one of them being entirely in the wrong. This last kind of tragedy seems to me far to surpass the other two, for it shows us the greatest misfortune, not as an exception, not as something occasioned by rare circumstances or monstrous characters, but as arising easily and of itself out of the actions and characters of men, indeed almost as essential to them, and thus brings it terribly near to us. In the other two kinds we may look on the prodigious fate and the horrible wickedness as terrible powers which certainly threaten us, but only from afar, which we may very well escape without taking refuge in renunciation. But in the last kind of tragedy we see that those powers which destroy happiness and life are such that their path to us also is open at every moment; we see the greatest sufferings brought about by entanglements that our fate might also partake of, and through actions that perhaps we also are capable of performing, and so could not complain of injustice; then shuddering we feel ourselves already in the midst of hell. This last kind of tragedy is also the most difficult of achievement; for the greatest effect has to be produced in it with the least use of means and causes of movement, merely through the position and distribution of the characters; therefore even in many of the best tragedies this difficulty is evaded. Yet one tragedy may be referred to as a perfect model of this kind, a tragedy which in other respects is far surpassed by more than one work of the same great master; it is *Clavigo*.[61] *Hamlet* belongs to a certain extent to this class, as far as the relation of Hamlet to Laertes and Ophelia is concerned. *Wallenstein*[62] has also this excellence. *Faust* belongs entirely to this class, if we regard the events connected with Gretchen and her brother as the principal action; also the *Cid* of Corneille,[63] only that it lacks the tragic conclusion, while on the contrary the analogous relation of Max to Thecla has it.[64]

[...]

The life of every individual, if we survey it as a whole and in general, and only lay stress upon its most significant features, is really always a tragedy, but gone through in detail, it has the character of a comedy. For the deeds and vexations of the day, the restless irritation of the

---

[59]**Franz Moor:** the villain of Friedrich Schiller's tragedy *The Robbers* (1781).

[60]*Trachiniæ*: *The Women of Trachis* (*c.*450–420 BCE), a tragedy by Sophocles. The unmarried women of Trachis are the Chorus in the play.

[61]*Clavigo*: the title of a 1774 tragedy by Johann Wolfgang von Goethe.

[62]*Wallenstein*: historical trilogy about the Thirty Years' War by Friedrich Schiller, performed in 1798–9.

[63]**The *Cid* of Corneille:** Pierre Corneille (1606–84) was one of the foremost dramatists of seventeenth-century Europe; one of his most famous tragedies was *Le Cid* (1636–7).

[64]**Max to Thecla:** Max and Thekla are tragic lovers in Schiller's *Wallenstein*.

moment, the desires and fears of the week, the mishaps of every hour, are all through chance, which is ever bent upon some jest, scenes of a comedy. But the never-satisfied wishes, the frustrated efforts, the hopes unmercifully crushed by fate, the unfortunate errors of the whole life, with increasing suffering and death at the end, are always a tragedy. Thus, as if fate would add derision to the misery of our existence, our life must contain all the woes of tragedy, and yet we cannot even assert the dignity of tragic characters, but in the broad detail of life must inevitably be the foolish characters of a comedy.

Further reading

Christopher Janaway, 'Knowledge and Tranquility: Schopenhauer on the Value of Art', in *Schopenhauer, Philosophy and the Arts*, ed. Dale Jacquette (Cambridge: Cambridge University Press, 1996).

Alex Neill, 'Schopenhauer on Tragedy and the Sublime', in *A Companion to Schopenhauer*, ed. Bart Vandenabeele (Oxford: Wiley-Blackwell, 2012), 206–18.

Dylan Trigg, 'Schopenhauer and the Sublime Pleasure of Tragedy', *Philosophy and Literature* 28, no. 1 (2004): 165–79.

4.5 PERCY BYSSHE SHELLEY, *A DEFENCE OF POETRY* (1821)

Percy Bysshe Shelley (1792–1822) was one of the foremost English Romantic poets. *A Defence of Poetry* (1821) was a response to Thomas Love Peacock's satirical essay 'The Four Ages of Poetry' (1820) which claimed that poetry's importance had been overtaken by science. Shelley's short career was marked what Michael Rossington has termed a 'compulsive absorption in Athenian drama', a determination to ensure that the classical standards of Greek theatre continued to be respected in the early nineteenth century; he is thought to have been travelling with his pocket copies of Aeschylus and Sophocles when he drowned on board his sailing boat, the Don Juan, in the Gulf of Spezia in July 1822.[65] Shelley's idea of tragedy, drawn from his understanding of ancient Greek theatre, emerged from his reading of A.W. Schlegel's treatment of moral freedom in tragedy – see extract 4.1 – which he developed into his own Romantic theory of poetry and the imagination. The tragedies of antiquity, as well as those of Shakespeare, Shelley argued, avoided all didacticism; but because of that, like good poetry, they were instrumental in expanding the imagination, and, in turn, enhanced our capacity for sympathy and understanding.

According to one mode of regarding those two classes of mental action, which are called reason and imagination, the former may be considered as mind contemplating the relations borne by one thought to another, however produced, and the latter, as mind acting upon those thoughts so as to color them with its own light, and composing from them, as from elements, other thoughts, each containing within itself the principle of its own integrity. ... Reason is the enumeration of qualities already known; imagination is the perception of the value of those qualities, both separately and as a whole. Reason respects the differences, and imagination the similitudes of things. Reason is to imagination as the instrument to the agent, as the body to the spirit, as the shadow to the substance.

Poetry, in a general sense, may be defined to be 'the expression of the imagination': and poetry is connate with[66] the origin of man. Man is an instrument over which a series of external and internal impressions are driven, like the alternations of an ever-changing wind over an Æolian lyre,[67] which move it by their motion to ever-changing melody.

[...]

[P]oetry acts in another and diviner manner. It awakens and enlarges the mind itself by rendering it the receptacle of a thousand unapprehended combinations of thought. Poetry lifts the veil from the hidden beauty of the world, and makes familiar objects be as if they were not familiar; it reproduces all that it represents, and the impersonations clothed in its Elysian light[68] stand thenceforward in the minds of those who have once contemplated them, as memorials of that gentle and exalted content which extends itself over all thoughts and actions with which it

---

[65]Michael Rossington, 'Tragedy: *The Cenci* and *Swellfoot the Tyrant*', in *The Oxford Handbook of Percy Bysshe Shelley*, ed. Michael O'Neill, Anthony Howe and Madeleine Callaghan (Oxford: Oxford University Press, 2013), 303; http://shelleysghost.bodleian.ox.ac.uk/edition-of-sophocles.

[66]**connate with:** born together with; twinned.

[67]**Æolian lyre:** wind harp, named after Aeolus, ancient Greek god of the wind.

[68]**Elysian light:** heavenly light; in Greek mythology Elysium was where the blessed went after death.

coexists. The great secret of morals is love; or a going out of our nature, and an identification of ourselves with the beautiful which exists in thought, action, or person, not our own. A man, to be greatly good, must imagine intensely and comprehensively; he must put himself in the place of another and of many others; the pains and pleasure of his species must become his own. The great instrument of moral good is the imagination; and poetry administers to the effect by acting upon the cause. Poetry enlarges the circumference of the imagination by replenishing it with thoughts of ever new delight, which have the power of attracting and assimilating to their own nature all other thoughts, and which form new intervals and interstices whose void forever craves fresh food. Poetry strengthens the faculty which is the organ of the moral nature of man, in the same manner as exercise strengthens a limb. A poet therefore would do ill to embody his own conceptions of right and wrong, which are usually those of his place and time, in his poetical creations, which participate in neither. By this assumption of the inferior office of interpreting the effect, in which perhaps after all he might acquit himself but imperfectly, he would resign a glory in a participation in the cause. There was little danger that Homer, or any of the eternal poets, should have so far misunderstood themselves as to have abdicated this throne of their widest dominion. ...

Homer and the cyclic poets[69] were followed at a certain interval by the dramatic and lyrical poets of Athens, who flourished contemporaneously with all that is most perfect in the kindred expressions of the poetical faculty; architecture, painting, music, the dance, sculpture, philosophy, and, we may add, the forms of civil life. For although the scheme of Athenian society was deformed by many imperfections which the poetry existing in chivalry and Christianity has erased from the habits and institutions of modern Europe; yet never at any other period has so much energy, beauty, and virtue been developed; never was blind strength and stubborn form so disciplined and rendered subject to the will of man, or that will less repugnant to the dictates of the beautiful and the true, as during the century which preceded the death of Socrates. Of no other epoch in the history of our species have we records and fragments stamped so visibly with the image of the divinity in man. But it is poetry alone, in form, in action, or in language, which has rendered this epoch memorable above all others, and the store-house of examples to everlasting time. For written poetry existed at that epoch simultaneously with the other arts, and it is an idle inquiry to demand which gave and which received the light, which all, as from a common focus, have scattered over the darkest periods of succeeding time. We know no more of cause and effect than a constant conjunction of events: poetry is ever found to coexist with whatever other arts contribute to the happiness and perfection of man. I appeal to what has already been established to distinguish between the cause and the effect.

It was at the period here adverted to that the drama had its birth; and however a succeeding writer may have equalled or surpassed those few great specimens of the Athenian drama which have been preserved to us, it is indisputable that the art itself never was understood or practised according to the true philosophy of it, as at Athens. For the Athenians employed language, action, music, painting, the dance, and religious institutions, to produce a common effect in the representation of the highest idealisms of passion and of power; each division in the art was made perfect in its kind by artists of the most consummate skill, and was

---

[69]**cyclic poets:** early Greek epic poets.

disciplined into a beautiful proportion and unity one towards the other. On the modern stage a few only of the elements capable of expressing the image of the poet's conception are employed at once. We have tragedy without music and dancing; and music and dancing without the highest impersonations of which they are the fit accompaniment, and both without religion and solemnity. Religious institution has indeed been usually banished from the stage. Our system of divesting the actor's face of a mask, on which the many expressions appropriated to his dramatic character might be moulded into one permanent and unchanging expression, is favourable only to a partial and inharmonious effect; it is fit for nothing but a monologue, where all the attention may be directed to some great master of ideal mimicry. The modern practice of blending comedy with tragedy, though liable to great abuse in point of practice, is undoubtedly an extension of the dramatic circle; but the comedy should be as in *King Lear*, universal, ideal, and sublime. It is perhaps the intervention of this principle which determines the balance in favour of *King Lear* against the *Oedipus Tyrannus* or the *Agamemnon*, or, if you will, the trilogies with which they are connected;[70] unless the intense power of the choral poetry, especially that of the latter, should be considered as restoring the equilibrium. *King Lear*, if it can sustain this comparison, may be judged to be the most perfect specimen of the dramatic art existing in the world; in spite of the narrow conditions to which the poet was subjected by the ignorance of the philosophy of the drama which has prevailed in modern Europe. Calderon, in his religious *autos*,[71] has attempted to fulfil some of the high conditions of dramatic representation neglected by Shakespeare; such as the establishing a relation between the drama and religion and the accommodating them to music and dancing; but he omits the observation of conditions still more important, and more is lost than gained by the substitution of the rigidly-defined and ever-repeated idealisms of a distorted superstition for the living impersonations of the truth of human passions.

[...]

The drama at Athens, or wheresoever else it may have approached to its perfection, ever co-existed with the moral and intellectual greatness of the age. The tragedies of the Athenian poets are as mirrors in which the spectator beholds himself, under a thin disguise of circumstance, stript of all but that ideal perfection and energy which every one feels to be the internal type of all that he loves, admires, and would become. The imagination is enlarged by a sympathy with pains and passions so mighty, that they distend in their conception the capacity of that by which they are conceived; the good affections are strengthened by pity, indignation, terror, and sorrow; and an exalted calm is prolonged from the satiety of this high exercise of them into the tumult of familiar life: even crime is disarmed of half its horror and all its contagion by being represented as the fatal consequence of the unfathomable agencies of nature; error is thus divested of its wilfulness; men can no longer cherish it as the creation of their choice. In a drama of the highest order there is little food for censure or hatred; it teaches rather self-knowledge and self-respect. Neither the eye nor the mind can see itself, unless reflected upon that which it resembles. The drama, so long as it continues to express poetry, is as a prismatic and many-sided mirror, which collects the brightest rays of human nature and divides and

---

[70]**trilogies … connected:** Sophocles wrote three Theban plays: *Antigone, Oedipus the King* and *Oedipus at Colonus; Agamemnon, The Libation Bearers* and *The Eumenides* are the three plays in *The Oresteia* by Aeschylus.
[71]**Calderon … autos:** Pedro Calderón de la Barca (1600–1681), Spanish poet-dramatist, famed for his *autos sacramentales*, or religious plays.

reproduces them from the simplicity of these elementary forms, and touches them with majesty and beauty, and multiplies all that it reflects, and endows it with the power of propagating its like wherever it may fall.

But in periods of the decay of social life, the drama sympathizes with that decay. Tragedy becomes a cold imitation of the form of the great masterpieces of antiquity, divested of all harmonious accompaniment of the kindred arts; and often the very form misunderstood, or a weak attempt to teach certain doctrines, which the writer considers as moral truths; and which are usually no more than specious flatteries of some gross vice or weakness, with which the author, in common with his auditors, are infected. Hence what has been called the classical and domestic drama. Addison's *Cato*[72] is a specimen of the one; and would it were not superfluous to cite examples of the other! To such purposes poetry cannot be made subservient. Poetry is a sword of lightning, ever unsheathed, which consumes the scabbard that would contain it. And thus we observe that all dramatic writings of this nature are unimaginative in a singular degree; they affect sentiment and passion, which, divested of imagination, are other names for caprice and appetite. The period in our own history of the grossest degradation of the drama is the reign of Charles II,[73] when all forms in which poetry had been accustomed to be expressed became hymns to the triumph of kingly power over liberty and virtue. Milton[74] stood alone illuminating an age unworthy of him. At such periods the calculating principle pervades all the forms of dramatic exhibition, and poetry ceases to be expressed upon them. Comedy loses its ideal universality: wit succeeds to humour; we laugh from self-complacency and triumph, instead of pleasure; malignity, sarcasm, and contempt, succeed to sympathetic merriment; we hardly laugh, but we smile. Obscenity, which is ever blasphemy against the divine beauty in life, becomes, from the very veil which it assumes, more active if less disgusting: it is a monster for which the corruption of society for ever brings forth new food, which it devours in secret.

[...]

Poets have been challenged to resign the civic crown to reasoners and mechanists.[75] ... It is admitted that the exercise of the imagination is most delightful, but it is alleged that that of reason is more useful. Let us examine as the grounds of this distinction, what is here meant by utility. Pleasure or good, in a general sense, is that which the consciousness of a sensitive and intelligent being seeks, and in which, when found, it acquiesces. There are two kinds of pleasure, one durable, universal and permanent; the other transitory and particular. Utility may either express the means of producing the former or the latter. In the former sense, whatever strengthens and purifies the affections, enlarges the imagination, and adds spirit to sense, is useful. But a narrower meaning may be assigned to the word utility, confining it to express that which banishes the importunity of the wants of our animal nature, the surrounding men with security of life, the dispersing the grosser delusions of superstition, and the conciliating such a degree of mutual forbearance among men as may consist with the motives of personal advantage.

---

[72]**Addison's *Cato*:** Joseph Addison's *Cato* (1713) was one of the most popular tragedies of the eighteenth century.
[73]**Reign of Charles II:** Charles II ruled England from 1660 to 1685.
[74]**Milton:** John Milton (1608–74), poet, pamphleteer, ardent Republican, and author of the epic poem *Paradise Lost* (1667).
[75]**resign ... to reasoners:** a reference to Thomas Love Peacock's satirical essay 'The Four Ages of Poetry' (1820) which claimed that poetry's place had been usurped by science.

Undoubtedly the promoters of utility, in this limited sense, have their appointed office in society. They follow the footsteps of poets, and copy the sketches of their creations into the book of common life. They make space, and give time. Their exertions are of the highest value, so long as they confine their administration of the concerns of the inferior powers of our nature within the limits due to the superior ones. But whilst the sceptic destroys gross superstitions, let him spare to deface, as some of the French writers have defaced, the eternal truths charactered upon the imaginations of men. Whilst the mechanist abridges, and the political economist combines labour, let them beware that their speculations, for want of correspondence with those first principles which belong to the imagination, do not tend, as they have in modern England, to exasperate at once the extremes of luxury and want. They have exemplified the saying, 'To him that hath, more shall be given; and from him that hath not, the little that he hath shall be taken away.'[76] The rich have become richer, and the poor have become poorer; and the vessel of the state is driven between the Scylla and Charybdis of anarchy and despotism. Such are the effects which must ever flow from an unmitigated exercise of the calculating faculty.

It is difficult to define pleasure in its highest sense; the definition involving a number of apparent paradoxes. For, from an inexplicable defect of harmony in the constitution of human nature, the pain of the inferior is frequently connected with the pleasures of the superior portions of our being. Sorrow, terror, anguish, despair itself, are often the chosen expressions of an approximation to the highest good. Our sympathy in tragic fiction depends on this principle; tragedy delights by affording a shadow of the pleasure which exists in pain. This is the source also of the melancholy which is inseparable from the sweetest melody. The pleasure that is in sorrow is sweeter than the pleasure of pleasure itself. And hence the saying, 'It is better to go to the house of mourning, than to the house of mirth.'[77] Not that this highest species of pleasure is necessarily linked with pain. The delight of love and friendship, the ecstasy of the admiration of nature, the joy of the perception and still more of the creation of poetry, is often wholly unalloyed.

Further reading

Jacqueline Mulhallen, *The Theatre of Shelley* (Cambridge: Open Book Publishers, 2010).
Michael Rossington, 'Tragedy: *The Cenci* and *Swellfoot the Tyrant*', in *The Oxford Handbook of Percy Bysshe Shelley*, ed. Michael O'Neill, Anthony Howe and Madeleine Callaghan (Oxford: Oxford University Press, 2013), 299–308.

---

[76]**'To him that hath … taken away':** Mark 4:25; Matthew 13:12.
[77]**house of mourning … house of mirth:** a mixing of two verses from Ecclesiastes 7: 'It is better to go to the house of mourning, than to go to the house of feasting'; 'The heart of the wise is in the house of mourning; but the heart of fools is in the house of mirth'.

4.6 G.W.F. HEGEL, *AESTHETICS: LECTURES ON FINE ART* (1823–9)

Georg Wilhelm Friedrich Hegel (1770–1831), German philosopher, was perhaps the most influential philosophical writer on tragedy since Aristotle. He argued that classical tragedy worked in a very different way to its modern (or, as he termed it, Romantic) descendants. What the structure of the former revealed, Hegel insisted, was less a drama centring exclusively on the fall of a once-great tragic hero, than on a tragic collision or conflict which was eventually resolved in the play's catastrophe; this collision is not between forces of good and bad, right and wrong, but between two sets of values or powers which are equally justified. Hegel thus posited a dialectical structure for tragedy – a thesis, followed by antithesis and resolving into synthesis which began the whole process again. This interpretation has proved extremely influential – see, for example, the English literary critic A.C. Bradley's Christianized version of such a dialectical pattern in *Shakespearean Tragedy* (1904) in extract 5.2. But Hegel's original theory enabled an important corrective to dominant understandings of the way that fate or the gods worked in tragedy from antiquity – blind fate or destiny crushing the will and being of a protagonist. He posited instead that classical tragedy revealed the rationality of destiny, that it represented a desolating but fundamentally understandable tempering of overweening or excessive values embodied by the protagonist. Modern tragedies for Hegel, by contrast, internalized this conflict, with character becoming its focal point. No matter in whose translation, it is frequently difficult to follow the arguments of *The Aesthetics*. The difficulty of Hegel's expression of his ideas in *The Aesthetics* is compounded by the fact that he never intended them for print publication in their current form. He originally delivered this material as a series of lectures in the 1820s and the text we have is based upon the transcription of his students' lecture notes.

(α) With respect to *tragedy* I will here confine myself to a consideration of only the most general and essential characteristics.

[...]

(αα) The genuine content of tragic action subject to the *aims* which arrest tragic characters is supplied by the world of those forces which carry in themselves their own justification, and are realized substantively in the volitional activity of mankind. Such are the love of husband and wife, of parents, children, and kinsfolk. Such are, further, the life of communities, the patriotism of citizens, the will of those in supreme power. Such are the life of churches, not, however, if regarded as a piety which submits to act with resignation, or as a divine judicial declaration in the heart of mankind over what is good or the reverse in action; but, on the contrary, conceived as the active engagement with and demand for veritable interests and relations. It is of a soundness and thoroughness consonant with these that the really tragical characters consist.[78] They are throughout that which the essential notion of their character enables them and compels them to be. They are not merely a varied totality laid out in the series of views of it proper to the epic manner; they are, while no doubt remaining also essentially

---

[78]**It … consists:** a clearer translation of this sentence runs 'A similar excellence belongs to the genuinely tragic characters'; T.M. Knox, *Aesthetics: Lectures on Fine Art by G.W.F. Hegel* (Oxford: Clarendon Press, 1975), 1194.

vital and individual, still only the one power of the particular character in question, the force in which such a character, in virtue of its essential personality, has made itself inseparably coalesce with some particular aspect of the capital and substantive life-content … and deliberately commits himself to that. It is at some such elevation, where the mere accidents of unmediated individuality vanish altogether, that we find the tragic heroes of dramatic art, whether they be the living representatives of such spheres of concrete life or in any other way already so derive their greatness and stability from their own free self-reliance that they stand forth as works of sculpture, and as such interpret, too, under this aspect the essentially more abstract statues and figures of gods, as also the lofty tragic characters of the Greeks more completely than is possible for any other kind of elucidation or commentary.

Broadly speaking, we may, therefore, affirm that the true theme of primitive tragedy is the god-like. But by godlike we do not mean the Divine, as implied in the content of the religious consciousness simply as such, but rather as it enters into the world, into individual action, and enters in such a way that it does not forfeit its substantive character under this mode of realization, nor find itself converted into the contradiction of its own substance.[79] In this form the spiritual substance of volition and accomplishment is ethical life. For what is ethical, if we grasp it, in its direct consistency – that is to say, not exclusively from the standpoint of personal reflection as formal morality – is the divine in its secular or world realization, the substantive as such, the particular no less than the essential features of which supply the changing content of truly human actions, and in such action itself render this their essence explicit and actual.

(ββ) These ethical forces, as also the characters of the action, are *distinctively defined* in respect to their content and their individual personality, in virtue of the principle of differentiation to which everything is subject, which forms part of the objective world of things. If, then, these particular forces, in the way presupposed by dramatic poetry, are attached to the external expression of human activity, and are realized as the determinate aim of a human pathos which passes into action, their concordancy[80] is cancelled, and they are asserted *in contrast* to each other in interchangeable succession.[81] Individual action will then, under given conditions, realize an object or character, which, under such a presupposed state, inevitably stimulates the presence of a pathos[82] opposed to itself, because it occupies a position of unique isolation in virtue of its independently fixed definition, and, by doing so, brings in its train unavoidable conflicts. Primitive tragedy, then, consists in this, that within a collision of this kind both sides of the contradiction, if taken by themselves, are *justified*; yet, from a further point of view, they tend to carry into effect the true and positive content of their end and specific characterization merely as the negation and violation of the other equally legitimate power, and consequently in their ethical purport and relatively to this so far fall under *condemnation*.

I have already adverted to[83] the general ground of the necessity of this conflict. The substance of ethical condition is, when viewed as concrete unity, a totality of *different* relations and forces, which, however, only under the inactive condition of the gods in their blessedness

---

[79]**contradiction of its own substance:** i.e. the opposite of itself.

[80]**concordancy:** harmony.

[81]**If … succession:** for Hegel, ethical life is characterized by differentiated but harmonious powers or forces; when such forces are embodied by human agents and their actions, they come into conflict.

[82]**pathos:** in this specific context 'pathos' means an ethical principle, value, or norm embodied by an individual; it is more than an individual passion or narrowly defined self-interest.

[83]**adverted to:** taken notice of.

achieve the works of the Spirit in enjoyment of an undisturbed life. In contrast to this, however, there is no less certainly implied in the notion of this totality itself an impulse to move from its, in the first instance, still abstract ideality, and transplant itself in the real actuality of the phenomenal world. On account of the nature of this primitive obsession, it comes about that mere difference, if conceived on the basis of definite conditions of individual personalities, must inevitably associate with contradiction and collision. Only such a view can pretend to deal seriously with those gods which, though they endure in their tranquil repose and unity in the Olympus and heaven of imagination and religious conception, yet, in so far as they are actual, viewed at least as the energic[84] in the definite pathos of a human personality, participate in concrete life, all other claims notwithstanding, and, in virtue of their specific singularity and their mutual opposition, render both blame and wrong inevitable.

(γγ) As a result of this, however, an unmediated[85] contradiction is posited, which no doubt may assert itself in the Real,[86] but, for all that, is unable to maintain itself as that which is wholly substantive and verily[87] real therein; which rather discovers, and only discovers, its essential justification in the fact that it is able to *annul* itself as such contradiction. In other words, whatever may be the claim of the tragic final purpose and personality, whatever may be the necessity of the tragic collision, it is, as a consequence of our present view, no less a claim that is asserted ... by the tragic resolution of this division.[88] It is through this latter result that Eternal Justice is operative in such aims and individuals under a mode whereby it restores the ethical substance and unity in and along with the downfall of the individuality which disturbs its repose. For, despite the fact that individual characters propose that which is itself essentially valid, yet they are only able to carry it out under the tragic demand in a manner that implies contradiction and with a one-sidedness which is injurious. What, however, is substantive in truth, and the function of which is to secure realization, is not the battle of particular unities, however much such a conflict is essentially involved in the notion of a real world and human action; rather it is the reconciliation in which definite ends and individuals unite in harmonious action without mutual violation and contradiction. That which is abrogated in the tragic issue[89] is merely the one-sided particularity which was unable to accommodate itself to this harmony, and consequently in the tragic course of its action, through inability to disengage itself from itself and its designs, either is committed in its entire totality to destruction or at least finds itself compelled to fall back upon a state of resignation in the execution of its aim in so far as it can carry this out.

We are reminded of the famous dictum of Aristotle that the true effect of tragedy is to excite and purify *fear* and *pity*. By this statement Aristotle did not mean merely the concordant or discordant feeling with anybody's private experience, a feeling simply of pleasure or the reverse, an attraction or a repulsion, that most superficial of all psychological states, which only in recent times theorists have sought to identify with the principle of assent or dissent as ordinarily expressed. For in a work of art the matter of exclusive importance should be

---

[84]**the energic:** the driving force.
[85]**unmediated:** unresolved.
[86]**the Real:** the real world.
[87]**verily:** truly.
[88]**In other words ... division:** Compare with Knox: 'However justified the tragic character and his aim, however necessary the tragic collision, the third thing required is the tragic resolution of this conflict'; *Hegel's Aesthetics*, II.1197.
[89]**abrogated in the tragic issue:** cancelled out in the denouement of tragedy.

the display of that which is conformable with the reason and truth of Spirit; and to discover the principle of this we have to direct our attention to wholly different points of view. And consequently we are not justified in restricting the application of this dictum of Aristotle merely to the emotion of fear and pity, but should relate it to the principle of the *content*, the appropriately artistic display of which ought to purify such feelings. Man may, on the one hand, entertain fear when confronted with that which is outside him and finite; but he may likewise shrink before the power of that which is the essential and absolute subsistency of social phenomena.[90] That which mankind has therefore in truth to fear is not the external power and its oppression, but the ethical might which is self-defined in its own free rationality, and partakes further of the eternal and inviolable, the power a man summons against his own being when he turns his back upon it. And just as fear may have two objectives, so also too compassion. The first is just the ordinary sensibility – in other words, a sympathy with the misfortunes and sufferings of another, and one which is experienced as something finite and negative. Your countrified cousin is ready enough with compassion of this order. The man of nobility and greatness, however, has no wish to be smothered with this sort of pity. For just to the extent that it is merely the nugatory[91] aspect, the negative of misfortune which is asserted, a real depreciation of misfortune is implied. True sympathy, on the contrary, is an accordant feeling with the ethical claim at the same time associated with the sufferer – that is, with what is necessarily implied in his condition as affirmative and substantive. Such a pity as this is not, of course, excited by ragamuffins and vagabonds. If the tragic character, therefore, just as he aroused our fear when contemplating the might of violated morality, is to awake a tragic sympathy in his misfortune, he must himself essentially possess real capacity and downright character. It is only that which has a genuine content which strikes the heart of a man of noble feeling, and rings through its depths. Consequently we ought by no means to identify our interest in the tragic *denouement* with the simple satisfaction that a sad story, a misfortune merely as misfortune, should have a claim upon our sympathy. Feelings of lament of this type may well enough assail men on occasions of wholly external contingency and related circumstance, to which the individual does not contribute, nor for which he is responsible, such cases as illness, loss of property, death, and the like. The only real and absorbing interest in such cases ought to be an eager desire to afford immediate assistance. If this is impossible, such pictures of lamentation and misery merely rack the feelings. A veritable tragic suffering, on the contrary, is suspended over active characters entirely as the consequence of their own act, which as such not only asserts its claim upon us, but becomes subject to blame through the collision it involves, and in which such individuals identify themselves heart and soul.

Over and above mere fear and tragic sympathy we have therefore the feeling of *reconciliation* which tragedy is vouched for in virtue of its vision of eternal justice, a justice which exercises a paramount force of absolute constringency on account of the relative claim of all merely contracted aims and passions; and it can do this for the reason that it is unable to tolerate the victorious issue and continuance in the truth of the objective world of such a conflict with and opposition to those ethical powers which are fundamentally and essentially concordant. ...[92]

---

[90]**essential and absolute subsistency of social phenomena:** i.e. the Absolute.

[91]**nugatory:** negative.

[92]**Over ... concordant:** Knox's translation renders this paragraph as: 'Above mere fear and tragic sympathy there therefore stands that sense of reconciliation which the tragedy affords by the glimpse of eternal justice. In its absolute

(β)In tragedy then that which is eternally substantive is triumphantly vindicated under the mode of reconciliation. It simply removes from the contentions of personality the false one-sidedness, and exhibits instead that which is the object of its volition, namely, positive reality, no longer under an asserted mediation of opposed factors, but as the real support of consistency. And in contrast to this in comedy it is the purely personal experience which retains the mastery in its character of infinite self-assuredness. And it is only these two fundamental aspects of human action which occupy a position of contrast in the classification of dramatic poetry into its several types. In tragedy individuals are thrown into confusion in virtue of the abstract nature of their sterling volition and character, or they are forced to accept that with resignation, to which they have been them-selves essentially opposed. In comedy we have a vision of the victory of the intrinsically assured stability of the wholly personal soul-life, the laughter of which resolves everything through the medium and into the medium of such life. ...

(c) 'The Concrete Development of Dramatic Poetry and Its Types' ...

In all these tragic conflicts, however, we must above all place on one side the false notion of *guilt* or *innocence*. The heroes of tragedy are quite as much under one category as the other. If we accept the idea as valid that a man is guilty only in the case that a choice lay open to him, and he deliberately decided on the course of action which he carried out, then these plastic figures of ancient drama are guiltless. They act in accordance with a specific character, a specific pathos, for the simple reason that they are this character, this pathos. In such a case there is no lack of decision and no choice. The strength of great characters consists precisely in this that they do not choose, but are entirely and absolutely just that which they will and achieve. They are simply themselves, and never anything else, and their greatness consists in that fact. Weakness in action, in other words, wholly consists in the division of the personal self as such from its content, so that character, volition and final purpose do not appear as absolutely one unified growth; and inasmuch as no assured end lives in the soul as the very substance of the particular personality, as the pathos and might of the individual's entire will, he is still able to turn with indecision from this course to that, and his final decision is that of caprice. A wavering attitude of this description is alien to these plastic creations. The bond between the psychological state of mind and the content of the will is for them indissoluble. That which stirs them to action is just in this very pathos which implies an ethical justification and which, even in the pathetic aspects of the dialogue, is not enforced in and through the merely personal rhetoric of the heart and the sophistry of passion, but in the equally masculine and cultivated objective presence, in the profound possibilities, the harmony and vitally plastic beauty of which Sophocles was to a superlative degree master. At the same time, however, such a pathos, with its potential resources of collision, brings in its train deeds that are both injurious and wrongful. They have no desire to avoid the blame that results therefrom. On the contrary, it is their fame to have done what they have done. One can in fact urge nothing more intolerable against a hero of this type than by saying that he has acted innocently. It is a point of honour with such great characters that they are guilty. They have no desire to excite pity or our sensibilities. For it is not the substantive, but rather the wholly personal deepening

---

sway this justice overrides the relative justification of one-sided aims and passions because it cannot suffer the conflict and contradiction of naturally harmonious ethical powers to be victorious and permanent in truth and actuality'; *Hegel's Aesthetics*, II.1198.

of the individual character, which stirs our individual pain. These securely strong characters, however, coalesce entirely with their essential pathos, and this indivisible accord inspires wonder, but does not excite heart emotions. The drama of Euripides marks the transition to that.

The final result, then, of the development of tragedy conducts us to this issue and only this, namely, that the twofold vindication of the mutually conflicting aspects are no doubt retained, but the *onesided* mode under which they were maintained is cancelled, and the undisturbed ideal harmony brings back again that condition of the chorus, which attributes without reserve equal honour to all the gods. The true course of dramatic development consists in the annulment of *contradictions* viewed as such, in the reconciliation of the forces of human action, which alternately strive to negate each other in their conflict. Only so far is misfortune and suffering not the final issue, but rather the satisfaction of spirit, as for the first time, in virtue of such a conclusion, the necessity of all that particular individuals experience, is able to appear in complete accord with reason, and our emotional attitude is tranquillized on a true ethical basis, rudely shaken by the calamitous result to the heroes, but reconciled in the substantial facts. And it is only in so far as we retain such a view securely that we shall be in a position to understand ancient tragedy.[93]

We have to guard ourselves therefore from concluding that a *dénouement* of this type is merely a moral issue conformably to which evil is punished and virtue rewarded, as indicated by the proverb that 'when crime turns to vomit, virtue sits down at table'.[94] We have nothing to do here with this wholly personal aspect of a self-reflecting personality and its conception of good and evil, but are concerned with the appearance of the affirmative reconciliation and with the equal validity of both the powers engaged in actual conflict, when the collision actually took place. To as little extent is the necessity of the issue a blind destiny, or in other words a purely irrational, unintelligible fate, identified with the classical world by many; rather it is the rationality of destiny, albeit it does not as yet appear as self-conscious Providence, the divine final end of which in conjunction with the world and individuals appears on its own account and for others, depending as it does on just this fact that the highest Power paramount over particular gods and mankind cannot suffer this, namely, that the forces, which affirm their self-subsistence in modes that are abstract or incomplete, and thereby overstep the boundary of their warrant, no less than the conflicts which result from them, should retain their self-stability. Fate drives personality back upon its limits, and shatters it, when it has grown overweening. An irrational compulsion, however, an innocence of suffering would rather only excite indignation in the soul of the spectator than ethical tranquility.[95]

From a further point of view, therefore, the reconciliation of *tragedy* is equally distinct from that of epic. If we look at either Achilles or Odysseus[96] in this respect we observe that both attain their object, and it is right that they do so; but it is not a continuous happiness with which they are favoured; they have on the contrary to taste in its bitterness the feeling of finite

---

[93]**tragedy./ We:** In breaking the paragraph here, we follow Knox's edition rather than Osmaston's translation as it aids comprehension; see Knox, *Hegel's Aesthetics* II. 1215.

[94]**'when crime turns to vomit, virtue sits down at table':** this quotation is the final line of Friedrich Schiller's polemical poem *Shakespeare's Shadow* (1797).

[95]**tranquility./ From:** This paragraph break is not in the Osmaston translation. It is introduced here to assist comprehension and follows Knox, *Hegel's Aesthetics*, II. 1216.

[96]**Achilles and Odysseus:** epic heroes, respectively, of Homer's *The Iliad* and *The Odyssey*.

condition, and are forced to fight wearily through difficulties, losses and sacrifices. It is in fact a universal demand of truth that in the course of life and all that takes place in the objective world the nugatory character of finite conditions should compel attention. So no doubt the anger of Achilles is reconciled; he obtains from Agamemnon[97] that in respect of which he had suffered the sense of insult; he is revenged upon Hector; the funeral rites of Patroclus are consummated, and the character of Achilles is acknowledged in all its glory. But his wrath and its reconciliation have for all that cost him his dearest friend, the noble Patroclus; and, in order to avenge himself upon Hector for this loss, he finds himself compelled to disengage himself from his anger, to enter once more the battle against the Trojans, and in the very moment when his glory is acknowledged receives the prevision of his early death. In a similar way Odysseus reaches Ithaca at last, the goal of his desire; but he does so alone and in his sleep, having lost all his companions, all the war-booty from Ilium,[98] after long years of endurance and fatigue. In this way both heroes have paid their toll to finite conditions and the claim of nemesis is evidenced in the destruction of Troy and the misfortunes of the Greek heroes. But this nemesis is simply justice as conceived of old, which merely humiliates what is everywhere too exalted, in order to establish once more the abstract balance of fortune by the instrumentality of misfortune, and which merely touches and affects finite existence without further ethical signification. And this is the justice of the Epic in the field of objective fact, the universal reconciliation of what is simply accommodation. The higher conception of reconciliation in tragedy is on the contrary related to the resolution of specific ethical and substantive facts from their contradiction into their true harmony.

[...]

Modern tragedy accepts in its own province from the first the principle of subjectivity or self-assertion. It makes, therefore, the personal intimacy of character – the character, that is, which is no purely individual and vital embodiment of ethical forces in the classic sense – its peculiar object and content. It, moreover, makes, in a type of concurrence that is adapted to this end, human actions come into collision through the instrumentality of the external accident of circumstances in the way that a contingency of a similar character is also decisive in its effect on the consequence, or appears to be so decisive.[99]

[...]

In modern tragedy it is not the substantive content of its object in the interest of which men act, and which is maintained as the stimulus of their passion; rather it is the inner experience of their heart and individual emotion, or the particular qualities of their personality, which insist on satisfaction. ...

In order to emphasize still more distinctly the difference which in this respect obtains between ancient and modern tragedy, I will merely refer the reader to Shakespeare's *Hamlet*. Here we find fundamentally a collision similar to that which is introduced by Aeschylus into his

---

[97]**Agamemnon:** in *The Iliad* the argument between Agamemnon and Achilles over the captive princess Briseis is one of the main drivers of the plot. Agamemnon eventually 'returns' Briseis to Achilles. But Achilles's sense of injury from his treatment at Agamemnon's hands means that he withdraws for a time from the Trojan war. During this period his closest friend Patroclus goes into battle in his stead but is killed by Hector in battle.

[98]**Odysseus ... Ilium:** this is a précis of the plot of *The Odyssey*. The poem recounts Odysseus' journeys from Ilium (Troy) to the Greek island of Ithaca.

[99]**It makes ... content:** Knox renders these sentences more clearly. 'Therefore it takes for its proper subject-matter and contents the subjective inner life of the character who is not, as in classical tragedy, a purely individual embodiment of ethical powers, and, keeping to this same type, it makes actions come into collision with one another as the chance of external circumstances dictates, and makes similar accidents decide, or seem to decide, the outcome'; *Hegel's Aesthetics*, II.1223.

Choephori and that by Sophocles into his *Electra*.[100] For Hamlet's father, too, and the King, as in these Greek plays, has been murdered, and his mother has wedded the murderer. That which, however, in the conception of the Greek dramatists possesses a certain ethical justification – I mean the death of Agamemnon – relatively to his sacrifice of Iphigeneia in the contrasted case of Shakespeare's play, can only be viewed as an atrocious crime, of which Hamlet's mother is innocent; so that the son is merely concerned in his vengeance to direct his attention to the fratricidal king, and there is nothing in the latter's character that possesses any real claim to his respect. The real collision, therefore, does not turn on the fact that the son, in giving effect to a rightful sense of vengeance, is himself forced to violate morality, but rather on the particular personality, the inner life of Hamlet, whose noble soul is not steeled to this kind of energetic activity, but, while full of contempt for the world and life, what between making up his mind and attempting to carry into effect or preparing to carry into effect its resolves, is bandied from pillar to post, and finally through his own procrastination and the external course of events meets his own doom.

If we now turn, in close connection with the above conclusions, to our second point of fundamental importance in modern tragedy – that is to say, the nature of the characters and their collisions – we may summarily take a point of departure from the following general observations.

The heroes of ancient classic tragedy discover circumstances under which they, so long as they irrefragably[101] adhere to the one ethical state of pathos which alone corresponds to their own already formed personality, must infallibly come into conflict with an ethical Power which opposes them and possesses an equal ethical claim to recognition. Romantic characters,[102] on the contrary, are from the first placed within a wide expanse of contingent relations and conditions, within which every sort of action is possible; so that the conflict, to which no doubt the external conditions presupposed supply the occasion, essentially abides within the character itself, to which the individuals concerned in their passion give effect, not, however, in the interests of the ethical vindication of the truly substantive claims, but for the simple reason that they are the kind of men they are. Greek heroes also no doubt act in accordance with their particular individuality; but this individuality, as before noted, if we take for our examples the supreme results of ancient tragedy, is itself necessarily identical with an ethical pathos which is substantive. In modern tragedy the peculiar character in its real significance, and to which it as a matter of accident remains constant, whether it happens to grasp after that which on its own account is on moral grounds justifiable, or is carried into wrong and crime, forms its resolves under the dictate of personal wishes and necessities, or among other things purely external considerations. In such a case, therefore, though we may have a coalescence between

---

[100]**Aeschylus … Electra:** In his reading of the motives for revenge in Aeschylus' *Choephori* (458 BCE), commonly referred to as *The Libation Bearers*, Sophocles' *Electra* (*c*.410–401 BCE), and Shakespeare's *Hamlet* (*c*.1600), Hegel claims to distinguish between classical and modern or Romantic forms of tragedy and to pinpoint the different kinds of conflict governing them. Agamemnon's death at the hands of his wife Clytemnestra is ethically justified since it is prompted by Agamemnon's sacrificing of their daughter Iphigeneia. Old Hamlet's murder by his brother Polonius, by contrast, is straightforwardly criminal. Hamlet's revenging of his father's death, therefore, is an act of heroic self-assertion against a manifest wrong, whereas Electra and Orestes' vengeance is complicated by the fact that they offer it in opposition to an act that already had some moral justification.

[101]**irrefragably:** stubbornly.

[102]**Romantic characters:** i.e. the protagonists of modern (as opposed to classical) tragedy.

the moral aspect of the object and the character, yet, for all that, such a concurrence does not constitute, and cannot constitute – owing to the divided character[103] of ends, passions, and the life wholly personal to the individual, the essential basis and objective condition of the depth and beauty of the tragic drama.

Further reading

Frederick C. Beiser (ed.), *The Cambridge Companion to Hegel and Nineteenth-Century Philosophy* (Cambridge: Cambridge University Press, 2008).

T.M. Knox, *Aesthetics: Lectures on Fine Art by G.W.F. Hegel* (Oxford: Clarendon Press, 1975).

Julian Young, *The Philosophy of Tragedy: From Plato to Žižek* (Cambridge: Cambridge University Press, 2013).

Michelle Zerba, *Tragedy and Theory: The Problem of Conflict since Aristotle* (Princeton: Princeton University Press, 2014).

---

[103]**character:** condition.

4.7 GEORGE ELIOT, '*THE ANTIGONE* AND ITS MORAL' (1856)

George Eliot was the pseudonym of Marian Evans (1819–80), one of the most important and best-selling English novelists of the nineteenth century. Eliot was a keen student of classical tragedy and its theories. The influence of contemporary German ideas of tragedy such as A.W. Schlegel's *Course of Lectures on Dramatic Art and Literature* (1809) – see extract 4.1 – and Philip August Böckh's *Der Sophokles Antigone: Griechisch und deutsch* (1843) can be seen in this short essay reviewing a school edition of Sophocles's *Antigone*. Even though her reading of that tragedy as consisting in the antagonism between valid claims sounds Hegelian (see extract 4.6), there is no evidence that she read Hegel extensively on this subject.[104] She did, however, study Aristotle's *Poetics* carefully at three important points in her career: in 1856, just before launching her first piece of fiction, 'Amos Barton' (1857); in 1865, while writing *Felix Holt the Radical* (1866); and again in 1873 in preparation for her final novel *Daniel Deronda* (1876). Her novels routinely make productive use of dramatic reversals in fortune, or peripeteia; her description of Maggie Tulliver, the heroine of her most tragic novel, *The Mill on the Floss* (1860), bears the hallmarks of an Aristotelian understanding of tragic heroism: 'a character essentially noble but liable to great error'.[105]

'Lo! Here a little volume but great Book' – a volume small enough to slip into your breast pocket, but containing in fine print one of the finest tragedies of the single dramatic poet who can be said to stand on a level with Shakspeare. Sophocles is the crown and flower of the classic tragedy as Shakspeare is of the romantic: to borrow Schlegel's comparison, which cannot be improved upon, they are related to each other as the Parthenon to Strasburg Cathedral.[106]

The opinion which decried all enthusiasm for Greek literature as 'humbug,' was put to an excellent test some years ago by the production of the Antigone at Drury Lane.[107] The translation then adopted was among the feeblest by which a great poet has ever been misrepresented; yet so completely did the poet triumph over the disadvantages of his medium and of a dramatic motive foreign to modern sympathies, that the Pit was electrified, and Sophocles, over a chasm of two thousand years, once more swayed the emotions of a popular audience. And no wonder. The Antigone has every quality of a fine tragedy, and fine tragedies can never become mere mummies for Hermanns and Böckhs[108] to dispute about: they must appeal to perennial human

---

[104]Avrom Fleishman, *George Eliot's Intellectual Life* (Cambridge: Cambridge University Press, 2010), 82.

[105]'a character…error': *The George Eliot Letters*, ed. Gorgon S. Haight, 7 vols. (New Haven and London: Yale University Press, 1954–6), III:318.

[106]**Parthenon to Strasburg Cathedral:** Eliot here misremembers a passage from one of Schlegel's lectures: 'The Pantheon is not more different from Westminster Abbey or the church of St Stephen at Vienna, than the structure of a tragedy of Sophocles from a drama of Shakespeare'; August William Schlegel, *A Course of Lectures on Dramatic Art and Literature*, trans. John Black (London: Henry G. Bohn, 1846), 23.

[107]**Drury Lane:** The performance took place on 1 May 1850; Antigone was played by Charlotte Vandenhoff.

[108]**Hermanns and Böckhs:** Johann Gottfied Jacob Hermann (1772–1848) classicist and philologist, and August Böckh (1785–1867) classicist and antiquarian, both of whom produced scholarly editions of works by Sophocles.

nature, and even the ingenious dulness of translators cannot exhaust them of their passion and their poetry.

E'en in their ashes live their wonted fires.[109]

We said that the dramatic motive of the Antigone was foreign to modern sympathies, but it is only superficially so. It is true we no longer believe that a brother, if left unburied, is condemned to wander a hundred years without repose on the banks of the Styx; we no longer believe that to neglect funeral rites is to violate the claims of the infernal deities. But these beliefs are the accidents and not the substance of the poet's conception. The turning point of the tragedy is not, as it is stated to be in the argument prefixed to this edition, 'reverence for the dead and the importance of the sacred rites of burial', but the *conflict* between these and obedience to the State. Here lies the dramatic collision: the impulse of sisterly piety which allies itself with reverence for the Gods, clashes with the duties of citizenship; two principles, both having their validity, are at war with each. Let us glance for a moment at the plot.

Eteocles and Polynices, the brothers of Antigone, have slain each other in battle before the gates of Thebes, the one defending his country, the other invading it in conjunction with foreign allies. Hence Creon becomes, by the death of these two sons of OEdipus, the legitimate ruler of Thebes, grants funeral honours to Eteocles, but denies them to Polynices, whose body is cast out to be the prey of beasts and birds, a decree being issued that death will be the penalty of an attempt to bury him. In the second scene of the play Creon expounds the motive of his decree to the Theban elders, insisting in weighty words on the duty of making all personal affection subordinate to the well-being of the State. The impulses of affection and religion which urge Antigone to disobey this proclamation are strengthened by the fact that in her last interview with her brother he had besought her not to leave his corpse unburied. She determines to brave the penalty, buries Polynices, is taken in the act and brought before Creon, to whom she does not attempt to deny that she knew of the proclamation, but declares that she deliberately disobeyed it, and is ready to accept death as its consequence. It was not Zeus, she tells him-it was not eternal justice that issued that decree. The proclamation of Creon is not so authoritative as the unwritten law of the Gods, which is neither of to-day nor of yesterday, but lives eternally, and none knows its beginning.

οὐ γάρ τι νῦν γε κἀχθές, ἀλλ᾽ ἀεί ποτε
ζῇ ταῦτα, κοὐδεὶς οἶδεν ἐξ ὅτου 'φάνη.[110]

Creon, on his side, insists on the necessity to the welfare of the State that he should be obeyed as legitimate ruler, and becomes exasperated by the calm defiance of Antigone. She is condemned to death. Haemon, the son of Creon, to whom Antigone is betrothed, remonstrates against this judgment in vain. Teiresias also, the blind old soothsayer, alarmed by unfavourable omens,

---

[109]**E'en ... wonted fires:** a quotation from later editions of Thomas Gray's 'Elegy Written in a Country Churchyard', l. 92.

[110]*οὐ γάρ... 'φάνη:* Eliot has just translated this Greek quotation from Sophocles' *Antigone* ll.456-7 in the previous sentence. A more modern translation runs: 'They are alive, not just today or yesterday: / they live forever, from the first of time, / and no one knows when they first saw the light'; Sophocles, *The Three Theban Plays*, trans. Robert Fagles (London: Penguin, 1984), 82.

comes to warn Creon against persistence in a course displeasing to the Gods. It is not until he has departed, leaving behind him the denunciation of coming woes, that Creon's confidence begins to falter, and at length, persuaded by the Theban elders, he reverses his decree, and proceeds with his followers to the rocky tomb in which Antigone has been buried alive, that he may deliver her. It is too late. Antigone is already dead; Haemon commits suicide in the madness of despair, and the death of his mother Eurydice on hearing the fatal tidings, completes the ruin of Creon's house.

It is a very superficial criticism which interprets the character of Creon as that of a hypocritical tyrant, and regards Antigone as a blameless victim. Coarse contrasts like this are not the materials handled by great dramatists. The exquisite art of Sophocles is shown in the touches by which he makes us feel that Creon, as well as Antigone, is contending for what he believes to be the right, while both are also conscious that, in following out one principle, they are laying themselves open to just blame for transgressing another; and it is this consciousness which secretly heightens the exasperation of Creon and the defiant hardness of Antigone. The best critics have agreed with Böckh in recognising this balance of principles, this antagonism between valid claims; they generally regard it, however, as dependent entirely on the Greek point of view, as springing simply from the polytheistic conception, according to which the requirements of the Gods often clashed with the duties of man to man.

But, is it the fact that this antagonism of valid principles is peculiar to polytheism? Is it not rather that the struggle between Antigone and Creon represents that struggle between elemental tendencies and established laws by which the outer life of man is gradually and painfully being brought into harmony with his inward needs. Until this harmony is perfected, we shall never be able to attain a great right without also doing a wrong. Reformers, martyrs, revolutionists, are never fighting against evil only; they are also placing themselves in opposition to a good-to a valid principle which cannot be infringed without harm. Resist the payment of ship-money, you bring on civil war;[111] preach against false doctrines, you disturb feeble minds and send them adult on a sea of doubt; make a new road, and you annihilate vested interests; cultivate a new region of the earth, and you exterminate a race of men. Wherever the strength of a man's intellect, or moral sense, or affection brings him into opposition with the rules which society has sanctioned, *there* is renewed the conflict between Antigone and Creon; such a man must not only dare to be right, he must also dare to be wrong-to shake faith, to wound friendship, perhaps, to hem in his own powers. Like Antigone, he may fall a victim to the struggle, and yet he can never earn the name of a blameless martyr any more than the society-the Creon he has defied, can be branded as a hypocritical tyrant.

Perhaps the best moral we can draw is that to which the Chorus points – that our protest for the right should be seasoned with moderation and reverence, and that lofty words – μεγάλοι λόγοι[112] – are not becoming to mortals.

---

[111]**ship money:** a tax levied by the English king Charles I on his subjects. It was extremely unpopular and resistance to its payment is often seen as one of the triggers for the English Civil War (1642–9).
[112]**μεγάλοι λόγοι:** grand or lofty words.

Further reading

P.E. Easterling, 'George Eliot and Greek Tragedy', *Arion: A Journal of Humanities and the Classics* 1, no. 2 (1991): 60–74.

Jeanette King, *Tragedy in the Victorian Novel: Theory and Practice in the Novels of George Eliot, Thomas Hardy and Henry James* (Cambridge: Cambridge University Press, 1978).

Darrel Mansell, 'George Eliot's Conception of Tragedy', *Nineteenth-Century Fiction* 22, no. 2 (1967): 155–71.

4.8 FRIEDRICH NIETZSCHE, *THE BIRTH OF TRAGEDY* (1872)

Friedrich Nietzsche (1844–1900) was a German philosopher, now regarded as one of the foremost thinkers of the nineteenth century. *The Birth of Tragedy* (1872), his first book, published when he was 27, created a critical controversy when it appeared. While it had enthusiastic defenders, such as its dedicatee Richard Wagner (1813–83), Nietzsche's detractors inveighed against its sometimes exaggerated, under-evidenced claims as well as its allusive, elliptical style. Nietzsche himself came to regard the book as 'somewhat strange and inaccessible'.[113] Part of its difficulty is that it presents itself as a familiar work of historically grounded literary criticism, scrutinizing the rise and fall of Greek tragedy under particular sociocultural circumstances, yet also continually probes the philosophical abstractions that Nietzsche saw as key to unriddling the meaning of human existence. At this stage of his career Nietzsche was a disciple of the pessimistic philosophy of Arthur Schopenhauer (1788–1860) – see extract 4.4 – and believed that all attempts to abstract lived experience, to make it conform to some clearly definable moral scheme or benign ordering principle, concealed the true nature of reality, which was an endless cycle of creation and destruction. Greek tragedy, Nietzsche thought, unlike contemporary bourgeois tragedy, exposed the true nature of this reality, and confronted the terrors inherent in experience rather than offering its audiences any obfuscatory moral or spiritual salve. Nietzsche saw classical Greek culture as riven by two equally important, productively opposed forces, which he read as metaphysical principles underpinning all reality. The Apolline, or Apollonian, concerned with appearances, the individual, order, and clarity, was associated with illusions and dreams; the Dionysiac, by contrast, tied to intoxication, loss of clarity, and the merging of individualities, enabled us to grasp the undifferentiated nature of reality without being destroyed by it.

§1

We shall have gained much for the science of aesthetics when we have succeeded in perceiving directly, and not only through logical reasoning, that art derives its continuous development from the duality of the *Apolline* and *Dionysiac*; just as the reproduction of species depends on the duality of the sexes, with its constant conflicts and only periodically intervening reconciliations. These terms are borrowed from the Greeks, who revealed the profound mysteries of their artistic doctrines to the discerning mind, not in concepts but in the vividly clear forms of their deities. To the two gods of art, Apollo and Dionysus,[114] we owe our recognition that in the Greek world there is a tremendous opposition, as regards both origins and aims, between the Apolline art of the sculptor and the non-visual, Dionysiac art of music. These two very different tendencies walk side by side, usually in violent opposition to one

---

[113]Friedrich Nietzsche, *The Birth of Tragedy: Out of the Spirit of Music*, ed. Michael Tanner, trans. Shaun Whiteside (New York: Penguin, 2003), 3.

[114]**Apollo and Dionysus:** sons of Zeus in Roman and Greek mythology. Apollo was god of light, poetry, prophecy, and healing; his brother Dionysus was god of theatre, wine, and religious ecstasy. In *The Birth of Tragedy* the former is associated with civilization and order, whereas the latter is ungovernable.

another, inciting one another to ever more powerful births, perpetuating the struggle of the opposition only apparently bridged by the word 'art'; until, finally, by a metaphysical miracle of the Hellenic 'will', the two seem to be coupled, and in this coupling they seem at last to beget the work of art that is as Dionysiac as it is Apolline – Attic tragedy.[115]

To reach a better understanding of these two tendencies, let us first conceive them as the separate art worlds of *dream* and *intoxication*, two physiological states which contrast similarly to the Apolline and the Dionysiac. It was in dreams, according to Lucretius,[116] that the wondrous forms of the deities first appeared before the souls of men; in dreams that the great sculptor first saw the delightful bodies of superhuman beings; and the Hellenic[117] poet, if questioned about the mysteries of poetic creation, would also have referred to dreams, and might have instructed his listeners much as Hans Sachs instructs us in *Die Meistersinger*:

> It is the poet's task, my friend,
> To note his dreams and comprehend.
> Mankind's most true delusion seems
> To be revealed to him in dreams:
> All poesy and versification
> Is merely dream interpretation.[118]

The beautiful illusion of the dream worlds, in the creation of which every man is a consummate artist, is the precondition of all visual art, and indeed, as we shall see, of an important amount of poetry. We take pleasure in the immediate apprehension of form, all shapes speak to us, and nothing is indifferent or unnecessary. But even when this dream reality is presented to us with the greatest intensity, we still have a glimmering awareness that it is an *illusion*. That is my experience, at least, and I could cite many proofs, including the statements of the poets, to vouch for its frequency, its normality. Men of philosophy even have a sense that beneath the reality in which we live there is hidden a second, quite different world, and that our own world is therefore an illusion; and Schopenhauer actually says that the gift of being able at times to see men and objects as mere phantoms or dream images is the mark of the philosophical capacity.[119] Thus the man who is responsive to artistic stimuli reacts to the reality of dreams as does the philosopher to the reality of existence; he observes closely, and he enjoys his observation: for it is out of these images that he interprets life, out of these processes that he trains himself for life. It is not only pleasant and agreeable images that he experiences with such universal understanding: the serious, the gloomy, the sad and the profound, the sudden restraints, the mockeries of chance, fearful expectations, in short the whole 'divine comedy' of life, the Inferno included, passes before him, not only as a shadow-play – for he too lives and suffers through these scenes – and yet also not without that fleeting sense of illusion; and

---

[115]**Attic Tragedy:** Greek tragedy of fifth-century BCE Athens.

[116]**Lucretius:** Titus Lucretius Carus (*c.*99–*c.*55 BCE), a Roman poet and philosopher who explored the relationship between sight, visions and dreams in Book IV of *De Rerum Natura* (*c.*49 BCE).

[117]**Hellenic:** Greek.

[118]*Die Meistersinger* … **interpretation:** this quotation is from the third act of Richard Wagner's opera *Die Meistersinger von Nürnberg* (1868). Hans Sachs is a cobbler and poet in the opera.

[119]**Schopenhauer … capacity:** Arthur Schopenhauer (1780–1860), German philosopher whose magnum opus, *The World as Will and Representation* (1818) was immensely influential on Nietzsche at this stage of his career.

perhaps many, like myself, can remember calling out to themselves in encouragement, amid the perils and terrors of the dream, and with success: 'It is a dream! I want to dream on!' Just as I have often been told of people who have been able to continue one and the same dream over three and more successive nights: facts which clearly show that our innermost being, our common foundation, experiences dreams with profound pleasure and joyful necessity.

This same joyful necessity of dream experiences was also expressed by the Greeks in the figure of Apollo: Apollo, the deity of all plastic forces, is also the soothsaying god. Etymologically the 'shining one', the deity of light, he also holds sway over the beautiful illusion of the inner fantasy world. The higher truth, the perfection of these states in contrast to imperfectly comprehensible daily reality, the deep awareness of nature healing and helping in sleep and dreams, is at the same time the symbolic analogue of soothsaying powers and of art in general, through which life is made both possible and worth living. But our image of Apollo must incorporate the delicate line that the dream image may not overstep without becoming pathological, in which case illusion would deceive us as solid reality; it needs that restraining boundary, that freedom from wilder impulses, that sagacious calm of the sculptor god. His eye must be sunlike, as befits his origin; even should it rage and show displeasure, it still bears the solemnity of the beautiful illusion. And thus we might say of Apollo what Schopenhauer said of man caught up in the veil of Maya:[120]

Just as the boatman sits in his little boat, trusting to his fragile craft in a stormy sea which, boundless in every direction, rises and falls in howling, mountainous waves, so in the midst of a world full of suffering the individual man calmly sits, supported by and trusting the *principium individuationis*.[121]

Indeed, it might be said of Apollo that the unshaken faith in that *principium* and the peaceful stillness of the man caught up in it have found their most sublime expression in him, and we might even describe Apollo as the glorious divine image of the *principium individuationis*, from whose gestures and looks all the delight, wisdom and beauty of 'illusion' speak to us.

In the same passage Schopenhauer has described the tremendous *dread* that grips man when he suddenly loses his way amidst the cognitive forms of appearance, because the principle of sufficient reason, in one of its forms, seems suspended. If we add to this dread the blissful ecstasy which, prompted by the same fragmentation of the *principium individuationis*, rises up from man's innermost core, indeed from nature, we are vouchsafed a glimpse into the nature of the *Dionysiac*, most immediately understandable to us in the analogy of *intoxication*. Under the influence of the narcotic potion hymned by all primitive men and peoples, or in the powerful approach of spring, joyfully penetrating the whole of nature, those Dionysiac urges are awakened, and as they grow more intense, subjectivity becomes a complete forgetting of the self. In medieval Germany, too, the same Dionysiac power sent singing and dancing throngs, constantly increasing, wandering from place to place: in these dancers of Saint John and Saint Vitus we can recognize the Bacchic choruses of the Greeks, with their prehistory in Asia

---

[120]**veil of Maya:** veil of illusion, from the Sanskrit word 'maya' for 'illusion' or 'unreality'.

[121]**Just as ...** ***principum individuationis:*** the quotation is from Arthur Schopenhauer, *The World as Will and Idea*, trans. R.B. Haldane and J. Kemp (London: Kegan Paul, 1909), I. 451–2; see extract 4.4. *Principium Individuationis* is Schopenhauer's term for the principle of individuation, that which identifies one thing or being from another. In Schopenhauer this principle is illusory, a fiction we impose on reality, which is infinitely more chaotic and difficult to comprehend.

Minor, as far back as Babylon and the orgiastic Sacaea.[122] Some people, either through a lack of experience or through obtuseness, turn away with pity or contempt from phenomena such as these as from 'folk diseases', bolstered by a sense of their own sanity; these poor creatures have no idea how blighted and ghostly this 'sanity' of theirs sounds when the glowing life of Dionysiac revellers thunders past them.

Not only is the bond between man and man sealed by the Dionysiac magic: alienated, hostile or subjugated nature, too, celebrates her reconciliation with her lost son, man. The earth gladly offers up her gifts, and the ferocious creatures of the cliffs and the desert peacefully draw near. The chariot of Dionysus is piled high with flowers and garlands; under its yoke stride tigers and panthers. If we were to turn Beethoven's 'Hymn of Joy'[123] into a painting, and not to restrain the imagination even as the multitudes bowed awestruck into the dust: this would bring us close to the Dionysiac. Now the slave is a free man, now all the rigid and hostile boundaries that distress, despotism or 'impudent fashion' have erected between man and man break down. Now, with the gospel of world harmony, each man feels himself not only united, reconciled, and at one with his neighbour, but *one* with him, as if the veil of Maya had been rent and now hung in rags before the mysterious primal Oneness.

Singing and dancing, man expresses himself as a member of a higher community: he has forgotten how to walk and talk, and is about to fly dancing into the heavens. His gestures express enchantment. Just as the animals now speak, and the earth yields up milk and honey, he now gives voice to supernatural sounds: he feels like a god, he himself now walks about enraptured and elated as he saw the gods walk in dreams. Man is no longer an artist, he has become a work of art: the artistic power of the whole of nature reveals itself to the supreme gratification of the primal Oneness amidst the paroxysms of intoxication. The noblest clay, the most precious marble, man, is kneaded and hewn here, and to the chisel-blows of the Dionysiac world-artist there echoes the cry of the Eleusinian mysteries, 'Do you bow low, multitudes? Do you sense the Creator, world?'[124]

[...]

§7

We must now call upon all the aesthetic principles we have so far discussed in order to find our way around the labyrinth, which is how we must refer to the *origin of Greek tragedy*. I do not think I am making an extravagant claim when I say that the problem of this origin has not yet even been seriously tackled, however many times the tattered rags of the classical tradition have been sewn together in their various combinations, and ripped apart again. This tradition tells us quite categorically *that tragedy arose from the tragic chorus*, and was originally only chorus and nothing else. This is what obliges us to penetrate to the core of this tragic chorus as the true primal drama, disregarding the usual aesthetic clichés: that it is the ideal

---

[122]**dancers of Saint John and Saint Vitus … Sacaea:** the dances of Saint John and Saint Vitor are historic examples of dancing mania in which thousands of people reputedly danced erratically until they collapsed; the dancing mania are reported to have taken place throughout medieval mainland Europe. Asia Minor is the western peninsula of Asia, roughly constituting modern Turkey. Sacaea was a five-day Babylonian festival marked by sexual licence and misrule.
[123]**Hymn to Joy:** The last movement of Ludwig Van Beethoven's Ninth Symphony (1824) which contains a setting of Friedrich Schiller's poem 'An die Freude'.
[124][**Translator's note:**] A quotation from Schiller's 'Hymn', the most solemn part of the last movement of Beethoven's Ninth Symphony.

viewer, or that it represents the populace as against the noble realm of the drama proper.[125] This latter interpretation, edifying as certain politicians may find it – suggesting that the immutable moral law of the democratic Athenians was represented in the popular chorus, always correct in its appraisal of the passionate misdeeds and extravagances of the kings – may indeed have been suggested by a phrase of Aristotle's:[126] it can have had no influence on the original formation of tragedy, whose purely religious beginnings rule out the very idea of contrasting the populace with the nobility, as indeed they exclude the whole area of political and social concerns; but with reference to the classical form of the chorus as we know it from Aeschylus and Sophocles, we should also consider it blasphemous to speak of the idea of a presentiment of the 'constitutional representation of the people', though others have not shrunk from such sacrilege. Constitutional representation of the people was unknown to the classical polities, and it is to be hoped that the ancient tragedies had no such 'presentiment' of it.

Much more celebrated than this political explanation of the chorus is the idea put forward by A.W. Schlegel,[127] who proposes that we should see the chorus as being to some degree the epitome and concentration of the mass of spectators, the 'ideal spectator'. This view, when seen alongside the historically traditional idea that the tragedy was originally only the chorus, reveals itself in its true colours, a crude and unscientific yet brilliant statement, but one whose brilliance has been preserved only through the concentrated form of its expression, the truly Germanic predilection for everything that is called 'ideal', and our momentary astonishment. We will be truly astonished once we compare the theatre audience – one which we know very well – with that chorus, and ask ourselves whether it is indeed possible to idealize from that audience anything resembling the tragic chorus. We inwardly deny this, and are just as amazed by the boldness of Schlegel's claim as by the totally different nature of the German audience. We had actually always believed that the true spectator, whoever he might be, must always remain aware that he is watching a work of art and not an empirical reality, while the tragic chorus of the Greeks is required to grant the figures on the stage a physical existence. The chorus of the Oceanides really believes that it is seeing the Titan Prometheus,[128] and thinks itself just as real as the stage god. And is that supposed to be the highest and purest kind of spectator, one who, like the Oceanides, believes that he sees Prometheus real and present in the flesh? And would it be a sign of the ideal spectator to run on to the stage and free the god from his tormentors? We had previously believed in an aesthetic audience, and seen the individual viewer as being all the more skillful the more capable he was of seeing the work of art as art, in an aesthetic way; and now Schlegel's pronouncement tells us that the perfect ideal viewer allows the world on stage to affect him not in an aesthetic way, but in a physically empirical way. 'Oh, those Greeks!' we sighed. 'They are turning our aesthetic on its head!' But once we had become accustomed to it, we repeated Schlegel's dictum every time the chorus was mentioned.

---

[125]**populace … drama proper:** Nietzsche here discredits the idea that the chorus in Greek tragedy represented the democratic voice of the people in opposition to the aristocratic or regal voices of the principal characters in Greek tragedies.
[126]**phrase of Aristotle's:** In the *Poetics*, Aristotle insisted that the Chorus 'should be regarded as one of the actors' which has occasionally been interpreted to mean that the chorus stood in for members of the general population in particular plays.
[127]**A.W. Schlegel:** August Wilhelm Schlegel (1767–1845), Romantic German poet and critic. He described the chorus of Greek tragedy as the ideal spectator in 'Lecture III' in his *Course of Lectures on Dramatic Art and Literature*, trans. John Black (Philadelphia: Hogan and Thompson, 1833), 44. See extract 4.1.
[128]**Oceanides … Titan Prometheus:** the Oceanides were water goddesses who featured as a chorus in *Prometheus Bound* (c.460–430 BCE), a Greek tragedy sometimes attributed to Aeschylus.

But the very emphatic tradition I mentioned before refutes Schlegel in this instance: the chorus as such, without the stage – the primitive form of tragedy, then – and the chorus of ideal spectators are incompatible. What sort of artistic genre would it be that took as its foundation the concept of the spectator, and whose actual form was 'the spectator as such'? The idea of the spectator without a play is an absurd one. I fear that the birth of tragedy may no more be explained with reference to respect for the moral intelligence of the masses than with reference to the concept of the spectator without a play, and I consider this problem too profound even to be touched on by such shallow interpretations.

An infinitely more valuable insight into the meaning of the chorus was put forward by Schiller in the famous preface to the *Bride of Messina*,[129] in which he sees the chorus as a living wall that tragedy pulls around itself to close itself off entirely from the real world and maintain its ideal ground and its poetic freedom.

Schiller uses this as his chief weapon in his fight against the commonplace concept of naturalism, against the illusionism commonly demanded from dramatic poetry. While, for Schiller, in the theatre the daylight itself is merely artificial, the architecture is merely symbolic and the metrical language is idealized, delusions still predominate; it is not enough, for Schiller, that we should only tolerate as a poetic liberty what is in fact the essence of all poetry. The introduction of the chorus is the crucial step towards the open and honest declaration of war on all naturalism in art. This is the kind of interpretation, it seems to me, for which our own age, convinced of its superiority, uses the dismissive catchword 'pseudo-idealism'. I fear, on the other hand, that in our idolization of the natural and the real we have arrived at the opposite pole from our idealism – the realm of the wax museums. These too are without art, like certain popular novels of the present day: I only ask that I should not be troubled with the claim that in this art Schiller's and Goethe's[130] 'pseudo-idealism' has been vanquished.

It is certainly the case, as Schiller rightly saw, that the ground walked upon by the Greek satyr chorus, the chorus of the original tragedy, is an 'ideal' ground, a ground lifted high above the real paths of mortal men. For this chorus the Greeks built the floating scaffold of an invented *natural state*, and placed upon it *natural beings* invented especially for it. It was on this foundation that tragedy arose, and it was indeed for this reason that it was excused from the start from precise depiction of reality. Yet this is not a world randomly imagined to fit in between heaven and earth; rather it is a world of equal reality and credibility, as Olympus with its inhabitants was for the Hellenes.[131] The satyr, the Dionysiac chorist, lives in a world granted existence under the religious sanction of myth and ritual. That tragedy begins with him, that the Dionysiac wisdom of tragedy speaks through him, is for us a phenomenon just as surprising as the very origin of tragedy out of the chorus. Perhaps we shall find a point of departure for our reflections in the claim that the satyr, the invented natural being, relates to cultural humanity as Dionysiac music

---

[129]**Bride of Messina:** *The Bride of Messina, or, the Hostile Brothers* (1803) is a tragedy by the German poet, philosopher, and playwright Friedrich Schiller (1759–1805) which combined classical Greek and nineteenth-century German theatrical techniques. His preface to the play, 'On the Employment of the Chorus in Tragedy', saw the chorus as a vital means of opposing naturalism in theatre. For a modern translation of the preface see https://www.schillerinstitute.org/fid_91-96/931_chorus_trag.html.
[130]**Goethe:** Johann Wolfgang von Goethe (1749–1832), poet, novelist, and dramatist, who was, for Nietzsche, the supreme German verbal artist.
[131]**Olympus ... Hellenes:** Mount Olympus is the highest mountain in Greece; it was thought to be home of the gods by the ancient Greeks, or Hellenes.

relates to civilization. Of the latter, Richard Wagner says that it is annulled by music as lamplight is annulled by the light of day.[132] In the same way, I believe, the Greek man of culture felt himself annulled in the face of the satyr chorus, and the immediate effect of Dionysiac tragedy is that state and society, the gulfs separating man from man, make way for an overwhelming sense of unity that goes back to the very heart of nature. The metaphysical consolation (with which, as I wish to point out, every true tragedy leaves us), that whatever superficial changes may occur, life is at bottom indestructibly powerful and joyful, is given concrete form as a satyr chorus, a chorus of natural beings, living ineradicably behind all civilization, as it were, remaining the same for ever, regardless of the changing generations and the path of history.

This chorus was a consolation to the Hellene,[133] thoughtful and uniquely susceptible as he was to the tenderest and deepest suffering, whose piercing gaze has seen to the core of the terrible destructions of world history and nature's cruelty; and who runs the risk of longing for a Buddha-like denial of the will. He is saved by art, and through art life has saved him for itself.

The ecstasy of the Dionysiac state, abolishing the habitual barriers and boundaries of existence, actually contains, for its duration, a lethargic element into which all past personal experience is plunged. Thus, through this gulf of oblivion, the worlds of everyday and Dionysiac reality become separated. But when one once more becomes aware of this everyday reality, it becomes repellent; this leads to a mood of asceticism, of denial of the will. This is something that Dionysiac man shares with Hamlet: both have truly seen to the essence of things, they have *understood*, and action repels them; for their action can change nothing in the eternal essence of things, they consider it ludicrous or shameful that they should be expected to restore order to the chaotic world. Understanding kills action, action depends on a veil of illusion – this is what Hamlet teaches us, not the stock interpretation of Hamlet as a John-a-dreams who, from too much reflection, from an excess of possibilities, so to speak, fails to act. Not reflection, not that! – True understanding, insight into the terrible truth, outweighs every motive for action, for Hamlet and Dionysiac man alike.[134] No consolation will be of any use from now on, longing passes over the world towards death, beyond the gods themselves; existence, radiantly reflected in the gods or in an immortal 'Beyond', is denied. …

Here, in this supreme menace to the will, there approaches a redeeming, healing enchantress – *art*. She alone can turn these thoughts of repulsion at the horror and absurdity of existence into ideas compatible with life: these are the *sublime* – the taming of horror through art; and *comedy* – the artistic release from the repellence of the absurd. The satyr chorus of the dithyramb[135] is the salvation of Greek art; the frenzies described above were exhausted in the middle world of these Dionysiac attendants.

[…]

---

[132]**Wagner … light of day:** A paraphrase from Richard Wagner's study *Beethoven* (1870); 'Let everyone see for himself how the whole modern world of appearances which, to his despair, everywhere encloses him on all sides, suddenly vanishes to nothing when he hears just the first bars of one of those divine [Beethoven] symphonies. … In a very real sense, it is the same effect that music has on our whole civilisation: music extinguishes it as daylight extinguishes lamplight'; *Richard Wagner's Beethoven (1870)*, trans. Roger Allen (Woodbridge: Boydell, 2014), 179–81.

[133]**Hellene:** Greek.

[134]**understanding … action:** This is a famous reading of Shakespeare's *Hamlet*. True knowledge of reality kills action because it is too 'terrible' to bear; we need illusions of reality, such as art, to function and act.

[135]**dithyramb:** an ancient choral hymn usually dedicated to Dionysus. They were sung and danced by choruses of fifty men or boys.

§10

It is an uncontested tradition that Greek tragedy in its oldest form dealt only with the sufferings of Dionysus, and that for a long time Dionysus was the only theatrical hero. But we may claim with equal certainty that, until Euripides, Dionysus never ceased to be the tragic hero, and that all the celebrated characters of the Greek stage – Prometheus, Oedipus and so on – are merely masks of that original hero, Dionysus. The fact that a divinity lurks behind all these masks is the major reason for the typical 'ideality' of those celebrated characters that has so often aroused astonishment. Someone, I do not know who, claims that all individuals, as individuals, are comic and consequently untragic: from which we can deduce that the Greeks were actually *unable* to bear individuals on the tragic stage. And they do seem to have felt that way, just as the Platonic distinguishing valuation of the 'idea' as against the 'idol' lies deep within the Hellenic spirit. But to use Plato's terminology, we might speak of the tragic figures of the Hellenic stage rather as follows: the one real Dionysus appears in a multiplicity of figures, in the mask of a warrior hero and, we might say, entangled in the net of the individual will. As the god on stage speaks and acts, he resembles an erring, striving, suffering individual: and the fact that he *appears* with this precision and clarity is the effect of Apollo, the interpreter of dreams, who shows the chorus its Dionysiac state through this symbolic appearance. In fact, however, this hero is the suffering Dionysus of the mysteries, the god who himself experiences the suffering of individuation, of whom marvellous myths relate that he was dismembered by the Titans and that, in this condition, he is worshipped as Zagreus.[136] This suggests that dismemberment, the true Dionysiac *suffering*, amounts to a transformation into air, water, earth and fire, and that we should therefore see the condition of individuation as the source and origin of all suffering and hence as something reprehensible. From the smile of this Dionysus were born the Olympian gods, from his tears mankind. In his existence as a dismembered god Dionysus had the dual nature of a cruel, savage daemon and a mild, gentle ruler. But the hope of the epopts[137] was the rebirth of Dionysus, which we can now interpret, with some foreboding, as the end of individuation: the roaring hymn of joy of the epopts celebrated the coming of this third Dionysus. This hope alone casts a ray of joy across the face of the world, torn and fragmented into individuals, mythically symbolized by Demeter,[138] sunk in eternal grief, who *rejoices* once more only when told that she can give birth to Dionysus *again*. In these ideas we already have all the component parts of a profound and pessimistic view of the world, and at the same time the *mystery doctrine of tragedy*: the basic understanding of the unity of all things, individuation seen as the primal source of evil, art as the joyful hope that the spell of individuation can be broken, as a presentiment of a restored oneness.

[...]

§25

Music and tragic myth are to an equal extent expressions of the Dionysiac capacity of a people, and they are inseparable. Both originate in a sphere of art beyond the Apolline. Both

---

[136]**Zagreus:** In Orphic myth, Zagreus was the child of Zeus and Persephone who was torn to pieces by the Titans. Zeus swallowed Zagreus's heart before impregnating Semele, mortal mother of Dionysus.

[137]**epopts:** initiates in the Eleusinian Mysteries, the most famous religious rites of ancient Greece.

[138]**Demeter:** the Greek goddess of earth, agriculture, and fertility. Her mythic story was perhaps the best known of the Eleusian Mystery cults. She was mother of Persephone and grieved for four months every year while her daughter was in the underworld; her story informed ancient understandings of seasonal renewal.

transfigure a region in whose chords of delight dissonance as well as the terrible image of the world charmingly fade away; they both play with the sting of displeasure, trusting to their extremely powerful magical arts; both use this play to justify the existence even of the 'worst world'. Here the Dionysiac, as against the Apolline, proves to be the eternal and original artistic force, calling the whole phenomenal world into existence: in the midst of it a new transfiguring illusion is required if the animated world of individuation is to be kept alive. If we could imagine dissonance becoming man – and what else is man? – then in order to stay alive that dissonance would need a wonderful illusion, covering its own being with a veil of beauty. That is the real artistic intention of Apollo, in whose name we bring together all those innumerable illusions of the beauty of appearance, which at each moment make life worth living and urge us to experience the next moment.

From the foundation of all existence, the Dionysiac substratum of the world, no more can enter the consciousness of the human individual than can be overcome once more by that Apolline power of transfiguration, so that both of these artistic impulses are forced to unfold in strict proportion to one another, according to the law of eternal justice. Where the Dionysiac powers have risen as impetuously as we now experience them, Apollo, enveloped in a cloud, must also have descended to us; some future generation will behold his most luxuriant effects of beauty.

Further reading

F.A. Lea, *The Tragic Philosopher: Friedrich Nietzsche* (London: Athlone Press, 1993).

M.S. Silk and J.P. Stern, *Nietzsche on Tragedy* (Cambridge: Cambridge University Press, 1981).

Michael Tanner, *Nietzsche: A Verse Short Introduction* (Oxford: Oxford University Press, 2000).

Lee Spinks, *Friedrich Nietzsche* (London and New York: Routledge, 2003).

CHAPTER 5
1900 TO 1968

In the wake of contentious nineteenth-century debates about tragedy's relation to moral order, the twentieth century's two world wars and mass killings prompted a cacophony of new ideas and arguments about the genre. In their responses to these new crises, modern theorists of tragedy explored variations on the essential questions posed since Plato and Aristotle: what is tragedy, and is it good for us or bad? Why do we seek it out, should we, and if so, in what forms? Twentieth-century thinkers approached these questions with both the advantages and the burdens of an enormous archive of previous reflections on tragedy. Beyond the original classical debates, and their early modern and eighteenth-century heirs, modern writers were inescapably shaped by the consequences of nineteenth-century philosophical debates about the genre, as well as by emerging concerns about the ethical status of these intellectual traditions themselves. In the context of new political and intellectual crises, modern enquiries into tragedy's possible benefits and dangers raised new questions about the political and social consequences of engaging with tragic drama. Looking backwards towards a genre originally rooted in the distant past, they asked with increasing urgency whether tragedy could still exist in the modern world, and what it could and should look like if so.

This chapter's survey of modern approaches to tragedy begins at the turn of the twentieth century with Sigmund Freud, who rooted the field of psychoanalysis in large part on his reading of Sophocles' *Oedipus Rex* (extract 5.1). Like Plato and Aristotle, Freud attributes tragedy's power especially to the identification that its suffering protagonists solicit. Oedipus, he argues, has maintained his magnetic pull on our imaginations across the centuries because he taps a universal male psychic instinct, while the interrogations that slowly uncover his true story represent the process of decoding signs and symptoms that psychoanalysis itself – like literary study – pursues.

Freud's emphasis on the tragic protagonist's interior workings built on, and revised, the pan-European Romantic fascination with the ways in which tragedy heightened individual emotional experience and our capacity to identify with others. The intellectual legacy of German idealism also resonated, albeit in different ways, in the work of British literary scholar A.C. Bradley, whose influential *Shakespearean Tragedy* (1904) similarly locates the literary power of Shakespeare's tragedies in the male protagonists that he terms tragic heroes (extract 5.2). Firmly indebted to Hegel's reading of classical tragedy, Bradley identifies the plays' electricity in the tensions between these heroes' greatness, on the one hand, and their calamitous decisions, which bring about their suffering and the suffering of others, on the other. In singling out character, rather than action, as tragedy's central feature, Bradley crucially and consequentially revises Aristotle's conception of *hamartia*, originally framed as an error (literally 'missing the mark') but now widely understood as a tragic flaw. In different ways, both Freud and Bradley praise tragedy for probing the inner recesses of the individual male psyche, and illuminating its motives and contradictions.

While Freud and Bradley turned to tragedy to shape their respective analytical disciplines, modernist writers reflected on tragedy with an eye to their own evolving literary experiments. For W.B. Yeats, influenced by Nietzsche's *Birth of Tragedy* (extract 4.8) and fascinated by mysticism, tragedy's value lies in undermining rather than underscoring individual selves. Eschewing the idea of character, which he criticizes as a bourgeois concept linked to the quotidian worlds of comedy, Yeats praises tragedy in 1910 as an overwhelmingly ecstatic, Dionysian force that dissolves the barriers between individuals (extract 5.3). In contrast to the confidence with which Freud, Bradley and Yeats declaim on the meanings of tragic texts, Virginia Woolf, who studied Greek, translated Aeschylus, and was influenced by Cambridge classical scholar Jane E. Harrison, insists on the fundamental impossibility of fully understanding texts so removed from us by time, language, and culture, even as she admires the apparently iconic types represented in Greek tragedies (extract 5.4). Also unlike Freud, Bradley, and Yeats, Woolf turns her attention especially to the complex suffering of female tragic protagonists, in keeping with her interest in developing nuanced female characters in her own fiction, and her feminist critique of literary production in *A Room of One's Own* (1929).

For all their substantial differences, Freud, Bradley, Yeats, and Woolf, writing in the early years of the twentieth century, shared an understanding of tragedy's terrain as primarily psychological, reflecting and shaping emotional experience within and between people, in keeping with their various debts to nineteenth-century German philosophical writing on tragedy.[1] These debts were to be sharply problematized by the middle of the twentieth century, as the horrors of the Holocaust complicated the legacy of German intellectual traditions. As Jaś Elsner has observed, *Bildung* – the German tradition of education, formation, and self-cultivation, deeply rooted in classical literature – 'was meant to make you a better person ethically', yet 'between 1933 and 1945, the nation that had supremely created and fostered this ideology … systematically and in the name of an insane racist nationalism disproved the link between *Bildung* and humanity, between cultural education and ethics, between the Classical tradition and anything we might want to value in human action'.[2] Given the centrality of Greek tragedy to shaping the German philosophical tradition, and vice versa, the terrible contradiction between this tradition's claims to humane goals and the inhumane political realities to which it gave rise complicated the horizon of possibilities for thinking about tragedy.

Many responses to these new ethical and political challenges emphasized looking outwards from tragedy's inner psychological landscapes to its historical and political settings and implications. Writing between the two world wars, the German Jewish philosopher Walter Benjamin, influenced by Marxist thought, contrasted classical tragedy with the modern German *Trauerspiel*, or mourning-play, to consider the significance of replacing mythic roots and aristocratic characters with the more familiar and realistic materials of history. His exploration of newer versions of tragedy rooted in increasingly contemporary settings and problems paved the way for larger questions about tragedy's place – or lack thereof – in the post-war world. Responding to similar concerns, in 1948 German playwright and director Bertolt Brecht

---

[1]See previous chapter; on German philosophy's centrality in shaping modern ideas of tragedy, see Joshua Billings, *Genealogy of the Tragic: Greek Tragedy and German Philosophy* (Princeton: Princeton University Press, 2014) and Miriam Leonard, *Tragic Modernities* (Cambridge, MA: Harvard University Press, 2015).

[2]Jaś Elsner, 'Reception and Redemption: Some Questions in Response to Charles Martindale's Call for a New Humanism', *Classical Receptions Journal* 5, no. 2 (2013): 212–7, 215.

attacked the Aristotelian idea of catharsis by arguing that empathetic responses to characters instilled passivity and complacency in audiences (extract 5.5). Brecht criticized what he saw as the genre's conventional form in political terms, for weakening audience members' sense of outrage and injustice by training them to see suffering as an inevitable feature of human existence, rather than a consequence of irresponsible decisions that can and must be fought.

Brecht proposed to replace tragedy's appeal to empathy with what he termed 'epic theatre', or 'dialectical theatre', which should estrange audiences from depictions of suffering rather than invite identification. Other mid-century playwrights suggested alternate ways to shatter theatrical conventions in the interests of challenging audiences' expectations and complacency. French surrealist poet and playwright Antonin Artaud imagined a Theatre of Cruelty, which should strip words of meaning and startle spectators into direct experience of pain. Jean Anouilh, Jean-Paul Sartre, Eugène Ionesco, and Samuel Beckett, whose plays have been identified alternately with existentialism, theatre of the absurd, and black comedy, developed bleak and sometimes apparently nonsensical forms of dramatic representations in the interests of rethinking the medium's intellectual, emotional, and ethical goals.[3]

These new theatrical experiments prompted questions about the limits of generic definitions. Alongside the ongoing questions inherited from antiquity about whether tragedy was harmful or beneficial, twentieth-century writers found themselves asking whether a form shaped by the mythical, quasi-magical, and historically alien realm of Greek antiquity could still flourish in a secular, capitalist, postcolonial world. In *The Death of Tragedy* (1961), literary scholar George Steiner vehemently and influentially insisted that tragedy was intrinsically a product of the ancient Greek world, and fundamentally inimical to the optimistic belief in progress inherent in a modern world shaped by the Enlightenment, Christianity, and Marxism (extract 5.7). Steiner has been criticized by many as conservative and restrictive in his account of what tragedy could be, but some writers typically seen as progressive also took similar views. The South African playwright Athol Fugard, known for his politically and formally daring dramatizations of his society's racial crises, suggested in 1963 that modern drama had lost its grasp on what he called the tragic dimension, which he identified as dependent on forms of certainty and absoluteness no longer available in the twentieth century (extract 5.8). Although Fugard's own plays include adaptations of Greek tragedies, his own hesitation over the term's continuing viability suggests that he might label his own versions of these plays by other names.

Despite the forcefulness and influence of Steiner's claims, many critics sharply disagreed with the assumption that tragedy must represent a specific literary model no longer accessible in the modern world. In 1955, the French novelist and philosopher Albert Camus suggested that the middle of the twentieth century was in fact uniquely congenial for the flourishing of a genre fundamentally rooted in the restless dissatisfaction linked with periods of cultural and political upheaval. Similarly, in an explicit response to Steiner, British scholar Raymond Williams described tragedy as a form that has constantly evolved in conversation with historic circumstances, and argued optimistically for the possibility of revolutionary tragedy (extract 5.9). Affinities between tragedy and resistance to unjust power date back at least as far as Athenian democracy's challenges to tyranny, and other twentieth-century philosophers turned to tragedy to discuss the possibility of political change. Philosopher Hannah Arendt, who

---

[3]See Martin Esslin, *Theater of the Absurd* (New York: Anchor, 1961).

escaped Nazi Germany, closed her 1963 *On Revolution* with two quotations from Sophocles' *Oedipus at Colonus*, using the play paradoxically as a mouthpiece for both optimistic and pessimistic views about the political future.[4]

While philosophers debated what could count as tragedy, and whether the genre was intrinsically conservative or flexible, playwrights wrestled with similar questions. In the spirit of the bourgeois tragedy developed by eighteenth-century playwright George Lillo (extract 3.2), in 1949 the American playwright Arthur Miller challenged Aristotle's claims about the greatness of the tragic hero by arguing that 'the common man is as apt a subject for tragedy in its highest sense as kings were.'[5] Miller's plays, especially *Death of a Salesman*, became icons of the tragic theatre in post-war America, as did the similarly everyday domestic worlds of Eugene O'Neill and Tennessee Williams. An even more modern and popularized genre, the urban gangster film, offered an alternative model for tragedy's evolving possibilities. In 1948 American film critic Robert Warshow described the gangster film as an acutely modern version of tragedy, one that allowed viewers to participate vicariously in the pleasurable freedoms of a dark underworld while maintaining the safety of their bourgeois positions on the right side of the law, both reflecting and enabling a distinctly American juxtaposition of rebellion and conformity (extract 5.6). Both Americans from Jewish immigrant families, Miller and Warshow – like Arendt – represent a new cultural challenge to the cultural ideas of tragedy fostered by German philosophical traditions.

Just as new voices increasingly challenged the long-standing convention that tragedy should depict the upper classes, emerging critiques began to challenge what many perceived as the genre's long-standing focus on male heroism. In 1949 Simone de Beauvoir wrote, in *The Second Sex*, that 'The *Eumenides* represents the triumph of the patriarchate over the matriarchate.'[6] Woolf had earlier complicated this criticism with her observations of the complex sympathies in Greek tragic portraits of female characters, insisting that 'Clytemnestra is no unmitigated villainess. 'δεινὸν τὸ τίκτειν ἐστίν' she says –'there is a strange power in motherhood.' It is no murderess, violent and unredeemed, whom Orestes kills within the house.'[7] These different, though not necessarily incompatible, readings of women's roles in tragedies developed a foundation for the more extended feminist debates about tragedy that would emerge in the wake of these critiques.

Opening with authoritative claims rooted in nineteenth-century philosophical traditions, twentieth-century theories of tragedy unfolded in new directions, both reflecting and shaping modernist experiments, and responding to the enormous ethical questions posed by the Holocaust's challenge to Europe's cultural achievements. As groups including playwrights, immigrants, Americans, and women added their voices to the developing conversations, assumptions about authority changed, as did expectations of what tragedy was or could be. Approaching another wave of social tumult in the 1960s, these conversations established foundations for the continuing changes and new questions discussed in the subsequent chapter.

---

[4]Hannah Arendt, *On Revolution* (New York: Viking, 1963), 281; see also Robert Pirro, *Hannah Arendt and the Politics of Tragedy* (DeKalb, IL: Northern Illinois University Press, 2000).
[5]Arthur Miller, 'Tragedy and the Common Man', *New York Times*, February 27, 1949, p. 1.
[6]Simone de Beauvoir, *The Second Sex*, trans. H.M. Parshley (New York: Vintage, 1952), 99.
[7]Virginia Woolf, 'On Not Knowing Greek', in *The Common Reader* (New York: Harcourt, Brace, 1925), 28; see extract 5.4. The Greek word '*tiktein*', which Woolf translates as 'motherhood', literally means 'to give birth'.

5.1 SIGMUND FREUD, *THE INTERPRETATION OF DREAMS* (1900)

Sigmund Freud (1856–1939) is known as the founder of psychoanalysis. Born to Jewish parents in what is now the Czech Republic, he became a doctor in Vienna until escaping the Nazis for England in 1938. Through observing and reflecting on his patients, he developed influential theories about the unconscious mind. Freud frequently turned to both Greek and Shakespearean tragedy to inspire and illustrate his theories. In *The Interpretation of Dreams* (1900), he develops one of his most famous theories through examining Sophocles' *Oedipus Rex*, which he sees as illuminating a universal (albeit exclusively male) childhood wish to marry one's mother and kill one's father. For Freud, literary texts, like dreams and jokes, offer privileged vehicles for expressing unconscious wishes and fears. Freud's arguments about Oedipus have prompted controversy, but his commitment to excavating hidden and conflicted meanings has had an influential role in shaping modern literary criticism.

According to my already extensive experience, parents play a leading part in the infantile psychology of all persons who subsequently become psychoneurotics. Falling in love with one parent and hating the other forms part of the permanent stock of the psychic impulses which arise in early childhood, and are of such importance as the material of the subsequent neurosis. But I do not believe that psychoneurotics are to be sharply distinguished in this respect from other persons who remain normal – that is, I do not believe that they are capable of creating something absolutely new and peculiar to themselves. It is far more probable – and this is confirmed by incidental observations of normal children – that in their amorous or hostile attitude toward their parents, psychoneurotics do no more than reveal to us, by magnification, something that occurs less markedly and intensively in the minds of the majority of children. Antiquity has furnished us with legendary matter which corroborates this belief, and the profound and universal validity of the old legends is explicable only by an equally universal validity of the above-mentioned hypothesis of infantile psychology.

I am referring to the legend of King Oedipus and the *Oedipus Rex* of Sophocles. Oedipus, the son of Laius, king of Thebes, and Jocasta, is exposed as a suckling, because an oracle had informed the father that his son, who was still unborn, would be his murderer. He is rescued, and grows up as a king's son at a foreign court, until, being uncertain of his origin, he, too, consults the oracle, and is warned to avoid his native place, for he is destined to become the murderer of his father and the husband of his mother. On the road leading away from his supposed home he meets King Laius, and in a sudden quarrel strikes him dead. He comes to Thebes, where he solves the riddle of the Sphinx, who is barring the way to the city, whereupon he is elected king by the grateful Thebans, and is rewarded with the hand of Jocasta. He reigns for many years in peace and honour, and begets two sons and two daughters upon his unknown mother, until at last a plague breaks out – which causes the Thebans to consult the oracle anew. Here Sophocles' tragedy begins. The messengers bring the reply that the plague will stop as soon as the murderer of Laius is driven from the country. But where is he?

> Where shall be found,
> Faint, and hard to be known, the trace of the ancient guilt?[8]

The action of the play consists simply in the disclosure, approached step by step and artistically delayed (and comparable to the work of a psychoanalysis) that Oedipus himself is the murderer of Laius, and that he is the son of the murdered man and Jocasta. Shocked by the abominable crime which he has unwittingly committed, Oedipus blinds himself, and departs from his native city. The prophecy of the oracle has been fulfilled.

The *Oedipus Rex* is a tragedy of fate; its tragic effect depends on the conflict between the all-powerful will of the gods and the vain efforts of human beings threatened with disaster; resignation to the divine will, and the perception of one's own impotence is the lesson which the deeply moved spectator is supposed to learn from the tragedy. Modern authors have therefore sought to achieve a similar tragic effect by expressing the same conflict in stories of their own invention. But the playgoers have looked on unmoved at the unavailing efforts of guiltless men to avert the fulfilment of curse or oracle; the modern tragedies of destiny have failed of their effect.

If the *Oedipus Rex* is capable of moving a modern reader or playgoer no less powerfully than it moved the contemporary Greeks, the only possible explanation is that the effect of the Greek tragedy does not depend upon the conflict between fate and human will, but upon the peculiar nature of the material by which this conflict is revealed. There must be a voice within us which is prepared to acknowledge the compelling power of fate in the *Oedipus*, while we are able to condemn the situations occurring in *Die Ahnfrau*[9] or other tragedies of fate as arbitrary inventions. And there actually is a motive in the story of King Oedipus which explains the verdict of this inner voice. His fate moves us only because it might have been our own, because the oracle laid upon us before our birth the very curse which rested upon him. It may be that we were all destined to direct our first sexual impulses toward our mothers, and our first impulses of hatred and violence toward our fathers; our dreams convince us that we were. King Oedipus, who slew his father Laius and wedded his mother Jocasta, is nothing more or less than a wish fulfilment – the fulfilment of the wish of our childhood. But we, more fortunate than he, in so far as we have not become psychoneurotics, have since our childhood succeeded in withdrawing our sexual impulses from our mothers, and in forgetting our jealousy of our fathers. We recoil from the person for whom this primitive wish of our childhood has been fulfilled with all the force of the repression which these wishes have undergone in our minds since childhood. As the poet brings the guilt of Oedipus to light by his investigation, he forces us to become aware of our own inner selves, in which the same impulses are still extant, even though they are suppressed. The antithesis with which the chorus departs: –

> ...Behold, this is Oedipus,
> Who unravelled the great riddle, and was first in power,
> Whose fortune all the townsmen praised and envied;
> See in what dread adversity he sank![10]

---

[8]**Where ... guilt:** Sophocles, *Oedipus Rex*, l. 108–9.
[9]***Die Ahnfrau***, or *The Ancestress*: 1816 tragedy by Austrian playwright Franz Grillparzer (1791–1872), in which the ghost of a woman killed by her husband for adultery haunts her former home and her descendants, prompting revelations and violence.
[10]**Behold ... sank:** Sophocles, *Oedipus Rex*, ll. 1524–7.

– this admonition touches us and our own pride, us who since the years of our childhood have grown so wise and so powerful in our own estimation. Like Oedipus, we live in ignorance of the desires that offend morality, the desires that nature has forced upon us and after their unveiling we may well prefer to avert our gaze from the scenes of our childhood.[11]

In the very text of Sophocles' tragedy there is an unmistakable reference to the fact that the Oedipus legend had its source in dream-material of immemorial antiquity, the content of which was the painful disturbance of the child's relations to its parents caused by the first impulses of sexuality. Jocasta comforts Oedipus – who is not yet enlightened, but is troubled by the recollection of the oracle – by an allusion to a dream which is often dreamed, though it cannot, in her opinion, mean anything: –

For many a man hath seen himself in dreams
His mother's mate, but he who gives no heed
To suchlike matters bears the easier life.[12]

The dream of having sexual intercourse with one's mother was as common then as it is to-day with many people, who tell it with indignation and astonishment. As may well be imagined, it is the key to the tragedy and the complement to the dream of the death of the father. The Oedipus fable is the reaction of phantasy to these two typical dreams, and just as such a dream, when occurring to an adult, is experienced with feelings of aversion, so the content of the fable must include terror and self-chastisement. The form which it subsequently assumed was the result of an uncomprehending secondary elaboration of the material, which sought to make it serve a theological intention.[13] The attempt to reconcile divine omnipotence with human responsibility must, of course, fail with this material as with any other.

Another of the great poetic tragedies, Shakespeare's *Hamlet*, is rooted in the same soil as *Oedipus Rex*.[14] But the whole difference in the psychic life of the two widely separated periods of civilization, and the progress, during the course of time, of repression in the emotional life of humanity, is manifested in the differing treatment of the same material. In *Oedipus Rex* the basic wish-phantasy of the child is brought to light and realized as it is in dreams; in *Hamlet* it remains repressed, and we learn of its existence – as we discover the relevant facts in a neurosis – only through the inhibitory effects which proceed from it. In the more modern drama, the curious fact that it is possible to remain in complete uncertainty as to the character of the hero has proved to be quite consistent with the overpowering effect of the tragedy. The play is based upon Hamlet's hesitation in accomplishing the task of revenge assigned to him; the text does not give the cause or the motive of this hesitation, nor have the manifold

---

[11]**[Freud's note]:** None of the discoveries of psychoanalytical research has evoked such embittered contradiction, such furious opposition, and also such entertaining acrobatics of criticism, as this indication of the incestuous impulses of childhood which survive in the unconscious. An attempt has even been made recently, in defiance of all experience, to assign only a 'symbolic' significance to incest. Ferenczi has given an ingenious reinterpretation of the Oedipus myth, based on a passage in one of Schopenhauer's letters, in *Imago*, i, 1912. The 'Oedipus complex', which was first alluded to here in *The Interpretation of Dreams*, has through further study of the subject, acquired an unexpected significance for the understanding of human history and the evolution of religion and morality. See *Totem und Taboo*.

[12]**For ... life:** Sophocles, *Oedipus Rex,* ll. 981–3.

[13]**[Freud's note]:** Cf. the dream-material of exhibitionism, p. 141.

[14]***Hamlet:*** *c.*1600 play by Shakespeare, in which the ghost of Hamlet's father asks his son to avenge his murder by his brother, who has since married Hamlet's mother.

attempts at interpretation succeeded in doing so. According to the still prevailing conception, a conception for which Goethe was first responsible, Hamlet represents the type of man whose active energy is paralysed by excessive intellectual activity: 'Sicklied o'er with the pale cast of thought.' According to another conception, the poet has endeavoured to portray a morbid, irresolute character, on the verge of neurasthenia. The plot of the drama, however, shows us that Hamlet is by no means intended to appear as a character wholly incapable of action. On two separate occasions we see him assert himself: once in a sudden outburst of rage, when he stabs the eavesdropper behind the arras, and on the other occasion when he deliberately, and even craftily, with the complete unscrupulousness of a prince of the Renaissance, sends the two courtiers to the death which was intended for himself. What is it, then, that inhibits him in accomplishing the task which his father's ghost has laid upon him? Here the explanation offers itself that it is the peculiar nature of this task. Hamlet is able to do anything but take vengeance upon the man who did away with his father and has taken his father's place with his mother – the man who shows him in realization the repressed desires of his own childhood. The loathing which should have driven him to revenge is thus replaced by self-reproach, by conscientious scruples, which tell him that he himself is no better than the murderer whom he is required to punish. I have here translated into consciousness what had to remain unconscious in the mind of the hero; if anyone wishes to call Hamlet an hysterical subject I cannot but admit that this is the deduction to be drawn from my interpretation. The sexual aversion which Hamlet expresses in conversation with Ophelia is perfectly consistent with this deduction – the same sexual aversion which during the next few years was increasingly to take possession of the poet's soul, until it found its supreme utterance in *Timon of Athens*.[15] It can, of course, be only the poet's own psychology with which we are confronted in *Hamlet*; and in a work on Shakespeare by Georg Brandes[16] (1896) I find the statement that the drama was composed immediately after the death of Shakespeare's father (1601) – that is to say, when he was still mourning his loss, and during a revival, as we may fairly assume, of his own childish feelings in respect of his father. It is known, too, that Shakespeare's son, who died in childhood, bore the name of Hamnet (identical with Hamlet). Just as *Hamlet* treats of the relation of the son to his parents, so *Macbeth*,[17] which was written about the same period, is based upon the theme of childlessness. Just as all neurotic symptoms, like dreams themselves, are capable of hyper-interpretation, and even require such hyper-interpretation before they become perfectly intelligible, so every genuine poetical creation must have proceeded from more than one motive, more than one impulse in the mind of the poet, and must admit of more than one interpretation. I have here attempted to interpret only the deepest stratum of impulses in the mind of the creative poet.[18]

---

[15]***Timon of Athens:*** *c.*1605 play by Shakespeare, probably collaboratively written with Thomas Middleton, in which a wealthy and generous Athenian descends into misanthropy, misogyny, madness, and death after his friends abandon him when he has given away all his money.

[16]**Georg Brandes:** Danish scholar and literary critic (1842–1927), whose work included an influential 1896 book on Shakespeare.

[17]**Macbeth:** in Shakespeare's play (*c.*1605), the childless Macbeth murders the king of Scotland but is eventually killed, with rule restored to the original king's son.

[18][**Freud's note, added 1919**] These indications in the direction of an analytical understanding of *Hamlet* were subsequently developed by Dr Ernest Jones, who defended the above conception against others which have been put forward in the literature of the subject. (*The Problem of Hamlet and the Oedipus Complex*, 1911.) The relation of the material of Hamlet to the 'myth of the birth of the hero' has been demonstrated by O. Rank. Further attempts at an

Further reading

Rachel Bowlby, 'Freud's Classical Mythologies', in *Freudian Mythologies: Greek Tragedy and Modern Identities* (Oxford: Oxford University Press, 2007), 14–46.

Cynthia Chase, 'Oedipal Textuality: Reading Freud's Reading of Oedipus', *Diacritics* 9, no. 1 (1979): 54–68.

André Green, 'Prologue: The Psycho-analytic Reading of Tragedy', in *The Tragic Effect: The Oedipus Complex in Tragedy*, trans. Alan Sheridan (Cambridge: Cambridge University Press, 1979), 1–34.

Miriam Leonard, 'Freud and Tragedy: Oedipus and the Gender of the Universal', *Classical Receptions Journal* 5, no. 1 (2013): 63–83.

analysis of *Macbeth* will be found in my essay on *Einige Charaktertypen, aus der psychoanalytischen Arbeit*, in *Imago*, iv, 1916 (*Ges. Schriften*, Bd. x), in L. Jekels's *Shakespeare's Macbeth*, in *Imago*, v, 1918; and in *The Oedipus Complex as an Explanation of Hamlet's Mystery: A Study in Motive* (*American Journal of Psychology*, Vol. xxi, 1910).

5.2 A.C. BRADLEY, *SHAKESPEAREAN TRAGEDY* (1904)

Albert Cecil Bradley (1851–1935) was a British literary scholar known for his study of Shakespeare's tragedies. Influenced by classical ideas of tragedy inherited from Aristotle (extract 1.2) as well as nineteenth-century German theorists of tragedy, especially G. W. F. Hegel (extract 4.6), he explores Shakespeare's conception of tragedy through analysing the conflicts and inner working of the plays' characters. In *Shakespearean Tragedy* (1904), Bradley defines Shakespeare's model of tragedy as focused on a single hero – invariably male – who experiences exceptional suffering, calamity, and ultimately death, not accidentally or passively but as a direct result of his own actions. Whether good or evil, the hero possesses greatness, and his distinctively extreme nature brings about his disastrous choices. For Bradley, the relationship between a character's psychology and action lies at the heart of the sublimity and awe that he attributes to Shakespeare's tragedy. Bradley has provoked mixed responses – he is both revered as the foundation of modern criticism, and criticized for treating fictional characters as actual people – but the debates themselves bear witness to the enduring influence of his legacy.

LECTURE I
THE SUBSTANCE OF SHAKESPEAREAN TRAGEDY

The question we are to consider in this lecture may be stated in a variety of ways. We may put it thus: What is the substance of a Shakespearean tragedy, taken in abstraction both from its form and from the differences in point of substance between one tragedy and another? Or thus: What is the nature of the tragic aspect of life as represented by Shakespeare? What is the general fact shown now in this tragedy and now in that? And we are putting the same question when we ask: What is Shakespeare's tragic conception, or conception of tragedy?

These expressions, it should be observed, do not imply that Shakespeare himself ever asked or answered such a question; that he set himself to reflect on the tragic aspects of life, that he framed a tragic conception, and still less that, like Aristotle or Corneille,[19] he had a theory of the kind of poetry called tragedy. These things are all possible; how far any one of them is probable we need not discuss; but none of them is presupposed by the question we are going to consider. This question implies only that, as a matter of fact, Shakespeare in writing tragedy did represent a certain aspect of life in a certain way, and that through examination of his writings we ought to be able, to some extent, to describe this aspect and way in terms addressed to the understanding. Such a description, so far as it is true and adequate, may, after these explanations, be called indifferently an account of the substance of Shakespearean tragedy, or an account of Shakespeare's conception of tragedy or view of the tragic fact.

Two further warnings may be required. In the first place, we must remember that the tragic aspect of life is only one aspect. We cannot arrive at Shakespeare's whole dramatic way of looking at the world from his tragedies alone, as we can arrive at Milton's way of regarding things, or at Wordsworth's or at Shelley's, by examining almost any one of their important

---

[19]**Corneille:** Pierre Corneille (1606–84), French tragic playwright; see extract 2.6.

works. Speaking very broadly, one may say that these poets at their best always look at things in one light; but *Hamlet* and *Henry IV* and *Cymbeline* reflect things from quite distinct positions,[20] and Shakespeare's whole dramatic view is not to be identified with any one of these reflections. And, in the second place, I may repeat that in these lectures, at any rate for the most part, we are to be content with his *dramatic* view, and are not to ask whether it corresponded exactly with his opinions or creed outside his poetry – the opinions or creed of the being whom we sometimes oddly call 'Shakespeare the man.' It does not seem likely that outside his poetry he was a very simple-minded Catholic or Protestant or Atheist, as some have maintained; but we cannot be sure, as with those other poets we can, that in his works he expressed his deepest and most cherished convictions on ultimate questions, or even that he had any. And in his dramatic conceptions there is enough to occupy us.

I

In approaching our subject it will be best, without attempting to shorten the path by referring to famous theories of the drama, to start directly from the facts, and to collect from them gradually an idea of Shakespearean Tragedy. And first, to begin from the outside, such a tragedy brings before us a considerable number of persons (many more than the persons in a Greek play, unless the members of the Chorus are reckoned among them); but it is pre-eminently the story of one person, the 'hero,'[21] or at most of two, the 'hero' and 'heroine.' Moreover, it is only in the love-tragedies, *Romeo and Juliet* and *Antony and Cleopatra*, that the heroine is as much the centre of the action as the hero. The rest, including *Macbeth*, are single stars. So that, having noticed the peculiarity of these two dramas, we may henceforth, for the sake of brevity, ignore it, and may speak of the tragic story as being concerned primarily with one person.

The story, next, leads up to, and includes, the *death* of the hero. On the one hand (whatever may be true of tragedy elsewhere), no play at the end of which the hero remains alive is, in the full Shakespearean sense, a tragedy; and we no longer class *Troilus and Cressida* or *Cymbeline* as such, as did the editors of the Folio.[22] On the other hand, the story depicts also the troubled part of the hero's life which precedes and leads up to his death; and an instantaneous death occurring by 'accident' in the midst of prosperity would not suffice for it. It is, in fact, essentially a tale of suffering and calamity conducting to death.

The suffering and calamity are, moreover, exceptional. They befall a conspicuous person. They are themselves of some striking kind. They are also, as a rule, unexpected, and contrasted with previous happiness or glory. A tale, for example, of a man slowly worn to death by disease, poverty, little cares, sordid vices, petty persecutions, however piteous or dreadful it might be, would not be tragic in the Shakespearean sense.

Such exceptional suffering and calamity, then, affecting the hero, and – we must now add – generally extending far and wide beyond him, so as to make the whole scene a scene of woe, are an essential ingredient in tragedy, and a chief source of the tragic emotions, and especially of pity. But the proportions of this ingredient, and the direction taken by tragic pity, will naturally

---

[20]**Hamlet … distinct positions:** Bradley juxtaposes three very different Shakespearean protagonists, from very different kinds of plays. *Hamlet* (c.1600) is a revenge tragedy, *Henry IV* (c.1597) is a history play, and *Cymbeline* (c.1611) is typically categorized as a romance, or tragicomedy.

[21][**Bradley's note:**] *Julius Caesar* is not an exception to this rule. Caesar, whose murder comes in the Third Act, is in a sense the dominating figure in the story, but Brutus is the 'hero'.

[22]**Folio:** Shakespeare's First Folio (1623) was produced seven years after his death under the auspices of his playing company, the King's Men.

vary greatly. Pity, for example, has a much larger part in *King Lear* than in *Macbeth*, and is directed in the one case chiefly to the hero, in the other chiefly to minor characters.

Let us now pause for a moment on the ideas we have so far reached. They would more than suffice to describe the whole tragic fact as it presented itself to the mediaeval mind. To the mediaeval mind a tragedy meant a narrative rather than a play, and its notion of the matter of this narrative may readily be gathered from Dante or, still better, from Chaucer. Chaucer's *Monk's Tale* is a series of what he calls 'tragedies'; and this means in fact a series of tales *De Casibus Virorum Illustrium* – stories of the Falls of Illustrious Men, such as Lucifer, Adam, Hercules and Nebuchadnezzar. And the Monk ends the tale of Croesus thus:

> Anhanged was Cresus, the proudè kyng;
> His roial tronè myghte hym nat availle.
> Tragédie is noon oother maner thyng,
> Ne kan in syngyng criè ne biwaille
> But for that Fortune alwey wole assaile
> With unwar strook the regnès that been proude;
> For whan men trusteth hire, thanne wol she faille,
> And covere hire brighte facè with a clowde.[23]

A total reverse of fortune, coming unawares upon a man who 'stood in high degree', happy and apparently secure, – such was the tragic fact to the mediaeval mind. It appealed strongly to common human sympathy and pity; it startled also another feeling, that of fear. It frightened men and awed them. It made them feel that man is blind and helpless, the plaything of an inscrutable power, called by the name of Fortune or some other name, – a power which appears to smile on him for a little, and then on a sudden strikes him down in his pride.

Shakespeare's idea of the tragic fact is larger than this idea and goes beyond it; but it includes it, and it is worth while to observe the identity of the two in a certain point which is often ignored. Tragedy with Shakespeare is concerned always with persons of 'high degree'; often with kings or princes; if not, with leaders in the state like Coriolanus, Brutus, Antony; at the least, as in *Romeo and Juliet*, with members of great houses, whose quarrels are of public moment. There is a decided difference here between *Othello* and our three other tragedies, but it is not a difference of kind. Othello himself is no mere private person; he is the General of the Republic. At the beginning we see him in the Council-Chamber of the Senate. The consciousness of his high position never leaves him. At the end, when he is determined to live no longer, he is as anxious as Hamlet not to be misjudged by the great world, and his last speech begins,

> Soft you; a word or two before you go.
> I have done the state some service, and they know it.[24,25]

---

[23]**Anhanged ... clowde:** Geoffrey Chaucer, 'The Monk's Tale', ll. 871–8, *The Canterbury Tales* (1387–1400).
[24]**Soft ... it:** *Othello*, 5.2.338–9.
[25][**Bradley's note:**] *Timon of Athens*, we have seen, was probably not designed by Shakespeare, but even *Timon* is no exception to the rule. The sub-plot is concerned with Alcibiades and his army, and Timon himself is treated by the Senate as a man of great importance. *Arden of Feversham* and *A Yorkshire Tragedy* would certainly be exceptions to

And this characteristic of Shakespeare's tragedies, though not the most vital, is neither external nor unimportant. The saying that every death-bed is the scene of the fifth act of a tragedy has its meaning, but it would not be true if the word 'tragedy' bore its dramatic sense. The pangs of despised love and the anguish of remorse, we say, are the same in a peasant and a prince; but, not to insist that they cannot be so when the prince is really a prince; the story of the prince, the triumvir, or the general, has a greatness and dignity of its own. His fate affects the welfare of a whole nation or empire; and when he falls suddenly from the height of earthly greatness to the dust, his fall produces a sense of contrast, of the powerlessness of man, and of the omnipotence – perhaps the caprice – of Fortune or Fate, which no tale of private life can possibly rival.

Such feelings are constantly evoked by Shakespeare's tragedies, – again in varying degrees. Perhaps they are the very strongest of the emotions awakened by the early tragedy of *Richard II*, where they receive a concentrated expression in Richard's famous speech about the antic Death, who sits in the hollow crown

That rounds the mortal temples of a king,[26]

grinning at his pomp, watching till his vanity and his fancied security have wholly encased him round, and then coming and boring with a little pin through his castle wall. And these feelings, though their predominance is subdued in the mightiest tragedies, remain powerful there. In the figure of the maddened Lear we see

A sight most pitiful in the meanest wretch,
Past speaking of in a king;[27]

and if we would realise the truth in this matter we cannot do better than compare with the effect of *King Lear* the effect of Tourgénief's parallel and remarkable tale of peasant life, *A King Lear of the Steppes*.[28]

2

A Shakespearean tragedy as so far considered may be called a story of exceptional calamity leading to the death of a man in high estate. But it is clearly much more than this, and we have now to regard it from another side. No amount of calamity which merely befell a man, descending from the clouds like lightning, or stealing from the darkness like pestilence, could alone provide the substance of its story. Job was the greatest of all the children of the east, and his afflictions were well-nigh more than he could bear; but even if we imagined them wearing him to death, that would not make his story tragic. Nor yet would it become so, in the Shakespearean sense, if the fire, and the great wind from the wilderness, and the torments of his flesh were conceived as sent by a supernatural power, whether just or malignant. The

---

the rule; but I assume that neither of them is Shakespeare's; and if either is, it belongs to a different species from his admitted tragedies. See, on this species, Symonds, *Shakspere's Predecessors*, chapter xi.

[26]*That ... king*: *Richard II*, 3.2.161.

[27]*A sight ... king*: *King Lear*, 4.6.193–4.

[28]*A King Lear of the Steppes*: short story by Russian writer Ivan Turgenev (1818–83), published in 1870, loosely adapting *King Lear* set in the Russian countryside.

calamities of tragedy do not simply happen, nor are they sent; they proceed mainly from actions, and those the actions of men.

We see a number of human beings placed in certain circumstances; and we see, arising from the co-operation of their characters in these circumstances, certain actions. These actions beget others, and these others beget others again, until this series of inter-connected deeds leads by an apparently inevitable sequence to a catastrophe. The effect of such a series on imagination is to make us regard the sufferings which accompany it, and the catastrophe in which it ends, not only or chiefly as something which happens to the persons concerned, but equally as something which is caused by them. This at least may be said of the principal persons, and, among them, of the hero, who always contributes in some measure to the disaster in which he perishes.

This second aspect of tragedy evidently differs greatly from the first. Men, from this point of view, appear to us primarily as agents, 'themselves the authors of their proper woe'; and our fear and pity, though they will not cease or diminish, will be modified accordingly. We are now to consider this second aspect, remembering that it too is only one aspect, and additional to the first, not a substitute for it.

The 'story' or 'action' of a Shakespearean tragedy does not consist, of course, solely of human actions or deeds; but the deeds are the predominant factor. And these deeds are, for the most part, actions in the full sense of the word; not things done "tween asleep and wake,'[29] but acts or omissions thoroughly expressive of the doer, – characteristic deeds. The centre of the tragedy, therefore, may be said with equal truth to lie in action issuing from character, or in character issuing in action.

Shakespeare's main interest lay here. To say that it lay in *mere* character, or was a psychological interest, would be a great mistake, for he was dramatic to the tips of his fingers. It is possible to find places where he has given a certain indulgence to his love of poetry, and even to his turn for general reflections; but it would be very difficult, and in his later tragedies perhaps impossible, to detect passages where he has allowed such freedom to the interest in character apart from action. But for the opposite extreme, for the abstraction of mere 'plot' (which is a very different thing from the tragic 'action'), for the kind of interest which predominates in a novel like *The Woman in White*,[30] it is clear that he cared even less. I do not mean that this interest is absent from his dramas; but it is subordinate to others, and is so interwoven with them that we are rarely conscious of it apart, and rarely feel in any great strength the half-intellectual, half-nervous excitement of following an ingenious complication. What we do feel strongly, as a tragedy advances to its close, is that the calamities and catastrophe follow inevitably from the deeds of men, and that the main source of these deeds is character. The dictum that, with Shakespeare, 'character is destiny' is no doubt an exaggeration, and one that may mislead (for many of his tragic personages, if they had not met with peculiar circumstances, would have escaped a tragic end, and might even have lived fairly untroubled lives); but it is the exaggeration of a vital truth.

---

[29]**'tween ... wake:** *King Lear*, 1.2.17.
[30]***The Woman in White*:** popular 1859 novel by Wilkie Collins featuring a sensational plot.

Further reading

John Russell Brown, 'Practical Study and Criticism', in *A.C. Bradley on Shakespeare's Tragedies: A Concise Edition and Reassessment* (New York: Palgrave Macmillan, 2006), 7–39.

G.K. Hunter, 'A.C. Bradley's *Shakespearean Tragedy*', *Essays and Studies* 21 (1968): 101–7.

Rene Wellek, 'A.C. Bradley, Shakespeare, and the Infinite', *Philological Quarterly* 54, no. 1 (1975): 85–103.

5.3 WILLIAM BUTLER YEATS, 'THE TRAGIC THEATRE' (1910)

William Butler Yeats (1865–1939), one of the most prominent writers of the twentieth century, was an Irish poet, playwright, essayist, and central figure in the Irish Literary Revival. Although he is best known for his poetry, for which he won the Nobel Prize for Literature in 1923, he considered his plays crucial to his literary achievements, and described his poetry as fundamentally dramatic. A co-founder of the Abbey Theatre in Dublin, he frequently wrote about theatre, and especially about tragedy. Strongly influenced by Nietzsche (see extract 4.8), Yeats described tragedy as a violent Dionysian force. In his 1910 essay 'The Tragic Theatre', he repeatedly likens it to a flood: 'tragedy must always be a drowning and breaking of the dykes that separate man from man'. Yeats argues that tragedy must transcend the mundane realms of realism and character, which he links with comedy, in order to encompass the more transformative possibilities of ritual, passion, and ecstasy.

I did not find a word in the printed criticism of Synge's *Deirdre of the Sorrows*[31] about the qualities that made certain moments seem to me the noblest tragedy, and the play was judged by what seemed to me but wheels and pulleys necessary to the effect, but in themselves nothing.

Upon the other hand, those who spoke to me of the play never spoke of these wheels and pulleys, but if they cared at all for the play, cared for the things I cared for. One's own world of painters, of poets, of good talkers, of ladies who delight in Ricard's portraits[32] or Debussy's music,[33] all those whose senses feel instantly every change in our mother the moon, saw the stage in one way; and those others who look at plays every night, who tell the general playgoer whether this play or that play is to his taste, saw it in a way so different that there is certainly some body of dogma – whether in the instincts or in the memory – pushing the ways apart. A printed criticism, for instance, found but one dramatic moment, that when Deirdre in the second act overhears her lover say that he may grow weary of her; and not one – if I remember rightly – chose for praise or explanation the third act which alone had satisfied the author, or contained in any abundance those sentences that were quoted at the fall of the curtain and for days after.

Deirdre and her lover, as Synge tells the tale, returned to Ireland, though it was nearly certain they would die there, because death was better than broken love, and at the side of the open grave that had been dug for one and would serve for both, quarrelled, losing all they had given their life to keep. 'Is it not a hard thing that we should miss the safety of the grave and we trampling its edge?' That is Deirdre's cry at the outset of a reverie of passion that mounts and mounts till grief itself has carried her beyond grief into pure contemplation. Up to this the play had been a Master's unfinished work, monotonous and melancholy, ill arranged, little more than a sketch of what it would have grown to, but now I listened breathless to sentences that may never pass away, and as they filled or dwindled in their civility of sorrow, the player, whose art had seemed clumsy and incomplete, like the writing itself, ascended into that tragic ecstasy which is the best that art – perhaps that life – can give. And at last when Deirdre, in the

---

[31]**Synge:** John Millington Synge (1871–1909) was a prominent Irish writer and co-founder of the Abbey Theatre. His play *Deirdre of the Sorrows* was left unfinished when he died; Yeats and Molly Allgood, Synge's fiancée, completed it.
[32]**Ricard:** Louis Gustave Ricard (1823–73) was a French painter known for his portraits.
[33]**Debussy's music:** Claude Debussy (1862–1918) was an influential French composer.

paroxysm before she took her life, touched with compassionate fingers him that had killed her lover, we knew that the player had become, if but for a moment, the creature of that noble mind which had gathered its art in waste islands, and we too were carried beyond time and persons to where passion, living through its thousand purgatorial years, as in the wink of an eye, becomes wisdom; and it was as though we too had touched and felt and seen a disembodied thing.

One dogma of the printed criticism is that if a play does not contain definite character, its constitution is not strong enough for the stage, and that the dramatic moment is always the contest of character with character.

In poetical drama there is, it is held, an antithesis between character and lyric poetry, for lyric poetry – however much it move you when read out of a book – can, as these critics think, but encumber the action. Yet when we go back a few centuries and enter the great periods of drama, character grows less and sometimes disappears, and there is much lyric feeling, and at times a lyric measure will be wrought into the dialogue, a flowing measure that had well befitted music, or that more lumbering one of the sonnet. Suddenly it strikes us that character is continuously present in comedy alone, and that there is much tragedy, that of Corneille,[34] that of Racine,[35] that of Greece and Rome, where its place is taken by passions and motives, one person being jealous, another full of love or remorse or pride or anger. In writers of tragi-comedy (and Shakespeare is always a writer of tragi-comedy) there is indeed character, but we notice that it is in the moments of comedy that character is defined, in Hamlet's gaiety, let us say; while amid the great moments, when Timon orders his tomb,[36] when Hamlet cries to Horatio 'Absent thee from felicity awhile,'[37] when Antony names 'Of many thousand kisses the poor last,'[38] all is lyricism, unmixed passion, 'the integrity of fire.' Nor does character ever attain to complete definition in these lamps ready for the taper, no matter how circumstantial and gradual the opening of events, as it does in Falstaff,[39] who has no passionate purpose to fulfil, or as it does in Henry V,[40] whose poetry, never touched by lyric heat, is oratorical; nor when the tragic reverie is at its height do we say, 'How well that man is realised! I should know him were I to meet him in the street,' for it is always ourselves that we see upon the stage, and should it be a tragedy of love, we renew, it may be, some loyalty of our youth, and go from the theatre with our eyes dim for an old love's sake.

I think it was while rehearsing a translation of *Les Fourberies de Scapin*[41] in Dublin, and noticing how passionless it all was, that I saw what should have been plain from the first line I had written, that tragedy must always be a drowning and breaking of the dykes that separate man from man, and that it is upon these dykes comedy keeps house. But I was not certain of the site of that house (one always hesitates when there is no testimony but one's own) till somebody told me of a certain letter of Congreve's.[42] He describes the external and superficial expressions of 'humour' on which farce is founded and then defines 'humour' itself – the foundation of comedy – as a 'singular and unavoidable way of doing anything peculiar to one

---

[34]**Corneille:** Pierre Corneille (1606–84), French tragic playwright; see extract 2.6.

[35]**Racine:** Jean Racine (1639–99), French tragic playwright.

[36]**Timon:** from Shakespeare's *Timon of Athens* (c.1605), probably collaboratively written with Thomas Middleton.

[37]**'Absent ... awhile':** Shakespeare, *Hamlet*, 5.2.345.

[38]**'Of ... last':** Shakespeare, *Antony and Cleopatra*, 4.15.20.

[39]**Falstaff:** comic character appearing in Shakespeare's *Henry IV, Parts One and Two* (c.1597–c.1598) and *The Merry Wives of Windsor* (1597), and eulogized in *Henry V* (1599).

[40]**Henry V:** protagonist of Shakespeare's *Henry V* (1599).

[41]*Les Fourberies de Scapin:* 1671 comedy by French playwright Moliere (1622–73).

[42]**Congreve:** William Congreve (1670–1729), English Restoration playwright.

man only, by which his speech and actions are distinguished from all other men,' and adds to it that 'passions are too powerful in the sex to let humour have its course,' or, as I would rather put it, that you can find but little of what we call character in unspoiled youth, whatever be the sex, for, as he indeed shows in another sentence, it grows with time like the ash of a burning stick, and strengthens towards middle life till there is little else at seventy years.

Since then I have discovered an antagonism between all the old art and our new art of comedy and understand why I hated at nineteen years Thackeray's novels[43] and the new French painting. A big picture of *cocottes*[44] sitting at little tables outside a café, by some follower of Manet,[45] was exhibited at the Royal Hibernian Academy while I was a student at a life class there, and I was miserable for days. I found no desirable place, no man I could have wished to be, no woman I could have loved, no Golden Age, no lure for secret hope, no adventure with myself for theme out of that endless tale I told myself all day long. Years after, I saw the *Olympia* of Manet at the Luxembourg and watched it without hostility indeed, but as I might some incomparable talker whose precision of gesture gave me pleasure, though I did not understand his language. I returned to it again and again at intervals of years, saying to myself, 'Some day I will understand'; and yet it was not until Sir Hugh Lane brought the *Eva Gonzales*[46] to Dublin, and I had said to myself, 'How perfectly that woman is realised as distinct from all other women that have lived or shall live,' that I understood I was carrying on in my own mind that quarrel between a tragedian and a comedian which the Devil on Two Sticks in Le Sage[47] showed to the young man who had climbed through the window.

There is an art of the flood, the art of Titian[48] when his *Ariosto*, and his *Bacchus and Ariadne*,[49] give new images to the dreams of youth, and of Shakespeare when he shows us Hamlet broken away from life by the passionate hesitations of his reverie. And we call this art poetical, because we must bring more to it than our daily mood if we would take our pleasure; and because it takes delight in the moment of exaltation, of excitement, of dreaming (or in the capacity for it, as in that still face of Ariosto's that is like some vessel soon to be full of wine). And there is an art that we call real, because character can only express itself perfectly in a real world, being that world's creature, and because we understand it best through a delicate discrimination of the senses which is but entire wakefulness, the daily mood grown cold and crystalline.

We may not find either mood in its purity, but in mainly tragic art one distinguishes devices to exclude or lessen character, to diminish the power of that daily mood, to cheat or blind its too clear perception. If the real world is not altogether rejected, it is but touched here and there, and into the places we have left empty we summon rhythm, balance, pattern, images that remind us of vast passions, the vagueness of past times, all the chimeras that haunt the edge of trance; and if we are painters, we shall express personal emotion through ideal form, a symbolism handled by the generations, a mask from whose eyes the disembodied looks, a style that remembers many masters that it may escape contemporary suggestion; or we shall leave out some element

---

[43]**Thackeray:** William Makepeace Thackeray (1811–63), British satiric novelist.

[44]*cocottes*: in context, courtesans.

[45]**Manet:** Édouard Manet (1832–83), French Impressionist painter.

[46]*Eva Gonzales*: Manet's *Portrait of Eva Gonzales* (1869–70). Gonzales (1849–83), a student of Manet, was also a French Impressionist painter.

[47]**The Devil on Two Sticks:** 1707 comic French novel by Alain-René Lesage (1668–1747).

[48]**Titian:** Tiziano Vecelli (*c*.1489–1576), Italian painter.

[49]*Ariosto, Bacchus and Ariadne*: paintings by Titian.

of reality as in Byzantine painting, where there is no mass, nothing in relief; and so it is that in the supreme moment of tragic art there comes upon one that strange sensation as though the hair of one's head stood up. And when we love, if it be in the excitement of youth, do we not also, that the flood may find no stone to convulse, no wall to narrow it, exclude character or the signs of it by choosing that beauty which seems unearthly because the individual woman is lost amid the labyrinth of its lines as though life were trembling into stillness and silence, or at last folding itself away? Some little irrelevance of line, some promise of character to come, may indeed put us at our ease, 'give more interest' as the humour of the old man with the basket does to Cleopatra's dying;[50] but should it come, as we had dreamed in love's frenzy, to our dying for that woman's sake, we would find that the discord had its value from the tune. Nor have we chosen illusion in choosing the outward sign of that moral genius that lives among the subtlety of the passions, and can for her moment make her of the one mind with great artists and poets. In the studio we may indeed say to one another, 'Character is the only beauty,' but when we choose a wife, as when we go to the gymnasium to be shaped for woman's eyes, we remember academic form, even though we enlarge a little the point of interest and choose 'a painter's beauty,' finding it the more easy to believe in the fire because it has made ashes.

When we look at the faces of the old tragic paintings, whether it is in Titian or in some painter of mediaeval China, we find there sadness and gravity, a certain emptiness even, as of a mind that waited the supreme crisis (and indeed it seems at times as if the graphic art, unlike poetry which sings the crisis itself, were the celebration of waiting). Whereas in modern art, whether in Japan or Europe, 'vitality' (is not that the great word of the studios?), the energy, that is to say, which is under the command of our common moments, sings, laughs, chatters or looks its busy thoughts.

Certainly we have here the Tree of Life and that of the Knowledge of Good and Evil which is rooted in our interests, and if we have forgotten their differing virtues it is surely because we have taken delight in a confusion of crossing branches. Tragic art, passionate art, the drowner of dykes, the confounder of understanding, moves us by setting us to reverie, by alluring us almost to the intensity of trance. The persons upon the stage, let us say, greaten till they are humanity itself. We feel our minds expand convulsively or spread out slowly like some moon-brightened image-crowded sea. That which is before our eyes perpetually vanishes and returns again in the midst of the excitement it creates, and the more enthralling it is, the more do we forget it.

August 1910

Further reading

Bernard O'Donoghue, 'Yeats and the Drama', in *The Cambridge Companion to W.B. Yeats*, ed. Marjorie Howe and John Kelly (Cambridge: Cambridge University Press, 2006), 101–5.

Paul Gordon, '"Troubled Ecstasy": Yeats's Tragic Vision', in *Tragedy after Nietzsche: Rapturous Superabundance* (Urbana: University of Illinois Press, 2001), 38–54.

Warren Leamon, 'Yeats, Synge, Realism, and "The Tragic Theatre"', *The Southern Review* 11, no. 1 (1975): 129–38.

---

[50]**Cleopatra's dying:** a scene in the final act of Shakespeare's *Antony and Cleopatra* (c.1606).

5.4 VIRGINIA WOOLF, 'ON NOT KNOWING GREEK' (1925)

British novelist and essayist Virginia Woolf (1882–1941) was one of the most prominent authors associated with literary modernism, known especially for her development of stream of consciousness writing and her feminist arguments on women's education and writing. Born into an eminent Victorian literary family, she was raised in London and attended King's College, London, where she studied Greek, Latin, and history. Along with the writer Leonard Woolf, whom she married in 1912, she established the Hogarth Press, which published important modernist writings including her own. A student and translator of Greek, Woolf reflected on Greek tragedy in her fiction as well as her essays. In 'On Not Knowing Greek' (1925), she insisted on the impossibility of fully understanding a literary realm as temporally and linguistically remote as that of Aeschylus, Sophocles, and Euripides, but simultaneously argued for the importance of the distinctive imaginative power embedded in their tragic worlds.

For it is vain and foolish to talk of knowing Greek, since in our ignorance we should be at the bottom of any class of schoolboys, since we do not know how the words sounded, or where precisely we ought to laugh, or how the actors acted, and between this foreign people and ourselves there is not only difference of race and tongue but a tremendous breach of tradition. All the more strange, then, is it that we should wish to know Greek, try to know Greek, feel for ever drawn back to Greek, and be for ever making up some notion of the meaning of Greek, though from what incongruous odds and ends, with what slight resemblance to the real meaning of Greek, who shall say?

[...]

Sophocles would take the old story of Electra, for instance, but would at once impose his stamp upon it.[51] Of that, in spite of our weakness and distortion, what remains visible to us? That his genius was of the extreme kind in the first place; that he chose a design which, if it failed, would show its failure in gashes and ruin, not in the gentle blurring of some insignificant detail; which, if it succeeded, would cut each stroke to the bone, would stamp each fingerprint in marble. His Electra stands before us like a figure so tightly bound that she can only move an inch this way, an inch that. But each movement must tell to the utmost, or, bound as she is, denied the relief of all hints, repetitions, suggestions, she will be nothing but a dummy, tightly bound. Her words in crisis are, as a matter of fact, bare; mere cries of despair, joy, hate:

οἲ ᾽γὼ τάλαιν᾽, ὄλωλα τῇδ᾽ ἐν ἡμέρᾳ.[52]

But these cries give angle and outline to the play. It is thus, with a thousand differences of degree, that in English literature Jane Austen shapes a novel.[53] There comes a moment – 'I will

---

[51]**Sophocles ... Electra:** Sophocles' *Electra* (*c*.410–406 BCE) depicts Electra's reunion with her brother Orestes, and their plan to kill their mother, Clytemnestra, in revenge for her murder of their father, Agamemnon.

[52]**οἲ ... ἡμέρᾳ:** 'Oh wretched me, I am destroyed today!' Sophocles, *Electra*, l.674.

[53]**Jane Austen:** a prominent English novelist (1775–1817) known for her depictions of social mores.

dance with you,' says Emma – which rises higher than the rest, which, though not eloquent in itself, or violent, or made striking by beauty of language, has the whole weight of the book behind it.[54] In Jane Austen, too, we have the same sense, though the ligatures are much less tight, that her figures are bound, and restricted to a few definite movements. She, too, in her modest, everyday prose, chose the dangerous art where one slip means death.

But it is not so easy to decide what it is that gives these cries of Electra in her anguish their power to cut and wound and excite. It is partly that we know her, that we have picked up from little turns and twists of the dialogue hints of her character, of her appearance, which, characteristically, she neglected; of something suffering in her, outraged and stimulated to its utmost stretch of capacity, yet, as she herself knows ('my behaviour is unseemly and becomes me ill'), blunted and debased by the horror of her position, an unwed girl made to witness her mother's vileness and denounce it in loud, almost vulgar, clamour to the world at large. It is partly, too, that we know in the same way that Clytemnestra is no unmitigated villainess. '[δεινὸν τὸ τίκτειν ἐστίν]' she says – 'there is a strange power in motherhood'.[55] It is no murderess, violent and unredeemed, whom Orestes kills within the house, and Electra bids him utterly destroy – 'Strike again.' No; the men and women standing out in the sunlight before the audience on the hill-side were alive enough, subtle enough, not mere figures, or plaster casts of human beings.

Yet it is not because we can analyse them into feelings that they impress us. In six pages of Proust[56] we can find more complicated and varied emotions than in the whole of the *Electra*. But in the *Electra* or in the *Antigone*[57] we are impressed by something different, by something perhaps more impressive – by heroism itself, by fidelity itself. In spite of the labour and the difficulty it is this that draws us back and back to the Greeks; the stable, the permanent, the original human being is to be found there. Violent emotions are needed to rouse him into action, but when thus stirred by death, by betrayal, by some other primitive calamity, Antigone and Ajax and Electra behave in the way in which we should behave thus struck down; the way in which everybody has always behaved; and thus we understand them more easily and more directly than we understand the characters in the *Canterbury Tales*. These are the originals, Chaucer's the varieties of the human species.

It is true, of course, that these types of the original man or woman, these heroic Kings, these faithful daughters, these tragic Queens who stalk through the ages always planting their feet in the same places, twitching their robes with the same gestures, from habit not from impulse, are among the greatest bores and the most demoralising companions in the world. The plays of Addison,[58] Voltaire,[59] and a host of others are there to prove it. But encounter them in Greek. Even in Sophocles, whose reputation for restraint and mastery has filtered down to us from the scholars, they are decided, ruthless, direct. A fragment of their speech broken off would, we feel, colour oceans and oceans of the respectable drama. Here we meet them before

---

[54]**'I will dance with you'**: Jane Austen, *Emma* (London: Penguin, 1966), 327–8.

[55]**δεινὸν ... motherhood**: Sophocles, *Electra*, 770.

[56]**Proust**: Proust: Marcel Proust (1871–1922) was a French novelist and essayist widely considered one of the most influential literary Modernists.

[57]**Antigone**: play by Sophocles (442 BCE) in which Antigone, daughter of Oedipus and Jocasta, defies her uncle Creon by burying her brother Polynices, whom Creon had declared an enemy of Thebes because of his role in the city's civil war.

[58]**Addison**: Joseph Addison (1672–1719), English poet, playwright and editor of *The Spectator*. Voltaire was an avid reader of *The Spectator* during his London years. See extract 3.1.

[59]**Voltaire**: François-Marie Arouet (1694–1778), known as Voltaire, French dramatist and philosopher; one of the foremost figures of the Enlightenment. See extract 3.3.

their emotions have been worn into uniformity. Here we listen to the nightingale whose song echoes through English literature singing in her own Greek tongue. For the first time Orpheus with his lute makes men and beasts follow him. Their voices ring out clear and sharp; we see the hairy, tawny bodies at play in the sunlight among the olive trees, not posed gracefully on granite plinths in the pale corridors of the British Museum. And then suddenly, in the midst of all this sharpness and compression, Electra, as if she swept her veil over her face and forbade us to think of her any more, speaks of that very nightingale: 'that bird distraught with grief, the messenger of Zeus. Ah, queen of sorrow, Niobe, thee I deem divine – thee; who evermore weepest in thy rocky tomb.'[60]

And as she silences her own complaint, she perplexes us again with the insoluble question of poetry and its nature, and why, as she speaks thus, her words put on the assurance of immortality. For they are Greek; we cannot tell how they sounded; they ignore the obvious sources of excitement; they owe nothing of their effect to any extravagance of expression, and certainly they throw no light upon the speaker's character or the writer's. But they remain, something that has been stated and must eternally endure.

Yet in a play how dangerous this poetry, this lapse from the particular to the general must of necessity be, with the actors standing there in person, with their bodies and their faces passively waiting to be made use of! For this reason the later plays of Shakespeare, where there is more of poetry than of action, are better read than seen, better understood by leaving out the actual body than by having the body, with all its associations and movements, visible to the eye. The intolerable restrictions of the drama could be loosened, however, if a means could be found by which what was general and poetic, comment, not action, could be freed without interrupting the movement of the whole. It is this that the choruses supply; the old men or women who take no active part in the drama, the undifferentiated voices who sing like birds in the pauses of the wind; who can comment, or sum up, or allow the poet to speak himself or supply, by contrast, another side to his conception. Always in imaginative literature, where characters speak for themselves and the author has no part, the need of that voice is making itself felt. For though Shakespeare (unless we consider that his fools and madmen supply the part) dispensed with the chorus, novelists are always devising some substitute – Thackeray speaking in his own person, Fielding coming out and addressing the world before his curtain rises.[61] So to grasp the meaning of the play the chorus is of the utmost importance. One must be able to pass easily into those ecstasies, those wild and apparently irrelevant utterances, those sometimes obvious and commonplace statements, to decide their relevance or irrelevance, and give them their relation to the play as a whole.

We must 'be able to pass easily'; but that of course is exactly what we cannot do. For the most part the choruses, with all their obscurities, must be spelt out and their symmetry mauled. But we can guess that Sophocles used them not to express something outside the action of the play, but to sing the praises of some virtue, or the beauties of some place mentioned in it. He selects what he wishes to emphasize and sings of white Colonus and its nightingale, or of love unconquered in fight. Lovely, lofty, and serene, his choruses grow naturally out

---

[60]**that bird ... tomb:** Sophocles, *Electra*, 149–52.

[61]**Thackeray ... rises:** William Makepeace Thackeray (1811–63) was a satirical English novelist best known for *Vanity Fair* (1847–8); Henry Fielding (1707–54), another satirical English novelist, was best known for *Tom Jones* (1749). Both writers established distinctive authorial voices that routinely interrupt and comment on the stories they narrate.

of his situations, and change, not the point of view, but the mood. In Euripides, however, the situations are not contained within themselves; they give off an atmosphere of doubt, of suggestion, of questioning; but if we look to the choruses to make this plain we are often baffled rather than instructed. At once in the *Bacchae* we are in the world of psychology and doubt; the world where the mind twists facts and changes them and makes the familiar aspects of life appear new and questionable. What is Bacchus, and who are the Gods, and what is man's duty to them, and what the rights of his subtle brain? To these questions the chorus makes no reply, or replies mockingly, or speaks darkly as if the straitness of the dramatic form had tempted Euripides to violate it, in order to relieve his mind of its weight. Time is so short and I have so much to say, that unless you will allow me to place together two apparently unrelated statements and trust to you to pull them together, you must be content with a mere skeleton of the play I might have given you. Such is the argument. Euripides therefore suffers less than Sophocles and less than Aeschylus from being read privately in a room, and not seen on a hill-side in the sunshine. He can be acted in the mind; he can comment upon the questions of the moment; more than the others he will vary in popularity from age to age.

If then in Sophocles the play is concentrated in the figures themselves, and in Euripides is to be retrieved from flashes of poetry and questions far flung and unanswered, Aeschylus makes these little dramas (the *Agamemnon* has 1663 lines; *Lear* about 2600) tremendous by stretching every phrase to the utmost, by sending them floating forth in metaphors, by bidding them rise up and stalk eyeless and majestic through the scene. To understand him it is not so necessary to understand Greek as to understand poetry. It is necessary to take that dangerous leap through the air without the support of words which Shakespeare also asks of us. For words, when opposed to such a blast of meaning, must give out, must be blown astray, and only by collecting in companies convey the meaning which each one separately is too weak to express. Connecting them in a rapid flight of the mind we know instantly and instinctively, what they mean, but could not decant that meaning afresh into any other words. There is an ambiguity which is the mark of the highest poetry; we cannot know exactly what it means. Take this from the *Agamemnon* for instance –

ὀμμάτων δ᾽ ἐν ἀχηνίαις ἔρρει πᾶσ᾽ Ἀφροδίτα.[62]

The meaning is just on the far side of language. It is the meaning which in moments of astonishing excitement and stress we perceive in our minds without words; it is the meaning that Dostoevsky[63] (hampered as he was by prose and as we are by translation) leads us to by some astonishing run up the scale of emotions and points at but cannot indicate; the meaning that Shakespeare succeeds in snaring.

Aeschylus thus will not give, as Sophocles gives, the very words that people might have spoken, only so arranged that they have in some mysterious way a general force, a symbolic power, nor like Euripides will he combine incongruities and thus enlarge his little space, as a small room is enlarged by mirrors in odd corners. By the bold and running use of metaphor he will amplify and give us, not the thing itself, but the reverberation and reflection which, taken

---

[62]ὀμμάτων ... Ἀφροδίτα: 'In the hunger of his eyes, all loveliness is departed'; Aeschylus, *Agamemnon*, ll. 418–19.
[63]**Dostoevsky:** Fyodor Dostoevsky (1821–81) was a Russian author of fiction, essays, and journalism, known especially for the searing explorations of psychology in his novels.

into his mind, the thing has made; close enough to the original to illustrate it, remote enough to heighten, enlarge, and make splendid.

For none of these dramatists had the licence which belongs to the novelist, and, in some degree, to all writers of printed books, of modelling their meaning with an infinity of slight touches which can only be properly applied by reading quietly, carefully, and sometimes two or three times over. Every sentence had to explode on striking the ear, however slowly and beautifully the words might then descend, and however enigmatic might their final purport be. No splendour or richness of metaphor could have saved the *Agamemnon* if either images or allusions of the subtlest or most decorative had got between us and the naked cry

> ὀτοτοτοῖ πόποι δᾶ.
> Ὤπολλον Ὤπολλον.⁶⁴

Dramatic they had to be at whatever cost.

[...]

But again (the question comes back and back), Are we reading Greek as it was written when we say this? When we read these few words cut on a tombstone, a stanza in a chorus, the end or the opening of a dialogue of Plato's, a fragment of Sappho, when we bruise our minds upon some tremendous metaphor in the *Agamemnon* instead of stripping the branch of its flowers instantly as we do in reading *Lear* – are we not reading wrongly? losing our sharp sight in the haze of associations? reading into Greek poetry not what they have but what we lack? Does not the whole of Greece heap itself behind every line of its literature? They admit us to a vision of the earth unravaged, the sea unpolluted, the maturity, tried but unbroken, of mankind. Every word is reinforced by a vigour which pours out of olive-tree and temple and the bodies of the young. The nightingale has only to be named by Sophocles and she sings; the grove has only to be called ἄβατον, 'untrodden', and we imagine the twisted branches and the purple violets. Back and back we are drawn to steep ourselves in what, perhaps, is only an image of the reality, not the reality itself, a summer's day imagined in the heart of a northern winter. Chief among these sources of glamour and perhaps misunderstanding is the language. We can never hope to get the whole fling of a sentence in Greek as we do in English. We cannot hear it, now dissonant, now harmonious, tossing sound from line to line across a page. We cannot pick up infallibly one by one all those minute signals by which a phrase is made to hint, to turn, to live. Nevertheless, it is the language that has us most in bondage; the desire for that which perpetually lures us back....

Then, spare and bare as it is, no language can move more quickly, dancing, shaking, all alive, but controlled. Then there are the words themselves which, in so many instances, we have made expressive to us of our own emotions, θαλασσα, θανατοζ, ανθοζ, αστηρ, σεληνη⁶⁵ – to take the first that come to hand; so clear, so hard, so intense, that to speak plainly yet fittingly without blurring the outline or clouding the depths, Greek is the only expression. It is useless, then, to read Greek in translations. Translators can but offer us a vague equivalent; their language is necessarily full of echoes and associations.

---

⁶⁴ὀτοτοτοῖ ... Ὤπολλον.: 'Woe, woe, woe! O Apollo, O Apollo!' Aeschylus, *Agamemnon*, 1072–3.
⁶⁵Θαλασσα ... σεληνη: Sea, death, flower, star, moon.

[…]

With the sound of the sea in their ears, vines, meadows, rivulets about them, they are even more aware than we are of a ruthless fate. There is a sadness at the back of life which they do not attempt to mitigate. Entirely aware of their own standing in the shadow, and yet alive to every tremor and gleam of existence, there they endure, and it is to the Greeks that we turn when we are sick of the vagueness, of the confusion, of the Christianity and its consolations, of our own age.

Further reading

Rowena Fowler, '"On Not Knowing Greek": The Classics and the Woman of Letters', *Classical Journal* 78 (1983): 337–49.

Yopie Prins, 'OTOTOTOI: Virginia Woolf and "The Naked Cry" of Cassandra', in *Agamemnon in Performance 458 BC to AD 2004*, ed. Fiona Macintosh et al (Oxford: Legenda, 2005), 163–87.

Angeliki Spiropoulou, '"On Not Knowing Greek": Virginia Woolf's Spatial Critique of Authority', *Interdisciplinary Literary Studies* 4, no. 1 (2002): 1–19.

5.5 BERTOLT BRECHT, *A SHORT ORGANUM FOR THE THEATRE* (1948)

Bertolt Brecht (1898–1956) was a German playwright, poet, and theatre director. A committed Marxist, he criticized conventional theatrical practices as apolitical and reactionary. Brecht objected in particular to the model of empathy that he saw in Aristotle's ideas about tragic pity and fear, which he saw as fostering acceptance of suffering, and of attributing it to individual psychology rather than social dysfunction. In his *A Short Organum for the Theatre* (1948), Brecht calls for a revolt against what he sees as bourgeois and complacent modes of drama. He proposes to replace them with 'epic theatre,' or 'dialectical theatre,' which should estrange audiences from depictions of suffering rather than invite identification. As a result, the viewing experience should prompt outrage at the social and political problems that give rise to suffering, and mobilize active responses to them.

PROLOGUE

The following sets out to define an aesthetic drawn from a particular kind of theatrical performance which has been worked out in practice over the past few decades. In the theoretical statements, excursions, technical indications occasionally published in the form of notes to the writer's plays, aesthetics have only been touched on casually and with comparative lack of interest. There you saw a particular species of theatre extending or contracting its social functions, perfecting or sifting its artistic methods and establishing or maintaining its aesthetics – if the question arose – by rejecting or converting to its own use the dominant conventions of morality or taste according to its tactical needs. This theatre justified its inclination to social commitment by pointing to the social commitment in universally accepted works of art, which only fail to strike the eye because it was the accepted commitment. As for the products of our own time, it held that their lack of any worthwhile content was a sign of decadence: it accused these entertainment emporiums of having degenerated into branches of the bourgeois narcotics business. The stage's inaccurate representations of our social life, including those classed as so-called Naturalism,[66] led it to call for scientifically exact representations; the tasteless rehashing of empty visual or spiritual palliatives, for the noble logic of the multiplication table. The cult of beauty, conducted with hostility towards learning and contempt for the useful, was dismissed by it as itself contemptible, especially as nothing beautiful resulted. The battle was for a theatre fit for the scientific age, and where its planners found it too hard to borrow or steal from the armoury of aesthetic concepts enough weapons to defend themselves against the aesthetics of the Press they simply threatened 'to transform the means of enjoyment into an instrument of instruction, and to convert certain amusement establishments into organs of mass communication' ('Notes to the opera *Mahagonny*' – [see No. 13]): i.e. to emigrate from the realm of the merely enjoyable. Aesthetics, that heirloom of a by now depraved and parasitic class, was in such a lamentable state that a theatre would certainly have gained both in reputation and in elbowroom if it had rechristened itself theatre.

---

[66]**Naturalism:** a literary movement of the late nineteenth and early twentieth centuries, named by French writer Emile Zola, that emphasized realism, simplicity, and often harsh subject matter.

And yet what we achieved in the way of theatre for a scientific age was not science but theatre, and the accumulated innovations worked out during the Nazi period and the war[67] – when practical demonstration was impossible – compel some attempt to set this species of theatre in its aesthetic background, or anyhow to sketch for it the outlines of a conceivable aesthetic. To explain the theory of theatrical alienation except within an aesthetic framework would be impossibly awkward.

Today one could go so far as to compile an aesthetics of the exact sciences. Galileo[68] spoke of the elegance of certain formulae and the point of an experiment; Einstein[69] suggests that the sense of beauty has a part to play in the making of scientific discoveries; while the atomic physicist R. Oppenheimer[70] praises the scientific attitude, which 'has its own kind of beauty and seems to suit mankind's position on earth'.

Let us therefore cause general dismay by revoking our decision to emigrate from the realm of the merely enjoyable, and even more general dismay by announcing our decision to take up lodging there. Let us treat the theatre as a place of entertainment, as is proper in an aesthetic discussion, and try to discover which type of entertainment suits us best.

1

'Theatre' consists in this: in making live representations of reported or invented happenings between human beings and doing so with a view to entertainment. At any rate that is what we shall mean when we speak of theatre, whether old or new.

2

To extend this definition we might add happenings between humans and gods, but as we are only seeking to establish the minimum we can leave such matters aside. Even if we did accept such an extension we should still have to say that the 'theatre' set-up's broadest function was to give pleasure. It is the noblest function that we have found for 'theatre'.

3

From the first it has been the theatre's business to entertain people, as it also has of all the other arts. It is this business which always gives it its particular dignity; it needs no other passport than fun, but this it has got to have. We should not by any means be giving it a higher status if we were to turn it e.g. into a purveyor of morality; it would on the contrary run the risk of being debased, and this would occur at once if it failed to make its moral lesson enjoyable, and enjoyable to the senses at that: a principle, admittedly, by which morality can only gain. Not even instruction can be demanded of it: at any rate, no more utilitarian lesson than how to move pleasurably, whether in the physical or in the spiritual sphere. The theatre must in fact

---

[67]**The war:** World War II (1939–45).

[68]**Galileo:** Italian scientist (1564–1642) who advocated the theory that the earth revolves around the sun, a controversial view that resulted in his conviction for heresy. A central figure in the seventeenth-century scientific revolution, he has been credited with the birth of modern astronomy, and was the subject of a 1938 play by Brecht.

[69]**Einstein:** German-born theoretical physicist (1879–1955) known for his contributions to modern physics, especially his theory of relativity.

[70]**R. Oppenheimer:** Robert Oppenheimer (1904–67) was an American theoretical physicist with a central role in the development of the atomic bomb during the Second World War.

remain something entirely superfluous, though this indeed means that it is the superfluous for which we live. Nothing needs less justification than pleasure.

4

Thus what the ancients, following Aristotle,[71] demanded of tragedy is nothing higher or lower than that it should entertain people. Theatre may be said to be derived from ritual, but that is only to say that it becomes theatre once the two have separated; what it brought over from the mysteries was not its former ritual function, but purely and simply the pleasure which accompanied this. And the catharsis of which Aristotle writes –cleansing by fear and pity, or from fear and pity – is a purification which is performed not only in a pleasurable way, but precisely for the purpose of pleasure. To ask or to accept more of the theatre is to set one's own mark too low.

5

Even when people speak of higher and lower degrees of pleasure, art stares impassively back at them; for it wishes to fly high and low and to be left in peace, so long as it can give pleasure to people.

6

Yet there are weaker (simple) and stronger (complex) pleasures which the theatre can create. The last-named, which are what we are dealing with in great drama, attain their climaxes rather as cohabitation does through love: they are more intricate, richer in communication, more contradictory and more productive of results.

7

And different periods' pleasures varied naturally according to the system under which people lived in society at the time. The Greek demos [literally: the demos of the Greek circus][72] ruled by tyrants had to be entertained differently from the feudal court of Louis XIV.[73] The theatre was required to deliver different representations of men's life together: not just representations of a different life, but also representations of a different sort.

8

According to the sort of entertainment which was possible and necessary under the given conditions of men's life together the characters had to be given varying proportions, the situations to be constructed according to varying points of view. Stories have to be narrated in various ways, so that these particular Greeks may be able to amuse themselves with the inevitability of divine laws where ignorance never mitigates the punishment; these French with the graceful self-discipline demanded of the great ones of this earth by a courtly code of duty; the Englishmen of the Elizabethan age with the self-awareness of the new individual personality which was then uncontrollably bursting out.

---

[71]**Aristotle:** see extract 1.2 for Aristotle's arguments about drama.
[72]**Literally ... circus:** translator's gloss.
[73]**Louis XIV:** King of France (1638–1715), known as the Sun King, with the longest recorded monarchical reign in European history, known for his increasingly centralized rule and lavish court at Versailles.

9

And we must always remember that the pleasure given by representations of such different sorts hardly ever depended on the representation's likeness to the thing portrayed. Incorrectness, or considerable improbability even, was hardly or not at all disturbing, so long as the incorrectness had a certain consistency and the improbability remained of a constant kind. All that mattered was the illusion of compelling momentum in the story told, and this was created by all sorts of poetic and theatrical means. Even today we are happy to overlook such inaccuracies if we can get something out of the spiritual purifications of Sophocles or the sacrificial acts of Racine[74] or the unbridled frenzies of Shakespeare, by trying to grasp the immense or splendid feelings of the principal characters in these stories.

10

For of all the many sorts of representation of happenings between humans which the theatre has made since ancient times, and which have given entertainment despite their incorrectness and improbability, there are even today an astonishing number that also give entertainment to us.

11

In establishing the extent to which we can be satisfied by representations from so many different periods – something that can hardly have been possible to the children of those vigorous periods themselves – are we not at the same time creating the suspicion that we have failed to discover the special pleasures, the proper entertainment of our own time?

12

And our enjoyment of the theatre must have become weaker than that of the ancients, even if our way of living together is still sufficiently like theirs for it to be felt at all. We grasp the old works by a comparatively new method – empathy – on which they rely little. Thus the greater part of our enjoyment is drawn from other sources than those which our predecessors were able to exploit so fully. We are left safely dependent on beauty of language, on elegance of narration, on passages which stimulate our own private imaginations: in short, on the incidentals of the old works. These are precisely the poetical and theatrical means which hide the imprecisions of the story. Our theatres no longer have either the capacity or the wish to tell these stories, even the relatively recent ones of the great Shakespeare, at all clearly: i.e. to make the connection of events credible. And according to Aristotle – and we agree there – narrative is the soul of drama. We are more and more disturbed to see how crudely and carelessly men's life together is represented, and that not only in old works but also in contemporary ones constructed according to the old recipes. Our whole way of appreciation is starting to get out of date.

13

It is the inaccurate way in which happenings between human beings are represented that restricts our pleasure in the theatre. The reason: we and our forebears have a different relationship to what is being shown.

---

[74]**Racine:** Jean Racine (1639–99), French tragic playwright.

14

For when we look about us for an entertainment whose impact is immediate, for a comprehensive and penetrating pleasure such as our theatre could give us by representations of men's life together, we have to think of ourselves as children of a scientific age. Our life as human beings in society – i.e. our life – is determined by the sciences to a quite new extent.

15

A few hundred years ago a handful of people, working in different countries but in correspondence with one another, performed certain experiments by which they hoped to wring from Nature her secrets. Members of a class of craftsmen in the already powerful cities, they transmitted their discoveries to people who made practical use of them, without expecting more from the new sciences than personal profit for themselves.

Crafts which had progressed by methods virtually unchanged during a thousand years now developed hugely; in many places, which became linked by competition, they gathered from all directions great masses of men, and these, adopting new forms of organization, started producing on a giant scale. Soon mankind was showing powers whose extent it would till that time scarcely have dared to dream of.

16

It was as if mankind for the first time now began a conscious and coordinated effort to make the planet that was its home fit to live on. Many of the earth's components, such as coal, water, oil, now became treasures. Steam was made to shift vehicles; a few small sparks and the twitching of frogs' legs revealed a natural force which produced light, carried sounds across continents, etc. In all directions man looked about himself with a new vision, to see how he could adapt to his convenience familiar but as yet unexploited objects. His surroundings changed increasingly from decade to decade, then from year to year, then almost from day to day. I who am writing this write it on a machine which at the time of my birth was unknown. I travel in the new vehicles with a rapidity that my grandfather could not imagine; in those days nothing moved so fast. And I rise in the air: a thing that my father was unable to do. With my father I already spoke across the width of a continent, but it was together with my son that I first saw the moving pictures of the explosion at Hiroshima.[75]

17

The new sciences may have made possible this vast alteration and all-important alterability of our surroundings, yet it cannot be said that their spirit determines everything that we do. The reason why the new way of thinking and feeling has not yet penetrated the great mass of men is that the sciences, for all their success in exploiting and dominating nature, have been stopped by the class which they brought to power – the bourgeoisie – from operating in another field where darkness still reigns, namely that of the relations which people have to one another during the exploiting and dominating process. This business on which all alike depended was performed without the new intellectual methods that made it possible ever illuminating the

---

[75]**Hiroshima:** site of the world's first nuclear bombing, by the United States, at the end of World War II, on 9 August 1945.

mutual relationships of the people who carried it out. The new approach to nature was not applied to society.

18

In the event people's mutual relations have become harder to disentangle than ever before. The gigantic joint undertaking on which they are engaged seems more and more to split them into two groups; increases in production lead to increases in misery; only a minority gain from the exploitation of nature, and they only do so because they exploit men. What might be progress for all then becomes advancement for a few, and an ever-increasing part of the productive process gets applied to creating means of destruction for mighty wars. During these wars the mothers of every nation, with their children pressed to them, scan the skies in horror for the deadly inventions of science.

19

The same attitude as men once showed in face of unpredictable natural catastrophes they now adopt towards their own undertakings. The bourgeois class, which owes to science an advancement that it was able, by ensuring that it alone enjoyed the fruits, to convert into domination, knows very well that its rule would come to an end if the scientific eye were turned on its own undertakings. And so that new science which was founded about a hundred years ago and deals with the character of human society was born in the struggle between rulers and ruled. Since then a certain scientific spirit has developed at the bottom, among the new class of workers whose natural element is large-scale production; from down there the great catastrophes are spotted as undertakings by the rulers.

20

But science and art meet on this ground, that both are there to make men's life easier, the one setting out to maintain, the other to entertain us. In the age to come art will create entertainment from that new productivity which can so greatly improve our maintenance, and in itself, if only it is left unshackled, may prove to be the greatest pleasure of them all.

21

If we want now to surrender ourselves to this great passion for producing, what ought our representations of men's life together to look like? What is that productive attitude in face of nature and of society which we children of a scientific age would like to take up pleasurably in our theatre?

22

The attitude is a critical one. Faced with a river, it consists in regulating the river; faced with a fruit tree, in spraying the fruit tree; faced with movement, in constructing vehicles and aeroplanes; faced with society, in turning society upside down. Our representations of human social life are designed for river-dwellers, fruit farmers, builders of vehicles and upturners of society, whom we invite into our theatres and beg not to forget their cheerful occupations while we hand the world over to their minds and hearts, for them to change as they think fit.

23

The theatre can only adopt such a free attitude if it lets itself be carried along by the strongest currents in its society and associates itself with those who are necessarily most impatient to make great alterations there. The bare wish, if nothing else, to evolve an art fit for the times must drive our theatre of the scientific age straight out into the suburbs, where it can stand as it were wide open, at the disposal of those who live hard and produce much, so that they can be fruitfully entertained there with their great problems. They may find it hard to pay for our art, and immediately to grasp the new method of entertainment, and we shall have to learn in many respects what they need and how they need it; but we can be sure of their interest. For these men who seem so far apart from natural science are only apart from it because they are being forcibly kept apart; and before they can get their hands on it they have first to develop and put into effect a new science of society; so that these are the true children of the scientific age, who alone can get the theatre moving if it is to move at all. A theatre which makes productivity its main source of entertainment has also to take it for its theme, and with greater keenness than ever now that man is everywhere hampered by men from self-production: i.e. from maintaining himself, entertaining and being entertained. The theatre has to become geared into reality if it is to be in a position to turn out effective representations of reality, and to be allowed to do so.

24

But this makes it simpler for the theatre to edge as close as possible to the apparatus of education and mass communication. For although we cannot bother it with the raw material of knowledge in all its variety, which would stop it from being enjoyable, it is still free to find enjoyment in teaching and inquiring. It constructs its workable representations of society, which are then in a position to influence society, wholly and entirely as a game: for those who are constructing society it sets out society's experiences, past and present alike, in such a manner that the audience can 'appreciate' the feelings, insights and impulses which are distilled by the wisest, most active and most passionate among us from the events of the day or the century. They must be entertained with the wisdom that comes from the solution of problems, with the anger that is a practical expression of sympathy with the underdog, with the respect due to those who respect humanity, or rather whatever is kind to humanity; in short, with whatever delights those who are producing something.

25

And this also means that the theatre can let its spectators enjoy the particular ethic of their age, which springs from productivity. A theatre which converts the critical approach – i.e. our great productive method – into pleasure finds nothing in the ethical field which it must do and a great deal that it can. Even the wholly anti-social can be a source of enjoyment to society so long as it is presented forcefully and on the grand scale. It then often proves to have considerable powers of understanding and other unusually valuable capacities, applied admittedly to a destructive end. Even the bursting flood of a vast catastrophe can be appreciated in all its majesty by society, if society knows how to master it; then we make it our own.

26

For such an operation as this we can hardly accept the theatre as we see it before us. Let us go into one of these houses and observe the effect which it has on the spectators. Looking about us, we see somewhat motionless figures in a peculiar condition: they seem strenuously to be tensing all their muscles, except where these are flabby and exhausted. They scarcely communicate with each other; their relations are those of a lot of sleepers, though of such as dream restlessly because, as is popularly said of those who have nightmares, they are lying on their backs. True, their eyes are open, but they stare rather than see, just as they listen rather than hear. They look at the stage as if in a trance: an expression which comes from the Middle Ages, the days of witches and priests. Seeing and hearing are activities, and can be pleasant ones, but these people seem relieved of activity and like men to whom something is being done. This detached state, where they seem to be given over to vague but profound sensations, grows deeper the better the work of the actors, and so we, as we do not approve of this situation, should like them to be as bad as possible.

27

As for the world portrayed there, the world from which slices are cut in order to produce these moods and movements of the emotions, its appearance is such, produced from such slight and wretched stuff as a few pieces of cardboard, a little miming, a bit of text, that one has to admire the theatre folk who, with so feeble a reflection of the real world, can move the feelings of their audience so much more strongly than does the world itself.

28

In any case we should excuse these theatre folk, for the pleasures which they sell for money and fame could not be induced by an exacter representation of the world, nor could their inexact renderings be presented in a less magical way. Their capacity to represent people can be seen at work in various instances; it is especially the rogues and the minor figures who reveal their knowledge of humanity and differ one from the other, but the central figures have to be kept general, so that it is easier for the onlooker to identify himself with them, and at all costs each trait of character must be drawn from the narrow field within which everyone can say at once: that is how it is.

For the spectator wants to be put in possession of quite definite sensations, just as a child does when it climbs on to one of the horses on a roundabout: the sensation of pride that it can ride, and has a horse; the pleasure of being carried, and whirled past other children; the adventurous daydreams in which it pursues others or is pursued, etc. In leading the child to experience all this the degree to which its wooden seat resembles a horse counts little, nor does it matter that the ride is confined to a small circle. The one important point for the spectators in these houses is that they should be able to swap a contradictory world for a consistent one, one that they scarcely know for one of which they can dream.

29

That is the sort of theatre which we face in our operations, and so far it has been fully able to transmute our optimistic friends, whom we have called the children of the scientific era, into a cowed, credulous, hypnotized mass.

30

True, for about half a century they have been able to see rather more faithful representations of human social life, as well as individual figures who were in revolt against certain social evils or even against the structure of society as a whole. They felt interested enough to put up with a temporary and exceptional restriction of language, plot and spiritual scope; for the fresh wind of the scientific spirit nearly withered the charms to which they had grown used. The sacrifice was not especially worth while. The greater subtlety of the representations subtracted from one pleasure without satisfying another. The field of human relationships came within our view, but not within our grasp. Our feelings, having been aroused in the old (magic) way, were bound themselves to remain unaltered.

31

For always and everywhere theatres were the amusement centres of a class which restricted the scientific spirit to the natural field, not daring to let it loose on the field of human relationships. The tiny proletarian section of the public, reinforced to a negligible and uncertain extent by renegade intellectuals, likewise still needed the old kind of entertainment, as a relief from its predetermined way of life.

32

So let us march ahead! Away with all obstacles! Since we seem to have landed in a battle, let us fight! Have we not seen how disbelief can move mountains? Is it not enough that we should have found that something is being kept from us? Before one thing and another there hangs a curtain: let us draw it up!

33

The theatre as we know it shows the structure of society (represented on the stage) as incapable of being influenced by society (in the auditorium). Oedipus, who offended against certain principles underlying the society of his time, is executed: the gods see to that; they are beyond criticism. Shakespeare's great solitary figures, bearing on their breast the star of their fate, carry through with irresistible force their futile and deadly outbursts; they prepare their own downfall; life, not death, becomes obscene as they collapse; the catastrophe is beyond criticism. Human sacrifices all round! Barbaric delights! We know that the barbarians have their art. Let us create another.

Further reading

Sean Carney, 'Brecht and Tragedy', in *Brecht and Critical Theory* (London and New York: Routledge, 2005), 152–84.

Angela Curran, 'Brecht's Criticisms of Aristotle's Aesthetics of Tragedy', *The Journal of Aesthetics and Art Criticism* 59, no. 2 (2001): 167–84.

Martin Revermann, 'Brecht and Greek Tragedy: Re-Thinking the Dialectics of Utilising the Tradition of Theatre', *German Life and Letters* 69, no. 2 (2016): 213–32.

5.6 ROBERT WARSHOW, 'THE GANGSTER AS TRAGIC HERO' (1948)

American film critic Robert Warshow (1917–55) was a member of the primarily Jewish, politically left wing (though anti-communist) group known as the New York Intellectuals, which included Lionel Trilling, Mary McCarthy, Edmund Wilson, and Hannah Arendt. In 'The Gangster as Tragic Hero' (1948), Warshow argues that gangster films offer a distinctively American version of tragedy, expressing the dark underside of a culture committed to happiness and success. With his violence, outlaw status, and inevitable fall from power, the gangster 'speaks for us, expressing that part of the American psyche which rejects the qualities and the demands of modern life, which rejects 'Americanism' itself'. Punished for his success through death, the gangster offers a sacrificial scapegoat for his audiences, who can participate vicariously in his dangerous rebellion while evading its risks.

America, as a social and political organization, is committed to a cheerful view of life. It could not be otherwise. The sense of tragedy is a luxury of aristocratic societies, where the fate of the individual is not conceived of as having a direct and legitimate political importance, being determined by a fixed and supra-political – that is, non-controversial – moral order or fate. Modern equalitarian societies, however, whether democratic or authoritarian in their political forms, always base themselves on the claim that they are making life happier; the avowed function of the modern state, at least in its ultimate terms, is not only to regulate social relations, but also to determine the quality and the possibilities of human life in general. Happiness thus becomes the chief political issue – in a sense, the only political issue – and for that reason it can never be treated as an issue at all. If an American or a Russian is unhappy, it implies a certain reprobation of his society, and therefore, by a logic of which we can all recognize the necessity, it becomes an obligation of citizenship to be cheerful; if the authorities find it necessary, the citizen may even be compelled to make a public display of his cheerfulness on important occasions, just as he may be conscripted into the army in time of war.

Naturally, this civic responsibility rests most strongly upon the organs of mass culture. The individual citizen may still be permitted his private unhappiness so long as it does not take on political significance, the extent of this tolerance being determined by how large an area of private life the society can accommodate. But every production of mass culture is a public act and must conform with accepted notions of the public good. Nobody seriously questions the principle that it is the function of mass culture to maintain public morale, and certainly nobody in the mass audience objects to having his morale maintained. At a time when the normal condition of the citizen is a state of anxiety, euphoria spreads over our culture like the broad smile of an idiot. In terms of attitudes towards life, there is very little difference between a 'happy' movie like *Good News*,[76] which ignores death and suffering, and a 'sad' movie like *A*

---

[76]***Good News***: 1947 American musical film directed by Charles Walter about undergraduates pursuing football and romance, based on a 1927 play; a 1930 black-and-white film version was no longer available in America by the 1940s because its innuendo violated the 1934 Motion Picture Production Code.

Tree Grows in Brooklyn,[77] which uses death and suffering as incidents in the service of a higher optimism.

But, whatever its effectiveness as a source of consolation and a means of pressure for maintaining 'positive' social attitudes, this optimism is fundamentally satisfying to no one, not even to those who would be most disoriented without its support. Even within the area of mass culture, there always exists a current of opposition, seeking to express by whatever means are available to it that sense of desperation and inevitable failure which optimism itself helps to create. Most often, this opposition is confined to rudimentary or semi-literate forms: in mob politics and journalism, for example, or in certain kinds of religious enthusiasm. When it does enter the field of art, it is likely to be disguised or attenuated: in an unspecific form of expression like jazz, in the basically harmless nihilism of the Marx Brothers,[78] in the continually reasserted strain of hopelessness that often seems to be the real meaning of the soap opera. The gangster film is remarkable in that it fills the need for disguise (though not sufficiently to avoid arousing uneasiness) without requiring any serious distortion. From its beginnings, it has been a consistent and astonishingly complete presentation of the modern sense of tragedy.

In its initial character, the gangster film is simply one example of the movies' constant tendency to create fixed dramatic patterns that can be repeated indefinitely with a reasonable expectation of profit. One gangster film follows another as one musical or one Western follows another. But this rigidity is not necessarily opposed to the requirements of art. There have been very successful types of art in the past which developed such specific and detailed conventions as almost to make individual examples of the type interchangeable. This is true, for example, of Elizabethan revenge tragedy and Restoration comedy.

For such a type to be successful means that its conventions have imposed themselves upon the general consciousness and become the accepted vehicles of a particular set of attitudes and a particular aesthetic effect. One goes to any individual example of the type with very definite expectations, and originality is to be welcomed only in the degree that it intensifies the expected experience without fundamentally altering it. Moreover, the relationship between the conventions which go to make up such a type and the real experience of its audience or the real facts of whatever situation it pretends to describe is of only secondary importance and does not determine its aesthetic force. It is only in an ultimate sense that the type appeals to its audience's experience of reality; much more immediately, it appeals to previous experience of the type itself: it creates its own field of reference.

Thus the importance of the gangster film, and the nature and intensity of its emotional and aesthetic impact, cannot be measured in terms of the place of the gangster himself or the importance of the problem of crime in American life. Those European movie-goers who think there is a gangster on every corner in New York are certainly deceived, but defenders of the 'positive' side of American culture are equally deceived if they think it relevant to point out that most Americans have never seen a gangster. What matters is that the experience of the gangster *as an experience of art* is universal to Americans. There is almost nothing we understand better or react to more readily or with quicker intelligence. The Western film, though it seems never

---

[77]*A Tree Grows in Brooklyn:* 1945 American film directed by Elia Kazan depicting a girl's coming of age in a struggling Brooklyn Irish-American immigrant family, based on a 1943 novel by Betty Smith.
[78]**Marx Brothers:** American vaudeville comedians, brothers from a German-Jewish immigrant family, who performed on stage and screen during the first half of the twentieth century.

to diminish in popularity, is for most of us no more than the folklore of the past, familiar and understandable only because it has been repeated so often. The gangster film comes much closer. In ways that we do not easily or willingly define, the gangster speaks for us, expressing that part of the American psyche which rejects the qualities and the demands of modern life, which rejects 'Americanism' itself.

The gangster is the man of the city, with the city's language and knowledge, with its queer and dishonest skills and its terrible daring, carrying his life in his hands like a placard, like a club. For everyone else, there is at least the theoretical possibility of another world – in that happier American culture which the gangster denies, the city does not really exist; it is only a more crowded and more brightly lit country – but for the gangster there is only the city; he must inhabit it in order to personify it: not the real city, but that dangerous and sad city of the imagination which is so much more important, which is the modern world. And the gangster – though there are real gangsters – is also, and primarily, a creature of the imagination. The real city, one might say, produces only criminals; the imaginary city produces the gangster: he is what we want to be and what we are afraid we may become.

Thrown into the crowd without background or advantages, with only those ambiguous skills which the rest of us – the real people of the real city – can only pretend to have, the gangster is required to make his way, to make his life and impose it on others. Usually, when we come upon him, he has already made his choice or the choice has already been made for him, it doesn't matter which: we are not permitted to ask whether at some point he could have chosen to be something else than what he is.

The gangster's activity is actually a form of rational enterprise, involving fairly definite goals and various techniques for achieving them. But this rationality is usually no more than a vague background; we know, perhaps, that the gangster sells liquor or that he operates a numbers racket; often we are not given even that much information. So his activity becomes a kind of pure criminality: he hurts people. Certainly our response to the gangster film is most consistently and most universally a response to sadism; we gain the double satisfaction of participating vicariously in the gangster's sadism and then seeing it turned against the gangster himself.

But on another level the quality of irrational brutality and the quality of rational enterprise become one. Since we do not see the rational and routine aspects of the gangster's behavior, the practice of brutality – the quality of unmixed criminality – becomes the totality of his career. At the same time, we are always conscious that the whole meaning of this career is a drive for success: the typical gangster film presents a steady upward progress followed by a very precipitate fall. Thus brutality itself becomes at once the means to success and the content of success – a success that is defined in its most general terms, not as accomplishment or specific gain, but simply as the unlimited possibility of aggression. (In the same way, film presentations of businessmen tend to make it appear that they achieve their success by talking on the telephone and holding conferences and that success *is* talking on the telephone and holding conferences.)

From this point of view, the initial contact between the film and its audience is an agreed conception of human life: that man is a being with the possibilities of success or failure. This principle, too, belongs to the city; one must emerge from the crowd or else one is nothing. On that basis the necessity of the action is established, and it progresses by inalterable paths to the point where the gangster lies dead and the principle has been modified: there is really only one possibility – failure. The final meaning of the city is anonymity and death.

In the opening scene of *Scarface*,[79] we are shown a successful man; we know he is successful because he has just given a party of opulent proportions and because he is called Big Louie. Through some monstrous lack of caution, he permits himself to be alone for a few moments. We understand from this immediately that he is about to be killed. No convention of the gangster film is more strongly established than this: it is dangerous to be alone. And yet the very conditions of success make it impossible not to be alone, for success is always the establishment of an *individual* pre-eminence that must be imposed on others, in whom it automatically arouses hatred; the successful man is an outlaw. The gangster's whole life is an effort to assert himself as an individual, to draw himself out of the crowd, and he always dies *because* he is an individual; the final bullet thrusts him back, makes him, after all, a failure. 'Mother of God,' says the dying Little Caesar, 'is this the end of Rico?'[80] – speaking of himself thus in the third person because what has been brought low is not the undifferentiated *man*, but the individual with a name, the gangster, the success; even to himself he is a creature of the imagination. (T.S. Eliot[81] has pointed out that a number of Shakespeare's tragic heroes have this trick of looking at themselves dramatically; their true identity, the thing that is destroyed when they die, is something outside themselves – not a man, but a style of life, a kind of meaning.)

At bottom, the gangster is doomed because he is under the obligation to succeed, not because the means he employs are unlawful. In the deeper layers of the modern consciousness, *all* means are unlawful, every attempt to succeed is an act of aggression, leaving one alone and guilty and defenseless among enemies: one is *punished* for success. This is our intolerable dilemma: that failure is a kind of death and success is evil and dangerous, is – ultimately – impossible. The effect of the gangster film is to embody this dilemma in the person of the gangster and resolve it by his death. The dilemma is resolved because it is *his* death, not ours. We are safe; for the moment, we can acquiesce in our failure, we can choose to fail.

1948

Further reading

David Denby, 'Robert Warshow: Life and Works', in Robert Warshow, *The Immediate Experience: Movies, Comics, Theatre and Other Aspects of Popular Culture*, ed. Sherry Abel, 3rd ed. (Cambridge, MA: Harvard University Press, 2001), ix–xxi.

Robert T. Eberwein, 'Robert Warshow', in *A Viewer's Guide to Film Theory and Criticism* (Metuchen: Scarecrow Press, 1979), 109–16.

Judith Hess Wright, 'Genre Films and the Status Quo', in *Film Genre Reader II*, ed. Barry Keith Grant (Austin: University of Texas Press, 1995), 41–9.

---

[79]*Scarface*: 1932 film directed by Howard Hawks featuring the rise and fall of gangster Tony Camonte (based on Al Capone), from a 1929 novel by pulp-fiction author Armitage Trail; the film was remade in 1983 by Brian DePalma.
[80]**Little Caesar**: protagonist of *Little Caesar*, a 1931 film directed by Mervyn LeRoy, adapted from 1929 novel by William Burnett, about the rise and fall of gangster Rico Bandello.
[81]**T.S. Eliot**: American-born Modernist poet (1888–1965); he reflected on Shakespeare especially in his essay 'Hamlet and His Problems' (1920) and throughout his *Essays on Elizabethan Drama* (1932).

5.7 GEORGE STEINER, *DEATH OF TRAGEDY* (1961)

Literary scholar George Steiner was born in France in 1929 to Jewish parents who had fled Vienna's rising Nazi presence. Raised multilingual, he went on to teach comparative literature in the United States, England, and Switzerland, and to write studies of Russian literature, translation, the Holocaust, and tragedy. In *The Death of Tragedy* (1961), Steiner presents the genre as a phenomenon rooted in ancient Greece, revived in Elizabethan England and seventeenth-century France, and now extinct. Unlike catastrophe, which persists regardless of circumstances, tragedy as a dramatic genre requires divinity, a mysterious inexorable force lacking rationality or justification, in the face of which humanity is not simply vulnerable but doomed. Although Steiner acknowledges that not all tragedies end badly, he does not accept Aristotle's subcategory, developed by Giraldi (extract 2.1), of tragedy with a happy ending. For him, tragedy is fundamentally pessimistic, reflecting the impossibility of human control; it accordingly cannot flourish in a modern world underpinned by faith in reason and progress.

I

We are entering on large, difficult ground. There are landmarks worth noting from the outset.

All men are aware of tragedy in life. But tragedy as a form of drama is not universal. Oriental art knows violence, grief, and the stroke of natural or contrived disaster; the Japanese theatre is full of ferocity and ceremonial death. But that representation of personal suffering and heroism which we call tragic drama is distinctive of the western tradition. It has become so much a part of our sense of the possibilities of human conduct, the *Oresteia*,[82] *Hamlet*, and *Phèdre*[83] are so ingrained in our habits of spirit, that we forget what a strange and complex idea it is to re-enact private anguish on a public stage. This idea and the vision of man which it implies are Greek. And nearly till the moment of their decline, the tragic forms are Hellenic.

Tragedy is alien to the Judaic sense of the world. The book of Job is always cited as an instance of tragic vision. But that black fable stands on the outer edge of Judaism, and even here an orthodox hand has asserted the claims of justice against those of tragedy:

So the Lord blessed the latter end of Job more than the beginning: for he had fourteen thousand sheep, and six thousand camels, and a thousand yoke of oxen, and a thousand she-asses.[84]

God has made good the havoc wrought upon His servant; he has compensated Job for his agonies. But where there is compensation, there is justice, not tragedy. This demand for justice is the pride and burden of the Judaic tradition. Jehovah is just, even in His fury. Often the balance of retribution or reward seems fearfully awry, or the proceedings of God appear

---

[82]*Oresteia:* 458 BCE trilogy of tragedies by Greek playwright Aeschylus, dramatizing the murders of Agamemnon and Clytemnestra.
[83]*Phèdre:* 1677 tragedy by French playwright Jean Racine based on Euripides' *Hippolytus.*
[84]**So ... she-asses:** Job 42:12.

unendurably slow. But over the sum of time, there can be no doubt that the ways of God to man are just. Not only are they just, they are rational. The Judaic spirit is vehement in its conviction that the order of the universe and of man's estate is accessible to reason. The ways of the Lord are neither wanton nor absurd. We may fully apprehend them if we give to our inquiries the clearsightedness of obedience. Marxism is characteristically Jewish in its insistence on justice and reason, and Marx repudiated the entire concept of tragedy. 'Necessity,' he declared, 'is blind only in so far as it is not understood.'[85]

Tragic drama arises out of precisely the contrary assertion: necessity is blind and man's encounter with it shall rob him of his eyes, whether it be in Thebes or in Gaza. The assertion is Greek, and the tragic sense of life built upon it is the foremost contribution of the Greek genius to our legacy. It is impossible to tell precisely where or how the notion of formal tragedy first came to possess the imagination. But the *Iliad* is the primer of tragic art. In it are set forth the motifs and images around which the sense of the tragic has crystallized during nearly three thousand years of western poetry: the shortness of heroic life, the exposure of man to the murderousness and caprice of the inhuman, the fall of the City. Note the crucial distinction: the fall of Jericho or Jerusalem is merely just, whereas the fall of Troy is the first great metaphor of tragedy. Where a city is destroyed because it has defied God, its destruction is a passing instant in the rational design of God's purpose. Its walls shall rise again, on earth or in the kingdom of heaven, when the souls of men are restored to grace. The burning of Troy is final because it is brought about by the fierce sport of human hatreds and the wanton, mysterious choice of destiny.

There are attempts in the *Iliad* to throw the light of reason into the shadow-world which surrounds man. Fate is given a name, and the elements are shown in the frivolous and reassuring mask of the gods. But mythology is only a fable to help us endure. The Homeric warrior knows that he can neither comprehend nor master the workings of destiny. Patroclus is slain, and the wretch Thersites sails safely for home.[86] Call for justice or explanation, and the sea will thunder back with its mute clamour. Men's accounts with the gods do not balance.

The irony deepens. Instead of altering or diminishing their tragic condition, the increase in scientific resource and material power leaves men even more vulnerable. This idea is not yet explicit in Homer, but it is eloquent in another major tragic poet, in Thucydides.[87] Again, we must observe the decisive contrast. The wars recorded in the Old Testament are bloody and grievous, but not tragic. They are just or unjust. The armies of Israel shall carry the day if they have observed God's will and ordinance. They shall be routed if they have broken the divine covenant or if their kings have fallen into idolatry. The Peloponnesian Wars,[88] on the contrary, are tragic. Behind them lie obscure fatalities and misjudgements. Enmeshed in false rhetoric and driven by political compulsions of which they can give no clear account, men go out to destroy one another in a kind of fury without hatred. We are still waging Peloponnesian wars.

---

[85]**'Necessity … understood'**: this quote is not actually by Marx; Engels quoted it, from Hegel, in *Anti-Dühring* (1878).
[86]**Patroclus … Thersites**: in legends of the Trojan war, Patroclus is a noble figure, beloved of Achilles, who dies in battle; Thersites, a Greek soldier depicted as vulgar and crude, survives the war.
[87]**Thucydides**: (*c*.460–*c*.400 BCE) was a Greek writer of prose history, rather than a tragic poet. Steiner uses this term to emphasize that Thucydides' account of the Peloponnesian Wars embodies the principles defined here as tragic.
[88]**Peloponnesian Wars**: extended war (431–404 BCE) in the ancient Greek world between the Peloponnesian League, led by Sparta, and the Delian League, led by Athens.

Our control of the material world and our positive science have grown fantastically. But our very achievements turn against us, making politics more random and wars more bestial.

The Judaic vision sees in disaster a specific moral fault or failure of understanding. The Greek tragic poets assert that the forces which shape or destroy our lives lie outside the governance of reason or justice. Worse than that: there are around us daemonic energies which prey upon the soul and turn it to madness or which poison our will so that we inflict irreparable outrage upon ourselves and those we love. Or to put it in the terms of the tragic design drawn by Thucydides: our fleets shall always sail toward Sicily although everyone is more or less aware that, they go to their ruin. Eteocles knows that he will perish at the seventh gate but goes forward nevertheless:

> We are already past the care of gods.
> For them our death is the admirable offering.
> Why then delay, fawning upon our doom?[89]

Antigone is perfectly aware of what will happen to her, and in the wells of his stubborn heart Oedipus knows also. But they stride to their fierce disasters in the grip of truths more intense than knowledge. To the Jew there is a marvellous continuity between knowledge and action; to the Greek an ironic abyss. The legend of Oedipus, in which the Greek sense of tragic unreason is so grimly rendered, served that great Jewish poet Freud as an emblem of rational insight and redemption through healing.[90]

Not that Greek tragedy is wholly without redemption. In the *Eumenides* and in *Oedipus at Colonus*,[91] the tragic action closes on a note of grace. Much has been made of this fact. But we should, I think, interpret it with extreme caution. Both cases are exceptional; there is in them an element of ritual pageant commemorating special aspects of the sanctity of Athens. Moreover, the part of music in Greek tragedy is irrevocably lost to us, and I suspect that the use of music may have given to the endings of these two plays a solemn distinctness, setting the final moments at some distance from the terrors which went before.

I emphasize this because I believe that any realistic notion of tragic drama must start from the fact of catastrophe. Tragedies end badly. The tragic personage is broken by forces which can neither be fully understood nor overcome by rational prudence. This again is crucial. Where the causes of disaster are temporal, where the conflict can be resolved through technical or social means, we may have serious drama, but not tragedy. More pliant divorce laws could not alter the fate of Agamemnon;[92] social psychiatry is no answer to *Oedipus*. But saner economic relations or better plumbing *can* resolve some of the grave crises in the dramas of Ibsen.[93] The distinction should be borne sharply in mind. Tragedy is irreparable. It cannot lead to just and material compensation for past suffering. Job gets back double the number of she-asses; so he

---

[89]**We ... doom:** Aeschylus, *Seven against Thebes*, ll. 702–4.

[90]**Oedipus ... Freud:** On Freud's reading of Oedipus, see extract 5.1.

[91]***Eumenides...Colonus***: The *Eumenides* was the final play in Aeschylus' Oresteia trilogy (458 BCE), in which the cycle of revenge is resolved at a trial overseen by the goddess Athena. **Oedipus at Colonus** was Sophocles' final Theban tragedy (c.406), dramatizing the end of Oedipus' life.

[92]**Agamemnon:** murdered by his wife Clytemnestra in retribution for his sacrifice of their daughter Iphigenia for the Trojan War.

[93]**Ibsen:** Norwegian playwright Henrik Ibsen (1828–1906), whose realist domestic tragedies explore contemporary social issues.

should, for God has enacted upon him a parable of justice. Oedipus does not get back his eyes or his sceptre over Thebes.

Tragic drama tells us that the spheres of reason, order, and justice are terribly limited and that no progress in our science or technical resources will enlarge their relevance. Outside and within man is *l'autre*,[94] the 'otherness' of the world. Call it what you will: a hidden or malevolent God, blind fate, the solicitations of hell, or the brute fury of our animal blood. It waits for us in ambush at the crossroads. It mocks us and destroys us. In certain rare instances, it leads us after destruction to some incomprehensible repose.

None of this, I know, is a definition of tragedy. But any neat abstract definition would mean nothing. When we say 'tragic drama' we know what we are talking about; not exactly, but well enough to recognize the real thing. In one instance, however, a tragic poet does come very near to giving an explicit summary of the tragic vision of life. Euripides' *Bacchae* stands in some special proximity to the ancient, no longer discernible springs of tragic feeling. At the end of the play, Dionysus condemns Cadmus, his royal house, and the entire city of Thebes to a savage doom. Cadmus protests: the sentence is far too harsh. It is utterly out of proportion with the guilt of those who fail to recognize or have insulted the god. Dionysus evades the question. He repeats petulantly that he has been greatly affronted; then he asserts that the doom of Thebes was predestined. There is no use asking for rational explanation or mercy. Things are as they are, unrelenting and absurd. We are punished far in excess of our guilt.

It is a terrible, stark insight into human life. Yet in the very excess of his suffering lies man's claim to dignity. Powerless and broken, a blind beggar hounded out of the city, he assumes a new grandeur. Man is ennobled by the vengeful spite or injustice of the gods. It does not make him innocent, but it hallows him as if he had passed through flame. Hence there is in the final moments of great tragedy, whether Greek or Shakespearean or neoclassic, a fusion of grief and joy, of lament over the fall of man and of rejoicing in the resurrection of his spirit. No other poetic form achieves this mysterious effect; it makes of *Oedipus*, *King Lear*, and *Phèdre* the noblest yet wrought by the mind.

From antiquity until the age of Shakespeare and Racine, such accomplishment seemed within the reach of talent. Since then the tragic voice in drama is blurred or still. What follows is an attempt to determine why this should be.

Further reading

Ruth Padel, 'George Steiner and the Greekness of Tragedy', in *Reading George Steiner*, ed. Nathan A. Scott Jr and Ronald A. Sharp (Baltimore: Johns Hopkins University Press, 1994), 99–133.

George Steiner, '"Tragedy", Reconsidered', *New Literary History* 35, no. 1 (2004): 1–15.

Graham Ward, 'Steiner and Eagleton: The Practice of Hope and the Idea of the Tragic', *Literature and Theology* 19, no. 2 (2005): 100–11.

---

[94] *l'autre*: the other, in French.

5.8 ATHOL FUGARD, 'ON *A VIEW FROM THE BRIDGE*' (1963)

Athol Fugard (born 1932) is a South African playwright, actor, and director known especially for using theatre to probe the human consequences of racial injustice. His opposition to apartheid spurred his commitment to multiracial theatre, and to dramatizing the rage, violence, and grief created by a corrupt political system. Although his plays are primarily set in contemporary South Africa, Fugard has frequently drawn on Greek tragedy with experimental versions of a Greek tragic chorus and of figures including Antigone and Orestes. In this extract, he reflects on the nature of tragedy after watching Arthur Miller's *A View from the Bridge*. Like Brecht, Fugard advocates theatre that will provoke outrage rather than catharsis; like Steiner, he suggests that the genre of tragedy cannot flourish in our rational, post-Enlightenment world. In particular, he suggests that his resistance to absolute finality – a resistance he sees also in other contemporary writers – prevents his own plays from being tragedies.

With Sheila[95] on Saturday night to see the film of Arthur Miller's *A View from the Bridge*.[96] Halfway through I was forced to turn to Sheila and whisper: 'It's going off the rails. It's getting lost.' Feelings, and a final disappointment, that almost parallel my reactions on reading *Death of a Salesman*.[97] Afterwards, we talked for a long time about Miller and the 'tragic' in modern playwriting. I can only remember the gist of the main thoughts.

The essence of Tragedy is surely Truth – and the recognition of it – and then, for all this recognition and understanding of where one is going, to *still* choose or be forced to take the path to the final catastrophe. For Eddie in *View from the Bridge* the final tragic crescendo should have started with a moment when he is told, 'You want her (Catherine)', to which he must reply, inwardly or outwardly, 'Yes. Yes! I want her. And if I can't have her, no-one has her.' Knowing what this means; seeing the shadow of a final catastrophe stretched across that way but still choosing to move because something bigger than he can contain is pulling the strings.

I say 'truth' – and that one word encompasses total awareness; light in the darkest quarter of man's soul; inevitability; madness; the collapse of reason; Finality; Morality.

Finality: an important word – a word that I cannot help feel points to the answer to the old, old talking-point: Why has the tragic dimension been lost in modern playwriting, where has it gone? At this moment I cannot help thinking, feeling, that we have lost it because of our confusion on moral issues – our clever uncertainty about right and wrong – and because of our assault on the concept of finality, the end – FINIS. This is certainly true of myself. With

---

[95]**Sheila:** Fugard was married at the time to Sheila Meiring Fugard, an actress who went on to become a poet and novelist.

[96]*A View from the Bridge:* 1955 play by American playwright Arthur Miller (1915–2005), made into a 1962 film directed by Sidney Lumet. Italian-American dock worker Eddie falls in love with his wife Beatrice's orphaned niece Catherine, who lives with them in Brooklyn. When Catherine falls in love with Beatrice's Italian cousin Rodolpho, who has come with his brother Marco to work illegally, an unhinged Eddie betrays Marco and Rodolpho to immigration officials, leading to violence.

[97]*Death of a Salesman:* 1949 play by Arthur Miller, in which traveling salesman Willy Loman struggles with the collapse of his dreams after the loss of his job and tensions with his sons.

God gone, how haven't I struggled to convince myself about 'life after death' – life on this planet, life in rockpools, life anywhere in the universe. But I have had to say to myself – It will go on. Even though I am dust, it will go on. This is a direct assault on finality. Had Macbeth said that to himself – or her – would their stories have ended the same way? I don't think so. For Shakespeare, for Sophocles, Life was a bridge from light to darkness and man had to face the enormous consequence of any act. By making life a circle I have removed consequence. By trying to eliminate 'THE END' I have unwittingly assaulted the tragic dimension.

My 'life after death' – no retribution is involved.

But to return to *A View from the Bridge* – it is Eddie's self-deception, his meaningless 'Give me back my name, Marco!' his refusal to recognise and face the consequences, that block the emergence of a tragic dimension – because the play in the final half certainly points in the right direction.

Another angle on the above: the light of twentieth century knowledge, scientific, that has banished the dark shadow of tragedy. Incompatibilities – tragedy and enlightenment.

Further reading

E.A. Mackay, 'Antigone and Orestes in the Works of Athol Fugard,' *Theoria* (1989): 31–43.

Marianne McDonald, 'The Return of Myth: Athol Fugard and the Classics', *Arion* 14, no. 2 (2006): 21–48.

Albert Wertheim, 'The Drama as Teaching and Learning: Trauerspiel, Tragedy, Hope and Race', in *The Dramatic Art of Athol Fugard: From South Africa to the World* (Bloomington: Indiana University Press, 2000), 117–53.

5.9 RAYMOND WILLIAMS, *MODERN TRAGEDY* (1966)

Raymond Williams (1921–88) was a British cultural materialist critic, known for exploring the literary implications of Marxist economic thought. In *Modern Tragedy* (1966), Williams challenges the idea, developed most forcefully by George Steiner, that tragedy can no longer flourish in the modern world. Like Brecht, Williams situates tragedy in relation to social and political events, rather than defining it through personal, interior experience. Because tragedy responds to political circumstances, he explains, we cannot look for a fixed, universal idea of the genre. Instead, the form of tragedy necessarily changes as society changes. Writing during the political and social turbulence of the 1960s, Williams identifies moments of upheaval as rich with potential for new cultural forms. Because tragedy responds to social disorder, he argues, it thrives not in times of stability but during periods of flux, uncertainty, and disorder. These moments also give rise to revolution, which also represents an outgrowth of disorder; tragedy, accordingly, is potentially a revolutionary genre.

Tragedy and Revolution

The most complex effect of any really powerful ideology is that it directs us, even when we think we have rejected it, to the same kind of fact. Thus, when we try to identify the disorder which is at the root of our tragic experiences, we tend to find elements analogous to former tragic systems, as the ideology has interpreted them. We look, almost unconsciously, for a crisis of personal belief: matching a lost belief in immortality with a new conviction of mortality, or a lost belief in fate with a new conviction of indifference. We look for tragic experience in our attitudes to God or to death or to individual will, and of course we often find tragic experience cast in these familiar forms. Having separated earlier tragic systems from their actual societies, we can achieve a similar separation in our own time, and can take it for granted that modern tragedy can be discussed without reference to the deep social crisis, of war and revolution, through which we have all been living. That kind of interest is commonly relegated to politics, or, to use the cant word, sociology. Tragedy, we say, belongs to deeper and closer experience, to man not to society. Even the general disorders, which can hardly escape the most limited attention, and which equally can hardly be said to involve only societies and not men, can be reduced to symptoms of the only kind of disorder we are prepared to recognize: the fault in the soul. War, revolution, poverty, hunger; men reduced to objects and killed from lists; persecution and torture; the many kinds of contemporary martyrdom: however close and insistent the facts, we are not to be moved, in a context of tragedy. Tragedy, we know, is about something else.

Yet the break comes, in some minds. In experience, suddenly, the new connections are made, and the familiar world shifts, as the new relations are seen. We are not looking for a new universal meaning of tragedy. We are looking for the structure of tragedy in our own culture. Once we begin to doubt, in experience and then in analysis, the ordinary twentieth-century idea, other directions seem open.

Tragedy and social disorder

Since the time of the French Revolution,[98] the idea of tragedy can be seen as in different ways a response to a culture in conscious change and movement. The action of tragedy and the action of history have been consciously connected, and in the connection have been seen in new ways. The reaction against this, from the mid-nineteenth century, has been equally evident: the movement of spirit has been separated from the movement of civilisation. Yet even this negative reaction seems, in its context, a response to the same kind of crisis. The academic tradition, on the whole, has followed the negative reaction, but it is difficult to hear its ordinary propositions and feel that they are only about a set of academic facts. They sound, insistently, like propositions about contemporary life, even when they are most negative and most consciously asocial. The other nineteenth-century tradition, in which tragedy and history were consciously connected, seems then deeply relevant. In experience and in theory we have to look again at this relation.

We must ask whether tragedy, in our own time, is a response to social disorder. If it is so, we shall not expect the response to be always direct. The disorder will appear in very many forms, and to articulate these will be very complex and difficult. A more immediate difficulty is the ordinary separation of social thinking and tragic thinking. The most influential kinds of explicitly social thinking have often rejected tragedy as in itself defeatist. Against what they have known as the idea of tragedy, they have stressed man's powers to change his condition and to end a major part of the suffering which the tragic ideology seems to ratify. The idea of tragedy, that is to say, has been explicitly opposed by the idea of revolution: there has been as much confidence on the one side as on the other. And then to describe tragedy as a response to social disorder, and to value it as such, is to break, apparently, from both major traditions.

The immediate disturbance is radical, for the fault in the soul was a recognition of a kind; it was close to the experience, even when it added its ordinary formulas. From the other position, from the recognition of social disorder, there is a habit of easy abstraction which the scale of the disorder almost inevitably supports. As we recognise history, we are referred to history, and find it difficult to acknowledge men like ourselves. Before, we could not recognise tragedy as social crisis; now, commonly, we cannot recognise social crisis as tragedy. The facts of disorder are caught up in a new ideology, which cancels suffering as it finds the name of a period or a phase. From day to day we can make everything past, because we believe in the future. Our actual present, in which the disorder is radical, is as effectively hidden as when it was merely politics, for it is now only politics. It seems that we have jumped from one blindness to another, and with the same visionary confidence. The new connections harden, and no longer connect.

What seems to matter, against every difficulty, is that the received ideas no longer describe our experience. The most common idea of revolution excludes too much of our social experience. But it is more than this. The idea of tragedy, in its ordinary form, excludes especially that tragic experience which is social, and the idea of revolution, again in its ordinary form, excludes especially that social experience which is tragic. And if this is so, the contradiction is significant. It is not a merely formal opposition, of two ways of reading experience, between which we can choose. In our own time, especially, it is the connections between revolution and

---

[98]**French Revolution:** political upheaval leading to the violent overthrow of the French monarchy, 1789–99.

tragedy – connections lived and known but not acknowledged as ideas – which seem most clear and significant.

The most evident connection is in the actual events of history, as we all quite simply observe them. A time of revolution is so evidently a time of violence, dislocation and extended suffering that it is natural to feel it as tragedy, in the everyday sense. Yet, as the event becomes history, it is often quite differently regarded. Very many nations look back to the revolutions of their own history as to the era of creation of the life which is now most precious. The successful revolution, we might say, becomes not tragedy but epic: it is the origin of a people, and of its valued way of life. When the suffering is remembered, it is at once either honoured or justified. That particular revolution, we say, was a necessary condition of life.

Contemporary revolution is of course very different. Only a post-revolutionary generation is capable of that epic composition. In contemporary revolution, the detail of suffering is insistent, whether as violence or as the reshaping of lives by a new power in the state. But further, in a contemporary revolution, we inevitably take sides, though with different degrees of engagement. And a time of revolution is ordinarily a time of lies and of suppressions of truths. The suffering of the whole action, even when its full weight is acknowledged, is commonly projected as the responsibility of this party or that, until its very description becomes a revolutionary or counter-revolutionary act. There is a kind of indifference which comes early whenever the action is at a distance. But there is also an exposure to the scale of suffering, and to the lies and campaigns that are made from it, which in the end is also indifference. Revolution is a dimension of action from which, for initially honourable reasons, we feel we have to keep clear.

Thus the social fact becomes a structure of feeling. Revolution as such is in a common sense tragedy, a time of chaos and suffering. It is almost inevitable that we should try to go beyond it. I do not rely on what is almost certain to happen: that this tragedy, in its turn, will become epic. However true this may be, it cannot closely move us; only heirs can inherit. Allegiance to even a probable law of history, which has not, however, in the particular case, been lived through, becomes quite quickly an alienation. We are not truly responding to this action but, by projection, to its probable composition.

The living alternative is quite different in character. It is neither the rejection of revolution, by its simple characterisation as chaos and suffering, nor yet the calculation of revolution, by laws and probabilities not yet experienced. It is, *rather, a recognition; the recognition of revolution* as a whole action of living men. Both the wholeness of the action, and in this sense its humanity, are then inescapable. It is this recognition against which we ordinarily struggle.

[…]

The tragedy of revolution

This idea of 'the total redemption of humanity' has the ultimate cast of resolution and order, but in the real world its perspective is inescapably tragic. It is born in pity and terror: in the perception of a radical disorder in which the humanity of some men is denied and by that fact the idea of humanity itself is denied. It is born in the actual suffering of real men thus exposed, and in all the consequences of this suffering: degeneration, brutalisation, fear, hatred, envy. It is born in an experience of evil made the more intolerable by the conviction that it is not inevitable, but is the result of particular actions and choices.

And if it is thus tragic in its origins – in the existence of a disorder that cannot but move and involve – it is equally tragic in its action, in that it is not against gods or inanimate things that its impulse struggles, nor against mere institutions and social forms, but against other men. This, throughout, has been the area of silence, in the development of the idea. What is properly called utopianism, or revolutionary romanticism, is the suppression or dilution of this quite inevitable fact.

There are many reasons why men will oppose such a revolution. There are the obvious reasons of interest or privilege, for which we have seen men willing to die. There is the deep fear that recognition of the humanity of others is a denial of our own humanity, as our whole lives have known it. There is the flight in the mind from disturbance of a familiar world, however inadequate. There is the terror, often justified, of what will happen when men who have been treated as less than men gain the power to act. For there will of course be revenge and senseless destruction, after the bitterness and deformity of oppression. And then, more subtly, there are all the learned positions, from an experience of disorder that is as old as human history and yet also is continually re-enacted: the conviction that any absolute purpose is delusion and folly, to be corrected by training, by some social ease where we are, or by an outright opposition to this madness which would destroy the world.

From all these positions, revolution is practically opposed, in every form from brutal suppression and massive indoctrination to genuine attempts to construct alternative futures. And all our experience tells us that this immensely complicated action between real men will continue as far ahead as we can foresee, and that the suffering in this continuing struggle will go on being terrible. It is very difficult for the mind to accept this, and we all erect our defences against so tragic a recognition. But I believe that it is inevitable, and that we must speak of it if it is not to overwhelm us.

In some Western societies we are engaged in the attempt to make this total revolution without violence, by a process of argument and consensus. It is impossible to say if we shall succeed. The arrest of humanity, in many groups and individuals, is still severe and seems often intractable. At the same time, while the process has any chance of success, nobody in his senses would wish to alter its nature. The real difficulty, however, is that we have become introverted on this process, in a familiar kind of North Atlantic thinking, and the illusions this breeds are already of a tragic kind.

Thus we seek to project the result of particular historical circumstances as universal, and to identify all other forms of revolution as hostile. The only consistent common position is that of the enemies of revolution everywhere, yet even they, at times, speak a liberal rhetoric. It is a very deep irony that, in ideology, the major conflict in the world is between different versions of the absolute rights of man. Again and again, men in Western societies act as counter-revolutionaries, but in the name of an absolute liberation. There are real complexities here, for revolutionary regimes have also acted, repeatedly and brutally, against every kind of human freedom and dignity. But there are also deep and habitual forms of false consciousness. Only a very few of us, in any Western society, have in fact renounced violence, in the way that our theory claims. If we believe that social change should be peaceful, it is difficult to know what we are doing in military alliances, with immense armament and weapons of indiscriminate destruction. The customary pretence that this organised violence is defensive, and that it is wholly dedicated to human freedom, is literally a tragic illusion. It is easy to move about in our own comparatively peaceful society, repeating such phrases as 'a revolution by due course of law', and simply failing to notice that in our name, and endorsed by repeated majorities, other peoples have been violently opposed in the very act of their own liberation. The bloody tale of the past is always conveniently discounted, but I am writing on a day when British military power is being used against 'dissident tribesmen' in South Arabia, and I know this pattern and its covering too well, from repeated examples through my lifetime, to be able to acquiesce in the ordinary illusion. Many of my countrymen have opposed these policies, and in many particular cases have ended them. But it is impossible to believe that as a society we have yet dedicated ourselves to human liberation, or even to that simple recognition of the absolute humanity of all other men which is the impulse of any genuine revolution. To say that in our own affairs we have made this recognition would also be too much, in a society powered by great economic inequality and by organised manipulation. But even if we had made this recognition, among ourselves, it would still be a travesty of any real revolutionary belief. It is only when the recognition is general that it can be authentic, for in practice every reservation, in a widely communicating world, tends to degenerate into actual opposition.

Further reading

Elizabeth Eldridge and John Eldridge, 'Drama and Literature: Williams' Analytical and Theoretical Approach', in *Raymond Williams: Making Connections* (London: Routledge, 2005), 111–38.

John Higgins, 'Cambridge Criticism 1962–73', in *Raymond Williams: Literature, Marxism and Cultural Materialism* (London: Routledge, 2013), 65–99.

Kenneth Surin, 'Raymond Williams on Tragedy and Revolution', in *Cultural Materialism: On Raymond Williams*, ed. Christopher Prendergast (Minneapolis: University of Minnesota Press, 1995), 143–72.

CHAPTER 6
POST-1968

Like the previous chapter, this one begins in the twentieth century, but it encompasses a very different intellectual terrain. After the tumult of 1960s social protests and the movements they spurred, approaches to tragedy took up new directions and questions, inflected especially by growing concerns about social, economic, and sexual inequality. As one of the oldest and most prestigious literary genres, tragedy has been perceived by many as a synecdoche for the Western literary tradition, and its considerable cultural capital has made it a lightning rod for debates about that tradition's achievements and failings. Accordingly, in variations on long-running questions about whether tragedy helped or harmed its audiences, after 1968 critics increasingly found themselves asking whether the genre challenges or fortifies the cultural privileges and hierarchies increasingly under suspicion. Is tragedy intrinsically elitist, capitalist, colonial, and misogynist, or can its violent upheavals offer lessons and even corrections for the problems it portrays?

The social, cultural, and political critiques explored in this chapter diverge from the stark emphasis on the interior experience of tragic protagonists observed in many of the previous chapter's extracts. At the same time, they build on other previous approaches. Just as both Brecht's model of epic theatre (extract 5.5) and Raymond Williams' idea of revolutionary tragedy (extract 5.9) drew on Marx's challenges to economic inequality, rising social protests led other writers to take up this mantle, including more voices from outside Europe and the United States. Brazilian activist, playwright, and director Augusto Boal drew on his own theatrical practices to argue that tragedy could and should be reconceived into a tool against political oppression (extract 6.2). In *Theatre of the Oppressed*, Boal joined Brecht in criticizing Aristotle's model of tragic catharsis as paralysing audiences into passivity and leading them to accept suffering rather than rage against it. In response, he argued that new theatrical practices should aspire to develop active spectators who reclaim agency through involving themselves directly in performances.

Tragedy's cultural and ritual contexts also attracted attention in this period from critics inspired by the structural anthropological theory associated with French scholar Claude Lévi-Strauss, which focused on recurring social structures that determine rules of marriage, kinship, and alliances.[1] Structuralist literary critics approached tragedy as representing communities' strategies for maintaining and reproducing themselves, with an eye to the genre's ritual contexts. Turning especially to the cultural milieu of the genre's Greek roots, influential French critic René Girard identified tragedy's origins in collective rituals of sacrifice, through which

---

[1] On structuralist thought, see especially Claude Lévi-Strauss, *Structural Anthropology*, trans. Claire Jacobson and Brooke Grundfest Schoepf (New York: Doubleday, 1963); on structuralist approaches to tragedy, see especially Jean-Pierre Vernant and Pierre Vidal-Naquet, *Myth and Tragedy in Ancient Greece*, trans. Janet Lloyd (Cambridge, MA: Zone Books, 1990).

communities identified a scapegoat that they could banish in order to restore the unity of their own social worlds (extract 6.1). Like sacrifice, Girard argues, tragedy identifies a surrogate victim whose suffering can both represent and avert that of the larger community. Tragedy's version of sacrifice, however, inevitably fails in its task of preserving a pre-existing integrity.

Structural anthropological readings of tragedy's social contexts focused exclusively on human societies, but the late twentieth century also saw rising attention to the effects of human society on the non-human world. In particular, growing concerns about the natural environment and the escalating threat of climate change gave rise to ecologically-informed literary approaches, now known as ecocriticism. In *The Comedy of Survival* (1974), American scholar Joseph Meeker argued that tragedy represents the most extreme version of anthropocentrism, the hubristic assumption that mankind is both different from and greater than the rest of the world (extract 6.3). Because tragic heroes romanticize their power even in downfall, and many have followed their lead – especially in the character-centred criticism popularized by A.C. Bradley (extract 5.2) – Meeker held that both the genre and the associated body of critical writings about it share culpability for our current environmental crisis.

Meeker's attack on tragedy as morally and politically dangerous rests on an entrenched set of assumptions that identify the genre itself not only with its protagonist – the so-called tragic hero – but also with a particular model of tragic hero, invariably identified as male. In the wake of questions, challenges, and protests raised by second-wave feminism beginning in the 1960s, these assumptions came under scrutiny. As observed by Virginia Woolf in the previous chapter, the original Greek plays – in which we typically locate tragic authority – in fact heavily feature female protagonists, whose complexity is at least as nuanced as that of their male counterparts (extract 5.4). While some feminist critics have built on Woolf's interest in underexplored female tragic protagonists, others have focused on a broader challenge to the largely male-written and male-centred literary canon, a phenomenon whose consequences were also observed by Woolf, in *A Room of One's Own* (1929).[2]

In keeping with developments in this period more broadly, the essays in this chapter build on Woolf's feminist challenges. In stark contrast to earlier chapters, this one features as many female writers as male, and most of these female writers direct themselves explicitly to the topic of women's place in tragedy, from a range of perspectives. Writing in the Marxist-inflected framework of cultural materialism, discussed in the previous chapter with reference to Raymond Williams, British literary critic Catherine Belsey developed a nuanced critique of what she described as the liberal humanist subject of tragedy by identifying this conventional tragic subject as insistently male, and contrasting it with the very different position of female figures in tragedy (extract 6.4). Other feminist critics developed in conversation with the structural anthropological theoretical approach linked with Girard and Lévi-Strauss. In *Tragic Ways of Killing a Woman* [originally *Façons Tragiques de Tuer une Femme*, 1985], French classical scholar Nicole Loraux explored patterns of female deaths in Greek tragedy to argue that the genre categorizes its female characters by their means of death, assigning them either

---

[2]For the former approach, see, for instance, Naomi Conn Liebler, ed., *The Female Tragic Hero in English Renaissance Drama* (Basingstoke: Palgrave, 2002); for the latter, see Linda Bamber, *Comic Women, Tragic Men: A Study of Gender and Genre in Shakespeare* (Stanford: Stanford University Press, 1982). Influential manifestos in feminist literary criticism include Elaine Showalter, *A Literature of Their Own* (Princeton: Princeton University Press, 1977).

the chaste sexual suppression of hanging or the masculine phallic power of stabbing, reflecting a broader system of understanding female agency and suffering (extract 6.5).

With its emphasis on sexuality and power, Loraux's structuralist account of women's tragic roles resonates with other French feminist literary theory from the 1980s. Others writing in this tradition, however, rooted their approaches especially in post-structuralist critiques of the universal assumptions shared by many structuralist theorists. The deconstructionist theory associated especially with Jacques Derrida, and the post-Freudian version of psychoanalysis linked with Jacques Lacan, were both important influences for French feminist scholars such as Julia Kristeva, Luce Irigaray, and Hélène Cixous. In 'Enter the Theater' (1999), Cixous reflects upon how her theatrical collaborations with Ariane Mnouchkine, founder and director of the Théâtre du Soleil in Paris, enabled her to explore the ways in which women's historical experiences might intersect with tragic dramatizations of the sufferings of mythic women from antiquity (extract 6.7). In unpicking or blurring apparently stable distinctions between history and myth, between contemporary Paris and ancient Athens, Cixous drew on her post-structuralist critico-theoretical work to produce a theatre that insisted that the sufferings of ordinary people uncovered and then forgotten by a contemporary rolling news cycle might be honoured, remembered and understood through theatrical tragedy.

Post-structuralist models of criticism also lie behind American gender theorist Judith Butler, whose social critiques challenge broader assumptions about sexuality and family structures. In *Antigone's Claim* (2000), Butler turns to Sophocles' portrait of Thebes' incest-muddled family to argue for the artificially constructed nature of all family structures. Exposing inherent contradictions in so-called conventional or traditional families, Butler suggests, offers liberating possibilities for reconceiving kinship structures (extract 6.8). Like Woolf, Butler turns to female tragic icons rather than more frequently lionized male figures such as Oedipus or Hamlet, and finds new questions and insights arising from the very different aspects of the genre that they typically represent.

Just as Butler's attention to the traditionally female-coded realm of the domestic sphere yields decidedly non-traditional insights and arguments, the American philosopher Martha Nussbaum similarly turns to the traditionally female-coded realm of emotion – especially the female-coded emotion of pity – to pursue a rigorous conversation with Plato and Aristotle about the moral consequences of tragedy's solicitation of emotions (extract 6.10). Nussbaum here follows a long tradition of Enlightenment, Romantic and post-Romantic debates (explored in chapters 3 and 4) over whether the passions provoked by tragedy might enable or inhibit moral action. She disagrees with Plato's contention that emotion interferes with rational decisions, arguing instead that emotion is and should be a crucial element to ethical action, but she also suggests that properly involving emotion in decisions is a complex and challenging skill, and one that tragedy helps us develop.

While concerns with social, economic, and sexual equality provoked Marxist and feminist critiques, world crises borne of racial and global inequality have spurred postcolonial literary adaptations of and inquiries into the genre.[3] Novelists and playwrights from throughout Africa,

---

[3] For studies of literary tragedy in postcolonial contexts see Ato Quayson, 'Tragedy and the Postcolonial Novel', in *The Cambridge Companion to the Postcolonial Novel*, ed. Ato Quayson (Cambridge: Cambridge University Press, 2015), 230–47; Timothy J. Reiss, 'Using Tragedy against Its Makers: Some African and Caribbean Instances', in *A Companion to Tragedy* ed. Rebecca Bushnell (Oxford: Blackwell, 2005), 505–36.

the Caribbean, Asia, and South America have productively returned to classical Greek tragedy in particular as a means of reassessing the relationships between once-colonized nations and their European former colonial powers. Just as Athol Fugard (extract 5.8), for instance, probed the intertextual possibilities of Sophocles's *Antigone* under the South African apartheid system in *The Island* (1973), so too Nigerian playwright, poet, and critic Wole Soyinka critiqued Eurocentric assumptions of Greek models of tragedy from an equally committed standpoint. In plays like *The Bacchae of Euripides* (1974) and *Death and the King's Horseman* (1975), he anatomized the relationship between Yoruba tragedy and culture, in which gods and rituals maintain an intimate and urgent presence. Classical tragedy has exercised a similarly transformative influence over the development of the postcolonial novel. For instance, Junot Diaz's examination of the relationships between individual agency, curses and fate in *Brief Wondrous Life of Oscar Wao* (2007) owes much to Sophocles's *Oedipus Rex*, and Yvonne Vera's novel about one woman's pursuit of love and illusory freedoms in Harare, *Without a Name* (1994), reconsiders Euripides's treatment of such issues in Euripides's *Medea*.[4]

Such flourishing of creative postcolonial responses to tragedy has been matched by a keen interest in the ideological investments of the theories of the genre. In his analysis of the theatre of Soyinka, Biodun Jeyifo argues that Aristotelian ideas about tragedy are simply too ahistorical and essentializing to do justice to the nature of postcolonial struggle or, indeed, to help make sense of the obsessively historical turn of much postcolonial tragedy (extract 6.6). He prefers instead to supplement an Aristotelian understanding with a Hegelian perspective (extract 4.6) which centres tragedy in an enduring conflict rather than in the errors or flaws of an enigmatic or isolated tragic protagonist. Hegel's reading of classical tragedy has also influenced political rather than literary studies of the postcolonial world. Greg Å. Graham's *Democratic Political Tragedy in the Postcolony* (2017), for instance, controversially insists that the catastrophic failure of radical schemes for social transformation in Jamaica and post-apartheid South Africa is due to the broad encroachment of, and particular leaders' susceptibility to, neoliberal ideology. He characterizes this development, in an explicit 'creolization' of Hegel's reading of tragedy, as 'democratic political tragedy' borne out of 'a defining tension and ultimately a politically paralysing conflict between … politically valid claims'.[5]

Hegel's reflections on the constitutive nature of conflict in tragedy as a means of viewing the disappointments of anti-colonial revolutions are, likewise, central to David's Scott's reading of the revised edition of C.L.R. James's history of the eighteenth-century Haitian revolution *The Black Jacobins* (1963), in *Conscripts of Modernity* (extract 6.9). However, Scott's emphasis is on the nature of genre as a means of comprehending postcolonial temporality. Scott refuses to accept the dominant genre assumptions of many works of anti-colonial and postcolonial theory – such as Frantz Fanon's *The Wretched of the Earth* (1961) – which implicitly or explicitly plot the nature of anti-colonial struggle as romance, charting a movement from oppression through resistance to liberation. Scott argues instead that tragedy, specifically 'the tragedy of colonial enlightenment', offers a much more fruitful way of accounting for the frustration, crushing or exhaustion of anti-colonial hopes. Tragedy, unlike romance, refuses to concede the pastness of the past – history and its ghosts always have recursive habits in tragedies – and, likewise, can

---

[4]For a rich discussion of Diaz's novel see Quayson, 'Tragedy and the Postcolonial Novel', 243.
[5]Greg A. Graham, *Democratic Political Tragedy in the Postcolony* (Abingdon and New York: Routledge, 2017), 4–5.

offer a more sceptical response to romantic assumptions about masterful nature of individual agency and the inevitability of progress.

It has been a commonplace since Shakespeare's *Hamlet* to observe that tragedy paints a picture of world in which phenomena do not quite connect, in which time is 'out of joint'. Postmodernity has demanded that we also pay attention to the ruptures, lacunae and instabilities that lurk beneath and structure our experiences of that world. As each of the extracts in this chapter show, whether from ecocritical, feminist, post-structuralist, or postcolonial perspectives, tragedy remains a vital means of trying to comprehend and respond to them.

6.1 RENÉ GIRARD, 'THE SACRIFICIAL CRISIS' (1972)

René Girard (1923–2015) was an influential French literary critic whose work is rooted in anthropological theory. Throughout his extensive and wide-ranging writings, he explores structural similarities within literary texts, and the forms of vicarious experience that they both reflect and cause. In his influential model of mimetic desire, Girard argues that we borrow our desires from others, leading to rivalry and violence. In this chapter from *Violence and the Sacred* [originally *La Violence et le Sacré*, 1972], he builds on this idea to explain the sacrificial rituals linked with the origins of tragedy. In order to regulate and deflect violence, Girard suggests, communities require a scapegoat who is similar enough to its members to become a surrogate victim, while separate enough to be cast out. As the privileged vehicle for the sacrificial crisis, tragedy dramatizes mimetic rivalry, culminating in a conflict between two mirror-image antagonists, which it resolves through the hero's sacrifice.

As we have seen, the proper functioning of the sacrificial process requires not only the complete separation of the sacrificed victim from those beings for whom the victim is a substitute but also a similarity between both parties. This dual requirement can be fulfilled only through a delicately balanced mechanism of associations.

Any change, however slight, in the hierarchical classification of living creatures risks undermining the whole sacrificial structure. The sheer repetition of the sacrificial act – the repeated slaughter of the same type of victim – inevitably brings about such change. But the inability to adapt to new conditions is a trait characteristic of religion in general. If, as is often the case, we encounter the institution of sacrifice either in an advanced state of decay or reduced to relative insignificance, it is because it has already undergone a good deal of wear and tear.

Whether the slippage in the mechanism is due to 'too little' or 'too much' contact between the victim and those whom the victim represents, the results are the same. The elimination of violence is no longer effected; on the contrary, conflicts within the community multiply, and the menace of chain reactions looms ever larger.

If the gap between the victim and the community is allowed to grow too wide, all similarity will be destroyed. The victim will no longer be capable of attracting the violent impulses to itself; the sacrifice will cease to serve as a 'good conductor', in the sense that metal is a good conductor of electricity. On the other hand, if there is *too much* continuity the violence will overflow its channels. 'Impure' violence will mingle with the 'sacred' violence of the rites, turning the latter into a scandalous accomplice in the process of pollution, even a kind of catalyst in the propagation of further impurity.

These are postulates that seem to take form a priori from our earlier conclusions. They can also be discerned in literature – in the adaptations of certain myths in classical Greek tragedy, in particular in Euripides' version of the legend of Heracles.

Euripides' *Heracles*[6] contains no tragic conflict, no debate between declared adversaries. The real subject of the play is the failure of a sacrifice, the act of sacrificial violence that suddenly

---

[6]***Heracles***: tragedy by Euripides (*c.*416 BCE) in which Heracles rescues his wife and children by killing Lycus, the King of Thebes, but after being stricken with madness ends up killing his wife and children himself.

goes wrong. Heracles, returning home after the completion of his labors, finds his wife and children in the power of a usurper named Lycus, who is preparing to offer them as sacrificial victims. Heracles kills Lycus. After this most recent act of violence, committed in the heart of the city, the hero's need to purify himself is greater than ever, and he sets about preparing a sacrifice of his own. His wife and children are with him when Heracles, suddenly seized by madness, mistakes them for his enemies and *sacrifices* them.

Heracles' misidentification of his family is attributed to Lyssa, goddess of madness, who is operating as an emissary of two other goddesses, Iris and Hera, who bear Heracles ill will. The preparations for the sacrifice provide an imposing setting for the homicidal outburst; it is unlikely that their dramatic significance passed unnoticed by the author. In fact, it is Euripides himself who directs our attention to the ritualistic origins of the onslaught. After the massacre, Heracles' father, Amphitryon, asks his son: 'My child, what happened to you? How could this horror have taken place? Was it perhaps the spilt blood that turned your head?'[7] Heracles, who is just returning to consciousness and remembers nothing, inquires in turn: 'Where did the madness overtake me? Where did it strike me down?' Amphitryon replies: 'Near the altar, where you were purifying your hands over the sacred flames.'[8]

The sacrifice contemplated by the hero succeeded only too well in polarizing the forces of violence. Indeed, it produced a superabundance of violence of a particularly virulent kind. As Amphitryon suggested, the blood shed in the course of the terrible labors and in the city itself finally turned the hero's head. Instead of drawing off the violence and allowing it to ebb away, the rites brought a veritable flood of violence down on the victim. The sacrificial rites were no longer able to accomplish their task; they swelled the surging tide of impure violence instead of channeling it. The mechanism of substitutions had gone astray, and those whom the sacrifice was designed to protect became its victims.

The difference between sacrificial and nonsacrificial violence is anything but exact; it is even arbitrary. At times the difference threatens to disappear entirely. There is no such thing as truly 'pure' violence. Nevertheless, sacrificial violence can, in the proper circumstances, serve as an agent of purification. That is why those who perform the rites are obliged to purify themselves at the conclusion of the sacrifice. The procedure followed is reminiscent of atomic power plants; when the expert has finished decontaminating the installation, he must himself be decontaminated. And accidents can always happen.

The catastrophic inversion of the sacrificial act would appear to be an essential element in the Heracles myth. The motif reappears, thinly concealed behind secondary themes, in another episode of his story, in Sophocles' *The Women of Trachis*.[9]

Heracles had mortally wounded the centaur Nessus, who had assaulted Heracles' wife, Deianira. Before dying, the centaur gave the young woman a shirt smeared with his sperm – or, in Sophocles' version, smeared with his blood mixed with the blood of a Hydra. (Once again, as in the *Ion*,[10] we encounter the theme of the two kinds of blood mingling to form one.)

---

[7]'**My child ... head**': Euripides, *Heracles*, ll. 1133–7.

[8]'**Near...flames**': Euripides, *Heracles*, ll. 1143–5.

[9]*The Women of Trachis:* tragedy by Sophocles (*c.*450–420 BCE), in which Heracles dies after wearing a robe dyed with the blood of the Centaur Nessus.

[10]*Ion:* tragedy by Euripides (*c.*414 BCE) in which Creusa, daughter of Erechtheus, nearly poisons her long-lost son Ion with the Gorgon's blood before realizing who he is.

The subject of the tragedy, as in Euripides' *Heracles*, is the return of the hero. In this instance Heracles is bringing with him a pretty young captive, of whom Deianira is jealous. Deianira sends a servant to her husband with a welcoming gift, the shirt of Nessus. With his dying breath the centaur had told her that the shirt would assure the wearer's eternal fidelity to her; but he cautioned her to keep it well out of the way of any flame or source of heat.

Heracles puts on the shirt, and soon afterward lights a fire for the rites of sacrificial purification. The flames activate the poison in the shirt; it is the rite itself that unlooses the evil. Heracles, contorted with pain, presently ends his life on the pyre he has begged his son to prepare. Before dying, Heracles kills the servant who delivered the shirt to him; this death, along with his own and the subsequent suicide of his wife, contributes to the cycle of violence heralded by Heracles' return and the failure of the sacrifice. Once again, violence has struck the beings who sought the protection of sacrificial rites.

A number of sacrifice motifs intermingle in these two plays. A special sort of impurity clings to the warrior returning to his homeland, still tainted with the slaughter of war. In the case of Heracles, his sanguinary[11] labors render him particularly impure.

The returning warrior risks carrying the seed of violence into the very heart of his city. The myth of Horatius,[12] as explicated by Georges Dumézil,[13] illustrates this theme: Horatius kills his sister before any ritual purification has been performed. In the case of Heracles the impurity triumphs over the rite itself.

If we examine the mechanism of violence in these two tragedies, we notice that when the sacrifice goes wrong it sets off a chain reaction of the sort defined in the first chapter. The murder of Lycus is presented in the Euripides play as a last 'labor' of the hero, a still-rational prelude to the insane outburst that follows. Seen from the perspective of the ritualist, it might well constitute a first link of impure violence.

With this incident, as we have noted, violence invades the heart of the city. This initial murder corresponds to the death of the old servant in *The Women of Trachis*.

Supernatural intervention plays no part in these episodes, except perhaps to cast a thin veil over the true subject: the sacrificial celebration that has gone wrong. The goddess Lyssa, Nessus' shirt – these add nothing to the meaning of the two stories; rather, they act as a veil, and as soon as the veil is drawn aside we encounter the same theme of 'good' violence turning into 'bad.' The mythological accompaniments of the stories can be seen as redundant. Lyssa, the goddess of madness, sounds more like a refugee from an allegorical tale than a real goddess, and Nessus' shirt joins company with all the acts of violence that Heracles carries on his back.

[...]

All the bloody events that serve as background to the plays – the plagues and pestilences, civil and foreign wars – undoubtedly reflect the contemporary scene, but the images are unclear, as if viewed through a glass darkly. Each time, for example, a play of Euripides deals with the collapse of a royal house (as in *Heracles*, *Iphigenia in Aulis*, or *The Bacchae*), we are convinced that the poet is suggesting that the scene before our eyes is only the tip of the iceberg, that the real issue is the

---

[11]**Sanguinary:** bloody.

[12]**Horatius:** a mythic Roman hero who defended Rome against the Curiatii brothers; he killed his sister when she grieved for one of the brothers, to whom she had been engaged.

[13]**Georges Dumézil:** French scholar of mythography (1898–1986), who discussed Horatius in *Les Mythes Romains: Horace et Les Curiaces* (1942).

fate of the entire community. At the moment when Heracles is slaughtering his family offstage, the chorus cries out: 'Look, look! The tempest is shaking the house; the roof is falling in.'[14]

If the tragic crisis is indeed to be described in terms of the sacrificial crisis, its relationship to sacrifice should be apparent in all aspects of tragedy – either conveyed directly through explicit reference or perceived indirectly, in broad outline, underlying the texture of the drama.

If the art of tragedy is to be defined in a single phrase, we might do worse than call attention to one of its most characteristic traits: the opposition of symmetrical elements. There is no aspect of the plot, form, or language of a tragedy in which this symmetrical pattern does not recur. The third actor, for instance, hardly constitutes the innovation that critics have claimed. Third actor or no third actor, the core of the drama remains the tragic dialogue; that is, the fateful confrontation during which the two protagonists exchange insults and accusations with increasing earnestness and rapidity. The Greek public brought to these verbal contests the same educated sense of appreciation that French audiences many centuries later evinced for their own classic drama – for Théramène's famous speech from the last act of *Phèdre*,[15] for example, or for almost any passage from *Le Cid*.[16]

The symmetry of the tragic dialogue is perfectly mirrored by the stichomythia, in which the two protagonists address one another in alternating lines. In tragic dialogue hot words are substituted for cold steel. But whether the violence is physical or verbal, the suspense remains the same. The adversaries match blow for blow, and they seem so evenly matched that it is impossible to predict the outcome of the battle. The structural similarity between the two forms of violence is illustrated by the description of the duel between the brothers Eteocles and Polyneices in Euripides' *Phoenician Women*.[17] There is nothing in this account that does not apply equally to both brothers: their parries, thrusts, and feints, their gestures and postures, are identical: 'If either saw the other's eye peer over the rim of his shield, He raised his spear.'[18]

Polyneices loses his spear in the fight, and so does Eteocles. Both are wounded. Each blow upsets the equilibrium, threatening to decide the outcome then and there. It is immediately followed by a new blow that not only redresses the balance but creates a symmetrical disequilibrium that is itself, naturally enough, of short duration. The tragic suspense follows the rhythm of these rapid exchanges, each one of which promises to bring matters to a head – but never quite does so. 'They struggle now on even terms, each having spent his spear. Swords are unsheathed, and the two brothers are locked in close combat. Shield clashes with shield, and a great clamor engulfs them both.'[19] Even death fails to tip the balance. 'They hit the dust and lay together side by side; and their heritage was still unclaimed.'[20]

The death of the brothers resolves nothing; it simply perpetuates the symmetry of the battle. Each had been his army's champion, and the two armies now resume the struggle, re-establish the symmetry. Oddly enough, however, the conflict is now transferred to a purely verbal

---

[14]'**Look ... in**': Euripides, *Heracles*, 904–5.

[15]***Phèdre**: 1677 tragedy by French playwright Jean Racine (1639–99), based on Euripides' *Hippolytus*.

[16]*Le Cid*: 1636 tragicomedy by French playwright Pierre Corneille (1606–84), based on the legend of a medieval Spanish warrior.

[17]*The Phoenician Women*: tragedy by Euripides (*c*.410 BCE) dramatizing the Theban civil war in which Polyneices and Eteocles – the sons of Oedipus and Jocasta – kill each other, spurring Jocasta to take her life.

[18]'**If...spear**': Euripides, *Phoenician Women*, ll. 1384–5.

[19]'**They struggle...both**': Euripides, *Phoenician Women*, ll. 1402–6.

[20]'**They hit...unclaimed**': Euripides, *Phoenician Women*, ll. 1423–4.

plane, transforming itself into a true tragic dialogue. Tragedy now assumes its proper function as a verbal extension of physical combat, an interminable debate set off by the chronically indecisive character of an act of violence committed previously:

> The soldiers then leapt to their feet, and the argument began. We claimed that our king had won; they claimed the victory for Polyneices. The captains quarreled, too. Some said that Polyneices had struck the first blow; others replied that death had snatched the palm of victory from both claimants.[21]

The indecisiveness of the first combat spreads quite naturally to the second, which then sows it abroad. The tragic dialogue is a debate without resolution. Each side resolutely continues to deploy the same arguments, emphases, goals; *Gleichgewicht* is Hölderlin's word for it.[22] Tragedy is the balancing of the scale, not of justice but of violence. No sooner is something added to one side of the scale than its equivalent is contributed to the other. The same insults and accusations fly from one combatant to the other, as a ball flies from one player to another in tennis. The conflict stretches on interminably because between the two adversaries there is no difference whatsoever.

The equilibrium in the struggle has often been attributed to a so-called tragic impartiality; Hölderlin's word is *Impartialität*.[23] I do not find this interpretation quite satisfactory. Impartiality implies a deliberate refusal to take sides, a firm commitment to treat both contestants equally. The impartial party is not eager to resolve the issue, does not want to know if there is a resolution; nor does he maintain that resolution is impossible. His impartiality-at-any-price is not unfrequently simply an unsubstantiated assertion of superiority. One of the adversaries is right, the other wrong, and the onlooker is obliged to take sides; either that, or the rights and wrongs are so evenly distributed between the two factions that taking sides is impossible. The self-proclaimed advocate of impartiality does not want to commit himself to either course of action. If pushed toward one camp, he seeks refuge in the other. Men always find it distasteful to admit that the 'reasons' on both sides of a dispute are equally valid – which is to say that *violence operates without reason*.

Tragedy begins at that point where the illusion of impartiality, as well as the illusions of the adversaries, collapses. For example, in *Oedipus the King*,[24] Oedipus, Creon, and Tiresias are each in turn drawn into a conflict that each had thought to resolve in the role of impartial mediator.

It is not clear to what extent the tragedians themselves managed to remain impartial. For example, Euripides in *The Phoenician Women* barely conceals his preference for Eteocles – or perhaps we should say his preference for the Athenian public's approval. In any case, his partiality is superficial. The preferences registered for one side or another never prevent the authors from constantly underlining the symmetrical relationship between the adversaries.

---

[21]**'The soldiers...claimants'**: Euripides, *Phoenician Women*, 1460–4.

[22]**Hölderlin**: Friedrich Hölderlin (1770–1843) was a German poet; *Gleichgewicht*: balance.

[23]*Impartialität*: impartiality, neutrality.

[24]**Oedipus the King**: tragedy by Sophocles (*c.*429 BCE) in which Oedipus, King of Thebes, learns that he is guilty of having killed his father and married his mother.

At the very moment when they appear to be abandoning impartiality, the tragedians do their utmost to deprive the audience of any means of taking sides. Aeschylus, Sophocles, and Euripides all utilize the same procedures and almost identical phraseology to convey symmetry, identity, reciprocity. We encounter here an aspect of tragic art that has been largely overlooked by contemporary criticism. Nowadays critics tend to assess a work of art on the basis of its *originality*. To the extent that an author cannot claim exclusive rights to his themes, his style, and his esthetic effects, his work is deemed deficient. In the domain of esthetics, singularity reigns supreme.

Such criteria cannot apply, of course, to Greek tragedy, whose authors were not committed to the doctrine of originality at any price. Nevertheless, our frustrated individualism still exerts a deleterious effect on modern interpretations of Greek tragedy.

It is readily apparent that Aeschylus, Sophocles, and Euripides shared certain literary traits and that the characters in their plays have certain characteristics in common. Yet there is no reason to label these resemblances mere stereotypes. It is my belief that these 'stereotypes' contain the very essence of Greek tragedy. And if the tragic element in these plays still eludes us, it is because we have obstinately averted our attention from these similarities.

The tragedians portray men and women caught up in a form of violence too impersonal in its workings, too brutal in its results, to allow any sort of value judgement, any sort of distinction, subtle or simplistic, to be drawn between 'good' and 'wicked' characters. That is why most modern interpretations go astray; we have still not extricated ourselves entirely from the 'Manichean'[25] frame of reference that gained sway in the Romantic era and still exerts its influence today.

In Greek tragedy violence invariably effaces the differences between antagonists. The sheer impossibility of asserting their differences fuels the rage of Eteocles and Polyneices. In Euripides' *Heracles* the hero kills Lycus to keep him from sacrificing his family, and next he does what he wanted to prevent his enemy from doing, thereby falling victim to the ironic humor of a Destiny that seems to work hand in glove with violence. In the end it is Heracles who carries out the crime meditated by his counterpart. The more a tragic conflict is prolonged, the more likely it is to culminate in a violent mimesis; the resemblance between the combatants grows ever stronger until each presents a mirror image of the other. There is a scientific corollary: modern research suggests that individuals of quite different make-up and back-ground respond to violence in essentially the same way.

It is the act of reprisal, the repetition of imitative acts of violence, that characterizes tragic plotting. The destruction of differences is particularly spectacular when the hierarchichal distance between the characters, the amount of respect due from one to the other, is great – between father and son, for instance. This scandalous effacement of distinctions is apparent in Euripides' *Alcestis*.[26] Father and son are engaged in a tragic dialogue; each accuses the other of fleeing from death and leaving the heroine to die. The symmetry is perfect, emphasized by the symmetrical interventions of the members of the Chorus, who first castigate the son ('Young

---

[25]**Manichean:** dualist, believing that the world is divided into good and evil, following the Persian philosopher Mani or Manichaeus (*c*.216–76 CE).
[26]*Alcestis*: tragedy by Euripides (438 BCE), in which Alcestis volunteers to die in place of her husband Admetus, whose grief prompts Heracles to retrieve her from the underworld and bring her back to life. After his wife dies, Admetus blames his father for not volunteering to replace him instead of his wife; his father in turn argues that Admetus should have accepted his death rather than letting his wife replace him.

man, remember to whom you are speaking; do not insult your father'[27]), and then rebuke the father ('Enough has been said on this subject; cease, we pray you, to abuse your own son.'[28]).

In *Oedipus the King* Sophocles frequently puts in Oedipus's mouth words that emphasize his resemblance to his father: resemblance in desires, suspicions, and course of action. If the hero throws himself impetuously into the investigation that causes his downfall, it is because he is reacting just as Laius did in seeking out the potential assassin who, according to the oracles, would replace him on the throne of Thebes and in the bed of the queen.

Oedipus finally kills Laius, but it is Laius who, at the crossroads, first raised his hand against his son. The patricide thus takes part in a reciprocal exchange of murderous gestures. It is an act of reprisal in a universe based on reprisals.

At the core of the Oedipus myth, as Sophocles presents it, is the proposition that all masculine relationships are based on reciprocal acts of violence. Laius, taking his cue from the oracle, violently rejects Oedipus out of fear that his son will seize his throne and invade his conjugal bed. Oedipus, taking his cue from the oracle, does away with Laius, violently rebuffs the sphinx, then takes their places – as king and 'scourge of the city', respectively. Again, Oedipus, taking his cue from the oracle, plots the death of that unknown figure who may be seeking to usurp his own position. Oedipus, Creon, and Tiresias, each taking his cue from the oracle, seek one another's downfall.

All these acts of violence gradually wear away the differences that exist not only in the same family but throughout the community. The tragic combat between Oedipus and Tiresias pits the community's chief spiritual leaders against one another. The enraged Oedipus seeks to strip the aura of 'mystery' from his rival, to prove that he is a false prophet, nothing more:

> Come tell us: have you truly shown yourself a prophet? When the terrible sphinx held sway over our countrymen, did you ever whisper the words that would have delivered them? That riddle was not to be answered by anyone; the gift of prophecy was called for. Yet that gift was clearly not yours to give; nor was it ever granted to you, either by the birds or by the gods.[29]

Confronted by the king's frustration and rage at being unable to uncover the truth, Tiresias launches his own challenge. The terms are much the same: 'If you are so clever at solving enigmas, why are you powerless to solve this one?'[30] Both parties in this tragic dialogue have recourse to the same tactics, use the same weapons, and strive for the same goal: destruction of the adversary. Tiresias poses as the champion of tradition, taking up the cudgels on behalf of the oracles flouted by Oedipus. However, in so doing he shows himself insolent to royal authority. Although the targets are individuals, it is the institutions that receive the blows. Legitimate authority trembles on its pedestal, and the combatants finally assist in the downfall of the very order they strove to maintain. The impiety referred to by the chorus – the neglect of the oracles, the general decadence that pervades the religion of the community – are surely

---

[27]'**Young man...father**': Euripides, *Alcestis*, ll. 673–74.
[28]'**Enough...son**': Euripides, *Alcestis*, ll. 706–7.
[29]'**Come...gods**': Sophocles, *Oedipus Rex*, ll. 390–6.
[30]'**If...one**': Sophocles, *Oedipus Rex*, l. 440.

part of the same phenomenon that works away at the undermining of family relationships, as well as of religious and social hierarchies.

The *sacrificial crisis*, that is, the disappearance of the sacrificial rites, coincides with the disappearance of the difference between impure violence and purifying violence. When this difference has been effaced, purification is no longer possible and impure, contagious, reciprocal violence spreads throughout the community.

The sacrificial distinction, the distinction between the pure and the impure, cannot be obliterated without obliterating all other differences as well. One and the same process of violent reciprocity engulfs the whole. The sacrificial crisis can be defined, therefore, as a crisis of distinctions – that is, a crisis affecting the cultural order. This cultural order is nothing more than a regulated system of distinctions in which the differences among individuals are used to establish their 'identity' and their mutual relationships.

In the first chapter the danger threatening the community with the decay of sacrificial practices was portrayed in terms of physical violence, of cyclical vengeance set off by a chain reaction. We now discover more insidious forms of the same evil. When the religious framework of a society starts to totter, it is not exclusively or immediately the physical security of the society that is threatened; rather, the whole cultural foundation of the society is put in jeopardy. The institutions lose their vitality; the protective façade of the society gives way; social values are rapidly eroded, and the whole cultural structure seems on the verge of collapse.

The hidden violence of the sacrificial crisis eventually succeeds in destroying distinctions, and this destruction in turn fuels the renewed violence. In short, it seems that anything that adversely affects the institution of sacrifice will ultimately pose a threat to the very basis of the community, to the principles on which its social harmony and equilibrium depend.

A single principle is at work in primitive religion and classical tragedy alike, a principle implicit but fundamental. Order, peace, and fecundity depend on cultural distinctions; it is not these distinctions but the loss of them that gives birth to fierce rivalries and sets members of the same family or social group at one another's throats.

Modern society aspires to equality among men and tends instinctively to regard all differences, even those unrelated to the economic or social status of men, as obstacles in the path of human happiness. This modern ideal exerts an obvious influence on ethnological approaches, although more often on the level of technical procedure than that of explicit principle. The permutations of this ideal are complex, rich in potential contradictions, and difficult to characterize briefly.

Further reading

Chris Fleming, 'Sacrificial Crisis and Surrogate Victimage', in *René Girard: Violence and Mimesis* (Cambridge: Polity Press, 2004), 41–69.

Richard Golsan, 'Sacrificial Violence and Scapegoat', in *René Girard and Myth: An Introduction* (London: Routledge, 2014), 29–60.

Wolfgang Palaver, 'Mimetic theories of religion and violence', in *The Oxford Handbook of Religion and Violence*, ed. Mark Juergensmeyer, Margo Kitts and Michael Jerryson (Oxford: Oxford University Press, 2013), 533–53.

6.2 AUGUSTO BOAL, *THE THEATRE OF THE OPPRESSED* (1974)

Brazilian theatre director, writer, and activist Augusto Boal (1931–2009) is known for his commitment to theatre as means of political liberation. In his influential *Theatre of the Oppressed* (1974) he criticizes Aristotle's model of the tragic theatre as coercive and repressive. Like Brecht, Boal argues that Aristotle's idea of catharsis relies on a close identification with the protagonist that encourages spectators to engage vicariously and passively, weakening their sense of agency. Boal suggests that Aristotelian catharsis purges the spectator not of pity and fear, but of antisocial reactions such as outrage and defiance. Through redirecting and expelling these traits, tragedy suppresses responses that could otherwise lead to action and revolt. Rather than challenging this model by promoting alienation from the theatre's action and emotion, like Brecht, Boal sought in his own theatrical practice to transform audiences into 'spect-actors', active participants in creating performance.

In What Sense Can Theatre Function as an Instrument for Purification and Intimidation?

We have seen that the population of a city is not *uniformly* content. If there is inequality, no one wants it to be to his disadvantage. It is necessary to make sure that all remain, if not uniformly satisfied, at least uniformly passive with respect to those criteria of inequality. How to achieve this? Through the many forms of repression: politics, bureaucracy, habits, customs – and Greek tragedy.

This statement may seem somewhat daring, but it is nothing more than the truth. Of course, the system presented by Aristotle in his *Poetics*, the functional system of tragedy (and all the forms of theater which to this day follow its general mechanism) is not *only* a system of repression. Other, more 'esthetic', factors clearly enter into it. And there are many other aspects that ought likewise to be taken into account. But it is important to consider especially this fundamental aspect: its repressive function.

And why is the repressive function the fundamental aspect of the Greek tragedy and of the Aristotelian system of tragedy? Simply because, according to Aristotle, the principle aim of tragedy is to provoke catharsis.

The Ultimate Aim of Tragedy

The fragmentary nature of the *Poetics* has obscured the solid connection existing among its parts, as well as the hierarchy of the parts within the context of the whole. Only this fact explains why marginal observations, of little or no importance, have been taken to be central concepts of Aristotelian thought. For example, when dealing with Shakespeare or the medieval theater, it is very common to decide that such and such a play is not Aristotelian because it does not obey the 'law of the three unities'.[31] Hegel's objection to this view is contained in his *The Philosophy of Fine Art*:

The inalterability of one exclusive *locale* of the action proposed belongs to the type of those rigid rules which the French in particular have deduced from classic tragedy and

---

[31]**Unities:** on the dramatic unities, often attributed to Aristotle but in fact developed and codified by Lodovico Castelvetro (1505–71), see extract 2.2.

the critique of Aristotle thereupon. As a matter of fact, Aristotle merely says that the duration of the tragic action should not exceed at the most the length of a day. He does not mention the unity of place at all....[32]

The disproportionate importance that is given to this 'law' is incomprehensible, since it has no more validity than would the statement that only the works that contain a prologue, five episodes and choral chants, and an exode are Aristotelian. The essence of Aristotelian thought cannot reside in structural aspects such as these. To emphasize these minor aspects is, in effect, to compare the Greek philosopher to the modern and abundant professors of dramaturgy, especially the Americans, who are no more than cooks of theatrical menus. They study the typical reactions of certain chosen audiences and from there extract conclusions and rules regarding how the perfect work should be written (equating perfection to box office success).

Aristotle, on the contrary, wrote a completely organic poetics, which is the reflection, in the field of tragedy and poetry, of all his philosophical contribution; it is the practical and concrete application of that philosophy specifically to poetry and tragedy.

For this reason, every time we find imprecise or fragmentary statements, we should immediately consult other texts written by the author. S.H. Butcher[33] does precisely this, with crystal clear results, in his book *Aristotle's Theory of Poetry and Fine Art*.[34] He tries to understand the *Poetics* from the perspective of the *Metaphysics, Politics, Rhetoric*, and above all, the three *Ethics*.[35] To him we owe mainly the clarification of the concept of catharsis.

Nature tends toward certain ends; when it fails to achieve those objectives, art and science intervene. Man, as part of nature, also has certain ends in view: health, gregarious life in the State, happiness, virtue, justice, etc. When he fails in the achievement of those objectives, the art of tragedy intervenes. This correction of man's actions is what Aristotle calls *catharsis*.

Tragedy, in all its qualitative and quantitative aspects, exists as a function of the effect it seeks, catharsis. All the unities of tragedy are structured around this concept. It is the center, the essence, the purpose of the tragic system. Unfortunately, it is also the most controversial concept. Catharsis is correction: what does it correct? Catharsis is purification: what does it purify?

Butcher helps us with a parade of opinions of such illustrious people as Racine, Milton, and Jacob Bernays.[36]

Racine.

In tragedy, he wrote:

the passions are shown only to reveal all the disorder of which they are the cause; and vice is always painted with colors that make us know and hate the deformity ... this is what the first tragic poets had in mind, more than anything else. Their theater was a

---

[32][**Boal's note:**] G.W.F. Hegel, *The Philosophy of Fine Art*, trans. F.P.B. Osmaston, 4 vols. (London: G. Bell and Sons, Ltd., 1920), 4:257.

[33]**S.H. Butcher:** Anglo-Irish classical scholar (1850–1910).

[34][**Boal's note:**] S.H. Butcher, *Aristotle's Theory of Poetry and Fine Art*, 4th ed. (New York: Dover Publications, Inc., 1951).

[35]*Metaphysics, Politics, Rhetoric, ... Ethics:* additional philosophical writings by Aristotle, which at some points touch on concerns he discusses in the *Poetics*.

[36]**Racine, Milton, and Jacob Bernays:** Jean Racine (1639–99) was a French tragic playwright; John Milton (1608–74) was an English poet, essayist, and pamphleteer; Jacob Bernays (1824–81) was a German classical scholar.

school where the virtues were taught fully as well as in the philosopher's schools. For this reason Aristotle wanted to provide rules for the dramatic poem; … It is to be desired that our works should be as solid and as full of useful instructions as the ones of those poets.[37]

As we see, Racine emphasizes the doctrinal, moral aspect of tragedy; and this is fine, but there is one correction to be made: Aristotle did not advise the tragic poet to portray vicious characters. The tragic hero should suffer a radical change in the course of his life – from happiness to adversity – but this should happen not as a consequence of vice, but rather as a result of some error or weakness (see Chapter 13 of the *Poetics*). Soon we shall examine the nature of this *hamartia*.[38]

It is necessary to understand also that the presentation of the error of weakness was not designed to make the spectator, in his immediate perception of it, feel repugnance or hatred. On the contrary, Aristotle suggested that the mistake or weakness be treated with some understanding. Almost always the state of 'fortune' in which the hero is found at the beginning of the tragedy is due precisely to this fault and not to his virtues. Oedipus is King of Thebes because of a weakness in his character, that is, his pride. And indeed the efficacy of a dramatic process would be greatly diminished if the fault were presented from the beginning as despicable, the error as abominable. It is necessary, on the contrary, to show them as acceptable in order to destroy them later through the theatrical, poetic processes. Bad playwrights in every epoch fail to understand the enormous efficacy of the transformations that take place before the spectators' eyes. Theater is change and not simple presentation of what exists: it is becoming and not being.

Jacob Bernays.

In 1857, Bernays proposed an intriguing theory: the word 'catharsis' would be a medical metaphor, a purgation which denotes the pathological effect on the soul, analogous to the effect of medicine on the body. Basing his argument on the definition of tragedy given by Aristotle ('imitation of human actions that excite pity or fear'), Bernays concludes that simply because these emotions are found in the hearts of all men, the act of exciting offers, afterward, a pleasant relaxation. This hypothesis seems to find confirmation in Aristotle himself, who declares that 'pity is occasioned by undeserved misfortune, and fear by that of one like ourselves…' (Chapter 13). (We will soon examine the meaning of the word 'empathy', which is based on those two emotions.)

The feelings stimulated by the spectacle, adds Bernays, are not removed in a permanent or definitive manner. But they remain calm for a certain time and all the system can rest. The stage thus offers harmless and pleasant discharge for the instincts that demand satisfaction and that can be tolerated much more easily in the fiction of the theater than in real life.[39]

---

[37][**Boal's note:**] 'Les passions n'y sont présentées aux yeux que pour montrer tout le désordre dont elles sont cause; et le vice y est peint partout avec des couleurs qui en font connaître et haïr la difformité … et c'est ce que les premiers poètes tragiques avaient en vue sur toute chose. Leur théâtre était une école où la vertu n'était pas moins bien enseignée que dans les écoles des philosophes. Aussi Aristote a bien voulu donner des règles due pòeme dramatique … Il serait à souhaiter que nos ouvrages fussent aussi solides et aussi pleins d'utiles instructions que ceux de ces poètes'; Cited in Butcher, 243–4, note.

[38]*Hamartia*: a key term in Aristotle's *Poetics*, often translated as 'tragic flaw,' though its Greek meaning is closer to error (literally, missing of the mark). For Aristotle, a protagonist's hamartia causes the reversal of fortune, typically from good fortune to bad.

[39][**Boal's note:**] Butcher, 245.

Bernays, therefore, permits the supposition that perhaps the purgation does not refer only to the emotions of pity and fear, but also to certain 'non-social' or socially forbidden instincts. Butcher himself, trying to understand what is the object of the purgation (that is, of what is one purged?), adds his own belief that it is the pity and terror we bring with us in our real life or, at least, those elements in our life which are disturbing.[40]

Is this clear? Perhaps that of which one is purged is not the emotions of pity or fear, but something contained in those emotions, or mixed with them. We must determine the identity of this foreign body which is eliminated by the cathartic process. In this case, pity and fear would only be part of the mechanism of expulsion and not its object. Here would reside the political significance of tragedy.

In Chapter XIX of the *Poetics* we read: 'The Thought of the personages is shown in everything to be effected by their language – in every effort to prove or disprove, to arouse emotion (pity, fear, anger, and the like), ...' We ask why purgation should not have been dealt with before in relation to 'like' emotions such as hatred, envy, pride, partiality in worship of the gods and in the obedience to laws, etc.? Why choose pity and fear? Why does Aristotle explain the obligatory presence of these emotions only?

Analysing some of the tragic characters, we see that they may be guilty of many ethical errors, but we can hardly say that any of them manifest either an excess or lack of pity or fear. It is never there that their virtue fails. Those emotions indeed play so little part that they cannot even be considered a characteristic common to all tragic characters.

It is not in the tragic characters that pity and fear manifest themselves – but rather in the *spectators*. *Through those emotions the spectators are linked to the heroes.* We must keep this clearly in mind: the spectators are linked to the heroes, *basically*, through the emotions of pity and fear, because, as Aristotle says, something *undeserved* happens to a character that *resembles ourselves*.

Let us clarify this a little more. Hippolytus[41] loves all the gods intensely, and this is good, but he does not love the goddess of love, and this is bad. We feel pity because Hippolytus is destroyed in spite of all his good qualities, and fear because perhaps we are liable to criticism for the same reason of not loving all the gods, as the laws require. Oedipus is a great king, the people love him; his government is perfect, and for this reason we feel pity that such a wonderful person is destroyed for having one fault, pride, which perhaps we also have: hence our fear. Creon defends the right of the State and seeing that he has to bear the death of his wife and son causes pity in us because, together with all the virtues he possesses, he has the fault of seeing only the good of the State and not that of the Family; this one-sidedness could also be a fault of ours, hence the fear.

Once again, let us remember the relationship between the virtues and the fortune of the characters, ending with their downfall: Because of haughtiness and pride Oedipus becomes a great king; because he scorns the goddess of love, Hippolytus loves the other gods more intensely; and by caring excessively for the good of the State, Creon was in the beginning a great chieftain, at the peak of happiness.

---

[40][**Boal's note:**] Butcher, 252–4.

[41]**Hippolytus:** protagonist of Euripides' *Hippolytus* (428 BCE), whose disdain for the goddess Aphrodite leads her to punish him by making his stepmother Phaedra fall in love with him; when she is rejected, Phaedra kills herself, leaving a letter to her husband Theseus in which she accuses Hippolytus of raping her.

We conclude, therefore, that pity and fear are the minimal specific form linking the spectator and the character. But these emotions are in no way the objects of purification (purgation). Rather, they are purified of something else which, at the end of the tragedy, ceases to exist.

Milton.

'Tragedy … said by Aristotle to be of power, by raising pity and fear, or terror, to purge the mind of those and such-like passions; that is to temper or reduce them to just measure with a kind of delight stirred up by reading or seeing those passions well imitated.' Up to here, Milton adds very little to what has already been said; but something better follows: '… in physick medicine, things of melancholick hue and quality are used against melancholy, sour against sour, salt to remove salt humours.'[42],[43] In effect, it is a kind of homeopathy[44] – certain emotions or passions curing analogous, but not identical, emotions or passions.

Besides his study of the views of Milton, Bernays and Racine, Butcher goes to Aristotle's own *Politics* to find the explanation of the word *catharsis* which is not to be found in the *Poetics*.[45] Catharsis is utilized there to denote the effect caused by a certain kind of music on patients possessed by a given type of religious fervor. The treatment 'consisted in applying movement to cure movement, in soothing the internal trouble of the mind by a wild and restless music'. According to Aristotle, the patients subjected to that treatment returned to their normal state, as if they had undergone a medical or purgative treatment – that is, cathartic.[46]

In this example we verify that through 'homeopathic' means (savage music to cure savage interior rhythms), the religious fervor was cured by means of an analogous exterior effect. The cure was brought about through the stimulus. As in the tragedy, the character's fault is initially presented as cause of his happiness – the fault is stimulated.

Butcher adds that, according to Hippocrates,[47] catharsis meant removal of a painful or disturbing element in the organism, purifying in this way what remains, free finally of the eliminated extraneous matter. Butcher concludes that applying the same definition to tragedy, one will arrive at the conclusion that 'pity and fear' in real life contain a morbid or disturbing element. During the process of tragic excitation this element, whatever it may be, is eliminated. 'As the tragic action progresses, when the tumult of the mind, first roused, has afterward subsided, the lower forms of emotion are found to have been transmuted into higher and more refined forms.'[48]

This reasoning is correct and we can accept it totally, except for its insistent attribution of impurities to the emotions of pity and fear. The impurity exists, no doubt, and it is in fact the object of purgation in the character's mind, or as Aristotle would say, in his very *soul*. But Aristotle does not speak of the existence of pure or impure pity, pure or impure fear. The impurity is *necessarily distinct from* the emotions which will remain once the spectacle of the

---

[42][**Boal's note:**] Cited in Butcher, 247–8.

[43]**in…humours:** for more context on this quotation from Milton, see extract 2.7.

[44]**homeopathy:** principle that 'like cures like,' and that illnesses should accordingly be treated with medicines that cause similar symptoms in a healthy person.

[45]**not to be found in the Poetics:** that is, Aristotle uses the term *catharsis* in the *Poetics*, but his explanation of the term appears only in the *Politics*.

[46][**Boal's note:**] Butcher, 248–9.

[47]**Hippocrates:** ancient Greek physician (*c*.460–*c*.370 BCE) known as the father of modern medicine.

[48][**Boal's note:**] Butcher, 254.

tragedy is ended. That extraneous matter – the eliminated impurity – can only be an emotion or passion other than the ones that remain. Pity and fear have never been vices or weaknesses or errors and, therefore, never needed to be eliminated or purged. On the other hand, in the *Ethics*, Aristotle points to numerous vices, errors, and weaknesses which do indeed deserve to be destroyed.

The impurity to be purged must undoubtedly be found among the latter. It must be something that threatens the individual's equilibrium, and consequently that of society. Something that is not virtue, that is not the greatest virtue, justice. And since all that is unjust is forseen in the laws, the impurity which the tragic process is destined to destroy is therefore something *directed against the laws*.

If we go back a little, we will be able to understand better the workings of tragedy. Our last definition was: 'Tragedy imitates the actions of man's rational soul, his passions turned into habits, in his search for happiness, which consists in virtuous behavior … whose supreme good is justice and whose maximum expression is the Constitution.'

We have also seen that nature tends toward certain ends, and when nature fails, art and science intervene to correct it.

We can conclude, therefore, that when man fails in his actions – in his virtuous behavior as he searches for happiness through the maximum virtue, which is obedience to the laws – the art of tragedy intervenes to correct that failure. How? Through purification, catharsis, through purgation of the extraneous, undesirable element which prevents the character from achieving his ends. This extraneous element is contrary to the law; it is a social fault, a political deficiency.

We are finally ready to understand how the tragic scheme works.

Further reading

Frances Babbage, *Augusto Boal* (London: Routledge, 2004).
Jan Cohen-Cruz and Mady Schutzman (eds), *A Boal Companion: Dialogues on Theatre and Cultural Politics* (London: Routledge, 2006).
Graham Ley, 'Towards a Theoretical History for Greek Tragedy', *New Theatre Quarterly* 31, no. 2 (2015): 144–63.

6.3 JOSEPH MEEKER, 'LITERARY TRAGEDY AND ECOLOGICAL CATASTROPHE' (1974)

Joseph Meeker (born 1932) is a literary scholar and early practitioner of ecocriticism, an analytical model focused on exploring the environmental implications of cultural activity. In this chapter from *The Comedy of Survival* (1974), Meeker argues that our current environmental crisis stems from a Western anthropocentric (human-centred) tradition of elevating man-made culture above nature. Meeker identifies the genre of tragedy as one of the crucial engines of this anthropocentric tradition. Like George Steiner (extract 5.7), Meeker identifies tragedy as a specific phenomenon rooted in Greece, and like A.C. Bradley (extract 5.2), he distinguishes tragedy from catastrophe by identifying tragedy as caused by deliberate human agency. A long-running tendency to romanticize the greatness of the tragic hero, Meeker argues, has reinforced the idea that destructive human actions not only represent heroic freedom, but give meaning to the world around us. If we are to redeem our relationship with the world we inhabit, he suggests, we must abandon the tragic mode and instead embrace the comic.

Literary Tragedy and Ecological Catastrophe

Artists and philosophers are generally assumed to be exempt from ecological guilt. While engineers exploit nature, the poets presumably praise its beauties and the philosophers interpret its moral lessons. Whatever errors may have been committed by means of human technology, the human spiritual tradition is regarded as one that all can take pride in. Plato and Jesus were not environmental exploiters, nor were Sophocles and Shakespeare. On the contrary, the message repeated over and over again by philosophy and literature seems to be that man does not live by bread and bulldozers alone, but must give thought to goodness, truth, and beauty, all of which are ecologically safe.

If it were true that the engineers are environmental villains while humanists are lovers and defenders of nature, Western culture would be even more fragmented than it is. Actually, the engineering mentality has always worked closely with that of the humanists: engineers enthusiastically perform only what the philosophers and artists have determined to be valuable and desirable. The humanities have given consistent intellectual support to the environmental exploitation which is the most distinctive product of Western civilization, and they began their work centuries before the engineers became clever enough to think up ways to implement their ideas.

Tragic literature is an appropriate source for information about the humanistic endorsement of ecological error, for tragedy is unusually inclusive of the values of civilization. No other literary form incorporates metaphysical, moral, social, and emotional attitudes in a matrix as tightly unified as tragedy's. None has more clearly expressed human ideals or explored their implications. Tragic literature is a mirror with impeccably sharp resolution and high selectivity. Its image of mankind is a genuine reflection of man's deepest and most significant qualities, but not of all of them. Like other mirrors, tragedy discriminates among available sources of imagery, selectively emphasizing those qualities it was created to display. Tragic writers, like engineers, have consistently chosen to affirm those values which regard the world as mankind's exclusive property.

Tragedy is not synonymous with catastrophe. Newspaper headlines notwithstanding, it is not a tragedy when train wrecks, floods, or earthquakes kill thousands or when an innocent child is run down by an automobile. Such accidents cause pain and death to many who do not deserve to suffer, but they are not tragic. Genuine tragic suffering is a consequence of deliberate choice. Tragic figures bring on their own suffering, for they have taken a course of action which must inevitably lead to their doom, even though they may not have been aware at an early stage of the consequences of their choice. They become tragic because they accept responsibility for their actions and face their pain with the full knowledge that they have brought it on themselves. Their courage is admired even while they are pitied for their suffering. Tragedy, unlike catastrophe, is comforting and flattering to man. It presents the world as an ordered place where some kind of justice or morality rules. The universe is shown to care enough about man to punish him when he goes astray, rather like a stern but compassionate judge. And man appears as a worthy object of love, for he has the capacity to grow and to learn, even to the point of transcending many of his own weaknesses and limitations. Tragic man is ennobled by his struggles, and mankind is ennobled through him.

Like the engineering mentality, the tragic view of life is a unique feature of Western civilization with no true counterpart in primitive or Oriental cultures. It was developed by the Greeks and later modified within the context of the Judeo-Christian tradition. Individual elements of the tragic view of life are present in many cultures, but the peculiar conglomeration of ideas and beliefs that constitutes literary tragedy is a distinctive feature of the West. Further, literary tragedy and environmental exploitation in Western culture share many of the same philosophical presuppositions. Neither tragedy nor ecological crisis could have developed as they have without the interweaving of a few basic ideas which have attained in the Western tradition an importance far greater than they carry in other cultures.

Three such ideas will illustrate the point: the assumption that nature exists for the benefit of mankind, the belief that human morality transcends natural limitations, and humanism's insistence upon the supreme importance of the individual personality. All are characteristic beliefs which appear implicitly and explicitly in tragic literature. Tragedy has gradually lost its power as these beliefs have been increasingly doubted or rejected.

Mankind's very own environment

Hebraic and Greek cultures have asserted from their beginnings that nature exists for the benefit of mankind. In the Genesis account of creation, plants and animals are created to be useful to Adam, and the Garden of Eden is supplied as a fit environment to meet human needs. Adam receives 'dominion over the fish of the sea, and over the fowl of the air, and over the cattle, and over all the earth, and over every creeping thing that creepeth upon the earth.'[49] Whether 'dominion' is to be interpreted to mean responsible stewardship or wanton exploitation is an old debate among theologians (lately revived by environmentalists), but at least exploitation is not clearly ruled out. Adam and his progeny have felt themselves licensed

---

[49]'dominion...earth': Genesis 1:26.

to use their dominion to their own advantage, for it is obvious that people are very important and creeping things aren't.

The Greeks saw nature more as a challenge to human ingenuity than as a god-given source of sustenance, but the superior status of man over nature was never doubted. The choral ode from Sophocles' *Antigone* elaborates the theme of human supremacy, emphasizing man's technological superiority over nature and the miracle of human mentality:

> Many the wonders but nothing walks stranger than man.
> This thing crosses the sea in winter's storm,
> making his path through the roaring waves.
> And she, the greatest of gods, the earth –
> ageless she is, and unwearied – he wears her away
> as the ploughs go up and down from year to year
> and his mules turn up the soil.
>
> Gay nations of birds he snares and leads,
> wild beast tribes and the salty brood of the sea,
> with the twisted mesh of his nets, this clever man.
> He controls with craft the beasts of the open air,
> walkers on hills. The horse with his shaggy mane
> he holds and harnesses, yoked about the neck
> and the strong bull of the mountain.
>
> Language, and thought like the wind
> and the feelings that make the town,
> he has taught himself, and shelter against the cold,
> refuge from rain. He can always help himself.
> He faces no future helpless. There's only death
> that he cannot find escape from. He has contrived
> refuge from illnesses once beyond all cure.
>
> Clever beyond all dreams
> the inventive craft that he has
> which may drive him one time or another to well or ill.
> When he honors the laws of the land and the gods' sworn right
> high indeed is his city; but stateless the man
> who dares to dwell with dishonor.[50]

Though the earth is 'the greatest of gods' rather than a garden created for man's use, yet man is greater still by virtue of his inventiveness and power. It is no accident that a rhapsody extolling man's conquests over nature appears at a crucial point in Greek tragic drama, for man's spiritual

---

[50][**Meeker's note**]: Sophocles, *Antigone*, in David Grene and Richmond Lattimore, *The Complete Greek Tragedies* (Chicago: University of Chicago Press, 1959), 2:170–1.

elevation above his natural environment is an essential tragic assertion. Mankind is here being praised at the expense of nature, and only man is of interest to the poet. Though the land is worn away by man's ploughs and the nations of birds presumably lose their gaiety once they are snared, there is no shame but only praise for the clever man who can inflict this damage for his own benefit. Human dignity is assumed to be independent of and superior to nature, though the conquest of nature is a necessary precondition for its realization. Sophocles has here made explicit man's assumed superiority over nature which is an essential feature of the tragic view of life. It is not that the struggle to control nature is itself tragic, for man is said to master his biological problems with relative ease. His real difficulties are social and metaphysical: how to live with the law and what to do about death, and to meet both problems with something called honor.

Honor and dignity, from either the Greek or the Hebrew perspective, depend upon spiritual states which transcend nature. In both cultures ethical laws which derive from metaphysical principles define the proper activities of man. For the Hebrews, obedience to divine law and devotion to God are supernatural allegiances which determine human excellence. For the Greeks, social order and intellectual integrity are the highest values. Both assume the elevation of man above the processes of nature.

Morality is unnatural

Corollary to the belief in human supremacy is the assumption of a metaphysical moral order which also transcends nature. Greek and Hebrew sources are again unanimous in this belief, though they vary in its application. Fate, destiny, the will of God, justice, salvation, honor, are just a few of the terms used to identify the nature of universal order. In modern attempts at tragedy order is more likely to be described in social terms. All these concepts share the supposition that the welfare of humanity depends upon man's ability to live up to a preexisting standard of virtuous behavior, and that this standard is essentially supranatural, the product of spiritual, intellectual, or social powers not governed by the processes of nature. Among the Greeks, violation of the moral order leads to tragedy; the Hebrews and Christians regarded such violations as sins leading to damnation.

Only humans can experience tragedy or damnation since the moral order specifically governs human affairs and does not apply to the rest of creation. Dogs may mate with their mothers without encountering the moral problems of Oedipus, lions may walk into traps without pondering the destiny that moved them to do so, and the many nearly extinct species of plants and animals are not questioners of divine justice as Job was when he saw disaster on every hand. We may feel pity for the sufferings of animals if we recognize that their pain resembles ours, but we cannot experience tragic emotions through them (nor, presumably, can they).

Tragedy is more concerned with moral pollution, an exclusively human phenomenon, than with the biologically universal experiences of disaster and pain. Only humans can sin by departing from the moral order, and humans alone can purify themselves by reestablishing their harmony with that order. 'Thy people which thou broughtest out of the land of Egypt have corrupted themselves,' says the Lord as he delivers the tables of the law into Moses' hands.[51]

---

[51][**Meeker's note**]: Exodus 32.

Better law is the typical Hebrew prescription for the disease of sin. The Ten Commandments undertake to purify the people by a more perfect regulation of their social behavior and by establishing ritual observances which will remind them of their dependence upon divine power. As prophets interpreted moral law for the Hebrews, so tragic dramatists interpreted it for the Greeks. Tragedy is a ritual purification, in Aristotle's term a catharsis,[52] which immerses us in moral corruption in order to free us from it. We see in the tragic hero the consequences of overstepping the boundaries of moral law; in the process the existence and validity of the law itself are demonstrated.

The Greeks were quite as insistent as the Hebrews that moral law originated above and beyond the sphere of natural existence. Plato's analogy of the cave in *The Republic*[53] is intended to demonstrate that men's perceptions are generally false, and that the source of both morality and truth is far removed from mundane experience. Platonic ideas of goodness, truth, and beauty are independent of experience and unalterable by human actions. All humans can do is to discover their existence and contemplate their meaning, which is what Plato recommends as the proper activity of philosophers. Tragic heroes, too, encounter these absolutes when the actions of their lives run contrary to moral law, and they suffer accordingly. Fate, the gods, and moral law are assumed to exist on a plane far removed from natural existence.

Further reading

Lawrence Buell, 'Introduction', in *The Environmental Imagination* (Cambridge, MA: Harvard University Press, 1995), 1–27.

Simon C. Estok, 'Doing Ecocriticism with Shakespeare', in *Early Modern Ecostudies*, ed. Ivo Kamps, Karen Raber and Thomas Hallock (New York: Palgrave Macmillan, 2008), 77–91.

Cheryll Glotfelty and Harold Fromm (eds), *The Ecocriticism Reader: Landmarks in Literary Ecology* (Athens, GA: University of Georgia Press, 1996), xv–xxxvii.

---

[52]**catharsis:** see Aristotle, extract 1.2.
[53]**analogy of the cave:** in Plato's *Republic* (c.380–360 BCE), Plato's Socrates describes a group of people chained in a cave, who can only see the world through the shadows cast on a wall in front of them. Socrates claims that humans are like these cave-dwellers, restricted to seeing only earthly reflections of pure forms, rather than the forms themselves; only philosophers recognize that there is a higher world and try to see it directly.

6.4 CATHERINE BELSEY, *THE SUBJECT OF TRAGEDY* (1985)

Catherine Belsey (born 1940) is a British literary critic known for her contributions to cultural and feminist literary theory. In *The Subject of Tragedy* (1985), she challenges the concept of tragic character envisioned by A.C. Bradley (extract 5.2) and others. Although 'the self' identified as the subject of tragedy has been understood as universal, essential, and interior, she argues, it is in fact a liberal humanist idea with a specific historical development. It is also an explicitly male self, as women have not been accorded the subjectivity, cohesiveness, or freedom identified with male tragic heroes. Belsey identifies the early modern period as a crucial moment in the development of the liberal humanist self, and early modern tragedies as playing a central role in constructing that self. Canonical plays such as *Hamlet* contribute conspicuously to this process, but examining the fragility of female figures in tragedy highlights the precariousness of the liberal humanist self.

6.1 An Uncertain Place

The subject of liberal humanism claims to be the unified, autonomous author of his or her own choices (moral, electoral and consumer), and the source and origin of speech. Women in Britain for most of the sixteenth and seventeenth centuries were not fully any of these things. Able to speak, to take up a subject-position in discourse, to identify with the 'I' of utterance and the uttering 'I' which always exceeds it, they were none the less enjoined to silence, discouraged from any form of speech which was not an act of submission to the authority of their fathers or husbands. Permitted to break their silence in order to acquiesce in the utterances of others, women were denied any single place from which to speak for themselves. A discursive instability in the texts about women has the effect of withholding from women readers any single position which they can identify as theirs. And at the same time a corresponding instability is evident in the utterances attributed to women: they speak with equal conviction from incompatible subject-positions, displaying a discontinuity of being, an 'inconstancy' which is seen as characteristically feminine. Legally the position of women was inherently discontinuous, their rights fluctuating with their marital status. From the discourses defining power relations in the state women were simply absent; in the definitions of power relations within the family their position was inconsistent and to some degree contradictory. While the autonomous subject of liberalism was in the making, women had no single or stable place from which to define themselves as independent beings. In this sense they both were and were not subjects.

Within the framework of a contest between absolutism and an emerging liberal humanism, and with no determinate subject-position for women, a clearly delineated feminism arguing for the 'equality' or the 'rights' of women is unthinkable. This does not imply that voices were not raised, including women's voices, on behalf of women, but in the general crisis of the period we can hardly expect to find a consistent, united women's liberation movement. What we do find, however, is a series of contests for the place of women in the family and in society, which may in turn be understood as struggles to install women as subjects. In the course of these struggles women found a number of forms of resistance which we should not now be anxious to identify as feminist. Alice Arden's crime[54] was one of these forms; witchcraft and inspired prophesying were others. Murderous or demonic, whores and saints, women were placed at the margins of the social body, while at the same time, in the new model of marriage they were uneasily, silently at the heart of the private realm which was its microcosm and its centre.

[…]

6.3 A Question of Patience

In *The White Devil*,[55] Bracciano says, 'Woman to man/Is either a god or a wolf' (iv.ii. 91–2). 'To man' is important: in a society where the circulation of discourses is controlled by men the definition of women is inevitably patriarchal and reductive. To what extent this definition is shared by women themselves it is always difficult to say. There is no space outside discourse from which women may silently intuit an alternative definition, but it is worth noting that *The Tragedy of Mariam* (1603–4?)[56], the one play of the early seventeenth century which we know to have been written by a woman, sharply problematizes patriarchal absolutism and women's speech. It is always possible to interrogate the dominant definitions, especially when these are themselves full of uncertainties, even though no coherent alternative may emerge from the process.

Bracciano's observation is additionally useful, however, in drawing attention to the way in which plays of this period tend to include contrasted female stereotypes, one saintly, submissive, faithful, forgiving and silent, and the other predatory, dominating, usually lustful, destructive and voluble. The contrast between the devilish Vittoria and the patient Isabella is to some degree reproduced in, for instance, the contrast between Goneril and Regan on the one hand and Cordelia on the other, Lady Macbeth and Lady Macduff, Cleopatra and Octavia, or Beatrice-Joanna and Isabella, at the centre of the main plot and sub-plot respectively in *The Changeling*.[57] As Marilyn French points out, female sexuality, kept under male control, guarantees masculine supremacy over nature and over time, ensuring the stability of the family and the legitimacy of heirs. Women's sexuality unleashed is seen as able to destroy all control, undermining the institutions of society by threatening their continuity (French, 1982).[58] Stereotypes define what the social body endorses and what it wants to exclude.

But the construction of stereotypes cannot ensure permanent stability, not only because the world always exceeds the stereotypical, but also in so far as the stereotypes themselves are inevitably subject to internal contradictions and so are perpetually precarious. This is

---

[54] **Alice Arden:** The main character of the anonymous 1592 domestic tragedy *Arden of Faversham* was based on a historical figure accused of murdering her husband.

[55] *The White Devil:* a 1612 revenge tragedy by John Webster.

[56] *The Tragedy of Mariam:* A closet drama, a play written to be read rather than performed, written *c.*1602 by Elizabeth Cary, Viscountess Falkland (1585–1639), regarded as the first extant original play (as opposed to a translation) written by a woman in early modern England.

[57] *The Changeling:* 1622 tragedy by Thomas Middleton and William Rowley exploring women's roles in marriage. In the main plot, Beatrice-Joanna arranges the murder of her fiancé in order to marry the man she loves, and in the subplot the doctor Alibius tests the loyalty of his new wife Isabella by asking a friend to watch her when he leaves her in charge of his madhouse, where she undergoes many attempted seductions.

[58] **French:** Marilyn French, *Shakespeare's Division of Experience* (London: Cape, 1982).

the case with the type of the faithful, forgiving and silent woman, which probably finds its purest formulation in this period in the figure of patient Griselda. Like Isabella[59] in *The White Devil*, Griselda is a wife who is infinitely patient in the multiple senses of the word: suffering, enduring, passive, submissive and uncomplaining. The story of a woman whose husband takes her children away, seems to have them murdered, sends her home to the humble cottage from which he took her, and then commands her to prepare a banquet for his new bride, can have appealed only, one would suppose, to the most vehemently misogynistic audience. That her 'reward' for enduring all this without protest is her reinstatement and reconciliation with her husband and her children, who have not been murdered after all but have been brought up by someone else, implies that for a woman an eventual place in the bosom of the (aristocratic) family is worth a lifetime of torment.

Further reading

Hugh Grady, 'On the Need for a Differentiated Theory of (Early) Modern Subjects', in *Philosophical Shakespeares*, ed. John J. Joughin (London: Routledge, 2000), 34–50.
Carol Thomas Neely, 'Constructing the Subject: Feminist Practice and the New Renaissance Discourses', *English Literary Renaissance* 18, no. 1 (1988): 5–18.
Alan Sinfield, 'From Bradley to Cultural Materialism', *Shakespeare Studies* 34 (2006): 25–34.

---

[59]**Isabella**: the martyred and eventually murdered wife of Duke Brachiano in Webster's *The White Devil*.

6.5 NICOLE LORAUX, 'THE ROPE AND THE SWORD' (1985)

French classical scholar Nicole Loraux (1943–2003) developed a feminist anthropological approach to Greek literature and culture. In this chapter from *Tragic Ways of Killing a Woman* (originally *Façons Tragiques de Tuer une Femme*, 1985), Loraux argues that Greek tragedy offered a public space for reflecting on the difference between the sexes, especially through representation of women's deaths. Men in tragedy die primarily through murder, but women typically die either through sacrifice, if virgins, or suicide, if married. In either case, women can choose whether to die heroically or passively, through either hanging (a feminine mode), or stabbing (masculine). In contrast to their near-invisibility in ancient Athens, women in tragedy can attain glory through death, but that glory will always be both anomalous and male; after blurring the boundary between the sexes, the plays reinforce them again. Loraux's analysis is philological, probing the associations of recurring Greek words, but she uses literary texts as windows into social and cultural codes.

The Rope and the Sword

A woman's suicide for a man's death

'For a woman it is already a distressing evil to remain at home, abandoned, without a husband. And when suddenly one messenger arrives, and then another, always bringing worse news, and all proclaiming disaster for the house …! If this man had received as many wounds [*traumatōn*] as were reported to his home through various channels, his body would now have more cuts [*tetrōtai*] than a net has meshes … Those were the cruel rumors which made me more than once hang my neck in a noose, from which I was wrenched only by force' (Aeschylus, *Agamemnon*, 861–76).

Beyond the lie that the queen handles with consummate skill, there is a truth, or at least an apparent truth, proper to tragedy, which is expressed in these words of Clytemnestra as she welcomes Agamemnon on his return to his palace. The death of a man inevitably calls for the suicide of a woman, his wife. Why should a woman's death counterbalance a man's? Because of the heroic code of honor that tragedy loves to recall, the death of a man could only be that of a warrior on the field of battle. Thus the children of Agamemnon in the *Choephoroe*[60] dream for a moment of what might have been their father's glorious death under the walls of Troy; and, on merely being told of her husband's death, his wife, immured in her home, would kill herself with a noose round her neck. It was as part of this tragic pattern that Hecuba in the *Troades*[61] (1012–4) was bitterly to rebuke Helen because nobody had ever 'surprised her in the act of hanging up a noose or sharpening a dagger as a noble-hearted woman [*gennaia gynē*] would have done in mourning her first husband.'

---

[60]***Choephoroe***: *The Libation Bearers* (458 BCE), the second tragedy in Aeschylus' *Oresteia* trilogy, in which Orestes kills his mother Clytemnestra as revenge for his father's death.
[61]***Troades***: *The Trojan Women* (415 BCE), tragedy by Euripides about the women of Troy after the war's end. Hecuba was the wife of Priam, King of Troy.

Of course Clytemnestra did not kill herself, any more than her sister Helen did. Not only was the queen no Penelope[62] (even though in her lying speech she speaks of her eyes burning with tears as she lay sleepless, crying for her absent husband), but she was also no ordinary tragic wife. Clytemnestra did not kill herself, and it was Agamemnon who was to die, ensnared in her veil and his body pierced with wounds. She turned death away from herself and brought it upon the king just as Medea, instead of killing herself, was to kill Jason indirectly through his children and his newly-wed wife.[63] In Clytemnestra, the mother of Iphigenia and the mistress of Aegisthus triumphed over the king's wife. The murdering queen denied the law of femininity, that in the extreme of misery a knotted rope should provide the way out.[64]

A death devoid of male courage

Finding a way out in suicide was a tragic solution, one that was morally disapproved in the normal run of everyday life. But, most important, it was a woman's solution and not, as has sometimes been claimed, a heroic act.[65] That the hero Ajax,[66] both in Sophocles and in the epic tradition, killed himself was one thing; that he killed himself in a virile manner was another, and I shall come back to this. But to infer from this example that in the Greek imagination all suicide was inspired by *andreia* (the Greek word for courage as a male characteristic) is a step we should not take. Heracles in Euripides without doubt conforms much more to the traditional ethic when, from the depths of his disasters, he agrees to go on living.[67] In the case of mere citizens, things are even clearer. Nothing was further from suicide than the hoplites'[68] imperative of a 'fine death,' which must be accepted and not sought.[69] We know that after the battle of Plataea the Spartan Aristodamus[70] was deprived by his fellow citizens of the posthumous glory of appearing on the roll of valor because he had sought death too openly in action. Whether he were a Spartan or not, a warrior committed suicide only when struck by

---

[62]**Penelope:** wife of Odysseus, one of the Greek warriors in the Trojan War; in the *Odyssey*, Homer depicts her faithfulness to her husband, for whom she waits for ten years after the war's end.

[63][**Loraux's note**]: Compare Euripides, *Medea*, 39–40 and 379.

[64][**Loraux's note**]: The knot of the rope (*brochos*) makes real the metaphorical knot of misfortune. Compare *Hippolytus*, 671 and 781.

[65][**Loraux's note**]: A. Katsouris ('The Suicide Motive in Ancient Drama', *Dioniso* 47 (1956): 5–36) asserts this, although he cannot avoid admitting (p. 9) that in tragedy the majority of suicides were committed by women.

[66]**Ajax:** Greek warrior in the Trojan War, whose suicide is depicted in Sophocles' tragedy *Ajax* (c.442 BCE).

[67][**Loraux's note**]: It is worth remembering that traditionally Ajax is the only male hero to carry a suicide through to the end. The interpretation of Heracles' choice proposed here contradicts that of Jacqueline de Romilly ('Le refus du suicide dans l'Héraclès d'Euripide', *Arkhaiognosia* 1 (1980): 1–10).

[68]**hoplites:** ancient Greek soldiers, named for *hopla*, shields in Greek.

[69][**Loraux's note**]: This shows all the difference between a wish of reason (*ethelō*) and an inclination (*boulomai*). See Nicole Loraux, *The Invention of Athens* (Cambridge, MA: Harvard University Press, 1986), 102–4, and, on Aristodamus (Herodotus, IX.71), 'La belle mort spartiate', *Ktema* 2 (1977): 105–20. It should be noted that, in *Le suicide* (new ed., Paris: Presses Universitaires de France, 1981, 374), Emile Durkheim interprets Aristodamus' death as a suicide. Othryadas: Herodotus, I.82; Pantites: Herodotus, VII.232.

[70]**Aristodamus:** Spartan warrior who fought heroically at Battle of Platea (479 BCE) during the second Persian invasion of Greece, but was not awarded honours because his fighting was viewed as suicidal in its zeal.

dishonor, as Othryadas[71] did in book I of Herodotus[72] and Pantites[73] in book VII. Plato in the *Laws* echoes these practices; he is prescribing laws but is loyal to civic conventions when he lays down that the suicide should be formally punished, 'for total lack of manliness,' by being buried in a solitary and unmarked grave on the edge of the city, in the darkness of anonymity (IX. 873c–d). I would add (and it is relevant) that the Greek language, in the absence of a special word for suicide, describes the act by resorting to the same words as are used for the murder of parents, that ultimate ignominy.[74]

Suicide, then, could be the tragic death chosen under the weight of necessity by those on whom fell 'the intolerable pain of a misfortune from which there is no way out.'[75] But in tragedy itself it was mainly a woman's death. There was one form of suicide – an already despised form of death – that was more disgraceful and associated more than any other with irremediable dishonor. This was hanging, a hideous death, or more exactly a 'formless' death (*aschēmōn*), the extreme of defilement that one inflicted on oneself only in the utmost shame.[76] It also turns out – but is it just chance? – that hanging is a woman's way of death: Jocasta, Phaedra, Leda, Antigone ended in this way, while outside tragedy there were deaths of innumerable young girls who hanged themselves, to give rise to a special cult or to illustrate the mysteries of female physiology.[77]

Hanging was a woman's death. As practiced by women, it could lead to endless variations, because women and young girls contrived to substitute for the customary rope those adornments with which they decked themselves and which were also the emblems of their sex, as Antigone strangled herself with her knotted veil. Veils, belts, headbands – all these instruments of seduction were death traps for those who wore them, as the suppliant Danaids explained to King Pelasgus.[78] To borrow Aeschylus' powerful expression, there was here a fine trick, *mēchanē kalē*, by which erotic *peithō* (persuasion) became the agent of the most sinister threat.

I am not going to dwell here on women's relation to *mētis*, that very Greek concept of cunning intelligence. Yet this is a good moment to recall that, even when a woman was armed with a sword to kill herself or another, every action of hers was likely to be covered by the

---

[71]**Othryadas:** warrior who was the last Spartan standing in the Battle of Thyreatis (*c.*545 BCE), and inscribed a victory trophy with his own blood before dying.

[72]**Herodotus:** Greek historian (*c.*484–*c.*425 BCE), proclaimed by Cicero 'the father of history'.

[73]**Pantites:** Spartan warrior who hanged himself in disgrace after failing to return from a mission to Thessaly in time to fight in the Battle of Thermopylae (480 BCE), in which his fellow soldiers were killed.

[74][**Loraux's note**]: For example, *autophonos* and *autocheir*. The overdetermination suicide/death in combat/family murder is particularly clear in the single combat between the sons of Oedipus. See Aeschylus, *Seven against Thebes*, 850; Sophocles, *Antigone*, 172; Euripides, *Phoenissae*, 880. Other examples are Aeschylus, *Agamemnon*, 1091; Euripides, *Orestes*, 947; and Sophocles, *Antigone*, 1175. See also the commentary of L. Gernet on book IX of Plato's *Laws* (Paris: Ernest Leroux, 1917), 162 (873c5–6).

[75][**Loraux's note**]: This is one of the extenuating circumstances envisaged by Plato in his condemnation of suicide (*Laws*, IX. 873c5–6).

[76][**Loraux's note**]: Shame: Plato, *Laws*, IX.873e6; ugliness of hanging: Euripides, *Helen*, 298–302; defilement: Sophocles, *Antigone*, 54 (*lōbē*), also Aeschylus, *Supplices*, 473 (*miasma* in a system of suicide as revenge); dishonor: Euripides, *Helen*, 134–6, 200–2, 686–7 (death of Leda).

[77][**Loraux's note**]: As it closes forever the too open bodies of women, hanging is almost latent in feminine physiology. See Nicole Loraux, 'Le corps étranglé', in *Le châtiment dans la cité*, ed. Y. Thomas (Rome and Paris: Ecole Française de Rome, 1984), 195–218.

[78][**Loraux's note**]: Sophocles, *Antigone*, 1220–2; Aeschylus, *Supplices*, 455–66.

vocabulary of cunning. Thus, in the *Agamemnon*, in order to suggest the murderous designs of Clytemnestra as she sharpened her sword for use against her husband, Cassandra quite unexpectedly resorts to the imagery of poison mixed in a cup. But the text of the *Oresteia* will soon substitute a very real snare, the garment that will imprison Agamemnon as in a net – a bold materialization of every metaphor concerning *mētis*. The same logic is at work in the *Trachiniae*.[79] Without meaning to, Deianira has caught Heracles in the poisoned trap of Nessus' shirt. She straightway turns to the sword for a quick death and her release, but even so her suicide can still be construed, if only momentarily, as the product of cunning intelligence.[80]

Against this ensnaring *mētis*, which works in the words and actions of women and weaves the meshes of death or busily tightens knots, tragedy sets up in contrast the weapons that cut and tear, those that draw blood. This brings us back to the Suppliants of Aeschylus and their drive toward hanging. As a last resort in their headlong flight from the sons of Aegyptus, the deadly rope would protect the Danaids against the violent desire of the male, just as hurling themselves from the top of a steep rock (something they dreamed for a moment of doing) would have kept them safe from marriage, that prison where the husband is only a master. But it is significant that they give this master the name of *daiktor*, which does not mean 'ravisher' (as an influential translation has it) but, very precisely, 'tearer.'[81] From this tearing – which clearly refers to rape or deflowering – there are only two ways of escape: either the death of the Danaids by the rope, resulting in defilement of the city, or their survival at the cost of a war that would spill the blood of men 'on behalf of women' (*Supplices*, 476–7). The Danaids did not hang themselves. We know the result – marriage arranged in the end, a wedding night ending in bloodshed, fatal for the husbands, and later punishment in Hades. But that is another story.

The gash in the man's body

If we are to believe Euripides. Thanatos (Death) was armed with a sword. This was certainly not pure chance. If death, the same for all, makes no distinction between its victims and cuts the hair of men and women alike, it was for Thanatos, the male incarnation of death, to carry the sword, the emblem of a man's demise.[82]

A man worthy of the name could die only by the sword or the spear of another, on the field of battle. The Menelaus of Euripides was an inglorious character, being the only warrior to come back from Troy without even a trace of a wound suffered in close combat, the only

---

[79] ***Trachiniae:*** or *Women of Trachis*, tragedy by Sophocles (*c*.450–420 BCE), in which Heracles dies after wearing a robe dyed with the blood of the Centaur Nessus.

[80] **[Loraux's note]:** Poison: *Agamemnon*, 1260–3. The veil as net: ibid., 1382–3, 1492, 1580, 1611; *Choephoroe*, 981–2, 998–1004; *Eumenides*, 460, 634–5. Deianira: Sophocles, *Trachiniae*, 883–4 (*emēsato*), 928 (*technomenēs*). The mixing of the 'straight path' of the sword and of *mētis* is at its height in *Medea*, 384–409 and 1278 (where the sword is a net).

[81] **[Loraux's note]:** Hanging rather than the male: Aeschylus, *Supplices*, 787–90; precipitation rather than the *daiktōr*: 794–9. Compare *daiktōr* with *gōos daiktēr*, *Seven against Thebes*, 917: a tearing sob, a doleful mourning in which one tears one's body in imitation of the torn bodies of the dead, in this case the sons of Oedipus, themselves *autodaiktoi*, 735. Finally, note that at line 680 of the *Supplices*, the verb *daizō* (tear) has made its first appearance, to characterize civil war as the tearer of the city. So there is no reason to turn 'tearer' euphemistically into 'ravisher'.

[82] **[Loraux's note]:** Euripides, *Alcestis*, 74–6. Other metaphors of death as cutting or bloody: 118 and 225. On Thanatos as the masculine form of death, see J.-P. Vernant, 'Figures féminines de la mort', forthcoming in a collective work *Masculin/Féminin en Grèce ancienne* (ed. Nicole Loraux).

wound that made a man complete.[83] Even in human sacrifice, an act that was corrupt from every point of view, the executioner had to be a man, especially when the victim was a male. There is proof of this in *Iphigenia in Tauris*,[84] where Orestes questions the sister whom he has not yet recognized: 'Would you, a woman, strike men with a sword?' and Iphigenia assures him in reply that there is a male killer (*sphageus*) in the sanctuary to carry out the task.[85]

Even suicide in tragedy obeys this firm rule, that a man must die at a man's hand, by the sword and with blood spilt. In Sophocles, as in Pindar, Ajax kills himself by the sword, faithful till the end to his status as a hero who lives and dies in war, where wounds are given and received in an exchange that, on the whole, is subject to rules. So Ajax kills himself, but in the manner of a warrior.[86] Pierced by the blade with which he identifies himself (*Ajax*, 650–1), he tears open his side on the sword that, in staging his own death, he makes into an actor: 'the killer [*sphageus*] is there,' he says, 'standing upright so that he can slice as cleanly as possible.'[87] Ajax's sword is a basic signifier in Sophocles' play, recurring at each step in the metaphorical texture of the tragedy and serving to bind it together. If it is the warrior's sword itself that becomes the healing blade that Ajax invokes in his prayers, there are also in a figurative sense many other swords in the *Ajax*, such as the words that have been sharpened like steel and 'cut the living flesh.' No wonder then that, at the sight of the hero's corpse, the sharp blade of grief pierced Tecmessa 'to the liver.'[88]

I shall say no more about Ajax's sword. Others before me have discussed it ably, sometimes brilliantly like Jean Starobinski.[89] Nor shall I dwell on the theme of spilt blood, even though it is central to the *Ajax*, for there is another of Sophocles' heroes to make the point that a man's suicide is inevitably bloody. This is the betrothed of Antigone, whose death is announced punningly in words that cannot adequately be translated. 'Haemon is dead; his own hand has drenched him in blood.'[90] It is enough to recall that the name Haemon is only too like the word for blood (*haima*). In this way the son of Creon, pierced by his own sword, fulfills the prophecy of his own name and dies like a man.

---

[83][**Loraux's note**]: Euripides, *Andromache*, 616: *oude trōtheis*. It is the scholiast who is right (as opposed to L. Méridier, the translator of the Belles Lettres edition). Menelaus in book IV of the *Iliad* was certainly wounded from afar by an arrow from Pandarus, but no wound was inflicted on him at close quarters, by a sword or a lance; and this was the sign of his dubious courage.

[84]***Iphigenia in Tauris***: play by Euripides (*c*.414 BCE) in which Iphigenia is unexpectedly reunited with her brother Orestes, after each believes the other to be dead.

[85][**Loraux's note**]: Euripides, *Iphigenia in Tauris*, 621–2. On the place given to the slaughterer at the heart of feminine sacrifice, see M. Detienne, 'Violentes Eugénies', in *La cuisine du sacrifice en pays grec*, ed. M. Detienne and J.-P. Vernant (Paris: Gallimard, 1979), 208.

[86][**Loraux's note**]: On this exchange, on which I have commented in 'Blessures de virilité' (*Le Genre Humain* 10 (1984): 38–56), see Pindar, *Nemean*, VIII.40 (also *Nemean*, VII.35 and *Isthmian*, IV.35). We must remember that in the tragedy of Sophocles, Hector's sword is a gift from the enemy. As for Ajax, he dies as a warrior 'falls' (*piptō*: *Ajax*, 828, 841, 1033).

[87][**Loraux's note**]: *Ajax*, 815, with the translation and commentary of J. Casabona, *Recherches sur le vocabulaire des sacrifices en Grèce* (Aix-en-Provence: Annales Fac. Lettres, 1966), 179. One will note that the sword is set upright (*hestēken*) as is usually a hoplite at his post. In 1026 Teucer speaks of his sword as a *phoneus*, a killer.

[88][**Loraux's note**]: The blade: *Ajax*, 581–2, in a context at once medical and sacrificial (cf. *Trachiniae*, 1032–3; *Antigone*, 1308–9); the sharpened tongue: 584; the flesh cut by words: 786; the misfortune that pierces the liver: 938.

[89][**Loraux's note**]: Jean Starobinski, 'L'épée d'Ajax', in *Trois fureurs* (Paris: Gallimard, 1974), particularly pp. 27–9 and 61. See also D. Cohen, 'The Imagery of Sophocles: A Study of Ajax' Suicide', *Greece and Rome* 25 (1978): 24–36, and Charles Segal, 'Visual Symbolism and Visual Effects in Sophocles', *Classical World* 74 (1981): 125–42.

[90][**Loraux's note**]: Haemon: *Antigone*, 1175 (see also 1239). On *haima* as a word for effusion of blood, see H. Koller, 'Haima', *Glotta* 15 (1967): 149–55.

Hanging or Sphagē

There is a word that must now be mentioned, because it is obsessively present in Greek tragedy and is insistently opposed to the language of hanging. This word is *sphagē*. which means sacrificial throat-cutting, and also the gash and the blood that flows from it. Together with the verb *sphazō* and its derivatives, it is of course used to indicate sacrifices—the sacrifice of Iphigenia in Aeschylus and Euripides, but also in Euripides that of Macaria in the *Heraclidae*, of Polyxena in the *Hecuba* and the *Troades*, of Menoeceus in the *Phoenissae*, and finally of the daughters of Erechtheus offered to their country by way of *sphagia* (*Ion*, 278). Up to this point there is nothing abnormal to note, or scarcely so. But, from Aeschylus through Sophocles to Euripides, *sphazō* and *sphagē* are also used to denote murder within the family of the Atreides. Moreover, the same words are used to describe a suicide when it is stained with blood, such as the suicides of Ajax, Deianira, and Eurydice. In order to justify this slight deviation from the usual meaning, can one call on some principle of semantic looseness in the character of tragic speech? Is *sphazō* to be lumped together with words that are more neutral or descriptive like *schizō* and *daizō*, which imply tearing of the body?[91] This would be a misunderstanding of the verbal rigor of Greek tragedy, which twists language only for a very definite purpose, such as to upset the normal categories. It is better to trust in the strong sacrificial sense of these words and to notice that *sphazō*, *sphagē*, and *sphagion*, terms laden with religious values, do not signify in tragedy just any throat-cutting murder or suicide, but the long series of 'murders that result from the application of the blood law' in the family of the Atreides, or the self-inflicted death of Eurydice at the foot of the altar of Zeus Herkeios.[92] More generally, *sphagē* is used to characterize death by the sword as a 'pure' death in opposition to hanging.[93]

No sooner have we recalled this difference between two modes of death, one male and the other female, than we are forced to admit that the distinction is in fact violated in the 'virile' deaths of Deianira and Eurydice, who plunge swords into their bodies. And in Euripides there is no lack of heroines who, as they contemplate death, prefer the sword to the rope. Thus Electra, as she mounts guard at the door of the house where Clytemnestra is being murdered, brandishes a sword, ready to turn it on herself if the enterprise should fail (*Electra*, 688, 695–6). (Conversely, in Euripides there are men who die fatally strangled, in the manner of women. Thus Hippolytus, entangled in the reins of his horses, was smashed against the rocks by the roadside.[94] However, as far as men were concerned, it must be said that this irregular form of death was evidently less frequent.)

---

[91][**Loraux's note**]: *Schismos*: Aeschylus, *Agamemnon*, 1149 (Cassandra); *schizō*: Sophocles, *Electra*, 99 (murder of Agamemnon). *Daizō*: Aeschylus, *Agamemnon*, 207–8 (sacrifice of Iphigenia), *Choephoroe*, 860, 1071 (murder).

[92][**Loraux's note**]: The blood law: Casabona, *Vocabulaire*, 160. Compare in Euripides' *Electra* the presence of sacrificial equipment (*kanoun*, *sphagis*) in the description of Clytemnestra's murder (1142; cf. 1222: *katarchomai*, commented on by P. Stengel, *Opferbräuche der Griechen*. Leipzig and Berlin: Teubner, 1910, p. 42). Eurydice is a *sphagion*: *Antigone*, 1291, with the commentary of Casabona, *Vocabulaire*, 187. See also the remarks in the text commentary by R.C. Jebb (Cambridge: Cambridge University Press, 1900) on *bōmia* (suicide at the foot of the altar) and the suicide's sword as sacrificial knife (1301).

[93][**Loraux's note**]: See, for example, Euripides, *Helen*, 353–9.

[94][**Loraux's note**]: *Hippolytus*, 1236–7, 1244–5. In his agony of pain, the dying Hippolytus, caught in a snare like Heracles, will ask for a flesh-cutting sword that will deliver him (1357; cf. Sophocles, *Trachiniae*, 1031–3).

The confusion in tragedy that consists in giving a man's death to a woman is not a matter of chance. Let us take the death of Jocasta in the *Phoenissae*.[95] In Sophocles, as we all know, as soon as Jocasta came to see the truth about Oedipus, she hanged herself, as a woman overwhelmed by a crushing misfortune. The Jocasta of Euripides did not hang herself. She survived the revelation of her incest and it was the death of her sons that killed her, as she turned on herself the sword that had killed them.[96] This was a remarkable departure from a tradition that had been well established since Homer and the hanging of Epicaste (Jocasta). Should one attribute this innovation, as some do, to a change in outlook that had become increasingly hostile to death by hanging?[97] There is really nothing to support this hypothesis: ever since the *Odyssey* (XXII. 462–4), the rope dealt the impurest of deaths, and one cannot see how attitudes could have developed on this point. But above all one should read the text of Euripides beside that of Sophocles, and one will see that the *Phoenissae* brings a whole new interpretation of the character of Jocasta. She is no longer, as she is in Sophocles, above all a wife; she is exclusively a mother,[98] and her manly death should be seen as a consequence of this critical reshaping of the tradition.

Starting from this example and several others, I offered in an earlier publication a generalization about women's deaths in tragedy, to the effect that hanging was associated with marriage – or rather, with an excessive valuation of the status of bride (*nymphē*) – while a suicide that shed blood was associated with maternity, through which a wife, in her 'heroic' pains of childbirth, found complete fulfillment.[99] I still abide by that reading. However, I shall not return to it, for it is simply the confusion as such that interests me here, and more particularly the many statements in Euripides that seem to assume that the rope and the sword come to the same thing.

The rope or the sword – in brief, death at any price, whatever the method. That is the way manlike women, who would in general prefer the sword, reason in a desperate situation. It is also the way women who are overfeminine boast when, like Hermione, they will not dare even to hang themselves. But, in either case, the way the text runs makes it perfectly clear what would be the real choice for the particular woman in despair – the sword or the rope. It is this choice that the chorus leaves to Admetus, in face of the imminent death of Alcestis, saying that 'a misfortune of this kind justifies cutting one's throat [*sphagē*] or slipping a noose round one's neck' – a simple way of indicating that, having avoided death, a womanish man would not be able to escape the distress that breaks women's spirits.[100]

---

[95]***Phoenissae:*** *Phoenician Women* (c.410 BCE), tragedy by Euripides in which Oedipus's wife Jocasta kills herself after witnessing the death of her sons Polynices and Eteocles.

[96][**Loraux's note**]: I deliberately use this phrase, which is logically impossible, for the text of the *Phoenissae* not only does not specify which of the two swords she uses, but even suggests in a general way that the common sword of the sons is involved (see 1456 and 1578).

[97][**Loraux's note**]: R. Hirzel, 'Der Selbstmord', *Archiv für Religionswissenschaft* 11 (1908): especially pp. 256–8.

[98][**Loraux's note**]: One can compare *Oedipus Tyrannus*, where. Jocasta is *pantelēs damar* (accomplished wife), and the *Phoenissae*, where Jocasta dies 'with' her sons and will be buried with them (1282, 1483, 1553–4, 1635). In the same way Eurydice is *pammētor*, entirely given to maternity (*Antigone*, 1282).

[99][**Loraux's note**]: 'Le lit, la guerre', *L'Homme* 21 (1981): 37–67. See also '*Ponos*. Sur quelques difficultés de la peine comme nom du travail', *Annali dell' Instituto Orientale di Napoli* 4 (1982): 171–92.

[100][**Loraux's note**]: Rope or sword: for Helen, if she had been a *gennaia gynē* (*Troades*, 1012–4); for Creusa, if her death plan should fail (*Ion*, 1063–5); for the manlike Electra (*Orestes*, 953), who would prefer the sword (1041, 1052); for the boastful Hermione (*Andromache*, 811–3, 841–4), whose nurse dreads above all her hanging herself (815–6); for Admetus (*Alcestis*, 227–9). See again *Andromache*, 412, as well as *Hercules Furens*, 319–20 and 1147–51.

Paradoxically, as these few examples have already suggested, the confusion even at its very height aims only to reinforce the standard opposition. So it is with Helen in the play that bears her name, summoning death in her prayers: 'I shall put my neck in a deadly, dangling noose, or in a mighty effort I shall sink the whole blade of a sword in my flesh, and its murderous thrust will open up a stream of blood from my throat, and I will sacrifice myself to the three goddesses' (353–7). As the final outcome indicates, the only possibility that Helen sees as truly worthy of her is *sphagē* but, on closer inspection, the choice was already revealed through the very words in which Helen spoke of hanging herself, and especially in the expression *phonion aiōrēma* (353), the untranslatable and contradictory 'gory suspension' that translators cover up as best they can, because in their view the distinctive feature of hanging is that no blood flows.[101] But it is precisely in this oxymoron that one can and must guess what the heroine's choice will be. For her no death can be considered that does not shed blood, and her words reject hanging at the very moment that she mentions its possibility. *Phonion aiōrēma*: proclaiming in advance the blood of the *sphagē*, Helen's language runs ahead of her thought.

At the end of this inquiry, therefore, the contrast between the rope and the sword stands more strongly than ever. But certain facts must be clearly understood. A man never hangs himself, even when he has thought of doing so;[102] a man who kills himself does it in a manly way. For a woman, however, there is an alternative. She can seek a womanly way of ending her life, by the noose, or she can steal a man's death by seizing a sword. Is this a matter of identification, of personal coherence in her character within the play? Perhaps. The imbalance is nonetheless obvious, proving, if proof were needed, that the genre of tragedy can easily create and control a confusion of categories, and also knows the limits it cannot cross. To put it another way, the woman in tragedy is more entitled to play the man in her death than the man is to assume any aspect of woman's conduct, even in his manner of death. For women there is liberty in tragedy – liberty in death.

In ordinary life an Athenian woman was allowed no accomplishments beyond leading a quiet and exemplary existence as wife and mother. Her glory was to have no glory. In Greek tragedy, however, women die violently and, through violence, master their own fate. It is a genre that delights in blurring the formal frontier between masculine and feminine.

Further reading

Roland Champagne, 'Loraux: The Myths of Death and Life', in *The Methods of the Gernet Classicists: The Structuralists on Myth* (London: Routledge, 2015), 139–60.

Mary Maxwell, 'A Lament for Loraux', *Arion* [3rd Series], 11, no. 3 (2004): 105–20.

Froma Zeitlin, 'Foreword', in Nicole Loraux, *The Children of Athena*, trans. Caroline Levine (Princeton: Princeton University Press, 1993), xi–xvii.

---

[101][**Loraux's note**]: I differ here from the interpretation of Casabona, *Vocabulaire*, 161. One should add that the verb *oregomai* used by the heroine is more suited to the act of wounding (frequent in the *Iliad*) than to that of knotting.

[102][**Loraux's note**]: Hanging is mentioned by Orestes (Aeschylus, *Eumenides*, 746; Euripides, *Orestes*, 1062–3) and by Oedipus (Sophocles, *Oedipus Tyrannus*, 1374; Euripides, *Phoenissae*, 331–4).

6.6 BIODUN JEYIFO, 'TRAGEDY, HISTORY AND IDEOLOGY' (1986)

Biodun Jeyifo (born in 1946 in Ibadan, Nigeria) is Professor of African, African-American Studies and Comparative Literature at Harvard University. Jeyifo has written or edited over 14 books on Anglophone African literature, theatre, or dramatists including *The Truthful Lie: Essays in a Radical Sociology or African Drama* (1985) and *Wole Soyinka: Politics, Poetics and Postcolonialism* (2003). Jeyifo's work combines Marxist and post-colonial approaches to the study of history, literature, and politics in order to probe and re-imagine the exclusionary critical practices of Anglo-American and European literary discourse. In this essay, he uses the writings of Hegel and Marx to critique enduring Aristotelian ideas of tragedy as essentializing and ahistorical; his analysis requires that our understanding of tragedy be broadened in order both to offer a more satisfying account of the emergence of the theatrical genre of African historical tragedy and to comprehend more fully the nature of historical and contemporary geopolitical struggle.

Dramatic theory and dramatic criticism have always sought to extend and enrich the mediation between the idea and form of tragedy – the 'highest' art of all – and life. In this theoretical and critical issue, 'life', itself an already over-generalized conception, confronts another conception – the idea and form of tragedy; many critics and theorists, particularly those of a materialist outlook, have thus situated this mediation in the realms of history and society. This paper is a resumption of this enquiry.

In Western theory and criticism we may identify, out of the rich, varied and multi-dimensional investigations into the nature of tragic art and its connections to history, three great *moments*: Aristotle; Hegel; Marx-Engels.[103]

Aristotle's great contribution consisted of a much needed *affirmation* and *definition*: affirmation against the powerful, influential but ultimately philistinic strictures of Plato against the art of tragedy; definition of the new realm of tragedy in the continent of drama. But speaking of tragedy *qua* history, as complete and comprehensive as his theory was, Aristotle's great deficiency was the furiously undialectical nature of his definitions. From the great classical practitioners of the tragic art Aristotle deduced the classic idea of tragedy: a spirit and a vision sublimated from life into an 'organic' form which is eternally 'true', and indifferent to the unfolding of 'life' in history. This classic idea Aristotle elaborated in the principal concepts with an unchanging essentiality: an archetypal tragic hero; and a tragic issue, equally essential, which inheres in the dramatic action. To enhance the purity of this idea, Aristotle suggested that it were much better for the playwright, in selecting a subject, to look to myth, a fantasized reality, than to history, a factual reality. In at least two subsequent periods of the resumption of the Aristotelian principles we see the congealment and sclerosis[104] of this *idea*: in Renaissance

---

[103][**Jeyifo's note**]: I refer readers to the essay 'The Concept of Tragedy in Marx and Engels' in *Art and Society* by Adolfo Sanchez Vasquez, Monthly Review Press, New York, 1973. The model I have outlined here is my own extension of some of Vasquez's interpretations.

[104]**sclerosis**: hardening.

Italy and in the mid-seventeenth, to early eighteenth-century France, during the hegemony of the so-called 'neo-classical' ideal.[105]

Hegel first directly opened the doors of the idea and form of tragedy to the insistent knockings of history. It must be emphasized that before Hegel there was no absence of efforts to refract the tragic form and idea through the prism of life and practice. But these efforts were in the main apologetic: if great playwrights such as Corneille and Shakespeare wrote great, moving tragedies, *against* the form and idea of the Aristotelian classic, then room must be made for enrichment, for revisions and extensions of the idea. Hegel's great contribution was to inject into the false organicism of the Aristotelian tragic idea the notion of the self-actualizing dialectic[106] (the dialectic of consciousness, of spirit, of being and becoming).

Tragedy is the highest art, averred Hegel, because it distilled the *necessary* collisions which the World-Historical spirit, in every age and in its manifestations in racial or national communities, must go through in its self-actualisation in history. Protagonist and antagonist forces are therefore both themselves and *more* than themselves; in the objective contents of their 'volitional' collisions they reflect the contradictions which must be 'annulled', be negated for Spirit to realize itself in an age or epoch. One may thus speculate, according to Hegelian analysis, that, had the confrontation of such African leaders as Idi Amin and Julius Nyerere[107] (to give a particularly trenchant example) resulted in a political-military contest of wills leading to the defeat of one man, the action would have symbolized, more than the confrontation of two opposing ethical and ideological outlooks, the self-actualizing activity of a spirit of history which selects contradictory human forces for its dialectical operations. If such a confrontation – always a possibility in the unstable sea of contemporary African politics – had resulted in the defeat of Nyerere and the sack of Tanzania by Amin's hordes, the Hegelian tragic issue would still have emerged intact, as shown by the following quote from Hegel himself:

> The true course of dramatic development is the annulment of *contradictions* viewed as such, in the reconciliation of the forces of human action, which alternately strive to negate each other in their conflict. Only so far is misfortune not the final issue but rather the satisfaction of spirit, as for the first time, in virtue of all that particular individuals experience, is able to appear in complete accord with reason, and our emotional attitude is tranquilized on a true ethical basis....[108]

---

[105][Jeyifo's note]: A major collection of Western dramatic theory and criticism is Bernard F. Dukore, *Dramatic Theory and Criticism: Greeks to Grotowski* (New York: Holt, Rinehart and Winston, Inc., 1974). All the quotations in this paper on theory and criticism are from this book.

[106]**dialectic:** Hegel's dialectical method of argument was central to all aspects of his philosophy. Dialectics are a mode of argument which relies on contradictory and conflicting determinations being dissolved or resolved into a third position.

[107]**Idi Amin and Julius Nyerere:** Idi Amin Dada (*c.*1925–2003), military commander and president of Uganda (1971–9); Julius Nyerere (1922–9) was president of neighbouring Tanzania who gave sanctuary to refugees fleeing Amin's regime. When Amin invaded Tanzania in 1979, Nyerere retaliated and, allied to the Uganda National Liberation Army, defeated him and forced him into exile.

[108][Jeyifo's note]: Dukore, *Dramatic Theory and Criticism*, 540.

Marx-Engels, in the famous conceit which everyone now knows, 'stood the dialectic on its feet', where Hegel had stood it 'on its head'.[109] To Hegel's *dialectic of consciousness* in which great forces of tragedy merely incarnated the self-actualizing, self-totalizing activity of Spirit, Marx-Engels opposed a *consciousness of the dialectic*. True tragedy – tragedy based on historical events – reflects the collisions of men and forces who are more or less conscious of the socio-historical roots of the tragic issue. More concentrated, more intense is the revolutionary historical tragedy where

> We are on historical ground and the conflict is not waged among individuals, or between individuals and the community but among social classes or forces.[110]

To sum up: between the three great *moments* of Western investigations into the connections between tragedy and history we have three *key points* along a chronological-theoretical *spectrum*. The first point is Aristotle's *idea* of tragedy. With all the enrichments and reformulations of this idea, it has remained largely intact. Its putative truth is poetic and it is indifferent to history. It is therefore held that it is far better to imagine or invent its story than to pluck it from 'banal' history. The second point is Hegel's dialectic of consciousness: whether or not tragedy uses a historical material, it reflects the dialectical activities of an immanent[111] consciousness, a world-historical spirit which actualizes itself in history. The third point is Marx-Engels: when tragedy confronts history it is on solid ground and loses its abstract, 'artistic' purity; protagonist and antagonist forces are not agents who carry an ineluctable 'tragic flaw' which destroys them. Rather they are individuals who carry the concrete goals and aspirations of social groups, forces or classes.

Any tragedy, historical, mythical or imagined, can be placed at approximate points along this spectrum, which has now lost its chronological perspective but retains the theoretical dimension. The important point to note is that we are here dealing with the nature of tragic epistemology and that this is elaborated in the two principal structures already identified: a tragic hero (or protagonist forces) and the tragic issue in an action. Such placement, based on penetrating textual and structural analysis yields ideological and political insights crucial for consciousness raising and political praxis. This is particularly true of the historical tragedy, that impure sub-genre of drama in which an exceptionally strongly articulated body of formalistic principles encounter perturbations from the real passions and struggles of real men.

[...]

That a tragedy and a tragic hero can express, symbolically, the basic myths and the psychic experience of a culture, has been amply demonstrated by great examples in Western literature. One thinks particularly of *Oedipus Rex* and *Hamlet*, in an extensive field which includes, apart from the great Greek classics, others such as Shakespeare's *Macbeth* and *Lear* and Brecht's *Galileo*.[112] How can the personal disaster or tragic destiny of one character come to express the

---

[109]**stood the dialectic ... on its head:** i.e. Marx and Engels took Hegel's dialectic and reversed it, grounding it in historical materialism rather than idealism.

[110]**[Jeyifo's note]:** Vasquez, *op. cit.*, 123.

[111]**immanent:** permanently pervading.

[112]**Brecht's *Galileo*:** Bertolt Brecht's play *Life of Galileo* (1947). Brecht preferred his play to be regarded as epic theatre rather than tragedy; see extract 5.5.

collective destiny of a people or a race? This question has never been wholly resolved. But, to refer back to our theoretical model, it seems that we are here at a point between Aristotle and Hegel. The actions and fate of a protagonist hero assume an essentiality and a representativeness both by virtue of *his* nature and the potentiality for symbolic reverberations carried by his goals and aspirations – which are defeated in the course of the tragic action. In other words, both in his person and in, the enterprise which he comes to assert and defend, a tragic hero of the kind we are discussing must embody the basic emotions and the collective will of a people.

In *Death and the King's Horseman*[113] both Elesin Oba and the other African characters of the play, excepting the native functionaries of the colonial machine, are made to express, consciously and with considerable lyrical force, the redemptive nature of Elesin Oba's intended ritual suicide. The lyrical and rhetorical aspect must be emphasized. The play never really dramatizes either the force of Elesin Oba's personality or the inevitability of his actions. We are simply presented these matters as given structures and the playwright compels our acceptance of them by the lyrical brilliance of his dramatic language, perhaps unsurpassed by any of his other plays.

[...]

... The extensive field of theory and criticism on tragedy usually makes no separation between the epistemological and the aesthetic-affective; rather it usually fuses them. By this operation the field of investigation and speculation is open and eternal, though it must be emphasized that the issues have remained constant, from Aristotle to the present, e.g. what constitutes the 'essence' of tragedy: the possibility of writing a 'true' tragedy in any particular period or for any particular culture; the contradictory or paradoxical nature of tragedy to, on the one hand, confront us sharply and hone our awareness of life and on the other, ultimately enervate or paralyse our human will, etc.[114]

It is my contention that when tragedy – the idea, the form – confronts history then we can broaden our analytical framework beyond the mainly technical and speculative vectors of discussing the art. If we get nothing else, we can uncover the playwright's, the theorist's or the critic's implicit ideological and political attitudes. I have therefore constructed what seems to me a possible model for the determinations of these issues: the Aristotle-Hegel-Marx spectrum. I advise that the reader return to my opening section before reading the following concluding remarks.

An African 'bourgeois' historical tragedy now exists in African drama and dominates the writings in this genre.[115] Its elaborated pattern and themes place it at some point between Aristotle and Hegel; near the former, in fact. The main impulse is to write according to an existent, received tragic idea, which idea dominates the historical material. Moreover, the protagonist heroes in these plays are scions of bourgeois individualism and solipsism: lone tragic heroes, proposed either as great historical personages or culture heroes and avatars

---

[113]**Death and the King's Horseman**: Wole Soyinka's tragedy *Death and the King's Horseman* (1975), perhaps the most widely read of Soyinka's plays, recounts the story of Elesin Oba, the king's horseman, expected to commit ritual suicide following the death of the king, but who only kills himself when it is revealed that his son, Olunde, has done so in his stead.

[114]**[Jeyifo's note]**: For a very interesting discussion of these issues with special regard to Soyinka see Andrew Gurr's 'Third World Drama: Soyinka and Tragedy', *The Journal of Commonwealth Literature* 10, no. 3 (April 1976): 45–52.

[115]**[Jeyifo's note]**: Other examples of this school are Ola Rotimi's *Kurunmi* and *Overamwen Nogbaisi*, and Seydou Badian's *The Death of Chaka*.

dominate the action; their connection to us is never dialectical; it is symbolic. This hero is always immersed in a recognisable, supposedly 'authenticating' African metaphysical or cosmogonic milieu; a static milieu. The oracle initiates the action of *Oedipus Rex*, the ghost of Hamlet's father, from the netherworld, sends him into the tragic fray: the supernatural or metaphysical element also serves in the bourgeois African tragedy as the external determining factor. Moreover, it also serves as the proof of 'Africanness' and the more dense and impenetrable the better. Conformism is the hallmark of this cultural and metaphysical immersion. *Death and the King's Horseman* is an example of this dominant school of the African historical tragedy; more than this, it is the greatest artistic realisation of the school.[116]

In Hussein's *Kinjeketile*[117] we confront a minority tradition of which the only other example I know is Aimé Césaire's *A Season in the Congo*.[118] Call this school the 'realist' or 'socialist' African historical tragedy if you like. Here the conception of the tragic hero, the archetypes of tragic action and the socio-cultural milieu are probed within the framework of real historical circumstances and confrontations. And the confrontation is not between individuals and society, but between individuals and forces which embody the irreconcilable goals and aspirations of social groups and classes or competing nations and alliances. Of especial interest is the treatment of the cultural, traditional milieu or metaphysical universe. The impulse is to demystify, to clarify, to show the dialectical operations between politics, material existence and the superstructural categories – the morality, the myths and the metaphysics of the society. There is not the need *merely* to 'authenticate', or celebrate the cultural milieu or reveal it as a cluster around a cultural hero.

I don't think I need emphasize here that the two patterns of the African historical tragedy discussed here return us to the lasting ideological and political query to art and drama: about whom, for whom?

Further reading

Biodun Jeyifo (ed.), *Perspectives on Wole Soyinka: Freedom and Complexity* (Jackson: University Press of Mississippi, 2001).

Ketu H. Katrak, *Wole Soyinka and Modern Tragedy: A Study of Dramatic Theory and Practice* (New York and London: Greenwood, 1986).

Kevin Wetmore, *The Athenian Sun in an African Sky: Modern African Adaptations of Classical Greek Tragedy* (Jefferson, NC: McFarland, 2002).

---

[116][**Jeyifo's note**]: I would go so far as to state that *Death and the King's Horseman* is one of the superior creations in the poetic drama in English. Not all of the play is in verse, of course, but the conception is poetic and some of the dialogue is cast in Soyinka's best dramatic poetry to date. But from our present angle, the play lacks any real historical perspective, and from this angle it cannot begin to approach the author's *The Road* which is, paradoxically, not a historical tragedy. In *Death and the King's Horseman* assimilating metaphysics and mythico-religious phenomena into social, economic and secular institutional life, he dramatizes the dialectical interplay of myth and history.

[117]**Hussein's *Kinjeketile***: Ebrahim Hussein (born 1943) is a Tanzanian playwright and poet whose historical tragedy *Kinjeketile* (1969) recounts the Maji–Maji rebellion against German colonial rule in present-day Tanzania.

[118]**Césaire … *Season in the Congo***: Aimé Césaire (1913–2008) was a Francophone Caribbean writer whose *A Season in the Congo* (1966) is a tragedy about the death of Patrice Lumumba, Congo's first elected prime minister.

6.7 HÉLÈNE CIXOUS, 'ENTER THE THEATRE (IN BETWEEN)' (1999)

Hélène Cixous (born 1937) is a Jewish, Algerian-French feminist writer. She is known to Anglo-American readers as a feminist philosopher and literary theorist, who, in her landmark essay 'The Laugh of Medusa' (1975) coined the term 'ecriture feminine', feminine writing, to describe forms of writing linked to the maternal body which resist patriarchal and hierarchical ordering principles to create alternative ways of experiencing the world. In France, Cixous is best known through her avant-garde fiction, poetry, and theatre. Cixous's tragic theatre insists that the classical, the historical, and the mythic have immediate and urgent political relevance. Her tragedy *La Ville Parjure* [The Perjured City] (1994) adapts the final play in Aeschylus's *Oresteia* trilogy, *The Eumenides*. Cixous explores a mother's grief for children dead from an unnamed plague, reflecting on a French scandal of the 1980s in which The National Centre for Blood Transfusions criminally distributed contaminated blood to haemophiliacs resulting in thousands of deaths. Cixous's plays show ordinary citizens' deaths to be as meaningful as those of the elevated protagonists of antiquity. In problematizing the distinctions between history and myth, she contends that tragedy does not merely aestheticize or inure us to pain but is a vital means of comprehending and responding to the sufferings of life. The text below is extracted from a guest lecture that Cixous gave in English at the University of Toronto on 30 September 1999.

Everything began in 1940 and up to 1948 in my very early childhood before consciousness, thought, with a play without an author, which was history itself, *Res gestae*,[119] the theatre of which was the centre of my native city Oran.[120] The *core* of Oran had by chance the shape of the Theatre, I only realized it fifty years later.

The scene was the Place d'Armes – to the right the Municipal Theatre, to the left the Military Club and the pharmacy. On the corner *Les Deux Mondes*, my aunt Deborah's tobacconist's which was Ali Baba's Cave and the first version of the chorus. I myself was in the upper circle of Philippe Street and I could see the history of the entire world played out before me. This history was structured by a twofold plot. One world was trying to annihilate one world. In the first plot Nazism plus Vichyism[121] and the fascisms were trying to destroy the wavering democracies, the champions of eternal moral values. In the second plot these same forces of good were divided and half evil, colonialist, misogynistic, repressive. From the upper circle where I climbed onto the rails, flanked by the hen, I wondered how in this entanglement of violent evil forces and good forces, and where it was impossible to separate a pure good from any kind of morbid or diabolical attack, anything other than a tragic ending could be expected. I could not see any possibility of this on the stage. I was three-and-a-half, four years old and searching with all my strength for a beyond. My German family was in the concentration

---

[119]*Res gestae*: events, circumstances.

[120]**Oran:** city in northwest Algeria.

[121]**Vichyism:** Vichy, a city in central France, was the centre of government during the German occupation of France during the Second World War. The term became a synonym for collaboration with the Nazis.

camps, my grandmother had just managed to escape. She had come to us in Algeria where we were witnesses and hostages to many major and secondary persecutions.

From everywhere there loomed the forms of exclusion, exile or massacre. I also saw Fortinbras de Gaulle[122] and the Allies enter the Place d'Armes. We were liberated but the Algerians were more enslaved than ever.

Democracy showed itself to be a dream, a word. There was no justice, no equality, no respect. Almost no courage. I was on the verge of despair. The world is tragic. If I did not give up hope, it was because my family was without sin and my father was a young doctor true-spirited and incorruptible. But then he died at thirty-nine. What are the gods doing meanwhile? And we who are small and threatened, what can we do?

'If there is a somewhere else,' I would say to myself, 'which can escape the infernal practice of repetition, then it is there that new worlds are written, dreamed, invented.'[123]

Such was my obsession and my need. Is there a somewhere else? Where? It has to be invented. This is the mission of poets. Assuming that there are any. And that they are not cast into the triturator[124] of history before they have even created.

Decades later I am attending the performance of my plays, and what do I see? That they had begun before I wrote, in Oran, Algeria.

In the meantime I have not stopped asking myself with growing astonishment what evil is, experiencing it in increasingly stupefying and painful ways, trying to understand its structure, machine, ineluctability. And feeling myself cast as the keeper of after-lives (I do not say lives – *after-lives*) or Night light. The mission entrusted to me by my father I would define as follows: I must do everything to ensure that I and the people around me are not swept away by oblivion, indifference, I must keep alive the qui vive[125] and preserve the dead, the murdered, the captive, the excluded, from the jaws of death. This is my mission. I do not claim to fulfil it: there would no longer be any problem. I live the tragic, I live myself tragically, I am totally occupied by the question of the tragic. Which in no way excludes happiness and the comic, on the contrary. But I live and breathe the sense of threat, imminence and betrayal within the very midst of happiness and the love of peace.

When I use the word *tragic*, I determine the word in a trivial and ordinary way, that is to say that on the one hand there is tragic theatre, with the goat, the rather Greek fatality of making the wrong choice. On the other, and rather freer from etymology and the Greek context, I see it as linked to the need of the double bind, that is, to the fatal rending of what I call the soul or the heart, to situations of divided loyalty, a quartering of the self. It is the irreconcilable as ineluctable: the situation in which I must accept the unacceptable, or renounce what is most dear and most necessary to me because there is no right answer or happy ending, you cannot expect any consolation or justice, I have looked for it, I have wanted justice, I have crossed generations and frontiers, I have spent my life doing this to the point of finding myself almost

---

[122]**Fortinbras de Gaulle:** Cixous characteristically conflates tragedy and history here. Fortinbras is the prince of Norway, rival-hero to Hamlet who attempts to establish a new order from the desolation at the close of Shakespeare's tragedy. Charles de Gaulle (1890–1970) was leader of French allied forces during the Second World War.

[123]**'escape the infernal practice of repetition'…:** the 'somewhere else' Cixous has in mind here is writing itself. This quotation is from one of her most famous essays, 'Sorties', in her book co-written with Catherine Clément *The Newly Born Woman* (London: I.B. Tauris, 1996), 72.

[124]**triturator:** a grinding or threshing machine.

[125]**qui vive:** a sentry's call meaning, in French, '(long) live who?'; a synonym for 'lookout' or 'sentinel'.

outside of myself – in vain, because consolation and justice do not exist. But even so it was the right thing to do: because it is in this search and this pursuit that the share of justice and consolation reserved for us is to be found. As I ran, searched, struggled, committed myself to action, something calm was being hollowed out in me, calm in opposition to dramatic, something with which there is no negotiation: since the tragic is, and since it is *implacable*, there is no decision that wins the day, it is unquestionable (questioning is Job[126] – Job is the theatre, is movement, protest, despair [that is wounded hope], anger).

No, I would have discovered in the end that *there isn't* and *that's the way it is, the irreconcilable* is the tragic. That's the way it is. That's why, because it is unquestionable, there is a certain 'serenity,' a stasis, an immobility. This conviction of *that's the way it is* is often worn in my plays by characters who are no doubt fairly close to the secret of my heart, for example Aeschylus in *La Ville Parjure*.[127] These are people who have lived a lot, thousands of years and of adventures.

The most incontestable example of the tragic, in my view, is *solitude*, the inescapable, unacceptable part of solitude, and which we experience to a minimal or major degree in all our human relationships, in family ties, and even in love: we do not understand one another *at the same time*. We are the subjects of misunderstanding. Even in the most successful love solitude is not overcome. You say to me: 'Do you understand what I am saying to you?' And I say to you: 'Yes, yes – of course.' And it is only the next day that I understand that when I thought I understood you I did not understand you at all. The lateness, the too late, the lag, the untimely arrival of the message, are our most common and our most painful experience. And it is that which, transposed, transfigured into a theatrical mainspring causes havoc in tragedies: we call it the *untimely letter*, it is sent too soon, too late, and someone is killed. Cordelia is not saved.[128] This solitude (this deafness, this disjunction of our rhythms) exists only if there is someone to make it appear. You have to imagine the conjunction of two conscious solitudes. One can be two in itself (see Kafka),[129] it is the incurable, the unsavable or the unsolvable. Or the impossible. We are impossible. And the contretemps.[130] The Theatre is acted upon, that is to say undermined by the contretemps.

The tragic is the insurmountable anachrony: the missed appointment. Even when it is not missed.

Sero te amavi:[131] Beauty, I have loved you too late, said St. Augustine to God. And Jacques Derrida repeats it at the beginning of his tragic text *Un verre à soie: Sero…*.[132] How can one *love too late?* It is TooLate who is the demon of the Theatre.

---

[126]**Job:** eponymous protagonist of a book of the Old Testament and Hebrew scriptures. Its recounting of Job's endurance in the face of myriad losses and sufferings has led some critics to regard the Book of Job as an archetype for tragedy.

[127]**Aeschylus in *La Ville Parjure*:** a reference to Cixous's own 1994 tragedy *La Ville Parjure* [The Perjured City]. Aeschylus is the name she gives to the character of the caretaker at the cemetery where the mother mourns the loss of her children.

[128]**Cordelia is not saved:** the innocent daughter of Shakespeare's *King Lear* who dies an unbearable and untimely death in the final scene of the tragedy. See extract 3.1 for the way this scene was interpreted in the eighteenth century.

[129]**Kafka:** Franz Kafka (1883–1924) Czech novelist; his novel *The Castle* (1926), for example, is preoccupied with the figure of the double, the two-in-one.

[130]**contretemps:** inopportune accident.

[131]*Sero te amavi*: 'Too late came I to love thee' from St Augustine's *Confessions*, X.27.

[132]**Derrida … Sero:** a reference to the French poststructuralist philosopher Jacques Derrida's essay 'Un Ver á Soie' in Hélène Cixous and Jacques Derrida, *Voiles* (Paris: Éd. Galilée, 1998).

But there is always an unpredictable element. Hazard, chance, a grain of sand in the works: the possibility that the tragic programming will break down, the grace of a totally unforeseen development. *That's the way it is*, it is necessary but at the same time, there is contingency.

But perhaps what is tragic, I fear and suspect, is the fact that it is only *from without*, by leaving society (*La Ville Parjure*) and even life (*La Ville Parjure, L'Histoire*[133]) that we can transgress, interrupt the practice of repetition. It is perhaps only the 'dead' – or poets – those whom Artaud calls 'the suicides of society'[134] – who manage to conceive of a something beyond vengeance, or resentment, or reprisal. But that requires passing *through death*, or through something equivalent: the consent of the I to renunciation. To expect nothing. To attain the state of *unexpectancy*. Another innocence. Is it possible?

[…]

A cruel, paradoxical, ludic, fateful question, abyss and wall into which my plays plunge in their slightly crazy course, since they present the tragic in a *performative manner* by asking questions about the tragic, calling into question the tragic, trying to interrupt the end, the teleological, trying to write History in which 'there is still some blank space' – still some indetermination. And this whiteness in *L'Histoire (qu'on ne connaîtra jamais)*[135] is a 'real' white, a Snow which covers everything with a page on which a poet yet to come could write what has just happened in another version.

And in *La Ville Parjure* it is a Night, a celestial starry fabric.

In each case, I try to engage the possibility of a theatrical writing which overflows tragedy – is it possible? – to write understanding the tragedy and at the same time overflowing it and asking in the play itself the question about the overflowing of tragedy? That is what I hope to do. And that is why my plays have such strange and such unfinal endings.

[…]

It is difficult, because for me, there is no final end. The spectators end up by observing, and I too, that often my plays do not have any conclusive end. But the play has to end, it will soon be time for the last metro, and this I don't forget because the public is an essential character in any play: it is there, everything is addressed to it, *and it is the watch* and it calls the tune.

Now from the beginning, the play has been seeking its end.

At the beginning we were already wondering, Ariane and myself:[136] how will it end? But this question conceals a concern. Deep down we probably wanted it to 'end well,' that is, not too badly. With all our strength the characters and myself try to break out of the mortal trap, the circle of blood, the ineluctable repetition. If we knew how to, there would be no play.

On our side, we want the end. Who would not want the end of a tragedy? It will be tragic but it will at least put an end to the agony. Everyone will be dead. Then Fortinbras will arrive

---

[133]*L'Histoire*: *L'histoire terrible mais inachivée de Norodom Sihanouk, roi du Cambodge* (*The Terrible but Unfinished Story/History of Norodom Sihanouk, King of Cambodia*) is a 1985 tragedy that Cixous wrote in response to the Khmer Rouge genocide in Cambodia.

[134]**Artaud… 'suicides of society':** Antonin Artaud (1896–1948) was a French experimental dramatist, theatre director and theorist; his controversial essay 'Is Suicide a Solution?' was published in *La Révolution Surréaliste*, no. 2, 15 January 1925.

[135]*L'Histoire (qu'on ne connaîtra jamais)*: *The History/Story (that we will never know)* is a 1994 history play centring upon Snorri Sturlluson, complier of Icelandic versions of Norse mythology.

[136]**Ariane and myself:** Cixous began collaborating with Ariane Mnouchkine, founder and director of the Théâtre du Soleil in Paris, in 1981.

and our mourning can begin. In a secret way even a bad end is always at the same time the beginning of a consolation.

One wants to see the end. I too. But as I have said to myself since the age of four in Oran, it is the sign itself of tragedy that *we shall not see the end*, it will come but we will no longer be there to greet it and for it to greet us. There will be no greeting and no salvation. The war will necessarily finish, but my grandfather the soldier died on the front without seeing the end. Hitler died without six million Jews knowing it, at least during their lifetime. I know Khmers who, although saved from the Khmer Rouge camps and living among us, were unable to resume their lives because, since Pol Pot was alive, they had not seen the end of their torture.

It will end nevertheless. But, before the end, I do not know how. At the Théâtre du Soleil, there is a tradition, it is not commented upon, it comes from the well of time: it is understood that I will not write the last scene until the last days of the rehearsal. And it is right. Thus we all experience uncertainty. The players are unable to plan, to cheat. They are in the present.

[…]

The mathematically elegant solution: you wipe everything out. After, we shall see. But it is terrible, cry the spectators. It is unbearable. Then God provides the spectators with an ark. But I am not God, and I was not able to save anyone. When everyone was dead, at the end of *La Ville Parjure*, and when for the first time the members of company discovered the last scene, they were paralyzed with terror and grief. It was worse than *The Eumenides*.[137] At the end of *The Eumenides*, everything is unbearable, the mother does not obtain justice, the matricidal son recovers his assets, and the old goddesses that called for vengeance let themselves be buried like old lambs under the earth. You come out of the theatre with a pang of anguish. But even so the old disappeared goddesses are immortal. Whereas we are mortal. At the sorrow caused by this ending, I, the author, allowed myself to add another scene. Because I, H.C., do not believe that the end ends and closes. Furthermore neither do the players, and the people at the Theatre believe in an end which encloses: they are by definition on the side of resurrection.

So we were all agreed that, after the end, there should be a continuation. Objectively, it happens *elsewhere* and *after* death. All our dead character friends reappear. From where they are, they have an extraordinary point of view over the Theatre of the Earth which they have just left. From this distance the Earth resembles an orange of soft light. They see, they see us. How small, agitated, threatened we are.

I must finish my account here now.

This continuation beyond the end had a very interesting fate: the public was split in two. Those who like us relished the suspension and the impossible. Those who did not tolerate this fantasy, this childishness. The latter came to see me and asked to cut and condemn to the wastepaper basket this moment of transgression, a caprice, an unreality. The Theatre, they said, must obey, it must not overflow. Once it's finished, it's finished. Remove from me this filth, this obscenity. It is outrageous. An insult to political frontiers.

And so the play overflowed into the hall and continued, the battle raged between those who had a conception of tragedy which obeyed the Graecophilosophical prescription programme, for whom history is an uninterrupted net, and those who like me can breathe only through its interruptions, going over the edge between the threads. For me the Theatre is itself the Proof of

---

[137] **Eumenides:** the final tragedy in the *Oresteia* by Aeschylus which Cixous freely adapted in *La Ville Parjure*.

the real transgressive force of the Dream, it is a meteor from the other world. The magical place of a story and a history which we will never know, which awaits us and promises always to exceed – all that we have ever feared, desired. It is the temple of our fortune. That is why 'at the end' of the play-without-end the players return for the final bow, salute and salvation. Ours.

Further reading

Frances Babbage, *Re-Visioning Myth: Modern and Contemporary Drama by Women* (Manchester and New York: Manchester University Press, 2011).

Eleftheria Ioannidou, *Greek Fragments in Postmodern Frames: Rewriting Tragedy 1970–2005* (Oxford: Oxford University Press, 2017).

Susan Sellers (ed.), *The Hélène Cixous Reader* (London and New York: Routledge, 1994).

6.8 JUDITH BUTLER, *ANTIGONE'S CLAIM* (2002)

Judith Butler (born 1956) is an American feminist literary critic known especially for her theory of gender performativity. In *Gender Trouble* (1990) she argues that gender is artificially constructed through a series of social performances that are repeated, revised, and consolidated until they are perceived as natural. In *Antigone's Claim* (2002), Butler turns to the figure of Antigone across three plays by Sophocles to argue that kinship relations are similarly constructed through repeated social performances, which similarly lead us to perceive certain family structures as natural. Because the intergenerational incest at the heart of Antigone's family complicates the plays' kinship relations, her mourning challenges conventional assumptions about natural family order. Critiquing anthropologists, psychoanalysts, and politicians who assume the universality of certain family structures, Butler argues that Antigone's challenges to these structures exposes their constructed nature, implicitly inviting us to consider alternative possibilities for kinship.

In George Steiner's study of the historical appropriations of *Antigone*, he poses a controversial question he does not pursue: What would happen if psychoanalysis were to have taken Antigone rather than Oedipus as its point of departure?[138] Oedipus clearly has his own tragic fate, but Antigone's fate is decidedly postoedipal. Although her brothers are explicitly cursed by her father, does the curse also work on her and, if so, through what furtive and implicit means? The chorus remarks that something of Oedipus' fate is surely working through her own, but what burden of history does she bear? Oedipus comes to know who his mother and father are but finds that his mother is also his wife. Antigone's father is her brother, since they both share a mother in Jocasta, and her brothers are her nephews, sons of her brother–father, Oedipus. The terms of kinship become irreversibly equivocal. Is this part of her tragedy? Does this equivocity of kinship lead to fatality?

Antigone is caught in a web of relations that produce no coherent position within kinship. She is not, strictly speaking, outside kinship or, indeed, unintelligible. Her situation can be understood, but only with a certain amount of horror. Kinship is not simply a situation she is in but a set of practices that she also performs, relations that are reinstituted in time precisely through the practice of their repetition. When she buries her brother, it is not simply that she acts from kinship, as if kinship furnishes a principle for action, but that her action is the action of kinship, the performative repetition that reinstates kinship as a public scandal. Kinship is what she repeats through her action; to redeploy a formulation from David Schneider, it is not a form of being but a form of doing.[139] And her action implicates her in an aberrant repetition of a norm, a custom, a convention, not a formal law but a lawlike regulation of culture that operates with its own contingency.

---

[138][**Butler's note:**] Steiner, *Antigones*, 18.
[139][**Butler's note:**] David Schneider, *A Critique of the Study of Kinship* (Ann Arbor: University of Michigan Press, 1984), 131.

If we recall that for Lacan[140] the symbolic, that set of rules that govern the accession of speech and speakability within culture, is motivated by the father's words, then the father's words are surely upon Antigone; they are, as it were, the medium within which she acts and in whose voice she defends her act. She transmits those words in aberrant form, transmitting them loyally and betraying them by sending them in directions they were never intended to travel. The words are repeated, and their repeatability relies on the deviation that the repetition performs. The aberration that is her speech and her act facilitates such transmissions. Indeed, she is transmitting more than one discourse at once, for the demands that are upon her come from more than one source: her brother also petitions her to give him a decent burial, a demand that in some ways conflicts with the curse that Oedipus has laid upon his son, to die at battle and be received by the underworld. These two demands converge and produce a certain interference in the transmitting of the paternal word. After all, if the father is the brother, then what finally is the difference between them? And what is to elevate the demand of Oedipus over the demand of Polyneices?

The words are upon her, but what does that mean? How does a curse come to inform the action that fulfills the prophecy inherent in the curse? What is the temporality of the curse such that the actions that she takes create an equivocation between the words that are upon her, that she suffers, and the act that she herself performs? How are we to understand the strange *nomos* of the act itself? How does the word of the Other become one's own deed, and what is the temporality of this repetition in which the deed that is produced as a result of the curse is also in some ways an aberrant repetition, one that affirms that the curse produces unanticipated consequences?

Oedipus, of course, unknowingly sleeps with his mother and slays his father, and is driven into the wilderness accompanied by Antigone. In *Oedipus at Colonus*[141] the two of them, along with a small party of followers, are given shelter by Theseus in a land governed by Athens. Oedipus learns, that his sons have explicitly forbidden his return to Thebes and also learns that they have turned against one another in a bitter battle for the throne. Toward the end of that play, the second of the trilogy, Polyneices[142] visits Oedipus and calls upon him to return. Oedipus not only refuses but levels a curse against Polyneices, that 'you shall never conquer in war your native land; … but shall perish by your brother's hand, and kill him who drove you out!' (1385–93).

Antigone stands by, importuning her father to show benevolence toward Polyneices, and fails. And it remains unclear whether the brother whose act will kill him is Eteocles who delivers the fatal blow, or Oedipus, whose curse both predicts and mandates the blow itself. Polyneices, despite Antigone's protest, decides nevertheless to go into battle with Eteocles, and Antigone is left, crying out 'My heart is broken!' She then speaks a line that prefigures her own knowing approach to her own fate: 'Brother, how can anyone *not* mourn, seeing you set out to death so clear before you go with open eyes to death!' (Grene 1645–9). Indeed, Antigone

---

[140]**Lacan:** Jacques Lacan (1901–81) was a French psychoanalyst who identified the development of the subject with the realms of the symbolic, the real, and the imaginary; linked with language, rules, and the father, the symbolic realm serves to organize the subject and make the psyche accessible.

[141]*Oedipus at Colonus:* tragedy by Sophocles, *c.*406 BCE, depicting the end of Oedipus' life.

[142]**Polyneices:** one of Oedipus' sons (and brothers) by Jocasta; the other is Eteocles.

will and – given the chronology of the plays – 'already has' undergone precisely the fate she predicts for her brother, to enter death knowingly.

Antigone not only loses her brother to her father's curse, words that quite literally yield the force of annihilation, but she then loses her father to death by the curse that is upon him. Words and deeds become fatally entangled in the familial scene. The acts of Polyneices and Eteocles seem to fulfill and enact the father's words, but his words – and his deeds – are also compelled by a curse upon him, the curse of Laius. Antigone worries over their fate even as she embarks upon her own course of action for which death is a necessary conclusion. Her desire to save her brothers from their fate is overwhelmed, it seems, by her desire to join them in their fate.

Before he dies, Oedipus makes several utterances that assume the status of a curse. He condemns her, but the force of the condemnation is to bind her to him. His words culminate in her own permanent lovelessness, one that is mandated by Oedipus' demand for loyalty, a demand that verges on incestuous possessiveness: 'From none did you have love more than from this man, without whom you will now spend the remainder of your life' (1617–9). His words exert a force in time that exceeds the temporality of their enunciation: they demand that for all time she have no man except for the man who is dead, and though this is a demand, a curse, made *by* Oedipus, who positions himself as her only one, it is clear that she both honors and disobeys this curse as she displaces her love for her father onto her brother. Indeed, she takes her brother to be her only one – she would risk defying the official edict for no kin but Polyneices. Thus she betrays Oedipus even as she fulfills the terms of his curse. She will only love a man who is dead, and hence she will love no man. She obeys his demand, but promiscuously, for he is clearly not the only dead man she loves and, indeed, not the ultimate one. Is the love for the one dissociable from the love for the other? And when it is her 'most precious brother' for whom she commits her criminal and honorable act, is it clear that this brother is Polyneices, or could it be Oedipus?

Knowing that he is dying, Oedipus asks, 'And will they even shroud my body in Theban soil?' (406) and learns that his crime makes that impossible. He is thus buried by Theseus out of everyone else's sight, including Antigone's. Then, Antigone, in the play by that name, mimes the act of the strong and true Theseus and buries her brother out of sight, making sure that Polyneices' shade is composed of Theban dust. Antigone's assertive burial, which she performs twice, might be understood to be for both, a burial that at once reflects and institutes the equivocation of brother and father. They are, after all, already interchangeable for her, and yet her act reinstitutes and reelaborates that interchangeability.

Although Sophocles wrote *Antigone* several years before *Oedipus at Colonus*,[143] the action that takes place in the former *follows* the action of the latter. What is the significance of this belatedness? Are the words that goad the action understandable only in retrospect? Can the implications of the curse, understood as extended action, be understood only retrospectively? The action predicted by the curse for the future turns out to be an action that has been happening all along, such that the forward movement of time is precisely what is inverted through the temporality of the curse. The curse establishes a temporality for the action it

---

[143]***Antigone…Oedipus at Colonus:*** Sophocles wrote *Antigone* in or before 441 BCE, well before *Oedipus the King* (429 BCE) or *Oedipus at Colonus* (c.406 BCE).

ordains that predates the curse itself. The words bring into the future what has always already been happening.

Antigone is to love no man except the man who is dead, but in some sense she is also a man. And this is also the title that Oedipus bestows upon her, a gift or reward for her loyalty. When Oedipus is banished, Antigone cares for him, and in her loyalty, is referred to as a 'man' (*aner*). Indeed, she follows him loyally into the wilderness, but at some point that following imperceptibly turns into a scene in which *she* leads *him*: 'Follow, follow me this way with your unseeing steps, father, where I lead you!' (183–4).

Indeed, she is at once cursed with a loyalty to a dead man, a loyalty that makes her manly, compels her to acquire the attribute that carries his approbation such that desire and identification are acutely confounded in a melancholic bind. Oedipus clearly understands gender as something of a curse itself, since one of the ways in which he condemns his sons is by leveling his accusation through the trope of an orientalizing gender inversion:

> Those two conform together to the customs that prevail in Egypt in their nature and the nurture of their lives! For there the males sit in their houses working at the loom, and their consorts provide the necessities of life out of doors. And in your case, my children, those who ought to perform this labour sit at home and keep the house like maidens, and you two *in their place* bear the burdens of your unhappy father's sorrows. (337–44, my emphasis)

Later, Oedipus maintains that Ismene[144] and Antigone have quite literally taken the place of their brothers, acquiring masculine gender along the way. Addressing his sons, he says:

> If I had not begotten these daughters to attend, me, I would not be living, for all you did for me. But as it is they preserve me, they are my nurses, they are men, not women, when it comes to working for me; but you are sons of some other, and no sons of mine. (1559–63)

His daughters thus become his sons, but these same children (Antigone and Ismene), he maintains earlier, are also his 'sisters' (328). And so we've arrived at something like kinship trouble at the heart of Sophocles. Antigone has, then, already taken the place of her brother; when she breaks with Ismene, it mirrors the break that Polyneices has made with Eteocles, thus acting, we might say, as brothers do. By the time this drama is done, she has thus taken the place of nearly every man in her family. Is this an effect of the words that are upon her?

[…]

The Antigonean revision of psychoanalytic theory might put into question the assumption that the incest taboo legitimates and normalizes kinship based in biological reproduction and the heterosexualization of the family. Although psychoanalysis has often insisted that normalization is invariably disrupted and foiled by what cannot be ordered by regulatory norms, it has rarely addressed the question of how new forms of kinship can and do arise on the basis of the incest taboo. From the presumption that one cannot—or ought not to—choose

---

[144]**Ismene:** Oedipus' daughter (and sister), Antigone's sister.

one's closest family members as one's lovers and marital partners, it does not follow that the bonds of kinship that *are* possible assume any particular form.

To the extent that the incest taboo contains its infraction within itself, it does not simply prohibit incest but rather sustains and cultivates incest as a necessary specter of social dissolution, a specter without which social bonds cannot emerge. Thus the prohibition against incest in the play *Antigone* requires a rethinking of prohibition itself, not merely as a negative or privative operation of power but as one that works precisely through proliferating through displacement the very crime that it bars. The taboo, and its threatening figuration of incest, delineates lines of kinship that harbor incest as their ownmost possibility, establishing 'aberration' at the heart of the norm. Indeed, my question is whether it can also become the basis for a socially survivable aberration of kinship in which the norms that govern legitimate and illegitimate modes of kin association might be more radically redrawn.

Antigone says 'brother', but does she mean 'father'? She asserts her public right to grieve her kin, but how many of her kin does she leave ungrieved? Considering how many are dead in her family, is it possible that mother and father and repudiated sister and other brother are condensed there at the site of the irreproducible brother? What kind of psychoanalytic approach to Antigone's act would foreclose in advance any consideration of overdetermination at the level of the object? This equivocation at the site of the kinship term signals a decidedly postoedipal dilemma, one in which kin positions tend to slide into one another, in which Antigone is the brother, the brother is the father, and in which psychically, linguistically, this is true regardless of whether they are dead or alive; for anyone living in this slide of identifications, their fate will be an uncertain one, living within death, dying within life.

One might simply say in a psychoanalytic spirit that Antigone represents a *perversion* of the law and conclude that the law requires perversion and that, in some dialectical sense, the law is, therefore, perverse. But to establish the structural necessity of perversion to the law is to posit a static relation between the two in which each entails the other and, in that sense, is nothing without the other. This form of negative dialectics produces the satisfaction that the law is *invested* in perversion and that the law is not what it seems to be. It does not help to make possible, however, other forms of social life, inadvertent possibilities produced by the prohibition that come to undermine the conclusion that an invariant social organization of sexuality follows of necessity from the prohibitive law. What happens when the perverse or the impossible emerges in the language of the law and makes its claim precisely there in the sphere of legitimate kinship that depends on its exclusion or pathologization?[145]

[...]

What is the contemporary voice that enters into the language of the law to disrupt its univocal workings? Consider that in the situation of blended families, a child says 'mother' and might expect more than one individual to respond to the call. Or that, in the case of adoption, a child might say 'father' and might mean both the absent phantasm she never

---

[145][**Butler's note:**] Here I am not suggesting that the perverse simply inhabits the norm as something that remains autonomous, but neither am I suggesting that it is dialectically assimilated into the norm itself. It might be understood to signal the impossibility of maintaining a sovereign lock on any claim to legitimacy, since the reiteration of the claim outside of its legitimated site of enunciation shows that the legitimate site is not the source of its effectivity. Here I am indebted to what I take to be Homi Bhabha's significant reformulation dispersed throughout his work of both speech act theory and the Foucaultian notion of discourse developed in the latter's *Archaeology of Knowledge*.

knew as well as the one who assumes that place in living memory. The child might mean that at once, or sequentially, or in ways that are not always clearly disarticulated from one another. Or when a young girl comes to be fond of her stepbrother, what dilemma of kinship is she in? For a woman who is a single mother and has her child without a man, is the father still there, a spectral 'position' or 'place' that remains unfilled, or is there no such 'place' or 'position'? Is the father absent, or does this child have no father, no position, and no inhabitant? Is this a loss, which assumes the unfulfilled norm, or is it another configuration of primary attachment whose primary loss is not to have a language in which to articulate its terms? And when there are two men or two women who parent, are we to assume that some primary division of gendered roles organizes their psychic places within the scene, so that the empirical contingency of two same-gendered parents is nevertheless straightened out by the presocial psychic place of the Mother and Father into which they enter? Does it make sense on these occasions to insist that there are symbolic positions of Mother and Father that every psyche must accept regardless of the social form that kinship takes? Or is that a way of reinstating a heterosexual organization of parenting at the psychic level that can accommodate all manner of gender variation at the social level? Here it seems that the very division between the psychic or symbolic, on the one hand, and the social, on the other, occasions this pre-emptory normalization of the social field.

I write this, of course, against the background of a substantial legacy of feminist theory that has taken the Lévi-Straussian[146] analytic of kinship as the basis for its own version of structuralist and poststructuralist psychoanalysis and the theorization of a primary sexual difference. It is, of course, one function of the incest taboo to prohibit sexual exchange among kin relations or, rather, to establish kin relations precisely on the basis of those taboos. The question, however, is whether the incest taboo has also been mobilized to *establish* certain forms of kinship as the only intelligible and livable ones. Thus one hears, for instance, the legacy of this tradition in psychoanalysis invoked by psychoanalysts in Paris in recent months against the prospect of 'contracts of alliance,' construed by conservatives as a bid for gay marriage. Although the rights of gay people to adopt children were not included in the proposed contracts, those who opposed the proposal fear that such contracts might lead to that eventuality and argue that any children raised in a gay family would run the immanent threat of psychosis, as if some structure, necessarily named 'Mother' and necessarily named 'Father' and established at the level of the symbolic, was a necessary psychic support against an engorgement by the Real. Similarly, Jacques-Alain Miller argued that whereas he was clear that homosexual relations deserve recognition, they should not qualify for marriage because two men together, deprived of the feminine presence, would not be able to bring fidelity to the relationship (a wonderful claim made against the backdrop of our presidential evidence of the binding power of marriage on heterosexual fidelity). Yet other Lacanian practitioners who trace the sources of autism in the 'paternal gap' or 'absence' similarly predict psychotic consequences for children with lesbian parents.

These views commonly maintain that alternative kinship arrangements attempt to revise psychic structures in ways that lead to tragedy again, figured incessantly as the tragedy of and

---

[146]**Lévi-Straussian:** Claude Lévi-Strauss (1908–2009) was a French anthropologist known for developing the theory of structuralism, which identifies meaning as produced by underlying structures of thought across cultures. Lévi-Strauss argued that kinship relations were structured especially by marriage alliances, also known as structures of exchange, and the incest taboo.

for the child. No matter what one ultimately thinks of the political value of gay marriage, and I myself am a skeptic here for political reasons I outline elsewhere,[147] the public debate on its legitimacy becomes the occasion for a set of homophobic discourses that must be resisted on independent grounds. Consider that the horror of incest, the moral revulsion it compels in some, is not that far afield from the same horror and revulsion felt toward lesbian and gay sex, and is not unrelated to the intense moral condemnation of voluntary single parenting, or gay parenting, or parenting arrangements with more than two adults involved (practices that can be used as evidence to support a claim to remove a child from the custody of the parent in several states in the United States). These various modes in which the oedipal mandate fails to produce normative family all risk entering into the metonymy of that moralized sexual horror that is perhaps most fundamentally associated with incest.

The abiding assumption of the symbolic, that stable kinship norms support our abiding sense of culture's intelligibility, can be found, of course, outside of the Lacanian discourse. It is invoked in popular culture, by psychiatric 'experts' and policy makers to thwart the legal demands of a social movement that threatens to expose the aberration at the heart of the heterosexual norm. It is quite possible to argue in a Lacanian vein that the symbolic place of the mother can be multiply occupied, that it is never identified or identifiable with an individual, and that this is what distinguishes it as symbolic. But why is the symbolic place singular and its inhabitants multiple? Or consider the liberal gesture in which one maintains that the place of the father and the place of the mother are necessary, but hey, anyone of any gender can fill them. The structure is purely formal, its defenders say, but note how its very formalism secures the structure against critical challenge. What are we to make of an inhabitant of the form that brings the form to crisis? If the relation between the inhabitant and the form is arbitrary, it is still structured, and its structure works to domesticate in advance any radical reformulation of kinship.[148]

The figure of Antigone, however, may well compel a reading that challenges that structure, for she does not conform to the symbolic law and she does not prefigure a final restitution of the law. Though entangled in the terms of kinship, she is at the same time outside those norms. Her crime is confounded by the fact that the kinship line from which she descends, and which she transmits, is derived from a paternal position that is already confounded by the manifestly incestuous act that is the condition of her own existence, which makes her brother her father, which begins a narrative in which she occupies, linguistically, every kin position *except* 'mother' and occupies them at the expense of the coherence of kinship and gender.

---

[147][**Butler's note:**] See my contribution, 'Competing Universalities', to Judith Butler, Ernesto Laclau, and Slavoj Žižek, *Universality, Hegemony, Contingency* (London: Verso, 2000).

[148][**Butler's note:**] It has been one strategy here to argue that the incest taboo does not always produce normative family, but it is perhaps more important to realize that the normative family that it does produce is not always what it seems. There is, for instance, clearly merit in the analysis offered by Linda Alcoff and others that heterosexual incest within heterosexually normative families is an extension rather than abrogation of patriarchal prerogative within heterosexual normativity. Prohibition is not fully or exclusively privative, that is, just as prohibition requires *and produces* the spectre of crime it bars. And for Alcoff, in an interesting Foucaultian move, the prohibition offers the cover that protects and abets the practice of incest. But is there any reason to check the productivity of the incest taboo here, at this dialectical inversion of its aim? See Linda Alcoff, 'Survivor Discourse: Transgression or Recuperation?' SIGNS 18, no. 2 (Winter 1993): 260–91. See also for a very interesting and brave Foucaultian discussion of the criminalization of incest, Vikki Bell, *Interrogating Incest: Feminism, Foucault and the Law* (London: Routledge, 1993).

Although not quite a queer heroine, Antigone does emblematize a certain heterosexual fatality that remains to be read. Whereas some might conclude that the tragic fate she suffers is the tragic fate of any and all who would transgress the lines of kinship that confer intelligibility on culture, her example, as it were, gives rise to a contrary sort of critical intervention: What in her act is fatal for heterosexuality in its normative sense? And to what other ways of organizing sexuality might a consideration of that fatality give rise?

[…]

Who then is Antigone within such a scene, and what are we to make of her words, words that become dramatic events, performative acts? She is not of the human but speaks in its language. Prohibited from action, she nevertheless acts, and her act is hardly a simple assimilation to an existing norm. And in acting, as one who has no right to act, she upsets the vocabulary of kinship that is a precondition of the human, implicitly raising the question for us of what those preconditions really must be. She speaks within the language of entitlement from which she is excluded, participating in the language of the claim with which no final identification is possible. If she is human, then the human has entered into catachresis:[149] we no longer know its proper usage. And to the extent that she occupies the language that can never belong to her, she functions as a chiasm[150] within the vocabulary of political norms. If kinship is the precondition of the human, then Antigone is the occasion for a new field of the human, achieved through political catachresis, the one that happens when the less than human speaks as human, when gender is displaced, and kinship founders on its own founding laws. She acts, she speaks, she becomes one for whom the speech act is a fatal crime, but this fatality exceeds her life and enters the discourse of intelligibility as its own promising fatality, the social form of its aberrant, unprecedented future.

Further reading

Derek Barker, 'Judith Butler's Postmodern Antigone', in *Tragedy and Citizenship: Conflict, Reconciliation, and Democracy from Haemon to Hegel* (Albany, NY: SUNY Press, 2009), 119–38.

David W. McIvor, 'Bringing Ourselves to Grief: Judith Butler and the Politics of Mourning', *Political Theory* 40, no. 4 (2012): 409–36.

Thomas Strong, 'Kinship between Judith Butler and Anthropology?', *Ethnos* 67, no. 3 (2002): 401–18.

---

[149]**Catachresis:** improper use (Greek); a figure of speech in which a word or phrase is used significantly differently from conventional usage. Butler uses the word here to suggest that identifying Antigone as human requires rethinking the word's meanings.

[150]**Chiasm:** crossing (Greek); a grammatical structure in which word-order is inverted in one of two parallel clauses. Butler borrows a grammatical term here to situate Antigone within a set of kinship structures, and to suggest that she complicates these structures.

6.9 DAVID SCOTT, *CONSCRIPTS OF MODERNITY* (2004)

David Scott (born in Jamaica, 1958) is Professor of Anthropology at Columbia University in New York. He researches Caribbean culture, history, and politics as well as postcolonial criticism and ideology more broadly. His first books *Refashioning Futures: Criticism after Postcoloniality* (1999) and *Conscripts of Modernity: The Tragedy of Colonial Enlightenment* (2004) scrutinize the ways in which the relationships between the colonial past and postcolonial present have been imagined and plotted. Genre, especially the differences between romance and tragedy, is central to Scott's reconceptualization of questions of politics and time. His analysis rejects the narrative trajectory of anti-colonial works like Frantz Fanon's *The Wretched of the Earth* (1961), which he characterizes as revolutionary romance, arguing that its teleological narrative of oppression though resistance to emancipation fails to account for the collapse or exhaustion of numerous anti-colonial movements and regimes. In *Conscripts of Modernity*, he offers a close-reading of the revised edition of C.L.R. James's landmark history of the eighteenth-century Haitian revolution, *Black Jacobins* (1963), to argue, instead, that tragedy offers the most viable way of making sense of traditional anti-colonial narratives.

Anticolonialism has been written in the narrative mode of Romance and, consequently, has projected a distinctive image of the past (one cast in terms of what colonial power denied or negated) and a distinctive story about the relation between that past and the hoped-for future (one emplotted as a narrative of revolutionary overcoming.) But after Badung,[151] after the end of anticolonialism's promise, our sense of time and possibility have altered so significantly that it is hard to continue to live in the present as though it were a mere transitory moment in an assured momentum from a wounded past to a future salvation. The horizon that made that erstwhile story so compelling as a dynamo for intellectual and political work has collapsed. It is now a superseded future, one of our futures past...

In my view we live in tragic times. Not meaningless times, not merely dark or catastrophic times but times that in fundamental ways are distressingly off-kilter in the specific sense that the critical languages in which we wagered our moral vision and our political hope (including, importantly, the languages of black emancipation and postcolonial critique) are no longer commensurate with the world they were meant to understand, engage, and overcome. And consequently, to reinvoke Raymond Williams's deeply poignant phrase, we are living with the 'slowly settling loss of any acceptable future'.[152] It seems to me, therefore, that a tragic sensibility is a particularly apt and timely one because, not driven by the confident hubris of teleologies that extract the future seamlessly from the past, and more attuned at the same time to the intricacies, ambiguities, and paradoxes of the relation between actions and their consequences,

---

[151]**Badung:** this refers to a mass suicide, known as the Puputan Badung, which took place in Indonesia on 20 September 1906. Rather than submit to Dutch colonial forces, the people of Badung killed themselves with knives or walked directly into enemy fire.
[152]**Raymond Williams's ... phrase:** the quotation is from the afterword to Raymond Williams's *Modern Tragedy* (London: Verso, 1979), 209. See extract 5.9.

and intentions and the chance contingencies that sometimes undo them, it recasts our historical temporalities in significant ways.

[...]

On Revolution is sometimes thought of as the third and final volume in Hannah Arendt's[153] trilogy on political theory. And indeed, anyone familiar with the first two, *The Origins of Totalitarianism* and *The Human Condition* (as well as the collection of essays that complements these monographs, *Between Past and Future*),[154] will easily recognize that although the mood and tone of each of these books is different ... the central preoccupations are much the same: the nature of freedom, the virtue of public action and speech, the idea of authority, the concept of politics and its distinctive realm, and so on.[155] In many ways, Arendt is pursuing an interconnected project of remarkable consistency and continuity. At the same time, however, *On Revolution* is its own profoundly original book. It is, above all, Arendt's lament for what she calls the 'lost treasure' of the revolutionary tradition.[156] All revolutions since the French Revolution (the constitutive point of origin of the revolutionary tradition) have been carried out in the name of freedom, but all of them, Arendt argues, have missed the opportunity to found freedom – that is to say, they have failed to give freedom an appropriate and durable political-institutional form. As a consequence, she maintains, the 'revolutionary spirit' embodied in the principles of 'public freedom, public happiness, and public spirit' (the principles that inspired and motivated the eighteenth-century revolutionaries) has faded not only from practice but even from memory. In *The Black Jacobins* too, ... James is also asking a question about the fate and the legacy of the eighteenth-century revolutionary tradition, how it shaped and how it doomed his tragic hero, Toussaint Louverture.[157]

[...]

For Arendt there are only two eighteenth-century revolutions, the French and the American. It is a paradoxical fact that she is unsparingly contemptuous of those who, with familiar Eurocentric hubris, have 'proceeded as though there never had occurred a revolution in the New World and as though there never had been any American notions and experiences in the realm of politics and government worth thinking about',[158] when she herself proceeds as though the American Revolution were the only revolution in the New World in the eighteenth century.

---

[153]**Hannah Arendt:** Hannah Arendt (1906–75), German-American philosopher and political theorist.

[154][Scott's note]: Hannah Arendt, *The Origins of Totalitarianism* (New York: Harcourt, Brace and Co., 1951); and idem., *Between Past and Future: Eight Exercises in Political Thought* (New York: Viking, 1961).

[155][Scott's note]: See Elisabeth Young-Bruehl, *Hannah Arendt: For Love of the World* (New Haven: Yale University Press, 1982), for some of the backgrounds and connections among these books. It is an interesting fact that of all of them it is *The Origins of Totalitarianism* that has seemed to many in our time the most pertinent and that has received the most systematic attention. See, for example, the recent issue of *Social Research* 69, no. 2 (Summer 2002), devoted to 'Hannah Arendt: *The Origins of Totalitarianism*: Fifty Years Later'.

[156][Scott's note]: It is an interesting fact that one of the inspirations for *On Revolution* was Rosa Luxemburg, with whom Arendt formed a strong identification and whose book *The Russian Revolution* she read while teaching at the University of California, Berkeley, in the mid-1950s. See Young-Bruehl, *Hannah Arendt*, 294. Many historians – Eric Hobsbawm among them – found *On Revolution* wanting in the way of proper social history. It was short, or misinformed, on the facts. But as Elisabeth Young-Bruehl has written: 'Hannah Arendt discussed revolutions not in order to outline their histories or distinguish their types but in order to present an ideal for practice' (406). For a discussion of responses to *On Revolution*, see Young-Bruehl, *Hannah Arendt*, 402–6.

[157]**Toussaint Louverture:** Toussaint Louverture, or François Dominique Toussaint (1743–1803), was the leader of the Haitian independence movement at the end of the eighteenth century. Scott suggests that he is figured as the tragic hero of James's *Black Jacobins*.

[158][Scott's note]: Arendt, *On Revolution*, 216.

It was as though Thomas Jefferson and James Madison and John Adams were the only citizens of the New World who had 'notions and experiences in the realm of politics and government worth thinking about', as though Toussaint Louverture were a minor or negligible figure on the world-historical stage.[159] This is precisely the kind of hubris against which *The Black Jacobins* is written. It is the meaning of James's boldly stated vindicationist claim in the preface that 'with the single exception of Bonaparte himself no single figure appeared on the historical stage more greatly gifted than this Negro, a slave till he was 45'.[160] But Arendt's oversight is all the more puzzling, and all the more disappointing, because what she is lamenting in *On Revolution* is precisely the failure of memory; she is in fact urging the importance of 'remembrance' to sustaining the spirit of the revolutionary tradition. Perhaps in this James's fidelity to memory as a resource of criticism commands a more profound regard.

Indeed there is an unforgettable moment in *The Black Jacobins* in which James seems to be responding to Hannah Arendt on just this question. The year is 1797. In France royalist and proslavery colonists have made a significant comeback with the reactionary Vaublanc[161] representing them in the newly elected legislature. They would be purged before the end of the year, but it is now clear to Toussaint that France can no longer be depended upon. In San Domingo,[162] the Jacobin and great liberator Léger-Félicité Sonthonax[163] names Toussaint commander-in-chief of the French republican army, but soon finds himself urged to return to France, ostensibly to assume his seat in the French legislature. For Toussaint, the game is up. He has so far played it with a resolute commitment to principle and honor. But the circle has slowly closed and he has finally come face to face with the insurmountable impossibility of simultaneously holding on to power (a power that would preserve the liberty of the former slaves) and loyalty to France. On November 5 he writes a letter to the Directory[164] in which, while carefully disavowing suspicion of their intentions and asserting his personal faithful attachment to France, he makes clear that any attempt to reenslave the blacks will be met with determined force: 'we have known how to face dangers to obtain our liberty, we shall know how to brave death to keep it'. For James, this is Toussaint Louverture's finest political and diplomatic moment. If the letter is a masterpiece it is James's commentary that deserves quoting at length:

> Pericles on Democracy, Paine on the Rights of Man, the Declaration of Independence, the Communist Manifesto, these are some of the political documents which, whatever the wisdom or weakness of their analysis, have moved men and will continue to move them, for the writers, some of them in spite of themselves, strike chords and awaken aspirations that sleep in the hearts of the majority of every age. But Pericles, Tom Paine,

---

[159][**Scott's note**]: It is not that blacks are invisible to Arendt. Though the question is far from adequately developed she is aware of the conundrum of race and black misery in the problem of the American Revolution. See *On Revolution*, 71–2. For some sense of her ambivalent relation to the Black Power movement of the 1960s, see Young-Bruehl, *Hannah Arendt*, 417–9.

[160][**Scott's note**]: C.L.R. James, *The Black Jacobins* (London: Secker and Warburg, 1938), vii; idem., *The Black Jacobins*, 2nd ed. rev. (New York: Vintage, 1963), x.

[161]**Vaublanc:** Vincent-Marie Viénot de Vaublanc (1756–1845), French royalist politician.

[162]**San Domingo:** the former, colonial-era name for Haiti.

[163]**Léger-Félicité Sonthonax:** Léger-Félicité Sonthonax (1763–1813) was a French abolitionist, Jacobin and opponent of the French royalist party who was tasked with preserving French control of Haiti.

[164]**the Directory:** the Directory was a committee which governed France between 1795 and 1799.

Jefferson, Marx and Engels, were men of a liberal education, formed in the tradition of ethics, philosophy, and history. Toussaint was a slave, not six years out of slavery, bearing alone the unaccustomed burden of war and government, dictating his thoughts in the crude words of a broken dialect, written and rewritten by his secretaries until their devotion and his will had hammered them into adequate shape. Superficial people have read his career in terms of personal ambition. This letter is their answer. Personal ambition he had. But he accomplished what he did because, superbly gifted, he incarnated the determination of his people never to be slaves again.

Soldier and administrator above all yet his declaration is a masterpiece of prose excelled by no other writer of the revolution. Leader of a backward and ignorant mass, he is yet in the forefront of the historical movement of his time. The blacks were taking their part in the destruction of European feudalism begun by the French Revolution and liberty and equality, the slogans of the revolution meant far more to them than to any Frenchman. That was why in the hour of danger Toussaint, uninstructed as he was, could find the language of Diderot, Rousseau, and Raynal, of Mirabeau, Robespierre, and Danton. And in one respect he excelled them all. For even these masters of the spoken and written word, owing to the class-complications of their society, had always to pause, to hesitate, to qualify. Toussaint could defend the freedom of the blacks without reservation, and this gave to his declaration a strength and a single-mindedness rare in the great documents of the time. The French bourgeoisie could not understand it. Rivers of blood were to flow before they understood that elevated as was his tone Toussaint had written neither bombast nor rhetoric but the simple and sober truth.[165]

This is C.L.R. James's answer to Hannah Arendt. It is a moment in which he shows Toussaint Louverture in the incomparable role of a political statesman and strategist, the embodiment of the *vita activa*, stepping into the political realm and acting with brilliant and eloquent decision.

However, if in all the conventionally recognizable ways Arendt was a Eurocentric, this is not all that she was; nor is it the only or the most important lesson to be drawn from *On Revolution*. The story of Toussaint Louverture in *The Black Jacobins* is, I believe, the sort of story of the tragedy of the revolutionary tradition that *On Revolution* wishes us to remember, a solemn story of the surrendering of freedom to necessity, of the political to the social. Or at least in my view one can read *The Black Jacobins* as a story about the distinction between liberation and freedom and the relation between these and tragedy. On this reading, the tragedy of Toussaint Louverture is the tragedy of a leader who (like Robespierre and Lenin) felt obliged to forgo the principles of public freedom, public happiness, and public spirit – however temporary he might have imagined the contingency to be. It is a memorable and central theme in James's narrative that the end of white domination and the tyranny of plantation slavery was one thing, the fashioning of a free black republic, the creation of a public and constitutional arena in which the newly emancipated black could *appear* and have her voice heard, quite another. All of Toussaint's later errors were committed within the conflicted space of this insurmountable conundrum. Faced with economic devastation, foreign military encirclement aiming to return the blacks to slavery, and an increasingly restless, hungry, and suspicious mass of emancipated

---

[165][**Scott's note**]: James, *The Black Jacobins*, 162–3 (1st ed.), 197–8 (2nd ed.).

slaves, Toussaint had precious little space within which to act. But act he had to. And when he did, he (again like Robespierre and Lenin) opted to secure the economic (necessity) over the risk of the political (freedom) on the calculated grounds that the former was at least a guarantee of the latter. Surely one of the sobering lessons of the story of the downfall of Toussaint Louverture is that nothing guarantees freedom but the political commitment to its founding – and even this, James is likely to have added, is often not enough.

What then is the sense of the tragic for our postcolonial time? Because tragedy has a more respectful attitude to the contingencies of the past in the present, to the uncanny ways in which its remains come back to usurp our hopes and subvert our ambitions, it demands from us more patience for paradox and more openness to chance than the narrative of anticolonial Romanticism does, confident in its striving and satisfied in its own sufficiency. The colonial past may never let go. This is a hard truth. Toussaint Louverture, James's magnificent hero, arrived at this insight by a long and difficult road and without the benefit of precedent to guide him. Nor were there second chances, the option of starting over. And Toussaint Louverture paid for the lesson of his insight with his life. The knowledge of our postcolonial selves this insight has enabled is Toussaint's gift to modernity's conscripts, and the price he paid for it is our debt to his doomed endeavor. The sense of the tragic for our postcolonial time is not the belief that we are likewise doomed, that change is futile, that in the end we are mere pawns of imperial tyranny. For *The Black Jacobins*, the sense of the tragic for our postcolonial time is an awareness of Toussaint's gift: the awareness that our own struggle for alternative futures, beginning as they do with the inheritance of what has gone before, has always to be tempered by our remembrance of his example.

Further reading

'David Scott by Stuart Hall', https://bombmagazine.org/articles/david-scott/.

Timothy J. Reiss, *Against Autonomy: Global Dialectics of Cultural Exchange* (Stanford, CA: Stanford University Press, 2002).

David Scott, 'The Tragic Vision in Postcolonial Time', *PMLA* 129, no. 4 (2014): 799–808.

6.10 MARTHA NUSSBAUM, 'THE "MORALITY OF PITY"' (2008)

Martha Nussbaum (born 1946) is an American philosopher who specializes in ancient philosophy, political philosophy, feminism, and ethics. Throughout her writings, she frequently turns to tragedy to reflect on ethical questions. In *The Fragility of Goodness: Luck and Ethics in Greek Tragedy and Philosophy* (1986), she explores the tension dramatized in Greek tragedy between the freedom to make choices and the constraints imposed on those choices by external forces. Recognizing vulnerability and human limitations, Nussbaum asserts, is crucial to acting ethically. In 'The "Morality of Pity"' (2008) she turns to Sophocles' tragedy *Philoctetes* to examine the emotion of pity. Arguing that pity is frequently justified and valuable in spurring action, Nussbaum acknowledges that it can also be unreliable and arbitrarily directed, and requires careful cultivation. Tragedy, she suggests, can help us become more ethical by making us appreciate the urgency of responding to suffering.

It was precisely here that I saw the beginning of the end, the dead stop, a retrospective weariness, the will turning against life, the tender and sorrowful signs of the ultimate illness: I understood the ever-spreading morality of pity that had seized even on philosophers and made them ill, as the sinister symptom of a European culture that had itself become sinister.

Nietzsche, Genealogy of Morals, Preface, Section 5

The savages in North America, we are told, assume upon all occasions the greatest indifference, and would think themselves degraded if they should ever appear in any respect to be overcome, either by love, or grief, or resentment. Their magnanimity and self-command, in this respect, are almost beyond the conception of Europeans.... When a savage is made prisoner of war, and receives, as is usual, the sentence of death from his conquerors, he hears it without expressing any emotion, and afterwards submits to the most dreadful torments, without ever bemoaning himself, or discovering any other passion but contempt of his enemies. When he is hung by the shoulders over a slow fire, he derides his tormentors.... After he has been scorched and burnt, and lacerated in all the most tender and sensible parts of his body for several hours together, he is often allowed, to prolong his misery, a short respite, and is taken down from the stake: he employs this interval in talking upon all indifferent subjects, inquires after the news of the country, and seems indifferent about nothing but his own situation.

Adam Smith, The Theory of Moral Sentiments, V.2.9

The Pity Debate

Pity is problematic. The emotion that lies at the heart of ancient Greek tragedy has provoked intense debate, both in Greco-Roman antiquity and in modern Europe. Some modern philosophers, embracing the general ethos of the ancient Greek tragic poets, hold that pity is a valuable social emotion without which it would be difficult to establish decent political communities. Jean-Jacques Rousseau,[166] devoting an entire book in *Emile* to pity and its social role, connects the emotion strongly to the very possibility of republican government, saying that it brings people together around the thought of their common weakness and vulnerability, in the process undermining hierarchies of title, rank, and wealth. Others, following Plato and the ancient Greek and Roman Stoics[167] – and adding some further arguments of their own – hold that pity saps the civic fabric and produces bad citizens, soft, sluggish, and effeminate.[168]

Sophocles' *Philoctetes*[169] is the pity play par excellence. If most extant fifth-century tragedies do indeed, as Aristotle claims, take the pitiable as their subject matter, showing heroic characters coming to grief in ways for which they are not (or not primarily) blameworthy, the *Philoctetes* appears to be constructed deliberately so as to highlight the prerequisites and workings of the emotion. As Stephen Halliwell puts it, it provides 'a remarkable and revealing case of an individual tragedy whose very action comes to revolve around the operation of pity.'[170] Pain, sickness, weakness, hunger, cold, isolation, unjust treatment – all these classical occasions for pity, recognized in Aristotle's analysis in the *Rhetoric*[171] (II.8), turn up as features of Philoctetes' life on the island, and they are mentioned again and again. Their seriousness receives great emphasis, especially in the remarkable scene in which Philoctetes suffers a debilitating attack of pain, a scene that may be unique in Greek tragedy, usually so reticent in its onstage depiction of bodily suffering. Similarly emphasized are Philoctetes' blamelessness and the fact, again central to Aristotle's analysis, that any human being might suffer a similar calamity.[172]

[...]

According to Aristotle, whose account of *eleos*[173] in *Rhetoric* II.8 is both a valuable philosophical guide in its own right and an excellent summation of much that we observe in Greek tragedy, pity involves three characteristic thoughts: that a serious bad thing has happened to someone else; that it was not (or not primarily) that person's own fault (the person

---

[166]**Rousseau:** Swiss-born Enlightenment philosopher (1712–78); see extract 3.6.

[167]**Plato...Stoics:** on the Greek philosopher Plato (c.429–347 BCE) and his suspiciousness towards emotions, see extract 1.1. The Stoics were ancient philosophers who believed that human flourishing required detachment from both painful and pleasurable emotions.

[168][**Nussbaum's note:**] I discuss the Platonic critique of pity with reference, as well, to the role of pity in Aristotle's *Poetics*, in 'Tragedy and Self-Sufficiency: Plato and Aristotle on Fear and Pity', in *Essays on Aristotle's Poetics*, ed. Amélie Rorty (Princeton: Princeton University Press, 1992), 261–90; the Stoic critique is discussed in *The Therapy of Desire: Theory and Practice in Hellenistic Ethics* (Princeton: Princeton University Press, 1994); the modern debate is analysed in a general way in *Upheavals of Thought: The Intelligence of Emotions* (New York: Cambridge University Press, 2001), chaps. 6 and 7. I analyse Nietzsche' debt to Stoic arguments in 'Pity and Mercy: Nietzsche's Stoicism', in *Nietzsche, Genealogy, Morality*, ed. Richard Schacht (Berkeley: University of California Press, 1994), 139–67, and Adam Smith's fascinating contribution in the forthcoming '"Mutilated and Deformed": Adam Smith on the Material Basis of Human Dignity', part of Nussbaum, *The Cosmopolitan Tradition* under contract to Yale University Press.

[169]**Sophocles' *Philoctetes*:** Greek tragedy (409 BCE) featuring the suffering of the Greek warrior Philoctetes during the Trojan War. Infected by a snakebite, Philoctetes becomes misanthropic after being abandoned on the island of Lemnos, but fellow Greek warriors Odysseus and Neoptolemus must win back his trust in order to lure him and the bow of Heracles – in his keeping – to return to Troy to win the war.

[170][**Nussbaum's note:**] Stephen Halliwell, *The Aesthetics of Mimesis* (Princeton: Princeton University Press, 2002), 208.

[171]**Aristotle's... Rhetoric:** fourth-century BCE treatise on the art of persuasion by the Greek philosopher; on Aristotle's theory of tragedy, see extract 1.2.

[172][**Nussbaum's note:**] See *anaxiou*, *Rhet.* 1385b14, and 'which he himself might expect to suffer, or someone he cares about', 1385b14–5.

[173]***eleos:*** pity (Greek).

is *anaitios*[174]); and, third, that it is the sort of thing 'that one might expect to suffer, either oneself or someone one cares about' (1385b14–5). Having devoted an entire chapter to these requirements in *Upheavals of Thought*,[175] I shall not dwell on them at length here, except to point out that Eagleton misdescribes my position when he says that I think that you cannot pity someone who brought suffering on him or herself. What I do say is that if we pity in such cases, it is because the magnitude of the suffering is overwhelmingly greater than the magnitude of the fault. Eagleton's own examples fit that analysis well.[176]

The thought of seriousness and the thought of nonfault seem to me just right; the requirement of similar possibilities strikes me as a very usual element in pity, but we should conclude that it is not absolutely necessary, since we pity nonhuman animals without imagining that they are similar in kind to us, and we imagine that a god with no needs pities human beings who are utterly different in kind.[177]

There is, however, another thought that needs to be added to these three in order to make the emotion complete. I call this thought the 'eudaimonistic judgment,' meaning by this the thought that the person who is the object of pity is an important part of one's own scheme of goals and ends, one's conception of one's own *eudaimonia*.[178] This does not mean that the person is seen as a mere instrument of personal ends: we love and benefit our friends and family members for their own sake. It does mean that the people who will be singled out for pity, as for other strong emotions, are those who are woven into the fabric of one's own life, a part of our sense of what is most important in it. Distant people can be of eudaimonistic relevance in several ways: because the pitier has managed already to concern herself strongly with their well-being; because the pitier attaches eudaimonistic importance to general principles of justice, according to which we have ethical duties to people at a distance; or because, during an episode of deliberation or imagination, the distant people *become* of strong concern to her, although they were not before.[179]

The occasions for pity that Aristotle enumerates read like a plot outline of Sophocles' play. They fall into two groups: painful and destructive things, and bad things for which luck is responsible. (The rationale for the division might be that the bad things in the first group can be deliberately inflicted by another person and need not be caused by luck; if so, old age is misplaced, as are several items in the second group.) In the first group are deaths, bodily damages (*aikeiai*), bodily afflictions (*sômatôn kakôseis*), old age, illnesses, lack of food. In the second group are friendlessness; having few friends; being separated from one's friends and relations; ugliness; weakness; deformity; getting something bad from a source from which you were expecting something good; having that happen many times; the coming of good after the worst has happened; that no good should befall someone at all; or that one should not be able to enjoy it when it does. Philoctetes has every item on this list except old age—including the

---

[174]*anaitios*: not the cause; without blame (Greek).

[175][**Nussbaum's note:**] Nussbaum, *Upheavals of Thought*, chap. 6.

[176][**Nussbaum's note:**] Eagleton, *Sweet Violence*, 154–5; see Nussbaum, 'Tragedy and Self-Sufficiency: Plato and Aristotle on Fear and Pity', in Rorty, *Essays on Aristotle's Poetics*, and Nussbaum, *Upheavals of Thought*, chap. 6. Eagleton is familiar with the former, though not, it seems, with the latter.

[177][**Nussbaum's note:**] See Nussbaum, *Upheavals of Thought*, chap. 6, where this point is developed at greater length.

[178]*eudaimonia*: happiness, human flourishing (Greek).

[179][**Nussbaum's note:**] See 'Précis' and 'Responses', in book symposium on Nussbaum, *Upheavals of Thought*, in *Philosophy and Phenomenological Research* 68 (2004): 443–9, 473–86, in reply to Deigh.

more unusual ones (getting something bad from a source from which you expected something good; having the good come when it is too late to enjoy it). It is as if Aristotle, who clearly knew the play (since he refers to it in the *Nicomachean Ethics* discussion of *akrasia*[180]) used it as a template for his own discussion. In any case, from this list we can see the extent to which the play provides us with a map of pity and its occasions, as well as the underlying thoughts (seriousness, blamelessness, similarity) that enter into the structure of the emotion.

Arguing against Pity

The philosophical tradition makes many arguments against the value and appropriateness of pity. We may, however, focus on four, which introduce most of the salient issues. As we shall see, three of the four arguments can already be found in Plato and the Stoics; the fourth chimes in with themes in Stoic ethics, but it is pressed, as such, only in the modern period.

1. Falsity: Pity involves an overestimation of the importance of external goods for people's lives. Pity revolves around various types of pain and deprivation, attributing to them considerable significance for a person's flourishing. So the question immediately arises: Are these matters really important, or not? Nobody, and certainly not Aristotle, would wish to deny that some things for which we pity others are actually trivial and not worthy of our intense concern. Slights to honor, insults, monetary losses – all these, Aristotle holds in his ethical writings, are frequently overvalued. It would consequently be right to criticize someone who asked for pity on account of such relatively trivial matters and to reprove the giver of pity. What is at issue, however, is whether the things that Aristotle lists as the major occasions for pity are worthy of such intense concern. Plato's *Republic*[181] III tells us that the spectacle of Achilles weeping over the death of his friend ought to be stricken from the education of the young in the ideal city, because a good person simply does not think such a calamity very important, believing himself to be sufficient unto himself for well-being (387DE). The Stoics famously develop this position much further, holding that none of life's calamities is properly seen as an occasion for strong emotion. The Stoic who loses a child, a friend, or a city, or who is stricken with pain, will not get upset at these predicaments. Nor will he want the pity of another, which would insult him by wrongly implying that he depends on the gifts of fortune. (The Stoic doctrine of suicide is closely linked to this line of argument, because it assures us that a person can always find an escape from pain if it becomes too intense. Thus, even in such severe cases, there is no occasion for pity.) Both Plato and various Stoic writers associate behavior that rises above pain with manliness, weeping and moaning with effeminacy (e.g., *Republic*, 388A).

In ancient Greece, these positions were contentious and, we might say, counter-cultural – although in the late years of the Roman Republic and the early Empire popular sentiments about misfortune and emotion seem much closer to Stoic norms, whether because of antecedent similarities or because of Stoic influence. In eighteenth-century Europe, as Lessing[182] observes, cultural norms have put the expression of strong emotion strictly off-limits for the respectable

---

[180]*akrasia*: lack of self-control, acting against better judgment (Greek).
[181]**Plato's *Republic*:** philosophical dialogue (*c.*380–360 BCE) about the government of the ideal city; see extract 1.1.
[182]**Lessing:** Gotthold Lessing (1729–81) was a German Enlightenment philosopher whose book *Lacoön* (1766) explored the different aesthetic effects of painting and poetry.

(noneffeminate) man. For some thinkers, who closely follow Stoic norms, the norm of self-command applies to the inner world as well as to outer displays; to others, somewhat more relaxed, it is all right to have the emotion, as long as one controls its outward expression. (This latter view need not endorse the strong Stoic repudiation of the worth of externals.) One thing that is clear, however, from Lessing's treatise and many other pieces of cultural evidence, is that the face distorted in pain was agreed to be ugly and deeply unheroic; even Lessing hastens to assure us that the Laocoon[183] is admirable because he does not display such a face.

Adam Smith[184] wrestles with these cultural norms, and with the Stoic texts that were his lifelong preoccupation, in a fascinating way. On the whole, he defends the Stoic position on external goods, holding, in consequence, that a good man will not think of life's calamities as occasions for weeping or for the pity of others. In the last edition of the *Theory of Moral Sentiments*, however, published shortly before his death in 1792, he argues that Stoicism goes too far when it urges us not to have pity for the sufferings of our friends and our family. By uprooting these sentiments, Stoicism undermines the bonds that hold families and communities together.

According to Smith, we ought to pity the sufferings of our dear ones. In our own calamities, however, he insists, it is right both to behave like a Stoic and to try to have a truly Stoic inner life.[185] To weep at a calamity is effeminate. Here Smith speaks disparagingly of the French and the Italians. The duc de Biron, he says with fine Scottish contempt, even disgraced himself by weeping on the scaffold.[186] Consider by contrast, he urges, the sublime behavior of the Native American 'savages,' who greet death with a mocking song and endure with equanimity all the most horrible tortures.[187] The passage that I have cited as an epigraph shows the extent of the fascination these Stoic 'savages' held for Smith, a lifelong hypochondriac and constant complainer. They exemplify a norm of manliness to which he is deeply drawn, possibly because it seems so difficult to attain in real life. The passage shows an odd melding of Smith's readings about Native Americans with Stoicism: for the description of how the savages behave during the respite from pain is so close to Tacitus's account of Seneca's behavior during the slow progress of his suicide[188] that it is difficult to think the two unconnected.[189]

Smith's asymmetry thesis is a notable attempt to salvage pity while sticking to Stoic notions of proper manliness. It is not very successful; indeed, it seems quite incoherent. If life's calamities are proper occasions for pity when they strike our friends and family, they are

---

[183]**Laocoon:** ancient sculpture showing the Trojan priest Laocoön and his sons being attacked by sea serpents; widely considered an iconic depiction of human agony.

[184]**Adam Smith:** Scottish Enlightenment political economist and moral philosopher (1723–90).

[185]**[Nussbaum's note:]** I discuss all the relevant texts in the forthcoming '"Mutilated and Deformed": Adam Smith on the Material Basis of Human Dignity', part of Nussbaum, *The Cosmopolitan Tradition*, under contract to Yale University Press.

[186]**[Nussbaum's note:]** Smith, *The Theory of Moral Sentiments*, 49.

[187]**[Nussbaum's note:]** Ibid., 205–6.

[188]**Tacitus's account of Seneca's...suicide:** in the 15th book of *The Annals* (*c.*115–7), Roman historian Tacitus (*c.*55–*c.*117 CE) describes the suicide of writer and statesman Lucius Annaeus Seneca (*c.*4 BCE–65 CE), carried out under Nero's orders, as an act of courage and a model of Stoicism.

[189]**[Nussbaum's note:]** Smith's source for the Native Americans was apparently a work by Lafitau called *Moeurs des sauvages amériquains*, which depicted the torture scene with a grisly illustration, reproduced in Ian Simpson Ross, *The Life of Adam Smith* (Oxford: Clarendon Press, 1995); it is possible, then, that Smith, focusing on the visual representation, narrates it with language of his own, and thus Seneca manages to creep in.

similarly important when they strike us, and we would be right to ask for and accept pity in such circumstances. But Smith's odd thesis is worth mentioning because many people hold it: going through life with dignity intact, for people who have encountered great calamities (people with severe physical disabilities, for example) is often thought to require an extreme Stoical attitude toward one's own misfortunes, while a 'softer' attitude is permitted toward the suffering of others.

2. *Pity does no good; it is useless moaning and groaning.* This objection, pressed often by Nietzsche, is strongly suggested, at least, by the Platonic-Stoic critique.[190] Seneca frequently insists that we do not need pity, or any other emotion, for proper conduct, conduct in accordance with duty. Emotion simply makes us soft and passive, less likely to act well.

3. *Pity is closely linked to revenge.* A particularly fascinating objection, evident in Seneca but developed most explicitly by Nietzsche, focuses on the commitments to external goods that underlie all the major emotions. If you love one of these uncertain externals, then you are all set up for fear lest it be lost, for grief when it is lost, for pity when others lose such a thing through no fault of their own, for gratitude, when someone helps you get such a thing – and for anger, when someone else willfully damages it. The posture of the pitier seems so nice, so helpful, so full of the milk of human kindness. Consider, however, a person who pities another because he has lost his child (let's say). Such a person is acknowledging in that very emotion that children are really very important. How will this person react if someone damages his own child? A culture of pity is in this way a culture of anger. Seneca knows what he is doing when he urges Nero to avoid the softness of pity, for it lies all too close to the troubling propensities to cruelty that the young man is already displaying. We can make the connection between pity and anger even more direct by thinking about the person who asks for pity: for that person is set up for anger directly, in the very intensity of his concern for the good things that life has taken from him.

4. *Pity is partial: it favors the close against the distant.* This objection is presaged in Stoicism, which urges an impartial concern for humanity as a whole, while depicting pity as focusing on incidents close to the self. Given the egalitarian concerns of eighteenth-century thinkers, however, it gets developed much more fully there, particularly by Smith. He introduces the famous example of an earthquake in China, which will be an object of pity to a 'man of humanity' in Europe – *until* he has occasion to worry about something that is really important to him close to home.[191] That worry might be trivial by comparison – the loss of his little finger, as compared to the deaths of 'a hundred millions of his brethren.' And yet it will extinguish all pity for the large but distant disaster: 'He will snore with the more profound security over the ruin of a hundred millions of his brethren, and the destruction of that immense multitude seems plainly an object less interesting to him, than this paltry misfortune of his own.' Life provides us with such examples every day.

My own analysis of pity explains this inconstancy in pity better, I believe, than Aristotle's can. In my view, pity requires the thought that the object is among one's most important goals and projects. Distant people can take on such importance through moral education – whether

---

[190][**Nussbaum's note:**] On Nietzsche, see 'Pity and Mercy: Nietzsche's Stoicism', in Schacht, *Nietzsche, Genealogy, Morality*. Nietzsche here plays on the German term *Mitleid*, noting that it (correctly) implies that there has been a reduplication of suffering, thus making a bad thing worse.

[191][**Nussbaum's note:**] Smith, *The Theory of Moral Sentiments*, 136.

in themselves or through an intense commitment to social justice as an end. But life does not naturally lead people in the direction of such attachments to the distant. We begin, typically, with intense love of a small number of people, and it is only gradually – if at all – that we broaden our emotional lives. For this reason, the morality of pity seems likely to remain an uneven inconstant morality, given to momentary flickers of concern for the distant, who seem really important to us when we hear a vivid story of their plight,[192] and to backsliding when our usual scheme of goals and ends, with ourselves and our loved ones (typically) at the center, reasserts itself.

[…]

The problem of generalizing pity, one of the greatest moral problems of our time, might be thought to be surmountable, since we now have forms of mass communication that make it possible to connect our imaginations to the sufferings of people anywhere in the world. And, despite much critical grumbling about 'compassion fatigue', I believe that we do see many good examples of this sort, in which the vivid awareness of distant peoples' plight (victims of an earthquake on the other side of the world, victims of hurricane Katrina, civilians and soldiers whose lives are blasted in war, victims of genocide, women whose lives are deformed by rape and other violence) leads to new concern and to helping action.

Sophocles' play, however, stands as a warning: it is easier for our imaginations to become fascinated by the sufferings of the famous and glamorous. This, indeed, the media also show us every day, as we watch famous trials and ignore the struggles of poor people for basic justice, as the media's choice of which murder victims are even worth our attention reflects antecedent biases of race and class.

How might the modern media solve the partiality problem? As Rita Felski eloquently writes, 'No longer a sacramental relic, a safely distanced object of veneration or disdain frozen in past time, the tragic is shown to persist … into the present.'[193] How, then, can a present in which the obtuseness of an Odysseus is still the norm and the moral sensitivity of a Neoptolemus[194] still the rare exception deal with the problem of pity's un-evenness? One easy but relatively superficial solution would be to make sure to focus on examples of suffering that cross lines of class, race, and nation, ensuring that these daily stories of deprivation are told with a vividness and artistry that draws the viewer in. (The films of Satyajit Ray are splendid examples of how a great artist can achieve this. Ray's genius is his ability to make ordinary suffering so utterly particular, so riveting, that a rich American in New York can be connected to the deepest strivings of a rural family in Bengal, despite the utter difference in social and political context that the film faithfully reveals to us.)

There is, however, a deeper problem that the *Philoctetes* and Daniel Batson's[195] work reveal, and we cannot solve it through such great modern democratic tragedies. The problem is that we ultimately need a great deal more than a series of interesting particular narratives if we are to build a world that is fair to the sufferings and the strivings of all. If the 'eudaimonistic

---

[192][**Nussbaum's note:**] For experimental evidence on this point, see C. Daniel Batson, *The Altruism Question* (Hillsdale, NJ: Lawrence Erlbaum Associates, 1991).

[193][**Nussbaum's note:**] Rita Felski, 'Introduction', in *New Literary History* 35, no. 1 (2004): xix.

[194]**Obtuseness…Neoptolemus:** returning to the example with which the essay starts, Nussbaum refers here to the traits shown by these characters in Sophocles' *Philoctetes*.

[195]**Daniel Batson:** American social psychologist (born 1943) known for research on empathy and altruism.

judgment' about the worth and seriousness of the suffering of distant others is ever to become a stable reality in people's lives, then we have to build structures of attention that ensure that pity will not fade when the story ends or grows stale.

Ultimately, this means that we need to build reliable global institutions.[196] Just as one cannot hope to run a nation on the basis of good emotions – we need a good tax system that will make people pay their fair share even when they are not feeling compassion – so too with the world as a whole: we need institutional ways of ensuring that the global economic order is fair to all and produces decent living conditions for all. That large topic, however, would take us beyond our present theme. What we can say here is that such institutions (like a good welfare system domestically) will never come into being or remain stable unless individual human beings do have, and have often, experiences that link them to the fates of distant people who suffer. Pity is needed to prompt the creation of good institutions and, once they have been created, to sustain them.

We are left with a political and educational challenge. Pity does seem to be both justified (in the central cases) and valuable in prompting appropriate action. It is, however, fickle and in league with hierarchy. How might a society take advantage of the good in pity while cultivating it in an evenhanded way? After all, the common objects of pity are indeed, as Rousseau argued, the common lot of all human beings. In that way the emotion itself gives us a head start. The task of cultivating a truly balanced and equal pity is a daunting one, one that we have not yet fulfilled and have barely attempted. But Sophocles' drama helps us get started, by reminding us that the body's needs for food, drink, shelter, and release from pain, and the bodily human being's needs for friendship, talk, and political voice are both universal and of central significance for all.

Further reading

Brian Carr, 'Pity and Compassion as Social Virtues', *Philosophy* 74, no. 3 (1999): 411–29.

Aaron Ridley, 'Tragedy and the Tender-Hearted', *Philosophy and Literature* 17, no. 2 (1993): 234–45.

David L. Roochnik, 'The Tragic Philosopher: A Critique of Martha Nussbaum', *Ancient Philosophy* 8, no. 2 (1988): 285–95.

---

[196][**Nussbaum's note:**] See Martha C. Nussbaum, *Frontiers of Justice: Disability, Nationality, Species Membership* (Cambridge, MA: Harvard University Press, 2006).

SUPPLEMENTARY READING

The items below are listed in addition to those mentioned in the 'Further Reading' sections accompanying each extract.

Agovi, Kofi. 'Is There an African Vision of Tragedy in Contemporary African Theatre?' *Présence Africaine* 39, no. 133–4 (1985): 55–74.

Bamber, Linda. *Comic Women, Tragic Men: A Study of Gender and Genre in Shakespeare*. Stanford, CA: Stanford University Press, 1982.

Barker, Francis. *The Culture of Violence: Tragedy and History*. Manchester: Manchester University Press, 1993.

Barker, Howard. *Arguments for a Theatre*. Manchester: Manchester University Press, 1997.

Barthes, Roland. *On Racine*. Trans. Richard Howard. Berkeley: University of California Press, 1992.

Basterra, Gabriela. *Seductions of Fate: Tragic Subjectivity, Ethics, Politics*. Basingstoke: Palgrave Macmillan, 2004.

Bayley, John. *Shakespeare and Tragedy*. London: Routledge, 1981.

Benjamin, Walter. *The Origin of German Tragic Drama*. Trans. John Osborne. London and New York: Verso, 1998.

Berry, Philippa. *Shakespeare's Feminine Endings: Disfiguring Death in the Tragedies*. London: Routledge, 1999.

Billings, Joshua. *Genealogy of the Tragic: Greek Tragedy and German Philosophy*. Princeton: Princeton University Press, 2014.

Billings, Joshua and Miriam Leonard, eds. *Tragedy and the Idea of Modernity*. Oxford: Oxford University Press, 2015.

Booth, Stephen. *King Lear, Macbeth, Indefinition and Tragedy*. New Haven: Yale University Press, 1983.

Braden, Gordon. *Renaissance Tragedy and the Senecan Tradition: Anger's Privilege*. New Haven: Yale University Press, 1985.

Bronfen, Elisabeth. 'Femme Fatale: Negotiations of Tragic Desire'. *New Literary History* 35, no. 1 (2004): 103–16.

Brown, Laura. 'The Defenseless Woman and the Development of English Tragedy'. *Studies in English Literature* 22, no. 3 (1982): 429–43.

Bushnell, Rebecca. *A Companion to Tragedy*. Malden, MA: Blackwell, 2005.

Bushnell, Rebecca. 'Tragedy and Temporality'. *PMLA* 129, no. 4 (2014): 783–89.

Callaghan, Dympna. *Women and Gender in Renaissance Tragedy: A Study of King Lear, Othello, The Duchess of Malfi and The White Devil*. London: Routledge, 1989.

Canfield, J. Douglas. *Heroes and States: On the Ideology of Restoration Tragedy*. Lexington: University Press of Kentucky, 2000.

Carter, D.M. 'Was Attic Tragedy Democratic?' *Polis* 21, no. 1–2 (2004): 1–25.

Carter, D.M., ed. *Why Athens?: A Reappraisal of Tragic Politics*. Oxford: Oxford University Press, 2011.

Chafe, Eric. *The Tragic and the Ecstatic: The Musical Revolution of Wagner's Tristan und Isolde*. Oxford: Oxford University Press, 2005.

Clark, T.J. 'For a Left with No Future'. *New Left Review* 74 (2012): 53–75.

Cooper, Barbara T. 'French Romantic Tragedy'. In *A Companion to Tragedy*, ed. Rebecca Bushnell, 452–68. Oxford: Blackwell Publishing, 2005.

Cox, Jeffrey N. *In the Shadow of Romance: Romantic Tragic Drama in Germany, England and France*. Athens: Ohio University Press, 1987.

Supplementary Reading

Cox, Jeffrey N. 'Romantic Redevelopment of the Tragic'. In *Romantic Drama*, ed. Gerald Gillespie,. 153–66. Amsterdam and Philadelphia: John Benjamins Publishing Company, 1993.

Csengei, Ildiko. *Sympathy, Sensibility and the Literature of Feeling in the Eighteenth Century*. Basingstoke: Palgrave Macmillan, 2012.

Debnar, Paula. 'Fifth-Century Athenian History and Tragedy'. In *A Companion to Greek Tragedy*, ed. Justina Gregory, 1–22. Oxford: Blackwell, 2005.

Dewar-Watson, Sarah. *Tragedy: A Reader's Guide to Essential Criticism*. Basingstoke: Palgrave Macmillan, 2014.

Dobrée, Bonamy. *Restoration Tragedy, 1660–1720*. Oxford: Clarendon Press, 1929.

Dillon, Janette. *The Cambridge Introduction to Shakespeare's Tragedies*. Cambridge: Cambridge University Press, 2007.

Dollimore, Jonathan and Alan Sinfield, eds. *Political Shakespeare*. Manchester: Manchester University Press, 1985.

Drakakis, John and Naomi Conn Liebler, eds. *Tragedy*. London: Longman, 1998.

Draper, Ronald P., ed. *Tragedy: Developments in Criticism; A Casebook*. London: Macmillan, 1980.

Eagleton, Terry. *Sweet Violence: The Idea of the Tragic*. Oxford: Blackwell, 2003.

Easterling, Patricia Elizabeth, ed. *The Cambridge Companion to Greek Tragedy*. Cambridge: Cambridge University Press, 1997.

Euben, Peter. *The Tragedy of Political Theory: The Road Not Taken*. Princeton: Princeton University Press, 1990.

Felski, Rita, ed. *Rethinking Tragedy*. Baltimore and London: Johns Hopkins University Press, 2008.

Foley, Helene P. *Female Acts in Greek Tragedy*. Princeton: Princeton University Press, 2001.

Foley, Helene P. and Jean E. Howard. 'The Urgency of Tragedy Now'. *PMLA* 129, no. 4 (2014): 617–34.

Fleming, Paul. *Exemplarity and Mediocrity: The Art of Average from Bourgeois Tragedy to Realism*. Stanford, CA: Stanford University Press, 2009.

Foster, Daniel H. *Wagner's Ring Cycle and the Greeks*. Cambridge: Cambridge University Press, 2010.

Garland, Robert. *Surviving Tragedy*. London: Duckworth, 2004.

Garner, Shirley Nelson and Madelon Sprengnether, eds. *Shakespearean Tragedy and Gender*. Bloomington: Indiana University Press, 1996.

Gellrich, Michelle. *Tragedy and Theory: The Problem of Conflict since Aristotle*. Princeton: Princeton University Press, 1988.

Gildenhard, Ingo and Martin Revermann, eds. *Beyond the Fifth Century: Interactions with Greek Tragedy from the Fourth Century BCE to the Middle Ages*. Berlin and New York: de Gruyter, 2010.

Golden, Leon. *Aristotle on Tragic and Comic Mimesis*. Atlanta: Scholars Press, 1992.

Goldhill, Simon. *Reading Greek Tragedy*. Cambridge: Cambridge University Press, 1986.

Gordon, Paul. *Tragedy after Nietzsche: Rapturous Superabundance*. Urbana: University of Illinois Press, 2001.

Gossip, Christopher J. *An Introduction to French Classical Tragedy*. London: Macmillan, 1981.

Gourgouris, Stathis. 'Democracy Is a Tragic Regime'. *PMLA* 129, no. 4 (2014): 809–18.

Graham, Greg A. *Democratic Political Tragedy in the Postcolony*. Abingdon and New York: Routledge, 2017.

Griffin, Jasper, ed. *Sophocles Revisited: Essays Presented to Sir Hugh Lloyd-Jones*. Oxford: Oxford University Press, 1999.

Hall, Edith. *Inventing the Barbarian: Greek Self-Definition through Tragedy*. Oxford: Clarendon Press, 1989.

Hall, Edith, Fiona Macintosh and Amanda Wrigley, eds. *Dionysus since 69: Greek Tragedy at the Dawn of the Third Millennium*. Oxford: Oxford University Press, 2004.

Halliwell, Stephen. 'Learning from Suffering: Ancient Responses to Tragedy'. In *A Companion to Greek Tragedy*, ed. Justina Gregory, 394–412. Oxford: Blackwell, 2005.

Hammond, Paul. *The Strangeness of Tragedy*. Oxford: Oxford University Press, 2009.

Hnatko, Eugene. 'The Failure of Eighteenth-Century Tragedy'. *Studies in English Literature* 11, no. 3 (1971): 459–68.

Hopkins, Lisa. *The Female Hero in English Renaissance Tragedy*. Basingstoke: Palgrave Macmillan, 2002.

Hoxby, Blair. *What Was Tragedy?: Theory and the Early Modern Canon*. Oxford: Oxford University Press, 2017.

Hulfeld, Stephan. 'Modernist Theatre'. In *The Cambridge Companion to Theatre History*, ed. David Wiles and Christine Dymkowski, 15–32. Cambridge: Cambridge University Press, 2012.

Hotson, Leslie. *The Commonwealth and Restoration Stage*. Cambridge, MA: Harvard University Press, 1928.

James, Susan. *Passion and Action: The Emotions in Seventeenth-Century Philosophy*. Oxford: Oxford University Press, 1999.

Jaspers, Karl. *Tragedy Is Not Enough*. London: Victor Gollancz, 1953.

Jeyifo, Biofran. *Wole Soyinka: Politics, Poetics and Postcolonialism*. Cambridge: Cambridge University Press, 2004.

Katrak, Ketu H. *Wole Soyinka and Modern Tragedy: A Study of Dramatic Theory and Practice*. Oxford: Greenwood, 1986.

Kaufmann, Walter. *Tragedy and Philosophy*. Princeton: Princeton University Press, 1968.

Kelly, Henry Ansgar. *Ideas and Forms of Tragedy from Aristotle to the Middle Ages*. Cambridge: Cambridge University Press, 1993.

Kerrigan, John. *Revenge Tragedy: Aeschylus to Armageddon*. Oxford: Clarendon Press, 1996.

Kierkegaard, Søren. *Either/Or: A Fragment of a Life*. Ed. Victor Eremita and trans. Alastair Hannay. London and New York: Penguin, 1992.

King, Jeannette. *Tragedy and the Victorian Novel: Theory and Practice in the Novels of George Eliot, Thomas Hardy and Henry James*. Cambridge: Cambridge University Press, 1978.

Knox, Bernard. *The Heroic Temper: Studies in Sophoclean Tragedy*. Berkeley: University of California Press, 1964.

Knowles, Ronald. 'Carnival and Tragedy in Thomas Hardy's Novels'. *Thomas Hardy Journal* 21 (2005): 109–24.

Knowles, Ronald. 'Thomas Hardy: Elements of the Tragic'. *Thomas Hardy Journal* 22 (2006): 223–34.

Kramer, Dale, ed. *Thomas Hardy: The Forms of Tragedy*. London: Macmillan, 1975.

Krell, David Farrell. *The Tragic Absolute: German Idealism and the Languishing of God*. Bloomington: Indiana University Press, 2005.

Lamb, Jonathan. *The Evolution of Sympathy in the Long Eighteenth Century*. London: Pickering and Chatto, 2009.

Lambropoulos, Vassilis. *The Tragic Idea*. London: Duckworth, 2006.

Leggatt, Alexander. *Shakespeare's Tragedies: Violation and Identity*. Cambridge: Cambridge University Press, 2003.

Leonard, Miriam. *Tragic Modernities*. Cambridge, MA: Harvard University Press, 2015.

Liebler, Naomi Conn. *Shakespeare's Festive Tragedy: The Ritual Foundations of Genre*. London: Routledge, 1995.

Lough, John. *Seventeenth-Century French Drama*. Oxford: Clarendon Press, 1979.

Lyne, Raphael. 'Neoclassicisms'. In *Tragedy in Transition*, ed. Sarah Annes Brown and Catherine Silverstone, 123–40. Malden, MA and Oxford: Wiley-Blackwell, 2007.

Lyons, John D. *Kingdom of Disorder: The Theory of Tragedy in Classical France*. West Lafayette: Purdue University Press, 1999.

MacKinnon, Kenneth. *Greek Tragedy into Film*. London: Croom Helm, 1986.

Macpherson, Sandra. *Harm's Way: Tragic Responsibility and the Novel Form*. Baltimore: Johns Hopkins University Press, 2010.

Manuwald, Gesine. *Roman Republican Theatre*. Cambridge: Cambridge University Press, 2011.

May, Keith M. *Nietzsche and the Spirit of Tragedy*. Basingstoke: Palgrave Macmillan, 1990.

McAlindon, Tom. *Shakespeare's Tragic Cosmos*. Cambridge: Cambridge University Press, 1991.

McDonald, Ronan. *Tragedy and Irish Literature: Synge, O'Casey, Beckett*. Basingstoke: Palgrave Macmillan, 2002.

McEachern, Claire, ed. *The Cambridge Companion to Shakespearean Tragedy*. Cambridge: Cambridge University Press, 2006.

Mehl, Dieter. *Shakespeare's Tragedies: An Introduction*. Cambridge: Cambridge University Press, 1986.

Supplementary Reading

Miller, Arthur. 'Tragedy and the Common Man'. *New York Times*, 27 February 1949, p. 1.

Miola, Robert S. *Shakespeare and Classical Tragedy: The Influence of Seneca*. Oxford: Clarendon Press, 1992.

Muir, Kenneth. *Shakespeare's Tragic Sequence*. London: Hutchinson, 1972.

Neill, Michael. *Issues of Death: Mortality and Identity in English Renaissance Tragedy*. Oxford: Clarendon Press, 1997.

Nussbaum, Martha. *The Fragility of Goodness: Luck and Ethics in Greek Tragedy and Philosophy*. Cambridge: Cambridge University Press, 1986.

Nussbaum, Felicity A. 'The Challenge of Tragedy'. In *The Oxford Handbook of the Georgian Theatre, 1737-1832*, ed. Julia Swindells and David Francis Taylor, 368–89. Oxford: Oxford University Press, 2014.

Nuttall, Anthony David. *Why Does Tragedy Give Pleasure?* Oxford: Clarendon Press, 1996.

Padel, Ruth. *In and Out of the Mind: Greek Images of the Tragic Self*. Princeton: Princeton University Press, 1992.

Palmer, Richard H. *Tragedy and Tragic Theory: An Analytical Guide*. Westport, CT and London: Greenwood Press, 1992.

Palmer, David, ed. *Visions of Tragedy in Modern American Drama: From O'Neill to the Twenty-First Century*. London: Bloomsbury, 2018.

Panoussi, Vassiliki. 'Polis and Empire: Greek Tragedy in Rome'. In *A Companion to Greek Tragedy*, ed. Justina Gregory, 413–27. Oxford: Blackwell, 2005.

Parish, Richard. *Racine: The Limits of Tragedy*. Seattle: Papers on French Seventeenth Century Literature, 1986.

Pinch, Adela. *Strange Fits of Passion: Epistemologies of Emotion, Hume to Austen*. Stanford, CA: Stanford University Press, 1996.

Pirro, Robert. *Hannah Arendt and the Politics of Tragedy*. DeKalb, IL: Northern Illinois University Press, 2000.

Pirro, Robert. 'Tragedy, Theodicy and 9/11: Rhetorical Responses to Suffering and Their Public Significance'. *Thesis Eleven* 98 (2009): 5–32.

Poole, Adrian. *Tragedy: A Very Short Introduction*. Oxford and New York: Oxford University Press, 2005.

Quayson, Ato. *Calibrations: Reading for the Social*. Minnesota: University of Minnesota Press, 2003.

Quayson, Ato. 'Tragedy and the Postcolonial Novel'. In *The Cambridge Companion to the Postcolonial Novel*, ed. Ato Quayson, 230–47. Cambridge: Cambridge University Press, 2015.

Rehm, Rush. *Radical Theatre: Greek Tragedy in the Modern World*. London: Bloomsbury, 2013.

Rehm, Rush. *Understanding Greek Tragic Theatre*. London: Routledge, 2016.

Reiss, Timothy J. *Tragedy and Truth: Studies in the Development of a Renaissance and Neoclassical Discourse*. New Haven: Yale University Press, 1980.

Reiss, Timothy J. 'Using Tragedy against Its Makers: Some African and Caribbean Instances'. In *A Companion to Tragedy*, ed. Rebecca Bushnell, 505–36. Oxford: Blackwell, 2005.

Rocco, Christopher. *Tragedy and Enlightenment: Athenian Political Thought and the Dilemmas of Modernity*. Berkeley: University of California Press, 1997.

Rosen, Stephen. *Samuel Beckett and the Pessimistic Tradition*. New Brunswick, NJ: Rutgers University Press, 1976.

Rosslyn, Felicity. *Tragic Plots: A New Reading from Aeschylus to Lorca*. Aldershot: Ashgate, 2000.

Rothstein, Eric. *Restoration Tragedy: Form and the Process of Change*. Madison: University of Wisconsin Press, 1967.

Schmidt, Dennis J. *On Germans and Other Greeks: Tragedy and Ethical Life*. Bloomington: Indiana University Press, 2001.

Scodel, Ruth. *An Introduction to Greek Tragedy*. Cambridge: Cambridge University Press, 2010.

Seaford, Richard. 'Tragic Tyranny'. In *Popular Tyranny: Sovereignty and Its Discontents in Ancient Greece*, ed. Kathryn Morgan, 95–115. Austin: University of Texas Press, 2003.

Scullion, Scott. 'Tragedy and Religion: The Problem of Origins'. In *A Companion to Greek Tragedy*, ed. Justina Gregory, 23–37. Oxford: Blackwell, 2005.

Segal, Charles. *Interpreting Greek Tragedy: Myth, Poetry, Text*. Ithaca and London: Cornell University Press, 1986.

Segal, Charles. *Tragedy and Civilization: An Interpretation of Sophocles*. Norman: University of Oklahoma Press, 1999.

Silk, M. and J.P. Stern. *Nietzsche on Tragedy*. Cambridge: Cambridge University Press, 1981.

Silk, M.S., ed. *Tragedy and the Tragic: Greek Theatre and Beyond*. Oxford: Clarendon Press, 1996.

Simon, Bennett. *Tragic Drama and the Family: Psychoanalytic Studies from Aeschylus to Beckett*. New Haven and London: Yale University Press, 1988.

Simon, Ulrich. *Pity and Terror: Christianity and Tragedy*. Basingstoke: Palgrave Macmillan, 1989.

Smith, Emma. *Shakespeare's Tragedies*. Oxford: Blackwell, 2004.

Sontag, Susan. *Regarding the Pain of Others*. New York: Picador, 2003.

Sourvinou-Inwood, Christiane. 'Greek Tragedy and Ritual'. In *A Companion to Tragedy*, ed. Rebecca Bushnell, 7–24. Oxford: Blackwell, 2005.

Soyinka, Wole. *Myth, Literature and the African World*. Cambridge: Cambridge University Press, 1997.

Staves, Susan. 'Tragedy'. In *The Cambridge Companion to British Theatre, 1730–1830*, ed. Jane Moody and Daniel O'Quinn, 87–102. Cambridge: Cambridge University Press, 2007.

Stinton, T.C.W. 'Hamartia in Aristotle and Greek Tragedy'. *Classical Quarterly* 25, no. 2 (1975): 221–54.

Szondi, Peter. *An Essay on the Tragic*. Trans. Paul Fleming. Stanford, CA: Stanford University Press, 2002.

Taplin, Oliver. *Greek Tragedy in Action*. London: Methuen, 1978.

Tarrant, Richard J. 'Senecan Drama and Its Antecedents'. *Harvard Studies in Classical Philology* 82 (1978): 213–63.

Taylor, Carole Anne. *The Tragedy and Comedy of Resistance: Reading Modernity through Black Women's Fiction*. Philadelphia: University of Pennsylvania Press, 2000.

Tobin, Ronald W. *Racine and Seneca*. Chapel Hill: University of North Carolina Press, 1971.

Tredell, Nicolas. *Shakespeare, The Tragedies: A Reader's Guide to Essential Criticism*. Basingstoke: Palgrave Macmillan, 2014.

Vernant, Jean-Pierre and Pierre Vidal-Naquet. *Myth and Tragedy in Ancient Greece*. Trans. Janet Lloyd. Cambridge, MA: Zone Books, 1990.

Walder, Dennis. *Athol Fugard*. Basingstoke: Palgrave Macmillan, 1984.

Wallace, Jennifer. *The Cambridge Introduction to Tragedy*. Cambridge: Cambridge University Press, 2007.

Wetmore, Kevin J. Jr. *The Athenian Sun in an African Sky: Modern African Adaptations of Classical Greek Tragedy*. Jefferson, NC: McFarland, 2002.

Wetmore, Kevin J. Jr. *Black Dionysus: Greek Tragedy and African American Theatre*. Jefferson, NC: McFarland and Co., 2003.

Wiles, David. *Tragedy in Athens: Performance Space and Theatrical Meaning*. Cambridge: Cambridge University Press, 1997.

Winkler, John and Froma Zeitlin, eds. *Nothing to Do with Dionysos?: Athenian Drama in Its Social Context*. Princeton: Princeton University Press, 1989.

Young, Julian. *The Philosophy of Tragedy: From Plato to Žižek*. Cambridge: Cambridge University Press, 2013.

Zimmerman, Susan, ed. *Shakespeare's Tragedies*. Basingstoke: Palgrave Macmillan, 1998.

Zink, Sidney. 'The Novel as a Medium of Modern Tragedy'. *The Journal of Aesthetics and Art Criticism* 17, no. 2 (1958): 169–73.

LIST OF SOURCES

Chapter 1

1.1 Plato, *The Republic*

Plato, *The Republic*, trans. Francis Cornford (Oxford: The Clarendon Press, 1941), 81–3, 85, 336–40 (3:392–5, 397 and 10:603–7).

1.2 Aristotle, *Poetics*

Aristotle, *On the Art of Poetry*, trans. Ingram Bywater (Oxford: Oxford University Press, 1920), sections 4 and 6–15.

1.3 Horace, *The Art of Poetry*

The Satires, Epistles, and Art of Poetry by Horace, trans. John Conington (London, Bell, 1902), 86–124, 275–84, 333–46, 391–411.

1.4 Longinun, *On the Sublime*

Longinus, *On the Sublime*, trans. W. Rhys Roberts (Cambridge: Cambridge University Press, 1907), chapters 8, 15, and 33; 57–9, 83–91, 127–31.

1.5 Evanthius, 'On Drama'

Evanthius, 'On Drama' [*De Fabula*], trans. O. B. Hardison Jr, in *Classical and Medieval Literary Criticism*, ed. Alex Preminger, O.B. Hardison Jr, and Kevin Kerrane (New York: Frederick Ungar, 1974), 301–2, 305.

1.6 Augustine, 'On Stage-Plays'

Augustine, *The Confessions of St Augustine*, trans. J.G. Pilkington (New York: Horace Liveright, 1927), Book Three.

Chapter 2

2.1 Giovan Battista Giraldi Cinthio, *Discourse or Letter on the Composition of Comedies and Tragedies*

Cinthio, '*Discourse or Letter on the Composition of Comedies and Tragedies*', trans. Daniel Javitch, in *Renaissance Drama* 39 (2011): 207–55, 208–18, 254.

2.2 Lodovico Castelvetro, *The Poetics of Aristotle*

Castelvetro on the *Art of Poetry*, ed. and trans. Andrew Bongiorno (Binghamton, NY: Medieval and Renaissance Texts and Studies, 1984), 19–20, 81–82, 87, 151–2, 162–3.

2.3 Stephen Gosson, *Plays Confuted in Five Actions*

Gosson, *Plays Confuted in Five Actions* (London, 1582), B4r–B4v, C5r–C6r, C7v–C8r, D8v–E1r, E8v–F1v, and G4r–G5v.

2.4 Philip Sidney, *Defense of Poetry*

Sidney, *Defense of Poetry* (London, 1595), F3v–F4, I4v–K3v.

2.5 Thomas Heywood, *The Apology for Actors*

Heywood, *The Apology for Actors* (London, 1612), B1r–B1v, B3r, B3v–B4r, G1r–G2v.

2.6 Pierre Corneille, *Three Discourses on Dramatic Poetry*

Corneille, 'On Tragedy and the Means of Treating It according to Verisimilitude or "the Necessary"' and 'On the Three Unities of Action, of Time, and of Place', in *Sources of Dramatic Theory: Plato to Congreve*, trans. Pia Kleber, in Michael Sidnell, ed. (Cambridge: Cambridge University Press, 1991), vol. 1, 244–51.

2.7 John Milton, 'Of That Sort of Dramatic Poem Which Is Called Tragedy'

Milton, *Paradise Regained. A Poem in IV Books. To Which Is Added Samson Agonistes* (London, 1671), sigs. $I2^r$–$I3^r$.

2.8 René Rapin, *Reflections on Aristotle's Treatise of Poesie*

Rapin, *Reflections on Aristotle's Treatise of Poesie, Containing the Necessary, Rational, and Universal Rules for Epick, Dramatick, and Other Sorts of Poetry*, trans. Thomas Rymer (London, 1674), sig. $b3^r$, 103–117.

2.9 John Dryden, 'The Grounds of Criticism in Tragedy'

Dryden, *Troilus and Cressida: Or, Truth Found Too Late* (London, 1679), sigs. a^v–$b2^v$.

Chapter 3

3.1 Joseph Addison and Richard Steele, *The Spectator*

The Spectator 39, 14 April 1711; 40, 16 April 1711; 418, 30 June 1712.

3.2 George Lillo, 'The Dedication' and 'Prologue' to *The London Merchant*

Lillo, *The London Merchant: Or, the History of George Barnwell* (London, 1731), sigs. $A2^r$–$A4^v$, $A6^r$.

3.3 Voltaire, 'Letter XVIII. On Tragedy'

Voltaire, *Letters Concerning the English Nation by Mr De Voltaire*, trans. John Lockman (London: C. Davis, 1733), 166–70, 177–80.

3.4 David Hume, 'Of Tragedy'

Hume, *Four Dissertations* (London: A. Millar, 1757), 185–200.

3.5 Edmund Burke, 'Sympathy', 'Of the Effects of Tragedy' and 'The Sublime'

Burke, *A Philosophical Enquiry into the Origin of Our Ideas of the Sublime and the Beautiful* (London, 1757), 21–30.

3.6 Jean-Jacques Rousseau, *Letter to M. D'Alembert on the Theatre*

Allan Bloom (trans. and ed.), *Jean-Jacques Rousseau Politics and the Arts* (Ithaca, NY: Cornell University Press, 1977), 22–7, 32–4.

3.7 Samuel Johnson, 'Preface to Shakespeare'

The Plays of William Shakespeare in Eight Volumes ... To Which Are Added Notes by Sam. Johnson (London, 1765), vol. 1, sigs. A5ʳ–A7ᵛ, B2ʳ, B4ʳ–B7ʳ.

3.8 Elizabeth Montagu, *An Essay on the Writings and Genius of Shakespeare*

Montagu, *An Essay on the Writings and Genius of Shakespeare, Compared with the Greek and French Dramatic Poets. With Some Remarks Upon the Misrepresentations of Mons. De Voltaire* (London, 1769), 28–30, 31–5, 37–40, 63–4.

3.9 Joanna Baillie, 'Introductory Discourse'

Baillie, *A Series of Plays: In Which It Is Attempted to Delineate the Stronger Passions of the Mind. Each Passion Being the Subject of a Tragedy and a Comedy* (London, 1798), 28–43.

Chapter 4

4.1 August Wilhelm Schlegel, *A Course of Lectures on Dramatic Art and Literature*

Schlegel, *A Course of Lectures on Dramatic Art and Literature*, trans. John Black (London: Henry Bohn, 1846), 66–77.

4.2 Charles Lamb, 'On the Tragedies of Shakespeare Considered with Reference for Their Fitness for Stage Representation'

The Complete Works in Prose and Verse of Charles Lamb, ed. R.H. Shepherd (London: Chatto and Windus, 1875), 255–6, 258, 261, 264–5.

4.3 William Hazlitt, *Characters of Shakespeare's Plays*

Hazlitt, *Characters of Shakespeare's Plays* (New York: Wiley and Puttenham, 1845), xii, 28–31, 105–6, 114–5.

4.4 Arthur Schopenhauer, *The World as Will and Representation*

Schopenhauer, *The World as Will and Idea*, trans. R.B. Haldane and J. Kemp (London: Kegan Paul, Trench, Trübner & Co., 1909), vol. I, 324–30, 415–6.

4.5 Percy Bysshe Shelley, *A Defence of Poetry*

Shelley, *Essays, Letters from Abroad, Translations and Fragments*. 2 vols (Philadelphia: Lea and Blanchard, 1840), vol. I, 37–8, 39–41, 51–3.

4.6 G.W.F. Hegel, *Aesthetics: Lectures on Fine Art*

The Philosophy of Fine Art by G.W.F. Hegel. 4 vols, translated, with notes, by F.P.B. Osmaston (London: G. Bell and Sons, 1920), vol. IV, 294–301, 320–7, 334–6.

4.7 George Eliot, 'The *Antigone* and Its Moral'

Eliot, 'The *Antigone* and Its Moral', *Leader* VII (29 March 1856): 306.

4.8 Friedrich Nietzsche, *The Birth of Tragedy*

Nietzsche, *The Birth of Tragedy: Out of the Spirit of Music*, ed. Michael Tanner and trans. Shaun Whiteside (New York: Penguin, 2003), 14–8, 35–40, 51–2, 116–7.

Chapter 5

5.1 Sigmund Freud, *The Interpretation of Dreams*

Freud, *The Interpretation of Dreams*, trans. A.A. Brill (New York: Modern Library, 1978), 159–64.

5.2 A.C. Bradley, *Shakespearean Tragedy*

Bradley, *Shakespearean Tragedy* (London: Macmillan, 1904, reprinted in 1952), 5–13.

5.3 William Butler Yeats, 'The Tragic Theatre'

Yeats, *Essays and Introductions* (New York: Macmillan, 1961), 238–45.

5.4 Virginia Woolf, 'On Not Knowing Greek'

Woolf, *The Common Reader* (New York: Harcourt, Brace, 1925), 24, 27–33, 36–7, 39.

5.5 Bertolt Brecht, *A Short Organum for the Theatre*

Brecht, *Brecht on Theatre*, ed. and trans. John Willet (London: Methuen, 1964), 179–89.

5.6 Robert Warshow, 'The Gangster as Tragic Hero'

Warshow, *The Partisan Review* 15, no. 2 (February 1948): 580–6.

5.7 George Steiner, *Death of Tragedy*

Steiner, *Death of Tragedy* (New York: Alfred A. Knopf, 1961), 3–10.

5.8 Athol Fugard, 'On *A View from the Bridge*'

Athol Fugard: Notebooks 1960–1977, ed. Mary Benson (London: Faber and Faber, 1983), 75–6.

5.9 Raymond Williams, 'Tragedy and Revolution'

Williams, *Modern Tragedy* (London: Chatto & Windus, 1966), 61–5, 77–9.

List of Sources

Chapter 6

6.1 René Girard, 'The Sacrificial Crisis'

Girard, *Violence and the Sacred*, trans. Patrick Gregory (Baltimore: Johns Hopkins University Press, 1977, reprinted in 1979), 39–42, 44–9.

6.2 Augusto Boal, *The Theatre of the Oppressed*

Boal, *The Theatre of the Oppressed*, trans. Charles A. and Maria-Odilia Leal McBride and Emily Fryer (London: Pluto Press, 2000), 25–32, 36–9.

6.3 Joseph Meeker, 'Literary Tragedy and Ecological Catastrophe'

Meeker, *The Comedy of Survival* (New York: Scriber, 1974), 41–7. Reprinted by the University of Arizona Press in 1997.

6.4 Catherine Belsey, *The Subject of Tragedy*

Belsey, *The Subject of Tragedy* (London and New York: Methuen, 1985), 149–50, 164–6.

6.5 Nicole Loraux, 'The Rope and the Sword'

Loraux, *Tragic Ways of Killing a Woman*, trans. Anthony Forster (Cambridge, MA and London: Harvard University Press, 1987), 7–17.

6.6 Biodun Jeyifo, 'Tragedy, History and Ideology'

Georg. M Gugelberger (ed.), *Marxism and African Literature* (Trenton, NJ: Africa World Press, 1986), 94–6, 100, 106–7.

6.7 Hélène Cixous, 'Enter the Theatre (in between)'

Hélène Cixous and Brian J. Mallett (trans.), *Modern Drama* 42, no. 3 (1999): 301–4, 308, 313–4.

6.8 Judith Butler, *Antigone's Claim*

Butler, *Antigone's Claim* (New York: Columbia University Press, 2000), 57–63, 66–8, 69–72, 82, 92–7.

6.9 David Scott, *Conscripts of Modernity*

Scott, *Conscripts of Modernity: The Tragedy of Postcolonial Enlightenment* (Durham and London: Duke University Press, 2004), 209–22.

6.10 Martha Nussbaum, 'The "Morality of Pity"'

Rita Felski (ed.), *Rethinking Tragedy* (Baltimore: Johns Hopkins University Press, 2008), 148–9, 152–7, 165–9.

PERMISSIONS ACKNOWLEDGEMENTS

Chapter 1

Evanthius, 'On Drama' [*De Fabula*], trans. O.B. Hardison Jr, in *Classical and Medieval Literary Criticism* (New York: F. Ungar, 1974), 301–2, 305. Reprinted with permission of the translator's Estate.

Chapter 2

G.B. Giraldi Cinthio, from *Discourse or Letter on the Composition of Comedies and Tragedies* (1554), translated by Daniel Javitch (2011), from *Renaissance Drama*, vol. 39. Copyright © The University of Chicago Press. Reprinted with permission.

Lodovico Castelvetro, 'The Poetics of Aristotle', from *Poetica d'Aristotele Vulgarizzata et Sposta* (1570), ed. and trans. Andrew Bongiorno (Binghamton, NY: Medieval and Renaissance Texts and Studies, 1984). Copyright © Arizona Board of Regents for Arizona State University. Reprinted with permission.

Pierre Corneille, 'On Tragedy and the Means of Treating It according to Verisimilitude or "the Necessary"' and 'On the Three Unities of Action, of Time, and of Place', in *Sources of Dramatic Theory: Plato to Congreve*, trans. Pia Kleber, in Michael Sidnell (ed.) (Cambridge: Cambridge University Press, 1991), vol. 1, 244–51. Reprinted with kind permission of Pia Kleber.

Chapter 3

From *Politics and the Arts: Letter to M. D'Alembert on the Theatre* by Jean-Jacques Rousseau, translated with Notes and Introduction by Allan Bloom. Copyright © 1960 by The Free Press; copyright © renewed 1988 by The Free Press. Reprinted with the permission of The Free Press, a division of Simon & Schuster, Inc. All rights reserved.

Chapter 4

'World as Will and Idea' by Arthur Schopenhauer (1844), translated by K.B. Haldane and J. Kemp. Printed by Ballantyne, Hanson & Co. at the Ballantyne Press, Edinburgh. Reprinted with permission of the publisher.

Excerpt from Friedrich Nietzsche, *The Birth of Tragedy*, translated by Shaun Whiteside. Copyright © 1993 Penguin Random House LLC. Reprinted with permission of the publisher.

Chapter 5

Bertolt Brecht, 'A Short Organum for the Theatre', from *Brecht on Theatre: The Development of an Aesthetic*, translated by John Willet. Copyright © 1957, 1963, and 1964 by Suhrkamp Verlag. Translation copyright © John Willett. Reprinted by permission of Bloomsbury Publishing and Hill and Wang, a division of Farrar, Straus and Giroux.

'The Gangster as Tragic Hero' by Robert Warshow, from *The Partisan Review*, February 1948, Vol. 15, No. 2. Reprinted with permission of Howard Gotlieb Archival Research Center.

George Steiner, *The Death of Tragedy* (New York: Alfred A. Knopf, 1961), 3–10. Copyright © 1961 and 1980 by George Steiner. Reprinted by permission of Georges Borchardt, Inc., for the author.

'Tragedy and Revolution', from *Modern Tragedy* by Raymond Williams. Published by Chatto & Windus, 1992. Reprinted with permission of The Random House Group Limited. Copyright © 1975.

'On *A View from the Bridge*', from *Notebooks 1960–1977* by Athol Fugard, ed. Mary Benson (London: Faber and Faber, 1983), 75–6. Copyright © 1983 by Athol Fugard. Used by permission of Alfred A. Knopf, an imprint of the Knopf Doubleday Publishing Group, a division of Penguin Random House LLC. All rights reserved.

Chapter 6

Augusto Boal, *The Theatre of the Oppressed*, trans. Charles A. and Maria-Odilia Leal McBride and Emily Fryer (London: Pluto Press, 2000). Reprinted with permission from the author's Estate.

René Girard, *Violence and the Sacred*, trans. Patrick Gregory (Baltimore: Johns Hopkins University Press, 1977, reprinted in 1979), 39–42, 44–9 © 1972 Editions Bernard Grasset. English translation © 1977 The Johns Hopkins University Press. Reprinted with permission of Johns Hopkins University Press.

'Literary Tragedy and Ecological Catastrophe', from *The Comedy of Survival* by Joseph W. Meeker. Copyright © 1997 Joseph W. Meeker. Reprinted by permission of the University of Arizona Press.

Catherine Belsey, *The Subject of Tragedy* (London and New York: Methuen, 1985), 149–50, 164–6. Copyright © 1985 Methuen, reproduced by permission of Taylor & Francis Books UK.

Biodun Jeyifo, 'Tragedy, History and Ideology', from *Marxism and African Literature*, ed. Georg. M Gugelberger (Trenton, NJ: Africa World Press, 1986), 94–6, 100, 106–7. Reprinted with kind permission of the author.

'The Rope and the Sword', from *Tragic Ways of Killing a Woman* by Nicole Loraux, translated by Anthony Forster (Cambridge, MA and London: Harvard University Press, 1987). Copyright © 1987 by the President and Fellows of Harvard College.

Hélène Cixous, 'Enter the Theatre', from Hélène Cixous and Brian J. Mallett (trans.), *Modern Drama* 42, no. 3 (Fall 1999): 301–4. Reprinted with permission of the author.

'Promiscuous Obedience', from *Antigone's Claim* by Judith Butler (New York: Columbia University Press, 2000), 57–63, 66–8, 69–72, 82, 92–7. Copyright © 2000 Columbia University Press. Reprinted with permission of the publisher.

INDEX

Index

Brodowski, Antoni
  Edyp i Antygona 1, 2
Buchanan, George 69
Burke, Edmund 34, 98, 137
  'Of the Effects of Tragedy' 121–2
  'The Sublime' 120, 122–5
  on sympathy 120–2
burlesque 143 n.111
Butcher, S.H.
  Aristotle's Theory of Poetry and Fine Art
      265–8
Butler, Judith
  Antigone's Claim 4, 253, 297–304
Byron, George Gordon, Lord 141

Cadmus 3–4, 31 n.78, 242
Caecilius of Caleacte 34, 35, 108 n.35, 121 n.64
Caesar, Augustus 81, 134 n.93
Caesar, Julius 56 n.22, 71, 134, 135 n.99
capitalism 203, 251
Caribbean 254. *See also* Haitian revolution
  Jamaica 254
Cary, Elizabeth, Lady
  The Tragedy of Mariam 276
Casaubon, Dorothea (fictional character: Eliot)
      147–8, 151
Casaubon, Edward (fictional character: Eliot) 147
Cassandra 3, 36, 281
Castelvetro, Lodovico 46, 79 n.101
  on endings 56–7
  on magnitude 58, 60–1
  on monarchy and tragedy 4
  The Poetics of Aristotle 55–61
  on subjects of poetry 55–6
  on tragic pleasure 59–60
  on unity of plot 58–9
catastrophe 6–7, 87, 118, 150, 214, 231, 239, 241–2,
      243, 257
  ecological 270–1
catharsis
  Addison on 105–6
  Aristotle's idea of 8, 9, 18, 19, 23, 59, 74,
      75, 80, 84, 88, 98, 137, 152, 153, 165,
      166–7, 181, 182, 226, 228, 264, 265,
      266, 268, 274
  Augustine on 10, 42
  Bernays on 266–7
  Boal on 251, 264, 268–9
  Brecht on 202–3
  Butcher on 266–8
  Castelvetro on 59–60
  Dryden on 88–92
  Giraldi on 52, 53, 54
  Hazlitt on 165
  Hippocrates on 268
  Lessing on 153–4
  Milton on 268
  Racine on 265–6

Rapin on 49, 83, 84–5, 90
Rousseau on 127–9
Schelgel on 153–4, 158–9
Sidney on 74–7
Cato the Younger (fictional character: Addison) 95–6,
      112, 113, 135
Cato the Younger (Roman statesman) 108, 121
Césaire, Aimé
  A Season in the Congo 290
character/s. *See also* female protagonists; hero/es;
      specific names
  Aristotle on 19–20, 27–8
  'character is destiny' 214
  comedy vs. tragedy 52–3
  condemnation of 75–7
  in Greek tragedies 152, 179–80
  and lyric poetry 217
  and manners 91–2
  mimetic rivalry 256, 261–3
  modern tragedies 87
  and moral goodness 90
  and passions 145
  representation of 14, 142–5, 171–2
  Shakespeare's 92, 93
  and social class 10, 51, 53, 68, 74–5, 107–8, 204,
      212–13
  verbal conflicts between 259–60, 261–2
  virtue and fortunes of 267–8
  Woolf on 221–2
  Yeats on 202, 217
Chaucer, Geoffrey 10, 45
  Canterbury Tales 221
  'The Monk's Tale' 212
Chimène (fictional character: Corneille) 74, 75
chorus 40, 211
  Aristotle on 24
  Bacchic 40, 194, 199
  in Euripides 78, 155, 223, 259, 261–2
  Horace on 155
  Milton on 81
  Nietzsche on 195–8
  Pareus on 80 n.104
  satyr 197–8
  Schiller on 197
  Schlegel on 155, 196
  Sophocles use of 222–3
  in *The Women of Trachis* 172 n.60
Chremes 29
Christianity 10–11, 45, 46, 48–9, 55, 70, 80, 175,
      203, 225, 271, 273. *See also* Augustine of
      Hippo, Saint
Chryses 12
Cibber, Theophilus 109
Cicero 115–16, 118, 280 n.72
Cinthio. *See* Giraldi, Giovanni Battista
Cixous, Hélène 2
  on endings 294–6
  'Enter the Theatre (in between)' 253, 291–6

Index

Index

Index